The Cambridge Companion to the Harpsichord

Written by fourteen leading experts in the field, this Companion
covers almost every aspect of the harpsichord – the history of the
instrument, tuning systems, the role of the harpsichord in
ensemble, its use in the twentieth and twenty-first centuries – and
includes chapters devoted to Domenico Scarlatti and to J. S. Bach
and Handel. Chapters featuring almost every national style are
written by authors with close connections to the countries about
which they are writing, including England, the Netherlands,
Germany, the Austro-Hungarian Empire, France, Italy, Portugal,
and Spain, as well as the less extensive harpsichord traditions of
Russia, the Nordic and Baltic countries, and colonial Spanish and
Portuguese America. With musical examples, illustrations,
a chronology, and lists of composers, reliable editions, and original
sources, this is the book is for all who love the harpsichord or want
to learn more about it.

MARK KROLL's distinguished career as a performer, scholar, and
educator spans a period of more than fifty years. He has appeared
worldwide as a harpsichordist and fortepianist, published
numerous books, chapters, articles and editions, made more than
forty recordings, and is Professor *emeritus* at Boston University,
where he served for twenty-five years as Professor of Harpsichord
and Chair of the Department of Historical Performance. He is
currently recording the complete *Pièces de clavecin* of François
Couperin.

Cambridge Companions to Music

Topics

The Cambridge Companion to Ballet
Edited by Marion Kant

The Cambridge Companion to Blues and Gospel Music
Edited by Allan Moore

The Cambridge Companion to Brass Instruments
Edited by Trevor Herbert and John Wallace

The Cambridge Companion to Choral Music
Edited by André de Quadros

The Cambridge Companion to the Concerto
Edited by Simon P. Keefe

The Cambridge Companion to Conducting
Edited by José Antonio Bowen

The Cambridge Companion to Eighteenth-Century Music
Edited by Anthony R. DelDonna and Pierpaolo Polzonetti

The Cambridge Companion to Electronic Music
Edited by Nick Collins and Julio D'Escriván

The Cambridge Companion to Film Music
Edited by Mervyn Cooke and Fiona Ford

The Cambridge Companion to French Music
Edited by Simon Trezise

The Cambridge Companion to Grand Opera
Edited by David Charlton

The Cambridge Companion to Hip-Hop
Edited by Justin A. Williams

The Cambridge Companion to Jazz
Edited by Mervyn Cooke and David Horn

The Cambridge Companion to Jewish Music
Edited by Joshua S. Walden

The Cambridge Companion to the Lied
Edited by James Parsons

The Cambridge Companion to Medieval Music
Edited by Mark Everist

The Cambridge Companion to the Musical
Edited by William Everett and Paul Laird

The Cambridge Companion to Opera Studies
Edited by Nicholas Till

The Cambridge Companion to the Orchestra
Edited by Colin Lawson

The Cambridge Companion to Percussion
Edited by Russell Hartenberger

The Cambridge Companion to Pop and Rock
Edited by Simon Frith, Will Straw, and John Street

The Cambridge Companion to Recorded Music
Edited by Eric Clarke, Nicholas Cook, Daniel Leech-Wilkinson, and John Rink

Instruments

The Cambridge Companion to the

HARPSICHORD

....

EDITED BY
Mark Kroll
Boston University

CAMBRIDGE
UNIVERSITY PRESS

CAMBRIDGE
UNIVERSITY PRESS

University Printing House, Cambridge CB2 8BS, United Kingdom

One Liberty Plaza, 20th Floor, New York, NY 10006, USA

477 Williamstown Road, Port Melbourne, VIC 3207, Australia

314–321, 3rd Floor, Plot 3, Splendor Forum, Jasola District Centre, New Delhi – 110025, India

79 Anson Road, #06–04/06, Singapore 079906

Cambridge University Press is part of the University of Cambridge.

It furthers the University's mission by disseminating knowledge in the pursuit of
education, learning, and research at the highest international levels of excellence.

www.cambridge.org
Information on this title: www.cambridge.org/9781107156074
DOI: 10.1017/9781316659359

© Cambridge University Press 2019

First published 2019

Printed in the United Kingdom by TJ International Ltd, Padstow, Cornwall

A catalogue record for this publication is available from the British Library.

Library of Congress Cataloging-in-Publication Data
Names: Kroll, Mark.
Title: The Cambridge companion to the harpsichord / edited by Mark Kroll.
Description: Cambridge, United Kingdom ; New York, NY : Cambridge University Press, 2019.
Identifiers: LCCN 2018027191 | ISBN 9781107156074
Subjects: LCSH: Harpsichord – History. | Harpsichord music – History and criticism.
Classification: LCC ML651 .C36 2019 | DDC 786.4–dc23
LC record available at https://lccn.loc.gov/2018027191

ISBN 978-1-107-15607-4 Hardback
ISBN 978-1-316-60970-5 Paperback

Contents

Figures

Music Examples

Contributors

João Pedro d'Alvarenga is an Integrated Researcher, Coordinator of the Early Music Studies Research Group, and Executive Secretary of CESEM (the Centre for the Study of the Sociology and Aesthetics of Music) at Lisbon Nova University. He was an FCT Investigator affiliated with CESEM (2013–2018), and Assistant Professor at the University of Évora (1997–2011). He was the commissioner for the planning and settling of the National Music Museum in Lisbon in 1993–1994 and was also charged with the organization of the Music Service at the National Library of Portugal, which he headed in the period 1991–1997.

Rebecca Cypess is Associate Professor of Music at the Mason Gross School of the Arts at Rutgers University. She is the author of *Curious and Modern Inventions: Instrumental Music as Discovery in Galileo's Italy*, as well as numerous articles on the history, interpretation, and performance practices of music in seventeenth- and eighteenth-century Europe. She is coeditor of the two-volume collection *Word, Image, and Song* and of *Sara Levy's World: Gender, Judaism, and the Bach Tradition in Enlightenment Berlin*.

Pieter Dirksen, harpsichordist, organist, conductor, and musicologist, earned his PhD with honors at Utrecht University and the Dutch Erasmus Prize for an exhaustive study of Sweelinck's keyboard music. His numerous publications include books on the *Art of Fugue*, the St. Matthew Passion, and the works of Sweelinck and Scheidemann, and critical editions of music by Bull, Sweelinck, Cornet, Scheidemann, Froberger, Buxtehude, and many others. He has recorded Sweelinck's organ and harpsichord music and Bach's Goldberg Variations and *Art of Fugue*.

Ton Koopman, a leading figure in early music and historically informed performance practice, has performed in the world's most prestigious concert halls and on Europe's most beautiful historical instruments as organist and harpsichordist. As a conductor, Mr. Koopman and his Amsterdam Baroque Orchestra and Choir recorded all the sacred and secular cantatas of J. S. Bach between 1994 and 2004, and he appears as guest conductor with the world's leading orchestras. As an educator, Koopman serves as Professor at the University of Leiden.

John Koster, after graduation from Harvard in 1971, made harpsichords and was a consultant to the Museum of Fine Arts, Boston. In 1990–1991 he held a Mellon Senior Fellowship at The Metropolitan Museum of Art in New York and from 1991 to 2015 was Professor of Music and Curator of Keyboard Instruments at the National Music Museum, the University of South Dakota. Koster has published extensively on the history of musical instruments and in 2016 received the American Musical Instrument Society's Curt Sachs Award for lifetime achievement.

Mark Kroll's distinguished career as a performer, scholar and educator spans a period of more than fifty years. He has appeared in concert worldwide, made numerous recordings (most recently the *Pièces de clavecin* of F. Couperin), and published biographies of J. N. Hummel and Ignaz Moscheles, a book on historical harpsichord technique, and chapters, articles, and scholarly editions on a variety of subjects and repertoire. Kroll, who has taught throughout the world, served for twenty-five years as Professor of Harpsichord and Chair of the Department of Historical Performance at Boston University.

Robert L. Marshall is Sachar Professor Emeritus of Music at Brandeis University. He is the coauthor, with Traute M. Marshall, of *Exploring the World of J. S. Bach* (2016), the author of two prize-winning Bach studes: *The Compositional Process of J. S. Bach* (1972) and *The Music of Johann Sebastian Bach: The Sources, the Style, the Significance* (1989). His writings on Bach and Mozart have appeared in numerous publications.

Anna Maria McElwain has master's degrees from SUNY Buffalo in piano performance and music theory, and in clavichord performance from the Sibelius Academy (Finland), where she also taught until 2010. She is cofounder and artistic director of the Nordic Historical Keyboard Festival, founder of the First International Clavichord Competition and International Clavichord Composition Competition, and recently made the first clavichord recording of Beethoven on an 1808 Lindholm instrument in Stockholm.

Larry Palmer, born in Ohio, holds degrees from Oberlin College and the Eastman School of Music (DMA) in Organ and Church Music. His teaching career of fifty-two years was spent in Virginia and Texas, including forty-five years as Professor of Harpsichord and Organ at Southern Methodist University, Dallas, from which he retired in 2015. Harpsichord Editor for *The Diapason* since 1969, he remains in that capacity and continues an active concert career as harpsichordist and organist.

Águeda Pedrero-Encabo is Professor of Musicology and Director of the postgraduate "Master in Hispanic Music" at the University of Valladolid, Spain. She has written a book about the sonata in Spain and published editions of previously unedited keyboard works by Spanish composers. Her numerous articles include a survey of sources on Domenico Scarlatti, and she is now focused on further research on Scarlatti and other Spanish keyboard composers, and new directions in musical analysis.

Pedro Persone began his harpsichord study at the Conservatório de Tatuí, received his Bachelor's degree in harpsichord at the University of Campionas (Unicamp), Brazil, and was awarded the DMA in historical performance from Boston University. He has received numerous awards and grants, including the FAPESP to conduct postdoctoral research on European music played in Imperial Brazil, and in 2010 joined the Faculty of the Universidade Federal de Santa Maria (RS) as Associate Professor.

Paul Poletti studied composition and organ at California State University, Northridge, and since 1978 has been restoring and making copies of Viennese classical pianos. He lectures regularly throughout Europe on a variety of topics including early piano actions, the design and analysis of string scales, the interpretation of string gauge markings, and historical temperaments. He is a Professor at the Escola Superior de la Mùsica de Catalunya (Barcelona) where he teaches acoustics, organology, and historical temperaments.

Marina Ritzarev, an Israeli musicologist of Russian background, is the author of *Eighteenth-Century Russian Music* and *Tchaikovsky's "Pathétique"and Russian Culture*, and has contributed to research in eighteenth-century Russian music, including biographies of Dmitry Bortniansky and Maxim Berezovsky. She serves as Professor emerita at Bar-Ilan University, Israel, and is coeditor of *Min-Ad: Israel Studies in Musicology Online*.

Andrew Woolley is at present an FCT (Portuguese Foundation for Science and Technology) Investigator and member of the Early Music Studies Research Group within CESEM (the Centre for the Study of the Sociology and Aesthetics of Music) at the Nova University of Lisbon. He is working on a project to catalogue Portuguese music manuscripts of the late seventeenth and early eighteenth centuries and is involved in preparing the keyboard volume of the revised Purcell Society Edition.

Acknowledgments

I express my gratitude to Dr. Victoria L. Cooper, former Senior Commissioning Editor, Music and Theatre, at Cambridge University Press, for her initial approval of the project, which came about as the result of a brief conversation at the 2014 meeting of the American Musicological Society. My sincere thanks to her successor in the position, Dr. Katharina Brett, who was no less enthusiastic and helpful. Her expert advice and guidance, and that of editorial assistant Eilidh Burrett, content manager Lisa Sinclair, and copy-editor Kilmeny MacBride were essential in putting all of the many parts of this book together and shepherding it to publication, as were Samantha Bassler's untiring efforts in formatting the index.

I am deeply grateful to my wife, violinist and professor Dr. Carol Lieberman, and my dear friend Professor Wendy Heller of Princeton University for reading my two chapters many times and for their advice and careful proofreading. They seem to have done this for everything I have written and published, and I hope they will still be willing to do so in the future. I am also indebted to Dr. Valerie Walden, my former student and now expert cellist and musicologist, whose work I cite, and who also carefully read my chapters. Finally, I would like to take this opportunity to thank all the contributors to this book. These distinguished scholars responded to all of my editorial questions, suggestions, and corrections with an equally inexhaustible amount of patience, expertise, and professionalism.

Chronology

1494   Spain and Portugal sign the Treaty of Tordesillas
Christopher Columbus first sights Jamaica
The House of Medici expelled from Florence
1517   Publication of Martin Luther's Theses
1534   Ignatius Loyola founds the Society of Jesus (Jesuits)
Cambridge University Press given Royal Charter by Henry VIII
English Reformation: Parliament passes the Act of Supremacy,
establishing Henry VIII as supreme head of the Church of England
1558   Elizabeth I becomes Queen of England
Gioseffo Zarlino publishes *Le Istitutioni Harmoniche*
1577   Birth of Peter Paul Rubens
1578   Birth of Johannes Ruckers
1583   Birth of Girolamo Frescobaldi
1598   Death of Hans Ruckers
Calvinists in Zürich introduce music into their services
1606   Birth of Rembrandt van Rijn
Trial and execution of Guy Fawkes for Gunpowder Plot
First Charter of Virginia established
1618   First performance of Claudio Monteverdi's *Orfeo*
Beginning of the Thirty Years' War
Publication of René Descartes's *Compendium Musicae*
1643   Louis XIV becomes King of France
1688   James II escapes to France
Bartolomeo Cristofori becomes keeper of Medici's musical
instruments
1701   War of Spanish Succession
1706   Publication of J.-P. Rameau's first book of *Pièces de clavecin*
Thomas Twining opens the first known tea room in London
Birth of Benjamin Frankiln
1707   John V becomes King of Portugal
George Frideric Handel meets Domenico Scarlatti
1712   Peter the Great moves Russian capital from Moscow to Saint
Petersburg
Birth of Frederick II of Prussia
1713   Publication of F. Couperin's first book of *Pièces de clavecin*
Foundation of the *Académie Royale de Danse* by Louis XIV
Treaty of Utrecht ends War of Spanish Succession

1719 J. S. Bach travels to Berlin to pick up Michael Mietke harpsichord for Köthen

Domenico Scarlatti takes up residence in Lisbon

British sink the Spanish Navy

1724 Publication of J.-P. Rameau's second book of *Pièces de clavecin*

Founding of Longman publishing house in England

Birth of Immanuel Kant

1730 Publication of F. Couperin's fourth book of *Pièces de clavecin*

1734 Publication of Voltaire's *The Age of Louis XIV*

Lutherans expelled from Salzburg by the Roman Catholic bishop

1735 Publication of J. S. Bach's *Clavierübung*, Part II (Italian Concerto and French Overture)

Austria signs peace treaty with France and Spain

Birth of Paul Revere

1738 Publication of D. Scarlatti's *Essercizi* in London

Great Britain declares war on Spain

1768 Pascal Taskin introduces the *Peau de buffle* to the harpsichord

Royal Academy founded in London

1789 French Revolution

George Washington becomes first President of the United States

Mutiny on the HMS *Bounty*

1837 Ignaz Moscheles performs music of Scarlatti on a harpsichord in London

Prussian Copyright Act established to protect composers' rights

Queen Victoria ascends the throne of England

1879 Birth of Wanda Landowska

First female students admitted to study for degrees at Oxford University

Births of Albert Einstein and Sir Thomas Beecham

1889 Paris Exposition

Inauguration of Eiffel Tower

Establishment of the *Wall Street Journal* in New York City

Edison Records introduces first prerecorded wax cylinders of music

1908 Births of Sylvia Marlowe, Herbert von Karajan, and Milton Berle

New York City passes Sullivan Ordinance, making it illegal for women to smoke in public

1911 Birth of Ralph Kirkpatrick

1952 Publication of Elliott Carter's *Sonata for Flute, Oboe, Cello and Harpsichord*

Elizabeth II is proclaimed Queen of the United Kingdom

Greece and Turkey join NATO

Introduction

The harpsichord has enjoyed a prominent role in virtually every musical style and genre for an almost unbroken period of 600 years. It is found as a solo instrument, in chamber ensembles, concertos, secular and sacred vocal works, and, more recently, in commercials, movies and television shows (*The Addams Family* being perhaps the best-known example). As a harpsichordist, I have long felt that we needed a comprehensive but user-friendly source of information about the instrument and its repertoire. I hope this book fulfills that need.

Written by the leading experts in the field, including many who come from or live in the countries of the national styles about which they are writing, it offers separate chapters on just about every aspect of the harpsichord, such as the history of the instrument and how to tune it, the role of the harpsichord in ensembles, its extensive use in the twentieth and twenty-first centuries, and almost every era or national style. Readers will find insights into the rich harpsichord traditions of England, the Netherlands, northern and southern Germany, the Austro-Hungarian Empire, France, Italy, Portugal, and Spain. A separate chapter is devoted to Domenico Scarlatti, another discusses the role of the harpsichord in the life and music of J. S. Bach and Handel, and several authors take us to places that are not often associated with extensive harpsichord music and performance, such as Russia, the Nordic and Baltic countries, and colonial Spanish and Portuguese America. Our suggestions for further reading at the end of each chapter will enable readers to explore the many subjects discussed in greater depth, and the appendices at the end of the book provides those who want to play the music with lists of composers, reliable editions, or original sources. In other words, let this book serve as a faithful companion for all who love the harpsichord and its music, and want to learn more about it, for many years to come.

1 History and Construction of the Harpsichord

JOHN KOSTER

"The harpsichord is lord of all the instruments in the world," wrote the Neapolitan composer Giovanni Maria Trabaci in *Il secondo libro de ricercate* (Naples, 1615). As with lords and their domains, however, there was at different times and places a wide variety of harpsichords quite dissimilar in character. Knowledge of the harpsichords available to composers can inform the player or scholar about how particular works were conceived and performed.

The history of harpsichords, virginals, spinets, and similar instruments, for which "quilled keyboards" will be used here as the generic term, can be divided into five eras: late medieval, Renaissance, baroque, classical, and revival. To be sure, certain characteristics of design and construction persisted among Italian harpsichords of all periods and other characteristics persisted among Flemish harpsichords. Nevertheless, shared qualities of tone and touch are evident among early instruments of both schools, as well as those from other regions, while later instruments show qualities characteristic of their own times.

Some familiarity with the design, construction, and function of harpsichords and other quilled keyboards is necessary for understanding their history.[1] The keyboard or manual, of which harpsichords often have two, consists of a set of levers to be pressed down in front so that the far end rises. Sound is produced by plucking the string with a plectrum traditionally cut from bird quill but occasionally of leather or metal (or plastic in most modern instruments), protruding from a small wooden tongue held by an axle in an upright slip of wood called a jack, which rests on the far end of the key lever. When the key is depressed, the jack is raised and the plectrum plucks the string. When the key is released, the falling tongue swivels to pass around the string and is returned to its resting position by a spring. A small cloth flag held in a slot at the top of the jack comes to rest on the string to damp it. A jackrail over the jacks limits their upward motion.

Harpsichords have the familiar wing shape from which the form of the modern grand piano was derived (see Figures 1.1, 1.3, 1.4, 1.7, 1.9, and 1.10). They may have only one choir (set of strings) but most often two or three, occasionally more. In terminology derived from organs, an 8-foot choir is at "normal" pitch, which historically could range from about a tone

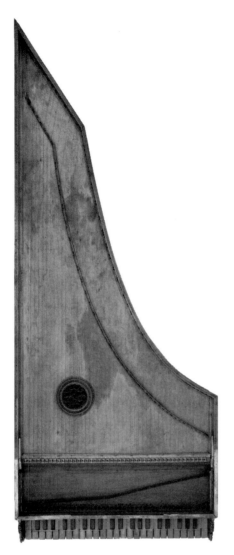

Figure 1.1 Harpsichord, maker unknown, Naples, about 1525 (National Music Museum, Vermillion, SD, cat. no. NMM 14408; photograph by Tony Jones, courtesy National Music Museum). For clarity, the jackrail has been removed for this and most other pictures.

lower than modern $a^1 = 440$ Hz to three-quarters of a tone above (i.e., with a^1 sounding from about 385 to 475 Hz). A 4-foot choir sounds an octave higher than an 8-foot; a 16-foot sounds an octave lower (the designation "foot" will occasionally be omitted, and only the number used, in some references to registration). Each choir is plucked by one set of jacks, or occasionally two with different plucking points. Strings plucked closer to their midpoints sound rounder or flutier, while those plucked closer to one end sound brighter or more nasal.

A harpsichord's major structural components are the walls (spine, tail, bentside, and cheekpiece); the bottom closing the entire underside of the instrument; the wrestplank; the nameboard; the guides to hold the jacks; the belly rail; the soundboard and often a soundhole in which a decorative rose is placed; and reinforcing inner supporting ribs under the soundboard and internal bracing of the walls.[2]

A "stop" or "register" consisting of a set of jacks can be turned off by moving its guide slightly to the right or left so that the plectra miss the strings as they rise. In many instruments, when a stop is off, dampers do not touch their strings, which are free to resonate sympathetically. Guides can be moved directly by hand, by stop levers on the wrestplank or protruding through the nameboard, or, exceptionally in historical instruments, by pedals or knee levers. In two-manual or "double" harpsichords, there is usually a provision to combine the two keyboards or their stops. This can be done by a shove coupler, in which the entire upper-manual keyboard (or occasionally, the lower manual) can be shoved back or pulled forward about 7 mm. In the shoved-back position, the back ends of the upper key levers are pushed up by upright "dogs" fixed to the lower-manual key levers. Another method of coupling is the dogleg jack, the front portion of which rests on the upper-manual key while a leg extends down from the jack to rest on the lower-manual key. When a dogleg stop is engaged, it can be played from both keyboards. A choir of strings may be provided with a buff ("lute" or "harp") stop, usually consisting of pads of soft leather that can be moved to touch the strings, thus eliciting a pizzicato tone.

Many early keyboards lacked accidentals at one or both extremes of their compasses. A common sixteenth-century compass of thirty-eight notes, for example, is written as F, G, A, to g^2, a^2 to indicate that F♯, G♯, and $g\sharp^2$ are not present. The common short-octave compass in which the lowest note, an apparent E, sounds C, apparent F♯ sounds D, and apparent G♯ sounds E, is indicated by C/E. Another short-octave arrangement, with apparent BB sounding GG, is indicated by GG/BB.

The overall dimensions and shape of a harpsichord are interdependent with the vibrating lengths of the strings, called the "scaling," and with the compass of the keyboard. The number of notes, with allowance for clearance at both ends of the keyboard, determines the width of the instrument, while the length of the instrument is that of the lowest string plus some expanse of soundboard beyond its far end and space for the tuning pins and keyboard(s) at the near end. Although the angle of the tail with the spine, which can be as blunt as 90 degrees or as sharp as 30 degrees, is somewhat arbitrary, the curve of the bentside is more or less parallel with that of the bridge, which is itself dependent on the lengths of the strings as they change from note to note.

Usually, the strings in the treble double in length for each lower octave. This is called "Pythagorean scaling," which in some instruments extends only down to about c^1 but in others much deeper into the tenor or bass. Below a certain point, however, the scaling is "foreshortened," so that the instrument will not become unreasonably long, that is, the strings are less than double the length of those an octave higher. According to modern convention, the length of the c^2 string (the longer 8 if there are two) is regarded as the basic scale of an instrument. The scaling of a harpsichord is closely related to its intended pitch and string material. The bass strings are always brass, and some harpsichords were designed for brass throughout their entire compass, while others were designed for iron strings from the tenor to the treble. Since the tone quality of a string is purer as it is pulled tauter, harpsichord makers traditionally made their scalings, at least in the treble, as long as the strings could bear without breaking, with a safety margin of a semitone or so. Care must be taken, however, if the treble scaling is non-Pythagorean. If, for example, c^3 is significantly longer than half of c^2, then one may regard twice the length of c^3 as the instrument's basic scale.

The principal alternative forms of quilled keyboards are the clavicytherium, which is a harpsichord turned upright; the virginal; and the spinet. In virginals the strings run from left to right within a rectangular or polygonal shape with the keyboard at the long front side (see Figures 1.2 and 1.6). Spinets resemble small harpsichords in which the long wall to the player's left has, together with all the strings, been rotated clockwise about 65

Figure 1.2 Virginal, maker unknown, Venice, 1540 (The Metropolitan Museum of Art, New York; photograph public domain).

degrees. Most common are "bentside spinets" (see Figure 1.8), to be distinguished from the very small spinets at octave pitch, which usually have a straight wall to the player's right.

Late-Medieval Origins

The harpsichord arose in what has jocularly been called the "Stone Age" of keyboard music.[3] Much of this repertoire, including the Robertsbridge Codex (ca. 1360), the Buxheim Keyboard Manuscript, and various early sixteenth-century sources, was, with the major exception of the Italian Faenza Codex (ca. 1420), written in the old German tablature, which favors a florid treble line. The earliest-known stringed keyboard instrument was the *eschequier*, first mentioned in French documents of the 1360s. Apparently invented in England but immediately transferred to France, the *eschequier* was, in all likelihood, some sort of clavichord. The harpsichord as we know it evidently originated in Vienna with Hermann Poll, who, passing through Padua in 1397, was recorded as having invented an instrument called the *clavicembalum*. No details are known, but the name indicates that it had keys (*claves*) and "bells," that is, the sound quality of small bells (*cymbala*), as the timbre of high-pitch undamped metal strings plucked by a hard material might well be described. Fifteenth-century depictions of harpsichords show small instruments that would often, in modern terms, have sounded at 4-foot pitch or higher.[4]

Knowledge of the instrument quickly spread throughout Europe. An illustrated description of a *clavisimbalum* in Henry Arnault de Zwolle's manuscript (Paris, Bibliothèque Nationale, ms. lat. 7295), produced in Dijon about 1440, provides extensive technical details. It was about 940 mm long and had a 35-note compass of B (then the usual lowest note of organ keyboards) to a^2. The three-octave measure (the width of twenty-one natural keys, typically 495 mm in modern pianos) was rather wide, about 530 mm, and the playing surfaces of the keys were very short. Several alternative rather cumbersome plucking actions, all lacking dampers, are shown.[5] None had a conventional jack, although the one Henry Arnault preferred had a tongue with a thin, narrow plectrum, presumably quill. Throughout the fifteenth century, harpsichords would generally have had just one choir of strings, although Henry suggested, somewhat impracticably, that a second string could be added directly above the first.

The oldest existing plucked keyboard, a late fifteenth-century south German clavicytherium (housed in the Royal College of Music, London), represents the next stage of development. Its jacks, plucking a single choir, are very nearly the standard type with quill plectra, but have no slot for dampers. The thin-walled instrument is still kept in its original outer case. The compass was originally forty notes – E, "E♯," F, G, G♯, A to g^2 – with the bass likely in some short-octave arrangement. The dimensions of the keyboard are similar to Henry Arnault's, with a three-octave measure of 529 mm and short natural heads. The scaling suggests that the instrument was tuned about a fourth or fifth above 8-foot pitch. Organs were made at alternative pitch levels roughly a fourth or fifth apart until well into the sixteenth century.[6] It is not surprising that harpsichords, often made by organ builders and played by organists, would also have been made at either pitch, neither of which was yet privileged as normal.

Late fifteenth-century depictions show that harpsichords approaching five or six feet (180 cm) in length, about the size of a typical sixteenth-century harpsichord at 8-foot pitch, were beginning to be made. These larger sizes would have resulted both from the expansion of the compass downward and from making some instruments at lower pitches than before. The overall lowering of the tonal center towards the bass led Italians occasionally to call the instrument a *gravicembalo*.

The rectangular form of plucked keyboard, already mentioned by Henry Arnault as a possibility, acquired the name *virginale* by about 1460. Within a few decades the virginal displaced the harpsichord as the most prevalent form of quilled keyboard in northern Europe. There is no harpsichord among the systematic illustrations of musical instruments in Sebastian Virdung's *Musica getutscht* (Basel, 1511).

The Renaissance

By 1500 an instrument originally evoking the ringing of little bells had reached a certain level of tonal and mechanical refinement. With a deeper voice and a more efficient action, the harpsichord in the age of Josquin des Prez was poised to assume its role as a medium for music making at the highest artistic level. "Renaissance," as used here in the context of quilled keyboards, includes the sixteenth century to approximately the first decade of the seventeenth in Italy, but extends later in other regions where older techniques of composition persisted (e.g., in England, to the mid-seventeenth century, or Spain arguably into the early eighteenth). Because of the overwhelming popularity of virginals north of the Alps, the paucity of northern harpsichords before the final decades of the sixteenth century compels us first to consider Italy, from which at least forty examples made before 1600 are known.[7]

Most sixteenth-century Italian plucked keyboards were made in two major centers, Naples and Venice.[8] Although the Venetian school is better known because its makers signed and dated their instruments, the Neapolitan school appears to have been established earlier. Common features of Italian plucked keyboards are: thin walls, with upper and lower edges surrounded by finely cut moldings; attachment of the walls around the edges of the bottom; jacks held by "box guides;" scrolls or carved key cheeks at the front ends of the spine and cheekpiece; and a separate outer case. All the harpsichords have just a single manual. Generally intended for brass strings throughout the compass, their Pythagorean scaling deep into the bass resulted in an elegant, slender outline.

Figure 1.1 shows a typical Neapolitan harpsichord as made from about 1515 into the seventeenth century. Prominent features are the sharp tail angle (33 degrees), the maple walls and spruce soundboard (fir or occasionally maple in later Neapolitan instruments), and the jack guide perpendicular with the spine. It has a single set of strings at 8-foot pitch (two known examples also had a 4-foot stop) and a compass of C/E to c^3. The dimensions of the keyboard, with three-octave measure of 495 mm, are similar to those of later centuries. Neapolitan harpsichords were widely distributed in Italy and imitated by Roman and Florentine makers. Neapolitan virginals, made at either 8- or 4-foot pitch, have rectangular cases, and their left-hand bridges lie on a solid wrestplank.

In Venice, harpsichords were commonly made with cypress soundboards and walls, although the latter were occasionally of ebony or other exotic woods. Tail angles are blunter than in Naples, about 45 to 60 degrees, and the guides are angled away from the player towards the bass. The keyboard is usually C/E to f^3 with the three-octave measure typically about 505 mm. The tails of the naturals, especially of the D-keys, are notably wide, facilitating playing between the sharps. Most Venetian harpsichords were made with a single 8+4, although a few instruments with a single 8 or with 2×8 are known, as well as the occasional octave instrument with 2×4. The scalings of many Venetian harpsichords are (or were originally) very long, with c^2 ranging from about 340 mm to 400 mm or more. Although they might have had iron strings tuned to 8-foot pitch, they were more likely designed for brass strings tuned a fourth or fifth lower. Although 8-foot pitch (albeit varying from place to place) came to be regarded as the central standard, instruments a fourth or fifth lower were useful for accompanying ensembles, which often performed at these lower transposed pitches.

Virginals were the principal Venetian form of quilled keyboard at 8-foot pitch. Scaled for iron strings in the treble, they were typically made in irregular pentagonal or hexagonal shape with the keyboard protruding from the long front side. With plucking points farther from the left-hand

Figure 1.3 Harpsichord, maker unknown, southern Germany, about 1630 (Bayerisches Nationalmuseum, Munich, Inv. Nr. Mu 78; photograph by the author). In addition to the three 8-foot registers typical of early German harpsichords, there are here a second nasal with metal plectra and a register with distant plucking points.

bridge, which is on active soundboard, the tone is rounder than that of Neapolitan virginals.

The earliest surviving northern-European harpsichord, made by Hans Müller in Leipzig, 1537, with thin walls surrounded by moldings, superficially resembles Italian instruments, but its design and construction are quite different.[9] As in most instruments made north of the Alps, the bottom is attached to the underside of the walls, and separate thin upper and lower guides hold the jacks. Two features, the extension of the

Figure 1.4 Harpsichord by Andreas Ruckers the Elder, Antwerp, 1607 (National Music Museum, Vermillion, SD, cat. no. NMM 7384; photograph by the author). A typical Ruckers single, substantially unaltered but with an eighteenth-century keyboard of larger compass than the original C/E to c^3.

soundboard towards the nameboard, such that the nut is acoustically active, and the presence of a nasal register, are frequent in early German instruments (see Figure 1.3).

Until the late seventeenth century Germanic harpsichords commonly had a single manual with compass C/E to c^3 and two 8-foot choirs plucked by three registers, two with normal plucking points, the third nasal. Often there was a buff stop, sometimes also a 4-foot stop. The short scalings of many instruments, c^2 about 310 mm, indicate that, with iron stringing in the treble, they were tuned to *Chorton*, a common organ pitch, about $a^1 =$ 465 Hz. Virginals were made at various pitches from 8-foot or a fourth or fifth above, to 4- or even 2-foot. The most usual compass was C/E to c^3, but

C/E to g^2, a^2 and F, G, A, to g^2, a^2 (a common organ compass) are found in some sixteenth-century examples. In addition to native instruments, there were imported instruments from Venice in southern Germany and from Antwerp in central and northern regions.

Plucked keyboard making in the region now encompassing Belgium and the Netherlands was dominated by Antwerp even before the advent of the supremely important Ruckers dynasty.[10] Throughout the sixteenth century primarily virginals were made, at first in the thin-walled manner seen in the Müller harpsichord of 1537, but the basic characteristics of the classic Flemish style of harpsichord and virginal making were fully developed by the time Hans Ruckers set up shop as a master in 1579.

Ruckers harpsichords as made until the mid-seventeenth century (most were later altered) have poplar walls about 13 mm thick with moldings cut into the top edge and were scaled for iron strings in the treble. Both single- and double-manual models had two choirs, an 8 and a 4. Each bridge was on a separate area of free soundboard, with a massive 4-foot hitch-pin rail between the 8- and 4-foot areas. Singles, with compass C/E to c^3, had two registers, while doubles had 8+4 on each keyboard. All Ruckers doubles were originally transposing instruments (Figure 1.5). The upper manual, compass C/E to c^3, was at 8-foot pitch, about $a^1 = 410$ Hz, but the lower, with compass C/E to f^3, plucking the same strings, was displaced so that

Figure 1.5 Harpsichord by Joannes Ruckers, Antwerp, 1638 (Musical Instrument Museum, University of Edinburgh; photograph by the author). A typical Ruckers double in its original state with transposing keyboards.

they sounded a fourth lower. Because engagement of the registers on one manual would damp the strings shared with the other manual, simultaneous use of the two keyboards was impossible. Transposing doubles amounted essentially to two single-manual harpsichords, one at 8-foot pitch, the other a fourth lower. In 1604, Jan Pieterszoon Sweelinck (1562–1621) traveled to Antwerp to oversee the purchase of a harpsichord for the city of Amsterdam, where he was the municipal organist. From its surviving lid (Rijksmuseum, Amsterdam) the instrument can be identified as a standard Ruckers transposing double. All Ruckers harpsichords had a buff stop for the 8 strings, divided between f^1 and $f\sharp^1$ (but $c^1/c\sharp^1$ on the upper manual of doubles). Their keyboards had a 500-mm three-octave measure and relatively narrow spaces between the sharps, making it difficult to play on the tails of *D, G,* and *A*.

The Ruckerses and their colleagues made two types of virginals, the *spinett* and the *muselar*. In the former, the strings are plucked near the left-hand bridge, which, deadened by a heavy plank under the soundboard, elicits a bright, almost nasal tone. In *muselars* the left-hand bridge is on active soundboard, and the jacks, plucking near the midpoints of the strings, generate a hollow tone. This could be modified in the lower part

Figure 1.6 Double virginal by Hans Ruckers, Antwerp, 1581 (The Metropolitan Museum of Art, New York; photograph public domain). The mother is a *muselar*; the child is shown halfway pulled out from its storage compartment.

of the compass (up to f^1) by advancing a batten with metal hooks towards the strings to cause a jarring sound. Virginals were made at several pitches, 8-foot and a tone, fourth, or fifth higher. A virginal at 8-foot pitch was often combined with a small virginal at 4-foot pitch to form a "mother and child" or "double virginal" (see Figure 1.6). The child could be stowed inside the mother, taken out and played separately, or, after the mother's jackrail was removed, placed on top to become an upper manual coupled to the mother's keyboard, which thus had an 8+4 registration. To judge from surviving instruments, the Ruckerses made approximately equal numbers of harpsichords and virginals.

In England harpsichords were so infrequent during the sixteenth century that *virginall* became the generic term for plucked keyboards. "Harpsichord" did not enter the language until about 1610. It is often assumed that "the majority of instruments in use in England at the time were imported, first from Italy and later from Flanders."[11] Although much of the English virginalists' repertoire is playable on continental instruments, many pieces require chromatic bass notes lacking on their short-octave keyboards. Numerous makers were active in England, and their earliest surviving instruments, a harpsichord by Lodewijk Theewes, London, 1579, and two anonymous virginals from about 1580–1600 have C to c^3 keyboards.[12] Because low C♯ is extremely rare in the repertoire, this key was probably tuned to AA, which occurs more frequently.

The Theewes harpsichord (Victoria and Albert Museum, London), combined with an organ underneath, is of supreme importance, as both Thomas Tallis and William Byrd had close connections with its owner. While the walls are thick like a Ruckers', the nuts, like Hans Müller's, are on active soundboard. There are three choirs and registers, 2×8+4. The pitch was approximately a^1 = 400 Hz. For each string of the second 8 choir, the bridge holds a brass fitting, very old if not original, apparently to cause a jarring sound. Although these could all be turned on or off, it seems reasonable to suppose that they were intended to be kept on permanently. The only other surviving harpsichord from the virginalist period, by John Hasard, London, 1622 (Knole House, Sevenoaks, Kent), is similarly complex, with three choirs and registers providing a variety of color. Although the soundboard and keyboard are missing, enough remains to reconstruct its basic features. Two of the stops, one of which was a close-plucked nasal, were an octave above the third. The compass was fifty-three notes, plausibly GG, AA to c^3, which, together with the estimated scaling, suggests that the lower-pitch choir was tuned a fourth below the prevailing English "quire pitch," which was about a^1 = 475 Hz.[13] A harpsichord by Charles Haward, London, 1683 (Hovingham Hall, Yorkshire), despite its late date, might well reflect earlier practices in addition to the archaic provision of four roses in the soundboard. With two choirs of 8-foot strings at quire pitch, there were originally three registers, two of them nasal.[14]

English virginals are similar to Flemish *spinetten*, but often with certain pre-Ruckers features including active left-hand bridges and multiple roses. Until about 1650 their compass was often C to c³. GG/BB to f³, found as early as 1644, was the most frequent of the wide compasses used after 1650. Most were scaled for quire pitch. The one known English double virginal, by Thomas White, London, 1638 (private collection), with only the child surviving, was scaled for a fourth below quire.

No French quilled keyboards survive from this period.[15] Documents indicate that virginals predominated during the sixteenth century. Many virginals in sixteenth-century inventories were only two and a half or three feet long and must have been tuned at octave pitch, but a drawing by Jacques Cellier, about 1585 (Paris, Bibliothèque Nationale, ms. fr. 9152), shows a larger instrument, compass C/E to a², generally similar to those of Antwerp and London. Double virginals were also known. Harpsichords begin to turn up in early seventeenth-century inventories. In the workshop of maker Jean Jacquet in 1632, there were two harpsichords, one with a single set of strings, the other with 100 strings. The latter presumably had a keyboard of fifty notes, likely GG/BB to c³, and two stops. An engraving of a harpsichord with these characteristics is in Marin Mersenne's *Harmonie universelle* (Paris, 1636–1637). The grouping of both sets of wrestpins, 8+4, just behind the nameboard, suggests that the wrestplank was narrow, as in the Müller and Theewes harpsichords, so that the nuts were acoustically active. One must be skeptical in considering other harpsichords mentioned by Mersenne, who, attempting to be comprehensive, described not only the commonplace and native but also the unusual and foreign, while adding his own theorizing. His passing remark about harpsichords with two or three keyboards and seven or eight *jeux*, that is, stops or combinations of stops, might refer to Ruckers transposing doubles, in which a third keyboard is occasionally present in a virginal built into the hollow of the bentside.

No Iberian quilled keyboard earlier than a harpsichord by Joseph Bueno, Valladolid, 1712, is known to survive, but documents show these instruments to have thrived in Spain and Portugal since the late fifteenth century.[16] By the early sixteenth, the carpenters' guilds in Valencia and Seville included makers of *clavicímbalos*, and twelve *carpinteiros de clavicórdios* (i.e., plucked keyboards, as clavichords would be called *monacórdios*) were recorded in Lisbon. Circumstantial evidence indicates that the early Iberian makers worked in a style related to that of the northern schools, not the Italian. Flemish harpsichords and virginals were well known in Spain and her colonies, and the migration of several

Antwerp masters to Spain towards the end of the sixteenth century provided further opportunities for northern influence. The Bueno harpsichord's musical resources match those of standard Ruckers singles: compass C/E to c^3 and a two-register 8+4 disposition with a buff for the 8. Archaic features of its design and construction, however, appear to have stemmed from pre-Ruckers practices. From various documents, several concerning *claviórganos* (harpsichords combined with organs), which were rather common, one can gather that sixteenth-century harpsichords were frequently made with just an 8-foot stop, that the usual compass was C/E to a^2 (with $g\#^2$, unlike instruments made elsewhere with this range), and that the pitch was usually about a^1 = 385 Hz. Possibly, the nuts in some instruments were on active soundboard, as in the Theewes and Müller harpsichords. In addition to the Low Countries, certain Italian territories, including Milan and Naples, were under Spanish sovereignty. While there is no evidence of Neapolitan instruments in Spain, a virginal in the distinctive heptagonal form made in Milan by Annibale dei Rossi and his son Ferrante was depicted by El Greco in his Annunciation of 1597–1600 (Museo del Prado, Madrid).

In summary, the actions, dispositions, and timbral characteristics of Renaissance quilled keyboards, although varied in form and detail, were well suited to the repertoire. Keys typically had balance (fulcrum) points relatively close to the front, such that players, feeling significant resistance in plucking the strings, would naturally apply a direct and vigorous touch befitting clear and precise performance of the prevalent textures of contrapuntal lines and brilliant diminutions, as well as the punchy chords of lively dances. Girolamo Diruta, in *Il Transilvano* (Venice, 1597), distinguished between the "striking" touch of those who played dances on quilled instruments and the "pressing" touch of good organists. Clarity and rhythmic precision were also enhanced by the instruments' acoustical properties, in particular the crystalline tone of the typical harpsichord's single 8, which could be enhanced in many instruments by a 4 or sometimes by a nasal 8. In 1648, Joannes Ruckers's nephew and successor, Jan Couchet, who had made a bespoke 2×8 harpsichord, wrote to the owner that he would prefer to make an instrument with a 4-foot which "goes quicker and sharper than the unison; it is sweet and lovely in sound."[17] Thus, Couchet still favored the original Renaissance tonal ideal of clarity rather than massiveness.

Finally, one should note that, except for double virginals or the contrivance of stacking a 4-foot virginal on top of an 8-foot instrument, no Renaissance plucked keyboard provided two manuals that could be played simultaneously or in rapid alternation.

The Baroque

After the Renaissance, the history of the harpsichord concerns various adjustments and additions to the basic designs, not fundamental changes. During the baroque period, techniques of performance, composition, and notation were developed to enhance the expressive possibilities of plucked instruments. François Couperin, for one, in *L'art de toucher le clavecin* (Paris, 1716), prescribed the "suppleness" and "gentleness of touch" (*souplesse* and *Douceur du Toucher*) with which, by subtle timing and articulation, the player could give "soul" (*L'âme*) to the harpsichord. To suit this gentler touch, keyboards were made with balance points farther back than in the Renaissance. This resulted in a less resistant sensation of plucking, which gave players more control over the attack and enabled a smoother musical flow when desired.

Parallel to these developments in the solo use of plucked keyboards was their use in a new manner of accompaniment, basso continuo, for which harpsichords had to provide a solid harmonic support. To enhance the requisite gravity of tone, harpsichords were now almost invariably made with two 8-foot choirs. Needless to say, 2×8 or 2×8+4 tutti also became indispensable for the solo repertoire. It is difficult to imagine the bold gestures of a Frescobaldi toccata or a French *sarabande grave* as sounding fully effective if played with a single 8, even when supplemented by a 4. It was a fairly simple matter to alter older harpsichords to update their musical resources by adding a second set of 8-foot strings (sometimes removing the original 4) and by altering or replacing their keyboards. Most extant Renaissance Italian and Ruckers harpsichords survive in their baroque states.

Italian harpsichords (see Figure 1.7), now typically made with two 8-foot stops, were still often constructed with thin walls and provided with separate outer cases, but the so-called "false-inner outer" manner, in which the instrument was built within a thick-walled case with cypress veneer and moldings to simulate the traditional appearance, became increasingly common. Compasses, occasionally still C/E to f^3, were most often C/E to c^3 although, towards the end of the seventeenth century, GG, AA to c^3 was not unusual. These compasses remained common during the first half of the eighteenth century, but later instruments tended to have larger compasses such as FF or GG to f^3. Although the tone of Italian harpsichords has been described as decaying rapidly, these instruments restored or reproduced according to the best modern standards are as resonant and sustaining as any.

By the early eighteenth century, the innovative Bartolomeo Cristofori, inventor of the piano, and other makers in Florence began to make overtly thick-walled instruments. In some of his harpsichords and pianos, he contrived a double-walled construction in which the thick outer wall

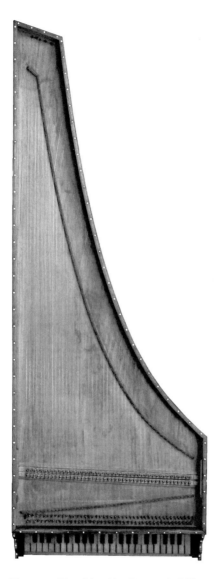

Figure 1.7 Harpsichord by Giacomo Ridolfi, Rome, ca. 1660–ca.1690 (National Music Museum, Vermillion, SD, cat. no. NMM 4657; photograph by the author).

bore the tension of the strings while the soundboard was attached to an unseen separate inner bentside and tail.[18] Florentine harpsichords usually had 90-degree tail angles. Otherwise, they and other Italian makers generally adhered to traditional principles of design, with scaling suitable for brass strings, Pythagorean deep into the bass.

New virginals were seldom made after about 1620 except in Naples where the leading maker, Onofrio Guarracino, continued to make them into the 1690s. Otherwise, to the extent that new small instruments at 8-

foot pitch were needed, makers turned to bentside spinets, the earliest-known example of which was made by Girolamo Zenti, Rome(?), 1637.

With few exceptions, French harpsichords – from the earliest known, by Jean Denis II, Paris, 1648 (Musée de l'Hospice Saint-Roch, Issoudun), to those made just before the storming of the Bastille in 1789 – have two manuals, with 8+4 on the lower, 8 on the upper, and a shove coupler.[19] The earliest unquestionable evidence of such doubles is in the first edition of the aforementioned Jean Denis's *Traité de l'accord de l'espinette* (Paris, 1643), which mentions "harpsichords with two keyboards for passing all the unisons, which the lute cannot do."[20] That is, with one hand on each keyboard with its separate 8-foot stop, the player can cross hands and sound simultaneous unisons. Except, however, for a handful of *pièces croisées*, the entire French harpsichord literature contains very few pieces in which this or any other two-manual registration is necessary. The great *claveciniste* Jean-Henry D'Anglebert, upon his death in 1691, owned four single-manual harpsichords but no double.[21] The two-manual harpsichord might primarily have thrived because it was useful for accompaniment. Saint-Lambert, in his *Nouveau traité de l'accompagnement du clavecin* (Paris, 1707), stated that a singer performing with a very weak "half voice" should be accompanied on the *petit jeu*, i.e., the upper manual, while all the stops should be used for a singer with a strong chest voice. To accommodate performers who issued varied degrees of loud and soft within a movement, the harpsichordist presumably would change manuals.

Seventeenth-century French harpsichords vary greatly in details of construction. Nevertheless, from the Denis of 1648 to about 1690, French harpsichords were quite standardized in their two-manual dispositions and in the details of their keyboards and actions. The compass was GG/BB to c^3, occasionally with one or both of the lowest sharps divided to provide C# and Eb in addition to the AA and BB of the short octave. Three-octave measures were very narrow, about 465 to 470 mm, such that an average hand could span the tenths occasionally required in the literature. Key levers and jacks were light and delicate, as presumably also was the voicing, in accordance with the refined grandeur of these instruments.

Towards the end of the seventeenth century Ruckers harpsichords were becoming so prized in France for their tone that they began to undergo *petit ravalement*, that is, updating with additional 8-foot choirs, and keyboards being modified or replaced. By the early eighteenth century, French makers had absorbed the major Flemish stylistic elements of construction, scaling, and soundboard layout, albeit expanded to suit extended compasses, typically GG to e^3 in the early decades, FF to e^3 into the 1750s, then FF to f^3. Eighteenth-century key levers and jacks were somewhat heavier and less delicate than those of the seventeenth century, and three-octave measures were slightly larger, about 475 mm. Buff stops were not usually included until the 1760s. In general, the tone of the eighteenth-century harpsichords could be characterized as more voluptuous than in those of the seventeenth-century. All along, Ruckers harpsichords underwent radical rebuilding – *grand ravalement* – with enlarged soundboards and cases to accommodate the wider compasses. Fake Ruckers instruments were also made. The very few known French single-manual harpsichords are disposed 2×8. More popular were bentside spinets, a fair number of which have survived from both the seventeenth and eighteenth centuries.

In Antwerp, the last known transposing doubles were made in 1646, after which only singles were produced until the eighteenth century. Although the Ruckers family began to make a few harpsichords with two 8 choirs as early as the mid-1630s, the last master of the Ruckers dynasty, Joseph Joannes Couchet, continued to make harpsichords with the traditional 8+4 until the end of his career, about 1680, albeit with compasses sometimes extended to nearly five octaves. A single by Joris Britsen III, Antwerp, 1681 (Museum Vleeshuis, Antwerp), had the compass GG/BB to c^3 with three choirs and registers, of which the second 8 was nasal. The most prominent eighteenth-century maker was Johann Daniel Dulcken, whose impressive surviving instruments date from 1745 to 1755. His doubles, all with compass FF to f^3, were usually disposed with 8+4 on the lower manual, 8-foot dogleg, and nasal 8-foot on the upper. Although registrations with an independent solo 8 on each manual were not possible, there were other interesting options.

Harpsichord making in the German-speaking areas was scattered among regional centers, not concentrated in national capitals like Paris and London. Styles varied from region to region, and musicians, such as J. S. Bach, who traveled among them would have encountered many different kinds of harpsichords.[22] Because many German harpsichords were made as a sideline by organ builders and virtually all professional harpsichordists were primarily organists, ideas from organ building had significant influence. In 1662 the prominent Westphalian organ builder Hans Henrich Bader made a large harpsichord with four registers, 2×8+4 and an *archispinetto*, presumably an 8-foot nasal stop, at the time a fairly normal disposition for German single-manual instruments. The contemporary account added, however, that "these stops can be interchanged in a special way or be used and played simultaneously on two keyboards."[23] This is the earliest evidence of a two-manual harpsichord in Germany. Bader, if he did not independently adopt the idea of multiple keyboards from the organ, must have been influenced at least indirectly by recent developments in France.

Ruckers harpsichords were well known in northern Germany, some, no doubt, brought there at the behest of J. P. Sweelinck's many German pupils. A group portrait by Johannes Voorhout, 1674 (Museum für Hamburgische Geschichte), includes Dietrich Buxtehude and Sweelinck's grand-pupil Johann Adam Reinken, with the latter seated at a Flemish double. Several Ruckers instruments that underwent *ravalement* in northern Germany are known, for example, a Joannes Ruckers double of 1618 (Kulturhistoriska Museet, Lund) rebuilt in Hamburg in 1724 by Johann Christoph Fleischer with aligned GG/BB to c^3 keyboards. Although the harpsichords made in Hamburg by members of the Fleischer and Hass families have S-shaped bentsides, they show the strong influence of Ruckers principles of scaling, design, and construction. Hamburg singles were usually 2×8+4, but as late as the 1720s, these builders did make some single-manual harpsichords with the same 8+4 disposition favored by the Ruckerses. Each of the surviving doubles by Hieronymus Albrecht Hass (1689–1752), with compasses from FF (or GG in one) to c^3, d^3, or f^3, has a different elaborate disposition: 2×8+4 on the lower manual and 8 on the upper, each 8 with its own strings; 16+8+4 on the lower, 8+4 on the upper; 16+8+4 on the lower, the upper with 8 and nasal 8 sharing the same strings; and one by his son, Johann Adolph Hass, with 16+8+4+2 on the lower, the upper with 8 and a 2 up to c^2.[24] The elder Hass's magnum opus was a three-manual instrument of 1740 (private collection), compass FF, GG to f^3, with 16+2 on the lower manual, 8+4 on the middle, and a dogleg 8 on the middle and upper, which also has a nasal 8. These instruments, which were also supplied with various couplers and buff stops, clearly show the influence of the organ aesthetic in the provision both of choruses consisting of stops at different octaves (16+8+4+2) and of colorful stops such as nasal registers. With one exception, the 16-foot strings of Hass harpsichords were provided with their own bridge, thus were longer and closer to their ideal lengths than if they shared the 8-foot bridge. Many North German harpsichords were exported to Scandinavia, where native makers worked in a similar style.

In Berlin, the leading maker, Michael Mietke (ca. 1656/1671–1719), reportedly sold some of his harpsichords as French imports. Presumably these had the standard French disposition, as does his one surviving double (Schloss Charlottenburg, Berlin), made about 1703–1713, originally with compass FF, GG, AA to c^3. His two known singles are disposed 2×8. The large two-manual Mietke harpsichord that Bach purchased for the Köthen court in 1719 might, like two other harpsichords Mietke is known to have made, have had a 16-foot stop.

From registrations indicated in C. P. E. Bach's Sonata in D minor (Wq69), composed in 1747 while he was court harpsichordist in Berlin, one can reconstruct the instrument's four-register disposition: lower manual with 8+4, upper with 8 and nasal 8 (probably with its own strings), coupler, and buff for the upper 8. The registrations in the final movement, a set of nine variations, are particularly imaginative, including the buffed upper 8 coupled to the 4; solo 4 accompanied by the buffed upper 8; and 2×8 on the upper manual accompanying 8+4 on the lower.

The Thuringian organist Jacob Adlung wrote in his *Anleitung zu der musikalischen Gelahrtheit* (Erfurt, 1758) that harpsichords, while they sometimes had one or four sets of strings, usually had two, most often 2×8 but occasionally 8+16, or three, presumably most frequently 2×8+4. Four-choired instruments were either 2×8+2×4 or 16+2×8+4, presumably spread over two manuals. He went on to describe doubles with two stops on the lower manual, one on the upper, and a coupler, and the possibility of adding extra registers to both manuals. An anonymous early eighteenth-century Thuringian 2×8 single (Bachhaus, Eisenach), has the archaic feature of the nut on active soundboard. An early eighteenth-century double by a member of the Harrass family in Großbreitenbach (Schlossmuseum, Sondershausen) has the standard French disposition while another (Musikinstrumenten-Museum, Berlin), once thought to have belonged to J. S. Bach, was originally made with 16+4 on the lower manual, 8 on the upper, with shove coupler, and later rebuilt with 16+8 on the lower manual, 8+4 on the upper.[25] As discussed in the chapter on Bach, its acceptance in the twentieth century as the "Bach" disposition has fallen out of favor. Nevertheless, a similarly disposed instrument advertised in a Leipzig newspaper in 1775 had been made by Zacharias Hildebrandt (1688–1757), who was closely associated with Bach during his Leipzig years.

Two-manual harpsichords made in Saxony by members of the Gräbner family in Dresden from the 1720s to 1780s and Gottfried Silbermann (1683–1753) in Freiberg, as well as by the latter's relatives in Strasbourg, mostly with compass FF to f^3, have the standard two-manual French disposition, although sometimes with a dogleg rather than shove coupler.[26] Among the Strasbourg Silbermanns, Gottfried's nephew Johann Heinrich (1727–1799), who made particularly beautiful spinets, also reportedly made a harpsichord with a 16-foot stop. Unlike North German harpsichords, those by Saxon and Thuringian makers show little if any Flemish influence.

As for southern Germany, Switzerland, and Austria, it seems that the typical harpsichord in these regions had a single manual with a 2×8 disposition, although there is a double with the standard French disposition by Peter Hellen, Bern, 1759 (Württembergisches Landesmuseum, Stuttgart).[27] From the late seventeenth century to about 1780, a distinctive style of harpsichord was made in Vienna.[28] Although certain features varied – some instruments had separate angled tails, others S-shaped bentsides – others were constant: the single-manual 2×8 disposition, scaling for brass strings throughout the compass, Italian-style box guides, and downward-sloping upper edges of spine and cheekpiece around the keyboard as in later Viennese pianos. Except in the two latest known examples, both made in 1778, with compass FF to f³, they had a "Viennese bass octave" beginning on FF; then a natural key divided into three front to back for GG, AA, and BB♭; a natural divided into two for C and BB♮; F; a divided sharp for D and F♯; G; a divided sharp for E and G♯; then in normal chromatic order. Any hand could play such widely spaced left-hand chords as the GG-G-b at the end of Joseph Haydn's Capriccio "Acht Sauschneider müssen sein" (HobXVII:1). The compasses end variously with c³, d³, e³, f³, and g³. Two spinets (technically, polygonal virginals with bentsides at the right) made by tuners to the imperial court theater in Vienna are known, dated 1799 and 1804.

More elaborate harpsichords were known in Vienna. Shortly after settling there in 1781, Mozart wrote to his father that "We have two *Flügel* in my residence, one for playing *Galanterie* and the other a machine with a lower octave throughout [i.e., 16-foot stop], like the one we had in London[!], therefore like an organ. On this, then, I've improvised and played fugues."[29] Although the term *Flügel*, referring to the form of the instruments, admits the possibility that the first of these had a hammer action, the second was doubtless a two-manual harpsichord. Imported English two-manual harpsichords were also known in Vienna.

In England, virginals fell out of fashion towards the end of the seventeenth century, their place taken by bentside spinets (Figure 1.8), at first modeled after French instruments. With burgeoning prosperity, the market for spinets, harpsichords, and eventually pianos was ever increasing. About 1690 a new style of single-manual harpsichord came into fashion.[30] Instead

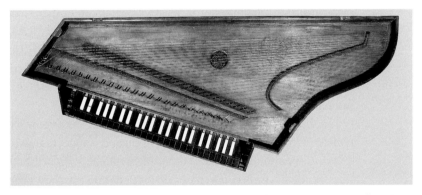

Figure 1.8 Spinet by Charles Haward, London, 1689 (National Music Museum, Vermillion, SD, cat. no. NMM 10773; photograph by Bill Willroth, Sr., courtesy National Music Museum).

of the colorful three-register dispositions of earlier English harpsichords, these, scaled for brass throughout the compass, have just two 8 stops. Some have S-shaped bentsides, others angled tails, a variability also found in spinets of the period. The earliest surviving example, by Thomas Barton, London, 1709 (Edinburgh University Collection) has a GG/BB to d^3 compass with the two lowest sharps divided, while the latest examples, made about 1725, have the GG to g^3 compass which by then and into the second half of the century was the usual compass of spinets. A portrait of George Frideric Handel painted by Philippe Mercier in the late 1720s (Handel House Museum, London) shows him seated by a harpsichord of this type. The earliest-known English two-manual harpsichord, by Joseph Tisseran, London, 1700 (Bate Collection, Oxford), with compass GG/BB to d^3, has 8 +4 on the lower manual and an 8-foot dogleg shared with the upper. A letter sent to the purchaser of this harpsichord in 1712 advised: the "three Setts of Strings . . . all together are only a thoroughbass to a Consort: for Lessons [i.e., solo pieces] any two sets of the three are more proper."[31] A harpsichord with this disposition but compass GG, AA to d^3, e^3 was made by Francis Coston, London about 1725 (Edinburgh University Collection).

The standard model of English double as made in large numbers from the 1720s to the end of the century has a substantial case with walls of oak handsomely veneered (see Figure 1.9). Unlike earlier English instruments, they show Ruckers influence in the overall manner of construction, soundboard structure, and scaling principles. The keyboards, with a three-octave measure of 485 mm, have the compass FF to f^3, without FF♯ until the 1770s. The disposition is 8+4 on the lower manual and an 8-foot dogleg shared with the upper, which has, in addition, a nasal 8 plucking the same strings; there is a buff stop for one of the 8 choirs. The two rival firms founded by Burkat Shudi (1702–1773) and Jacob Kirckman (1710–1792) dominated English harpsichord making until its demise. Shudi occasionally made doubles with keyboards extending down to CC. His and Kirckman's single-manual harpsichords, all FF to f^3 in compass, are usually disposed 2×8+4, sometimes just 2×8, rarely also with a nasal 8. The tone of these instruments, single or double, is more brilliant than that of the French instruments, direct and imposing rather than sensuous and subtle. One might similarly compare the harpsichord suites of Handel with those of François Couperin.

In some regions of Spain, very old-fashioned harpsichords continued to be made, for example, a single by Zeferino Fernández, Valladolid, 1750 (Fundación Joaquín Díaz, Urueña), compass GG/BB to c^3 (8+4).[32] Elsewhere, however, more progressive instruments are known, although none with two manuals. Examples include a harpsichord attributed to Francisco Pérez Mirabal, Seville, 1734 (private collection, England), GG/

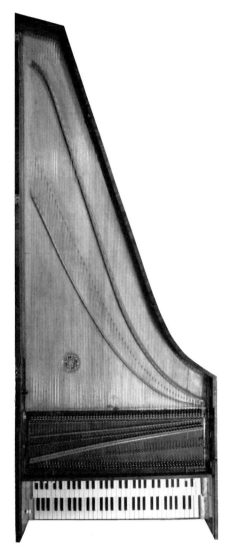

Figure 1.9 Harpsichord by Joseph Kirckman, London, 1798 (National Music Museum, Vermillion, SD, cat. no. NMM 3328; photograph by the author).

BB to c^3, 2×8 scaled for iron in the treble, with an S-shaped bentside; another, possibly made in Salamanca province (private collection, USA), with the same characteristics but scaled for brass throughout; an anonymous instrument (Museo Arqueológico Nacional, Madrid), compass C to c^3, 2×8+4, buff to one 8, also with an S-shaped bentside. A harpsichord by Salvator Bofill, Barcelona, 1743 (Museo de Arte Sacro, Bilbao), C/E to c^3, 2×8, closely resembles Italian instruments.

The growing influx of Italian musicians to Spain and Portugal, epitomized by Domenico Scarlatti's arrival in Lisbon in 1719, had a profound effect on

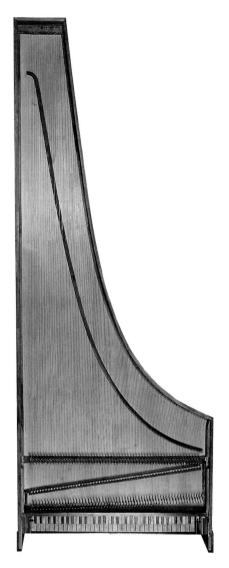

Figure 1.10 Harpsichord by José Calisto, Portugal, 1780 (National Music Museum, Vermillion, SD, cat. no. NMM 6204; photograph by Bill Willroth, Sr., courtesy National Music Museum).

Iberian harpsichord making.[33] Florentine instruments by Bartolomeo Cristofori and his followers came to the Portuguese court, then to Spain upon Scarlatti's transferal there along with his pupil, Princess Maria Barbara. She owned nine harpsichords at the time of her death in 1758, of which only one, a Flemish instrument with three sets of strings, doubtless 2×8+4, might have had two manuals. Most of the others were made by the Madrid-based Diego Fernández (1703–1775), who worked for the Spanish royal family from 1722 until his death. As Ralph Kirkpatrick noted, "The only instruments in the Queen's possession on which the full five-octave sonatas of Scarlatti could have been played were the three Spanish harpsichords with sixty-one notes and two registers!"[34] The one surviving harpsichord attributable to Fernández (Smithsonian Institution, Washington) closely resembles Florentine models in scaling and layout, but the materials and details of construction demonstrate its Spanish origin.[35] With GG to g^3 compass, the instrument is disposed 2×8, with no provision to turn either register off, entirely consistent with Kirkpatrick's observation that "Scarlatti sonatas do not seem to call for a harpsichord with a wide variety of registers; his writing itself is too colorful."[36]

Similar Florence-inspired harpsichords were made in Portugal, for example, one by José Calisto, 1780 (Figure 1.10). In this instrument, the back 8-foot register can be turned off, leaving on the permanently engaged front 8, for which there is a buff stop.

The Classical Era

The harpsichord was as familiar as the piano to musicians of Haydn and Mozart's generation, and many fine harpsichords insignificantly different from earlier instruments were made throughout Europe during the 1780s and 1790s. Inevitably, however, there were efforts to render the harpsichord more capable of that manner of expressivity which relies on actual, rather than feigned, shadings of loud and soft. Further, there was a gradual change of taste towards roundness of tone. Charles Burney (1726–1814), writing near the end of his life, noted that the tone of grand pianos had so improved towards the end of the eighteenth century that "the harsh scratching of the quills of a harpsichord can now no longer be borne."[37]

Leaving aside efforts that fundamentally altered the nature of the instrument – most notably Cristofori's invention of the piano by substituting hammers for jacks – we may also dismiss the many one-time creations of no lasting import, such as a harpsichord with four choirs, five registers, and ten pedals made by Diego Fernández in response to a whim of Queen Maria Barbara. A consequential innovation, developed by the prominent French maker Pascal Taskin in 1768, was a register with plectra of *peau de buffle*, a thick soft leather. According to a contemporary account:

> From the effect of this leather on the string of the instrument there resulted delicious and velvety sounds. One increased the sound at will by pressing more or less hard on the keyboard. By this means one obtained rich, pithy, and suave tones, voluptuous to the most epicurean ear ... The *buffle* obeys the pressure of the finger; it does not pluck any more but caresses the string.[38]

Taskin and other Parisian makers usually installed the *peau de buffle* as an addition to the three quilled stops of standard doubles and included a mechanism to control the registers by knee to vary the timbre and volume as one played.

Most late eighteenth-century English harpsichords had a pedal, the "machine stop," which, pushed down, effected a decrescendo on the lower manual and exchanged the dogleg for the nasal 8 on the upper. In 1769 Burkat Shudi introduced the Venetian swell, a set of louvers over the strings that could be opened by a pedal to create a crescendo effect. After the mid-1770s Shudi's successor John Broadwood often made plectra of soft leather faced with a thin layer of glove leather for the lower-manual 8-foot register (or the back 8 in singles).[39] Similar plectra are described in a pamphlet published in Rome in 1775. The anonymous author, calling his invention the *cembalo angelico*, recommended that each jack be provided with two tongues facing in opposite directions, one with leather plectra, the other with quill. A register moved in one direction or the other by a pedal would sound alternatively with hard or soft plectra. Two harpsichords by Vincenzio Sodi, Florence, 1782 and 1798, have such double-tongued jacks; late Italian makers sometimes used hard sole leather instead of quill.

Revival

Except for a few virginals outwardly resembling square pianos made in northern Italy as late as 1839, production of plucked keyboards ceased by 1810. Increased interest in early music towards the end of the nineteenth century led to a revival of the harpsichord, but because the traditions of harpsichord making had been lost during the intervening decades, it fell to piano makers to produce new ones. In doing so, they applied their own techniques of design and construction, such that most harpsichords made from the late nineteenth century to the 1950s were saddled with ponderous keyboards, massive cases, and thick, heavily ribbed soundboards like those of modern pianos. As if to compensate for the deficient tone issued by the unresonant soundboards, hard steel strings, and leather plectra of these "plucked pianos," the larger models were provided with 16-foot stops and pedals to change registrations while playing. Although such devices were known during the eighteenth century, the early revivalists applied them out of all proportion to historical precedent, and performers generally employed them without regard to chronology or style. Instruments such as the Pleyel harpsichords promoted by Wanda Landowska, however, retain a certain interest as the media for which composers including Francis Poulenc, Manuel de Falla, and Frank Martin conceived significant works. Enhanced by amplification and manipulative recording techniques, harpsichords of the early modern type have found much use in pop and rock music and for special effects in film and television scores.

After the Second World War, harpsichord makers began to produce instruments designed and constructed like those of the historical masters, and by the 1960s these were favored by leading performers of the era. For the past half-century, most new harpsichords have been copied, at least nominally, after historical models.

Notes

1. General surveys include Raymond Russell, *The Harpsichord and Clavichord: An Introductory Study*; Frank Hubbard, *Three Centuries of Harpsichord Making*; Donald H. Boalch, *Makers of the Harpsichord and Clavichord, 1440–1840*; and John Koster, "Reflections on Historical Harpsichord Registration" (see further reading).
2. Further details about these structural elements can be found in Hubbard, *Three Centuries of Harpsichord Making*; and "Harpsichord" in *The New Grove Dictionary of Music and Musicians*, second edition, Stanley Sadie and John Tyrrell, eds. (London: Macmillan Publishers, 2001).
3. Matters in this section are discussed further in Koster, "Toward a History of the Earliest Harpsichords," in *Das österreichische Cembalo: 600 Jahre Cembalobau in Österreich*, Alfons Huber, ed. (Tutzing: Hans Schneider, 2001), pp. 17–33, and "The Harpsichord Actions of Henry Arnault de Zwolle in Their Developmental Context," in *Unisonus: Musikinstrumente erforschen, bewahren, sammeln*, Beatrix Darmstädter and Ina Hoheisel, eds. (Vienna: Praesens, 2014), pp. 167–196.
4. See Edmund A. Bowles, "A Checklist of Fifteenth-Century Representations of Stringed Keyboard Instruments," in *Keyboard Instruments: Studies in Keyboard Organology, 1500–1800*, Edwin M. Ripin, ed. (Edinburgh: Edinburgh University Press, 1971), pp. 11–17.
5. Henry also described a striking action, but this was seldom if ever made.
6. The matters in this section are discussed further in John Koster, "Pitch and Transposition Before the Ruckers," in *Kielinstrumente aus der Werkstatt Ruckers* (Bericht über die Internationale Konferenz, September 1996; Schriften des Händel-Hauses in Halle, 14), Christiane Rieche, ed. (Halle an der Saale: Händel-Haus, 1998), pp. 73–94; "Transposition and Tuning from Schlick to Sweelinck," *The Organ Yearbook* 41 (2012), 59–90; and "Questions of Keyboard Temperament in the Sixteenth Century," in *Interpreting Historical Keyboard Music: Sources, Contexts and Performance*, Andrew Woolley and John Kitchen, eds. (London: Ashgate, 2013), pp. 115–130.
7. Denzil Wraight, *The Stringing of Italian Keyboard Instruments c.1500 – c.1650* (PhD diss., The Queen's University of Belfast, 1996/1997), provides a thorough survey of Italian harpsichord making.
8. See Koster, "The Early Neapolitan School of Harpsichord Making," in *Domenico Scarlatti en España / Domenico Scarlatti in Spain*, Luisa Morales, ed. (Garrucha, Almería, Spain: Asociación Cultural LEAL, 2009), pp. 47–80.

9.   Early German harpsichords are surveyed in John Henry van der Meer, "Beiträge zur Cembalobau im deutschen Sprachgebiet bis 1700," *Anzeiger des Germanischen Nationalmuseums* (Nuremberg) 1966, pp. 103–133.

10.   See Grant O'Brien, *Ruckers: a Harpsichord and Virginal Building Tradition* (Cambridge: Cambridge University Press, 1990); Jeannine Lambrechts-Douillez and Koster, "Master Joos Karest and the Rise of Clavecimbel Making in Antwerp," *Musique-Images-Instruments* 6 (2004), pp. 116–131; and Koster, "The Musical Uses of Ruckers Harpsichords in Their Own Time," in *The Golden Age of Flemish Harpsichord Making: A Study of the MIM's Ruckers Instruments*, Pascale Vandervellen, ed. (Brussels: Musical Instruments Museum, 2017), pp. 50–69 and 399–404.

11.   Hubbard, *Three Centuries*, p. 133.

12.   Recent publications about the early English school are Malcolm Rose, "Further on the Lodewijk Theewes Harpsichord," *Galpin Society Journal* 55 (2002), pp. 279–309, Darryl Martin, *The English Virginal* (PhD diss., University of Edinburgh, 2003), and Rose, "The History and Significance of the Lodewijk Theewes Claviorgan," *Early Music* 32, no. 4 (November 2004), pp. 577–593.

13.   See Bruce Haynes, *A History of Performing Pitch: The Story of "A"* (Lanham, Maryland: Scarecrow Press, 2002), pp. 88ff.

14.   See Darryl Martin, "The Native Tradition in Transition: English Harpsichords circa 1680–1725," in *The Historical Harpsichord, volume five: Aspects of Harpsichord Making in the British Isles*, John Koster, ed. (Hillsdale, NY: Pendragon Press, 2010), pp. 1–115, specifically 36ff.

15.   Matters in this and the following paragraphs are discussed further in Koster, "The Harpsichord in Seventeenth-Century France," in *Cembalo, Clavecin, Harpsichord: Regionale Traditionen des Cembalobaus*, Christian Ahrens and Gregor Klinke, eds. (Munich and Salzburg: Musikverlag Katzbichler, 2011), pp. 10–42.

16.   Matters in this paragraph are discussed further in Koster, "Traditional Iberian Harpsichord Making in Its European Context," *Galpin Society Journal* 61 (2008), pp. 3–78.

17.   O'Brien, *Ruckers*, p. 306.

18.   See Kerstin Schwarz, *Bartolomeo Cristofori: Hammerflügel und Cembali im Vergleich* (*Scripta Artium* 2, Universität Leipzig, 2001; Halle an der Saale: Verlag Janos Stekovics, 2002).

19.   Matters in this and the following paragraphs are discussed further in Koster, "The Harpsichord in Seventeenth-Century France." Two provincial instruments have only a doglegged 4 on the upper manual.

20.   Translation adapted from Hubbard, *Three Centuries*, p. 123; original text on p. 17 of the 1643 edition and p. 13 of the 1650 edition.

21.   See Hubbard, *Three Centuries*, p. 315.

22.   See Koster, "The Harpsichord Culture in Bach's Environs," in *Bach Perspectives* 4, *The Music of J.S. Bach: Analysis and Interpretation*, David Schulenberg, ed. (Lincoln, NE: University of Nebraska Press, 1999), pp. 57–77.

23.   Hugo Wohnfurter, *Die Orgelbauerfamilie Bader 1600–1742* (Kassel: Bärenreiter, 1981), p. 193.

24. Hass harpsichords are described in Lancelot Whitehead, *The Clavichords of Hieronymous and Johann Hass* (PhD diss., University of Edinburgh, 1994), pp. 321–333.

25. Dieter Krickeberg and Horst Rase, "Beiträge zur Kenntnis des mittel- und norddeutschen Cembalobaus um 1700," in *Studia Organologica: Festschrift für John Henry van der Meer zu seinem fünfundsechzigsten Geburtstag*, Freidemann Hellwig, ed. (Tutzing: Hans Schneider, 1987), pp. 294–302.

26. See John Phillips, "The 1739 Johann Heinrich Gräbner Harpsichord – an Oddity or a *Bach-Flügel*?," in *Das deutsche Cembalo*, Christian Ahrens and Gregor Klinke, eds. (Munich and Salzburg: Musikverlag Katzbichler, 2000), pp. 123–139, and Philippe Fritsch, *Les ateliers alsatien et saxon de la dynastie Silbermann: étude des "Claviers" et du répertoire musical, leur influence réciproque* (PhD diss., Université François-Rabelais, Tours, 1995).

27. See Michael Latcham, "The Musical Instruments *en forme de clavecin* by, and Attributed to, the Workshop of Johann Ludwig Hellen," *Musique-Images-Instruments* 6 (2004), pp. 68–94.

28. See Huber, *Das österreichische Cembalo* and Richard Maunder, *Keyboard Instruments in Eighteenth-Century Vienna* (Oxford: Clarendon Press, 1998).

29. *Mozarts Briefe*, Ludwig Kohl, ed. (Salzburg, 1865), p. 302.

30. See Martin, "The Native Tradition."

31. Hubbard, *Three Centuries*, p. 153.

32. Matters in this paragraph are discussed further in Koster, "Traditional Iberian Harpsichord Making."

33. See Koster, "Towards an Optimal Instrument: Domenico Scarlatti and the New Wave of Iberian Harpsichord Making," *Early Music* 35, no. 4 (November 2007), pp. 575–604.

34. Ralph Kirkpatrick, *Domenico Scarlatti* (Princeton: Princeton University Press, 1953), p. 179.

35. See Koster, "A Spanish Harpsichord from Domenico Scarlatti's Environs," *Early Music* 39, no. 2 (May 2011), pp. 245–251, and "A Harpsichord by Diego Fernández?," *Galpin Society Journal* 64 (2011), pp. 5–48.

36. *Scarlatti*, p. 177.

37. Abraham Rees, ed., *The Cyclopædia*, Vol. 17 (London, 1819), s.v. "Harpsichord."

38. Hubbard, *Three Centuries*, p. 252.

39. John Barnes, "Boxwood Tongues and Original Leather Plectra in Eighteenth-Century English Harpsichords," *Galpin Society Journal* 54 (April 2001), pp. 10–15.

Further Reading

Boalch, Donald H. *Makers of the Harpsichord and Clavichord, 1440–1840*. Third revised edition by Charles Mould. Oxford: Clarendon Press, 1995.

Hubbard, Frank. *Three Centuries of Harpsichord Making*. Cambridge, MA: Harvard University Press, 1965.

Koster, John. "Reflections on Historical Harpsichord Registration." *Keyboard Perspectives* 8 (2015), pp. 95–131.

Russell, Raymond. *The Harpsichord and Clavichord: An Introductory Study*. London: Faber and Faber. 1959.

2 The Virginalists

PIETER DIRKSEN

The first half of the sixteenth century witnessed a great flowering of organ composition in England, consisting mainly of music based on liturgical melodies. However, this development was for the greater part cut short by the Reformation, to be continued only in an idealized way by musicians such as John Blitheman, John Bull, and Thomas Tomkins. By ca. 1570 the genre was largely replaced by secular keyboard music for plucked keyboard instruments, a repertoire that would develop into an even more important tradition. We have only a few pieces from before that period that provide the background for the flowering afterwards, such as the handful of secular pieces found in the manuscripts "RA 58" and "Mulliner." Most notable are the three works from "RA 58," all of them grounds that include a vigorous *Hornpipe* by Hugh Aston (ca. 1485–1558). More substantial is the "Dublin Virginal Manuscript" that originated around 1570 in London, at a time when William Byrd's novel keyboard approach must already have been in full swing. It consists of thirty dances: pavans, galliards, almandes and corantos often based on Franco-Flemish and Italian ground patterns and, as a rule, set with a florid treble supported by a simple rhythmically enlivened left-hand part.

There can be little doubt that the term "virginals" was used generically in England for all plucked instruments, including the harpsichord. Henry VIII possessed many, such as a "longe virginalls made harp fashion"; that is, a harpsichord.[1] However, the actual virginal as described below seems to have been the instrument of choice. For example, there is the eloquent testimony in *Parthenia* that it contains "the first musicke that ever was printed for the virginalls" as the title page has it, along with a depiction of a woman playing the instrument. There also survives a fine Venetian virginal made by Giovanni Antonio Baffo that belonged to Queen Elizabeth.

Regarding the instrument itself, it is important to note that English (and Italian) virginals were all of the "spinet" type, with a plucking point close to the bridge, as opposed to the Flemish "*muselars*," with a central plucking point and a much different sound. It is indeed surprising how the repertoire comes alive on these simple instruments with only a single set of strings and no registrational possibilities. Byrd remains rather conservative in his demands of the range, often being content with the old-fashioned thirty-eight-note keyboard of F, G, A to g^2, a^2 or forty-two-note C/E to a^2, though a few pieces use F♯ and G♯ in the bottom octave as well. C, D, E to a^2 remained the standard range with the later virginalists, occasionally using the low AA as well. The standard tuning for the repertoire was meantone, in all likelihood of the ⅕-comma type with slightly larger than pure major thirds, and with a choice of either E♭s or D♯s.[2] This seems to be confirmed by the fact that many virginalist pieces (especially those of Byrd) have a final harmony with the major third in the treble.

Virginalists and Sources

The most important composer for the virginal by far was William Byrd (1540–1623). A pupil of Thomas Tallis, Byrd was organist at Lincoln from 1563–1572 and in 1573 became Gentleman at the Chapel Royal in London, where from 1575 onwards he served as organist. In this capacity he developed into the leading English composer of his time, becoming equally proficient in writing for the Roman Catholic rites (masses and motets) and those of the Reformed church (anthems and services), as well as secular songs, madrigals, and instrumental music. The result was a vast oeuvre without parallel in its day in terms of scope and variety. While many of Byrd's continental peers were also expert keyboard improvisers, Byrd was the first of the "mainstream" composers to give equal status and importance to both keyboard and polyphonic vocal music. The sonic potential of the harpsichord and virginal allowed him to develop a very personal and expressive keyboard style, while still paying lip service to the cantus-firmus tradition for organ in his early pieces. However, Byrd soon abandoned strictly polyphonic music idiomatic to the organ and developed a freer approach eminently suited for plucked instruments, applying this new style to as many genres as were available to him: pavans and galliards, variations, grounds, fantasias, hexachord settings, and smaller dances. Considering Byrd's renown, it is not surprising that his music can be found in many sources, the most important of which are Nevell, Fitzwilliam, *Parthenia*, Forster, and Weelkes. *My Ladye Nevells Booke* (Nevell) was written under his supervision and completed in 1591; its forty-two pieces form an anthology of his best keyboard music written up to that date. He is, moreover, the best-represented composer in the other sources, which all date from well after 1600.

Although other virginalist-composers were heavily influenced by Byrd, their output does not compare to their aged mentor in terms of quality and depth. Nevertheless, almost all of them managed to produce a number of masterpieces, particularly John Bull (ca. 1563–1628), the only virginalist who left a keyboard oeuvre of comparable size to Byrd's. Between 1574 and 1582, Bull was Child at the Chapel Royal, where his organ tutor was John Blitheman, whom he succeeded in 1591. In those years he was no doubt also taught by Byrd. In 1613 Bull was forced to flee England because of a sex scandal and spent a brief period at the Brussels Archducal court before moving on to Antwerp, where he became cathedral organist in 1617. Here he continued to write keyboard music, although Flemish sources of his music are not very reliable and are thus the main impediment in establishing the authenticity of his keyboard works.[3] The foremost keyboard virtuoso of his day, Bull composed very little beyond this realm, thus explaining why many of his pieces demand a high degree of technical proficiency by the player. His music, moreover, reveals an interesting mixture of the old organ style of his teacher Blitheman and the new one of Byrd, combined with some highly personal idiosyncratic and sometimes even eccentric tendencies. The main sources for his pre-1613 music are the probably holograph manuscript Paris 1185, containing seventy pieces, and the Fitzwilliam, with about fifty pieces.

Bull had been confronted by a serious rival during his final years at the Chapel Royal, in the person of the Oxfordian Orlando Gibbons (1583–1625), who was appointed in 1605 as Bull's organist colleague. Although considered by some as "the best finger of that age," comparatively little remains of Gibbons's keyboard music that, with its emphasis on learned contrapuntal work and controlled keyboard virtuosity, represents perhaps the most direct continuation of Byrd's style.[4] In contrast with the other major virginalists, the source situation for Gibbons's keyboard music is less than ideal. No autographs or other manuscripts close to the composer have been preserved, and he is only poorly represented in Fitzwilliam – a fact that has been attributed to the Catholic bias of its compiler, Francis Tregian. Only the Cosyn Manuscript contains a fair amount of his keyboard music. On the other hand, he was in all likelihood the editor of the 1613 *Parthenia*, which includes six outstanding pieces by him.

Thomas Tomkins (1572–1656) was a pupil of Byrd from 1594–1596, and subsequently organist and choirmaster at Worcester Cathedral, a post he held for a full half-century. In 1646 the Civil War reached the city, resulting in the suspension of services and the destruction of the organ. Tomkins also worked as Gentleman Extraordinary and from 1625 was Gibbons's successor as organist at the Chapel Royal. Like Byrd and Gibbons, his main focus as a composer was on vocal polyphony. Not much keyboard music from his early years survives – principally the five brilliant pieces included in Fitzwilliam. We would have been in an even worse situation than we are with Gibbons had it not been for the chance survival of a very late autograph (Paris 1122, in itself the sole survivor of a whole set of keyboard manuscripts) that contains music written by Tomkins at a very advanced age, between 1647 and 1654. These pieces show a staunchly conservative composer reviving the grand virginalist tradition in a very personal way.

Byrd's pupil Thomas Morley (ca. 1558–1602), a famous madrigalist and the author of an important treatise (*A Plaine and Easie Introduction to Practicall Musicke*, 1597), left a dozen or so pieces of varying quality. More important are the works of another early Byrd pupil, Peter Philips (1560/61–1628). He left England as a Catholic recusant as early as 1582 and, after much traveling, settled in the southern Netherlands in 1590, becoming principal organist at the Archducal court in Brussels in 1597. His keyboard music contains a fascinating mixture of English, Italian, and Flemish elements. An "amateur" composer of considerable merit was Giles Farnaby (ca. 1563–1640), a wood joiner and probably virginal maker by trade. He is well represented in the Fitzwilliam, and his music shows him to be an ardent follower of Bull, though with a distinctly personal if not whimsical touch. The same cannot be said of Benjamin Cosyn (ca. 1590–1653) who was a true Bull epigone by taking many models and melodies treated by Bull and expanding upon them ad infinitum. Through Cosyn's hands survive two major manuscripts: Paris 1185, the primary source for Bull, and the Cosyn Manuscript, which transmits not only his own works but also a significant portion of those by Gibbons.

The composers mentioned above were surrounded by a host of minor figures who left behind at most a handful of works for the virginal: John Mundy, Richard Farnaby (son of Giles), John Tomkins (brother of Thomas), William Inglott, William Tisdale, William Brown, John Lugge, Ferdinando Richardson, Thomas Weelkes, Martin Peerson, and others.

Pavans and Galliards

An especially striking feature of the Dublin Virginal Manuscript is the focus on pavan and galliard pairs. No fewer than six such pairs are specifically mentioned as such, and the collection places four of them at the head, beginning with a weighty "Passing Measures" setting. This genre remained central throughout the virginalist era and nowhere more so than with William Byrd, who enriched this basically homophonic style with a thoroughly polyphonic approach, particularly in the pavans. According to Byrd's pupil Morley, the pavan is "a kind of staide musicke, ordained for grave dauncing, and most commonlie made of three straines, whereof everie straine is plaid or song twice; a straine they make to containe 8.

Table 2.1 *William Byrd, Pavans and Galliards in Nevell (1591)*

1. Pavan and Galliard c1[5]	
2. Pavan and Galliard G2	
3. Pavan and Galliard a1	
4. Pavan and Galliard C1	
5. Pavan and Galliard c2	
6. Pavan and Galliard C2	Kinborough Good
7. Pavan G6	Canon: 2 in 1
8. Pavan a4	
9. Pavan and Galliard g1	Passing Measures
10. Pavan and Galliard g2	William Petre

12. or 16. semibreves as they list ... in this musicke you must cast your music by foure ... After every pavan we usually set a galliard ... This is a lighter and more stirring kinde of dauncing then the pavane, consisting of the same number of straines."[6] Byrd emphasized the prime importance of this genre in Nevell by numbering them consecutively from one to ten – the only genre thus treated and therefore indeed forming the heart of the collection (see Table 2.1).

The original plan was a series of nine works crowned by the monumental double setting of the *passamezzo antico* ("Passing Measures"), found as a closed entity as numbers 10–25 in the manuscript, only to be augmented towards the end of the book by a freshly composed pair (numbers 39–40). Byrd clearly thought highly of this pair, as can be seen by its inclusion in *Parthenia* twenty-two years later, with only minor revisions and the addition of a trendy little prelude. That we are dealing here with a chronological ordering is confirmed by the nature of the first pair, which, according to an annotation by Tregian in Fitzwilliam, formed "the first that ever hee made," and in addition was arranged from a consort original. All galliards except number nine are built from eight-bar strains, as are two of the pavans (numbers two and four). The latter are obviously made to try out a lighter type of pavan since, other than number nine, all are constructed with sixteen-bar strains (the "Passing Measures" pair greatly exceeds this scheme with 6×32 and 9×16 bars respectively). Most surprising, the cycle includes no fewer than two sets in C minor, in which the composer seems to rely on the possibility of retuning the G♯s into A♭s. A particularly beautiful work is the second of these (Pavan and Galliard c2), which takes full advantage of what is a rather exotic key within the meantone system, as described in Table 2.2.

Table 2.2 *Byrd's Pavan and Galliard c2, Sketch of Harmonic Development*

Strain	Pavan	Galliard
I.	c – (B♭) – G / c – C	c – G / c – (B♭) – C
II.	F – g – D / B♭– d – G	F – c – g – G / g – (d) – c – G
III.	E♭– B♭– G / c – C	g – c – C / c – G – C

While the finals of all strains are the standard ones, the extent of harmonic development of both pieces is rather wide, while also related to a great extent. All strains consist of two longer phrases (the so-called twin-cadence scheme), the clearest being in the galliard. Both movements open with a strain in which tonic and dominant are firmly exposed. The second strains are much more adventurous and colorful in their own way, although the opening and closing harmonies are identical. In the pavan, this rich harmonic palette spills over into the third strain to such an extent that the tonic of C minor is barely touched upon before the tonic major is reached. It thus seems that the pavan is not conceived as a self-sufficient movement, as its harmonic tension is only resolved in the galliard, which in its third strain completely restores the tonic minor before concluding in the major. Though far from being variations, the opening melodic lines of both pieces are closely related, while both third strains are characterized by a striking imitative motif. The particular liveliness of the galliard is in no small measure attributable to the systematic exploration of two types of hemiolas: one over two bars (first and third strains) and the other within the bar (second strain).

Although the Nevell cycle is rich in content, it still does not do justice to the full range of Byrd's achievement in this genre, as a host of further pairs and individual movements transmitted elsewhere testify. Most of them appear to have been written after 1591 and right up to the 1613 publication of *Parthenia*. New territories are explored, as in a fine set in the unusual key of B♭ and a pair (Pavan and Galliard G5) exploring the felicities of echo writing – a compositional technique very common around 1600, particularly in poetry. Also new is Byrd's willingness to enter into a creative discourse with his contemporaries, such as in the Pavans and Galliards C3 and F2, in which pavans by Bull (*Lord Lumley*) and Morley (*Pavan* in F) respectively seem to have been used as a springboard. Byrd even created a pair by arranging in very ornate fashion two dances by differing composers: John Dowland's famous *Lachrymae Pavan*, coupled with a galliard by James Harding. Byrd's activity in this field reaches its conclusion in two rather opposite pieces composed (it seems) especially for *Parthenia*: the Pavan with two Galliards a2, and the Galliard C4. The former piece is dedicated to the memory of the Earl of Salisbury (Robert Cecil), who died in May 1612. The Pavan employs an unusually simple style in its first two movements, further emphasized by the restriction to two eight-bar strains and the relinquishing of the usual ornamented repeats. The second galliard, perhaps an afterthought, restores the three-strain format but still does without the varied repeats. By contrast, the Mary Brownlow Galliard C4 forms Byrd's most ornate exemplar in this genre, incorporating frequent sixteenth-note writing (as became standardized in the galliards of his younger contemporaries such as Bull or Gibbons) that has been shown to form a comment upon Bull's *Prince's Galliard*, in itself a fine and brilliant work. Byrd's subtle mastery of the rhythmic possibilities of the galliard is much in evidence here, as is his wonderful command of melody, turning this "parody" into a very personal, affective composition.

Byrd's practice of strictly following a structure in "foures" (as described by Morley) in his pavans and galliards was often considerably relaxed by his successors, and nowhere more so than in the many examples by John Bull, who was more often than not remarkably successful in creating original music within this mold. The best, which are mostly provided with suggestive titles, include the *Fantastic, Melancholy, Lord Lumley* and *Chromatic* pavan-galliard pairs. The latter is alternatively known as "Queen Elizabeth's Pavan" (and Galliard) and was thus probably written in commemoration of the Queen's death in March 1603. In the pavan, Bull achieves maximum differentiation of his strains (made out of 16 + 18 + 16 bars, which along with the ornamented repeats results in the "perfect" number of 100 measures). The opening strain, a distant echo of Dowland's *Lachrymae*, features a wonderfully expressive upper line that climbs to the high a^2 in its middle and then slowly descends again by means of affective "suspiratio" figures. In the second strain the ascending chromatic lines soon give way to a sorrowful descending chromaticism, while the third strain forms a complete contrast, remaining in A major throughout and incorporating a high-pitch "cantus firmus" as well as much use of the subdominant harmony (a characteristic of Bull, which also appears in the major), giving the impression of a long drawn-out plagal cadence. The galliard (12 + 8 + 12 bars) adopts a different strategy by reserving the chromaticism for the last strain. The first two strains are dominated by dotted rhythms and the mapping out of the normal degrees within the mode used here, which is the ninth mode on A (I, III, IV, V and VII). The third strain, however, is completely modulatory in character, spiraling from the dominant (V), with the help of chromatic cross dominants via the supertonic to the sharpened median degree (VI), or F♯ major. Since the rest of the pair remains within the bounds of meantone tuning (with D♯s), it may very well be that the striking modulations in the third strain were meant to deliberately sound out of tune. The effect appears indeed dramatic and entirely appropriate within the context of this pair, making the rapid modulation returning to a bright A major all the more conclusive and triumphant.

The most "virginalistic" works of the exile Peter Philips are his pavans and galliards. A single-standing *Pavan in G*, apparently written while still in England in 1580, became one of the most famous pieces of the repertoire, its cantus firmus-like third strain a much-copied feature, similar to the Bull pavan described above. Philips's *Pavan and Galliard Dolorosa* from 1593, written during a brief spell in a Dutch prison (he dabbled in acts of espionage), and the one on the *passamezzo antico* stand out as well, the latter pair forming some sort of modernization of Byrd's "Passing Measures" set.[7] The pavans of Orlando Gibbons, on the other hand, have been shown to be inspired by Dowland's *Lachrymae* – especially the one in G minor, which might have been written as an epitaph for the young Prince Henry, who died in November 1612.[8] Another, in A minor, was written on the death of Lord Salisbury, who, as we have noted, died in May of the same year. One of the high points of virginal music, it was included in *Parthenia* and complemented by an equally impressive galliard.

Important too are the pavans and galliards by Tomkins. Though copied out separately in Fitzwilliam, the large chromatic Pavan in A (an arrangement of a consort original) and the sprightly *Hunting Galliard* in the same key may very well have been intended as a pair. For the other pavans and galliards, we have to turn to the late autograph which contains three pairs as a well as a series of single-standing pavans. Famous among the latter is the *Sad Pavan for these distracted Tymes*, completed on 14 February 1649 and written at a point when the Royalist cause was lost and King Charles I had been executed. It foregoes not only the varied repeats but surprisingly also any chromatic writing; instead there is consort-like polyphony and an introverted mood. A masterpiece of a very different nature is the *Earl Strafford Pavan and Galliard* from 1647, in which the dense imitative writing of the main strains is countered with elaborate figurations in the repeats, also encompassing exhilarating long sequences and (in the galliard) vigorous rhythmical playfulness.

Grounds and Variations

The variation is clearly the dominant principle in the virginalist repertoire. Its main genres – excluding the fantasia (see below) – are all based on it, such as the varied repeats in the dances as well as the grounds and melodic variation sets. Sometimes genres are blurred: the *passamezzo* sets can be seen as both pavan and galliard pairs and as grounds, while several of Byrd's pieces in particular are both grounds and (partial) melodic variations. *Fortune my foe* (set by Byrd and Thomas Tomkins), moreover, uses the *passamezzo antico* as harmonic basis, while the *passamezzo moderno* ("Quadran") can be recognized below the tune of "John come kiss me now" (set by Byrd and John Tomkins).

As has been seen, the ground was one of the main traditional techniques of secular keyboard music and, as a consequence, plays an important role in Byrd's early keyboard music. This is clearest in the early *Hornpipe*, obviously written in emulation of Hugh Aston's piece of that name. In what appears to be Byrd's last "traditional" ground, he uses yet another of Aston's bass patterns, but in this case the direct model has been lost. *Hughe Ashtons Grownde*, entered towards the end of Nevell, forms a powerful large-scale work. There is, however, no question that his two *passamezzo* pairs represent the pinnacle in this field. At some point during the decade after Nevell, his setting of the *passamezzo antico* (Nevell cycle no. 9) was followed by a Pavan and Galliard on the "moderno" bass ("Quadran"), which forms an even richer work. It was probably written as a response to Bull's first *Quadran Pavan* (solely preserved in Fitzwilliam), a piece of exactly the same structure and length as Byrd's.[9] Bull in his turn might have answered Byrd's great setting with an even more densely written and virtuosic version (named *Variation of the Quadran Pavan* in Fitzwilliam). Tomkins aptly characterized the rival settings as "excellent for the hand" (Bull) and "excellent for matter" (Byrd).[10]

In contrast with the ground and the fantasia, Byrd continued to write melodic variations until the end of his career, though, for some unknown reason, none were included in *Parthenia*. The range is very wide, showing the composer's sensitivity to the chosen melodies. There are vigorous early dance sets (*Gypsies'* and *Sellinger's Rounds*); colorful, rustic settings of folk tunes (*The Carman's Whistle, The Woods so wild*); understated lyricism (*All in a Garden Greene, Callino casturame*); and late-period exuberance (*Go from my window, John come kiss me now*). The most outstanding, however, is *Walsingham* (already appearing in Nevell), a lengthy but inexhaustible work consisting of twenty-two variations. Its most conspicuous feature is its constantly migrating tune, almost always moving in each variation between treble and tenor. Byrd even manages two bass and alto variations each, the latter achieved by using the same pitch as the treble variations while adding a free-ranging high soprano above the alto.

The large number of thirty variations which make up John Bull's famous *Walsingham* was no doubt meant to outdo Byrd's set, but the aim was rather different than Bull's reaction to Byrd's *Quadran Pavan*, Byrd's motivic and polyphonic refinement here being replaced by great virtuosity and a certain harmonic brilliance. Bull did not copy Byrd's method of alternating pitches but rather placed these firmly in the treble, while also setting the piece in the more brilliant key of A minor instead of Byrd's quite subdued G minor. In contrast with the other virginalists, however, Giles Farnaby clearly preferred more modern if not raucous tunes, and it is here that his most valuable contributions to the repertoire are to be found, as in pieces like *Rosasolis* or *Woody-Cock*.

Fantasias and Hexachords

A particularly fascinating part of Byrd's keyboard oeuvre is formed by the fantasias. Here Byrd did break with a European tradition of the fantasia as a special art of the organist's ability to improvise imitative (four-part) counterpoint – a secret art preferably not written down. In his seven written-out fantasias, Byrd reinterprets the fantasia as an eclectic concept in which imitation remains central but also incorporates elements of the canzona, song variation, ostinato and dance. As his pupil Morley explains (no doubt mimicking his much-revered master), in a fantasia the composer "selects a theme and wresteth and turneth it as he list, making either much or little of it according as shall seem best to his own conceit. In this more art may be showne than in any other musicke, because the composer is tide to nothing but that he may adde, diminish and alter at his pleasure," and uses "bindings with discords, quicke motions, slow motions, proportions, and what you list."[11]

Again, Byrd demonstrates an astonishing ability to craft highly sophisticated and individual pieces from this rather open and liberal concept. A case in point are the two mature "Fancies" copied out in close proximity towards the end of Nevell. Of comparable length and structure, their character could hardly be more different. The one in the Dorian mode (Fantasia d1) is a rather somber work, opening motet-like, followed by figuration that seems to "crash" into the polyphony. The Ionian work is lighter in touch, which is not only the result of the contrasting mode but also because of the generally higher tessitura and more clearly delineated sections with greater tonal variety. Whereas Fantasia d1 is laid out in four sections that all cadence on the tonic, Fantasia C2 exhibits a classical three-section form with a more differentiated construction and using subtle thematic metamorphoses and greater tonal variety (see the right-hand column in Table 2.3 and Example 2.1).

A solid point of departure is the opening theme A, which starts with a very instrumental ascending scale (x) and finishes with a few descending gestures (y) and a simple cadence (z). All elements are recycled in the course of the composition. Motif z is transformed into theme B for a very madrigalian, contrasting section. The instrumental and vocal aspect are then combined in another exordial section, in which a free inversion and

Table 2.3 *Byrd's Fantasia C2*

Measures	Length (mm.)	Section	Texture	Key(s)
Exordium (67)				
A 1–27	27	exposition	imitative, instrumental	C–C
B 28–47	20	interlude	quasi-homophonic, vocal	C–C
C 48–67	20	counter-exposition	imitative, vocal/instrumental	C–D
Medium (67)				
D 68–79	12	interlude	freely imitative, vocal	G–A
E 80–103	24	development	figuration, instrumental	a–C
F 104–134	31	sequential	instrumental, second half developing into running figuration	a
Finis (27)				
G 135–159	25	sequential	imitative, vocal, then instrumental	a–C
H 160–161	2	codetta		C

augmentation of y (the vocal element) is juxtaposed with a variant of the instrumental scale x. This contrasting and subsequent combination of both polarities remains the central theme of the fantasia. The *medium* (which is exactly as long as the *exordium*) thus opens "vocally" with an augmented and inverted variant of x in stretto fashion (D) and is further devoted to instrumental variants: a partly diminished and shortened variant of x (see E) develops into some free figuration alternating quavers with semiquavers, which runs into a playful variant of x (motif F) treated sequentially, followed by more free figuration, now principally in continuous semiquavers. As befits the succinct *finis*, a synthesis and conclusion are reached, combining all previous elements. Thus at its outset, sequential writing is combined with imitation in close stretto (G), and the whole thirteen-bar paragraph is then repeated, overlayed with rapid figuration based on x. The verbatim repeat (a technique also used in Fantasia d1) makes the vocal/instrumental synthesis easily perceptible while also achieving a satisfying conclusion. The little codetta appended to it (H) hides a final eloquent variant of y.

The level of sophistication demonstrated in Fantasia C2 (and d1) is rare even for Byrd, as a comparison with some of the (earlier) other and much longer fantasias, such as a2 and G2, demonstrates. While rich in content and polyphony (the lengthy but exciting Fantasia a2 in particular), the structure is somewhat diffuse. Indeed, in contrast with the other genres it was not a concept easily continued by the following generations. There is

Example 2.1 William Byrd, *Fantasia C2* (motivic analysis)

one fantasia in grand virtuoso style by John Bull from his English period (d3), which is exceptionally loosely written. More convincing as a rounded piece are two fantasias, which are principally written in two parts (d1–2), especially the first. It opens with a string of lively imitations leading, in the second half, to an obsessive bass ostinato with increasingly agitated right-hand extemporizations; the accumulated tension is resolved in a triumphantly imitative four-part conclusion.

Bull's influence is clearly evident in Farnaby's eight fantasias, usually rambling improvisatory affairs; the longest one in G minor is perhaps the most rewarding in its lively and playful succession of ideas. An opposite approach to the fantasia is found with Orlando Gibbons, who reserved virtuoso figurations mainly for his variations and galliards. Indeed, the most successful examples have no sixteenth-note passages at all, only smooth counterpoint. Outstanding among these is the big *Fantazia of foure parts* in *Parthenia*, which shows a similar subtlety of motivic relations similar to Byrd's Fantasia C2, but here concentrated on strict four-part polyphony and densely imitational writing. As with Gibbons, wide experience in the writing of consort music informs Tomkins's strictly polyphonic fantasias, which are exclusively to be found in his retrospective autograph.

Although routinely classified as fantasias, the hexachord settings of the virginalists survive exclusively under the title *Ut re mi fa sol la*, thus clearly forming a self-contained genre. Byrd was again the trendsetter here, with two compositions in this category. In the first setting, the hexachord appears as a treble ostinato "to be playd by a second person," under which the principal player weaves a tapestry of freely roaming imitations and figurations while managing to incorporate two folksongs along the way.[12] The other (included in Nevell) uses the hexachord not only on the three principal degrees (G, C, and F) but also on three "exotic" pitches (D, A, and Bb), along with dense polyphony resulting in a rich work with the maximum of tonal variety achievable within the bounds of meantone tuning.

The idea behind both pieces was developed, if not radicalized, in two particularly brilliant pieces by Bull. In a lengthy treble ostinato setting, Bull does away with Byrd's third hand, putting the main thrust of the often very virtuosic and dense writing in the left hand, resulting in one of the most difficult pieces in the entire repertoire. It no doubt stands as an emphatic demonstration of Bull's keyboard prowess. A demonstration piece of a wholly different nature is present in the "chromatic" *Ut re mi fa sol la*. Here Bull takes up the challenge of Byrd's second setting and doubles the number of degrees of the older work, thereby arriving at all twelve degrees of the chromatic scale, leading to radical modulations and enharmonic writing. Naturally, meantone tuning is no longer possible for such a work, and some sort of circular tuning has to be presumed. To make his intentions clear, he copies Byrd's number of hexachord entries (17) as well as again taking G as the principal key. He covers all chromatic degrees in two sets of six entries in whole-tone distance (G-A-B-Db-Eb-F, then Ab-Bb-C-D-E-F♯) and concludes with five more entries on the tonic. Here digital virtuosity is replaced by compositional virtuosity of an experimental nature.[13]

While Farnaby poked fun at the somewhat ponderous hexachord tradition in the satirical *His Humour*, Cosyn and Tomkins produced lengthy ostinato settings, similar to Bull's first setting. However, the hexachord tradition established by Byrd and Bull would be more rewardingly continued by the great keyboardists on the continent, such as Sweelinck, Scheidt, Hassler, or Frescobaldi.

Descriptive Pieces and Miniatures

In the field of descriptive music and small-scale pieces, Byrd was again the pioneer, not only introducing small dances such as corantos, almans, jigs, and voltas but creating in *The Battle* the first British cyclical keyboard piece. Byrd thought highly enough of the work to include it in Nevell, but he made sure to frame the actual nine-movement *Battle* sequence, with its blatant insistence on the C major harmony, with two musically more rewarding pieces (both in G): a *March before the Battle* and the *Galliard for the Victory*. A lively string of dance-like vignettes forms the similarly descriptive *Barley Break*, illustrating an open-air ball game popular in the 1580s. The much later *Bells* is both descriptive and with a ground (actually taking one element out of his *Hornpipe*), Byrd meets the challenge of being tied to just two adjacent notes treated as a ground with immense ingenuity.

A welcome side aspect of Bull the virtuoso is the many smaller pieces, some of them lyrical jewels such as the *Duke of Brunswicks Alman*, the various "Toys," the *Dutch Dance*, as well as "autobiographical" pieces such as *My Grief* and *My Self*. His principal contribution to descriptive music is the celebrated *King's Hunt*: a vigorous harpsichord piece whose exhilarating effect is enhanced by its original variation form: the two paragraphs are immediately repeated (AA^1BB^1), and this mold is then extended into two further variations. The whole structure thus actually consists of six dovetailed variations. The tradition of writing attractive character pieces ran through the virginalist era with a variety of contributions, such as Peerson's *The Fall of the Leafe*, John Mundy's *Weather* Fantasia, Farnaby's *Humour* and *Dreame*, and Tomkins's *Lady Folliot's Galliard* and *Perpetual Round*, the latter forming the very last virginalist piece in existence, dated 8 September 1654.

Parthenia at the Crossroads

The 1613 *Parthenia* appears to be seminal not only because of it being the solitary print and combining the three principal masters Byrd, Bull, and Gibbons in a historically conscious way, but also because it appears to mark a real turning point in the history of virginal music. There is no evidence that Byrd wrote any more keyboard music in the remaining ten years of his life. Bull was to flee to the southern Netherlands later that year, altering his style almost beyond recognition while living there. Gibbons seems to have discontinued the production of keyboard music in the "grand" style after *Parthenia*, and no music survives by Farnaby beyond the Fitzwilliam, which was completed ca. 1617.[14] Indeed, Gibbons's apparent turn to smaller fare – mainly corantos and almans – has a parallel with the content of the modest sequel to *Parthenia*, the much smaller *Parthenia In-Violata* from

1624–1625. This set the tone for a notably more modest repertoire in British keyboard music in which the French influence becomes more and more apparent, lasting well into the Restoration period: simple settings of popular tunes and short dances. Only the long-lived Tomkins refused to give in to these new trends, instead creating in old age a remarkable but completely isolated revival of the golden age of English keyboard music.

Key to Source Citations

Cosyn	*GB-Lbl*, R.M.L. 23.1.4 (Cosyn autograph, 1620 and earlier)
Dublin	*EIR-Dtc*, TCD MS D.3.30 (Dublin Virginal Manuscript, ca. 1570)
Forster	*GB-Lbl*, R.M.L. 24.d.3 (Will Forster's Virginal Book, 1624)
Fitzwilliam	*GB-Cfm*, Mus. MS 168 (Fitzwilliam Virginal Book, written by Francis Tregian, ca. 1612–1619)
Mulliner	*GB-Lbl*, Add. MS 30513 (Thomas Mulliner, ca. 1550–1575)
Nevell	*GB-Lbl*, MS Mus. 1591 (My Ladye Nevells Booke, 1591)
Paris 1122	*F-Pn*, c, Rés. 1122 (Tomkins autograph, 1647–54)
Paris 1185	*F-Pn*, Fonds du Conservatoire, Rés. 1185 (Bull autograph[?])
Parthenia	*Parthenia or the maydenhead of the first musicke that ever was printed for the virginalls* (London, 1612/13)
RA 58	*GB-Lbl*, MS Roy. App. 58 (ca. 1530)
Weelkes	*GB-Lbl*, Add. MS 30485 (Weelkes Manuscript, ca. 1610)

Notes

1. Inventory of 1547. See *GB-Lbl* Harley MS 1419; see also Alan Brown, "England," in *Keyboard Music before 1700*, ed. Alexander Silbiger (New York: Routledge, 2004), p. 27.
2. See John Koster, "Questions of Keyboard Temperament in the Sixteenth Century," in *Interpreting Historical Keyboard Music*, ed. Andrew Woolley and John Kitchen (Farnham: Ashgate, 2013), pp. 115–130, here pp. 120–122 and 127ff.
3. Pieter Dirksen, "Towards a Canon of the Keyboard Music of John Bull," in *Aspects of Early English Keyboard Music to c.1630*, ed. David J. Smith (London and New York: Routledge, in press, 2019).
4. See John Harley, *Orlando Gibbons and the Gibbons Family of Musicians* (Aldershot: Ashgate, 1999), p. 71.
5. I use here the ordering system established in Oliver Neighbour, *The Consort and Keyboard Music of William Byrd* (Berkeley: University of California Press, 1978).

6.   Thomas Morley, *A Plaine and Easie Introduction to Practicall Musicke* (London, 1597), p. 181.
7.   Rachelle Taylor and Frauke Jürgensen, "Politics, Religion, Style and the Passamezzo Galliards of Byrd and Philips: A Discussion of Networks Involving Byrd and his Disciples," in *Networks of Music and Culture in the Late Sixteenth and Early Seventeenth Centuries. A Collection of Essays in Celebration of Peter Philips's 450th Anniversary*, ed. David J. Smith and Rachelle Taylor (Aldershot: Ashgate, 2013), pp. 71–89.
8.   John Harley, *Orlando Gibbons and the Gibbons Family of Musicians*, (Aldershot: Ashgate, 1999), pp. 87–90.
9.   Oliver Neighbour, "John Bull, 5. Works," in *The New Grove* 2, 1980, pp. 588f.
10. Found in the front matter of Paris 1122.
11. Cited in Brown, "England," pp. 180ff.
12. See Tomkins, in Paris 1122, p. 4.
13. On this subject, see Gary Verkade, "John Bull: 'Ut re mi fa sol la': A Performer's Investigation," *The Diapason* 94, no. 1 (2003), pp. 16–18 and 94, no. 2 (2003), pp. 15–17.
14. Pieter Dirksen, "Orlando Gibbons's Keyboard Music: The Continental Perspective," in Taylor and Jürgensen, *Networks*, pp. 157–168.

Further Reading

Brown, Alan. "England," in *Keyboard Music before 1700*, ed. Alexander Silbiger. New York: Routledge, rev. 2004, pp. 23–146.

Caldwell, John. *English Keyboard Music before the Nineteenth Century*. Oxford: Oxford University Press, 1973.

Cunningham, Walker. *The Keyboard Music of John Bull*. Ann Arbor, MI: UMI Research Press, 1984.

Harley, John. *British Harpsichord Music*. 2 volumes. Aldershot: Scolar Press, 1992–1994.

  William Byrd – Gentleman of the Chapel Royal. Aldershot: Ashgate, 1999.

  Orlando Gibbons and the Gibbons Family of Musicians. Aldershot: Ashgate, 1999.

Neighbour, Oliver. *The Consort and Keyboard Music of William Byrd*. London: Faber & Faber, 1978.

Smith, David J. *The Instrumental Music of Peter Philips*. PhD dissertation. Oxford, 1994.

Stevens, Denis. *Thomas Tomkins 1572–1656*. London: Macmillan, rev. 1967.

von Streit, Anna Elisabeth. *Pavanen und Galliarden in der englischen Virginalmusik des ausgehenden 16. und beginnenden 17. Jahrhunderts*. PhD dissertation. Augsburg, 1998.

3 England

ANDREW WOOLLEY

This chapter surveys solo music for harpsichord-type instruments composed in England, and in some cases elsewhere in the British Isles, between ca. 1630 and the late eighteenth century. It concentrates on the types of keyboard music often referred to in the sources as "lessons," the collective term for binary-form airs modeled on dances, settings of popular tunes, or grounds, usually written for one or more instruments of the same type and range without accompanying bass instrument.[1] Between ca. 1650 and ca. 1760, lessons were organized into suites, often called "suites ['suits' or 'setts'] of lessons" on title pages. Later, "lesson" was simply another word for a sonata. Although numerous eighteenth-century collections of lessons or sonatas for solo harpsichord contain fugues, they were distinct from collections concentrating on organ music, such as Thomas Roseingrave's *Voluntaries and Fugues Made on Purpose for the Organ or Harpsicord* (1728).

The difficulties of distinguishing late eighteenth-century harpsichord music from piano music are well known.[2] Although the Kirckman firm continued to make harpsichords into the first decade of the nineteenth century, this chapter is limited to music by composers born before 1750, the youngest of whom were educated in the 1760s when mentioning "piano forte" on title pages remained infrequent.[3] In the eighteenth century, various types of ensemble music were considered suitable for performance as solo harpsichord music, including solo sonatas written for a high melody instrument and continuo, keyboard concertos, and sonatas for keyboard with obbligato accompanying part(s).[4] There are also important stylistic affinities between seventeenth- and eighteenth-century solo keyboard and ensemble music. Nevertheless, due to the large size of the repertoire, this chapter will be concerned mostly with original keyboard music or arranged music that has undergone significant transformation.

The Followers of Orlando Gibbons: John Cobb, Hugh Facy, and Others

An enduring model for seventeenth-century English composers was the keyboard and consort music of Orlando Gibbons (1583–1625), copied widely into manuscripts after Gibbons's death.[5] Several composers born around 1600 were his students, among them Randall Jewett of Chester (ca. 1603–1675). However, much of what survives consists of simple airs and arrangements of masque tunes.[6] Only a few dances and grounds approach the virtuoso style of earlier composers, although some simple airs have divisions, by Hugh Facy (1598–1649) and John Cobb (ca. 1600–after 1654), and there are also several grounds by the Oxford organist Arthur Phillips (1605–1695). By contrast, contemporary instrumental ensemble music emanating from the royal court, such as William Lawes's (1602–1645), is replete with sophisticated and elaborate divisions.[7]

An important source for harpsichord music by Cobb, Facy, Phillips, and their contemporaries is the Thomas Heardson manuscript, copied in the 1650s, mainly by Heardson (fl. 1637–1650s), an organist of Ludlow before the Civil War.[8] Included are Heardson's own almain-corant pairs, some with divisions, sometimes copied next to pieces by other composers in the same key to form larger units. Recent research has shown that Facy was active at the English College at Douai in present-day northern France.[9] Though interesting for their divisions, his harpsichord pieces are rather mechanical and a disappointment compared with some imaginative organ pieces we have by him. On the other hand, Cobb, an organist of the Chapel Royal, wrote a small number of high-quality pieces, including two that are anonymous but attributable on stylistic grounds.[10] Two almains, one of forty-two measures, the other of thirty-

Example 3.1 John Cobb (ca. 1600–after 1654), Almain [and Division], mm. 28–36 (*English Keyboard Music 1650–1695*, ed. Woolley, no. 15)

six, have divisions in the manuscript of the Oxford organist William Ellis (d. 1680).[11] The inventive divisions are built out of small germinating figures.

Cobb's pieces are arranged into almain-corant pairs in the Heardson manuscript, while in Ellis's sarabands are attached, forming some of the earliest suites in English keyboard sources. Possibly the earliest English keyboard suite is a group by Lawes called "The Golden Grove," consisting of an almain and several associated corants and sarabands, although it survives partially in consort versions and was probably not written for keyboard originally.[12] Other pieces by Lawes, with consort originals surviving, are found in several English keyboard sources of the 1650s and 1660s, including John Playford's anthology of short airs and dances, *Musick's Hand-Maid*, originally published ca. 1660 and reprinted in enlarged forms in 1663 and 1678.[13]

The Heardson and Ellis manuscripts contain several pieces by French lutenists in England, among them John Mercure (ca. 1600–before 1661), who was active 1641–1642 at the English court.[14] Mercure's widely copied Almain in A minor has elements of the lute-derived idiom known by the modern term *stile brisé*, characterized by such features as repeated-note figures and rhythmically dislocated part writing.[15] The sources preserve a number of slightly different versions, which probably reflect how several keyboard players adopted the piece and performed it. Another French musician represented in these sources is La Barre, whose first name is never given. He may also have been a lutenist, since the source texts vary to a similar degree; he has been termed the "English" La Barre to distinguish him from others belonging to the French family of musicians.[16]

The same sources contain many of the pieces by Jonas Tresure (fl. 1650s). However, it has been argued that Tresure probably originated from the Low Countries and is more likely to have written original harpsichord music.[17] A piece called "Allemand Tresoor" in a Dutch source is found in English sources in similar versions, presumably stemming from Tresure himself, and the conflicting ascriptions to the "English" La Barre for several of the pieces might have arisen if Tresure made some of the keyboard versions. The Heardson and Ellis manuscripts contain mostly French-style corants, while others preserve an attractive group of A minor pieces.[18] An Almain-Corant-Saraband Suite in E minor, unique to a source copied by Matthias Weckmann (1616–1674), has full, four-voice textures that are uncharacteristic of the other pieces.[19]

Matthew Locke, John Roberts, Albertus Bryne, and Their Contemporaries

The quantity of surviving pieces from the late 1650s to the 1670s is higher, in part because of Matthew Locke's important anthology *Melothesia, or, Certain General Rules for Playing upon a Continued Bass* (John Carr: 1673), which contains most pieces by Locke (ca. 1622–1677) and some by John Roberts (fl. 1650s–1670s).[20] There are, however, a number of important contemporaries of these composers not represented in this collection, including Albertus Bryne (ca. 1621–1668), Benjamin Rogers (1614–1698), and the Norwich organist Richard Ayleward (?1626–1669), whose sixty pieces are mostly preserved in a copy of a lost seventeenth-century manuscript by the pianist and writer Edward Dannreuther (1844–1905).[21] Christopher Gibbons (1615–1676), Orlando Gibbons's son and an organist of the Chapel Royal, belongs with this group, but the few surviving pieces suggest he wrote little harpsichord music. Additionally, high-quality anonymous pieces, similar in style to Locke's and Roberts's, are found in a manuscript associated with the English Jesuit College at St Omer.[22]

French influence on English composers active between ca. 1650 and ca. 1680 is apparent in their adoption of *stile brisé* idioms and a melody-oriented, rather than contrapuntal manner, especially in corants. *Stile brisé* tends to be most pronounced in four-voice almains, which are often highly intricate rhythmically, and in Ayleward's case unusual syncopated patterns even extend to imitative bass parts. The melody-oriented manner may have originated in a type of music for social dancing, known in England as "French Dances," which was published as single melodic lines by John Playford, initially within editions of *The Dancing Master* in the 1650s and 1660s.[23] Locke, Roberts, Bryne, and others were also influenced by French harpsichord music directly; a few suites by Locke and Roberts are headed by preludes in imitation of French unmeasured preludes.[24] There are otherwise few preludes based on chordal elaboration in English sources before Purcell's, although such preludes may have been extemporized.

Locke's style combines French elements with a fondness for angular melodic lines and duet-like writing between an active bass and the upper part. His *Melothesia* pieces are grouped into suites of four or more pieces. Other composers, including Rogers and Bryne, wrote four-movement suites consisting of an almain, corant, saraband, and jig-almain.[25] However, Locke's are of more miscellaneous character, often ending with a country dance or hornpipe, thus anticipating later suites by John Blow, Purcell, and William Croft (see below). The basic guiding principle of Locke and his

Example 3.2 John Roberts (fl. 1650s–1670s), Almain [and Division], mm. 32–39 (*The Collected Works*, ed. Bailey, no. 10)

contemporaries seems to have been a gradual increase in tempo, since French-style corants were slower than sarabands or hornpipes.

Nothing is known biographically about Roberts; his high-quality pieces feature elements from Locke's music but also look back to the division technique of earlier composers.[26] Roberts's French-style *doubles* (in *Melothesia* called "La double") combine *stile brisé* textures with flowing right-hand eighth notes in an attractive manner. In one Almain from the Heardson manuscript, division-like material breaks into 32nd notes and combines with an implied four-part contrapuntal texture with striking results (Example 3.2).[27]

There are at least twenty-nine pieces by Bryne, organist of St Paul's Cathedral before the Civil War and later organist of Westminster Abbey, surviving mainly in copies that seem to be autograph.[28] His pieces are also found in numerous posthumous sources and were apparently influential on later English composers; one such source, an early eighteenth-century manuscript copied by the north-eastern English musician Nicholas Harrison, includes variant versions of the D major pieces and ascribes them to Blow, Bryne's successor at Westminster Abbey, perhaps because they reflect revisions by Blow.[29] The elegant four-part *style brisé* textures in the Almain from this suite (and other Bryne almains) anticipates similar textures in some of Purcell's almands, such as Z.667/1.

John Blow, Henry Purcell, Giovanni Battista Draghi, and Their Contemporaries

Of the three major English composers of keyboard music in the 1680s and 1690s – John Blow (1649–1708), Henry Purcell (1658 or 1659–1695), and Giovanni Battista Draghi (ca. 1640–1708) – Blow stands out as the most prolific and arguably the most important. This is unsurprising considering his lengthy involvement in teaching as Master of the Children of the Chapel Royal: as in other periods and countries, keyboard pieces were often composed for instruction purposes. The early eighteenth-century music historian Roger North (1651–1734) noted how "great performers upon organs will doe voluntary, to a prodigy of wonder, and beyond their owne skill to recover and set downe," while the publisher John Young observed how the harpsichord's "neatness & easiness in Playing on hath so particularly Recommended it to the Fair Sex, that few Ladys of Quality Omitt to Learn on it, And for their Sake it is that ye Masters from time to time Com[m]unicate Their Compositions."[30]

Important sources of Blow's harpsichord music include the portion of a large manuscript copied ca. 1680–1685 by the Rochester and later Canterbury Cathedral organist, Daniel Henstridge (ca. 1650–1736), and one now in Brussels copied by an anonymous English professional musician around 1700.[31] A collection of Blow's harpsichord music containing some of his finest suite movements was published by John Walsh and John Hare in 1698, but this does not include the large-scale grounds that lie at the center of his harpsichord output, most of which appear to date from before 1690. "Ground in Elami," one of the longest, may be an early piece (one of its sources is the Henstridge manuscript) and achieves its length partly because of a bipartite ground of eight measures. Others, such as "Morlake Ground," adopt bass patterns characteristic of French orchestral chaconnes of the 1680s and sometimes juxtapose a French-style idiom with English division technique, notably in the spectacular "Chacone in Faut."[32]

Purcell's posthumous *A Choice Collection of Lessons for the Harpsichord or Spinnet* (1696, reprinted with additions in 1699 as the "third edition") was clearly a model for Blow's. It contains eight suites plus a supplement of four or six arrangements of ensemble music (the number varies between exemplars).[33] It was evidently compiled from several sources, possibly by Frances Purcell (d. 1706), the composer's widow, who dedicated the volume to the future Queen Anne.[34] Most of Purcell's harpsichord music likely dates from the 1690s, the period he was engaged by several wealthy families as a teacher.[35] It has been shown recently that the inscription "Bell Barr" above the Almand in

D minor (Z.668/1) was the name given to a summer residence of the Howard family.[36] The contrapuntal preludes in *A Choice Collection* (Z.661/1, 662/1, and 666/1) appear as independent compositions in organ manuscripts and were perhaps added to the suite movements by its compiler. Harpsichord manuscripts often contain substitutes, as in a Purcell autograph discovered in 1993 (London, British Library, MS Mus. 1), where a measured-notation transcription of an anonymous French prelude appears instead of Z.666/1.[37] Indeed, the suites have the appearance of being unbalanced and come across more effectively when supplemented by contemporary arrangements of Purcell's theater airs, songs, and vocal grounds.[38]

Draghi's ninety keyboard pieces are preserved in numerous contemporary manuscripts and a representative printed collection of six suites (1707); the manuscripts include MS Mus. 1, which contains seventeen autograph pieces at the opposite (inverted) end from the Purcell.[39] Giovanni Battista may have been a brother of the opera composer Antonio Draghi (1634 or 1635–1700); he arrived in London in the 1660s and eventually became a leading musician there.[40] Draghi's harpsichord music, surviving in sources mostly dating from the 1690s and later, is more French-influenced than that of English contemporaries, to judge from its elaborate ornamentation, suite groupings of six or more movements, and 3/2-meter corants. The remarkable B minor group, preserved in the large Charles Babel (d. 1716) manuscript, includes four extra pieces following a "core" suite of five, perhaps intended as optional additions or replacements to be incorporated at the performer's discretion.[41] However, some of Draghi's more flamboyant preludes or toccatas seem indebted to his compatriots such as Bernardo Pasquini (1637–1710), whose music is found in a manuscript housed at the Library of Congress, Washington, DC, and other sources of English origin.[42]

The harpsichord pieces of Francis Forcer (1649–1705) and Robert King (ca. 1660–?1726) are occasionally short-winded, but some seem worthy of revival.[43] Four partially autograph manuscripts reflect Forcer's activity as a teacher of amateurs, although his suite movements are mostly preserved in the Henstridge and Washington manuscripts.[44] Like Forcer, King was active for much of his career as a theater composer and teacher. Unusually for an English composer, he seems to have adopted the almand-corant-saraband-jig pattern consistently, while his French-style imitative jigs in 6/8 are similar to Draghi's in the way they employ flowing quaver patterns.

Followers of Blow and Purcell: William Croft, Jeremiah Clarke, Philip Hart, and Others

In the 1690s, a new technique for music engraving was adopted (i.e., the use of punches) and it seems publishing keyboard music became more commercially viable.[45] Much of the music to be considered next survives in the various printed anthologies and single-author collections that appeared between 1697 and 1711, although manuscript sources continue to be important. Indeed, manuscripts preserve some of the higher-quality pieces, including the majority of William Croft's (1678–1727), some of another Blow pupil, Raphael Courteville (d. ca. 1735), and William Davis of Worcester's (ca. 1675/6–1745).[46] The printed sources range in quality and significance, from composer-initiated single-author collections, such as Philip Hart's (?1674–1749), to publishers' anthologies, such as the publisher John Young's *A Choice Collection of Ayres* (1700), which contains suite movements by Blow and his followers, including Croft, Francis Pigott (1666–1704), Jeremiah Clarke (ca. 1674–1707), and John Barrett (ca. 1676–?1719).[47]

The most significant figure in this group is undoubtedly Croft, who succeeded Blow as Master of the Children and as organist of Westminster Abbey in 1708. His harpsichord music, both voluminous and of high quality, was probably written early on in his career; some of the more modern-looking, Italianate pieces, such as the Almand, Corant and Saraband of the E major suite, were copied into one manuscript dating to ca. 1700.[48] The almands make much use of chromaticism, bass parts in imitative dialogue with the upper part that recall Locke, and often intricate three-part writing (Example 3.3). Copyists probably selected Croft's pieces from a larger pool to create the suites

Example 3.3 William Croft (1678–1727), Slow Almand, opening (*Complete Harpsichord Music*, ed. Ferguson and Hogwood, no. 6a)

found in their manuscripts; the pieces are grouped differently in several authoritative sources, and it is possible to discern no fewer than eight groupings for those in C minor, all of which have some degree of authority.[49]

Clarke, who succeeded to the post of Chapel Royal organist jointly with Croft after the death of Piggot, is best know today for "Prince of Denmark's March," a keyboard arrangement of which is in *A Choice Collection of Ayres*.[50] However, the principal source of his harpsichord music is the posthumous single-author *Choice Lessons for the Harpsichord or Spinett* (1711). Its title page states it was "Carefully Corrected by Himself [Clarke] Being what he Design'd to Publish," and that it was "printed for & sould [sic] by" Charles King, the composer's brother-in-law and successor at St Paul's Cathedral, as well as for Young and John Hare; its spacious oblong format gives it the appearance of a composer-initiated publication.[51] The pieces are graceful and melodious, although uneven in quality, with rather repetitive use of *stile brisé* in the B minor, C minor, and C major almands. The seven-movement C major suite by Pigott in Young's anthology also deserves the attention of modern players; its Jig, built out of two small elements, which are combined in various permutations and inverted, is notable.

Philip Hart's *Fugues for the Organ or Harpsichord: with Lessons for the Harpsichord* (1704) stands out for its dedication to a patron, John Jeffries of Llywell, and fine-quality engraving from the workshop of Thomas Cross junior. Two slightly later collections that may have been inspired by this one – Abiell Whichello's *Lessons for the Harpsichord or Spinnet* (1707) and William Richardson's *Lessons for the Harpsichord or Spinet* (1708) – have title pages similar in appearance and also seem to have been engraved in the Cross workshop.[52] The collection survives in two states, one with two extra suites, in C minor and D major.[53] The first of the three fugues, in A major, with its arpeggio prelude, seems suited to the harpsichord, while the lessons employ a distinctive, highly ornamented idiom derived from Blow. The late eighteenth-century historian Sir John Hawkins pointed out that Hart "entertained little relish for those refinements in music which followed the introduction of the Italian opera into this country," while at the same time criticizing his playing for being overornamented. However, the style of ornamentation is not much dissimilar from what is encountered in some of Blow's harpsichord music.

Handel's Contemporaries: Thomas Roseingrave, John Baptist Loeillet "of London," Richard Jones, and Others

An important influence on English harpsichord music composed between ca. 1710 and ca. 1730 was Arcangelo Corelli's Op. 5 solo sonatas for violin (1700). Esteemed for their formal perfection, these sonatas were used widely as compositional models, while in performance they were associated with a new virtuosic style of ornamentation. Corelli's music was performed in public by violinists and recorder players who were also keyboard players, among them William Babell (1688–1723), the son of Charles; Charles Dieupart (ca. 1670–ca. 1740), whose harpsichord music was composed before he arrived in England; and John Baptist Loeillet "of London" (1680–1730). As members of the orchestra at the Haymarket theater, they would also have been familiar with the extensive ornamentation used in Italian opera, the spirit of which may have been captured in the flamboyant arrangements of Handel's and other composers' arias by Babell, John Reading (?1685–1764), and others.[54] Later, Francesco Geminiani (1687–1762), who came to London in 1714 and spent most of the remainder of his career in the British Isles, and the theater violinist Richard Jones (d. 1744), arranged their solo sonatas for violin or wrote keyboard music in a violinistic idiom. The former was regarded as Corelli's disciple in England.

Representative of the new Italianate style of the second and third decades of the eighteenth century is Loeillet's *Six Suits of Lessons for the Harpsicord or Spinnet* (1723). Loeillet, born in Ghent, was a recorder and oboe player in the Haymarket orchestra, held a concert series at his house, and, according to Hawkins, was a "teacher of the harpsichord, and an excellent composer for that instrument."[55] The regular construction of each suite (each consists of allemande, corente, *sarabanda*, gavotte or common-time "aria," minuet and giga) recalls his colleague Dieupart's *Six suittes de clavessin* (1701), which contains suites of similar makeup but with the addition of overtures. Loeillet's English contemporaries emulated him through borrowing, notably from a Minuet in A minor, which appears to have originated in a suite that was never published and, according to Hawkins (writing in the late eighteenth century), was "a great favourite with the ladies of the last age"; its opening figure was reused several times by Loeillet himself as well as by other composers (see Example 3.4).[56] Loeillet's influence is also apparent from collections such as Anthony Young's *Suits of Lessons for the Harpsicord or Spinnet* (1719), where Italianate pieces sit rather uneasily alongside dances in the style of Blow or Croft.[57] A more effective synthesis of English and Italianate elements is found in John

Example 3.4 a) John Baptist Loeillet (1680–1730), Minuet in A minor; (*Suite in A minor*, ed. Woolley, no. 5); b) Loeillet, Saraband in C minor (*Six Suits*, p. 22); c) Loeillet, Minuet in C minor (*Six Suits*, p. 27); d) Loeillet, Minuet in G minor (*Six Suits*, p. 8); e) Minuet from "Suite of Lessons By Geo: Spencer" (London, Foundling Museum, Gerald Coke Handel Collection, MS 1576, fol. 28v); f) John Sheeles (1695–1765), Minuet in E minor(*Suites of Lessons* [Vol. 1], p. 12)

Sheeles's (1695–1765) *Suites of Lessons for the Harpsicord or Spinett* (1724) and a similarly titled second collection (ca. 1730).[58] In the first collection, three of the suites contain Corellian fugues, while in the second, two suites (called "sett") begin with a French overture. A chaconne concluding the second collection's Fourth Sett, headed "To an old Ground," uses the eight-bar bass pattern from a harpsichord piece known in the late eighteenth century as "Purcell's Ground" (Z. S122).

A new benchmark had been reached in 1720 with the publication of Handel's suites, and a few harpsichord collections of the 1720s and 1730s may have attempted to rival these highly influential pieces. The most ambitious is Thomas Roseingrave's (1690/1–1766) *Eight Suits of Lessons for the Harpsicord or Spinnet* (1728).[59] In offering eight suites it matched Handel's plan, and its contents were evidently conceived as a set, with major and minor, and flat and sharp keys, more or less balanced. In common with Handel, Roseingrave spent a period in Italy (sometime between 1709 and 1712), where he encountered Domenico Scarlatti and was deeply impressed. Hawkins thought his style was "harsh and disgusting," though he admired its learnedness. Roseingrave's experimental approach to harmony and structure could have stemmed from his contact with Scarlatti; he was later responsible for *XLII Suites de pièces . . . composées par Domenico Scarlatti* (1739), an expanded edition of Scarlatti's [30] *Essercizi per gravicembalo* (1738 or 1739). Roseingrave's pieces often combine harmonic twists and turns with complex counterpoint, as in the piece called "Chacone" concluding the First Sett where four stepwise notes of the chaconne bass are enmeshed in a three-part texture full of inversions. Allemandes adopt an unusual formal design, found in at least one Scarlatti sonata (K52), where the second halves begin with a tonic chord instead of the dominant.

It is not clear whether some pieces in Richard Jones's *Suits or Setts of Lessons for the Harpsichord* (1732) originated in solo sonatas for violin; their frequent violinistic leaps, sometimes extending to almost two octaves in the middle of right-hand passagework, suggest so, and there was precedent in Giovanni Bononcini's *Divertimenti da camera traddotti pel cembalo* (London, 1722), later published as Bononcini's *Suites de pièces pour le clavecin* (ca. 1735). Jones's highly inventive pieces possess a concerto-like expansiveness and encompass a diverse range of styles.[60] Around the same time, the Neapolitan Francesco Mancini's *XII Sonatas* for recorder and basso continuo (1724) were advertised on their title page as "proper Lessons for the Harpsicord. / carefully Revis'd and Corected / By Mr: Geminiani." However, Geminiani's *Pièces de clavecin* (1743) and *The Second Collection of Pieces for the Harpsichord* (1762), containing arrangements of pieces selected mostly from his Op. 1 (1716), Op. 4 (1739), and Op. 5 (1747), are idiomatic transcriptions to rival the *pièces* of French composers as well as Handel's suites. A revised version of Geminiani's Op. 1 solo sonatas was published in 1739, and the impressive *stile antico* fugue from the sixth was expanded considerably in the process. In the 1743 keyboard transcription, the four-part texture is presented on a three-stave score; the player is advised to perform the music that appears on the two lower staves using the left hand.[61]

Thomas Chilcot, James Nares, Maurice Greene, and Their Contemporaries

The harpsichord music to be considered next was written between ca. 1730 and ca. 1765 by composers who were born mostly within the first two decades of the eighteenth century. This was a period that saw the expansion of regional musical centers in Britain, where burgeoning concert societies provided employment for musicians as performers and teachers.[62] Several English keyboard composers of this period built their careers outside of London, among them Barnabas Gunn of Birmingham (d. 1753), Thomas Chilcot of Bath (ca. 1707–66), James Nares (1715–1783) – organist of York for over twenty years before an appointment at the Chapel Royal – and John Alcock of Lichfield (1715–1806). Handel's assistant John Christopher Smith (born Johann Christoph Schmidt) (1712–1795), Chilcot, and Nares chose to make their mark early in their careers by offering a collection of harpsichord lessons in the manner of Handel's 1720 collection, while Thomas Arne (1710–1778) and Joseph Kelway (ca. 1702–1782) issued their pieces later in life and may have composed them over a longer period. Several of these composers took advantage of the rise of John Johnson's publishing firm in the 1740s, which issued harpsichord music on high-quality paper in a spacious format, upright or oblong.

A style associated with solo sonatas continued to be adopted in English harpsichord music of the 1730s. The textures in Alcock's *Six Suites of Easy Lessons for the Harpsicord or Spinnet with a Trumpet Piece* (1741), for example, are overwhelmingly in two parts,[63] although the lighter-textured pieces that appear towards the end of Walsh's unauthorized "Second Volume" of Handel's harpsichord music (1733) were undoubtedly among Alcock's models: the Courant from Alcock's "Third Suite" (C minor) is directly modeled on one of these pieces (HWV 441/3; G major).[64] Chilcot's *Six Suites of Lessons for the Harpsicord or Spinnet* (1734) has a number of pieces that are similarly thin-textured, but many are also longer and more impressive.[65] The first suite, consisting of a Handelian French overture followed by five dances, is notable. Handel's influence is also evident in the second movement of "Suite the Second," which relates to a keyboard arrangement (HWV 428/6) of the final movement of the overture to *Il Pastor Fido* (1712).[66] The mid-century *galant* style starts to make its appearance in Chilcot's pieces, notably in the sarabands with their triplet figures and in the minuet conclusions to several of the suites.

While retaining a formal plan in three or four movements, English composers of the 1740s started to adopt some of the signature traits of Scarlatti's one-movement sonatas, such as rapid repeated notes, rapid hand crossings, and special harmonic effects. The change is illustrated clearly in Smith's pieces. His first two collections (1732, 1735) look like student exercises and contain several pieces modeled directly on Handel's. In contrast, his later collections, *Six Suits of Lessons for the Harpsicord*, Op. 3 (1755), *A Collection of Lessons for the Harpsicord*, Op. 4 (1757), and, to some extent, *XII Sonatas for the Harpsicord*, Op. 5 (1765) are arguably the most Scarlatti-influenced of any English composer; some of their pieces are harmonically and formally quite experimental, and the first halves of two movements from Lessons VIII and XI

Example 3.5 John Christopher Smith (1712–1795), Lesson XI, first movement, mm. 1–16, from *A Collection of Lessons for the Harpsicord*, Op. 4 (1757)

in Op. 4 even close in the subdominant (Example 3.5). Nares's *Eight Setts of Lessons for the Harpsichord* (1747) and a follow-up volume, *These Lessons for the Harpsichord ... are Humbly Dedicated to ... The Countess of Carlisle*, Op. 2 (1759), feature Scarlattian acrobatics in equal measure and are effectively written but are mostly in a more harmonically straightforward style (with the exception of the chromatic "Larghetto" from Lesson V). In the prefatory text to Op. 2, Nares calls rising chromatic-scale figures in sixteenth notes, which occur with some frequency in Smith's Opp. 3 and 4 (see Example 3.5), "wanton and improper," although he does not identify the music to which he is referring; similar figures appear in Sonata VII from Domenico Paradies's (1707–1791) *Sonate di gravicembalo* (London, 1754). It is not clear why the historian Charles Burney denigrated Kelway's *Six Sonatas for the Harpsicord* (1764) as "perhaps, the most crude, aukward [*sic*], and unpleasant pieces of the kind that have ever been engraved"; he may have been put off by old-fashioned features, such as movements closely resembling the old dance prototypes (one is actually called "Allemande") and harmonic complexity in both slow and fast movements.[67]

Around 1750 a simpler type of harpsichord music modeled on Domenico Alberti's Op. 1 sonatas (1748) started to appear, characterized by melody-oriented textures and left-hand accompaniments consisting of arpeggio figuration or tremolo basses in eighth notes. A similar style was adopted by Maurice Greene (1696–1755) in *A Collection of Lessons for the Harpsichord* (1750) and by the clergyman William Felton

(1715–1769) in his Op. 3 and Op. 6 *Suits of Easy Lessons for the Harpsichord* (1752, 1757).[68] Later in the eighteenth century these types of collection were labeled "easy" or "progressive" with greater frequency, although Arne's *VIII Sonatas or Lessons for the Harpsichord* (1756), Elizabeth Turner's (d. 1756) *A Collection of Songs … with Six Lessons for the Harpsichord* (1756), and Smith's Op. 5 belong in the same category. There is little evidence of Scarlattian influence in Arne's. Turner's lessons each begin with a substantial toccata-like movement, while the dances that follow sometimes recall the two-part idioms of Alcock and Chilcot.[69]

The Late Eighteenth Century: John Jones, John Worgan, Jacob Kirckman, and Others

A large number of collections of harpsichord music were published in Britain between ca. 1760 and ca. 1785, which from the 1770s onwards were increasingly publicized on title pages as suitable "for harpsichord or piano forte" (for discussion of this phrase, see below).[70] Many reflect the tastes of this period, which gave preference to simple harmonies and brilliant effects. Alberti's sonatas introduced a two-movement structure, which was also used by Paradies and Baldassare Galuppi (1706–1785), opera composers resident in London in the 1750s. Paradies's twelve *Sonate* and Galuppi's Opp. 1 and 2 *Sonate per cembalo* (1756, 1759) both offered the winning combination of singing melodies and toccata-like passagework.[71] Two-movement form was adopted by several English composers, including Charles Burney (1726–1814), whose *Six Sonatas for the Harpsichord* (1761) appends examples of improvised preludes to each pair of movements. Later generations of Italians in Britain, such as Tommaso Giordani (ca. 1733–1806), the violinist Felice Giardini (1716–1796), and the castratos Giusto Ferdinando Tenducci (ca. 1735–1790) and Venanzio Rauzzini (1746–1810) also published solo harpsichord music but tended to concentrate on sonatas with obbligato parts or concertos. As the title of Giordani's *Six Progressive Lessons for the Harpsichord or Piano Forte Calculated for the Improvement of Young Performers* (1780) suggests, their solo music, although often charming, was written for teaching beginners or intermediate players. More ambitious sonatas were written by John Christian Bach (1735–1782), youngest son of Johann Sebastian, and Jacob Kirckman (1746–1812), as well as by English organists, such as John Worgan (1724–1790), John Jones (1728–1796) and George Berg (1730–1775).[72]

Worgan's *Six Sonatas for the Harpsicord* (1768) mixes styles in a way that is characteristic of late eighteenth-century English solo harpsichord collections. The first three sonatas are modern sinfonia-like pieces in three movements, while the remainder recall earlier music by incorporating movements based on a gavotte and a sarabande (Sonata VI is a "Sarabande with Variations"). The fourth sonata is a Scarlattian piece in two movements; its second movement, marked "Bizzaria," begins in slow 2/4 tempo, but has varied repeats written out in the sixteenth notes and 3/8 meter of the first movement. Worgan studied with Roseingrave, edited a collection of Scarlatti sonatas, and possessed more in manuscript.[73] Ostensibly, Jones's *Eight Setts of Lessons for the Harpsichord* (1754), and his two-volume *Lessons for the Harpsichord* (1761), harken back to collections of suites. However, within each key group there is clearly an attempt to create a unified, sonata-like whole from diverse elements. Lesson V (E♭) from the 1754 volume is representative in its synthesis of different moods, keys, and textures; it begins with a weighty prelude (Andante Moderato), followed by an Allmand and Corrante, then an Andante in C minor, which begins with an adapted version of the theme from the first movement, followed by a light-hearted Minuet. The 1761 volumes include such things as extended evocations of accompanied recitative (Vol. 1, pp. 28–29), and a suite based on horn idioms (Vol. 1, pp. 33–36).

Although the title-page expression "for the harpsichord or piano forte" could indicate that the two instruments were considered alternatives, it also seems to have been used to describe collections combining sonatas for harpsichord and sonatas for piano, as well as for collections containing mostly or entirely harpsichord music. Bach's Op. 5, published by Welcker as *Sonatas for the Piano Forte or Harpsichord* (1766), but self-published as *Six sonates pour le clavecin ou le piano*, features crescendo markings in Sonatas I–IV, which may have been intended for piano, but not in Sonatas V–VI, which lack dynamic indications and may have been written for harpsichord.[74] On the other hand, *Eight Lessons for the Harpsichord or Piano Forte*, Op. 7 (ca. 1771) and *Six Lessons for the Harpsichord or Piano Forte* (ca. 1772), by theater composers Samuel Arnold (1740–1802) and Charles Dibdin (1745–1814) respectively, seem suited to harpsichord throughout; many of the *piano* and *forte* contrasts in Arnold's can be accommodated by a double-manual instrument, while Dibdin's lacks dynamic markings and has a dedication to Miss Louisa Chauvet describing

Example 3.6 Jacob Kirckman (1746–1812), Fugue in F minor, opening of fugue subject, from *Six Lessons for the Harpsichord or Piano Forte*, Op. 3 (ca. 1780), p. 8; Jean-Philippe Rameau, "Canon, à la quinte" ("Ah! loin de rire"), subject, from *Traité de l'harmonie* (1722), p. 360, transposed to F minor

it as "a Set of Harpsicord Sonatas, which were compos'd for your use." Similarly, Berg's *Ten Sonatas for the Harpsichord or Piano Forte*, Op. 7 (1768) contains works that may have been intended for the harpsichord, although diminuendo and crescendo markings appear sporadically. In common with several other Johnson-firm publications, Berg's Op. 7 includes the text of a royal privilege, designed to protect it from unauthorized reprinting, brought out initially to protect the composer's Op. 3 sonatinas (1759).

A late collection of special interest is the *Six Lessons for the Harpsichord or Piano Forte*, Op. 3 (ca. 1780) of Jacob Kirckman, nephew and namesake of the harpsichord and piano maker.[75] Its date is uncertain, but it appeared before 19 March 1783, when Longman and Broderip advertised it among music "this day ... republished," and it is presumably later than Kirckman's *Six Sonatas for the Harpsichord or Piano Forte* (without opus number), an edition of which was issued by James Blundell, who was active between ca. 1778 and ca. 1782.[76] The collection juxtaposes three grand two-movement sonatas, with three Handel-inspired groups that include fugues; it culminates in a Prelude-Fugue-Allemande-Courante-Gigue suite in E minor. The Lesson II fugue is headed "The Subject No.1 by desire is taken from an Air of Rameau," perhaps because its first subject was suggested to Kirckman by the collection's dedicatee, the fifth Earl of Plymouth, Other Windsor (1751–1799), who was a member of the Noblemen and Gentlemen's Catch Club in 1775. The theme is uncharacteristic of Rameau but resembles the subject from the "Canon, à la quinte" ("Ah! loin de rire") from Rameau's influential *Traité de l'harmonie* (1722) (Example 3.6). If this canon was the source, Kirckman has added a head motif (fifth degree of the scale to first degree) and continuation, presumably to make it suited to the fugal context, although the changes transform it in a way that make it almost unrecognizable. These pieces doubtless reflect the interest in what was known at the time as "ancient" music and the veneration of classic composers such as Rameau and Handel that came with it.[77]

Notes

Biographical information has been obtained from *Oxford Music Online: Grove Music Online*, ed. Deane L. Root (www.oxfordmusiconline) and the *Oxford Dictionary of National Biography* (www.oxforddnb.com/). Where obtained from elsewhere, the source is cited. All printed sources were consulted in the British Library, London, or via the IMSLP/Petrucci Music Library (http://imslp.org/). Secondary literature on manuscripts has been given where unavailable or incomplete in modern editions. Musical examples from modern editions have been checked against the original sources. I am indebted to the existing studies, especially those listed in "Further Reading." I am grateful to Michael Talbot for helpful comments on a draft.

1. John Caldwell, "Lesson," in *Oxford Music Online*, ed. Root. The term was associated with mixed consorts in the late sixteenth century and retained an association with consort music modeled on dances before 1700.
2. John Harley, *British Harpsichord Music* 2 vols. (Aldershot: Scholar Press, 1992, 1994), Vol. 2, pp. 118–144.
3. For a chronological list of publications, see Harley, *British Harpsichord Music*, Vol. 1.
4. *English Keyboard Concertos, 1740–1815*, ed. Peter Lynan, Musica Britannica, Vol. 94 (London: Stainer and Bell, 2013); Ronald R. Kidd, "The Emergence of Chamber Music with Obligato Keyboard in England," *Acta Musicologica* 44 (1972), pp. 122–144, especially p. 131.
5. Orlando Gibbons, *Keyboard Music*, ed. Gerald Hendrie, Musica Britannica, Vol. 20, third edition (London: Stainer and Bell, 2010).
6. See, for example, *English Pastime Music 1630–1660*, ed. Martha Maas, Collegium Musicum, Yale University, 2nd series, Vol. 4 (Madison: A-R Editions, 1974). Other editions based on single sources are listed in Virginia Brookes, *British Keyboard Music to c.1660* (Oxford: Clarendon, 1996), xii–xiii, abbreviated to "BPBV," "BVPB," "CER," "DPIV," "CEKM, xix" and "FCVB."
7. John Cunningham, *The Consort Music of William Lawes, 1602–1645* (Woodbridge: Boydell and Brewer, 2010).
8. Heardson's location at the time he copied this manuscript is not known. See Bruce Gustafson, *French Harpsichord Music of the 17th Century: A Thematic Catalogue of the Sources with Commentary*, 3 vols. (Ann Arbor: UMT Press, 1979), Vol. 1, pp. 63–65, Vol. 2, pp. 133–40, and Candace Bailey, "New York Public Library Drexel MS 5611: English Keyboard Music of the Early Restoration," *Fontes Artis Musicae* 47 (2000), pp. 51–67, and the further literature cited.
9. Andrew Cichy, "Lost and Found: Hugh Facy," *Early Music* 42 (2014), pp. 95–104; Brookes, *British Keyboard Music*, p. 309.
10. See *English Keyboard Music 1650–1695: Perspectives on Purcell*, ed. Andrew Woolley, Purcell Society Companion Series, Vol. 6 (London: Stainer and Bell, in press), nos. 7A–17.
11. Gustafson, *French Harpsichord Music*, Vol. 1, pp. 62–63, Vol. 2, pp. 123–132; Candace Bailey, "William Ellis and the Transmission of Continental Keyboard Music in Restoration England," *Journal of*

Musicological Research 20 (2001), pp. 211–242; John Milsom, *Christ Church Library Music Catalogue*, http://library.chch.ox.ac.uk/music.

12. Barry Cooper, "The Keyboard Suite in England before the Restoration," *Music & Letters* 53 (1972), pp. 309–319, especially p. 312.

13. *Musick's Hand-Maid*, ed. Thurston Dart (London: Stainer and Bell, 1969); Peter Alan Munstedt, *John Playford, Music Publisher: A Bibliographical Catalogue* (PhD diss., University of Kentucky, 1983), pp. 225–227; Brookes, *British Keyboard Music*, pp. 339–342.

14. *Œuvres des Mercure*, ed. Monique Rollin and Jean Michel Vaccaro (Paris: Centre National de la Recherche Scientifique, 1977); Brookes, *British Keyboard Music*, no. 1948.

15. On this style of keyboard writing, see David J. Buch, "*Style brisé, Style luthé,* and the *Choses luthées,*" *The Musical Quarterly* 71 (1985), pp. 52–67, and David Ledbetter, *Harpsichord and Lute Music in 17th-Century France* (London: Macmillan, 1987).

16. Gustafson, *French Harpsichord Music*, Vol. 1, pp. 58–60; *Harpsichord Music Associated with the Name La Barre*, ed. Bruce Gustafson and R. Peter Wolf, The Art of the Keyboard, Vol. 4 (New York: The Broude Trust, 1999).

17. Gustafson, *French Harpsichord Music*, Vol. 1, pp. 64–65.

18. Andrew Woolley, "The Harpsichord Music of Richard Ayleward, an 'Excellent Organist' of the Commonwealth and Early Restoration," *Journal of Seventeenth-Century Music* 15 (2009) (www.sscm-jscm.org/v15/no1/woolley.html), section 5.2 and Table 2.

19. In Matthias Weckmann, *Sämtliche freie Orgel- und Clavierwerke*, ed. Siegbert Rampe, third edition (Kassel: Bärenreiter, 2003), Appendix II, nos. 1–3.

20. *Matthew Locke: Melothesia*, ed. Christopher Hogwood (Oxford: Oxford University Press, 1987); Matthew Locke, *Thirteen Pieces*, ed. Terence Charlston (Hebden Bridge: Peacock Press, 2004).

21. Benjamin Rogers, *Complete Keyboard Works*, ed. Richard Rastall (London: Stainer and Bell, 1973); Richard Ayleward, *Harpsichord Music*, ed. Andrew Woolley, Web Library of Seventeenth-Century Music, Vol. 27 (2013), www.sscm-wlscm.org/index.php/.

22. *The Selosse Manuscript: Seventeenth-Century Jesuit Keyboard Music*, ed. Peter Leech, second edition (Launton: Edition HH, 2009). The contents of a related source are in *"Fitt for the Manicorde." A Seventeenth-Century English Collection of Keyboard Music*, ed. Christopher Hogwood (Launton: Edition HH, 2003).

23. See *English Keyboard Music 1650–1695*, ed. Woolley, Preface (discussion of nos. 27–29).

24. Candace Bailey, "Des préludes 'non mesurés' en Angleterre?", *Revue de Musicologie*, 87 (2001), pp. 289–305. See also *English Keyboard Music 1650–1695*, ed. Woolley, no. 43.

25. A type of jig notated in common time probably performed as if written in compound time.

26. John Roberts, *The Complete Works*, ed. Candace Bailey, The Art of the Keyboard, Vol. 8 (New York: The Broude Trust, 2003).

27. *The Complete Works*, ed. Bailey, no 10.
28. Albertus Bryne, *Keyboard Music for Harpsichord and Organ*, ed. Terence Charlston and Heather Windram (Oslo: Norsk Musikforlag, 2008); *English Keyboard Music 1650–1695*, ed. Woolley, nos. 33–36.
29. Bryne, *Keyboard Music*, ed. Charlston and Windram, nos. C3–C5.
30. *Roger North on Music*, ed. John Wilson (London: Novello, 1959), p. 139n; *A Choice Collection of Ayres* (London: John Young, 1700), 1 ("The Publisher to the Reader").
31. John Blow, *Complete Harpsichord Music*, ed. Robert Klakowich, Musica Britannica, Vol. 73 (London: Stainer and Bell, 1998); Peter Holman, "A New Source of Restoration Keyboard Music," *Royal Musical Association Research Chronicle* 20 (1986/1987), pp. 53–57. For the Henstridge manuscript (London, British Library, Add. MS 31403) see also *English Keyboard Music 1650–1695*, ed. Woolley.
32. Blow, *Complete Harpsichord Music*, nos. 42, 60, and 46.
33. Christopher Hogwood, "The 'Complete Keyboard Music' of Henry Purcell," in *The Keyboard in Baroque Europe*, ed. Christopher Hogwood (Cambridge: Cambridge University Press, 2003), pp. 67–89, where modern editions are cited; Peter Holman, *Henry Purcell* (Oxford: Oxford University Press, 1994), pp. 93–98.
34. Thurston Dart, "Purcell's Harpsichord Music," *The Musical Times* 100 (1959), pp. 324–325.
35. The manuscript sources are considered in Robert Shay and Robert Thompson, *Purcell Manuscripts: The Principal Musical Sources* (Cambridge: Cambridge University Press, 2000), pp. 276–290. See also Andrew Woolley, *English Keyboard Sources and Their Contexts, c. 1660–1720* (PhD diss., University of Leeds, 2008), pp. 179–197.
36. Robert Thompson, "'A particular Friendship': Bell Barr, Annabella Howard and Sarah Churchill," *Early Music* 43 (2015), pp. 213–223.
37. Illustrated in Hogwood, "The 'Complete Keyboard Music,'" pp. 76–77. A digital reproduction of MS Mus. 1 is available at www.bl.uk/manuscripts/FullDisplay.aspx?ref=MS_Mus._1. It is discussed in Shay and Thompson, *Purcell Manuscripts*, pp. 278–282, where further literature is cited.
38. See, for example, Terence Charlston, *Purcell: Suites and Transcriptions* (Naxos, 8.553982: 1993), and Kenneth Gilbert, *Purcell: Harpsichord Suites* (Harmonia Mundi, HMA1951496: 1994). Modern editions of arrangements include *The Second Part of Musick's Hand-Maid*, ed. Thurston Dart (London: Stainer and Bell, 1969) and *Twenty Keyboard Pieces. Henry Purcell and One Piece by Orlando Gibbons*, ed. Davitt Moroney (London: Associated Board of the Royal Schools of Music, 1999). See also Henry Purcell, *Keyboard Music*, ed. Christopher Hogwood, David J. Smith and Andrew Woolley, The Complete Works of Henry Purcell, Vol. 6 (in preparation).
39. Giovanni Battista Draghi, *Harpsichord Music*, ed. Robert Klakowich, Recent Researches in the Music of the Baroque Era, Vol. 56 (Madison: A-R Editions, 1986); *English Keyboard Music 1650–1695*, ed. Woolley, nos. 106–122.

40. Peter Holman, "The Italian Connection: Giovanni Battista Draghi and Henry Purcell," *Early Music Performer* 22 (2008), pp. 4–19, reprinted in *Purcell*, ed. Holman, The Baroque Composers (Farnham: Ashgate, 2010), chapter 2.

41. London, British Library MS Add. 39569 ("Babell MS"), facsimile with an introduction by Bruce Gustafson (New York: Garland, 1987), pp. 24–31; Draghi, *Harpsichord Music*, ed. Klakowich, nos. 65–73.

42. Washington, DC, Library of Congress, MS M21.M185 case, facsimile with introduction by Alexander Silbiger (New York: Garland, 1989).

43. *English Keyboard Music 1650–1695*, ed. Woolley, nos. 49–58, 94–95, 101–105.

44. One Forcer autograph is edited as nos. 51 and 59–75 in *English Keyboard Music 1650–1695*.

45. Punches were initially developed for frequently reoccurring symbols, such as noteheads and clefs; they obviated the need to use a stylus for these symbols and were used on specially prepared plates. See H. Edmund Poole, "Engraving," in *Music Printing and Publishing*, ed. D. W. Krummel and Stanley Sadie (New York: W. W. Norton, 1990), pp. 40–53, especially pp. 43–44, and Richard Hardie, "'All Fairly Engraven'?: Punches in England, 1695 to 1706," *Notes* 61 (2005), pp. 617–633.

46. John Brian Hodge, *English Harpsichord Repertoire: 1660–1714* (PhD diss., 3 vols., University of Manchester, 1989), Vol. 2, pp. 34–35; Davis, *Keyboard Suite in C Minor*, ed. David Newsholme (York: York Early Music Press, 2016).

47. For Barrett, see Hodge, *English Harpsichord Repertoire*, Vol. 2, pp. 8–12.

48. William Croft, *Complete Harpsichord Works*, 2 vols., ed. Howard Ferguson and Christopher Hogwood, rev. Peter Holman (London: Stainer and Bell, 1982), Vol. 1, pp. 31–33.

49. Andrew Woolley, "An Unknown Autograph of Harpsichord Music by William Croft," *Music & Letters* 91 (2010), pp. 149–170, especially pp. 168–169.

50. Charles Cudworth and Franklin B. Zimmerman, "The Trumpet Voluntary," *Music & Letters* 41 (1960), pp. 342–348.

51. Jeremiah Clarke, *Seven Suites*, ed. John Harley (London: Stainer and Bell, 1985) and *Miscellaneous Keyboard Pieces*, ed. John Harley (London: Stainer and Bell, 1988).

52. The two engravers of the Whichello collection are not identified on its title page; all but the first page was engraved by the same person who engraved Richardson's, the title page of which is inscribed "T. Cross Junr. Sculp." Hart's collection is also inscribed "T. Cross Junr. Sculp." but neither of these engravers was responsible for it. For Cross-associated engravers, see Hardie, "'All Fairly Engraven'?", pp. 621–624.

53. Barry Cooper, *English Solo Keyboard Music of the Middle and Late Baroque* (New York: Garland, 1989), p. 160. For manuscript sources of Hart's pieces, see Woolley, *English Keyboard Sources*, pp. 60–68.

54. Babell's arrangements are considered in detail in Sandra Mangsen, *Songs Without Words: Keyboard Arrangements of Vocal Music in England, 1560–1760* (Woodbridge: Boydell and Brewer, 2016),

pp. 59–155. A manuscript of anonymous keyboard music containing eleven toccatas, two suites, and seven preludes, partially concordant with known works by Babell, has recently come to light in the Biblioteca Musicale Gaetano Donizetti, Bergamo, and appears to be a collection of Babell's keyboard music. See Andrew Woolley, "New Light on William Babell's Development as a Keyboard Composer," *Early Music*, 46 (2018), pp. 251–270.

55. *A General History of the Science and Practice of Music* [1776], 2 vols. (London: Novello, 1853), Vol. 2, p. 823.

56. Loeillet, *Suite in A minor for Harpsichord*, ed. Andrew Woolley (Hebden Bridge: Peacock Press, 2009).

57. Cooper, *English Solo Keyboard Music*, pp. 251–252.

58. Andrew Pink, "John Sheeles: Eighteenth-Century Composer, Harpsichordist, and Teacher," *Early Music Performer* 30 (2012), pp. 18–20; Michael Talbot, "More on the Life and Music of John Sheeles (1695–1765), Part 1: Origins and Early Years," and "More on the Life and Music . . . Part 2: Later Years and Legacy," *Early Music Performer*, 42 (2018), pp. 3–10 and 43 (2018), pp. 3–9.

59. Thomas Roseingrave, *Complete Keyboard Music*, ed. H. Diack Johnstone and Richard Platt, Musica Britannica, Vol. 84 (London: Stainer and Bell, 2006).

60. Richard Jones, *Lessons for the Harpsichord*, ed. Stoddard Lincoln (Paris: L'Oiseau-Lyre, 1974).

61. See *12 Sonatas for Violin and Figured Bass (1716) (H. 1–12): 12 Sonatas for Violin and Figured Bass (Revised, 1739) (H. 13–24)*, ed. Rudolf Rasch (Bologna: Ut Orpheus, 2015) and *12 Sonatas for Violin and Figured Bass Op. 4 (1739) (H. 85–96)*, ed. Mark Kroll (Bologna: Ut Orpheus, 2016). These are Vols. 1A and 4A respectively in the Francesco Geminiani Opera Omnia.

62. Jenny Birchell, *Polite or Commercial Concerts? Concert Management and Orchestral Repertoire in Edinburgh, Bath, Oxford, Manchester, and Newcastle, 1730–1799* (New York: Garland, 1996).

63. Alcock, *Six Suites of Easy Lessons*, ed. Richard Jones (London: Associated Board of the Royal Schools of Music, 1985). The "Trumpet Piece" is a keyboard piece imitating a natural trumpet.

64. On the doubtful authenticity of HWV 441, see Terence Best, "How Authentic Is Handel's G-major Suite HWV 441?," in *"Critica musica:" Studien zum 17. und 18. Jahrhundert: Festschrift Hans Joachim Marx zum 65. Geburtstag*, ed. Nicole Ristow, Wolfgang Sandberger and Dorothea Schröder (Stuttgart: Metzler, 2001), pp. 1–11, and Woolley, "New Light on William Babell's Development."

65. Chilcot, *Six Suites of Lessons for the Harpsichord*, ed. Davitt Moroney (Paris: L'Oiseau-Lyre, 1981). Keyboard manuscripts have recently been identified as being in Chilcot's hand; see Gerald Gifford, "Some Recently Identified Sources of Handelian Keyboard Music at the Fitzwilliam Museum, Cambridge," *The Consort* 65 (2009), pp. 46–59, and the catalogue at www.idiscover.lib.cam.ac.uk/.

66. Chilcot, *Six Suites*, ed. Moroney.
67. *A General History of Music*, 4 vols. (London: Payne & Son, et al., 1776–89), Vol. 4 [1789], p. 665.
68. H. Diack Johnstone, "Maurice Greene's Harpsichord Music: Sources and Style," in *Music in Eighteenth-Century Britain*, ed. David Wyn Jones (Aldershot: Ashgate, 2000), pp. 261–281.
69. Margaret Yelloly, "'The Ingenious Miss Turner': Elizabeth Turner (d. 1756), Singer, Harpsichordist and Composer," *Early Music* 33 (2005), pp. 65–79.
70. See the list in Harley, *British Harpsichord Music*, Vol.1.
71. Donald C. Sanders, "Sunday Music: The Sonatas of Domenico Paradies," *The Musical Times* 145 (2004), pp. 68–74.
72. For Berg, see George Berg, *Twelve Sonatinas Op. 3*, 2 vols., ed. Michael Talbot (Launton: Edition HH, 2017), and *Eight Suites of Lessons, Op. 5*, 2 vols., ed. Michael Talbot (Launton: Edition HH, 2017 and 2018).
73. Todd Decker, "'Scarlattino, the Wonder of His Time': Domenico Scarlatti's Absent Presence in Eighteenth-Century England," *Eighteenth-Century Music* 2 (2005), pp. 273–298, especially pp. 275, 278–279.
74. Richard Maunder, "J. C. Bach and the Early Piano in London," *Journal of the Royal Musical Association* 116 (1991), pp. 201–210. See also Gerald Gifford, "Burton, John," in *Oxford Music Online*, ed. Root.
75. Medea Bindewald, "Jacob Kirckman: Portrait of a Little Known Composer," *Sounding Board* 10 (2016), pp. 26–31.
76. *Morning Chronicle and London Advertiser*, Wednesday 19 March 1783; Frank Kidson, *British Music Publishers, Printers and Engravers* (London: W. E. Hill, 1900), pp. 13–14.
77. Guy Boas, Harald Christopherson, and Herbert Gladstone, *Noblemen and Gentlemen's Catch Club: Three Essays Towards Its History* (London: Cypher Press, 1996), p. 109. I am grateful to Graham Sadler for suggesting a possible connection to Rameau's treatises. In 1763, Rameau sent the manuscript of a "Méthode pour faire les canons" to the NGCC, which is likely to have contained "Ah! Loin de rire;" see Graham Sadler, *The Rameau Compendium* (Woodbridge: Boydell and Brewer, 2014), entry for "Noblemen and Gentlemen's Catch Club."

Further Reading

Bailey, Candace. *Seventeenth-Century British Keyboard Sources*. Warren, MI: Harmonie Park Press, 2003.

Brown, Alan. "England." *Keyboard Music Before 1700*. Edited by Alexander Silbiger. Second edition. New York: Routledge, 2004, pp. 23–89.

Caldwell, John. *English Keyboard Music Before the Nineteenth Century*. Oxford: Blackwell, 1973; New York: Praeger, 1973.

Cooper, Barry. *English Solo Keyboard Music of the Middle and Late Baroque*. New York: Garland, 1989.

Gustafson, Bruce. *French Harpsichord Music of the 17th Century: A Thematic Catalogue of the Sources with Commentary*, 3 vols. Ann Arbor: UMI Press, 1979.

Harley, John. *British Harpsichord Music*, 2 vols. Aldershot: Scolar Press, 1992, 1994.

4 The Netherlands and Northern Germany

TON KOOPMAN

The Netherlands, flourishing in the seventeenth and eighteenth centuries, was home to several important composers of harpsichord music. Besides Sweelinck, Cornet, and Bustijn, there have been many others who were born in Germany and came to work in the Netherlands in the eighteenth century, such as Lustig and Hurlebusch.[1] From the southern Netherlands during this period we know of Fiocco, Boutmy, and Loeillet, to give a few examples. But, of course, the Netherlands remains the smaller neighbor of Germany. When a harpsichordist thinks of Germany, the first composer to spring to mind is obviously Johann Sebastian Bach. His genius is the subject of another chapter in this book. Here I will focus on northern Germany, from which we have an abundance of excellent music for harpsichord by Buxtehude, Scheidemann, Böhm, Reincken, Weckmann, Tunder, Flor, and many others. A very rich repertoire indeed.

All of these composers wrote keyboard music, but it not always clear for what instrument: harpsichord, organ, or clavichord? Such distinctions might not have been very relevant to these composers, or the choice might have been determined by practical circumstances. For us it is good to know that in the seventeenth and eighteenth centuries, an organist was almost always a harpsichordist as well (and vice versa). The French Jacques Duphly is the only eighteenth-century harpsichordist I know of who thought organ playing would have a negative effect on his harpsichord playing, and he was definitely an exception.[2]

My advice for modern harpsichordists (and organists) is to approach the music with an open mind: if it sounds good on a harpsichord, then please feel free to play it! For instance, chorale partitas often sound wonderful on the harpsichord. Works with a pedal part or with "pedaliter" in the title are obviously meant for the organ, but in many North German works the choice to play with or without pedal has been left open or added later. When certain intervals exceed the span of the hand, that is, of course, a good reason to use the organ pedal. It is not always necessary to follow the choices of modern editors about what instrument to use (or to play "*manualiter*" or "*pedaliter*"). Everyday musical practice was less consistent and less strict than we are now led to believe. In Germany there were harpsichords and clavichords with a pedal as well. And one long "pedal" note can often still be played with hands only. If the long note dies out, you can play it again. The techniques of playing the organ and playing the harpsichord were actually almost the same. So, the choice of instrument is now up to us. Ask yourself which instrument would be best for a certain work. Or, if you don't play the organ yourself but do play the harpsichord, please feel free to perform all these wonderful works on your own instrument. Try them and hear if it works for that particular piece of music. And try them on an organ too, just for fun!

For some composers, more organ works than works for harpsichord have survived, but does that really reflect the musical practices of the seventeenth and eighteenth centuries? Organ works enjoyed more attention because the organ is a public instrument, while the harpsichord played a domestic role for a long time. It was only during the eighteenth century that the instrument began to move from the private sphere of the salon into the concert room – first as a continuo instrument and later also as a "concertante" instrument.

In this chapter, I will first speak about harpsichord music from the Netherlands, as this is a part of music history that, in my opinion, has too often been neglected. Then I will turn my attention to the rich harpsichord repertoire of northern Germany. Of course, my list of composers and works cannot be anywhere near complete within the scope of this one chapter, but, in addition to the obvious highlights, I will also pay attention to some composers that are not as well known. By doing that I hope to persuade harpsichordists to explore less familiar repertories.

Harpsichord Music of the Netherlands

The first source of keyboard music from the northern Netherlands is the *Susanne van Soldt MS* (on which I shall elaborate later) that was written before 1599. The high point follows directly after that with the works of Jan Pieterszoon Sweelinck (1562–1621). However, the first printed harpsichord music from the Netherlands is by Henderick Speuy (ca. 1575–1625), a contemporary of Sweelinck. Speuy's *De Psalmen Davids, gestelt op het Tabulatuer van het Orghel ende Clavecymmel* was published in Dordrecht in 1610, one year before the famous English collection titled *Parthenia* of 1611. We find a setting of Psalm 42 by Speuy in the *Bartfa MS* (before 1630?), which is also a unique source for some Sweelinck works. Speuy's music sounds particularly good on the virginal.[3]

Sweelinck (see Figure 4.1) is, without a doubt, the most important keyboard composer from the Netherlands. He was famous during his lifetime as an organist of the Oude Kerk in Amsterdam, where he worked for almost half a century, and as a widely respected teacher of organists. We are grateful that so many of his works have survived, although none come down to us in autograph but rather as copies in other (and often later) hands. There are, moreover, no extant sources of Sweelinck's music in the Netherlands; most are in Berlin. A number of important and reliable manuscript copies date from after Sweelinck's death, but such sources are often problematic, especially if they contain works that are only known from that one manuscript. This is the case with the *Bartfa MS* mentioned above.

Following the first edition of Sweelinck's keyboard works by Max Seiffert in 1894, three important editions have been published by Gustav Leonhardt, Alfons Annegarn, and Frits Noske (1968, reprinted in 1974); Siegbert Rampe (Bärenreiter, 2003–2010); and Pieter Dirksen and Harald Vogel (Breitkopf & Härtel, 2004–2007). Much has happened since Seiffert's edition. At first, more and more anonymous works were attributed to Sweelinck, but Alan Curtis refuted many of these claims in his book *Sweelinck's Keyboard Music* (1969), information that became the foundation for the Leonhardt edition.[4] Pieter Dirksen, in his dissertation, and his edition with Harald Vogel, attempted to establish a more correct and complete list of works. For anyone interested in Sweelinck, Dirksen's book on Sweelinck's keyboard music, in which he meticulously lists all sources, is highly recommended. And, especially in Sweelinck's case, these sources really matter. When playing Sweelinck, I recommend reading the critical commentary in the Dirksen-Vogel or Rampe editions for information on the sources and their importance.

There is no clear distinction between Sweelinck's works for organ and for harpsichord, unless there is a pedal part. As I said before, I prefer to try it and listen to what sounds good on which instrument. The echo fantasias and toccatas might be problematic in some cases. John Henry van der Meer begged to perform echo fantasias on a "mother and child" virginal.[5] The "mother" is a large 8-foot virginal, and the "child" a 4-foot instrument that fitted inside the "belly" of the larger "mother" and could be coupled to it or removed. That is, when lifting the jackrail of the mother virginal and putting the smaller instrument on the jackrail of the larger, one could use the combination of both instruments as an early double-manual harpsichord. On such combination, the echos would not sound in the same octave but an octave higher than indicated in the score (unless you play them an octave lower). However, in my opinion, the mother and child virginal is not the most suitable instrument for Sweelinck's intricate echo compositions. The distance between the two keyboards is quite large, and there is the problem of the octave transposition, so I prefer to play the echo fantasias on the organ. However, it is quite possible to perform the fantasias that have echos within the same octave on a virginal. The normal

8+4 Ruckers-type seventeenth-century harpsichord is of course an ideal Sweelinck instrument.

Sweelinck's toccatas do not have anything to do with the later Frescobaldi toccatas but are more closely related to those of his predecessors from Venice, Andrea and Giovanni Gabrieli, and in this context can be regarded as an improvisation, an exploration of the possibilities of the keyboard instrument (see Michael Praetorius's description in his *Syntagma Musicum III,* 1619).[6]

Sweelinck's fantasias are for the most part substantial works, based on a central theme that is developed in various forms. All of his fantasias are well suited for the harpsichord, the *Chromatic Fantasia* being the most famous of all. It is all the more remarkable because of Sweelinck's use of a meantone temperament in which he deliberately uses intervals that will sound out of tune in this tuning system. Michelangelo Rossi later uses the same effect in an even more extreme fashion in his famous Toccata VII.[7]

Sweelinck's "Hexachord Fantasia" is another breathtaking work of art that can be especially admired for its contrapuntal complexity, while remaining a true pleasure to perform. When you play it, be amazed at its construction! One of the most difficult choices with the elaborate fantasias is the tempo. If you start too fast, you will be forced to slow down later, which seriously damages the architectural qualities of the work. So you'll have to find the courage to start so slowly that each of the long notes at the beginning (almost) dies out before you go to the next. You will be grateful for this tempo later on. If you always keep the polyphonic structure in mind as your guide, the more improvisatory parts will fit in logically. It also helps to play fantasias by Byrd – they teach you a lot about the logic of Sweelinck's.

Sweelinck was an excellent improviser, and his spontaneous way of making music is tangible in his variations on secular songs of his time, such as "Est-ce mars," "Engelsche Fortuyn," "Mein junges leben hat ein End," "Ick voer al over Rijn," and others. Considerable keyboard technique is often required to perform these variations, but it is music that every listener can enjoy, especially when it is performed with early fingering and the appropriate articulation. I believe these variations sound good on an organ, but the virginal or the Ruckers-type harpsichord with 1×8 and 1×4 are ideal. The settings of sacred songs might be more suited for the organ, but *Puer nobis nascitur* and *Allein Gott in der Höh sei Ehr* work quite well on the harpsichord.

Dirksen attributes Sweelinck's *Ballo del Granduca* to Samuel Scheidt, but I don't agree with him on only that count.[8] There are certainly stylistic discrepancies in both the *Malle Symen* and *Ballo,* which can probably be explained by the way they have come down to us. They might not fit in Sweelinck's oeuvre very well, but they surely don't fit in anyone else's either. I am reluctant to remove a work from a certain composer's list unless we are absolutely certain who did write it. The result of the removal from an oeuvre will be that nobody will play it anymore. This is what happened when the smaller *Echo Fantasia in D minor* was moved to the Appendix of "Incomplete, dubious, attributed and misattributed works" in the Leonhardt edition.[9] Suddenly one of Sweelinck's most popular works was banished and was hardly ever heard again. Fortunately, Pieter Dirksen restored it to Sweelinck's impressive body of works.[10]

Figure 4.1 Jan Harmensz. Muller (1571–1628), *Portrait of Jan Pietersz. Sweelinck* (1624), copper engraving on paper, collection Ton Koopman.

Peeter Cornet (ca. 1575–1633) was an important Flemish composer of keyboard music. He was organist at the Archducal court in Brussels, with famous keyboard colleagues such as Peter Philips and John Bull. Cornet belongs to the generation that does not distinguish clearly between harpsichord and organ works, though his works with Latin titles seem to be more appropriate for the organ. Cornet's music has only survived through a unique single source for each work. The manuscript that contains most of his works had been missing from the Berlin library since the Second World War, thus explaining why the 1969 edition of Cornet's works by Willi Apel, which was based on a poor-quality microfilm, contained a lot of guesswork and some quite strange editorial conclusions.[11] However, with a turn of great fortune, the long-lost Berlin manuscript resurfaced again in the early 1980s in the University Library of Krakow.[12] It is in excellent condition too! Then it became clear that the Guilmant edition from 1910 (Guilmant's first edition of early music!) had actually been quite accurate.[13] Today we have a good edition by Dirksen and Ferrard, with even more works by Cornet and also some anonymous works that might be attributed to Cornet (e.g., the *Aria del Granduca*).

There are some striking similarities between Sweelinck and Cornet. The quality of work is high for both, but Cornet tends to be a bit more free in his fantasias and toccatas, and his style is more improvisatory, whereas Sweelinck is more focused on musical architecture.

All of Cornet's fantasias, toccatas, and even short individual courantes are written with sophistication and countrapuntal skill. All require a keyboard with a short octave, such as those in Ruckers harpsichords, which is not surprising, since Johannes Ruckers and Peeter Cornet worked at the same court in Brussels and must have known each other.

It is difficult to understand why Cornet's excellent music has remained so little known to this day. Whoever explores his work will be pleasantly surprised by this inventive and creative Flemish master.

Pieter Bustijn (1649–1729) was a Dutch composer of whom only one printed collection has been preserved: *IX Suittes pour le clavessin*, Op. 1, published by Roger in Amsterdam around 1712. Bustijn lived and worked in Middelburg and, like most Dutch organists, played the harpsichord, organ, and carillon. He was also probably the leader of the Middelburg Collegium Musicum, like his predecessor Remigius Schrijver (?–1681). Bustijn's nine suites for the harpsichord are well composed, pleasant to play, and offer many opportunities to improvise and to be creative with added diminutions. Most contain the same set of dances: preludio, allemanda, corrente, sarabanda, giga, but some suites end with an aria and variations or a tempo di gavotta.

Rynoldus Popma van Oevering (1692–ca. 1781) was from "Fryslân," the northernmost part of the northern Netherlands. He and some other colleagues were responsible for commissioning a new organ for the Grote Kerk in Leeuwarden from the famous German organ builder Christian Müller, and Popma van Oevering was one of the first to play on this beautiful instrument (the organ still exists!).[14]

We don't know much about Popma van Oevering's life. However, around 1710, when van Oevering was about eighteen years old, his *VI Suittes voor 't clavier* were published by Roger in Amsterdam. A scan of this edition can be found on the internet, but it would be a good idea to publish it in a facsimile edition so that this Frisian harpsichord music can be regularly played and enjoyed again.[15]

Anthoni van Noordt (ca. 1619–1675) came from a musical family. In 1659 he published his *Tabulatuurboeck*, in which we find many works for organ but also some *manualiter* fantasias that work very well on the harpsichord. There is only one surviving copy of this printed edition.[16] The fantasias bear a resemblance to Sweelinck fantasias. For example, van Nordt's Fantasia 12 quotes from Sweelinck's *Chromatic Fantasia* (no. 1 in the Leonhardt edition, page 1 in the Rampe edition published by Bärenreiter), but, in general, van Nordt's are smaller in scale.[17] Sybrandus van Noordt (1659–1705), the son of Anthoni's brother, was organist in the Oude Kerk in Amsterdam from 1679 to 1692 (where Sweelinck had worked most of his life) and from 1692 served in the Bavo in Haarlem. He published his Opus 1, *Sonate per il cimbalo appropriate al flauto & violino* in Amsterdam in 1690, with a beautiful engraved title page featuring musical instruments. It contains only one sonata for harpsichord, an adventurous work that tells us that Sybrandus van Noordt was an interesting composer. The *Sonata a cimbalo solo* features a basso continuo in the left hand, and thus resembles a flute or violin sonata, but it is actually an early (or the earliest?) example of a Dutch solo harpsichord sonata.

Quirinus van Blankenburg (1654–1739), son of an organist, followed in his father's footsteps when he was sixteen, first in Rotterdam, Gorinchem, and then the Waalse Kerk in Den Haag; in 1699 he was appointed organist at the Nieuwe Kerk in Den Haag. Van Blankenburg matriculated at the University of Leiden and became a well-known teacher of music. His earliest work for harpsichord, a *Preludium* full of ornaments and sudden changes in tempo, is found in the London Babell MS (British Library Add. MS 39569) from 1702. None of his earlier works have survived, though it seems likely that he would have started to write music early in his life. From the works that we know now he comes across as an experienced composer.

Van Blankenburg published three works toward the end of his life, though it is possible that he wrote them earlier. His *Clavicimbal en orgelboek* from 1732 is a beautifully printed keyboard edition of psalm settings, the melodies adapted to the contemporary taste, with abundant ornaments. Intended for private use, these psalms are now an almost-forgotten chapter in the history of harpsichord repertoire, but they are well composed and deserve to be played. The title reminds us again that there was not such a clear distinction between music for the organ and harpsichord. The majority of van Blankenburg's keyboard works are short, the most elaborate being the *Fuga obligata*, published in his treatise *Elementa musica*, 1739, which covers basso continuo and other subjects, including details about enlarging the *ambitus* of harpsichords.[18] Interestingly, a fugue with the same theme had been published by G. F. Handel in 1735, and, although the autograph of this fugue dates from around 1720, van Blankenburg accused Handel of plagiarism! He seems to be the first in the Netherlands to mention overlegato, which he calls "tenue," and his fingerings are based on those found in François Couperin's *L'art de toucher le clavecin* (1716).

Jacob Wilhelm Lustig (1706–1796), born in Hamburg (Germany), was a pupil of Johann Mattheson, Georg Philipp Telemann, and others. In 1728 Lustig was appointed organist of the Martinikerk in Groningen (the Netherlands), where he worked for more than half a century until his death in 1796. Lustig published several musical treatises, and also translated important exemplars into Dutch, such as J. J. Quantz's *Versuch* and Charles Burney's travel diaries.[19] However, he did not hesitate to add his own views and even criticism to the works he translated. He wrote exceptionally well in Dutch, which was remarkable considering it was not his native language; his writings became quite popular and are still a pleasure to read. As a composer, he focused mainly on the harpsichord. His *Six sonates pour le clavecin*, Op. 1 was published around 1734 by the Dutch publisher G. F. Witvogel, and a second edition (Leclair, Paris 1742) contains two additional sonatas. Lustig's sonatas tell us that meantone temperament was no longer prevalent in the Netherlands by the 1730s. For example, he regularly uses notes like D♯, A♯, E♯ and D♭, A♭, and C♭, which would have been impossible in meantone but no problem in a Werckmeister temperament. In 1994 a manuscript copy of *24 Capricetten voor 't clavier, uit ieder Grontoon één* (24 capricettos for the keyboard, one for every key) was rediscovered. These works wander through all twenty-four keys, similar to Bach's *Wohltemperierte Clavier*. Unfortunately, we don't know the date of composition of the *Capricetten*.

Lustig's best harpsichord music can be found among his sonatas. They are inventive works that give you a sense of joy in playing. Creativity is called for in the slower movements, in order to give all small-printed ornaments their own place and character. "*Con discrezione*" (i.e., use your own creativity) is not specifically indicated, but it applies here and in the best North German style. Some works are virtuoso pieces as well, where we feel Handel is looking over Lustig's shoulder. Lustig's notation is interesting, since it is more precise than one would perhaps expect in 1734. For example, he accurately prints sixteenth-note upbeats, thus indicating that Lustig and many other composers from his time could write exactly what they wanted. I therefore urge you to respect the composer's wishes and not to "overdot" unless it is clearly indicated.

Another regular feature of Lustig's music is the use of hand crossing, such as one would find in the sonatas of Domenico Scarlatti. In fact, I believe that Scarlatti's Sonata in C major, K 95 was actually composed by Lustig as the first movement of his Sonata II of Opus 1. Perhaps this quite simple work has been attributed to Scarlatti because of the cross-hand technique.

Conrad Friedrich Hurlebusch (1691–1765) was born in Braunschweig (Germany). One of his teachers was Buxtehude's pupil A. Coberg. Hurlebusch traveled from Braunschweig to Vienna, Hamburg, Venice, and Stockholm and was eventually appointed organist of the Oude Kerk in Amsterdam in 1743, where he worked for the remainder of his life. A substantial number of his works have survived, both vocal and instrumental, including arias from (lost) operas, songs, cantatas, orchestral music, and even a harpsichord concerto in A minor.

Hurlebusch's principal compositions for solo harpsichord include the *Opera scelte per il clavicembalo*, Op. 1 (Amsterdam, ca. 1733) and *Compositioni musicali per il cembalo* (Hamburg, ca. 1735). The *Compositioni musicali* was a corrected and enlarged edition of the *Opera scelte*. It was available for sale at Mr. J. S. Bach's house in Leipzig (one wonders what Bach thought of the somewhat elementary fugues in this edition)! There are also Hurlebusch's *De 150 Psalmen Davids met der zelver lofgezangen, gemaakt voor het clavier en orgel* (Amsterdam, 1746), another fine example of psalm settings for keyboard. Both editions of the *Psalmen Davids* (1746 and 1766) are meant for either the "clavier" and/or organ, but, despite the lengthy and ongoing discussion about the meaning of the word "clavier," I believe either clavichord or harpsichord can be used, without favoring one or the other.

There are two books of harpsichord sonatas by Hurlebusch that, to my knowledge, are not available in modern editions or facsimiles: *VI Sonate di cembalo*, Op. 5 and *VI Sonate di cembalo*, Op. 6. In the *Keyboard Book of Quirijn and Jacoba Elizabeth van Bambeek van Strijen* (1752), we find ten harpsichord works by Hurlebusch that were preserved in manuscript. Hurlebusch was a good composer, not a brilliant one, but was capable of some fine variety and invention.

Gerardus Havingha (1696–1753) was organist of the St. Laurenskerk in Alkmaar beginning in 1722. Besides playing the church organ and carillons (as did all Dutch organists), Havingha was keeper of the city's harpsichord. During summers he kept it at home, where he probably directed the local Collegium Musicum, for which he wrote music that is lost. His only harpsichord music that has been preserved is the printed edition of *VIII Suittes gecomponeerd voor de clavecijmbal off spinet* (Michel le Cène, Amsterdam, 1724).

Between 1723 and 1725, Havingha initiated a major rebuilding of the organ in Alkmaar that involved tuning in a "modern" temperament, making it possible to play in all tonalities. This tempered tuning was not the equal temperament we know today, but it made modulations "per omnos tonos" possible, as opposed to the old meantone temperament. This modernization met with fierce resistance in Alkmaar, forcing Havingha to defend his position wth the publication in 1727 of *Oorspronk en Voortgang der Orgelen*.[20]

It is therefore not surprising that we find remarkable tonalities in Havingha's harpsichord suites, such as the keys of B♭ minor and A♯ minor! These works are also technically quite demanding, but the musical quality is not always very high, although there are occasionally special moments. It is interesting to note that much of what a harpsichordist would want to improvise is already written out in detail by Havingha, something Scheibe had criticized in the works of J. S. Bach.[21]

Jean-Baptiste (John) Loeillet (1680–1730) was born in a family of musicians from Ghent and died famous in London. After moving from the southern Netherlands to England, probably around 1705, he called himself John instead of Jean-Baptiste and added "of London" to his family name, to prevent confusion with his cousin Jean-Baptiste Loeillet of Ghent.

John Loeillet published two sets of lessons: *Lessons for the harpsichord or spinet* (London, 1712) and *Six Suits of Lessons for the harpsichord or spinnet* (London, 1723). He was one of the famous harpsichordists of his day, which is absolutely clear from his excellent harpsichord music, in which he skillfully mixes French and Italian styles. Fortunately, both works are available in a clear and very legible facsimile edition, and they are warmly recommended to play and perform.

Josse Boutmy (1697–1779) was organist at the royal chapel in Brussels. A well-known pedagogue, he published three books of *Pièces de clavecin: Livre I* (1738), *Livre II* (1740–44), *Livre III* (ca. 1750), the third book containing an impressive list of subscribers that clearly reveals his Flemish roots and connections. Boutmy writes mostly in the French style, sometimes also in the "les goûts réunis" mixture of French and

Italian styles. He is a skillful composer. Some of his works are really interesting, others somewhat less original.

His second son Guillaume Boutmy (1723–1791) published *Sei sonate per il cembalo* around 1770. The left hand, which is written only in figured bass, requires harmonic realizations. Some movements are spectacular, others not bad. The music of both Boutmys is now seldom heard. Harpsichordists looking for lesser-known repertoire will find a treasure trove of well-composed music here, full of ornaments and written with an excellent sense of harmony.

Joseph-Hector Fiocco (1703–1741) was "Singmeester" (choir master) in the Cathedral of Antwerp, and later worked in Brussels until his sudden death at the age of thirty-eight. Fiocco composed excellent sacred vocal music. His only works for harpsichord are the *Pièces de clavecin*, Op. 1 (Brussels, 1730), containing two suites in which French and Italian elements are brought closely together. His models were François Couperin and Antonio Vivaldi. Fiocco stated in the preface to this edition that if these suites were well received, he would publish two more, but as far as we know that never happened. Too bad, because personally I regard these suites by Fiocco to be the highlight of eighteenth-century harpsichord music from the southern Netherlands. We find character pieces reminiscent of Couperin and a most remarkable four-movement sonata in the style of Vivaldi. This is an impressive work, in a sense a culmination of European harpsichord music. The two fast movements have bravura passages, and the third (slow) movement is exceptionally touching. In the second suite we hear echos not only of Couperin but also of the young Rameau. Fiocco deserves his rightful place in the repertoire of harpsichord music.

Christian Ernst Graf (Graaf) (1723–1804) was born in Germany and came to the Netherlands around 1750. He was an influential master who composed beautiful symphonies. In 1767 he was appointed "Kapelmeester" at the court of Prince William V in The Hague, and composed some harpsichord works for four hands that are fairly simple and well suited for teaching. His chamber music, often containing an obbligato harpsichord part, deserves to be performed again, but, in many cases, there is no modern edition available, and it is quite hard to find complete sets of parts for his works in the antiquarian market.

Graf (or Graaf as he was known in the Netherlands) was an internationally respected composer of instrumental music, and many of his works were published during his lifetime, not only in The Hague, but also in Berlin, Paris, and London. It should also be noted that even at the end of the eighteenth century, when much of his music was published, the harpsichord is still mentioned as the designated instrument on the title pages: first harpsichord and then the new and fashionable "forte-piano."

Johann August Just (ca. 1750–1791) was born in Germany, where he might have studied with Bach's pupil J. Ph. Kirnberger. He only came to the Netherlands in his late teens and mainly worked in Den Haag. He was well known as a keyboard player and taught at court. He composed concertos for harpsichord and strings and, a clever businessman like C. P. E. Bach, published them as violin concertos as well. His other published works include sonatinas, sonatas, and divertissements for harpsichord with a violin or harpsichord solo. Not all are very interesting, but the harpsichordist can find one or two attractive pieces in most sets. From his Opus 6 onwards, Just mentions the harpsichord *or* the forte-piano on his title pages. His harpsichord concertos are not difficult to play, can be quite original, and feature many printed indications for articulation, dynamics, and places to change manuals.

Speaking about the harpsichord as a solo instrument in a concerto, we should not overlook the concertos by Johan Nicolaas Lentz (1720?–1782). Lentz was probably not born in the Netherlands but came to Rotterdam to work as an organist at some point in his life. In 1749 he married the daughter of a wine merchant and succeeded his father-in-law in that business, combining the wine trade with his musical career. Lentz's two concertos for harpsichord, solo violin, and strings were published in Rotterdam around 1750.[22] They are pleasant and attractive works, technically not too demanding, and written with good musical taste: a worthy addition to the well-known concerto repertoire.

Keyboard Books

Besides printing, a normal method of disseminating music has always been by copying it by hand. Such handwritten keyboard books make very interesting sources. Sometimes they are teaching materials for (aristocratic or rich) pupils, sometimes they are a selected collection of favorite pieces for music amateurs.

In 1961 Alan Curtis published a volume of keyboard music from four important manuscripts from the Netherlands: the previously mentioned *Susanne van Soldt MS* in its entirely, and pieces from the Leningrad, Camphuysen, and Gresse manuscripts.

The *Susanne van Soldt MS* mentioned earlier is a unique and very early source for Dutch keyboard music. The members of the van Soldt family were Protestants from Antwerp who fled to London, where Susanne was born. She was given the manuscript as a young girl of twelve or thirteen.

It contains a number of notable features. In the *Brande champanje* we find one line with what must be the oldest preserved fingering from the Netherlands. Equally remarkable is a leap with one finger in the very first bar. The fifth finger is also used in a scale figure. The collection contains dances and psalm settings, one of the more elaborate pieces being a setting of Orlando di Lasso's *Susanne un jour.*

The Camphuysen MS, which contains many settings of songs from the very popular *Stichtelijke Rijmen* by D. R. Camphuysen from 1624, is important and unique, especially for its anonymous *Daphne* with variations: a virtuoso and excellent apogee of seventeenth-century keyboard music. In the *Gresse MS*, a collection from the second half of the seventeenth century, French influences prevail.

Godelieve Spiessens and Irène Cornelis have published a volume of music from three keyboard books from the southern Netherlands (Leuven, 1998). The keyboard books of Arendonk, Dimpna Isabella, and Maria Therese Reijnders are from the seventeenth century. They contain various settings of *Daphne* and several *Batailles*, which are mostly short and simple and seem to be meant for teaching. It is interesting that we also find fingerings here as well.

A significant source of Dutch harpsichord music from the eighteenth century is the keyboard book of Quirijn and Jacoba Elizabeth van Bambeek van Strijen (1752), a young brother and sister pair from a rich patrician family of Amsterdam. The manuscript, which can be found in Twickel Castle, was published in a modern edition by Rudolf Rasch in 2001.[23] The writer of the manuscript copied out ten works by Hurlebusch, mostly unpublished at that time. There is a remarkable *Menuet* with variations by Locatelli, a reworking of a movement from one of his flute sonatas.

Rudolf Rasch suggests that the writer of the manuscript could be Leonhard Frischmuth (ca. 1725–1764), a pupil of Hurlebusch and publisher of an interesting treatise about harpsichord playing: *Gedagten over de beginselen en onderwyzingen des clavecimbaals* (Thoughts on the Principles and the Teaching of the Harpsichord, Amsterdam, 1758). Not many of Frischmuth's harpsichord works have been preserved, but those we do have, such as his harpsichord arrangements of Giuseppe Tartini's *Concerti* Opus 4, are the work of a good keyboard master.

Harpsichord Music from Northern Germany

In northern Germany we first find talented Sweelinck pupils like Heinrich Scheidemann, Paul Siefert, and Melchior Schildt, and important composers in the generation after that: Matthias Weckmann, Franz Tunder, Dieterich Buxtehude, Georg Böhm, and many others.

Melchior Schildt (1592–1667), who studied with Sweelinck in Amsterdam, did not write much for harpsichord, or perhaps very little of it has been preserved. His *Paduana Lachrymae*, variations on John Dowland's "Flow my tears," however, are remarkable. Both Sweelinck and Scheidemann wrote variations on this "hit song" of the early 1600s, but in my opinion Schildt's variations are the most impressive. We find them in the *Voigtlander MS*, one of the many important German keyboard books that contains everything from simple lessons to great masterpieces. A few others in this category are the *Andreas Bach Book*; the *Möller MS*; the *Hintze MS*; and the *Celler Clavierbuch*.[24]

Some of these manuscripts also contain fingerings that show us how people played. The central aim of these early fingerings is to achieve a clear articulation. Modern keyboard players are often trained from their first piano lessons with a system that seeks to create a completely legato style. Before the nineteenth century, however, the central aim of fingering was to articulate, not to glue everything together. For example, in the *Voigtlander MS* and *Celler Clavierbuch* we find a fingering in which the third finger is central: you ascend 3–4–3–4–3–4 and descend 3–2–3–2–3–2 with the right hand (it is the opposite for the left hand). It is worth the effort to seriously try to play with these early fingerings (be careful not to twist your hands too much and overdo it) and listen to the effect. Adapting early fingerings is not as hard as it might seem at first, and the result in articulation is essential in this repertoire.

Dieterich Buxtehude (ca. 1637–1707) was born in Denmark or Sweden, depending on the exact year of his birth, although he regarded himself as Danish. In 1668 he was appointed successor to Franz Tunder as organist of the Marienkirche in Lübeck in Germany. Buxtehude is one of the most important North German composers of his time. His music belongs to the *stylus phantasticus,* the free keyboard style. The central feature of this style is that there are no tempo relations between the various sections of a composition, the player being free to choose a different tempo for each section. This idea is based on Girolamo Frescobaldi's Preface to his *Primo Libro di Toccate* (second edition from 1616), in which he makes the comparison to modern madrigals (of Monteverdi, for instance), that do not have a basic pulse or tempo for the whole work; rather, the tempo should be inspired by the text or music of a particular section. Contrast is therefore a very important factor.[25] Buxtehude is a true master of this style, a prime example being his *Preludium manualiter in G minor* (BuxWV 163), one of the best harpsichord works of the era.

Besides these free works, Buxtehude also wrote about twenty harpsichord suites, some with unique features. For example, there are suites with two and three sarabandes, others without a gigue (or are they incomplete?), and doubles (i.e., ornamented repeats). Then there are Buxtehude's variation works, *La Capricciosa* (BuxWV 250) being the most famous example and his longest work in this style. It is an aria with over 30 variations, displaying a great musical and technical variety without ever leaving the key of G major. Particularly noteworthy is the chromatic variation twelve (which is actually the eleventh, since the aria itself is numbered 1).

A very important issue in dealing with Buxtehude's music is what edition to use. There are several to choose from. Some editors find errors in the music and correct them, but what is an error? We have no autographs for Buxtehude's keyboard works, his works coming down to us in manuscript copies or copies of copies (the only keyboard music by Buxtehude that was printed in the seventeenth or eighteenth centuries was discovered by Pieter Dirksen in a Roger edition of 1710).[26] We have, for instance, the Ihre tabulature (from 1679 and later), and the *Frankenberger MS* in Den Haag (written by J. G. Walther).[27] When there is only one source for a particular piece, it can be very difficult to determine what is correct, what might be wrong, and what is impossible. Knowledge of the style is necessary, but it is not enough. I advise everyone to make their own decisions, by looking at the sources, including the increasing number of important manuscripts becoming available online. And let's not be too quick in determining that something is an error when it's only something unusual.

The chorale variations *Auf meinen lieben Gott* BuxWV179 is truly unique in that its movements have dance titles like allemande, sarabande, and gigue.[28] It should also be added that much of Buxtehude's keyboard music has been preserved in tabulature, a very precise notation for over-dotting and sixteenth-note upbeats. So we should be precise in playing rhythms as they are written (in tabulature or normal notation), in order to respect the composer's wishes.

A brief remark about temperament: many of Buxtehude's keyboard works do not work with meantone temperament, since he frequently writes D♯, A♯ and A♭. On a harpsichord it is of course possible to adjust your tuning before playing a particular piece. But I think it would make more sense to use a Werckmeister III temperament for Buxtehude's works. We know that Buxtehude and Andreas Werckmeister were friends, and Buxtehude had the organs in his Marienkirche in Lübeck tuned in Werckmeister temperament as well.

Heinrich Scheidemann (ca. 1595–1663) was one of Sweelinck's most brilliant pupils and became, like Sweelinck, a teacher of many organists himself (see Figure 4.2). For most of his working life Scheidemann was organist of the Catharinenkirche in Hamburg. He died during an outbreak of the plague in Hamburg in 1663.

Scheidemann was a great composer. See, for instance, his Gagliarda in D minor. His early works follow in Sweelinck's footsteps, but his later works stand firmly on their own. Scheidemann mainly wrote for the organ,

Figure 4.2 Johann Friedrich Fleischberger (1631–1665), *Portrait of Heinrich Scheidemann* (1652), engraving on paper, collection Ton Koopman.

and only little for the harpsichord. Of course, we can play some of his organ works on the harpsichord (or vice versa). What instrument sounds better for that particular work? Pieter Dirksen, in his edition of Scheidemann's keyboard works published by Breitkopf, points out that at least we have more harpsichord music by Scheidemann than by any of the other North German pupils of Sweelinck. Most of Scheidemann's works have come down to us in copies that were made during his lifetime, which is usually a good indication of their reliability. Personally, I find Scheidemann's six courantes with doubles very interesting. There is even a courante with *two* doubles!

Johann Adam Reincken (1643–1722) was born in Deventer, the Netherlands. He began organ lessons with Scheidemann in Hamburg at the age of ten. At fourteen he was back in Deventer and became organist of the Bergkerk. In 1658 he returned to Hamburg, eventually succeeding his master Scheidemann in the Catharinenkirche and marrying one of Scheidemann's daughters.

We know what Reincken looked like because of a painting from 1674 by the Dutch painter Johannes Voorhout, who portrays Reincken sitting behind a double-manual harpsichord, wearing a beautiful silk coat. Clearly Reincken was not a poor man!

It is odd that Mattheson, in his *Critica Musica,* describes Reincken as being twenty years older than he actually was. Perhaps he acted on Reincken's own request, because Reincken wanted to be taken seriously as a musician and probably thought a more respectable age would enhance his reputation. J. G. Walther describes him as a famous musician in his *Lexicon* of 1732.[29]

Reincken's music has been preserved in unique sources, with only two exceptions, about which there has been considerable discussion concerning authorship: two fugues, which have been attributed to Reinicken by J. H. Buttstett in Beckmann's edition, the manuscript having been lost during the Second World War.[30] For harpsichord, Reincken wrote eight suites, a toccata, and three variation works. I personally prefer the toccata in *stylus phantasticus.* Reincken's harpsichord music resembles Buxtehude's, although it is a little less exciting.

Georg Böhm (1661–1733) succeeded Christian Flor as organist of the Johanniskirche in Lüneburg in 1698. Johann Sebastian Bach was one of his pupils. This apprenticeship had long been suspected but could not be proven until Michael Maul and Peter Wollny found a fragment of a copy in young Johann Sebastian Bach's own hand of Reincken's *An Wasserflussen Babylon,* on which he had written that he copied it at Böhm's house (and on Böhm's paper).[31]

Böhm was a prominent and highly respected composer. Only the works with a pedal part are exclusively for organ, the rest being playable on either organ or harpsichord. "Manualiter" chorale settings sound excellent on harpsichord, organ, or clavichord! The suites are idiomatic harpsichord pieces. Besides these, the most unique work for harpsichord by Böhm is the *Preludium in G minor*, with remarkable ornaments on the second beat. This is *stylus phantasticus* in pure form. A bold composition that is already great without demanding much inspiration from the performer, it can sound truly fantastic if played creatively. Unfortunately, no autographs of Böhm's works have been preserved, so all are known from copies. Beckmann and others are concerned that the sources, often being the sole exemplars for a particular work, are not sufficiently authentic to be true representations of Böhm's works.[32] However, I feel it is still preferable to make a decision based on an authentic source rather than to guess what Böhm mght have wanted. Also remarkable is the fact that some of his works have come down to us without any ornaments at all, while others are full of embellishments. I regard the abundance of ornaments as authentic. Only keyboard players who find it hard to play them complain that there are too many ornaments (the solution lies in practice!). The lack of ornaments might also reflect the choice of the copyist. Was it too much trouble to copy them? Or was it easier to improvise them while playing? I am convinced that the music needs the ornaments, especially on the harpsichord.

Like many of his contemporaries, the Böhm repertory contains a number of "doubtful or spurious" works. Nevertheless, if you find they are interesting works, please do play them. As mentioned earlier, once someone has marked them as "anonymous" they will probably hardly be heard again. Böhm's works deserve to be heard much more often.

Matthias Weckmann (1616?–1674) was organist of the Jacobikirche in Hamburg, and fortunately he survived the plague that took his colleague Scheidemann's life. Besides magnificent organ works, Weckmann has left us *manualiter* canzonas, toccatas, and partitas that are suitable for the harpsichord. The six toccatas that have been preserved are written in full *stylus phantasticus*. Virtuosic works of genius, they sound equally well on a harpsichord as on a beautiful historical organ.

Franz Tunder (1614–1667) was Buxtehude's predecessor in the Marienkirche in Lübeck. He was the one who initiated the tradition of public concerts in the church, which he called *Abendmusiken*. Mattheson claims in his *Ehrenpforte* that Tunder studied in Italy with Girolamo Frescobaldi. Tunder became so famous during his lifetime that he is even mentioned in a book about the highlights of the city of Lübeck from 1666.[33]

For the harpsichord, Tunder wrote a cheerful *Canzona in G manualiter* on a theme of F. della Porte. There is a great contrast between this happy work and Tunder's serious chorale preludes for organ, which are wonderful and ingenious works, though determining their registration is not a simple task.

Christian Flor (1626–1697) was organist in Lüneburg. There is a manuscript in the *Ratsbücherei Lüneburg* that contains ten *Suites for Harpsichord*. Arndt Schnoor has attributed them to Flor.[34] One of these suites is also found in the Möller MS, which also contains an eleventh suite. These suites are written in the French style, with many doubles, here called "Variatio." In the same Lüneburg manuscript are anonymous chorale settings that are also by Flor. Short and well composed, these are very well suited to the harpsichord.

Of course, my list cannot be exhaustive, but I would like to conclude with just a few more names that are somewhat less familiar. Vincent Lübeck, Sr. (1654–1740), organist in Stade, wrote music for both organ and harpsichord – as did his son Vincent Lübeck, Jr. – good music, and enjoyable to play. Organist Delphin Strungk (Strunck) (1601–1694) and his son Nicolaus Adam Strungk (Strunck) (1640–1700) both composed for the harpsichord. The latter not only played the organ and harpsichord but the violin as well; he also composed operas and traveled to Italy. The Lowell Mason Codex, a very important and the earliest dated source for the works of Buxtehude, contains nine works by N. A. Strungk, including a *Capriccio in E minor* (for harpsichord?) and a beautiful ricercare written on the death of his mother (1685).[35] And finally, the music of another father and son pair – J. R. Radeck (ca. 1610–1663) and J. M. Radeck (1630?–1684) – can be found in the *Voigtlander MS*: the father wrote a courante with three variations and an *engellischer Mascharada* (with fingering!), and the son contributed a nice suite with an interesting *ciacona*.

The harpsichord repertoire of northern Germany is obviously a great treasure trove of many well-known gems and masterpieces by famous composers and hundreds of works that are hardly ever performed. There is still a lot to be (re)discovered and to be enjoyed!

Notes

All translations are the author's.

1. Full names and dates of composers, sources, and editions cited can be found throughout the chapter and in Appendix 1.
2. Cited in Friedrich Wilhelm Marpurg, *Historisch-kritische Beyträge zur Aufnahme der Musik, Band I* (Berlin 1754), p. 459. The statement reads: "Mr. Duphly, a student of Dagincourt only plays the harpsichord, in order, as he says, to not let the organ ruin his hand."

3. Országos Széchényi Könyvtár, Budapest (Hungarian National Library, Budapest), MS. Bártfa 27.

4. See Appendix 2 for information about this and other literature mentioned in the text.

5. See J. H. van der Meer, "Per ogni sorte di stromenti da tasti," *Tijdschrift van de Vereniging voor Nederlandse Muziekgeschiedenis* 19, nos. 1/2 (1960–1961), pp. 67–79.

6. Michael Praetorius, *Syntagma Musicum, Band III: Termini Musici* – Wolfenbüttel 1619. Faksimile-Nachdruck ed. Wilibald Gurlitt (Kassel: Bärenreiter, 1958), Vol. 1, chapter 10 "Von den Praeludiis zur Motetter oder Madrigalien: als die Toccaten," p. 23 (printed as p. 25, but there is an error in the page numbering).

7. Michelangelo Rossi, *Toccate e correnti d'intavolatura d'organo e cimbalo* (Rome, 1657). There is an extremely chromatic section at the end of the seventh Toccata, where Rossi deliberately plays with and stretches the limits of meantone temperament.

8. Dirksen, Pieter, *The Keyboard Music of Jan Pieterszoon Sweelinck. Its Style, Significance and Influence* (Utrecht: Koninklijke Vereniging voor Nederlandse Muziekgeschiedenis, 1997), p. 643: *Ballo del Granduca* is in the list of spurious works, in which Dirksen adds: "(Scheidt?)"

9. In the Seiffert edition of 1894/1943, the *Echo Fantasia in D minor* is included in Sweelinck's oeuvre as number 15, but the Leonhardt edition of 1974 has moved it to the appendix and listed it as dubious, number 34.

10. See Pieter Dirksen, *The Keyboard Music of Jan Pieterszoon Sweelinck*, p. 641.

11. Pieter Cornet, *Collected Keyboard Works*, ed. Willi Apel, *Corpus of Early Keyboard Music* Vol. 26 (California: American Institute of Musicology, rep. Holzgerlingen: Hänssler-Verlag, 1969).

12. Before 1941 the Berlin shelfmark for this manuscript was Mus. MS 40316. The manuscript is now housed in Krakow, Poland, in the *Biblioteka Jagiellonska*.

13. *Pièces de Peter Cornet* (ed. Alexandre Guilmant, André Pirro) in *Archives des maîtres de l'orgue*, Vol. 10 (Paris: Durand, 1910).

14. This organ was built between 1724 and 1727.

15. http://hdl.handle.net/2027/mdp.39015080972253.

16. This sole remaining copy is in the *Biblioteka Jagiellonska* in Krakow and can now be accessed online: www.jbc.bj.uj.edu.pl/publication/387034/content

17. See Anthoni van Noordt, *Tabulatuur-boeck van Psalmen en Fantasyen* 1659, ed. Max Seiffert, 1896, rep. Amsterdam 1957, Amsterdam, 2005, ed. Willem van Beaumont.

18. Quirinus van Blankenburg, *Elementa musica of Niew Licht tot het welverstaan van de Musiec en de Bascontinuo* ('s Gravenhage: Laurens Berkoske, 1739).

19. Lustig's translations include: J. J. Quantz, *Grondig onderwijs van den aardt en de regte behandeling der Dwarsfuit* [. . .] (Amsteldam: Olofsen, 1754); C. Burney, *Rijk gestoffeerd verhaal van de eigenlijke gesteldheid der hedendaagsche Toonkonst. Of Karel Burney's, Doctor in de Musiekkunde,*

Dagboek van zijne, onlangs gedane, musikale reizen door Frankrijk, Italie en Duitsland (Groningen: J. Oomkens, 1786); and F. W. Marpurg, *Aanleiding tot het clavier-speelen volgens de hedendaagsche luisterryker manier van uitvoering* (Amsterdam: Hummel, 1760).

20. G. Havingha, *Oorspronk en Voortgang der Orgelen. Met de Voortreffelykheid van Alkmaars Groote Orgel* (Alkmaar: J. van Beyeren, 1727, facs. ed., Buren: F. Knuf, 1985).

21. J. A. Scheibe published some critical notes about the music of Johann Sebastian Bach in his periodical *Der critische Musicus*. One of the comments was that Bach spelled out all embellishments. See *Der critische Musicus*, Vol. 1, part 6, 14 May 1737, second edition (Leipzig: B. C. Breitkopf, 1745), p. 62.

22. *Concerto per il cembalo concertato, due violini, viola, violoncello, e sonata a violino e cembalo obligato* (Amsterdam – Rotterdam, A. Olofsen & I. Hutte, 1753). *II. Concerti a sei stromenti, cembalo obligatro, tre violini, alto viola & violoncello* (Rotterdam: Alexis Magito, n.d.).

23. *Het klavierboek van Quirijn en Jacoba Elizabeth Bambeek van Strijen (1752)*, Rudolf Rasch, ed., Muziek uit de Republiek 5 / *The Keyboard Book of Quirijn and Jacoba Elizabeth van Bambeek van Strijen (1752)*, Music from the Dutch Republic 5 (Utrecht: Koninklijke Vereniging voor Nederlandse Muziekgeschiedenis, 2001).

24. The Voigtländer MS is a tablature manuscript bound with a copy of Gabriel Voigtländer's *Erster Theil Allerhand Oden vnd Lieder* (Sorø, 1642) in *Det Kongelige Bibliotek København* Mu 6610–2631. The *Andreas Bach Book* is an early eighteenth century keyboard manuscript from the Bach family. The Möller MS (or Möllersche MS) also originates in the Bach family. The Hintze MS (New Haven, Yale Ma.21 H 59) is a seventeenth-century German collection of music in French style; Weckmann is one of the copyists. The *Celler Clavierbuch* contains works by Scheidemann, Sweelinck, and others (Celle, *Bomann-Museum* DO 618).

25. Johann Gottfried Walther describes the *stylus phantasticus* in his *Lexicon* (1732) as "a completely free way of composing, without any constraint." The freedom is not only important for the composer but also for the performer. It is a personal way of playing, involving an individual approach that is essential for a performance. In music of the *stylus phantasticus* we often find the words *"con discrezione,"* which can be translated as "as you like it." This is not about tempo alone; it is about the freedom to use personal musical taste, rubato, and fantasy to bring the music to life.

26. *VI Suittes, divers airs avec leurs variations et fugues pour le clavessin, Amsterdam 1710*, Pieter Dirksen, ed., Muziek uit de Republiek 2 / Music from the Dutch Republic 2 (Utrecht: Koninklijke Vereniging voor Nederlandse Muziekgeschiedenis, 2004).

27. Ihre Tab.: Uppsala University Library Instr.mus.i.hskr.285; Frankenberger MS: Nederlands Muziek Instituut, Den Haag.

28. An examination of the manuscript and the new edition by Christoph Wolff reveals that the last line under the Allemande actually belongs to a different piece! This has often been played and recorded incorrectly. See

the Frankenberger MS at the Nederlands Muziek Instituut, Den Haag, which has also been available online: www.nederlandsmuziekinstituut.nl.

29. J. Mattheson, *Critica Musica* (Hamburg, 1722). On p. 255 Mattheson gives Reincken's birthdate as 27 April 1623. J. G. Walther quotes Mattheson on the birthdate in his *Musikalisches Lexicon* (Leipzig: W. Deer, 1732), p. 517, and states that Reincken was an extraordinarily famous organist on p. 360.

30. See the preface of J. A. Reincken, *Sämtliche Werke für Klavier / Cembalo.* Klaus Beckmann (ed.) (Wiesbaden: Breitkopf & Härtel, 1982), p. iv, and K. Beckmann, *Die Norddeutsche Schule II* (Mainz: Schott, 2009), pp. 226–227.

31. See *Weimarer Orgeltabulatur. Die frühesten Notenhandschriften Johann Sebastian Bachs sowie Abschriften seines Schülers Johann Martin Schubart. Mit Werken von Dietrich Buxtehude, Johann Adam Reinken und Johann Pachelbel.* Michael Maul, Peter Wollny, eds. Faksimile-Reihe Bachscher Werke und Schriftstücke Neue Folge Band III, Documenta Musicologica Zweite Reihe Band XXXIX (Kassel: Bärenreiter, 2007).

32. See G. Böhm, *Sämtliche Werke für Klavier / Cembalo*, Klaus Beckmann, ed. (Wiesbaden: Breitkopf & Härtel, 1985), Preface, p. iv.

33. Kunrat v. Höveln, *Der Kaiserl. Freien Reichs-Stadt Lübeck Glaub- und Besähewürdige Herrlichkeit* (Lübeck, 1666); see Wilhelm Stahl, *Franz Tunder und Dietrich Buxtehude. Ein Biographischer Versuch* (Leipzig: Kistner & Siegel, 1926), p. 29, fn. 1.

34. Arndt Schnoor, "Neue Cembalowerke von Christian Flor (1626–1697). Entdeckungen zu seinem 300. Todesjahr in Lüneburg," *Die Musikforschung* 50, no. 1 (1997), pp. 74–77.

35. Yale University Music Library, New Haven, CT, LM 5056.

Further Reading

Beckmann, K. *Die Norddeutsche Schule. Orgelmusik im protestantischen Norddeutschl zwischen 1517 und 1755.* 2 volumes. Vol. 1, *Die Zeit der Gründerväter 1517–1629.* Vol. 2, *Blütezeit und Verfall 1620–1755.* Mainz: Schott, 2005, 2009.

Curtis, A. *Sweelinck's Keyboard Music: A Study of English Elements in Seventeenth-Century Dutch Composition.* Leiden: Leiden University Press, 1969.

Dirksen, P. *The Keyboard Music of Jan Pieterszoon Sweelinck. Its Style, Significance and Influence.* Utrecht: Koninklijke Vereniging voor Nederlandse Muziekgeschiedenis, Utrecht, 1997.

Heinrich Scheidemann's Keyboard Music. Transmission, Style and Chronology. Aldershot: Ashgate, 2007.

Grijp, L. P., et al., editors. *Een muziekgeschiedenis der Nederlanden.* Amsterdam: Amsterdam University Press-Salox, 2001.

Rasch, R., *Geschiedenis van de muziek in de Republiek der Zeven Verenigde Nederlanden 1572–1795.* Mijn werk op internet Deel Een. www.let.uu.nl /~Rudolf.Rasch/personal/Republiek/Republiek.htm.

Snyder, K. J., *Dieterich Buxtehude. Organist in Lübeck.* New York: Schirmer, 1987.

5 Southern Germany and the Austro-Hungarian Empire to 1750

PIETER DIRKSEN

Apparently longer than most other styles, the South German and Austrian keyboard tradition showed little inclination to differentiate between the organ and the harpsichord. Whereas, for example, the virginalists and Frescobaldi and his school were predominantly oriented to the harpsichord, the Spanish and North German schools can be viewed in the context of the typical organ tradition. From the 1620s, French keyboard music already showed clear signs of conceiving a separation between organ and harpsichord, a conception that would become strictly formalized later in the century. This is, however, not yet the case in the music of such important South Germans as Hans Leo Hassler (1564–1612), Christian Erbach (ca. 1570–1635), or Johann Ulrich Steigleder (1593–1635). If anything, their music shows a primary orientation to the organ, and clear exceptions are rare. An important early harpsichord work can be found in Hassler's variations on *Ich ging einmal spatieren* – a melody that would later become more famous as the sacred contrafactum *Von Gott will ich nicht lassen*. A set of thirty variations became the ideal after John Bull's famous *Walsingham* variations. Although in this lengthy piece Hassler's Italianate, broad, and somewhat forbidding contrapuntal manner stands in the foreground, much of it seems idiomatic, as in the play with different short motives and ranges in variation 10, the "suspiratio" motive in variation 11, the complementary writing in variation 18 and the "syncopatio" in variation 21.

While Steigleder's *Tabulatur Buch Dass Vatter Vnser* from 1627 is, of course, first and foremost an organ publication, the fortieth and final variation is "auff Toccata Manier," which during this period meant "in the harpsichord way." That seems indeed to be the case here. To make this implication clear, Steigleder opens with two written-out arpeggios – indeed found nowhere else in the book – to which he expressly draws attention with a note within the musical text. It is a vigorous and lengthy piece freely modeled on the Venetian scheme: toccata (mm. 1–44), imitation (mm. 44–112), and toccata (mm. 113–37). The middle section, which is made of a succession of often very free imitations on the six individual chorale lines, has the same length (sixty-nine measures) as the framing parts combined. A sharper separation between organ and harpsichord is only to be found in the music of the Nuremberg organist Johann Erasmus Kindermann (1616–1655). His *Harmonia organica*, which appeared in 1645, consists entirely of organ music, but a collection of harpsichord dances has been preserved in manuscript (*PL-Kj*, Mus. Ms. 40147). One can recognize a number of three-movement suites here; although the Italianate trias *ballet – courante – sarabanda* is still predominant, three suites already replace the ballet with an allemande.

Vienna [1]: Johann Jacob Froberger

It is, however, only with Kindermann's peer, Johann Jacob Froberger (1616–1667), that we find an outspoken harpsichord composer and, together with Gottlieb Muffat, the most important encountered in this chapter. Born in Stuttgart, he probably learned his craft from Johann Ulrich Steigleder, but as a Viennese organist, Froberger, the Catholic convert, managed to obtain a stipend from Emperor Ferdinand III to complete his studies in Rome with the famous Frescobaldi. He did so between 1637 and 1641. On his return, Froberger was duly added to the imperial payroll as an organist, which he remained intermittently until 1657. His legendary travels as a virtuoso and probably also as some sort of secret diplomat carried him through Europe; longer stays can be presumed in Brussels and Paris. His friendly competition with Matthias Weckmann at the Dresden court at the beginning of 1653 is famous.[1] After Ferdinand's death in April 1657, Froberger apparently fell out of favor at the Vienna court and was dismissed for political reasons by the new Emperor Leopold I – even though the latter turned out to be an even greater music lover than his father and became the protégé of many musicians and composers, including several central ones for the keyboard, as we shall see shortly. But Froberger's dedication of two important keyboard works to him remained fruitless. Froberger thus went back to Stuttgart and Paris and eventually found shelter as the teacher of Countess Sibylla of Württemberg-Montbéliard, living quietly in her castle in Héricourt during the last years of his life.

Although he principally served as an imperial organist, Froberger was above all a harpsichordist. We now know that he went to Frescobaldi specifically to study "cembalo," for which the Italian's playing was particularly renowned.[2] A diplomat in Vienna in 1649 described Froberger as "un homme très-rare sur les espinettes" ("a man with a rare talent for the harpsichord").[3] And it is beyond doubt that the harpsichord suites, together with the *tombeaus*, form the most important category in

Froberger's oeuvre. More idiomatic music for the harpsichord is indeed hardly imaginable – and the same is true for most of the toccatas. It is furthermore striking that the large hexachord fantasia (FbWV201), which Kircher incorporated in score notation as a textbook example of a composition in "stylus phantasticus" in his *Musurgia universalis* (1650), was inscribed, no doubt at Froberger's instigation, "Clauicymbalis accomodata" ("made for the harpsichord").[4] In this fine tribute to the long-standing north-European tradition of ambitious keyboard fantasias on the hexachord, Froberger gives ample testimony of his contrapuntal prowess.

A particularly fascinating field of research with Froberger's music concerns the sources. Froberger himself stated at the end of his life that he was against the wide dissemination of his music since others could only spoil it without his specific personal instructions.[5] In spite of this, his music is encountered in a large quantity of sources and was copied well into the eighteenth century. Furthermore, the appearance of several prints proffering a fair sampling of his keyboard music in the 1690s (thus long after his death), including ten suites in an Amsterdam print, is highly unusual for the era. But pride of place must go to the three autograph collections preserved in the imperial archive in Vienna. This is especially true for the two surviving volumes from a set of four, the *Libro Secondo* from 1649 and the *Libro Quarto* from 1656, which present immaculate texts of Froberger's cosmopolitan keyboard program (the lost first and third volumes must have been from ca. 1645 and 1653, respectively); the *Libro Quarto* in particular is a lavishly produced volume. Each volume contains six each of toccatas, suites, and fugal pieces in *stile antico* (fantasias and ricercares, respectively) and *stile moderno* (canzonas and capriccios). Three recently discovered sources of gradually increasing importance primarily concern the suites. A manuscript copy from ca. 1675, which turned up in the late 1990s, contains copies allegedly taken directly from the autographs of no fewer than fourteen suites.[6] Another important manuscript from about the same period came to light a few years later, as part of the resurfaced *Singakademie* collection.[7] This manuscript contains only harpsichord music (toccatas, suites, and *tombeaus*) in clear texts with several important musical additions. Finally, a completely unknown autograph from Froberger's final years turned up at auction in 2006; among its thirty items are found eighteen new pieces,[8] which include a suite, a *tombeau*, and a *méditation*. Unfortunately, at present it is still unavailable for either study or editing.

As befits a disciple of Frescobaldi, Froberger wrote the majority of his toccatas for the harpsichord. Froberger here refers to the Neapolitan-Roman tradition, in which only special forms of the toccata such as the toccata "alla levatione" and "sopra gli pedali" are destined for the organ, while the nonspecific ones are (primarily) written for the harpsichord. While the pedal toccata, a standard item in the later South German tradition, was foreign to Froberger's mercurial temperament, and thus absent from his oeuvre, one finds three *Elevatione* toccatas which are indeed clearly written for the sustained organ sound.[9] The strong connection of the remaining toccatas with the harpsichord is confirmed by their close kinship with Louis Couperin's unmeasured harpsichord preludes. One can discern three stages. The first one can be found in the 1649 *Libro secondo*. Not only the two organ toccatas FbWV105–106 appear paired but the four harpsichord ones too. Thus two weighty minor-key works are followed by a pair of notably shorter and lighter works in major keys.[10] From this group, the second one in D minor has become justly famous, with its dark tone and densely written imitative sections based on the descending chromatic fourth. A second group, which can tentatively be associated with the lost *Libro terzo* from 1653, comprises the six works FbWV113–116, 118, and 121. They are marked by a mature sense of form and by imitative sections in which the theme proper is often replaced by motivic interplay. The third group, found in the *Libro quarto* of 1656 (FbWV107–112), is generally more compact, with imitative sections of almost laconic brevity.

It has long been recognized that Froberger's suites form his most original contribution to the keyboard repertoire. Furthermore, research has shown that Mattheson's observation that Froberger adapted the "Französische Lautenmanier von Galot und Gaultier" to the harpsichord should be taken at face value; by combining the brilliant Italian style with the subtle French lute manner, he developed a new, very personal "vermischten, angenehmen Styl."[11] In order to clarify Froberger's epochal creations here, it is important to eliminate a host of spurious and questionable attributions from the "anonymous" repertoire that clutters the recent *Froberger-Werkeverzeichnis.*[12] The newly discovered sources if anything demonstrate that the number of suites must have been relatively limited, but that they always maintain an immediately recognizable profile and high quality. Another striking aspect of this corpus is the great number of programmatic pieces (principally the allemandes) found here (see Table 5.1).[13]

Many of Froberger's most enduring compositions are found among these pieces. With few exceptions (i.e., FbWV606, 611 and 615), the subject matter is usually a sad one, ranging from a depiction of a perilous Rhine-crossing (FbWV627) to passionate outbursts of grief over the death of someone obviously close to the composer (FbWV632 and 633). The latter work, the *Tombeau sur la tres douloureuse Mort de sa majeste imperiale le troisiesme Ferdinand,* which, because of its three rather

Table 5.1 *Froberger's "Programmatic" Suites and Tombeaus*

FbWV	Key	Dating	Inscription
Suites			
606	G major	1649	Partita "Auff die Meyerin"
611	D major	1653 (May–August)	Allemande = on the coronation of Ferdinand IV as "Roy des Romains"
			Courante = on the birth of a princess
			Saranbande = on the coronation of Empress Eleonora Gonzaga
612	C major	1654 (July)	Allemande = Lamento on the death of Ferdinand IV
613	D minor	1652 (autumn)	Gigue = "Le retour de Mazarin"
614	G major	1653?	Allemande = "Lamentation sur ce que j'ay esté volé"
615	A minor	1658 (July–August)	Allemande = "faict sur le Couronnement de Sa Majesté Imperiale [Leopold I] à Franckfurt"
616	G major	<1654 (summer)?	Allemande = "Un chemin montaigneux"
620	D major	1660	Allemande = "Meditation faict sur ma mort future"
627	E minor	<1653 (spring)?	Allemande = Rhine passing ("Wasserfall")
630	A minor	ca. 1651?	Allemande = "Plaincte faite à Londres pour passer la Melancolie"
[657	F major	>1661?	Allemande = "Afligée"]*
Tombeaus			
632	C minor	1652 (November)	Tombeau on the death of Charles Fleury, Sieur de Blanrocher
633	F major/minor	1657 (April)	Tombeau on the death of Ferdinand III
[658	G minor	1666?	"Meditation faict à Madrid sur la Mort future de Madame Sybille"]*
[659	D minor	1662	Tombeau on the death of Count Leopold Friedrich of Würtemberg]*

* = Unica from the as yet inaccessible "London" autograph.

than two sections, should be considered a pavan, arguably forms Froberger's masterpiece, written for the most important patron in his life.[14] In this work of deeply felt sorrow, Froberger incorporated much symbolism. The basic key of F of course refers to the mourned one's name, and the three sections to his imperial number. Modulations as a rule occur within the flat region (f, c, g, A♭), which makes the sudden turn to A major (Example 5.1a), achieved with an enharmonic change from B♭ minor, all the more striking.

The piece opens with a festive F major "style brisé" figure, which is, however, immediately darkened into F minor (Example 5.1b); this is

Example 5.1 a) Froberger, *Tombeau faict sur la tres douloureuse Mort de sa Majeste Imperiale le Troisiesme Ferdinand*, FbWV633, mm. 29–30; b) Froberger, *Tombeau faict sur la tres douloureuse Mort de sa Majeste Imperiale le Troisiesme Ferdinand*, FbWV633, mm. 1–3; c) Froberger, *Tombeau faict sur la tres douloureuse Mort de sa Majeste Imperiale le Troisiesme Ferdinand*, FbWV633, mm. 34–37

emphasized by an immediate repeat of the phrase a fourth higher. The ending is similarly striking (Example 5.1c). After arriving at a bleak, unresolved dominant seventh chord, there is a protracted, chromaticized cadence featuring a prolonged cadential appoggiatura whose "brisé" repeats on the neighboring notes F and G clearly evoke the tolling of death bells. The final resolution into a widely spread F major chord is thus a real transformation from darkness into the bright light of heaven, where the monarch is duly received by the triple sounding of the high f^2 ("Ferdinand III"). The three sections consist of thirteen, eleven, and again thirteen bars; the number thirteen played a significant role in Froberger's life and rather pessimistic worldview.[15] What is more, the striking opening and closing passages shown in Example 5.1b and 5.1c imply by their nature that they and thus their corresponding sections are not to be repeated, and this in contrast with the central section, which is emphasized by the presence of "first-" and "second-time" bars for bar 24.[16] This results in a total of 2 x 13 plus 2 x 11 = 48 bars, which was the age reached by Ferdinand III at his death.

Vienna [2]: Ebner, Kerll, Poglietti, Richter

Froberger's senior organist colleague at the Vienna court, Wolfgang Ebner (1612–1665), who sought to use nepotism to turn the Imperial organist posts into a family affair and may have been behind Froberger's downfall, left a small but distinguished oeuvre in which he shows a clear penchant for variations. Foremost is the *Aria Augustissimi . . . XXXVI modis variata ac pro cimbalo accomodata*, printed in Prague in 1648 with a dedication to Ferdinand III, the author of the short aria. The variations are divided into three groups of a dozen variations each, inscribed Courante (vars. 13–24), Sarabande (vars. 25–36) and by analogy [Allemande] (vars. 1–12).

Johann Caspar Kerll (1627–1693) was probably at some point a pupil of Froberger, since they were apparently both at the archducal court in Brussels at the end of the 1640s. If so, it is remarkable that Kerll's four surviving suites are so modest in comparison to his teacher's and that there is little if any trace of a direct Froberger influence. Kerll's remaining keyboard music (apart from the one published work for organ, the *Modulatio organico* from 1686) is notably more ambitious, particularly his cycle of eight toccatas. These do not imitate the alternation of free and fugal sections characteristic of the Froberger type, but seem directly dependent on Italian models, notably those of Frescobaldi and later Italians. Two of them are by their typology clearly destined for the organ, namely numbers 4 ("durezze e ligature") and 6 ("con pedali"; i.e., with long pedal points). Since Toccata 2 is also marked by a lengthy opening pedal point, it appears that the even-numbered toccatas are for organ, while the odd-numbered ones seem to be written for harpsichord. Indeed, the latter includes a Toccata (no. 5) marked "tutti di salti," and is thus exquisitely idiomatic to the harpsichord, while the exploration of rhythmical problems and advanced keyboard virtuosity of Toccata 3 seems clearly inspired by Frescobaldi's famous virtuoso Toccata *nona* (*Libro* 2). Extroverted harpsichord music is also present in Kerll's well-known *Capricio sopra il cucu* and in two ostinato compositions: a bouncing major-key Ciacona (in C) consisting of twenty variations and a more dramatic Passacaglia, in

D minor, with twice the number of variations. This set the tone for ostinato pieces of many subsequent South German keyboardists, who often copied this major/minor constellation (e.g., Georg and Gottlieb Muffat, Johann Philipp Krieger, Fischer, and Fux).

A particularly fascinating figure in Vienna was the rather enigmatic Alessandro Poglietti (d. 1683), about whom little is known prior to his appointment as an organist at the imperial court in 1661; he in all probability hailed from Tuscany. Much admired by Leopold I, Poglietti's keyboard music, other than a learned and much-copied collection of twelve ricercares, is marked by lively virtuosity and a preference for programmatic and picturesque writing. He seems also the first composer to begin his harpsichord suites (of the standard order allemande – courante – sarabande – gigue) with a two-part introduction in the improvisatory-imitative style, such as a toccata with canzona. The essence of his harpsichord music is found in a remarkable autograph dedicated in 1677 to Emperor Leopold I and his third wife Eleonora Magdalena, whom he had just married: the celebrated *Rossignolo*.[17] Expressly designated on the title page as written for "cembalo," it contains a fascinating mixture of the serious and the comic.

The double title page sports an ingenious allegory of musical time, vanity, and eternal happiness wished for the imperial couple. Its thirty-six pieces – an allusion to the emperor's age – offer a generous sampling of all contemporary harpsichord genres, ordered into three categories: a suite (opening with a toccata and canzona); an aria with variations; and an "appendix" which supplies specimens of the two imitative genres hitherto missing (ricercare and capriccio); and two pieces directly imitating the nightingale. The variation principle is omnipresent: not only in the twenty variations of the central aria part but also in the doubles added to all dances of the suite (in the case of the allemande, two doubles); also notable is the fact that the imitative pieces in part three are conceived as variations. The ricercare is followed by a "Syncopatione del Ricercar" and a more loosely related "Capriccio sopra il Ricercar." Both variations enliven the subject with repeated notes and thus smoothly progress to the culmination of the collection: the two free bird pieces ("Arie Bizarre"), with their frantic note repetitions and tremolos. Hand-in-hand with this thorough exploration of the variation comes a strong emphasis on unabashed virtuosity. Thirty-second figuration, for example, is found in the toccata, three of the doubles, several of the aria variations, and the two concluding pieces. One also finds, hidden in the first two parts, many allusions to the bird of the title, in the form of repeated notes, repetitions, and tremolos. Another striking feature is the often very full chordal writing. The peculiar technical demands are reminiscent of the music of John Bull, and there is indeed evidence that Poglietti was familiar with Bull's music.

In the central "Aria Allemagna con alcuni variation" specifically written for the birthday of the new Empress Eleonora (6 January 1677), Poglietti delights in the imitation of folk instruments such as the hurdy-gurdy (var. 5), the Bohemian bagpipe (var. 8), the Dutch flageolet (var. 9), the Bavarian shawm (var. 11), or the Hungarian fiddle (var. 19), as well as other pictorial moments such as a procession of old women (var. 13), French kisses (var. 15), or a rope dance (var. 16). But he was also careful to exhibit the "learned" side of his musicianship, which is clearly visible in variation 4 with the theme in the bass and, especially, with the use of traditional score notation for the two ricercare movements.[18]

A similar, if much more sober collection of harpsichord music, the *Toccate, Canzoni, Ricercari et altre Galanterie* (*A-Wn*, Mus. Hs. 19167) by Franz Matthias Techelmann (ca. 1649–1714), was dedicated to Leopold I (ca. 1684), who duly rewarded Techelmann in 1685 with a post as a second court organist. It contains two cycles (in A minor and C major), each consisting of a toccata, canzona, ricercare, and suite; the first cycle adds an aria with thirty variations. The only programmatic piece is the Allemande in C, "dell'Allegrezze alla Liberazione di Vienna," in celebration of the liberation from the Turkish invasion in 1683, which had cost the life of Techelmann's predecessor, Poglietti.

The Würzburg organist Ferdinand Tobias Richter (1651–1711) came to Vienna in 1675 and was sent by the Emperor to Rome in 1679 for further studies with Bernardo Pasquini. In 1683 he became court organist and later tutor to the royal children. His fame as a keyboard player was such that Johann Pachelbel dedicated his *Hexachordum Apollonis* of 1699 to him (along with Buxtehude). It is therefore all the more regrettable that no autographs from his work in royal courts are extant. All that survives seems written for the harpsichord: principally five suites (a sixth is only a small fragment), which are always introduced by a toccatina, sometimes with an additional capriccio as well. One finds evidence of the lively imagination of the composer everywhere in, for example, a dashing passacaglia in F major, or the wayward fugal subjects and free development of the two capriccios. However, what may be regarded as Richter's most important harpsichord piece has remained unrecognized thus far. A Berlin manuscript (*D-B*, Mus. ms. 30318) contains two separate movements in D minor (a capriccio and a little further down a toccata), which appear in reverse order and united as a "Toccata" in the so-called Benisch Manuscript (*US-NH*, LM 5056, p. 222–27) attributed to Bernardo Pasquini, which is clearly a mistake.[19] The sparkle and variety of this large piece of 107 measures makes it one of the most attractive harpsichord compositions of the Viennese school.

Nuremberg: Schultheiss, the Kriegers, the Pachelbels

The suites of the Viennese masters encountered so far all remained in manuscript during their author's lifetime (as did the suites of Georg Muffat and Fux). It was thus left to the rather obscure Nuremberg organist Benedict Schultheiss (1653–1693) to receive the honor of having published the first harpsichord suites in Germany. They appeared in two installments in his hometown in 1679–1680, as *Muth- und Geist-ermuntrender Clavier-Lust*. They consolidate the "classic" quartet of dances allemande – courante – sarabande – gigue in ten competently written, if rather modest suites, the first four of which are prefaced by lively preludes.

Schultheiss must have rubbed shoulders with his peer and townsman Johann Pachelbel (1653–1706), both having been taught by Georg Caspar Wecker. Remarkably, the Lutheran Pachelbel sought to further his craft in Catholic Vienna, where he stayed between 1673 and 1675 and was probably tutored by Kerll, but he eventually found employment in Thuringia, notably 1678–1690 in Erfurt. After brief stints in Stuttgart and Gotha, he finally returned in 1695 to his native Nuremberg. This renowned teacher was of course first of all a great master of the Lutheran organ chorale and other typical organ forms, such as the pedal toccata and the verset fugue, but there still remains a substantial amount of his music that seems to be primarily destined for the harpsichord. There is even one category of chorale arrangement – the chorale partita – that appears to have been conceived in terms of a stringed keyboard rather than the organ. A lost print, the *Musicalischen Sterbens-Gedancken*, published in Erfurt in 1683 after the plague had taken away his wife and son, contained four such cycles for "Clavier." Its content has been preserved in manuscript and consisted of partitas on consolatory chorales, such as *Alle Menschen müssen sterben* and *Herzlich tut mich verlangen*.

A secular counterpart to this was published in Nuremberg in 1699, the famous *Hexachordum Apollinis*. According to the title page it was written for "organo pneumatico, vel clavato cymbalo," although the extensive use of *style brisé* throughout the collection – actually much more so than in both the *Sterbensgedancken* and five further aria sets preserved in manuscript – points rather exclusively to the latter instrument. These six cycles on original themes – more accurately, the bass lines, making them closely akin to the ciacona – show careful planning. The first five are neatly arranged in ascending fashion: D minor, E minor, F major, G minor, and A minor. The sixth set would naturally have been in B♭, and Pachelbel indeed duly notates two flats in the key signature. However, the piece is really in F minor, necessitating the constant application of additional flats. Apart from the unusual key, the Aria *sexta* also stands out from the rest because of its higher number of variations (eight instead of five or six), the use of the ciacona-like 3/4 meter instead of common time, and the addition of a title, "Aria Sebaldina" – the latter doubtlessly an affective reference to the church where he ended his career, St. Sebaldus in Nuremberg. This melancholic work is, if anything, even more refined and varied than the other sets.

Two of Pachelbel's ciaconas – he uses the term indiscriminately for both major- and minor-mode pieces – are almost aria variations as well, based as they are on a binary bass theme of 2 × 4 bars. These two pieces, both of them in D, are, however, much more schematic in their variation manner. The real high point of the genre (apart from the well-known one in D minor for organ with pedal) is found in two works discovered jointly in a late Brussels source (*B-Br*, Ms. II 3911 Mus.). They are complementary in both key and mood. The Ciacona in F major (forty-one variations on a four-bar ostinato) is exuberant and probably represents Pachelbel's most virtuosic keyboard work. The one in F minor (based on the descending tetrachord) exhibits a character closely akin to the "Aria Sebaldina": refined and melancholic. Only three suites survive under Pachelbel's name, and of these one has been reattributed to Froberger. This suite, a fine extended one in E minor (Allemande – Courante – Sarabande – Double – Gigue) from a now lost Nuremberg source is, however, entirely plausible as a Pachelbel composition. Though some Froberger mannerisms are certainly present, Pachelbel was certainly capable of emulation, and some stylistic traits point to the late seventeenth century, such as the style of the Double or the rolling motive in the second half of the Gigue. The two other suites, in F major and G minor, are more modest in scope and dispense with a gigue.

Pachelbel's son Wilhelm Hieronymus (1686–1764), who remained in Nuremberg all his working life, apparently wrote a great quantity of keyboard music that is mostly lost. The outspoken style of what survives – notably found in two small prints he brought out ca. 1725 – can only be explained as a reaction to his father's rather subdued manner. Wilhelm's preludes, fantasias, and fugues are extroverted and virtuosic, with a good dose of the *galant* and the concertante.

The careers of the brothers Johann Philipp (1649–1725) and Johann (1652–1735) Krieger followed a similar course to that of Johann Pachelbel. Both keyboardists and composers were trained in Nuremberg, but sought to further their careers in more northern regions, ending up with half-century tenures as Kapellmeisters in the middle German cities of Weissenfels and Zittau, respectively. The elder Krieger, who was ennobled in Vienna by Leopold I after hearing him play in 1675, soon concentrated on vocal sacred music, and only a handful of his keyboard music remains. His Passacaglia in D minor is clearly inspired by the work by Kerll of the same name. Johann Krieger on the other hand appears to be much more of a keyboard specialist. Towards the end of the century he managed to bring out two important, complementary keyboard collections printed in Nuremberg: the *Sechs musicalische Partien* (1697) and, two years later, the *Anmuthige Clavier-Übung*. The *Sechs musicalische Partien* was published without proper supervision by the composer, resulting in some confusion about the number of suites, but it is clear that the work indeed consists of six cycles grouped in ascending fashion: C major, D minor, F major, G major, A major and B♭ major. While the first three suites restrict themselves to the classic core of dances (the first one preceded by a lengthy fantasia), the last three are extended by "Galanterien" derived from the ballet suite.

That the "Liebhabern des Claviers" to which Krieger dedicated his *Anmuthige Clavier-Übung* encompassed both harpsichordists and organists is made clear by the nature of the two imposing final pieces: a big "ciacona" in G minor for (two-manual!) harpsichord and a toccata in C major for organ pedaliter. The three preceding single-standing free pieces seem destined for the organ too, but the rest of the collection, consisting of eight two-movement works, are true *manualiter* works for either harpsichord or organ. The printer again made a mess of it, often printing the prelude after the fugue or ricercare, and the order seems also otherwise to have been confused. Krieger, however, clearly intended a cycle spanning the eight most common keys. If one accepts that he would have started this learned collection in the *primus tonus*, the coherent cycle shown in Table 5.2 results.

As in the *Musicalische Partien*, the opening of the collection is now marked by a fantasia, while it climaxes in an imposing quadruple fugue of 203 bars. The latter work, which actually consists of four fugues, each

Table 5.2 *Restored Opening Cycle of Johann Krieger's* Anmuthige Clavier-Übung

1. Fantasia & Fuga in D minor
2. Praeludium & Ricercar in E minor
3. Praeludium & Ricercar in F major
4. Praeludium & Fuga in G major
5. Praeludium & Ricercar in G minor
6. Praeludium & Ricercar in A minor
7. Praeludium & Ricercar in B♭ major
8. Praeludium & Quadrupelfuga in C major

treating its own theme before these are combined in a fifth fugue, was justly celebrated in its own day. The other fugues and ricercares, however, which are all monothematic and make extensive use of such learned devices as inversion and stretto, are equally demonstrative of Krieger's contrapuntal skill. In conjunction with the varied character of the preludes and the fact that the pieces do no longer consist of (organ) miniatures, it is clear that this cycle forms an important predecessor of the *Wohltemperiertes Clavier*.

Southern Germany: Georg Muffat, Fischer

The Alsatian Georg Muffat (1653–1704) studied both French and Italian music in their principal havens: Paris and Rome. Therefore, like Froberger, Muffat was in the unique position to combine in his music the most important European trends of the day – personified by the names of Lully and Corelli respectively – which indeed informs his fine and influential music for strings. He became court organist in Salzburg in 1678, and finally *Hofkapellmeister* in Passau in 1690. The source situation with regard to his harpsichord music has notably improved recently through the reemergence of the Berlin *Singakademie* collection, which not only yielded a great number of unknown suites by Muffat's son Gottlieb (see below), but also produced a manuscript (*D-Bsak*, SA 4581) with six harpsichord suites by Georg, three of which were hitherto completely unknown. The high expectations from his well-known music for strings or organ are amply satisfied, especially with regard to the rich invention displayed in the core dances, which are longer than usual (especially the courantes and sarabandes). Georg Muffat's harpsichord masterpiece is, however, to be found in the *Apparatus musico-organisticus* from 1690. The main content of this seminal work consists of twelve organ toccatas to which he added three harpsichord pieces: a variation set ("Nova Cyclopeias Harmonica"), a short Ciacona in G major, and, most importantly, an extended Passacaglia in G minor. The latter abounds in fantastic harpsichord writing, consisting of an amalgam of Italian, German, and French elements – the latter above all visible in the fourfold recurrence of the arresting opening "theme" in the sense of a "passacaille en rondeau." Such an appendix with harpsichord music is found more often in organ publications of the 1690s, such as the 1693 *Ars magna consoni et dissoni* by the Augsburg organist Johann Speth (i.e., three very Italianate arias with variations) or the 1696 *Octi-tonium novum organicum* by the Munich organist Franz Xaver Anton Murschhauser (i.e., four Christmas carols with variations and a suite).

The exceptionally long-lived Johann Caspar Ferdinand Fischer (1662–1746) represents something of an outsider here, since he does not fit in with the master–pupil–colleague matrix encountered with the other composers in this chapter. Born in the Bohemian city of Schlackenwerth, he was a lifetime Kapellmeister of the reigning house of Baden, moving in 1715 from his native town to the court of Rastatt in Baden itself. Fischer was equally at home in vocal and instrumental music, but, as a renowned keyboard virtuoso, it is not surprising that his keyboard music takes pride of place, appearing in no fewer than four publications. Two of those contain harpsichord suites: *Les Pieces de clavessin* from 1696 (reissued two years later as *Musicalisches Blumen-Büschlein*), and the *Musicalischer Parnassus* from 1738. As an experienced composer of orchestral suites in the French manner, a selection of which appeared as early as 1695, Fischer treats the tradition rather freely. Thus, both the innovative content and the high quality of the 1696 print explains his great reputation. The *Parnassus* collection, despite the huge time gap, hardly differs stylistically from the earlier collection, and thus appears rather conservative for its date. It even retains the use of the traditional short-octave C/E to c^3 keyboard, already rather old-fashioned in 1696, suggesting that the *Parnassus* suites were composed long before their publication. In the earlier collection, the traditional core of dances is only present in Suites 1 (Allemande – Courante – Sarabande) and 6 (Allemande – Courante – Sarabande – Gigue); the others are either ballet suites (nos. 2, 3, 4, and 7) or single variation works (nos. 5 and 8). The ravishing Ciacona in G of the latter that concludes the volume stands out. A corresponding impressive Passacaglia in D minor comes at the end of the *Parnassus*. Despite the number of suites (nine) and title inscriptions with the names of the nine muses, it apparently bears no relation to Greek mythology. Only the first and last suites use the traditional core of Allemande – Courante – Sarabande – Gigue, the others usually restricting themselves to A–G plus a plethora of "Galanterien." Specific mention should be made of the great variety of preludes prefacing all seventeen suites, some of them direct precursors of those in Bach's *Wohltemperiertes Clavier* I.

Vienna [3]: Fux, Gottlieb Muffat

The longtime Hofkapellmeister at the Vienna court Johann Joseph Fux (1660–1741) was first and foremost a composer of vocal music, both sacred and secular, as well as of instrumental ensemble music. His keyboard music forms only a small niche in his enormous oeuvre, but what exists is of remarkable quality. In an anecdote transmitted by Marpurg,

Table 5.3 *Fux's Capriccio K 404*

1. Praelude	G minor
2. Fuga – allegretto-adagio-allegretto	G minor
3. *La superba* – allegretto	B♭ major
4. Arietta – gustuoso	G minor
5. *L'humilta* – tempo giusto	G minor
6. *La vera pace* – affettuoso	E♭ major
7. Finale – allegro	G minor

a harpsichord student of Gottlieb Muffat confessed that she was a greater lover of fine Fux suites than everything else, shunning the works of Kuhnau, Graupner, and even Handel.[20] Five such "Fuxpartien" have survived, along with some smaller fare as well as a Ciacona in D major, a large work which features an outstanding fusion of French and German manners. The suites indeed contain much fine music, and their varied style suggests a rather wide range of dates of origin. His keyboard masterpiece may be seen in a sixth "Suite" that, apparently because of its rather liberal makeup, was named "Capriccio." It opens with an arpeggiated prelude familiar in Austrian harpsichord music since the works of Richter and others. This serves as the introduction to a six-movement symmetrical structure (Table 5.3).

Two tersely structured "absolute" movements – a fugue on a double subject and a finale of Handelian allure – frame a group of four character pieces, the outer of which are in related major keys (the parallel and the mediant respectively). At the same time, a steady alternation of fast and slow is utilized. Dance seems absent here, however, except for *La superba* ("the proud one"), a fierce courante. The complementing *L'humilta* ("the humble one"), with its constantly descending arpeggios and melodic patches, is a character piece in almost nineteenth-century pianistic mode, while the Arietta is a pure *pièce de clavecin*.

Rather surprising for the author of the celebrated counterpoint treatise *Gradus ad Parnassum*, traditional imitative forms like the ricercare and canzona are absent from his keyboard music. This lacuna was, however, amply filled by his most prominent pupil, the equally long-lived Gottlieb Muffat (1690–1770), who produced an enormous number of such pieces, along with a plethora of toccatas, capriccios, and preludes. Although much of this no doubt belongs to the domain of the organ, which is borne out by the many pieces with pedal, his collection of thirty-nine ricercares and nineteen canzonas – a clear sign of the composer's conservatism and awareness of Viennese traditions, plus a retrospective nod to Frescobaldi – may very well be seen as harpsichord music too, particularly the lively canzonas. Also traditional is their notation in score format.

As the son of Georg Muffat, Gottlieb no doubt received a thorough early training in keyboard playing as well as composition. After the death of his father in 1704, Gottlieb left his native Passau for Vienna, becoming an organ scholar and pupil of Fux. In 1717, he became imperial court and chamber organist and was finally promoted to first imperial organist in 1741. Like Froberger, Gottlieb was a typical keyboard specialist, expressing hardly any compositional ambition beyond the harpsichord and the organ. He clearly was content to live and work outside the limelight of the opera and other more public genres. This is reminiscent of the second part of the career of his great contemporary Domenico Scarlatti, who then likewise wrote an enormous harpsichord oeuvre in the backrooms of an illustrious court. Moreover, both brought out a single seminal sampling of their work,

Table 5.4 *Content of the* Componimenti musicali

	Key	Introduction	Traditional Core	"Galanterien"	Conclusion
I	C major	Ouverture	Allemande Courante	Air (in C minor) Rigaudon Menuet & Trio (in A minor) Adagio	Finale
II	G minor	Prélude	Allemande Courante Sarabande (in G major)	Rigaudon Menuet & Trio (in E♭ major) Fantaisie	Gigue
III	D major	Fantaisie	Allemande Courante Sarabande (in B minor)	Menuet Rigaudon bizarre, Air (in D minor),	Finale
IV	B♭ major	Fantaisie [& Fuga]	Allemande Courante Sarabande (in B♭ minor)	*La hardiesse* Menuet & Trio (in G minor) Air Hornpipe	Gigue
V	D minor	Ouverture	Allemande Courante Sarabande	Menuett Rigaudon Menuet & Trio (in D major)	Gigue
VI	G major	Fantaisie [& Fuga]	Allemande Courante Sarabande (in E minor)	*La coquette*, Menuet & Trio (in G minor) Air	Gigue Menuet: *Cor de chasse*
VII	G major	Chaconne (38 variations)			

which happened to appear almost simultaneously, in 1739. Indeed, Muffat's *Componimenti musicali per il cembalo* can easily stand comparison with Scarlatti's much more famous *Essercizi per gravicembalo*. The successor to a much smaller 1726 print with organ versets, Muffat spared no effort to make his publication a sumptuous one both in content and presentation: an intricate title engraving, extensive prefaces in both Italian and German, a generous table of ornaments, and the music done in beautiful and meticulous calligraphy.[21] Its contents can be summarized as shown in Table 5.4.

Georg Friedrich Handel was greatly impressed by the *Componenti musicali*, of which he acquired a copy soon after its publication in 1739, raiding its musical ideas in the fall of that year for his *Ode for St Cecilia's Day* and the *Concerti Grossi*, Op. 6, as well as other music in the following decade. Muffat, on his side, made complete transcriptions in 1736 of Handel's Eight Suites (HWV 426–433) and Six Fugues (HWV605–610), adapting them to his own peculiar way of notating and ornamenting, while the Ciacona in G major that concludes the *Componimenti* seems modeled after Handel's chaconne in the same key (HWV435, first published in 1735).

Handel's admiration for the *Componimenti* is easy to understand: the music is inspired throughout, the workmanship is first-class, and many ideas are arresting indeed. It can be seen as a conservative publication in that Muffat retains the traditional core of four dances (Allemande – Courante – Sarabande – Gigue), though once replacing the sarabande by an air, and the gigue by a finale in two instances, while a more progressive element is found in the fact that the sarabande usually appears in the parallel key. Among the "Galanteriestücke" one always finds at least one minuet and often a rigaudon as well. The two French-titled character pieces (they are, in fact encountered throughout Muffat's suites) reflect the strong French influence; indeed, the elegance of the music and its publication and its meticulous ornamental system reminds one of François Couperin's *Livres*. Not surprisingly for the son of Georg Muffat, however, he strove for a synthesis of styles. Many of the courantes, for example, have a strong Italianate concertante slant to them. The fine contrapuntal finish everywhere could thus be seen as a "German" element. A feature that also strongly reminds one of Bach's partitas, published about a decade earlier, concerns the introductory movements.[22] Rather than using the short arpeggiated prelude here (which dominates the manuscript suites), Muffat developed more ambitious structures, obviously specifically for this publication, and varied them as much as possible. The only format repeated here is the ouverture, while the three fantasias become progressively longer, consisting of one, two, and three sections respectively. The last of these additional sections in fantasias IV and VI consist of two weighty four-part fugues, and together with the more fleeting fast fugues of the two ouvertures, Muffat is able to present a wide range of his expertise in this field.

As fine as the *Componimenti* suites are, it is important to emphasize that they form only a selection from a large corpus of such works. Prior to the year 2000, next to the six suites from the print, nineteen more were known from manuscript sources. However, the resurfacing of the collection of the Berlin Singakademie in that year yielded no fewer than twenty-five additional suites, thus doubling Muffat's contribution to this field and, moreover, predominantly in the form of holograph manuscripts. However, no sources datable beyond ca. 1741 are to be found, suggesting that Gottlieb Muffat ceased to compose after that date. Perhaps his *Componimenti* was judged out of date as soon as it appeared, since indeed a new generation of keyboard composers specializing in the *galant*, generally less-demanding harpsichord style came to the fore with prints, such as those of Franz Anton Hugl, Franz Anton Maichelbeck, Raimund Wenzel Pirck, or Georg Christoph Wagenseil. The wholly new, much more bourgeois aesthetic they reflected was far removed from the courtly world inhabited by (Habsburg) "Kenner" as known by Muffat, and for which he wrote his quintessentially aristocratic harpsichord music.

Notes

1. See Pieter Dirksen, "Johann Jacob Froberger in Dresden," *Schütz-Jahrbuch* 39 (2017), pp. 20–28.
2. See Marko Deisinger, "Johann Jacob Frobergers Karriere als Organist Kaiser Ferdinands III. im Lichte neuer Quellen," in *Avec discretion. Rethinking Froberger*, ed. Markus Grassl and Andreas Vejvar (Vienna: Wiener Veröffentlichungen zur Musikgeschichte 14, 2018), pp. 179–161.
3. Rudolf Rasch, "Froberger and the Netherlands," in *The Harpsichord and Its Repertoire, Proceedings of the International Harpsichord Symposium Utrecht 1990*, ed. Pieter Dirksen (Utrecht: STIMU Foundation for Historical Performance Practice, 1992), p. 121.
4. Athanasius Kircher, *Musurgia universalis* (Rome, 1650), p. 466.
5. Rudolf Rasch, "The Huygens – Froberger – Sibylla Correspondence," in *The Harpsichord and Its Repertoire*, p. 241.
6. D-Dl, Mus. 1-T-595. See Pieter Dirksen and Rudolf Rasch, "Eine neue Quelle zu Frobergers Cembalosuiten," in *Musik in Baden-Württemberg – Jahrbuch 2001* (Stuttgart, 2001), pp. 133–153.
7. D-Bsak, SA 4450. See Johann Jakob Froberger, *Toccaten, Suiten, Lamenti: Die Handschrift SA 4450 der Sing-Akademie zu Berlin, Faksimile und Übertragung*, ed. Peter Wollny (Kassel: Bärenreiter, 2004).
8. See Simon Maguire, *Johann Jacob Froberger: A Hitherto Unrecorded Autograph Manuscript* (auction brochure), London 2006, www.sscm-jscm .org/v13/no1/maguire.html; Bob van Asperen, "A New Froberger

Manuscript," *Journal of Seventeenth-Century Music* 13, no. 1 (2007), www.sscm-jscm.org/jscm/v13/no1/vanasperen.html.

9. FbWV 105, 106, and 111.

10. FbWV 101–102 and FbWV 103–104.

11. Johann Mattheson, *Grundlage einer Ehren-Pforte* (Hamburg 1740), ed. Max Schneider (Berlin 1910), p. 88; Pieter Dirksen, "Johann Jacob Froberger und die frühen Clavecinisten," in *Avec discretion. Rethinking Froberger*, pp. 223–237.

12. Johann Jacob Froberger, *Complete Works*, Vol. 7, ed. Siegbert Rampe (Kassel: Bärenreiter, 2015.).

13. See especially David Schulenberg, "Crossing the Rhine with Froberger: Suites, Symbols, and Seventeenth-Century Musical Autobiography", in *Fiori Musicali: Liber Amicorum Alexander Silbiger*, ed. Claire Fontijn and Susan Parisi (Michigan: Harmonie Park Press, 2010), pp.271–302.

14. Formerly known with the title "Lamentation," but thus titled in the "London" autograph.

15. Henning Siedentopf, *Johann Jakob Froberger – Leben und Werk* (Stuttgart: Stuttgarter Verlagskontor, 1977), pp. 78ff.

16. These observations as well as the musical examples are principally based on the version of the piece in *A-Wm*, Ms. XIV 743. It should however be mentioned that both *D-Bsak*, SA 4450 and the "London" autograph have first- and second-time bars for the third section as well (for the latter source, see the images in Maguire, *Johann Jacob Froberger*, pp. 5ff.), which is, however, rather suspect from a rhetorical perspective, since the deceased Emperor can only be accepted once into heaven.

17. *A-Wn*, Mus. Hs. 19248 Mus. See also http://data.onb.ac.at/rec/AC14017777.

18. The learned side of Poglietti comes emphatically to the fore in his collection of twelve ricercars; see the edition by Friedrich Wilhelm Riedel (Lippstadt: Kistner & Siegel, 1975).

19. It is edited under Pasquini's name in *Werke für Tasteninstrumente aus dem Codex E.B. von 1688 des Emanuel Benisch (um 1655–1725)*, ed. Raimund Schächer (Stuttgart: Cornetto Verlag, 2002), pp. 11–15.

20. Alison J. Dunlop, *The Life and Music of Gottlieb Muffat* (Vienna: Hollitzer, 2013), p. 161.

21. See https://search.onb.ac.at/primo_library/libweb/action/dlDisplay.do? vid=ONB&docId=ONB_alma21378773210003338&fn=permalink.

22. See Karl Heller, "Johann Sebastian Bach und Gottlieb Muffat: Zum stilistischen Profil der Componimenti Musicali, gesehen aus der Perspektive der Klaviersuiten Bachs," in *Bachs Musik für Tasteninstrumente. Bericht über das 4. Dortmunder Bach-Symposion 2002*, ed. Martin Geck, *Dortmunder Bachforschungen*, Bd. 6 (Dortmund: Klangfarben-Musikverlag, 2003), pp. 251–264.

Further Reading

Annibaldi, Buckley, Ruggeri Massip, et al. *Froberger musicien européen*. Paris: Klincksieck, 1998.

Apel, Willi. *The History of Keyboard Music before 1700.* Bloomington: Indiana University Press, 1972.

Dunlop, Alison J. *The Life and Music of Gottlieb Muffat.* Vienna: Hollitzer, 2013.

Rudolf, Walter. *Johann Caspar Ferdinand Fischer: Hofkapellmeister der Markgrafen von Baden.* Frankfurt and New York: P. Lang, 1990.

Somer, Avo. *The Keyboard Music of Johann Jakob Froberger.* PhD dissertation, University of Michigan, 1963.

Vinke, Linda Frances. *The Influence of the Madrigali Moderni on Johann Jacob Froberger's Keyboard Music.* PhD dissertation, University of the Free State (South Africa), 2011.

Welter, Kathryn Jane. *Johann Pachelbel. Organist, Teacher, Composer. A Critical Reexamination of His Life, Works, and Historical Significance.* PhD dissertation, Harvard University, 1998.

Wollenberg, Susan. "The Keyboard Suites of Gottlieb Muffat (1690–1770)." *Proceedings of the Royal Musical Association* 102 (1975–1976), pp. 83–91.

6 France

MARK KROLL

Jean-Laurent Lecerf de La Viéville, the noted seventeenth-century commentator on French society and culture, described the elements of French music in the most colorful of terms:

> Imagine a clever old coquette covered in rouge and white powder, and overloaded with bows, which are applied with absolutely all the care and skill possible. Hiding the wrinkles in her face and the defects of her figure by make-up that is equally magnificent as it is complete; smiling and grimacing in the finest prudence ... and without heart, soul or sincerity ... *Voilà*: Italian Music. Now imagine, on the other hand, a young woman of noble but modest bearing, of grand but slender figure without excess; neat, always dressed with a galant propriety, but preferring to be informal rather than overdressed, and magnificent only on certain days ... With lovely natural coloring, far removed from all that is false or imitation; a bow or two from time to time, or perhaps an occasional bit of rouge to cover some tiny flaw; smiling and gracious as appropriate, but never the coquette or crazily playful; ... speaking well without flattering herself that she is a great speaker and without wanting to speak all the time ... This is a lady that you should easily recognize; she is French Music.[1]

Lecerf's description of the difference between French and Italian music might have offended some of his female acquaintances, but it is perceptive and essentially correct, in stylistic terms at least. French baroque composers did choose a different path from those of their contemporaries in Italy and, for that matter, Germany and England. Why they remained faithful to this "noble" and "modest" woman, what they viewed as "excess," and how they maintained this style for almost two hundred years is the subject of this chapter.

The Elements of the Style

This fidelity is apparent in the most basic stylistic features of French harpsichord music: a two- or three-voice texture predominates, featuring, on the one hand, an elegant, richly ornamented melodic line, and on the other a simple accompaniment. Learned devices, intricate contrapuntal writing, or full-voice chordal homophony are avoided, and many of the genres typically found in the other national styles of the baroque, such as fugues, ricercares, fantasias, and sonatas, are rare in France. The French harpsichord composer achieved maximum expressive effect by the resonant spacing of parts, sensitivity to sonorities, extremely precise notation, and a rich harmonic language. Virtuoso keyboard displays were kept to a minimum, and techniques such as the extensive arpeggiation found in J. S. Bach's *Chromatic Fantasy* (BWV903) and Handel's *Lessons* or the rapid scale passages, repeated notes, and hand crossings of Domenico Scarlatti do not generally appear in France until the middle of the eighteenth century.

Lecerf's emphasis on propriety and nobility illuminates the aesthetic values upon which this unique style is built, which have their roots in the principles of *bon goût* (good taste or style), *politesse* (noble etiquette), and the *honnête homme* (the ideal gentleman) that dominated French thinking and behavior for the entire period.[2] The *honnête homme* was expected to make his tasteful behavior appear absolutely natural and effortless, Nicolas Faret explaining that the he must act with " ... a certain negligence that hides artifice and shows that nothing is done with forethought or any kind of effort."[3] François Couperin applied this sense of nonchalance to musical performance: "The player must have an easy air at his harpsichord ... without fixing his gaze on any one object."[4]

Thus, *les honnêtes gens* were expected to refrain from overt display and emotional excess.[5] Nothing could be further from this ideal than Italian music, as Charles Saint-Evremond describes:

> The Italians have a false, or at least outrageous expression, because they do not accurately understand the nature or degree of the passions. They break out laughing instead of singing when they express some joyful sentiment; if they want to sigh, one hears sobs that are violently formed in the throat rather than sighs that escape secretly from the passion of an amorous heart; from a painful reflection they make the strongest exclamations; tears of absence are funeral lamentations; the sad becomes the gloomy in their mouths; they cry out instead of complaining in sadness, and sometimes they express the languor of the passion as a weakness of nature.[6]

In consequence, to avoid what French composers would consider poor taste and empty bourgeois technique, they developed a compositional approach and mode of performance that distinguished their music from any other national styles, the Italian in particular and, as described earlier, remained remarkably consistent to it for almost two centuries.

Ornamentation

The most notable, or at least noticeable, feature of the style is the extensive use of ornamentation. Listeners and performers (and my students) today often express astonishment (or chagrin) at the number and variety of ornaments in *Pièces de clavecin*, and similar reservations were voiced by many commentators from the period, such as Charles Burney, who wrote:

> The great Couperin . . . was not only an admirable organist but, in the style of the times, an excellent composer for keyed instruments . . . tho' his pieces are so crowded and deformed by beats, trills, shakes, that no plain note was left to enable the hearer of them to judge whether the tone of the instrument on which they were played was good or bad.[7]

However, this "crowd" of "beats, trills [and] shakes," although appearing somewhat contradictory to the espoused principles of restraint or *politesse*, are not the familiar improvised or written-out Italianate divisions, embellishments, or other similar devices with which the performer adds notes and figurations to a melodic line and that Lecerf found so artificial. French ornaments are more like the rich and sumptuous decorations added to French furniture and architecture of the period, without which they would be simple tables, chairs, and walls. In music, these ornaments are meticulously notated and applied to create an astonishing range of nuance, color, and dynamics on the harpsichord. French harpsichords of the period are marvels of construction and refinement, and the *agréments* of *Pièces de clavecin* can be perfectly realized on their sensitive keyboards. The ornaments, moreover, are not optional or improvisatory, but rather an integral part of the composition.

Example 6.1a Jean-Baptiste Henry D'Anglebert, *Pieces [sic] de clavecin* (Paris, 1680), "Marques des Agrements"

One only has to play a French melody with ornaments removed to fully understand their crucial impact on the music.

This helps explain why so many French composers expressed concern that the ornaments they wrote should be played exactly as they were notated. Couperin was particularly adamant about the subject in the preface to his third book of *Pièces de clavecin* (1722):

Example 6.1b Jean-Philippe Rameau, *Pièces de clavecin* (Paris, 1724), Table of Ornaments

I am always surprised, after the care I have taken to indicate the ornaments which are appropriate to my pieces ... to hear people who have learned them without making sure that they were following the correct method. It is an unpardonable negligence, especially since it is not at the discretion of the players to place such ornaments where they want them.[8]

It also explains why most composers usually included a table of ornaments at the beginning of the published pieces. Two representative examples are the tables from books of harpsichord pieces by D'Anglebert and Rameau (see Examples 6.1a and 6.1b).

Style Luthée

Another striking characteristic of French harpsichord music is the so-called *style luthée* (lute style) or *style brisé* (broken style), in which the composer writes in an arpeggiated style to create a kaleidoscopic palate of rich sonorities and implied polyphony (see Example 6.2).

As the name implies, the *style luthée* recalls lute practice, but it is particularly effective on the harpsichord, since the instrument can sustain one or more "voices." *Style luthée* can surely be found in the works of the French lutenists, but, as we will discuss below, the commonly held assumption that the French harpsichord tradition developed directly from the French lute school is somewhat misleading.

Inégalité or *Notes Inégales*

In addition to the proper realization of the ornaments and *style brisé*, *inégalité* is yet another feature of French keyboard music that lies at the heart of the style. Simply stated, the term refers to the technique in which passages written with equal note values are performed in unequal rhythm,

Example 6.2 François Couperin, *Les charmes*, Book II, *Ordre* 9, mm. 1–19

according to a number of clearly defined rules. The basic principles are relatively straightforward: inequality is applied to notes with the smallest rhythmic values that move in stepwise melodic motion and, as Saint-Lambert writes, the common practice "is to make them alternately long and short, because this inequality gives them more grace."[9]

Performers of all seventeenth- and eighteenth-century keyboard music were of course allowed and sometimes obligated to alter the notated rhythm and use *tempo rubato*. The same is true for all music in every period. The principle of French *inégalité*, however, is different and remains a source of confusion and misinterpretation. François Couperin described the problem in his *L'art de toucher le clavecin*:

> In my view, there are faults in our way of writing music that correspond to the ways of writing our language. We write differently from the way we perform, which makes foreigners play our music less well than we play theirs. On the other hand, the Italians write their music in the true values they have conceived. For example, we dot several successive conjunct quavers, but write them as equal notes. Our custom has enslaved us, and we persist in it.[10]

This seems clear on the surface, but the question remains as to the degree of inequality: how much longer or shorter does one perform the notated rhythm? Most commentators of the period urge a subtle, almost unnoticeable application of *inégal*. Nivers writes in 1665 that inequality is best applied by making the alteration "as though half-dots [are added] after the 1st, 3d, 5th, and 7th eighth notes . . . that is to say, to augment ever so slightly the aforementioned eighths, and to diminish ever so slightly in proportion those that follow." He adds that this should be "practiced according to discretion, and many other things which prudence and the ear have to govern."[11]

Bénigne de Bacilly concurred in 1668, emphasizing that since *notes inégales* should be executed so delicately that it is not apparent, "it has been deemed appropriate not to mark them, for fear that one might accustom himself to execute them by jerks."[12] Indeed, the concern over playing *inégal* by "jerks" (i.e., excessively dotted) was considerable. Jean-Jacques Rousseau warned in 1687 to "take care not to mark [passages played unequally] too roughly."[13] Michel Pignolet de Montéclair expresses the same concern, while also confirming that inequality is almost always applied to stepwise motion, writing: "Notes in disjunct intervals are ordinarily equal." He added that it is necessary to distinguish notes played *inégal* from those that are notated in dotted rhythm, which is always a larger rhythmic alteration.[14]

There are many other rules for a variety of different circumstances, but the overriding principles are confirmed by almost every French writer and composer of the period: alter notes written in equal rhythm to make a long–short pattern, but do it with the widest range of subtle expression, based on the character of the piece and, of course, *bon goût*.

Nevertheless, an inappropriate use of *inégal* persists to this day, particularly by applying it to both conjunct and disjunct motion or creating uniformly dotted rhythms. Although such dotting is, to be sure, a possible realization, it is only one of an infinite range of rhythmic interpretations (and a rare one at that). Composers were certainly able to notate such dotted rhythms clearly and without ambiguity, and they often appear side by side with evenly notated passages.[15]

Let us allow Saint-Lambert to have the last word on the subject: "It is a matter of taste to decide if they should be more or less unequal. There are some pieces in which it is appropriate to make them very unequal and others in which they should be less so. Taste is the judge of this, as of tempo."[16]

Inégalité essentially remained within the borders of France. It should be obvious by this point that it was not regularly used in Italy, as Michel Corrette tells us: "in Italian music the quavers are played equally."[17] Composers of other nationalities were certainly aware of the existence of this performance practice, but it is dangerous to assume that it should be applied to their music unless these non-French composers indicated it specifically or were self-consciously writing in the French style.

The Use of Rhetoric

Another important aspect of the French style involves the use of the principles of classical rhetoric. Again, this is true for music of all eras, but as we have seen in our discussion about the roots of *politesse* and the *honnête homme*, it is particularly germane to the *clavecinistes*. Saint-Lambert describes the concept with his usual clarity:

> A piece of music somewhat resembles a piece of rhetoric, or rather it is the piece of rhetoric which resembles the piece of music, since harmony, number, measure, and the other similar things which a skillful orator observes in the composition of his works belong more naturally to music than to rhetoric. In any case, just as a piece of rhetoric is a whole unit which is most often made up of several parts, each of which is composed of sentences, each having a complete meaning, these sentences being composed of phrases, the phrases of words, and the words of letters, so the melody of a piece of music is a whole unit which is always composed of several sections. Each section is composed of cadences which have a complete meaning and are the sentences of the melody.
> The cadences are often composed of phrases, the phrases of measures, and the measures of notes. Thus, the notes correspond to the letters, the measures to

words, the cadences to sentences, the sections to parts, and the whole to the whole.[18]

This connection to the spoken and written word helps explain the painstaking attention to detail in the manner in which French composers, François Couperin in particular, notated note values, rests, and articulations.

The Lute and the Harpsichord: *Frères,* or *Père* and *Fille*

As mentioned in our discussion of *style luthée,* many questions have been raised about the connection of the lute to the development of the French harpsichord style. The lute certainly enjoyed a golden age in France during the final decades of the sixteenth century and early years of the seventeenth. The names of the great families of lute virtuoso composers, such as Mouton, Gaultier, and Denis, have long been recognized for their importance in the history of the instrument, not only in France but in other countries as well. For example, the music of the French lutenists Denis Gaultier (ca. 1597–1672) and John Mercure (ca. 1600–before 1661) was well known in England, and members of the renowned Richard family were in residence at the English court.

A plucked keyboard instrument, however, was not unknown during the reign of the lutenists. *Joueurs d'espinet* flourished, as early as the 1540s, and by the second half of the sixteenth century, there were usually two or three in the service of the French kings. They included Michel Nollu, Jacques Gerofe, Gabriel Dumas, Guillaume Raguenet, Pierre Marchand, and Jean Dugue, to mention just a few.[19] Most spinet players earned the bulk of their income as organists, which they supplemented by giving lessons or serving in an aristocratic household. This is true of Nicolas de la Grotte, Thomas and Jacques Champion, Claude Chabanceau de la Barre, Joachim de Lescot, Robert Ballard, and Ennemond Gaultier.[20]

Spinets were also used to accompany viol consorts, usually by doubling the parts. In addition, keyboard players would adapt all these parts to be played as a solo composition. Mersenne described the practice, praising the qualities of the keyboard instrument: "As for using the spinet, it is excellent in that one man can play all the parts of a consort, which it has in common with the organ and the lute [but] one can play several parts more easily on the spinet than on the lute."[21]

In fact, a number of viol publications specify this option, such as the fantasias of Eustache du Caurroy (1549–1609) and Charles Guillet (1575–1654). Du Caurroy states in his dedication that the fantasias were also intended for keyboard instruments "as custom has required, and the greatest masters in the profession have considered necessary," and Guillet writes that his pieces are for viols *or* organ ("tant pour les violes que pour l'orgue").[22]

The popularity of the lute began to fade during this time, and more precipitously in the 1620s, as Jean Titelouze described in a letter to Mersenne: "I remember having seen in my youth everybody admiring and being delighted by a man playing lute, and badly enough at that . . . now I see many lutenists more skilled than him who are hardly listened to."[23] By the 1650s, lute playing was gradually eclipsed by the harpsichord, with the appearance and rise of Jacques Chambonnières, Louis Couperin, and Jean-Henry d'Anglebert. This development reflects a major shift in tastes and profound changes in the political and economic conditions in France, the most important being the ascent of Louis XIV to the throne. La Fontaine's observation in his *Epître à M. Niert* of 1677 describes the situation:

> The time of Raymon and Hilaire is past: nothing pleases now but twenty harpsi-chords, a hundred violins, no longer do we look for the flutes and oboes of amorous shepherds. The charming theorbo, which we wished to hear only in the most refined salons, accompanying a tender voice, following and supporting with expressive chords a few choice and melodious airs, Boisset, Gaultier, Hernon, Chambonnieres, La Barre, all have gone out of fashion, and are no longer prized.[24]

Thus, rather than viewing the lute as the predecessor of the harpsichord in France, it would be more accurate to describe the development as the sharing of a common musical language and an act of borrowing and adapting between similar instruments. As David Ledbetter writes:

> It was the *clavecinistes*' familiarity with lute style that prompted them to appro-priate some of the conveniences of tablature notation to the keyboard. In the case of D'Anglebert, whose keyboard style most thoroughly absorbed that of the lute, this naturalisation of lute tablature extended to the notation of ornaments and even the characteristic *séparé* and *ensemble* signs. The notation was a natural consequence of a similarity of technical means and expressive aims.[25]

Forms and Genres

Three major genres can be found in French harpsichord music: dance movements, character or descriptive pieces, and dedicatory works.

The French suite usually consists of a core of four dances – allemande, courante, sarabande, and gigue – which are often preceded by an overture or an improvisatory piece, such as a prélude. The order of the dances would sometimes vary, and other dances might be also added. Minuets and gavottes are the most common, but the list includes chaconnes, *passacailles*, *rigaudons*, and *tambourins*.

The dance forms were similar to those found in other national styles. That is, the allemande was in duple meter, usually preceded by an upbeat; courantes were somewhat faster and could be in either simple triple or compound 3/2 meter; and the sarabande was a slow and serious dance in triple meter, with an emphasis placed on the second beat of some measures. Gigues could be composed in the Italian style, with a rapid tempo and a meter of either 6/8 or 12/8, while the French gigue was somewhat slower and rhythmically more complex, with a 6/4 time signature and predominant dotted rhythm. Nevertheless, exceptions were not uncommon, particularly in the eighteenth century. For example, Gaspard Le Roux's *Sarabande in D major* carries the tempo indication "Gaye."

The French *prélude non mesuré*, commonly known as the whole-note prelude, however, is unique to the style. Every nationality has a genre that is improvisatory in nature. The Italian toccata and the German præambulum, for example, allow the player considerable rhythmic and expressive freedom, but the *clavecinistes* took the approach to a new level by writing them either completely in whole notes without any rhythmic indication, or with a mixture of rhythmic and nonrhythmic values. They also often adopted their personal system of notation. The preludes of Louis Couperin are written entirely in whole notes, which are provided with slurs of varying lengths, the meaning of which is still open to interpretation.[26] Most other French composers, such as Nicolas Lebègue, were clearly aware that the French prelude might pose difficulties for inexperienced or foreign players. He wrote in his first book of harpsichord pieces (1677): "I have tried to present the preludes as simply as possible, in order to conform to harpsichord technique . . . if some things are found to be a little difficult or obscure, I ask the intelligent gentleman to please supply what is missing, considering the great difficulty of rendering this method of preluding intelligible enough for everybody."[27]

Louis Marchand, J. P. Rameau, Louis-Nicolas Clérambault, and others also attempted to achieve clarity, often by mixing unmeasured whole notes with notated rhythms, or adding dotted lines or other notational devices (see Example 6.3).[28] François Couperin's explanation evoked the principles of rhetoric and literary genres: "play [these preludes] without attaching too much precision to the movement; at least where I have not expressly written the word *measured*; thus, one may hazard to say that, in many ways, music (compared to poetry), has its prose and its verse."[29] Ultimately, French composers gradually imposed increasing limits on the performer's freedom until the form itself was ultimately abandoned by the middle of the eighteenth century.

Character or descriptive pieces appeared infrequently in the seventeenth century but became prevalent in the eighteenth. Inspired by extramusical ideas such as people, places, and things, they reflected the French belief that music should express something other than itself. By the creative use of keyboard figures, distinctive rhythms, or unusual harmonies, the *claveciniste* might depict natural phenomena, political or social situations, scenes from the theater or from the folk heritage, emotions or states of mind, or paintings and other works of art. For example, F. Couperin could create the impression of waves with gently undulating scale passages (e.g., *Les ondes*, Book I, *Ordre* 5); the chaotic disruption of a troupe of entertainers by a rapid tremolo figure in the left hand (*Les fastes de la grande et anciénne Mxnxstrxndxsx,* Book III, *Ordre* 11); or the pompous march of a noble order by thick chords and square rhythms (*La marche des grisvêtus,* Book I, *Ordre* 4).

Dedicatory pieces were written to honor or acknowledge famous, influential, or generous people and patrons, and carried the name of the dedicatee in the title, such as F. Couperin's *La logivière* (Book I, *Ordre* 5) and *La Verneüil* (Book III, *Ordre* 18). This genre was usually abstract in nature, but occasionally they contained subtle hints as to the character traits of the dedicatee and might also take the form of a dance movement (e.g., both *La logivière* and *La Verneüil* are allemandes).

Les Clavecinistes

It would not be an exaggeration to claim that the French harpsichord tradition begins with the works of Jacques Chambonnières, whose name appears in court records in 1624, but is only first mentioned as a spinet player in 1644. The end of the tradition, however, is not as easily defined. Bruce Gustafson and David Fuller suggest that it can be marked by the appearance between 1778 and 1783 of "Jean-François Tapray's four *Symphonies Concertantes,* [making these works] the last French music in which harpsichord was indispensable."[30] Yet, many harpsichords were found as late as 1793 in the workshop of the illustrious builder Pascal Taskin, proving that the instrument was still played (or at least purchased). Moreover, the harpsichord is listed as a solo instrument at the *Concert Spirituel* from 1777 until 1787, the same year as the appearance of Claude Balbastre's *La d'Esclignac,* which was listed as a *pièce de clavecin par M. Balbastre,* and still retains idiomatic harpsichord figuration.

Therefore, for our purposes, we will mark the death of Balbastre in 1799 as the end of the French harpsichord tradition.[31]

Jacques Champion de Chambonnières (1601–1672)
As founder of the French school of harpsichord playing, Chambonnières was greatly admired for his skill at what was called *le jeu coulant*, a smooth and self-controlled manner of playing, as opposed to the *jeu brilliant*, a more virtuosic style. Le Gallois described Chambonnières's attributes, especially his skill at ornamentation and embellishment, in a letter to Mademoiselle Regnault de Solar: "whenever [Chambonnières] played a piece he added new beauties by means of grace notes, passages and various ornaments, with double cadences. In short, he so varied them with all these different beauties that new graces were always to be found in them."[32]

It is therefore unfortunate that few compositions of Chambonnières survive. This is explained by the fact that he was reluctant to publish them, complaining about the numerous mistakes he found and the negative effects on his reputation.[33] Chambonnières finally succumbed to the pressure from his colleagues and listeners by publishing a single volume in 1670.

The Couperin Family
Similar to the Bach family in Germany, the members of the Couperin family played a major role and occupied the most important musical positions in France throughout much of the seventeenth and eighteenth centuries, including those at the royal court and the Eglise St. Gervais. The most notable are Louis and François *Le Grand* (1668–1733).

Louis Couperin (ca. 1626–1661)
The music of Louis Couperin has been justly hailed as the work of a master harpsichord composer who exerted a considerable influence on the *clavecin* style, his French contemporaries and successors (notably his nephew François *Le Grand*), and also on composers of other nationalities, such as J. J. Froberger. Recent research, however, has led us to question whether Louis was actually the composer of all of this great music. Glen Wilson, for example, presents a convincing argument that much of it might actually have been written by François *Le Grand's* other uncle, François (i) (ca. 1631–ca. 1710), or his father, Charles (ii) (1638–1679).[34] This does not diminish the superb quality and richness of this music, no matter which Couperin wrote it, but such investigations deepen our understanding of the history of the repertoire and the context and circumstances under which it was written. Harpsichordists are urged to "stay tuned" for further developments.

François Couperin (1668–1733)

Couperin published four books of *pièces de clavecin*, in 1713, 1716–1717, 1722 and 1730 respectively, but there is some evidence that many of the pieces in Book I were probably written earlier. There are no unmeasured préludes in any of the four books, although Couperin does suggest in his *L'art de toucher le clavecin* that the eight préludes in this publication could be played before an *ordre* in the corresponding key.[35]

The *ordres* of Book I are dominated by dance pieces, but from Book II on we see a growing preference for dedicatory or character pieces. This should come as no surprise. Not only did this reflect the changing nature of French society and tastes, but, as we discussed above, Couperin always believed that music should inspire the deepest feelings and thoughts and represent something other than itself. He made this clear in the Preface to the 1713 collection: "In composing these pieces, I have always had an object in view ... Thus the titles reflect ideas which I have had ... the pieces which bear them are a kind of portrait which, under my fingers, have on occasion been found fair enough likenesses."

Jean-Henry D'Anglebert (1629–1691)

D'Anglebert can be considered the greatest composer of *pièces de clavecin* between Louis and François Couperin. He published a beautifully engraved collection of four harpsichord suites in 1689 that also contained his arrangements of orchestral music by Lully. The table of ornaments (see Example 6.1a) in his collection influenced not only future French composers, but also J. S. Bach, who used it as a model for the *Explication unterschiedlicher Zeichen* in the *Clavier-büchlein vor Wilhelm Friedmann Bach*.[36]

Charles Dieupart (ca. 1670–1740)

The first eighteenth-century publication of *pièces de clavecin* by a French composer was perhaps the least typical, and hardly French: Dieupart's *Six suittes de clavessin* (1701). They were, in fact, never published in France, but are listed in Etienne Roger's catalogue in Amsterdam in 1702. The music has unmistakably French features, but strong foreign influences can be felt as well, such as the use of Italian-style gigues and Germanic contrapuntal textures. Dieupart also published his suites in an alternative instrumental version, rather than following the practice of merely suggesting the option. The upper part of the harpsichord part was assigned to "violin or flute" and a simplified figured version of the bass line to "bass viol and archlute." The names of the ornaments are given in both English and French.

Dieupart's suites were more widely known outside of France than other French harpsichord music, perhaps because the Parisian-born "François" spent most of his professional life in England as Charles and his publisher was Dutch.[37] This might help explain how Bach came to know and admire Dieupart's music and even copied out some of the pieces.

Louis Marchand (1669–1732)

Marchand published two books of *pièces de clavecin* in 1702, although Book I first appeared in 1699. Each book contains only one suite, although the term is not actually used. Book I consists of eight dances and a prelude written with both whole notes and rhythmic notation, while Book II is more conservative, and the individual dances are on a smaller scale. An elegant poetic dedication by Saint-Lambert opens the book, followed by a prélude similar in compositional technique to that of Book I, and then seven standard dances.

Louis-Nicolas Clérambault (1676–1749)

Clérambault was a member of a distinguished family of musicians who had served the kings of France since the fifteenth century. He occupied numerous organist positions and served as supervisor of the concerts of Mme. de Maintenon for Louis XIV. In 1704 Clérambault published his only book of *pièces de clavecin*, consisting of two suites in C major and C minor. The opening prélude of the first suite uses the mixture of *non-mesuré* and notated rhythms similar to Marchand, but Clérambault also employs vertical dotted lines to indicate when the right and left hands should play together, or separately.

Example 6.3 Louis-Nicolas Clérambault, *Pièces de clavecin* (Paris, 1704), *Suite* I, Prélude, opening measures

Jean-François Dandrieu (ca. 1682–1738)

Titon du Tillet compared Dandrieu favorably with Couperin and Rameau, but other critics, such as Pierre Louis d'Aquin de Chateau-Lyon, were more reserved in their appraisal.[38] A significant problem in the study of Dandrieu's harpsichord works is the chronology. His first book was published in approximately 1704, and the second and third books were not published but appeared between 1710 and 1720 (and probably written earlier). Dandrieu then published three more books of harpsichord pieces, publishing them in 1724, 1728, and 1734, respectively. His obvious intention was to replace the earlier harpsichord volumes, perhaps thinking their style too youthful or archaic, but many of the works in these later books are simply reworkings of earlier pieces, often changed merely by adding descriptive titles. Dandrieu's compositional style is similar to that of his contemporaries and generally follows common practice, but Book III has a didactic purpose, Dandrieu adding fingerings to many of the pieces.

Elisabeth Jacquet de La Guerre (b. 1665–1667, d. 1729)

Elisabeth Jacquet de La Guerre was by all accounts a child prodigy, the *Mercure* proclaiming in July 1677: "for four years a wonder has appeared here. She sings at sight the most difficult music. She accompanies herself ... at the harpsichord ... She composes pieces and plays them in all the keys asked of her ... and she is still only 10 years old."[39] Jacquet de La Guerre was a favorite of Louis XIV, who fostered her career, and she remained an active figure in the Parisian musical scene until retiring from public appearances in 1717. Her first book of harpsichord pieces appeared in 1687 (it is now lost); the second book was published in 1707. Her approach is fairly conventional in its arrangement of the dances and in the use of ornamentation and *style brisé*, but Jacquet de La Guerre also employs homophonic textures more often than most of her contemporaries. In conformity with common practice, she indicates in the preface that the works may be performed with instrumental accompaniment (in this case a violin), but a separate part is not provided for that instrument. The *Chaconne in D major* is one of the longest examples from the early part of the century.

Gaspard Le Roux (b. mid-17th Century, d. 1705–1707)

Although Le Roux's *Pièces de clavessin* were probably written at the end of the seventeenth century, both stylistic evidence and their 1705 publication date allow us to include him among the composers of the eighteenth. Little is known about his life, and the lack of a dedication in his *Pièces de clavessin* may imply that he was independent of means and did not need patronage.[40]

Le Roux follows earlier seventeenth-century practice in that a large number of dance movements are randomly grouped into suites by tonality. The préludes also look backwards, in so far as they are all written in the whole-note style. However, Le Roux's compositional technique is particularly sumptuous and well developed and presages some of the best writing of F. Couperin and later composers. Some striking examples include the rich harmonic language of the Sarabande in G minor with twelve couplets and the subtle treatment of texture in the *Courante luthée*. The gigues reflect an Italian influence. Three pieces are significant: *La pièce sans titre, La favoritte and La bel-ebat*, since they are the first examples in the French style of nondance pieces with fanciful titles. Most of Le Roux's pieces are given an alternative arrangement for two melody instruments and figured bass, but six are arranged for two harpsichords.

Jean-Philippe Rameau (1683–1764)

Although Rameau's reputation is based primarily on his operas and theoretical works, his harpsichord collections contain some of the most exciting and idiomatic French harpsichord music of the era.

He received his early musical training in his birthplace, Dijon, from his father and from the Jesuits. In 1706 he moved to Paris, but in 1709–1715 returned to Dijon to succeed his father at the Cathedral of Notre Dame. From 1715 to 1722 Rameau served as organist at Clermont Cathedral, where he wrote his organ works and the *Traité de l'harmonie réduite à ses principes naturels* (Paris: Ballard, 1722). He returned to Paris in 1722 but was still unable to secure a suitable organist position, even after the publication of his later harpsichord collections.

Rameau's harpsichord music includes three solo collections (published in 1706, 1724, and 1729 or 1730); transcriptions from his opera *Les Indes galantes* (1735); *La Dauphine* (ca. 1747); and the accompanied harpsichord music of the *Pièces en Concert* (1741). Book I (1706) fits comfortably into the stylistic tradition of Marchand and Clérambault. The opening prélude is written in both whole-note style and notated rhythms; however, it also includes a gigue-like section in 12/8. The remaining pieces are traditional dances, plus a single character piece, *La Vénitienne*.

The collection of 1724 contains two suites in the keys of E and D respectively. The Suite in E maintains an equal balance between dances and descriptive pieces. Included among the latter is the portrayal of the warble of birds, *Le rappel des oiseaux*. The pieces in D contain some of the century's finest descriptive and idiomatic harpsichord music. They include compositions inspired by natural phenomena (e.g., *Les tourbillons*, or whirlwinds); by the theater (*Les cyclopes*, which might refer to the one-

Example 6.4 Jean-Philippe Rameau, *Pièces de clavecin* (Paris, 1724), *Les cyclopes*, mm. 16–31

eyed giant in Lully's *Persée*, revived in 1722); and those evoking moods or states of mind (e.g., *Les tendre plaintes, Les soupirs*). Rameau acknowledges his intentions in a letter of 25 October 1727: "You have only to come and hear how I have characterized the song and dance of the savages who appeared at the Theatre Italien two years ago, and how I have rendered the titles *Les soupirs, Les tendres plaintes, Les cyclopes, Les tourbillons* (that is to say the swirls of dust raised by high winds)."[41] The 1724 collection also features some highly virtuosic and progressive keyboard writing, such as the revolutionary left-hand figure in *Les cyclopes,* which Rameau called *batteries.*

Rameau returns again to dance movements in the collection of 1729/ 1730, but he has also written a wide range of descriptive pieces as well, such as *Les trois mains*, an appropriate title for this virtuoso tour-de-force, and *La poule*, the repeated notes and keyboard figures graphically depicting the barnyard sounds of chickens (Rameau even writes beneath the opening notes the onomatopoetic "co co co co co co co dai").[42]

Musical Bouchers?

The composers of the generation after Couperin and Rameau were certainly productive and active, and a substantial quantity of harpsichord music was published. Unfortunately, the range in quality was also wide, and the standard extended from a high artistic level to examples of crude amateurism. Wilfrid Mellers considers the composers of this final period to be "musical Bouchers" in which "emotional indulgence reduces the art to (very charming) sensory titillation … They write to please."[43] Although there is some truth in Mellers' statement, his judgment is unduly harsh, both to the composers and the artist François Boucher. French society itself was rapidly changing, the aristocracy was in decline, and it is natural that the composers would write to suit the tastes of a growing, increasingly heterogeneous middle class. The style was also undergoing natural evolution, and the economy of expression and refinement of Couperin were often replaced by extroverted virtuosity and broad humor. Alberti basses and other Italian figuration appeared more frequently, as did sonata form (not surprisingly in parallel with the ascendency of the fortepiano). Nevertheless, harpsichord music worthy of inclusion in the classical litera- ture of the French *clavecinistes* was being written by composers such as Michel Corrette (1709–1795), Jean-François Tapray (1738–ca. 1819), Jean- Jacques Beauvarlet-Charpentier (1734–1794), the F. Couperin student Nicolas Siret (1663–1754), Armand-Louis Couperin (1727–1789), and others. The most interesting composers of this generation were Jacques Duphly, Claude Balbastre, and Joseph Nicolas Pancrace Royer.

Jacques Duphly (1715–1789)
In 1752, Duphly moved to Paris and earned his living there as a respected teacher. In that year, D'Aquin de Chateau-Lyon wrote admiringly about Duphly's "lightness of touch, and a certain softness which, sustained by ornaments, marvelously render the character of his pieces." He goes on to describe Duphly's congenial disposition: "in general his pieces are sweet and amiable: they take after their father."[44]

Duphly published four books of harpsichord pieces, in 1744, 1748, 1758, and 1768. Several dances appear in the first three books, but the vast majority of pieces are descriptive or dedicatory. Duphly's music earned him a small international reputation. Richard Fitzwilliam studied with him in 1765, and Wilhelm Marpurg tells us that he was the teacher of the leading families in Paris. Marpurg published two rondos from Duphly's first book in 1757, and we also learn from him that, as Ton Koopman tells us in Chapter 4, he "is the only eighteenth-century harpsi- chordist I know of who thought organ playing would have a negative effect on his harpsichord playing."[45]

Claude Balbastre (1727–1799)
Balbastre probably received his first organ lessons in Dijon from his father. He went to Paris at the age of twenty-three, studied and became friends with Rameau, and achieved great fame as an organist and harpsichordist. Balbastre appeared often at the *Concert Spirituel* until 1782, playing his own works or transcriptions of operas by Rameau or Mondonville, and became a popular figure in Parisian musical circles. His flamboyant per- forming style, particularly his *Noëls en variations* at the Eglise St. Roc, attracted such large crowds that the archbishop was forced to forbid him from playing. Burney described this style when he visited Paris in 1770: "When the Magnificat was sung, he played likewise between each verse several minuets, fugues, imitations and every species of music, even to

hunting pieces and jigs, without surprising or offending the congregation, as far as I was able to discover."[46]

In 1776 Balbastre was appointed organist to the future Louis XVIII, taught harpsichord to Marie Antoinette and the Duke of Chartres, and served as organist at the royal chapel. He was also teacher to foreign visitors, including Thomas Jefferson. The French Revolution, however, treated Balbastre poorly and he lived afterwards in poverty until his death.

Balbastre published his first book of *pièces de clavecin* in 1759. Several other harpsichord pieces appeared later in miscellaneous collections, including one of the last unmeasured preludes of the century. He also wrote music for organ and piano (including a *Marche des Marseillais et l'air Ça-ira arrangés pour le forte piano par le citoyen C. Balbastre aux braves défenseurs de la Republique*). One of Balbastre's last performances included this arrangement, on the deconsecrated organ at Notre Dame.

Like Duphly, Balbastre's harpsichord publications contain some of the best and some of the weakest music written for the instrument. And even more than his older colleague, Balbastre attempted to accommodate a wide divergence of approaches, including French, Italian, and the nascent classical piano styles. *La d'Héricourt*, a grand *tombeau* in C minor, exploits the lower register of the harpsichord and is worthy to be included with Couperin's *La ténébreuse* in the same key. The Italian influence manifests itself in *La Lujeac*, an irrepressible gigue-like piece in the spirit of Domenico Scarlatti. *La Malesherbe* brings us almost into the world of early Mozart, complete with an Alberti bass and a periodic phrase structure in the *galant* style.

Joseph Nicolas Pancrace Royer (ca. 1705–1755)

Born in Turin and the son of a Burgundian gentleman, Royer was trained for a career in the military. He moved to Paris in 1725 and was master of music at the Opéra from 1730–1733. In 1748 he took over the direction of the failing *Concert Spirituel*, had an organ installed, expanded the orchestra and chorus, and instituted major renovations in the hall. During his tenure Royer introduced symphonies of C. H. Graun, Hasse, and Stamitz, and in 1753 premiered Pergolesi's *Stabat Mater*. His own compositions include operas, ballets, and vocal and instrumental works.

Royer published one book of *pièces de clavecin* in 1746, although there are reports of additional harpsichord works that are now lost. Some of these pieces are among the most inspired and attractive in the literature – and also the most eccentric. Royer's keyboard works retain all the characteristics of the French clavecin tradition, but also clearly show the change in style and taste which occurred after the death of the Sun King. The most striking are *Le vertigo* and *La marche des scythes*. One can imagine that the

Example 6.5 J. N. P. Royer, *Pièces de clavecin* (Paris, 1746), *La marche des scythes*, mm. 54–66

repeated chords and dramatic leaps of *Le vertigo* or the slapstick humor and outrageous hysteria of *La marche des scythes* would not have found an appreciative audience in the Versailles of Louis XIV.

The Influence of the French Style Beyond the Borders of France

The dissemination of French harpsichord music throughout Europe was uneven and many composers were not known outside Paris. As we have noted, Dieupart and LeRoux did enjoy international recognition, probably because of their Dutch publishers, and Rameau and Duphly were known in England.[47] Francois Couperin's music was never printed outside of France, but copies of the books of *pièces de clavecin* were widely distributed. He was not well known in England, and Burney's comment about the ornaments gives an indication of the prevailing critical view of Couperin's style in that country.

A number of collections of miscellaneous French pieces appeared in Germany, such as the *Nebenstunden der berlinischen Musen in kleinen Clavierstücken* (1762), and Marpurg's *Clavierstücke mit einem practischen Unterricht für Anfänger und Geübtere* (1762–1763), which contains a transcription of Couperin's *Le réveil-matin* and works by Clérambault and Dandrieu. Composers like Krebs and Mattheson reportedly copied the music by hand.[48] Nevertheless, in 1771, Grimm described Couperin's music as "empty music and empty gardens."[49]

Similar criticism in Germany persisted into the nineteenth century. For example, in a letter to Goethe of June 9, 1827, Karl Friedrich Zelter calls Couperin's music "pretty little delicate pieces . . . with all their wildly curly notation," and describes the ornamentation as "curly French wigs."[50]

It is possible that Handel was aware of French harpsichord music, but it had little effect on his compositions, other than general stylistic elements such as the French overture and *style brisé*.

French music did play an important role in Bach's output, as we have seen in the use of D'Anglebert's table of ornaments. Bach was certainly familiar with the style, as is evident from his *Ouverture in the French Manner* (BWV831) and the version of *Les bergeries* titled Rondeau that appears in the *Notebook for Anna Magdalena Bach*, although it was probably not transcribed from a Couperin publication. According to Hans-Joachim Schulze, Bach probably first became familiar with the style during his visit to the court of Celle while he was attending the Michaelisschule in Lüneburg (1700–1702).[51] Traute Marshall, however, argues convincingly that it was the town of Ebstorf in which Bach enjoyed his first exposure to French music.[52]

French harpsichord music continued to have an influence in the Francophile atmosphere of the court of Frederick the Great, in particular the music of C. P. E. Bach. A strong connection can also be made, at least on stylistic grounds, to the keyboard works of the generation after C. P. E. Bach, including Haydn and Mozart. The classical piano style shares many traits in common with French harpsichord music, such as the preference for two-voice textures, the simple accompaniment figures, and regular phrase structure.

Les clavecinistes even maintained a presence in the minds of French composers in the twentieth century. This includes Claude Debussy, who couldn't decide whether to dedicate his *Études* for piano (L 136) to Couperin or Chopin, writing on 28 August 1915 to his publisher Jacques Durand: "You haven't given me an answer about the dedications: Couperin or Chopin."[53] In 1913, Debussy had expressed his surprise at the neglect of *les clavecinistes*, F. Couperin in particular, bestowing upon him the ultimate compliment by comparing him to another great French artist of the eighteenth century, Antoine Watteau. He called Couperin "the most poetic of our harpsichordists, whose tender melancholy is like that enchanting echo that emanates from the depths of a Watteau landscape filled with plaintive figures."[54]

Notes

All translations are the author's unless otherwise noted.

1. Jean-Laurent Lecerf de La Viéville, *Comparaison de la musique italienne et da la musique françoise* (1704–1705), Vol. 1, p. 147, trans. Don Fader, "The Honnête Homme as Music Critic: Taste, Rhetoric, and Politesse in the 17th-Century French Reception of Italian Music," *The Journal of Musicology* 20, no. 1 (Winter, 2003), pp. 3–44, here pp. 5–6.

2. The term *honnête* comes from the Latin *honestus* and the works of Cicero and Quintilian, *honnête* denoting one who was not only upright and virtuous but charming, pleasant, and well mannered. See Michael A. Bane, "*Honnêtes gens*, Amateur Musicianship, and the 'Easy Air' in France: The Case of Francesco Corbetta's Royal Guitars," *Journal of Seventeenth-Century Music* 20, no. 1 (2014), pp. 1–35, here p. 4.

3. Nicolas Faret, *L'Honeste-homme ou, l'art de plaire à la cour*, ed. Maurice Magendie (Paris: Presses Universitaires de France, 1925), pp. 34–35, trans. Bane, *Honnêtes gens*, p. 7.

4. François Couperin, *L'art de toucher le clavecin* (Paris: Boivin, Le Clerc, 1717, rep. Geneva: Minkoff, 1986), pp. 5–6.

5. Nevertheless, the original source of many of the principles of *politesse* was Italian – Baldesar Castiglione's *Il libro del cortegiano* (Venice: Aldine Press, 1528), which had been translated and disseminated in France at this time. See Baldesar Castiglione, *The Book of the Courtier*, trans. George Bull (London: Penguin Books, 1967), and Peter Burke, *The Fortunes of the Courtier: The European Reception of Castiglione's Cortegiano* (University Park, PA: The Pennsylvania State University Press, 1996).

6. Charles de Marguetel de Saint Denis de Saint-Evremond, "Sur les opéra à Monsieur le Duc de Bouquinquan," quoted in *Oeuvres en prose*, ed. René Ternois (Paris: Didier, 1966), Vol. 3, p. 157, trans. Fader, "The Honnête Homme", p. 33–34.

7. Charles Burney, *A General History of Music*, 2 vols. (London: Author, 1776–1789), reprint of 2nd ed. (New York: Dover, 1957), Vol. 2, p. 996.

8. It should be mentioned that a number of contemporary commentators took a more flexible view on the subject. The most notable was the eminently practical Saint-Lambert, who wrote: "the performer is extremely free in the choice of agréments ... he may play them in places where they are not indicated, remove those that are there if he finds that they don't suit the piece, and add others to his liking. He may even ... compose other new ones himself in accordance with his own taste, if he believes himself capable of inventing ones that are more beautiful." M. Saint-Lambert, *Les Principes du clavecin* (Paris, 1702; facs. Geneva, 1974), p. 14, English translation in *Principles of the Harpsichord by Monsieur de Saint-Lambert*, trans. and ed. Rebecca Harris-Warwick (Cambridge, 1984), p. 98.

9. Saint-Lambert, *Principles*, p. 46.

10. F. Couperin, *L'art de toucher de clavecin*, pp. 39–40, trans. David Chung, "Revisiting 'le bon goût': Observations on the Irregularities and Inconsistencies of French Harpsichord Music 1650–1730," *Music and Letters* 92, no. 2 (May 2011), pp. 183–201.

11. Guillaume Gabriel Nivers, *Premier livre d'orgue* (Paris, 1665, facs. Courlay, France: Jean Marc Fuzeau, 1996), p. 114, cited in Stephen Hefling, *Rhythmic Alteration in Seventeenth- and Eighteenth-Century Music* (New York: Schirmer, 1993), p. 5.

12. Bénigne de Bacilly, *Remarques curieuses sur l'art de bien chanter* (Paris: 1668, facsimile Geneva: Minkoff, 1971, trans. and ed. Austin Caswell as *Commentary Upon the Art of Proper Singing* (Brooklyn, NY: The Institute of Mediaeval Music, 1968), pp. 235–236.

13. Jean-Jacques Rousseau, *Dictionaire de musique* (Paris, 1768), "Pointer," cited in Beverly Jerold, "*Notes Inégales*: A Definitive New Parameter," *Early Music* 42, no. 2 (2014), pp. 243–289, here p. 277.

14. Michel Pignolet de Montéclair, *Nouvelle methode pour apprendre la musique* (Paris: L'Auteur, 1709/1736, facs. of 1736 ed. Geneva: Minkoff, 1972), p. 15.

15. See, for example, F. Couperin's *La Bersan*, *Ordre* 6, Book II, mm. 23–24.

16. Saint-Lambert, *Principles*, p. 46.

17. Michel Corrette, *Méthode pour apprendre facilement à jouer du pardessus de viole à 5 et à 6 cordes* (Paris, 1738/r1983), pp. 13–14, cited in Jerold, *Notes Inégales*, p. 277.

18. Saint-Lambert, *Principles*, pp. 32–33, trans. David Chung, "Revisiting 'Le bon gout,'" pp. 186–187.

19. For information on these spinet players, see David Ledbetter, *Harpsichord and Lute Music in 17th-Century France* (Bloomington, IN: University of Indiana Press, 1987), p. 5 and *passim*.

20. Ledbetter, *Harpsichord and Lute Music in 17th-Century France*, pp. 5–6 and *passim*.

21. Ledbetter, *Harpsichord and Lute Music in 17th-Century France*, p. 18.

22. Ledbetter, *Harpsichord and Lute Music in 17th-Century France*, p. 19.

23. Ledbetter, *Harpsichord and Lute Music in 17th-Century France*, p. 8.

24. Ledbetter, *Harpsichord and Lute Music in 17th-Century France*, pp. 12–13.

25. Ledbetter, *Harpsichord and Lute Music in 17th-Century France*, p. 140.

26. See Colin Tilney, *The Art of the Unmeasured Prelude for Harpsichord* (London: Schott, 1985), and Davitt Moroney, "The Performance of Unmeasured Harpsichord Preludes," *Early Music* 4, no. 2 (April, 1976), pp. 143–151.

27. Nicolas Lebègue, "Extrait du Privilege," *Les pièces de clavecin* (Paris, 1677).

28. The preludes in Le Roux's first and fifth suites differ from other examples of the form, however, in that they occasionally include what look like thoroughbass figures.

29. Couperin, *L'art de toucher le clavecin*, p. 60.

30. Bruce Gustafson and David Fuller, *A Catalogue of French Harpsichord Music, 1699–1780* (Oxford: Clarendon Press, 1990), p. 1.

31. There is a large literature on *les clavecinistes* and their music. It includes Carol Henry Bates, "French Harpsichord Music in the First Decade of the 18th Century," *Early Music* 17, no. 2 (May, 1989), pp. 184–196; David Fuller, "French Harpsichord Playing in the 17th Century: After Le Gallois," *Early Music* 4 (1976), pp. 22–26; Bruce Gustafson, *French Harpsichord Music of the 17th Century: A Thematic Catalog of the Sources*

with Commentary (Ann Arbor: UMI Press, 1977); and Mark Kroll, "The French Masters: French Keyboard Music," in *Eighteenth-Century Keyboard Music*. ed. Robert Marshall (New York: Schirmer, 1994, rep. New York: Routledge, 2003), pp. 124–153. See also the biographies of individual composers.

32. Ronald Broude, "Composition, Performance, and Text in Solo Music of the French Baroque," *Text: An Interdisciplinary Annual of Textual Studies* 15 (2003), pp. 19–49, here p. 29.

33. See Rebecca Cypess, "Chambonnières, Jollain and the First Engraving of Harpsichord Music in France," *Early Music* 35, no. 4 (2007), pp. 539–553.

34. Glen Wilson, "The Other Mr Couperin," *Early Keyboard Journal (The Historical Keyboard Society of North America)* 30, (2017), pp. 7–25.

35. F. Couperin, *L'art de toucher le clavecin*, p. 51.

36. See Mark Kroll, "L'Ornement mystérieux," *Early Music* 45, no. 2 (2017), pp. 297–309, here pp. 307–308.

37. John Hawkins, who chronicled many of Dieupart's activities in London, wrote: "In the latter part of his life he grew negligent, and frequented concerts performed in ale-houses, in obscure parts of town . . . He died . . . in very necessitated circumstances." John Hawkins, *A General History of the Science and Practice of Music* (London, 1776, rep. New York: Dover Publications, 1963), p. 822.

38. See Évrard Titon du Tillet, *Le Parnasse françois* (Paris, 1732), and Pierre Louis d'Aquin de Chateau-Lyon, *Lettres sur les homes célèbres . . . sur le regne de Louis* XV (Paris and Amsterdam, 1752).

39. *Mercure galant,* July 1677, p. 109–110, cited in *Elisabeth-Claude Jacquet de La Guerre, The Collected Works for Harpsichord, Part I,* ed. and trans. Arthur Lawrence (New York: The Broude Trust, 2008), p. v, fn. 3.

40. For a provocative discussion about the possible real identity of Le Roux, see Pascal Tufféry, "In Search of Gaspard Le Roux," *Early Music America* 22, no. 3 (September 2016), pp. 26–29. Tufféry theorizes that the composer "Le Roux" might have actually been "le Roi" himself; that is, Louis XIV.

41. Letter of 25 October 1727, cited in Kroll, "The French Masters," p. 142.

42. For some intriguing studies on the relationship between the compositional styles of Rameau and Domenico Scarlatti, particularly with regard to the virtuoso and progressive keyboard techniques they both used, see João Pedro d'Alvarenga, "Domenico Scarlatti in the 1720s: Portugal, Travelling and the Italianization of the Portuguese Musical Scene," in *Domenico Scarlatti Adventures: Essays to Commemorate the 250th Anniversary of His Death*, Massimiliano Sala and W. Dean Sutcliffe, eds. (Bologna: Ut Orpheus, 2008), pp. 17–68; and Graham Sadler, "When Scarlatti Met Rameau? Reflections on a Probable Encounter in the 1720s," in *The Worlds of Harpsichord and Organ: Liber Amicorum David Fuller*, ed. Bruce Gustafson (Hillsdale, NY: Pendragon Press, 2018).

43. Wilfred Mellers, *François Couperin and the French Classical Tradition* (London: Faber, 1987), pp. 248–249.

44. Cited and trans. in Yonit Lea Kosovske, *Historical Harpsichord Technique* (Bloomington: Indiana University Press, 2011), p. 67.

45. Cited in Friedrich Wilhelm Marpurg, *Historisch-kritische Beyträge zur Aufnahme der Musik, Band I* (Berlin 1754), p. 459. Koopman writes: "The statement reads: 'Mr. Duphly, a student of Dagincourt only plays the harpsichord, in order, as he says, to not let the organ ruin his hand.'"

46. See Charles Burney, *The Present State of Music in France and Italy* (London, 1773), second edition, p. 38.

47. For example, in 1751, Charles Avison was reportedly the first to introduce to England Rameau's *Pièces de clavecin en concert*, in the programs of Avison's Newcastle Music Society. See Jenny Burchell, *Polite or Commercial Concerts?* (New York: Garland Publishing Co., 1996), p. 283, and *Charles Avison: Concerto Grosso Arrangements of Geminiani's Opus 1 Violin Sonatas*, Mark Kroll, ed. (Middleton, Wisconsin: A-R Editions, 2010), Introduction.

48. See Kroll, "The French Masters," p. 135.

49. *Correspondance, littéraire, philosophique et critique par Grimm . . .* Vol. 9 (Paris: Garnier Frères, 1879), Juillet 1771, p. 347.

50. See H.-J. Schulze, "The French Influence in Bach's Instrumental Music," *Early Music* 13, no. 2 (May, 1985), pp. 180–184, here p. 180.

51. Schulze, "The French Influence in Bach's Instrumental Music," p. 181.

52. See Traute Marshall, "Wo hat Bach die Celler Hofkapelle gehört," in *Bach-Jahrbuch* 102 (2016), pp. 115–124, and Robert L. Marshall and Traute M. Marshall, *Exploring the World of J. S. Bach: A Traveler's Guide* (Urbana-Champagne: University of Illinois Press, 2016), pp. 24, 113. Further evidence of Bach's familiarity with French music can be seen in the inclusion of a suite by Marchand in the *Andreas Bach Book* (I am grateful to Robert Marshall for this information).

53. See *Debussy Letters*, selected and edited by François Lesure and Roger Nichols, trans. Roger Nichols (Cambridge, MA: Harvard University Press, 1987), pp. 300–301.

54. Cited in the *Bulletin of the Société Internationale de Musique*, January 15, 1913, and *Debussy on Music*, François Lesure, ed, trans. and ed. Richard Langham Smith (New York: Knopf, 1977), p. 273.

Further Reading

Bates, Carol Henry. "French Harpsichord Music in the First Decade of the 18th Century." *Early Music* 17, no. 2 (May, 1989), pp. 184–196.

Fuller, David and Bruce Gustafson. *A Catalogue of French Harpsichord Music, 1699–1780.* Oxford: Clarendon Press, 1990.

Kroll, Mark. "The French Masters: French Keyboard Music," in *Eighteenth-Century Keyboard Music*, ed. Robert Marshall. New York: Schirmer, 1994, rep. New York: Routledge, 2003.

Ledbetter, David. *Harpsichord and Lute Music in 17th-Century France.* Bloomington: University of Indiana Press, 1987.

Mellers, Wilfred. *François Couperin and the French Classical Tradition.* London: Faber, 1987.

7 Italy

REBECCA CYPESS

Esordio: On the Ideal of Variety in the Italian Harpsichord Repertory

Harpsichords were everywhere in early modern Italy: in church, at court, in the theater and the opera house, in the homes of patricians and aristocrats, and, from the turn of the early eighteenth century, in the homes of the nascent middle class. Cultivated in independent city-states ruled by wealthy and despotic families, in the cosmopolitan trade center of Venice, and in the courts of cardinals in Rome, harpsichords were as varied as the venues in which they were found: from small spinets to long, wing-shaped instruments; some with a normal twelve-note subdivision of the octave and others with split keys to accommodate more nuanced systems of temperament and intonation; those with metal strings and those strung with gut; some plain in appearance and some lavishly decorated.

This variety in instrument construction and social usage was matched by the diverse genres and styles that composers employed in writing for them. The Neapolitan composer Giovanni Maria Trabaci (1575–1647) considered the harpsichord capable of practically anything. Introducing his set of variations on the theme known as the "Zefiro," Trabaci indicated that even those variations not designated expressly for the harpsichord could still be played on that instrument. As he wrote, "let it be known that although some items in this book are labeled for the harp, the harpsichord should not be excluded, for the harpsichord is the lord of all the instruments in the world, and with it one can play everything with ease."[1]

During the sixteenth and seventeenth centuries, the versatility of the harpsichord observed by Trabaci allowed for the flourishing of a great variety of genres – dance pieces, contrapuntal and imitative works, variation sets, and works that mimic or demand improvisation. While the early eighteenth century witnessed a consolidation of these genres, the new *galant* style that emerged at that point embraced an overall aesthetic of variety, thus perpetuating the characterization, articulated by Trabaci, of the harpsichord's versatility and flexibility.

It is partly as a result of these characteristics that the construction of a history of Italian harpsichord music presents special challenges. Precisely because harpsichords were seen as capable of rendering music in such a wide range of genres and styles, the harpsichord repertory overlaps with that of other instruments – especially, in the sixteenth and seventeenth centuries, with that of the organ. Clavichords were also found in Italy throughout the early modern era, and the emergence of the Cristofori piano in 1700 means that repertory for that new instrument – conceived of as an adaptation of the harpsichord – intersects with that of the harpsichord.

In this chapter, I construct a history of harpsichord music in Italy that oscillates between the general and the specific. I rely on the conceit of a rhetorical presentation (a model in line with musical thought of early modern Italy) to expound on issues related to the sound of the instruments, notated texts, genres, and specific examples.[2] My introduction (*esordio*) is followed by a section on the harpsichord's *elocuzione* – the definition and articulation of the instrument's voice by composers and performers, which may allow us to define the harpsichord repertory in contrast to that of the organ in the years prior to 1700. I then discuss a series of *invenzioni* (inventions, ideas), by which I mean the genres that defined the compositional and performative roles before the late seventeenth century. If these discussions of genre offer a bird's-eye view of the development of the harpsichord repertory, they are also necessarily incomplete. I therefore supplement this general overview with a series of *esemplari* – case studies in the repertory that bring individual works into focus.[3] My discussion of the *galant* sonata in the early eighteenth century takes the form of an *invenzione con figure*, in which I identify some of the main tropes and gestures incorporated into the harpsichord sonata in the eighteenth century. (The music of Domenico Scarlatti will be discussed in this volume in Chapter 10.) My *preludio* and *perorazione* frame the story of the harpsichord repertory in Italy by exploring its outer reaches in the medieval era and in the age of the nascent pianoforte.

Elocuzione: Locating an Italian Harpsichord Repertory Before 1700

Past histories of keyboard music in early modern Italy have tended to conflate the harpsichord repertory with that of the organ. To some extent, this is reasonable: professional players in the sixteenth and seventeenth centuries were expected to be flexible, rendering music on whatever instrument was in front of them. (The distinction between harpsichords and pianos in the eighteenth century is less problematic, since the sound qualities of the two instruments were quite similar; this is a point to which I shall return). Nevertheless, there is much to be gained by attempting to locate a repertory that was ideally suited to (rather than merely "playable on") the harpsichord. As Alexander Silbiger has written:

> It is one matter to assert that performers played the same music indiscriminately on any keyboard instrument, and quite another to assert that a composer never had a specific instrument in mind when writing a particular work ... [S]tyles more appropriate to one or another instrument can be recognized already in many 16th-century compositions, even if such works were frequently played on different types of instruments.[4]

Distinctions between the harpsichord repertory and that of other instruments may be discerned through a variety of criteria. *Il Transilvano*, a monumental treatise on organ playing by Girolamo Diruta (1595–1647) issued in two parts in 1593 and 1609, respectively, devotes only a few pages to the harpsichord, but these are illuminating. One hint about the harpsichord repertory appears in Diruta's discussion of genre: "The sacred Council of Trent has prohibited the playing of *passamezzi* and other dances, and also lascivious and indecent songs on church organs. It is not fitting to mix the profane with the sacred."[5] Diruta goes on to explain that dance music of this sort is best suited to the "istrumenti da penna" (quilled instruments – i.e., harpsichords).[6] Moreover, harpsichords were considerably more likely than organs to be found in the homes of the aristocracy. As a result, dances and settings of secular songs are overall more likely to have been written with harpsichords in mind. This may be true even in cases where the title page of a given volume calls for performance on *organo*. For example, the *Frottole intabulate da sonare organi* (1517) compiled by Andrea Antico (1480–1538), which consists of keyboard intabulations (idiomatically embellished arrangements) of secular songs, bears a frontispiece that shows a player at the harpsichord, not the organ. If the famous *Libro del cortegiano* (Book of the Courtier) of Baldassare Castiglione (1478–1529) celebrated the "most perfect consonance" and "harmony" afforded by "all keyed instruments" (*tutti gl'instrumenti da tasti*), the frontispiece of Antico's collection links both the repertory and the ideal of courtly sociability with the harpsichord.[7]

Other criteria that may guide us in identifying music designed primarily for the harpsichord relate to the idiomatic treatment of the instrument – a factor that became increasingly important at the start of the seventeenth century.[8] Diruta again provides an important description: In answer to the question, "Why is it that many organists do not succeed in playing serious music on quilled instruments as well as they do on the organ?," he addresses the idiomatic properties of the harpsichord – especially its quickly decaying sound:

> When you play a breve or semibreve on the organ, do you not hear the entire sound without striking the key more than one time? But when you play such a note on a quilled instrument more than half the sound is lost. So it is necessary to compensate for such a defect by lightly striking the key many times with quickness and dexterity of the hand.[9]

The toccatas included in Diruta's treatise (including some by the author and some by other composers) provide a testing ground for keyboardists to adapt their performance practices to suit both organs and harpsichords. However, the first editions of the toccatas of Girolamo Frescobaldi (1583–1643), which will be discussed further below, specify the harpsichord as the intended medium, and Frescobaldi provided guidelines for their performance that echo Diruta's approach to harpsichord playing.[10] The toccatas of Frescobaldi and his successors consist primarily of elaborations of schematic chordal frameworks, often with idiomatic figuration; this style offers an opportunity to exploit the harpsichord's capacity for lush arpeggiation – something impossible on the organ.

Another feature of composition that seems closely linked to the harpsichord is the use of angular or irregular rhythms, syncopations, and other surprising rhythmic effects. The clear articulation of the harpsichord was, until the late eighteenth century, considered one of its great advantages, making it well suited to the accompaniment of dance and operatic recitative, and rendering it an ideal medium for the organization of an ensemble. While organists could also, obviously, play rhythmically irregular passages, these generally emerge more clearly on the harpsichord and may serve as an indicator that the latter instrument was the intended medium of a given piece of music.

The criteria that I have suggested here for locating an Italian harpsichord repertory apply until the last quarter of the seventeenth century, when composers began to focus their attentions to a greater extent on amateur musicians who would play in domestic settings; at that point, a clearer distinction grew between the harpsichord repertory and that of the organ. Moreover, even in the period before ca. 1675, these criteria are not definitive. A sense of idiomatic harpsichord writing emerges from an extended relationship with both the instruments and the music.

Preludio: Imagining the Earliest Harpsichord Music in Italy

Stringed keyboard instruments had a long history in Europe, and it is therefore difficult to arrive at a clear starting point for the history of Italian harpsichord music. The earliest-known written reference to a "clavicembalum" (the Latin equivalent of "harpsichord") appears in a Paduan source

in 1397.[11] A detailed diagram and description survive in the manuscript of
the Franco-Flemish physician Arnaut de Zwolle (late 14th/early 15th
century–1466, treatise ca. 1440), and David Catalunya and Paul Poletti
have shown that by the time of Arnaut's writing, stringed keyboard
instruments were in widespread use across the continent, including in
Italy.[12] Catalunya has argued for the performance of Italian repertory – in
particular, compositions preserved in the so-called Faenza codex – on
reconstructions of the stringed keyboard instruments in Arnaut's manuscript. In particular, the articulate attack of the stringed instruments
renders clearly the complex rhythms of the Faenza repertory – rhythmic
patterns characteristic of the Italian *Trecento* (1300s). Thus, despite the
recent claim that the Faenza repertory was intended solely for organ, the
possibility of performance on ancestors of the harpsichord cannot be ruled
out.[13]

Invenzione: Contrapuntal Genres

Perhaps more than any other instrument category, keyboard instruments
were valued for their capacity to coordinate and embody multiple voices.
To judge from the surviving repertory of the sixteenth and seventeenth
centuries, this was a highly prized compositional and performative skill.
Organists would have studied counterpoint and contrapuntal composition
as part of their early training.[14] Perhaps because of this association between
counterpoint and musicians educated within the church, or perhaps
because of the later association of counterpoint with an "austere" or
"churchly" style, it would be easy to assume that contrapuntal genres
writ large were intended for the organ rather than the harpsichord.
While such works played a significant role in liturgical situations, counterpoint was also an important part of the harpsichordist's art. Genres such as
the ricercare, fantasia, canzona, and capriccio allowed both composers and
performers to display their artistry and ingenuity, and these ideals found
their place as much in homes or academies – settings in which harpsichords were likely to be found – as they did in church.

   From around the middle of the sixteenth century, the ricercare was
treated as a thoroughly contrapuntal genre, and, as Robert Judd has
observed, "ricercars are among the first Western art music to eschew
reference to words and to rely entirely on sound."[15] Without words as a
structuring device, composers such as Andrea Gabrieli (1532/3?–1585)
used a variety of contrapuntal techniques, including inversion, augmentation, and stretto, to endow their ricercares with a sense of variety and
flexibility. In addition, these works are sometimes heavily decorated in the

"diminution" style, in which long notes are subdivided into shorter ornamental figures of varying melodic and rhythmic content; this figuration
can occur in every voice in the texture and sounds very much at home on
the harpsichord.[16] Posthumous collections of Gabrieli's music, including
settings of secular songs, indicate that they could be executed on "ogni
sorte di stromenti da tasti" (any type of keyboard instrument).

The canzona, sometimes called *canzona francese*, began as an adaptation of the polyphonic Franco-Flemish *chanson*, but, by the late sixteenth
century, it diverged from this vocal model. Instead, Italian composers for
keyboard and other instruments used aspects of these *chansons* to create
new works in the same style. Features that were taken over into the
independent instrumental canzona include the opening dactylic rhythmic
motto ♩♩♩ and a sectional organization that alternates between counterpoint and homophony, often with light, triple-meter sections included for
contrast with stately duple-meter opening and closing sections.[17] While
canzonas were often published by professional instrumentalists employed
in churches, their basis in secular *chansons* – and, in many cases, their
adherence to the *chanson* as a model – suggests that performance on
harpsichord was at least as likely as performance on the organ.[18]

The term "fantasia" might seem to imply the utmost freedom of
composition, but during this seventeenth century this did not negate the
genre's contrapuntal character. Keyboardists were expected to improvise
counterpoint, as noted, for example, by Adriano Banchieri (1568–1634),
and their fully-composed fantasias demonstrate their ability to negotiate
the boundary between tradition and invention.[19] The capriccio was often
characterized by a sectional organization in which the opening contrapuntal material is subjected to variation procedures in successive sections.
In its ever-changing treatment of the opening section, it displayed its
"capriciousness" while engaging with formal counterpoint.

Girolamo Frescobaldi, a towering figure whose keyboard music dominated Italy throughout the seventeenth century, contributed to all of these
contrapuntal genres, and in most cases he printed them in open score.
While, in earlier generations, this open-score format might have been used
to adapt a contrapuntal piece for instrumental ensemble, by Frescobaldi's
day, its purpose seems to have been the cultivation of an intellectual
understanding of the counterpoint. A virtuoso organist, Frescobaldi nevertheless embraced the harpsichord through idiomatic treatment in a number of his works. His prefatory note to the *Primo libro delle capricci* (1624)
includes a recommendation that the player arpeggiate dissonant chords,
which suggests that performance on the harpsichord was valid as on the
organ. In those works, moreover, he notes that there are sections where the

counterpoint breaks down, and where the execution must be governed by the "feeling of that passage" (*l'affetto di quel passo*).

Since the turn of the seventeenth century, strict counterpoint had been seen as coming into conflict with the looser principles adopted for basso continuo playing and the lighter genres associated with the *stile moderno*.[20] Frescobaldi demonstrated his keen interest in and mastery of contrapuntal styles as well as lighter, less strict genres (including chamber music with basso continuo and the toccata, which will be addressed below). His influence in this respect was lasting.[21] By the third quarter of the seventeenth century, however, practitioners of strict counterpoint found themselves increasingly overshadowed by composers who embraced the lighter *galant* style, influenced by the chamber sonatas of Arcangelo Corelli (1653–1713) and his peers. Luigi Battiferri (b. 1600–1610, d. 1682 or after) lamented the neglect of keyboard counterpoint in open score, writing in frustration that "those who play a simple *basso continuo* are esteemed valorous; what might be played in the space of an hour serves them for years." Instead, he argued, keyboardists should attempt to become "immortalized . . . in particular by attending to the playing of the *ricercare*, this being the most learned genre of playing."[22] The contrapuntal works of Bernardo Pasquini (1637–1710), preserved in an autograph manuscript, are among the most momentous of the late seventeenth century, showing a mastery over contrapuntal devices that Pasquini combines and extends over a long duration.[23] These pieces, however, did not reach publication, and they became overshadowed by public reception of lighter genres in the late seventeenth century. (Pasquini also composed such lighter fare, including suites of dance movements.) Aspects of the contrapuntal genres were folded into the "*galant* synthesis," but the heyday of the *ricercare* for which Battiferri longed had passed.

Esemplare: Claudio Merulo, *Ricercari* (1567)

The first *esemplare* to which I turn, which illustrates the Italian contrapuntal genres for harpsichord, reaches back into the sixteenth century. Victor Coelho and Keith Polk have observed a shift in notated music in the latter decades of the sixteenth century. Whereas earlier composers focused predominantly on lute repertory as a medium for expression and musical self-fashioning, the latter half of the sixteenth century saw a new focus on the composition of keyboard music. Coelho and Polk propose the *Ricercari* of 1567 by Claudio Merulo (1533–1604) as a turning point in the development of keyboard music.[24] Merulo was organist at San Marco in Venice, and Girolamo Diruta's descriptions of his professional role associate him primarily with the organ. Indeed, the organization of many of Merulo's contrapuntal works according to the church tones suggest that he conceived them with liturgical usage in mind. However, two factors identified by Coelho and Polk suggest that performance on the harpsichord was entirely appropriate, and the works could be adapted to a stringed keyboard instrument without much difficulty. First, they observe the strong relationship between the keyboard ricercare of the later sixteenth century and the lute ricercare of the 1520s onward. The timbre and performance practices of the lute are more closely related to the harpsichord than to the organ. In addition, they note Merulo's connection to the Venetian aristocracy, suggesting that his music would have been heard in domestic settings as well as churchly ones. While small organs were no doubt found in some homes, as noted above, it is likely that these contrapuntal works were also played on the harpsichord and adapted to suit the harpsichord in performance – especially through the restriking of chords and tied dissonances, and through the execution of idiomatic ornaments. The ricercares in this collection lend themselves to such readings readily, with room for creative arpeggiation, as well as for the addition of ornaments idiomatic to the harpsichord. These pieces are quite substantial in length in comparison to previous essays in the genre.

While these works may certainly be performed on the organ as well as the harpsichord, they underscore the liminal position of contrapuntal music in particular, with its adaptability to various instrumental idioms. If Polk and Coelho are correct in their understanding of this music as having found a place in social environments where the harpsichord flourished, then Merulo's works underscore his commitment – and that of others of his generation – to creating a harpsichord repertory that matched their conception of the instrument's import.

Invenzione: Harpsichord Works Based on Vocal Models

Instrumental composers in sixteenth-century Italy frequently drew on vocal compositions as models for their own work. The aesthetic motivations for this link were articulated in numerous sources, among them the treatise *Il Fontegara*, by Silvestro Ganassi (1492–mid-sixteenth century): "You must know that all musical instruments, in comparison to the human voice, are lacking; therefore we must attempt to learn from it and imitate it."[25]

Ganassi was a professional wind player (and also produced an important early treatise on string playing), but manifestations of this principle are evident in the keyboard repertory as well. Like other instrumentalists, keyboardists viewed the imitation of the human voice as an aesthetic ideal, but they adapted vocal works to suit the idiomatic capacities of their instruments. Composers produced keyboard intabulations of madrigals, *frottole*, and other popular vocal genres, creating a rich texture of arpeggiation and figuration that serves as filigree adorning the original vocal piece. In keyboard intabulations of this period, a consistent four- or five-voice texture would be maintained throughout, and elaboration through diminution can be found in each voice in turn. The association of these intabulations with secular songs suggests that the harpsichord was the intended medium. This conjecture is further supported by the complex rhythmic figuration in works like Claudio Merulo's setting of Orlando di Lasso's *Susanne un jour*, which an intricate rhythmic profile well suited to the harpsichord's articulate attack.

As new instrumental genres emerged in the seventeenth century and composers began to treat their instruments in more idiomatic ways, their direct reliance on vocal models lessened.[26] However, seventeenth-century settings of vocal polyphony still appeared, even if less frequently. These intabulations adopt the textural and expressive vocabulary of music specially designated for the harpsichord. Despite instrumental composers' decreased reliance on vocal works as direct models for their compositions in the eighteenth century, the overall aesthetic that mandated imitation of the human voice persisted. For much of the seventeenth century, it was the violin that embodied the spirit of the voice; this inspiration can be heard readily in the sonatas and concertos of Corelli and his Bolognese contemporaries in the later decades of the century. As keyboard sonatas began to adopt aspects of these chamber sonatas, they often incorporated the tropes of vocal music.

Esemplare: Three Settings of Arcadelt's "Ancidetemi pur"

Three seventeenth-century keyboard settings of a madrigal by Jacques Arcadelt (1507–1568) highlight changes in style and aesthetic purpose. Ascanio Mayone (1565–1627) was part of the Neapolitan school active at the turn of the seventeenth century. Like his contemporary Trabaci, he saw the harpsichord as more closely related to the harp or lute than to the organ.[27] There can be no question, however, that his intabulation of "Ancidetemi pur" was written with the harpsichord in mind. Mayone used the diminution style to elaborate on the framework of the madrigal, and his setting exploits the full range and capacities of the harpsichord in an idiomatic manner. Of special note are the wide leaps that he undertakes, sometimes with irregular or surprising rhythmic figuration.

Alexander Silbiger has discussed Frescobaldi's setting of "Ancidetemi pur," showing that the piece diverges substantially from Arcadelt's original madrigal. As he writes, "Frescobaldi's intabulation is essentially a free interpretation of the madrigal, and ... an interpretation not only of its notes but also of its words."[28] In contrast to earlier intabulations, which adopt the diminution style of ornamentation, Frescobaldi's is much closer in style to his revolutionary toccatas (to be addressed below), in which the integrity of the voice leading assumes secondary importance or is abandoned purposefully in favor of idiomatic figuration and the expressive use of dissonance akin to *seconda prattica* vocal music.[29] As Silbiger shows, Frescobaldi used his free ornamental keyboard idiom to differentiate and interpret aspects of the text that are treated in a straightforward manner by Arcadelt himself.

By the time that the setting of "Ancidetemi pur" by Gregorio Strozzi (1615–1687) appeared in print, in 1687, the genre of the madrigal intabulation was archaic, to be sure. He was among the harpsichord composers who continued to display the imprint of Frescobaldi's work in the latter decades of the seventeenth century, and in some respects his treatment of "Ancidetemi" is an homage to Frescobaldi, especially in its opening trilled gesture. More than Frescobaldi's setting, which adopts the rhapsodic and capricious manner of his toccatas, Strozzi's distinguishes each line of the poem with a separate musical style. Thus, despite his reliance on Frescobaldi's model, Strozzi seems to have been intent on leaving his own mark on Arcadelt's work.

Invenzione: The Harpsichord Toccata and the Posture of Improvisation

It must be assumed that keyboardists – at least those who were professionally trained or perhaps were highly-skilled amateurs – were engaged in improvisation long before the notation of genres such as the toccata, which seem designed to project aspects of an improvised style through the written or printed medium.

By the late sixteenth century, organs in Venice were apparently used to accompany the practice of polyphonic recitation of chant known as *falsobordone*.[30] In such works, the keyboard takes over the embellishment of a plainchant line in the diminution style from a singer. The Venetian toccata apparently emerged as an independent genre from this medium, and it crystallized as an ornamental elaboration of a schematic harmonic framework. Diruta featured works of this type in *Il Transilvano*, including some that he had composed himself, as well as others by Merulo, Andrea Gabrieli, and others whose art he admired. The ornamental passagework in the diminution style found in these Venetian toccatas hints at the virtuosity that would become a hallmark of the genre in the hands of Frescobaldi and his successors. In this type of toccata, the voices pass the ornamental role among one another, with each assuming the spotlight in turn; the texture is thus quite similar to that of the madrigal intabulation.

At the same time, an idiom more obviously suited to plucked instruments, including the harpsichord, lute, and harp, was being cultivated among composers in Ferrara and Naples. Of the generation before Frescobaldi, these included Giovanni de Macque (b. 1548–1550, d. 1614) and Ercole Pasquini (b. mid-sixteenth century, d. ca. 1619), whose music Frescobaldi knew but whose toccatas remained unpublished during their lifetimes.[31] Neapolitan composers including Trabaci and Mayone took a special interest in *durezze e ligature* (harsh sonorities and suspensions), which embraced heightened chromaticism for expressive purposes. This interest in chromaticism may have been related to the humanist interest in ancient Greek modal theory and the resulting exploration of various systems of tuning and temperament. While the *durezze e ligature* can sound extremely biting in the meantone system that dominated late-Renaissance Italy, composers such as Mayone also contributed to experiments with split-keyed instruments that enabled differentiation of sharp and flat notes.[32] Although not all of these pieces were labeled with the genre title "toccata," the chromatic explorations of this school had a marked influence on the toccata style of Frescobaldi.

Indeed, Frescobaldi seems to have had all of these models in mind when he composed and published his revolutionary toccatas in lavishly engraved editions for the first time in 1615. This was followed by a second book of toccatas in 1627; both volumes were reprinted multiple times during the seventeenth century.[33] Frescobaldi was aware of the novelty of his toccata style, and this novelty lay in part in his idiomatic treatment of the harpsichord, which was specified (to the exclusion of the organ) on the title page of the first editions of his *Tocccate e partite . . . libro primo*.[34] As Frescobaldi wrote in the dedicatory letter of his first book, "Having composed my first book of musical compositions upon the keyboard [*sopra i tasti*], I dedicate it devotedly to you, who in Rome deigned with frequent commands to excite me to the practice of these works, and to show that this style of mine was not unacceptable."[35] The phrase *sopra i tasti* suggests that Frescobaldi had written down his toccatas as a crystallization of the act of improvisation and also that the act of improvisation was fundamentally tactile, related to the touch and feel of the instrument before him. This idiomatic approach is confirmed in his well-known preface (the expanded version of which appeared in the 1616 edition), where he emphasized the need for performers to respond to the specific properties of the instrument. Echoing Diruta's statements about performance on the harpsichord as distinct from the organ, Frescobaldi advises harpsichordists on idiomatic execution: "Let the beginnings of the toccatas be done slowly, and arpeggiated: and in the ties, or dissonances, as also in the middle of the work they will be struck together, in order not to leave the instrument empty: which striking will be repeated at the pleasure of the player."[36] Perhaps the most famous aspect of this preface is the composer's instruction that the toccatas "should not remain subject to the beat, as we see practiced in the modern madrigal." The flexibility implied by this statement is matched by the capricious nature of the music itself, which moves easily from one texture or pattern of figuration to another. Chord progressions peppered with dissonances give way to fast scalar passages; these are complemented by imitative figures that mimic the vocal ornaments of the *stile moderno* madrigal. Although carefully planned in their formal design, these compositions assume the pretense of improvisation according to the fantastical imagination of the player.[37] Moreover, through his performance instructions, Frescobaldi makes it clear that the notation is insufficient to capture the works' improvisatory spirit, and players are responsible for elaborating on the score in accordance with their tastes and the responses of the instruments that they are using.

Toccatas published after Frescobaldi's include works by Michelangelo Rossi (1601/2–1656), Bernardo Storace (fl. mid-seventeenth century), Bernardo Pasquini, and Gregorio Strozzi, among others; Silbiger has explored the manuscript tradition that complements these sources. While these later composers retained essential aspects of Frescobaldi's style, toward the end of the century, they tended to define the sections of their toccatas more clearly by style, often incorporating a more rigorous contrapuntal approach in some sections than Frescobaldi had done. The idea of the toccata as a vehicle for the exploration of the idiomatic capacities of the harpsichord persisted, and composers after Frescobaldi often incorporated brilliant figuration and virtuosic passagework that emphasize technical skill as much as the improvisatory spirit. The cultivation of ease and virtuosity at the keyboard forms an overt motivation for the toccatas of Alessandro Scarlatti (1660–1725), which had a clear pedagogical purpose. His toccatas are arranged in separate movements including quasi-improvised material, fugal material, and sometimes dance sections.[38] In the eighteenth century, the posture of improvisation was incorporated in toccatas, fantasies, and preludes, the last category including opening movements of sonatas.

Esemplare: Bernardo Pasquini's "Toccata con lo scherzo del cucco"

Both virtuosity and the improvisational posture stand at the center of Bernardo Pasquini's celebrated "Toccata con lo scherzo del cucco." Imitations of nature – and birdsong in particular – had been a source of fascination and play by composers across Europe in the sixteenth and seventeenth centuries. Pasquini's toccata starts with an off-beat falling-third motive (E–C♯), which imitates the sound of the cuckoo. The motive is imitated in the tenor and bass registers, complemented by sixteenth-note scalic figuration. The cuckoo quickly gives way to an arpeggio section reminiscent of Frescobaldi's block chords, which are likewise meant to be elaborated by the player. The cuckoo motive returns but is again over-taken by skeletal harmonic progressions that call for arpeggiated elabora-tion. When the cuckoo returns for a third time, the virtuosity of the accompanimental figuration intensifies, as the player sounds driven to maintain the same patterns for an extended time, propelled by the now obsessive birdsong. The wit in this scene reaches a new level of intensity at the section marked "Duo," in which two cuckoo birds chirp their minor-third motive around the idiomatic figuration. Finally, the left hand begins to trill on a tenor-range A, while the cuckoos repeat their song; the trill moves up to the right hand, and the toccata ends in a staged scene of chaos, as the cuckoo's call becomes ever more frequent.

If this toccata, with its representational content, seems to stand apart from other works with the same generic designation, its embrace of virtuosity and the pretense of invention on the spur of the moment – as

Example 7.1 Bernardo Pasquini, "Toccata con lo scherzo del cucco," mm. 85–93 if the player were being driven forward by an unwieldy chorus of cuckoos – means instead that it forms a delightful manifestation of principles at play in numerous other Italian toccatas.

Invenzione: Variations and Dance Pieces

The art of variation on a basic melodic or chordal framework was a skill that professional musicians would have learned through apprenticeship or study. Professional keyboardists trained in church often learned techniques of variation through their simultaneous training as choirboys, though they generally knew how to read music in the sixteenth century at a higher rate than instrumentalists of other sorts, including string and wind players.[39] In the sixteenth century, especially the 1580s–1590s, such procedures of variation were notated in the diminution manuals by composer-performers including Ganassi and Diruta, among numerous others.[40] Among amateur academicians or members of the nobility, such as the characters depicted in the *Libro del cortegiano*, the ability to vary an instrumental formula or a musical-poetic recitation could be a mark of erudition and accomplishment. Poetry was often recited, with the accompaniment of a lute or viol, to *arie* (musical "modes," melodic formulas, or harmonic progressions) such as the romanesca or Ruggiero, or to formulas newly invented for the purpose, and each stanza could be varied through musical embellishment.[41] Thus amateur keyboardists in the sixteenth century might likewise have learned – whether through experience or instruction – to vary the chord progressions that they played. For musicians accompanying dance, progressions such as the *folia* and the *passamezzo* (literally, "a step and a half," named for an aspect of its choreography), as well as folksongs including the "Monica," would have constituted music for entertainment and dance, and these, too, called for elaboration.

In the sixteenth century and, in greater numbers, in the seventeenth, composers began to notate fully worked-out variation sets in large numbers for the first time. Keyboard composers were among these: Andrea Gabrieli's extended set of variations on the *Passamezzo antico* is one example. Frescobaldi included variation sets (*partite*) in his first and second books of toccatas, as did the many keyboard composers who built on the traditions that he established. At first, both vocal and instrumental composers focused their energies in the composition of variations on progressions such as the romanesca and the Ruggiero; in these, an extended formula (the equivalent of four or eight bars in modern notation) comes to a full cadence before the formula starts again. Later they would turn to the ciaccona and the passacaglia – two genres in which one iteration of the progression elides into the next – of which Frescobaldi provided the first published examples for keyboard. Silbiger has noted that Frescobaldi treated these genres in a manner quite distinct from the approach of composers of vocal settings or settings for instrumental ensemble.[42] Most obvious in Frescobaldi's settings is the absence of a true ostinato bass line; instead, each progression occurs without a repeating bass and is, in fact, subject to harmonic digression and other forms of variation. In the monumental *Cento partite sopra passacagli*, which appeared in the *Aggiunta* (addendum) to the 1637 reprint of the *Secondo libro di toccate*, some of the variations are actually labeled "ciaccona," and Silbiger argues that Frescobaldi purposefully sets the two genres against one another.[43] He observes: "the piece is in constant flux. It moves not only through different genres but also through different keys, modes, and tempos ... The work ends in a key different from that in which it began; but, after hearing a 'hundred' couplets of tonal wandering, who will remember?"[44]

Eliding formulas such as the ciaccona and passacaglia, and to some extent the earlier long forms as well, retained their position as important vehicles for elaboration in later Italian harpsichord music. Beyond Frescobaldi, Bernardo Storace included variations on the romanesca, Ruggiero, and *passamezzo*, as well as the ciaccona and passacaglia, in his published volume of 1664. Pasquini composed numerous variation sets. Gregorio Strozzi, who, as we have already seen, tended toward conservatism, likewise wrote variations on both long- and short-form progressions. Strozzi's romanesca variations interpolate short "tenori" and "ritornelli" between iterations of the romanesca formula. While each variation applies diminution-style elaboration to the romanesca progression, these interludes are comprised of block chords that require elaboration in the manner of toccatas.

Variation procedures were, of course, used in a wide array of genres aside from the variation set per se. Canzonas and capriccios often used similar procedures from one section to the next, thus creating a sense of organization through variety and contrast. It is no coincidence that some of the formulas described above also functioned as dance pieces: this was true, for example, of the *passamezzo* – a kind of pavan. Variation procedures were also applied to other dance genres: throughout the sixteenth and seventeenth centuries, *balletti*, *correnti*, and *gagliarde* with skeletal melodies were elaborated through improvised ornamentation in the division style. This practice may be seen in the 1551 collection *Intabolatura nova*, which is filled with *gagliarde*, *passamezzi*, and other dance genres. Although the highest voice is generally more heavily ornamented than the others, there is ample room for elaboration on repeated performance. Frescobaldi elevated individual dances to a new level, endowing them with a craft not seen in previous manifestations of the genre; his dances likewise can accommodate elaboration and variation in repeated sections. The *Balli d'arpicordo* of Giovanni Picchi (1572–1643), published in 1621, have largely been dismissed in previous literature, but their interesting variations on dance formulas display a level of rhythmic intricacy that may be instructive for the ornamentation of less elaborately notated dances, including the ten short *correnti* published in a collection by Michelangelo Rossi, likely in the 1630s.[45]

As with other musical genres and procedures of the sixteenth and seventeenth century, aspects of dance genres and variation procedures became part of the Italian *galant* sonata in the eighteenth century, a point to be pursued further below.

Esemplare: Frescobaldi's Romanesca Variations

As mentioned above, Frescobaldi's *Toccate e partite . . . libro primo* was issued in two editions in quick succession: the first in 1615 and the second in 1616. Beyond expansion of the preface, the musical composition most heavily revised from the first printing to the second was the variation set on the romanesca. This effect of this revision, as I have argued elsewhere, was to solidify the link between the romanesca variations and the style of the toccatas found in the same volume.[46] In the original set, the opening few variations seem to place a premium on variety and contrast, while the revised set introduces a clear sense of progression in complexity. The revised fourth variation is quite free in style – evocative of the toccata – while the original fourth variation was more strictly contrapuntal. The fifth through eleventh variations are the same in both versions.

In the original romanesca set, Frescobaldi ended with the twelfth variation, replete with intricate counterpoint, and a monument to the harpsichordist's ability to coordinate voices, bringing together disparate ideas and melodies into a single, unified whole. In the revised set, however, Frescobaldi changed the twelfth variation to one that represents a pinnacle of the toccata style, with sweeping scales that cover a wide range of the instrument in an impressive display of virtuosity. As in the toccatas, these runs are not supported by intricate contrapuntal motion, but by long notes that provide a harmonic foundation for the rhapsodizing solo voice. In the newly composed thirteenth and fourteenth variations, Frescobaldi backs away from this virtuosic toccata language, reverting instead to the more understated style of the first two variations in the piece. In this reserved ending, the

Example 7.2 Girolamo Frescobaldi, Variation 14 "Partite sopra l'aria della Romanesca," revised version (1616)

original object – the melodic-harmonic *modo* of the romanesca – reappears in a form stripped of all virtuosity. The last two variations are characterized by rhythmic displacements that require an affected interpretation; they seem to cast the player as hesitant – reluctant, perhaps, to bring the process of discovery to a close.

Invenzione Con Figure: The Eighteenth-Century Sonata and the "Galant Synthesis"

The term "sonata" had been applied to keyboard works prior to the late seventeenth century. As Gregory Barnett has shown, the term was used (usually in the manuscript tradition) in two ways: it could replace a specific genre designation such as "ricercare" or "toccata," or it could serve as a catch-all for a collection of genres.[47] Barnett traces the development of the keyboard sonata from its little-known usage in the manuscript context to the exceedingly popular genre that emerged in the early to mid-eighteenth century. At the heart of this story, he shows, is the tension, discussed above, between learned counterpoint and the nascent *galant* style that found its origins in the age of Corelli.[48] In the last quarter of the seventeenth century, keyboard composers (usually writing for the harpsichord) began to imitate the multimovement form of sonatas by Corelli and his contemporaries writing for chamber groups, also adopting the light textures, including simplified counterpoint, that those chamber composers applied.

Here we may recall the words of Giovanni Maria Trabaci early in the seventeenth century: the harpsichord, he claimed, was "lord of all the instruments in the world, and with it one can play everything with ease." This ideal of variety found further realization in the early eighteenth-century harpsichord sonata, which embraces an overall aesthetic of variety, most often packaged neatly in works of technical simplicity that would be widely accessible to amateur players. While Daniel E. Freeman has emphasized that the keyboard sonata was not yet considered a "serious" genre in the early eighteenth century,[49] Gregory Barnett has, more recently, shown that a compromise was reached between various pulls and contradictions that had defined the keyboard sonata. He has identified the Opus 3 sonatas of Benedetto Marcello (1686–1739) (which may or may not actually have appeared in print during the eighteenth century) as "crucial in the early history of the keyboard sonata in mediating between a series of contrasts during the late seventeenth and early eighteenth centuries: Frescobaldian tradition versus violin-influenced innovation; counterpoint versus homophony; virtuosity versus accessibility; professional versus recreational use; mostly manuscript versus mostly printed dissemination."[50]

In any case, the eighteenth-century Italian harpsichord sonata served important social and musical functions, employing both idiomatic harpsichord gestures and references to the nonkeyboard world. Composers such as Benedetto Marcello (1686–1739), Giovanni Benedetto Platti (before 1692–1763), Baldassare Galuppi (1706–1785), Domenico Alberti (1710–1746), and Giovanni Marco Rutini (1723–1797) crafted sonatas to suit these purposes, and their works survive in both printed editions and manuscript. Freeman has emphasized their wide referential frame: "the best Italian composers sought to enhance the expressive range of their keyboard sonatas by adopting the characteristic gestures of the 'more important' genres – opera, symphony, concerto – which were associated with public performance, lofty artistic goals, and greater musical virtuosity."[51] Exploration of some of these references, along with gestures that emerge from the medium of the harpsichord itself, give a sense of how the aesthetic of variety assumed primary importance and manifested itself in ways that Trabaci could hardly have anticipated at the start of the preceding century.

Most eighteenth-century Italian sonatas are made up of two or more movements, the first of which is usually a slow movement. The individual movements of these sonatas are most often in a binary form of one kind or another – either "rhyming" (in which the two halves start in a similar fashion) or "rounded" (involving a recapitulation of themes toward the end).[52] In any case, it is unhelpful to compare these works with the later Viennese classical sonata; even in the late eighteenth century, the Viennese model was by no means the only one in use. More to the point is to consider what these binary forms accomplished for those who used them; among other things, they provided a sense of motivic unity at the opening of each half, while exploring two alternative methods of continuation. Harmonic and motivic excursions in both halves should be judged by the aesthetic ideal of balance between unity and variety – a yardstick very much at the center of eighteenth-century musical thought.

Figura: The Alberti Bass

Perhaps the most widely known contribution of the Italian keyboard sonata – one later adopted by composers in Paris, Vienna, and indeed, across Europe – is the Alberti bass, named after the composer Domenico Alberti. This method of bass-register arpeggiation essentially forms a written-out realization of harmonies that would, in chamber music of the same period, be realized through use of basso continuo. At the same time, it maintains the polarized soprano–bass texture that was so essential to the *galant* style. In addition, through its active rhythmic profile, it provides a sense of momentum and energy that balances the sometimes slow harmonic rhythm of the soprano-range melodies. On modern pianos, players are often taught to quiet the Alberti bass so as not to drown out the singing melody, but on harpsichords (as well as eighteenth-century pianos) such a quieting effect is impossible and, in any case, undesirable, as it robs the figuration of its energy.[53]

Figura: Two First-Movement Topoi: The Toccata and the French Ouverture

Among numerous other types, two marked topoi emerge in first movements of numerous Italian sonata composers of the early eighteenth century. The first, an example of which may be seen in Benedetto Marcello's Sonata in A minor (S740), is the toccata type. Although it is not marked with that genre designation, this movement employs a quick repeated pattern that runs up and down the keyboard, followed by a section of chords that require an *arpeggiando* execution. With its characteristic ties and dissonances, this latter section traces its roots to the toccata style of Frescobaldi and altered through the prism of his successors.

Another topos that appears with some frequency in first movements of Italian sonatas of the eighteenth century is the French ouverture, characterized by recurring dotted rhythms and quick, ornamental runs; an example is the extended and interesting opening movement of Galuppi's Sonata in D major (I31). The incorporation of this trope in the work of Italian composers is a signal of the growing awareness of national styles and the attempt to fuse them into a single "mixed style," notwithstanding later attempts by German composers to take full credit for that ideal.[54]

Figura: "Light" Counterpoint

As in the chamber works of Corelli, keyboard sonatas did not abandon counterpoint entirely. The counterpoint appears, however, in reduced texture, with fewer voices and less intricacy overall than was found in the works of Pasquini, for example. This thinning out of the contrapuntal texture was fully in keeping with the *galant* aesthetic, which favored the soprano–bass polarity rather than an equal treatment of voices all across the registers of the keyboard. The same sonata by Marcello (S740) offers an example of this treatment: The third movement, marked "Allegro," contains a simple but rhythmically active subject stated first in the soprano register and accompanied by a descending bass line; the bass takes over the subject in measure 6 and is accompanied by off-beat motives in the right

Example 7.3 Benedetto Marcello, Sonata in A minor, S740, third movement, mm. 1–13. The use of countersubjects in parallel thirds is not shown here

hand. Nowhere does this "fugue" achieve more than two independent voices, but the effect of a more complex texture is created through the use of sixteenth-note arpeggiated figuration passed between the two hands, as well as countersubjects played occasionally in parallel thirds.

Figura: Dance Genres and Variations

Composers of the keyboard sonata in the early eighteenth century continued to incorporate dance genres within their multimovement compositions; in this respect, too, they were in lockstep with composers of chamber sonatas, whose *sonate da camera* relied heavily on dance. Giovanni Benedetto Platti's Op. 1, no. 3 incorporates a Sarabanda, Minuet and Trio, and Giga in immediate succession, thus juxtaposing three dances that employ triple or compound meter with different tempos and affects. Whether Platti had this model in mind or not, this choice may be considered analogous to the pairing of dances with different tempos and characters in previous centuries – for example, the balletto and gagliarda.

Variation procedures continued to be applied to dance genres as well as other forms. Benedetto Marcello composed a set of variations on the ciaccona, as did others of his generation. Individual movements – especially dance movements – by composers such as Domenico Alberti and Baldassare Galuppi (for example, his Sonata in D major, I8) often encompassed *variazioni* on a basic scheme – in this case a minuet. Although apparently far removed from the sixteenth-century origins of the diminution style, these works often involve the same principle: the subdivision of melodies in longer note values into more intricate melodies with shorter note values. In this aspect as well, the Italian keyboard sonata of the eighteenth century mirrored developments in chamber music of other sorts.

Figura: "Concerto-Like" Slow Movements

Slow movements of Italian harpsichord sonatas were often modeled after the slow movements of solo concertos. The middle movement of Platti's Op. 1, No. 4 is one such example. Its gentle, repeating eighth-note figuration in the left hand is reminiscent of concertos by Antonio Vivaldi that employ the same figuration, and the rhapsodic, expressive right-hand part assumes the role of a solo violinist.

Figura: Light Finales

Eighteenth-century Italian sonatas frequently conclude with a light, quick finale. In some cases, such a movement might be in a dance genre – for example, a minuet or giga. In others, the generic finale is in a light meter such as 3/8 or 2/4. In most cases, composers seem to have been concerned with the project of a sense of contrast with preceding movements.

Perorazione: Lodovico Giustini's *Sonate Da Cimbalo Di Piano E Forte* and the "Baroque Piano"

Instrument builders in Italy had long recognized that the harpsichord had limitations. In particular, the harpsichord's inability to render nuanced dynamic levels that would change with the force of the player's touch must have been frustrating enough to prompt builders to seek solutions. (Clavichords, of course, can make such dynamic adjustments, but they are significantly quieter than harpsichords.) Thus, in or just before 1700, Bartolomeo Cristofori (1655–1732) invented an action for a pianoforte, advertised in an article by Scipione Maffei in 1711, in which the instrument is called a "gravecembalo col piano e forte" (harpsichord [that plays] loud and soft).[55] This title suggests that the early pianoforte was considered a subset of the *cembalo* – a harpsichord with special features, rather than a completely separate instrument category.

In 1732, Lodovico Giustini (1685–1743) published a set of twelve sonatas, each in four or five movements, some comprised of dance genres (in the manner or a *sonata da camera*) and some of nondance genres (after the *sonata da chiesa*). While these pieces are peppered with dynamic markings that show the composer's interest in the instruments of the Cristofori school, the pieces are entirely playable on other types of *cembali* – that is, on "ordinary" Italian harpsichords. Organologist and instrument builder David Sutherland has suggested that pianos built by Cristofori and his Italian contemporaries were more common in eighteenth-century Italy than is commonly assumed.[56] Giustini's sonatas of 1732 were the first and only works designated specifically for the piano until some thirty years later, but the boundaries separating both instruments and repertory remained fluid: Music written for *cembalo* would have been suitable for *gravicembalo col piano e forte*, and Giustini's "piano" sonatas may be executed successfully on an ordinary *cembalo*.

Therefore, even though it is difficult if not impossible to make a definitive distinction between repertory for the Cristofori piano and Italian harpsichords of the eighteenth century, the practical implications of this problem are quite small. The timbre and rate of decay on the two instruments are similar, meaning that the repertory and performance practices were, in most respects, identical. For our purposes, Giustini's sonatas and Cristofori's invention serve as yet another marker of the rich keyboard culture that flourished in Italy for centuries.

Notes

I wish to express my thanks to Mark Kroll for his encouragement and careful reading. In addition, I owe a great debt to Alexander Silbiger, both for his extraordinary generosity in sharing ideas and responses to drafts of this chapter and for his support and mentorship over the past several years.

1. Giovanni Maria Trabaci, *Il secondo libro de ricercate, & altri varii capricci* (Naples: Giovanni Giacomo Carlino, 1615), p. 117.
2. The bibliography on music and rhetoric is too extensive to list here, but an overview is in Claude V. Palisca, "Music and Rhetoric," in *Music and Ideas in the Sixteenth and Seventeenth Centuries*, with a foreword by Thomas J. Mathiesen (Urbana, IL: University of Illinois Press, 2006), pp. 203–233.
3. A thorough survey of the Italian harpsichord repertory is impossible in the context of the present volume; indeed, such surveys have been written in the past. General histories of the keyboard literature, encompassing both harpsichords and organs, may be found, for example, in Willi Apel, *The History of Keyboard Music to 1700*, trans. and rev. by Hans Tischler (Bloomington and London: Indiana University Press, 1972) and in Robert Judd, "Italy," in *Keyboard Music Before 1700*, ed. Alexander Silbiger (New York: Schirmer Books, 1995), pp. 235–311. On the eighteenth-century Italian keyboard sonata, see Daniel E. Freeman, "Johann Christian Bach and the Early Classical Italian Masters," in *Eighteenth-Century Keyboard Music*, ed. Robert L. Marshall (New York: Schirmer Books, 1994), pp. 230–269. See also Alexander Silbiger's overview of the repertory of solo instrumentalists in the seventeenth century in *The Cambridge History of Seventeenth-Century Music*, ed. Tim Carter and John Butt (Cambridge: Cambridge University Press, 2004), pp. 426–478.
4. Alexander Silbiger, *Italian Manuscript Sources of 17th-Century Keyboard Music* (Ann Arbor, MI.: UMI Research Press, 1976), pp. 25–26.
5. Girolamo Diruta, *"The Transylvanian" (Il Transilvano)*, ed. Murray C. Bradshaw and Edward J. Soehnlen (Henryville, Ottawa, and Binningen: Institute of Mediaeval Music, 1984), Vol 1, p. 54, citing Diruta, *Il Transilvano: Dialogo sopra il vero modo di sonar organi, & istromenti da penna* (Venice: Vincenti, 1597/R), Vol. 1, p. 12.
6. Diruta, *"The Transylvanian,"* p. 12.
7. Baldesar Castiglione, *Il libro del cortegiano* (Milan: Società Tipografica de' Classici Italiani, 1803), p. 121, trans. Charles S. Singleton, *The Book of the Courtier* (New York: Doubleday, Inc., 1959), p. 105.
8. On the rise of an idiomatic approach to instruments and instrumental composition in early seventeenth-century Italy, see Rebecca Cypess,

Curious and Modern Inventions: Instrumental Music as Discovery in Galileo's Italy (Chicago: University of Chicago Press, 2016).

9. Diruta, "*The Transylvanian*," Vol. 1, p. 54.

10. Frescobaldi's performance instructions for the toccatas and other works are reprinted and translated in Frederick Hammond, *Girolamo Frescobaldi: A Guide to Research* (New York: Garland, 1988); see also the discussion below.

11. The builder of this instrument was one Hermann Poll.

12. David Catalunya and Paul Poletti, "Late Medieval Strung Keyboard Instruments: New Reflections and Attempts at Reconstruction," *Journal of the Alamire Foundation* 4 (2012), pp. 145–159. On Arnaut de Zwolle, see Stewart Pollens, *The Early Pianoforte* (Cambridge: Cambridge University Press, 1995), pp. 7–26.

13. The instrumentation of the Faenza codex has long been a subject of debate. See, for example, Richard Robinson, "The Faenza Codex: The Case for Solo Organ Revisited," *Journal of Musicology* 34, no. 4 (2017), pp. 610–646, especially p. 631, fn. 81; and Alexander Silbiger, "Introduction: The First Centuries of European Keyboard Music," in *Keyboard Music Before 1700,* p. 20, fn. 4.

14. See, for example, the educational program laid out in Adriano Banchieri, *Cartella musicale*, third edition (Venice: Vincenti, 1614), translated by Clifford A. Cranna, *Adriano Banchieri*'s Cartella musicale *(1614): Translation and Commentary* (PhD diss., Stanford University, 1981).

15. Judd, "Italy," p. 252. Judd observes that the 1523 *Ricercari* of Marc'Antonio Cavazzoni (ca. 1490–ca. 1560) and others before ca. 1540 take a different approach, which relies less heavily on counterpoint.

16. On styles of ornamentation in the sixteenth and seventeenth centuries, see Bruce Dickey, "Ornamentation in Early Seventeenth-Century Italian Music," in *A Performer's Guide to Seventeenth-Century Music*, ed. Stewart Carter, revised and expanded by Jeffery Kite-Powell (Bloomington: Indiana University Press, 2012), pp. 293–316.

17. An overview of these aspects of the (ensemble) canzona is in Gregory Barnett, "Form and Gesture: Canzona, Sonata, and Concerto," in *The Cambridge History of Seventeenth-Century Music*, pp. 479–532.

18. Eleanor Selfridge-Field, "Canzona and Sonata: Some Differences in Social Identity," *International Review of the Aesthetics and Sociology of Music* 9 (1978), pp. 111–119.

19. Edoardo Bellotti has documented the formulaic improvisational patterns – including contrapuntal principles – that lay behind a wide array of compositional and performative practices in the late Renaissance; see, for example, Edoardo Bellotti, "Counterpoint and Improvisation in Italian Sources from Gabrieli to Pasquini," *Philomusica on-line* 12 (2012), pp. 50–61.

20. See Bellotti, "Counterpoint and Improvisation," p. 53.

21. On Frescobaldi's influence, see Alexander Silbiger, "The Roman Frescobaldi Tradition, 1640–1670," *Journal of the American Musicological Society* 33, no. 1 (1980), pp. 42–87.

22. Luigi Battiferri, *Ricercari a Quattro, a cinque, e a sei*, Op. 3 (Bologna: Monti, 1669), 4, translated in Gregory Barnett, "The Early Italian Keyboard Sonata:

Origins, Influences, and Dissemination," in *The Early Keyboard Sonata in Italy and Beyond*, ed. Rohan H. Stewart-MacDonald (Brepols: Turnhout, 2016), p. 17.

23. The most recent study of Pasquini's music is Arnaldo Morelli, *La virtù in corte: Bernardo Pasquini (1637–1710)* (Lucca: Libreria Musicale Italiana, 2016). Chapter 5 deals with Pasquini's keyboard music.

24. Victor Coelho and Keith Polk, *Instrumentalists and Renaissance Culture, 1420–1600: Players of Function and Fantasy* (Cambridge: Cambridge University Press, 2016), pp. 109–113.

25. Ganassi, *Il Fontegara* (Venice, 1535), pp. 2–3. See also Anthony Rooley, "Ficino, and the Supremacy of Poetry Over Music," in *Le concert des voix et des instruments à la Renaissance: Actes du XXXIVe colloque internationale d'études humanistes Tours, Centre d'Études Superieures de la Renaissance, 1–11 juillet 1991*, ed. Jean Michel Vaccaro, Paris: CNRS 1995, pp. 51–56; and Howard Mayer Brown, "The Instrumentalist's Repertory in the Sixteenth Century," in *Le concert des voix et des instruments*, pp. 21–32.

26. See, however, Rebecca Cypess, "'Esprimere la voce humana': Connections between Vocal and Instrumental Music by Italian Composers of the Early Seventeenth Century," *Journal of Musicology* 27, no. 2 (2010), pp. 181–223.

27. Trabaci wrote keyboard intabulations as well, but his setting of "Ancidetemi pur" was written for harp.

28. Alexander Silbiger, "From Madrigal to Toccata: Frescobaldi and the *Seconda Prattica*," in *Critica Musica: Essays in Honor of Paul Brainard*, ed. John Knowles (Amsterdam: Gordon and Breach Publishers, 1996), p. 408.

29. On the relationship between vocal and instrumental music in the age of the *seconda prattica*, see Cypess, "Esprimere la voce humana" and *Curious and Modern Inventions*, and Andrew Dell'Antonio, *Syntax, Form, and Genre in Sonatas and Canzonas, 1621–1635* (Lucca: LIM, 1997).

30. Murray C. Bradshaw, "The Influence of Vocal Music on the Venetian Toccata," *Musica disciplina* 42 (1988), pp. 157–198.

31. Anthony Newcomb, "Frescobaldi's Toccatas and Their Stylistic Ancestry," *Proceedings of the Royal Musical Association* 111 (1984–1985), p. 32. See also Silbiger, *Italian Manuscript Sources*, p. 3.

32. See, for example, Naomi J. Barker, "Music, Antiquity, and Self-Fashioning in the Accademia dei Lincei," *The Seventeenth Century* 30, no. 4 (2015), pp. 375–390, and Christopher Stembridge, "Music for the Cimbalo Cromatico and the Split-Keyed Instruments in Seventeenth-Century Italy," *Performance Practice Review* 5, no. 1 (Spring, 1992), pp. 5–43.

33. On the publication history see the critical commentary in Girolamo Frescobaldi, *Toccate e partite d'intavolatura di cimbalo . . . libro primo*, ed. Christopher Stembridge and Kenneth Gilbert (Kassel: Bärenreiter, 2010) and in Girolamo Frescobaldi, *Il secondo libro di toccate* (Kassel: Bärenreiter, 2013). See also Etienne Darbellay, "Liberté, variété, et 'affetti cantabili' chez Girolamo Frescobaldi," *Revue de musicologie* 61, no. 2 (1975), pp. 197–243 and Darbellay, *Le toccate e i capricci di Girolamo Frescobaldi: Genesi delle edizioni e apparato critico*, supplement to vols. 4, 5, and 8 of *Opere complete di Girolamo Frescobaldi* (Milan: Edizioni Suvini Zerboni, 1988).

34. The second book of toccatas (1627) includes some pieces expressly for the organ. The relationship to a plucked idiom in the other toccatas of Frescobaldi, however, is emphasized by Victor Coelho, "Frescobaldi and the Lute and Chitarrone Toccatas of 'Il Tedesco della Tiorba,'" in *Frescobaldi Studies*, ed. Alexander Silbiger (Durham: Duke University Press, 1987), pp. 137–156.

35. Girolamo Frescobaldi, *Toccate e partite d'intavolatura di cimbalo, nuovamente da lui date in luce . . . libro primo* (Rome: Nicolò Borboni, 1615 and Rome: Nicolò Borboni, 1616).

36. Ibid., translated in Hammond, *Girolamo Frescobaldi: A Guide to Research*, pp. 188–189. See also Luigi Ferdinando Tagliavini, "The Art of 'Not Leaving the Instrument Empty': Comments on Early Italian Harpsichord Playing," *Early Music* 11, no. 3 (1983), pp. 299–308.

37. On the formal planning of the toccatas, see Anthony Newcomb, "Guardare e ascoltare le toccate," in *Girolamo Frescobaldi nel IV centenario della nascità: Atti del convegno internazionale di studi (Ferrara, 9–14 settembre 1983)*, ed. Sergio Durante and Dinko Fabris (Florence: Olschki Editore, 1986), pp. 281–300.

38. Roberto Pagano et al., "Scarlatti," *Oxford Music Online: Grove Music Online*, Oxford University Press, www.oxfordmusiconline.com.proxy .libraries.rutgers.edu/subscriber/article/grove/music/24708pg1.

39. See Lynette Bowring, *Orality, Literacy, and the Learning of Instruments: Professional Instrumentalists and Their Music in Early Modern Italy* (PhD diss., Rutgers University, 2017).

40. These sources are discussed in Dickey, "Ornamentation in Early Seventeenth-Century Italian Music," as well as Howard Mayer Brown, *Embellishing Sixteenth-Century Music* (London: Oxford University Press, 1976).

41. On the use of such formulas for poetic recitation, see, for example, Robert Nosow, "The Debate on Song in the Accademia Fiorentina," *Early Music History* 21 (2002), pp. 175–221; Jeanice Brooks, "Catherine de Médicis, nouvelle Artémise: Women's Laments and the Virtue of Grief," *Early Music* 27, no. 3 (1999), pp. 419–435; and Suzanne Cusick, *Francesca Caccini at the Medici Court: Music and the Circulation of Power* (Chicago: University of Chicago Press, 2009), chapter 6, "Voice Lessons: Introducing the *Primo libro delle musiche*."

42. Alexander Silbiger, "On Frescobaldi's Recreation of the Chaconne and the Passacaglia," in *The Keyboard in Baroque Europe*, ed. Christopher Hogwood (Cambridge: Cambridge University Press, 2002), pp. 3–18.

43. On Frescobaldi's use of the ciaccona and passacaglia together, see Alexander Silbiger, "Passacaglia and Ciaccona: Genre Pairing and Ambiguity from Frescobaldi to Couperin," *Journal of Seventeenth-Century Music* 2, no. 1 (1996), www.sscm-jscm.org/v2/no1/silbiger.html.

44. Silbiger, "On Frescobaldi's Recreation," p. 13.

45. This dating is demonstrated in Alexander Silbiger, "Michelangelo Rossi and his *Toccate e correnti*," *Journal of the American Musicological Society* 36 (Spring, 1983), pp. 18–38.

46. This section is a summary of the argument that I present in Rebecca Cypess, "Frescobaldi's *Toccate e partite . . . libro primo* (1615–1616) as a Pedagogical Text: Artisanship, Imagination, and the Process of Learning," *Recercare* 27, no. 1–2 (2015), pp. 103–138.
47. Barnett, "The Early Italian Keyboard Sonata," pp. 12–13 and *passim.*
48. On the emergence of the *galant* style and its manifestations throughout Europe in the nineteenth century, see Daniel Heartz, *Music in European Capitals, 1720–1780* (New York: W. W. Norton, 2003).
49. Freeman, "Johann Christian Bach," p. 232.
50. Barnett, "The Early Italian Keyboard Sonata," p. 56.
51. Freeman, "Johann Christian Bach," p. 232.
52. Freeman, "Johann Christian Bach," p. 241.
53. Freeman's assessment of Alberti bass figurations as a "symptom" of "neutralization" of "melodic and rhythmic interest of bass lines" (p. 239) seems to me unhelpful. Alberti bass lines remained in use for decades across Europe, and thus must have been meaningful to the people who used them.
54. On the use of a "mixed taste" by composers before J. S. Bach, see David Ledbetter, "*Les goûts réunis* and the music of J. S. Bach," *Basler Jahrbuch für historische Musikpraxis* 28 (2004), pp. 63–80. A recent account of Galuppi's keyboard sonatas is in Rohan H. Stewart-MacDonald, "The Keyboard Sonatas of Baldassare Galuppi: Textures, Topics, and Structural Shapes," in *The Early Keyboard Sonata in Italy and Beyond*, pp. 69–108.
55. The article appears in English translation in Pollens, *The Early Pianoforte*, pp. 57–62, and in the original Italian on pp. 238–243. Pollens's fascinating account of the surviving Cristofori instruments and other historical evidence is in chapter 3, "The *Gravecembalo col piano e forte* of Bartolomeo Cristofori," pp. 43–95. On Giustini's sonatas see Daniel E. Freeman, "Lodovico Giustini and the Emergence of the Keyboard Sonata in Italy," *Anuario musical* 58 (2003), pp. 111–138.
56. Some of Sutherland's research on the numbers of pianos that might have existed in early eighteenth-century Italy appears in David Sutherland, "On the Production of Pianos in Florence, 1700–1750," *Early Keyboard Journal* 27–29 (2013), pp. 47–76.

Further Reading

Carter, Stewart. *A Performer's Guide to Seventeenth-Century Music.* Edited, revised and expanded by Jeffery Kite-Powell. Bloomington, IN: Indiana University Press, 2012.
Cypess, Rebecca. *Curious and Modern Inventions: Instrumental Music as Discovery in Galileo's Italy.* Chicago, IL: University of Chicago Press, 2016.
Judd, Robert. "Italy," in *Keyboard Music Before 1700*, ed. Alexander Silbiger. New York: Schirmer Books, 1995.
Silbiger, Alexander. Introduction to *The Cambridge History of Seventeenth-Century Music*, ed. Tim Carter and John Butt. Cambridge: Cambridge University Press, 2004.
"The Roman Frescobaldi Tradition, 1640–1670." *Journal of the American Musicological Society* 33, no. 1 (1980), pp. 42–87.

8 Portugal

JOÃO PEDRO D'ALVARENGA

Historical Overview

References to the harpsichord in Portugal can be traced back to the late fifteenth century. In his chronicle of King João II (b. 1455; r. 1481–1495), Garcia de Resende (1470–1536) refers to an ambassador of the King of Naples whom the Portuguese king heard performing several times in Torres Vedras in 1493 as "the greatest harpsichord and organ player then known."[1] It is therefore safe to assume that harpsichords existed and were in use at the court in the early 1490s.

In 1523, King João III (b. 1502; r. 1521–1557) appointed a craftsman named Copym (or Copy) de Holanda – thus probably of Flemish birth – as "master of building our harpsichords" with responsibility for their maintenance, stringing, and tuning, assigning him an annual salary and later granting him extra pensions.[2] In January 1544, Cardinal *Infante* Dom Henrique (1512–1580), King João III's younger brother and the archbishop of Évora since 1540,[3] took into his service the organ builder Heitor Lobo (ca. 1495–after 1571) for the purpose of having repaired and tuned "the musical instruments of reeds and harpsichords" existing in his house.[4] There are also a number of references to the instruments owned by Catherine of Austria (1507–1578), the queen consort of King João III. Three harpsichords and their repairing by Diogo de Aranda in late December 1538 are mentioned on January 3, 1539 in the book of expenditures of Queen Catherine.[5] On March 5, 1556, another payment was ordered by the queen to the same Diogo de Aranda for repairing and stringing a claviorgan and three harpsichords.[6] These were possibly the same three harpsichords already existing in late 1538. The claviorgan was probably the instrument commissioned in May 1511 by Juan de Santa Maria on behalf of King Manuel I of Portugal (b. 1469; r. 1495–1521) from the renowned builder Mahoma Mofferiz, known as the Moor of Zaragoza.[7] On September 27, 1552, António do Valle, a harpsichord player, was paid for the lessons he had given to one of the queen's maids, Joana da Costa, and her sister.[8] Two years later, on August 11, 1554, a payment was made to Pantaleoa Afonso, the widow of Jorge Gonçalves, "master of making harpsichords," for a choir of strings he had made for one of the queen's instruments.[9] According to an inventory dated between late 1555 and

1557, there were three stringed keyboard instruments in the chambers of Queen Catherine at the royal palace in Lisbon: "a large claviorgan inside of a case of maple," "a clavichord inside of a case of maple," and "a small square harpsichord covered with leather of [a] scabbard-maker," probably a virginal.[10] Nothing is known about the characteristics of these instruments and, with the exception of the claviorgan (possibly the one made to order in 1511), their origins are unclear, although a number of the existing harpsichords from this time were probably imported from Flanders,[11] Portugal's main supplier of luxury goods, until at least the middle of the sixteenth century.[12] Others may have been built locally, given the fact that a Lisbon census from 1551 lists three organ builders, four clavichord makers, and twenty professional keyboard players.[13] Also the merits of the workshop of musical instruments – namely harpsichords, clavichords, viols, and guitars – in the Augustinian monastery of Santa Cruz in Coimbra earned the visit of King João III in 1550.[14]

The harpsichord was regularly used for solo and chamber music. For instance, reporting on the visit of the four famous Japanese boys to the palace of the Dukes of Bragança in Vila Viçosa in September 1584 on their way to Rome,[15] Luís Fróis (1532–1597) tells us in his *Historia de Japam* that the duke, Teodósio II (1568–1630), ordered for a harpsichord and some viols to be sent to his chambers and that all present marveled at seeing the young men playing and improvising with a viol and the harpsichord.[16] Regular practice of a stringed keyboard instrument – more often the clavichord, because it was portable and built at a low cost, but also the harpsichord – was also part of the daily life in Benedictine, Cistercian, and Canons Regular monasteries.[17]

A significant number of harpsichords found their way to the Portuguese overseas settlements and possessions starting in the early decades of the sixteenth century, to be used primarily by the Jesuits in their missions, seminaries, and colleges on the coasts of Africa and Brazil and in the Far East. All types of keyboard instruments often served an ambassadorial role, since they were presented to local authorities as exemplars of Western technology.[18] It also appears that it was fairly common for the harpsichord to be used in liturgical music outside European Portugal, at times taking over the function of the organ.[19]

The discovery of gold in Brazil in the late seventeenth century; the reestablishment of the Atlantic trade in sugar, tobacco, and tropical woods for the growing market for luxury goods in Europe; and the exportation of slaves from West Africa to Brazil, allowed King João V (b. 1689; r. 1706–1750) to develop a complex political and diplomatic program designed to bring the kingdom to modernity while at the same time legitimizing the absolutist power of the Portuguese Crown. One of the main objectives of such a program was the endorsement of Rome, the center of international prestige and global influence. As a result, significant cultural changes occurred in Portugal in the 1710s and 20s that accelerated the process of "Italianization" begun in the late sixteenth century – that is, the process whereby Italian models that gradually merged into Portuguese culture, including music, were assimilated, processed, and adapted.[20] This had a positive effect on the local manufacture and use of the harpsichord.

Domenico Scarlatti (1685–1757), although often absent traveling, was in Lisbon in the service of the Portuguese Crown between late November 1719 and early February 1727, returning for a short period in late September 1729 before going permanently to Spain. The *Infante* Dom António (1695–1757), King João V's younger brother, seems to have been a key figure in the history of stringed keyboard instruments in Portugal during the first half of the eighteenth century. He became a student of Domenico Scarlatti and achieved a professional level as a harpsichord player.[21] Dom António also promoted connections with the Florentine workshops of stringed keyboard instruments, allowing Lisbon to join Florence as an important center in the development of the early pianoforte.[22]

It should be noted here that the harpsichord and the pianoforte were named with the same term at this time, "*cravo*" (harpsichord), owing to the similar design of the outer case, but often with a qualification referring to the type of mechanical action: "*cravo de penas*" (harpsichord with quills); "*cravo de martelos*" (harpsichord with hammers); and also "*cravo de martelinhos*" (harpsichord with little hammers). In the 1790s, both instruments would almost always be mentioned with their different names. However, in the latter half of the eighteenth century, the harpsichord and the pianoforte coexisted and were used indistinctively and often also interchangeably so that the music written for one was considered suitable for the other. Differentiation of their respective idioms was primarily a matter of performing technique. This can be seen for instance in the many pieces having such indications as "per cembalo o piano forte"[23] and in the announcements of new pieces published in the periodical *Gazeta de Lisboa*.

Nevertheless, even as the pianoforte increased in popularity, the harpsichord remained a favorite in the houses of the nobility throughout the eighteenth century and beyond. English instruments were increasingly present from the 1780s onwards. For example, a harpsichord ordered by the prince regent, later King João VI (b. 1767; r. 1816–1826), for his wife, Carlota Joaquina de Bourbon (1775–1830), arrived from London in September 1799.[24] Customs records tell us that harpsichords were still exported and imported – and thus built and kept in use in Portugal – until at least the early 1840s.[25]

Repertory and Sources

It is usually assumed that keyboard repertories composed in Portugal before the early decades of the eighteenth century were primarily intended for the organ. Chronologically, the first known source for this is Gonçalo de Baena's *Arte nouamente inuentada pera aprender a tãger* (newly devised art for learning how to play), printed in Lisbon in 1540.[26] Although its title page depicts a keyboard and the pipes of an organ, the colophon uses the generic "keyboard instrument" and the prologue refers to the clavichord (*monocordio*) throughout. The intabulations in this collection – using a unique alphabet-based system – can therefore be performed on any keyboard instrument available during the first half of the sixteenth century, including the harpsichord. Most of the pieces fit within the compass of short octave C/E (described on page 4) to e2, as in the keyboard shown on the title page, but a few can only be accomodated within the larger compass of C/E (this short octave lacking the F#) to g2. As shown on the woodcut illustration in Virdung's 1511 treatise,[27] this is presumably the usual range of early sixteenth-century northern-European harpsichords. On the whole, the intabulations in Baena's *Arte* follow the vocal originals closely but he also tells the performer to add ornamentation at his discretion as long as it is "done with skill and not at whim."[28]

The next relevant Portuguese source for keyboard (and consort) music is P-Cug MM 242, a manuscript in open-score format copied and used in the Augustinian monastery of Santa Cruz in Coimbra and dated to the third quarter of the sixteenth century. It contains more than 265 pieces, including textless *chansons*, madrigals, and motets possibly intended to be provided with *glosa* and performed by a consort or a keyboard instrument, or more likely for study; ricercares, *tentos*, and *fantasias*; psalm-tone versets, *fabordões*, and other instrumental pieces based on chant; and *glosa* and cadential formulas. Many pieces in this manuscript were copied from Italian, Flemish, and Spanish prints dating from between 1547 and 1556.[29] This manuscript includes three instrumental pieces by Heliodoro de Paiva, an Augustinian canon regular who died in 1552, and reworkings of seven of Jacques Buus's ricercares from his 1547 *Libro primo*.[30] Four pieces in this manuscript bear unequivocal attributions to António Carreira ("A. car.," "carreira," and "A. carreira"), commonly identified as António Carreira the Elder, master of the Portuguese Royal Chapel.[31] One of these pieces is a version of the *canción Con qué la lavaré* for solo voice with four-part accompaniment, which can be played by a consort or on the keyboard.[32] Another has the attribution "A.c." and fifteen other pieces are headed "ca." Although in one case "ca." is known to stand for Antonio de

Cabezón,[33] most of these pieces, including some without attribution, may also be the work of Carreira, as first suggested by Santiago Kastner.[34] Charles Jacobs, however, included them in his edition of Cabezón's music, while admitting that the issue of their authorship remains open.[35] All the instrumental works attributed to Carreira fall into the genres of the polythematic *tento*, with up to five independent subjects presented in imitation with a motet-like polyphonic texture and structure; and the monothematic *fantasia*. The more these pieces use melodic diminution and have relatively wide-ranged parts, the more instrumental they are in character. Not all pieces are suited for keyboard performance, but some, particularly those making use of eighth-note-based *glosa* patterns in long-running segments and avoiding awkward part crossings, are certainly natural to the harpsichord.[36] One example is a fully written out glossed version of an unidentified *chanson* of likely Franco-Flemish origin featuring block-chord segments, motifs with repeated notes, and varied patterns of *glosa* mostly in the upper part and the bass. Although anonymous, Kastner assigns this work to António Carreira on stylistic grounds.[37]

Manuel Rodrigues Coelho (ca. 1555–ca. 1635) took the late sixteenth-century keyboard *tento* to its peak in his *Flores de mvsica*. Though collected before 1617 and including older pieces probably spanning the composer's entire career that began in the early or mid-1570s,[38] this volume was printed in Lisbon in 1620.[39] Coelho uses the open-score format throughout, which became common for the notation of keyboard music in Portugal until the early eighteenth century. In the title and the prologue to his collection, the composer refers to "the keyboard instrument, and the harp." Only in the individual titles of specific liturgical pieces is the organ mentioned.[40]

The twenty-four *tentos* in the *Flores de mvsica* cannot easily be characterized as a unified whole, but the writing is always idiomatic for the keyboard, including fluent figuration arranged in sequences, and *glosa* is now fully incorporated into the texture, rather than serving as decoration superimposed on the polyphonic fabric. The opening subject, sometimes accompanied by a second countersubject, even if in long notes, has an abstract instrumental quality and is treated fugally. Subsequent entries, also normally introduced by overlapping points of imitation, are often derived from the first subject through metrical diminution, augmentation, or variation. Some of the *tentos*, however, develop different unrelated subjects. Diminution passages, taking on a variety of rhythmic profiles in short note values including dotted rhythms, eighth-note triplets, and other figuration in *sesquialtera* proportion, can suddenly occur and also provide materials for more or less extended "free fantasia" segments or motivic interplay. A substantial section in triple time may be interpolated or, more frequently, would conclude the piece. Musical materials are freely invented, so that the *tento* is not strictly a liturgical genre, though it could be – and was – used during liturgy. Late manuscript copies of individual sections from Coelho's *tentos* were clearly intended to fulfill such a function.[41]

The four pieces that Coelho entitled "*Susana grosada a 4 sobre a de 5*," that is, the four glossed versions of Lassus's *Susanne un jour*, supplement the *tentos* and summarize the composer's methods for glossing, which are not very different from the "*modo di paseggiari alla bastarda*" explained and exemplified by Francesco Rognoni in his *Selva de varii pasaggi*.[42] The openings of Coelho's four *Susanas* retain most of Lassus's contrapuntal disposition; although excluding the original *quinta pars* (tenor II), the first and third *Susanas* are essentially based on Lassus's bass part, and the second and fourth are almost entirely limited to the original bass part. As in the *tentos*, long diminutions are achieved through the joining of two simple *glosa* formulas, which can be further extended through sequential arrangement.

Glossed versions of Lassus's *Susanne un jour* appear in the most important Iberian prints of keyboard music, becoming a paramount vehicle for the art of diminution, as they were throughout Europe in the late sixteenth and early seventeenth century.[43] Other such settings are also found in late seventeenth-century Portuguese manuscript sources.[44] One of these is the *Susana* or *Obra de 2.º tom* by Pedro de Araújo in the composite manuscript *P-BRp* Ms. 964.[45] As distinct from Coelho's, Araújo's version follows the contrapuntal structure of Lassus's *chanson* closely (though reducing it to four parts), alternating extensive soloist *glosa* in the upper part and the bass.

Setting aside the pieces specifically intended for the organ with divided keyboard including soloist parts for the right or the left hand calling for horizontal reed stops *en chamade* (that is, the "*meio registo*" and the "*batalha*"), we find in the works of Pedro de Araújo pieces with terms such as *tento*, *obra*, and *fantasia*.[46] This probably reflects the variety of influences converging in his keyboard style, which is nevertheless in the lineage of Rodrigues Coelho, Aguilera de Heredia (1561–1627), and Correa de Arauxo (1584–1654). Pedro de Araújo's harmonic language is colorful, at times suggestive of the Italian *durezze e legature*, and elements of the toccata style and the *style brisé* are not infrequent especially in his fantasias, which are particularly suited to the harpsichord. A sense of coherency arises from the thematic and motivic treatment, as a main subject is usually present throughout a piece, often in diminution or augmentation, also generating new contrasting motifs and minimal chromatic motifs frequently developing in sequences.

The first repertories appearing in Portuguese sources that are commonly acknowledged as specifically conceived for the harpsichord are Italian.[47] They consist of small collections of dances, airs, and sets of variations, including the *Partite sopra la aria della folia da Espagna* by Bernardo Pasquini (1637–1710). The first pieces in these collections are labeled "foreign or Italian" (*estrangeiras ou italianas*) and some are nevertheless assigned to the organ or harp. Their origin is Roman, as stated on the manuscript itself.[48] Indeed, two of the pieces in P-BRp Ms. 964, the *Ballo del Ciclope di Frascati* and the *Aria dello Organo di Frascati*, are the only likely examples of the music for the panpipes of the statue of Cyclope and the automatic organ in the *Stanza di Apollo o del Parnaso* at Villa Aldobrandini in Frascati, near Rome.[49]

The emergence of the binary sonata for keyboard instruments in Portugal is probably related to the process of accelerated "Italianization" mentioned previously, but the genre was certainly already known to Portuguese composers before the arrival of Domenico Scarlatti in Lisbon in late November 1719.[50] One of those composers – by far the most noted and prolific in his time – was Carlos Seixas.[51]

Seixas's surviving sonatas are contained in eleven manuscript sources dating from between around 1750 (P-Ln MM 5015) and the late 1790s (P-Ln CIC 110). Ninety-four – or indeed one hundred and seven, if we take the second movements occurring as separate pieces within certain sources – are considered authentic. To these we must add another twenty-seven pieces (nineteen sonatas and eight minuets) that are conjecturally attributed to him in modern editions.[52] However, since only thirty-four of the sonatas considered authentic have an individual attribution, further careful assessment of authorship issues will undoubtedly reduce these numbers.[53]

Almost all of Seixas's sonatas were written to be played on a keyboard instrument, and primarily the harpsichord. Only four are specifically assigned to the organ, and two others could have been imagined for a melodic instrument and continuo or at least could have been played as such. The composer, or clearly the copyists in some cases, favored structures with two or more movements, the last, with only a few exceptions, being a minuet.

Seixas displays an impressive diversity in the handling of form.[54] In two-reprise movements, he usually seeks for the establishment of functional, clearly defined component parts and searches for coordination between the tonal and thematic-motivic plans. This ultimately results in a peculiar type of a symmetrical convergence around the structural points of modulation on each side of the double bar, which involves parallelism not only of the postmodulation material, but also of the material immediately preceding it (e.g. no. 6–6/i in D minor). Many of his sonata movements reflect the simple textures of the first *galant* style, but they also feature technical display such as the interplay of hands (e.g. no. App. 15–1 in G major), repeated notes (e.g. no. 16–1/i in G minor; no. 16–8/i in G minor), extended leaps (e.g. no. 5–3/i in D major; no. 6–6/i in D minor; no. 12–3 in F minor; no. 19–4/i in A major), the crossing of hands combined with leaps (e.g. no. 5–3/i in D major; no. 15–3 in G major), synchronized thirds and sixths (e.g. no. 21–3/i in B♭ major; no. 1–6/i in C major; no. 19–4/i in A major) and carefully notated rhythmical articulation (e.g. no. 10–1 in E minor). On the whole, these sonata movements show an independently developed and highly demanding keyboard technique.[55]

Seixas's harpsichord concertos in A major and G minor should also be mentioned. Both are three-movement works ending with a gigue and therefore belong to the group of early Italian keyboard concertos. The A major concerto is undoubtedly one of the earliest if not the very first in this group, testifying to the absorption of Vivaldian models. Its briefness, thematic uniformity, melodic writing largely in the *Fortspinnung* style and the somewhat old-fashioned open-ended middle movement suggest a date of composition no later than the mid-1730s. The G minor concerto is a longer piece in the *galant* style. Its last movement, despite the tutti–solo alternation, essentially constitutes an extended two-reprise form in which material and tonality converge around the structural points of modulation on each side of the double bar. This unique feature is a Seixas hallmark. The fact that it introduces elements of binary structure within the concerto ritornello form, following southern-European trends of the early 1740s, suggests that this concerto was probably composed shortly before the composer's death in 1742.[56]

The three surviving one-movement binary sonatas by Jacinto do Sacramento (b. 1712), Seixas's near contemporary and a friar of the Order of St. Paul, reveal a different approach. They are basically monothematic, with frequent broken-chord figuration, fuller texture created by four-part block chords in the left hand and extensive passages in parallel thirds and sixths in the right. The harmony is richer and more chromatic than one finds in a typical Seixas work, particularly because of Sacramento's use of secondary dominants.[57]

In summary, variety in the internal arrangement of form, the mixture of local and foreign elements, and a stylistic balance between late-baroque, post-baroque and *galant* idioms are characteristics of the Portuguese keyboard sonata in the first half of the eighteenth century. Much of the Portuguese keyboard repertory from the latter half of the eighteenth century, however, remains unexplored, even if some pieces are available in modern editions. Among the harpsichord music from this period are the nine extant sonatas by Pedro António Avondano (1714–1782);[58] the five sonatas by José Joaquim dos Santos (ca. 1747–1801);[59] the four sonatas by Manuel Elias (fl. 1767–1805);[60] and the four sonatas and fourteen minuets by João Cordeiro da Silva (fl. 1756–1808).[61]

The most popular genres found in this last period include the sonata in one, two, or three movements; the minuet (often presented in sets); and, later in the century, variations on popular dance and song themes, marches, contredanses, rondos, and waltzes. Good examples are two collections of keyboard sonatas printed between the mid-1760s and the mid-1770s: the *Sei sonate* by Alberto José Gomes da Silva (fl. 1758–1795) and the *Dodeci sonate* by Francisco Xavier Baptista (d. 1797).[62]

Portuguese composers also began to lean towards full *galant* and early classical forms and styles. Among Seixas's authenticated sonatas, there were already a couple of examples of a formal type quite common in the works of "transitional," mid-century composers such as Johann Joachim Quantz (1697–1773), Giovanni Benedetto Platti (before 1692–1763), Carl Philipp Emanuel Bach (1714–1788), and Johann Christian Bach (1735–1782). This is characterized by having the initial material restated right after the double bar in the dominant key and again fully or partially restated after the return modulation in the tonic, the whole structure being further balanced by parallel closings.[63] Occurrences of this and similar formal types became usual in Portuguese keyboard sonatas of the 1760s and 1770s. Some of the earliest datable examples are the first movements of Francisco Xavier Baptista's Sonatas II, V, and XI from his *Dodeci sonate*.

Movements with an overall ternary disposition also occur after the 1760s. For instance, in a sonata wrongly attributed to Seixas, No. App. 19–2 in A major,[64] the first movements of Baptista's Sonatas IX and X,[65] and the one-movement Sonatas in B♭ major and C major by João Cordeiro da Silva,[66] we find ternary thematic organization with a simple polar-type tonal plan; highly contrasting thematic materials in complementary key areas, restatement of the first theme in the tonic arriving early in the second part of the movement after a brief development or a separate idea, varied reprises, and parallel closings restricted to the very last bars. This type of structure also became frequent in more or less extensive rounded-binary minuets as, for instance, in Manuel Elias's Minuet in D major.[67] In minuets, however, and in a number of sonatas like Pedro António Avondano's Sonata in C major,[68] the tonic incipit is more often restated at the end of the second part, opening the final cadential phrase. This late restatement occurs when a separate idea, a longer elaboration of previously heard motifs, or an exercise for technical display (usually the crossing of hands) immediately follows the double bar.

Nevertheless, binary forms of varying types remained in use throughout the second half of the eighteenth century. There was also a growing tendency towards periodicity, the use of the Alberti bass and similar accompaniment figures, a relatively slow harmonic rhythm, motivic repetition and symmetry, delicate chromaticism, and melodic writing that implied ornamentation by the performer. A prime example of these features is the only keyboard work assuredly attributed to the Neapolitan-trained João de Sousa Carvalho (1745–ca. 1800)[69] – a three-movement Sonata in D major probably written around 1785.[70] Most of the keyboard music of the ensuing generation of composers like António Leal Moreira (1758–1819) and Marcos Portugal (1762–1830), by relying on a more songful sort of melodic writing and on marked agogic and dynamic variation, is already unmistakably of the realm of the pianoforte.[71]

Notes

1. Garcia de Resende, "Vida e feytos d'el-rey Dom João Segundo," in *Lyuro das obras de Garcia de Resēde* (Lisbon: Luís Rodrigues, 1545), fols. [viii]v–456r, at fol. 105v, available at http://purl.pt/14664 (February 5, 2016). Resende was a chamberlain (*moço da câmara*) to King João II in 1490 and his private secretary (*moço de escrevaninha*) from the following year until the king's death in 1495.
2. P-Lant Chancelaria de D. João III, Liv. 3, fol. 54v, Liv. 14, fol. 3r, and Liv. 16, fol. 53v; see the transcripts in Sousa Viterbo, *Subsidios para a Historia da Musica em Portugal* (Coimbra: Imprensa da Universidade, 1932), pp. 284–285.
3. Cardinal *Infante* Dom Henrique was archbishop of Braga (1533–1540) and head of the Portuguese Inquisition (1539–1578). He ruled the archdiocese of Évora between 1540 and 1564 and again between 1575 and 1578. In the interim, he was archbishop of Lisbon (1564–1570), acting also as regent for his grand-nephew, Sebastião (b. 1554; r. 1557–1578), until he reached his majority in 1568; he was himself later made king following the death of the young monarch in the disastrous battle of El-Ksar-El-Kebir in Morocco on August 4, 1578.
4. In Easter 1543, Heitor Lobo had been put into the service of Évora Cathedral with the duty of maintaining and tuning "the organs he has built and will build," working there until late February 1553. See P-EVp Cód. CVII/1–29, *Liuro da fazemda do If.^{te} don Amrrique q' começou em Janj.^{ro} do ano de quinhemtos trimta e oito annos*, fols. 93r, 140r, 162r, and 203r; see also Armando Nobre de Gusmão, "Cantores e Músicos em Évora nos anos de 1542 a 1553," *Anais da Academia Portuguesa de História*, 2nd series, 14 (1964), pp. 95–121, here pp. 117–118.
5. See the transcript of the register in Viterbo, *Subsidios*, p. 57.
6. *P-Lant* Corpo Cronológico, Parte I, maço 97, doc. n.º 97.

7. See Pedro Calahorra Martinez, *La Música en Zaragoza en los siglos XVI y XVII*, Vol. 1, *Organistas, organeros y órganos* (Zaragoza: Institución "Fernando El Católico," 1977), pp. 100 and 104, available at http://ifc.dpz.es /recursos/publicaciones/06/53/_ebook.pdf; see also Carmen Morte García, "Mahoma Moferriz, maestro de Zaragoza, constructor de claviórganos para la corte de los Reys Católicos," *Aragón en la Edad Media* 14–15, no. 2 (1999), pp. 1115–1124.

8. *P-Lant* Corpo Cronológico, Parte I, maço 88, doc. n.º 132.

9. *P-Lant* Corpo Cronológico, Parte I, maço 93, doc. n.º 48.

10. *P-Lant* Códices e documentos de proveniência desconhecida, no. 64, *olim* Casa Forte, no. 64, fol. 58v. This manuscript consists of an inventory of the wardrobe of Queen Catherine of Austria including items possibly housed in adjoining chambers. The instruments are listed under the header "*crauos*" (harpsichords). An eighteenth-century copy exists in *P-La* Ms. 50-V-26, with the erroneous title *Livro da Recamara dos Reis Dom João 3º de Portugal e Dª Cnª*. See Annemarie Jordan, *The Development of Catherine of Austria's Collection in the Queen's Household: Its Character and Cost* (PhD diss., Brown University, 1994), pp. 174–175.

11. For instance, three harpsichords from Flanders are listed in the postmortem inventory of the Duke of Bragança, Teodósio I (d. 1563); see Bernadette Nelson, "Music in the Chapel of the Dukes of Braganza during the 16th Century," in *Da Flandres: Os azulejos encomendados por D. Teodósio I, 5º Duque de Bragança (c.1510–1563)*, edited by M. A. Pinto de Matos and A. N. Pais (Lisbon: Museu Nacional do Azulejo and Fundação da Casa de Bragança, 2012), pp. 21–24, here p. 24.

12. Portugal had an important factory in Flanders, which was first located in Bruges and, from 1498, in Antwerp. Portuguese representatives mediated in the regular commissioning and purchase of Flemish art for Portuguese patrons. The factory was officially closed in 1549 but remained active until 1795 when it completely disappeared.

13. Cristóvão Rodrigues de Oliveira, *Lisboa em 1551: Sumário em que brevemente se contêm algumas coisas assim eclesiásticas como seculares que há na cidade de Lisboa (1551)*, apresentação e notas de José da Felicidade Alves (Lisbon: Livros Horizonte, 1987), pp. 94–95.

14. See Ernesto Gonçalves de Pinho, *Santa Cruz de Coimbra, centro de actividade musical nos séculos XVI e XVII* (Lisbon: Fundação Calouste Gulbenkian, 1981), pp. 153–157.

15. The four noble Japanese youths were representatives of three of the most important Christian feudal lords in western Japan. They left Nagasaki on February 20, 1582, reaching Lisbon on August 11, 1584, and traveled through Portugal, Spain, and Italy for two years before returning to Lisbon, from where they finally set sail on April 13, 1586 for Nagasaki, where they arrived on July 21, 1590. See Derek Massarella, "The Japanese Embassy to Europe (1582–1590)," *The Journal of the Hakluyt Society* (February, 2013), pp. 1–12, at www.hakluyt.com/journal_index.htm.

16. "[M]andou vir alli cravo, e violas a sua camara; m.tº se admirarão todos de os ver tanger, e descantar cõ viola, e cravo." *La première ambassade du Japon en Europe, 1582–1592. Première partie: Le traité du Père Frois (texte*

portugais), edited by J. A. Abranches Pinto, Yoshitomo Okamoto, and Henri Bernard, Monumenta Nipponica 6 (Tokyo: Sophia University, 1942), p. 53.

17. For the Benedictine nuns and the Ursulines, see Elisa Lessa, "A música no quotidiano das monjas nos séculos XVII e XVIII – Mosteiros de beneditinas e ursulinas em Portugal," *Revista Portuguesa de Musicologia* 7–8 (1997–98), pp. 47–58, available at www.rpm-ns.pt/index.php/rpm/article/view/156/267.

18. For an overview on the subject of the role of music and musical instruments in the Portuguese expansion, see Manuel Carlos de Brito and Luísa Cymbron, *História da Música Portuguesa* (Lisbon: Universidade Aberta, 1992), pp. 63–77. On the diplomatic function of keyboard instruments, see Ian Woodfield, "The Keyboard Recital in Oriental Diplomacy, 1520–1620," *Journal of the Royal Musical Association* 115, no. 1 (1990), pp. 32–62; see also Victor Anand Coelho, "Music in the New Worlds," in *The Cambridge History of Seventeenth-Century Music*, ed. Tim Carter and John Butt (Cambridge: Cambridge University Press, 2005), pp. 88–110, especially pp. 96–98.

19. For some references on this use of the harpsichord, see Gerhard Doderer and John Henry van der Meer, *Portuguese String Keyboard Instruments of the 18th Century: Clavichords, Harpsichords, Fortepianos and Spinets* (Lisbon: Fundação Calouste Gulbenkian, 2005), pp. 309–310.

20. On the musical aspects of this process, see particularly João Pedro d'Alvarenga, "Domenico Scarlatti in the 1720s: Portugal, Travelling, and the Italianisation of the Portuguese Musical Scene," in *Domenico Scarlatti Adventures: Essays to Commemorate the 250th Anniversary of his Death*, ed. Massimiliano Sala and W. Dean Sutcliffe, Ad Parnassum Studies 3 (Bologna: Ut Orpheus Edizioni, 2008), pp. 17–68, especially pp. 42–57; d'Alvarenga, "'To Make of Lisbon a New Rome': The Repertory of the Patriarchal Church in the 1720s and 1730s," *Eighteenth-Century Music* 8, no. 2 (2011), pp. 179–214; and d'Alvarenga, "*Allo stile dei musici di questa nazione*: Balancing the Old and New in Portuguese Church Music from the 1720s and 1730s," *Basler Jahrbuch für Historische Musikpraxis* 38 (2014; published 2018), pp. 33–53.

21. Dom António had received his literary education and musical training in the monastery of Santa Cruz in Coimbra. Upon arrival in Lisbon, Domenico Scarlatti was assigned to his service.

22. See Stewart Pollens, "The Early Portuguese Piano," *Early Music* 13, no. 1 (1985), pp. 18–27 and *The Early Pianoforte* (Cambridge: Cambridge University Press, 1995), pp. 118–156. The *Infante* Dom António was the dedicatee of Ludovico Giustini da Pistoia's collection of twelve *Sonate da cimbalo di piano, e forte detto volgarmente di martelletti*, printed in Florence in 1732. On January 17 that year, Niccolò Susier, a theorbo player at the court of the Medicis, reported in his diary on the death of Bartolomeo Cristofori that King João V had paid the astounding sum of two hundred gold louis for some of Cristofori's pianofortes.

23. Among several possible examples, two are the *Concerto o sia quintetto per cembalo o piano forte con due violini, violetta, e basso* (P-Ln MM 209//1)

and the *Duetto per cembalo o piano forte e violino* (P-Ln MM 247//7) by José Palomino (1755–1810), whose copies are dated 1785. Palomino was a Spanish violinist who settled in Lisbon in 1774.

24. P-Lant Ministério dos Negócios Estrangeiros, Liv. 365, *Passaportes, 1794–1809.*

25. See Michel'Angelo Lambertini, "Industria instrumental portugueza (apontamentos)," *A Arte Musical* 16 (1914), pp. 141–144, 150–154, here pp. 151–152, quoted in Doderer and van der Meer, *Portuguese String Keyboard Instruments*, p. 316. On the trade of music and musical instruments in the latter half of the eighteenth century and the first decades of the nineteenth century, see Vanda de Sá, *Circuitos de Produção e Circulação da Música Instrumental em Portugal entre 1750–1820* (PhD diss., Universidade de Évora, 2008), pp. 329–354.

26. Gonçalo de Baena, *Arte nouamente inuentada pera aprender a tāger* (Lisbon: Germã Galharde, 1540); only known copy in *E-Mp* VIII/1816. On the author (a player of the viol and chamber musician at the Portuguese court between the late 1490s and sometime after 1552), the context for this printing and the repertory it contains, see *Gonçalo de Baena: Arte para tanger* (Lisbon, 1540*)*, ed. Tess Knighton (Lisbon: Colibri and Centro de Estudos de Sociologia e Estética Musical, 2012).

27. Sebastian Virdung, *Musica getutscht und aussgezogē* (Basel: Michael Furter, 1511), fol. [G i].

28. As an example, Juan de Badajoz's three-voice setting of the *Pange lingua* shows a mixture of contrapuntal writing and extensive scalic *glosa* patterns. The same kind of glossing also features in the two-voice elaborations of hymn chants included in Baena's collection. See *Gonçalo de Baena: Arte*, ed. Knighton, pp. 234–236 (no. 34) and 164–172 (*Contrapuntos*, nos. 16, 17, and 18) respectively.

29. *P-Cug* MM 242 is closely related to P-Cug MM 48, a manuscript also in open-score format and dating from the 1550s or 1560s, whose contents include many textless vocal pieces likewise copied from Italian and Flemish prints dating from between 1539 and 1547. On these manuscripts, see Owen Rees, *Polyphony in Portugal c. 1530–c. 1620: Sources from the Monastery of Santa Cruz, Coimbra* (New York and London: Garland, 1995), pp. 271–282 and 325–364 respectively; and Filipe Mesquita de Oliveira, *A génese do tento para instrumentos de tecla no testemunho dos manuscritos P-Cug MM 48 e MM 242* (PhD diss., Universidade de Évora, 2011), chapter 2. It is now generally agreed that both MM 48 and MM 242 most probably had a didactic function, some of the pieces they contain clearly being compositional exercises, and were not used in actual music performance. See Bernadette Nelson, "The Chansons of Thomas Crecquillon and Clemens non Papa in Sources of Instrumental Music in Spain and Portugal, and Sixteenth-Century Keyboard Traditions," in *Beyond Contemporary Fame: Reassessing the Art of Clemens non Papa and Thomas Crecquillon*, edited by Eric Jas (Turnhout: Brepols, 2005), pp. 167–189, especially pp. 177–185.

30. *Recercari di M. Iacqves Bvvs Organista in Santo Marco di Venetia da cantare, et sonare* d'organo *& altri* stromēti nouamente *posti in luce. Libro*

primo a qvatro voci (Venice: Antonio Gardano, 1547). On the reworkings in *P-Cug* MM 242, see Oliveira, *A génese do tento*, chapter 4.

31. On António Carreira the Elder, see Rui Vieira Nery, "António Carreira, o Velho, Fr. António Carreira e António Carreira, o Moço: Balanço de um enigma por resolver," in *Livro de Homenagem a Macário Santiago Kastner*, ed. Maria Fernanda Cidrais Rodrigues, Manuel Morais, and Rui Vieira Nery (Lisbon: Fundação Calouste Gulbenkian, 1992), pp. 405–430 and João Pedro d'Alvarenga, *Polifonia portuguesa sacra tardo-quinhentista: estudo de fontes e edição crítica do* Livro de São Vicente, *manuscrito P-Lf FSVL 1P/H-6* (PhD diss., Universidade de Évora, 2005), Vol. 1, pp. 197–236 and addenda, including a discussion of the vocal works attributed to António Carreira the Elder and his son, Fr. António Carreira (d. 1599).

32. A modern edition of these four pieces is in *Antologia de organistas do século XVI*, edited by Cremilde Rosado Fernandes with an introductory study by Macario Santiago Kastner, Portugaliae Musica 19 (Lisbon: Fundação Calouste Gulbenkian, 1969), nos. 1, 5, 19b, and 21. Editions in this volume are to be used with caution because of the many uncorrected errors.

33. There is a concordance in Luis Venegas de Henestrosa, *Libro de cifra nveva, para tecla, harpa, y vihvela, en el qual se enseña breuemente cantar canto llano, y canto de organo, y algunos auisos para contrapunto* (Alcalá de Henares: Ioan de Brocar, 1557).

34. Thirteen of the "*ca.*" pieces attributed to Carreira and the piece headed "*A. c.*" are published in modern edition in *Antologia de organistas*, nos. 2, 3, 4, 6, 7, 8, 10, 12, 13, 14, 15, 16, 17, and 23. One of the "*ca.*" pieces, the longest one, was not published because Kastner believed it might be a motet; see *Antologia de organistas*, p. lxi; see also the inventory of P-Cug MM 242 in Rees, *Polyphony in Portugal*, pp. 326–337. The piece not included in *Antologia de organistas* is no. 140 in Rees's inventory; it is published along with three other conjecturally attributed pieces in Pedro Crisóstomo, *António Carreira: 4 peças inéditas para órgão* (MA diss., Universidade de Évora, 2013).

35. *The Collected Works of António de Cabezón*, edited by Charles Jacobs, Vol. 5, *Intabulations and opera incerta* (Brooklyn, NY: Institute of Mediaeval Music, 1986). The discussion of the authorship issue in Nery, "António Carreira, o Velho," pp. 417–421, is also inconclusive.

36. According to Rees (*Polyphony in Portugal*, pp. 357, 360, and 364 fnn. 16–18), *Antologia de organistas* nos. 1 and 5, featuring complex voice-crossing and occasional unison doubling in imitative entries, are likely to be consort pieces; no. 8, because of its restricted range and lack of instrumental ornamentation, is possibly a vocal piece, even if textless. M. S. Kastner (*Três compositores lusitanos para instrumentos de tecla* [Lisbon: Fundação Calouste Gulbenkien, 1979], p. 26) suggests a connection of this latter piece with Jacob Clemens's motet *Erravi sicut ovis*.

37. *Antologia de organistas*, no. 9, originally entitled "*canção.*" It should be noted that Kastner's perception of the style of Carreira is rather circular, as it derived from the study of the pieces he believed to be attributed to the composer.

38. Manuel Rodrigues Coelho was born in Elvas near the Spanish border
     probably around 1555. He was a substitute organist at Badajoz Cathedral
     between 1573 and 1577. In the 1580s and 1590s, he held the post of organist
     at Elvas Cathedral, moving to Lisbon Cathedral in 1602 or 1603. Coelho
     was appointed a chaplain and organist of the royal chapel in Lisbon
     on February 25, 1604. He retired on 13 October 1633.

39. Manuel Rodrigues Coelho, *Flores de mvsica: pera o instrvmento de tecla, &*
     harpa (Lisbon: na officina de Pedro Craesbeeck, 1620); copy in P-Ln CIC 95
     V. digitized at www.purl.pt/68; modern edition in *Manuel Rodrigues*
     Coelho: Flores de musica pera o instrumento de tecla & harpa, ed. Macario
     Santiago Kastner, Portugaliae Musica 1, 2 (Lisbon: Fundação Calouste
     Gulbenkian, 1961). The most recent and comprehensive study of Coelho's
     Flores de mvsica is Edite Rocha, *Manuel Rodrigues Coelho "Flores*
     de música": Problemas de interpretação (PhD diss., Universidade de Aveiro,
     2010).

40. This collection is representative of the genres of keyboard music then in use
     in Portugal. It includes twenty-four *tentos* (three in each of the eight church
     modes, though using on the whole ten different tonal types); four glossed
     versions of Lassus's *Susanne un jour* (which Coelho also calls *tentos*); four
     cantus-firmus settings of *Pange lingua*, and four other similar settings of
     Ave maris stella; a set of five versets on phrases of the *Ave maris stella* chant;
     eight sets of verses from the Magnificat and the Nunc dimittis "to be sung
     with the organ"; eight more sets of versets for *alternatim* performance of
     the *Magnificat* and the *Benedictus*; and seven sets of Kyrie versets following
     the order of the tones from C-*sol fa ut* to B-*fa*, thus implying transpositions
     with up to two flats.

41. In *P-BRp* Ms. 964; see below.

42. Francesco Rognoni, *Selva de varii pasaggi*, parte seconda (Milano: Filippo
     Lomazzo, 1620), pp. [2] and 63–65; see Rocha, *Manuel Rodrigues Coelho*,
     pp. 207–230.

43. Two settings by Hernando de Cabezón are included in his father's *Obras*
     (1578); four settings in Coelho's *Flores de mvsica* (1620), as just seen; and
     one more setting in Francisco Correa de Arauxo's *Facultad organica* (1626).

44. For instance, in the *Liuro de obras de Orgaõ juntas pella coriosidade do*
     P. P. Fr. Roque da Cõceicão Anno de 1695, P-Pm Ms. 43, *olim* Ms. 1607, fols.
     130v–131v; modern edition in *Fr. Roque da Conceição: Livro de obras de*
     órgão, edited by Klaus Speer, Portugaliae Musica 11 (Lisbon: Fundação
     Calouste Gulbenkian, 1967), No. 65.

45. Pedro de Araújo was a teacher at the St. Peter and St. Paul's Seminary in
     Braga between 1662 and 1668. He was also second organist at Braga
     Cathedral until 1665, when he was given a benefice at the Church of the
     Divine Saviour in Joane (south of Braga in the nearby of Famalicão). His
     activities are documented up to 1704 in *P-BRp* Ms. 964, fols. 136v–139r.
     This manuscript is the subject of Gerhard Doderer's 1975 doctoral
     dissertation, later published as *Orgelmusik und Orgelbau im Portugal des*
     17. Jahrhunderts: Untersuchungen an Hand des Ms 964 der Biblioteca
     Pública in Braga (Tutzing: Hans Schneider, 1978), with an incomplete
     inventory at pp. 20–29. The contents of *P-BRp* Ms. 964 were partially

published in modern edition in *Obras selectas para órgão: Ms 964 da Biblioteca Pública de Braga*, edited by Gerhard Doderer, Portugaliae Musica 25 (Lisbon: Fundação Calouste Gulbenkian, 1974). Araújo's *Obra de 2.º tom* is no. 18 in this edition.

46. Thirteen keyboard works bear explicit authorship attribution to Pedro de Araújo in manuscripts *P-BRp* Ms. 964 and P-Pm Ms. 43. Six other works in both sources can be attributed to him on stylistic grounds. All these are published in modern edition in *Obras selectas para órgão*, ed. Doderer, and *Fr. Roque da Conceição*, ed. Speer. See also Sérgio Rodrigues da Silva, *Os tentos de meio-registo e as batalhas de Pedro de Araújo: questões de autoria e edição crítica* (MA diss., Universidade de Évora, 2010).

47. These were copied into two of the later fascicles of manuscript P-BRp Ms. 964 (fols. 216r–230v and 253r–259r), which can be provisionally dated to around 1715–1720.

48. *P-BRp* Ms. 964, fol. 224v: "continue the foreign pieces that came from Rome."

49. Another fascicle in *P-BRp* Ms. 964 (fols. 146r–161v), also datable to around 1715–1720, contains a number of verses from the Lamentations and the *Miserere* for solo singing with the accompaniment either of the organ or harp.

50. Late seventeenth- and early eighteenth-century Italian and possibly also South and Central German repertories of chamber and keyboard music are found in manuscript sources from Santa Cruz in Coimbra; see Fernando Miguel Jalôto, *Música de câmara da 1.ª metade do século XVIII nas fontes do Mosteiro de Santa Cruz de Coimbra: Os códices P-Cug MM 62 e MM 63* (MA diss., Universidade de Aveiro, 2006). *P-Cug* MM 60, a composite manuscript also from Santa Cruz in Coimbra, contains a number of organ and harpsichord works by Alessandro Scarlatti (1660–1725) which were most probably acquired without his son's mediation; see *Alessandro Scarlatti: Toccatas and Various Compositions (Biblioteca Geral da Universidade de Coimbra, Secção dos Reservados, Ms. MM 60)*, ed. Andrea Macinanti and Francesco Tasini, Complete Works for Keyboard 3 (Bologna: Ut Orpheus, 2007).

51. José António Carlos de Seixas was born in Coimbra on June 11, 1704. At the age of fourteen he succeeded his father as organist of Coimbra Cathedral and moved to Lisbon in early 1721, being appointed organist of the Royal Chapel and Patriarchal Church, a post he held for the rest of his life. He was made a knight of the Order of Christ in 1738 and died in Lisbon on August 25, 1742.

52. The most influential of these editions are *Cravistas portuguezes*, edited by Macario Santiago Kastner (Mainz: B. Schott's Söhne, 1935); *Cravistas portuguezes II*, edited by Macario Santiago Kastner (Mainz: B. Schott's Söhne, 1950); *Carlos Seixas: 80 Sonatas para instrumentos de tecla*, ed. Macario Santiago Kastner, Portugaliae Musica 10 (Lisbon: Fundação Calouste Gulbenkian, 1965); Carlos Seixas: *25 Sonatas para instrumentos de tecla*, ed. Macario Santiago Kastner and João Valeriano, Portugaliae Musica

34 (Lisbon: Fundação Calouste Gulbenkian, 1980); and Carlos Seixas: *12 Sonatas*, ed. João Pedro d'Alvarenga (Lisbon: Musicoteca, 1995).

53. A first approach to the problems of authorship attribution of Seixas's keyboard works – certainly requiring further research – is found in Alvarenga, "Some Preliminaries in Approaching Carlos Seixas' Keyboard Sonatas," *Ad Parnassum: A Journal of Eighteenth- and Nineteenth-Century Instruments* (April 2009), pp. 95–128, including a list of sources, important modern editions and a preliminary catalogue of the sonatas at pp. 110–123. Of the ninety-four sonatas considered authentic, one – no. 2–1 in the catalogue – is in fact the 2nd movement of a C minor sonata by Francesco Durante (1684–1755) in *GB-Lbl* Ms. Add. 14248, fols. 2v–4v. One of the conjecturally attributed sonatas – no. App. 2–1 in the catalogue – is partially by Francesco Geminiani (1687–1762), as its 2nd, 3rd and 4th movements appear in the same positions in "Sonata VII" from this composer's *Sonate a violino, violone, e cembalo*, Op. 1 (1716). Also no. App. 19–2, because of its ternary disposition, cannot be the work of Seixas, as argued in João Pedro d'Alvarenga, "Handling of Form, Style Markers and Authorial Identity: Two Case Studies around the Work of Carlos Seixas," in *Anais do IV Encontro de Musicologia de Ribeirão Preto*, ed. Rodolfo Coelho de Souza (Ribeirão Preto, São Paulo: Laboratório de Teoria e Análise Musicais, 2012), pp. 288–295, here pp. 293–295; corrected version at www.academia.edu/1902471.

54. On the forms and style of Seixas's keyboard sonatas, see the seminal study by Klaus F. Heimes, *Carlos Seixas's Keyboard Sonatas* (PhD diss., University of South Africa, 1967).

55. On the harpsichord style of Carlos Seixas and the supposed influence of Scarlatti on his keyboard technique, see Klaus F. Heimes, "Carlos Seixas's Keyboard Sonatas: The Question of Domenico Scarlatti's Influence," *A Arte em Portugal no século XVIII: Actas do Congresso, III, Bracara Augusta* 28, no. 65–66 (1974), pp. 447–471.

56. On Seixas's harpsichord concertos, see João Pedro d'Alvarenga, "Carlos Seixas's Harpsichord Concerto in G Minor: An Essay in Style Analysis and Authorship Attribution," *Ad Parnassum: A Journal of Eighteenth- and Nineteenth-Century Instrumental Music* 10, no. 19 (2012), pp. 27–50. Noncommercial editions of the A major concerto at www.academia.edu /13817944 and the G minor concerto at www.academia.edu/13818038.

57. These are published (with many inaccuracies) in *Sonatas para tecla do século XVIII*, edited by Janine Moura, Macario Santiago Kastner and Rui Vieira Nery, Portugaliae Musica 38 (Lisbon: Fundação Calouste Gulbenkian, 1982).

58. The main sources for Avondano's keyboard sonatas are manuscripts *F-Pn* Vm^7 4874 (late eighteenth century) and *P-Ln* MM 337 (third part, dated 1774–1775). A two-movement Sonata in D major was printed in London in around 1775 with the title *A Favourite Lesson for the Harpsicord* (also in manuscripts D-B Mus. Ms. 936 and *F-Pn* Vm^7 4874, no. 11). This was published in modern edition as *Pedro António Avondano: Tocatta per cembalo* (Lisbon: AvA Musical Editions, 2015). All other works are unpublished.

59. The five keyboard sonatas by José Joaquim dos Santos appear in manuscript *F-Pn* Vm^7 4874 (one also in *P-Ln* MM 4529); all are unpublished.

60. Sources are *P-Ln* MMs 40//57, MM 338, MM 951, MM 4329 and *F–Pn* Vm^7 4874; modern editions (not wholly reliable) in *Sonatas para tecla do século XVIII*, ed. Moura, Kastner and Nery, nos. 6, 7, 8, and 9.

61. Cordeiro da Silva's keyboard sonatas appear in manuscripts *F-Pn* Vm^7 4874, *P-Ln* MM 951, MM 4521 and MM 4530; all are unpublished. A set of twelve *Minueti per cembalo* is in *P-Ln* MM 69//10. This was published in modern edition as *João Cordeiro da Silva: 12* minueti *per* cembalo, edited by Cândida Matos and José Lourenço (Lisbon: AvA Musical Editions, 2007); the first minuet in the set is also published in *Portugiesische Sonaten, Toccaten und Menuette des 18. Jahrhunderts*, edited by Gerhard Doderer, Organa Hispanica 2 (Heidelberg: Willy Müller, Süddeutscher Musikverlag, 1972), No. 8. Two more unpublished minuets are in manuscripts *P-Ln* MM 69//11 and MM 2284.

62. Alberto José Gomes da Silva, *Sei sonate per cembalo: opera 1 composte per il Sigre. Alberto Giuseppe Gomes da Silva maestro e compositore di musica* (Lisbona: si vendono in casa del Sigre., n. d.); copies in *GB-Lbl* d.8 and *P-Ln* CIC 87 V.; and Francisco Xavier Baptista, *Dodeci sonate variazioni minuetti per cembalo: opera 1 composti da Francesco Zav^o Battista Maestro e compositore di musica, stampati a spese degli sigr. assinanti* (Lisbona: sculpte. da Francesco D. Milcent, stampati da Francesco Manuel, n.d.); copy in *P-La* 137-I-13, no. 1. Modern editions in *Francisco Xavier Baptista (d. 1797): 12 sonatas para cravo (Lisboa, ca. 1770),* edited by Gerhard Doderer, Portugaliae Musica 36 (Lisbon: Fundação Calouste Gulbenkian, 1981), and *Alberto José Gomes da Silva (+ 1795): Sei Sonate per Cembalo, Lisboa ca. 1770*, edited by Gerhard Doderer and Mafalda Nejmeddine (Mollerussa, Lleida: Scala Aretina, 2003). With the exception of Sonata III in three movements and Sonata XII in a single movement, Baptista's sonatas have two movements. Sonatas I and II conclude with a theme and variations. The remaining two-movement sonatas end with a minuet. Four of Gomes da Silva's sonatas have two movements, the last one being a minuet. Sonatas I and II are three-movement works, the first one starting with a *Sinfonia–Allegro* and the second one beginning with a *Preludio–Allegro assai*. The minuet of Sonata IV in E minor is headed "*Nell stille della chitara Portughese.*" Although intended for the "*cembalo*" on their respective title pages, pieces in both collections were certainly imagined for all kind of "harpsichords" then in use in Portugal, including the one-manual and the two-manual harpsichord "with quills" and the harpsichord "with hammers."

63. See Seixas's Sonatas Nos. 20–3 in A minor for organ and No. 9–1 in E major.

64. See Alvarenga, "Handling of Form," pp. 293–295.

65. Baptista's Sonata IX appears in a longer, possibly earlier version and coupled with a different minuet in the first part of manuscript *P-Ln* MM 338, dating from around 1765 (the minuet in *P-Ln* MM 338 is published in *Portugiesische Sonaten, Toccaten und Menuette*, ed. Doderer, no. 7). This is preceded by a two-movement Sonata in D major also attributed to Baptista.

The second part of manuscript *P-Ln* MM 337 consists of a two-movement Sonata in F major whose title page reads: "*Tocata per cemballo del Sig^re Francisco Xavier Baptista Alle Dame 1765.*" Four other movements from Baptista's *Dodeci sonate* appear in different versions in manuscript *P-Ln* MM 4510, also datable to the mid- or late 1760s. The extant keyboard output of Francisco Xavier Baptista also includes a set of seven minuets (P-Ln MM 1297) and a two-movement Sonata in G major for harpsichord and violin (P-Em Ms. 138); this latter piece was published as *Francisco Xavier Baptista: Sonata em Sol maior para violino e cravo (piano)*, edited by Ivo Cruz (Lisbon: Conservatório Nacional, 1971). Recent research by Mafalda Nejmeddine ("O género sonata em Portugal: Subsídios para o estudo do repertório português para tecla de 1750 a 1807" [PhD diss., Universidade de Évora, 2015], pp. 316–329) revealed that Francisco Xavier Baptista was Known in the 1780s by the surname "Bachixa" (also spelled "Baxixa", a word that in Spanish America refers to the Italian people and the Italian language, undoubtedly deriving from the apheresis of the proper name "Giambattista" through its Genoese version, "Baciccia" – thus a possible clue for Baptista's ancestry). Consequently, the two single-movement sonatas with attribution to "*Francisco Xavier Bachixa*" in *F-Pn* Vm^7 4874 (no. 30, in D major, and no. 31, in F major) are also his work.

66. *F-Pn* Vm^7 4874, nos. 25 and 27 respectively.

67. *Minuete de Fr. Manuel Elias, P-Ln* MM 86//15; modern edition in *Portugiesische Sonaten, Toccaten und Menuette*, ed. Doderer, no. 9.

68. No. 4 in manuscript *P-Ln* MM 337 and no. 2 in manuscript *F-Pn* Vm^7 4874.

69. Sousa Carvalho studied with Carlo Cotumacci (ca. 1709–1785) at the Conservatorio di Sant'Onofrio a Capuana in Naples, where he enrolled on January 15, 1761 thanks to a royal grant. On returning to Portugal in 1767, he was appointed professor of counterpoint in the Patriarchal Seminary. He succeeded the renowned Neapolitan David Perez as music teacher to the royal family in 1778. Perez (1711–1778) had been hired in 1752 on the orders of King José I (b. 1714; r. 1750–1777) for the purpose of running court opera productions. Three harpsichord sonatas of a marked *galant* idiom by David Perez, probably composed in Lisbon, survive in manuscripts *P-Ln* MM 337 and *F-Pn* Vm^7 4874.

70. *P-Ln* MM 321, no. 2, fols. 6v-10r. The piece has the overall range AA–d^3, which fits within the compass of GG–g^3 found only in instruments from the 1780s. Noncommercial modern edition at www.academia.edu/13835355 (March 16, 2016). For the critical commentary and a reference to other editions of this piece, see João Pedro d'Alvarenga, "Sobre a autoria das obras para tecla atribuídas a João de Sousa Carvalho," *Revista Portuguesa de Musicologia* 4–5 (1994–1995), pp. 115–145, at pp. 144–145, available online at www.rpm-ns.pt/index.php/rpm/article/view/149/152. Delicate melodic chromaticism can be seen especially in an anonymous one-movement Sonata in C minor from manuscript P-Ln MM 338 published in *Portugiesische Sonaten, Toccaten und Menuette*, ed. Doderer, no. 3.

71. See for instance, Moreira's two-movement Sonata in B♭ major (*P-Ln* CN 145 no. 5) and Portugal's Sonata in D major (*US-Wc* M23.P794S6; coupled with a Rondo in C major and a set of variations in E♭ major), this latter

published as *Marcos Antonio Portugal: Sonata y variaciones (sonata e variacoens) para piano*, edited by Alfred E. Lemmon (Madrid: Unión Musical Española, 1976; reprinted Niedernhausen: Edition Kemel, 2009).

Further Reading

d'Alvarenga, João Pedro. "Domenico Scarlatti in the 1720s: Portugal, Travelling, and the Italianisation of the Portuguese Musical Scene," in *Domenico Scarlatti Adventures: Essays to Commemorate the 250th Anniversary of his Death*, ed. Massimiliano Sala and W. Dean Sutcliffe, Ad Parnassum Studies 3. Bologna: Ut Orpheus Edizioni, 2008.

Coelho, Victor Anand. "Music in the New Worlds," in *The Cambridge History of Seventeenth Century Music*, ed. Tim Carter and John Butt. Cambridge: Cambridge University Press, 2005, pp. 88–110.

Pollens, Stewart. "The Early Portuguese Piano." *Early Music* 13, no. 1 (1985), pp. 18–27.

The Early Pianoforte. Cambridge: Cambridge University Press, 1995.

9 Spain

ÁGUEDA PEDRERO-ENCABO

The *Libro de cifra nueva para tecla, harpa y vihuela* (1557), compiled by Luis Venegas de Henestrosa (ca. 1510–1570), and the *Obras de música para tecla, harpa y vihuela* (1578) by Antonio de Cabezón (1510–1566) are the earliest books of keyboard music printed in Spain.[1] Except for some strictly liturgical organ pieces, they contain multipurpose repertoire meant for all sorts of keyboards – organ, clavichord, harpsichord, spinet, etc. – as well as for harp and vihuela.[2] The genres include dances, *diferencias* (i.e., variations), and *glosados* (diminutions). Cabezón's command of counterpoint, melodic diminutions, and masterful variation technique gives his works special distinction.[3] Among these are the *diferencias* based on a given melodic/harmonic structure (e.g., *Diferencias sobre las vacas,* on a bass pattern akin to the romanesca); dances (*Pavana italiana, Gallarda milanesa*); and popular tunes (*La dama le demanda,* the villancico *¿Quién te me enojó, Isabel?*, or the *Canto llano del cavallero,* based on the famous love song, *Dezidle al cavallero*) (see Example 9.1).[4]

The *glosados* on chansons and madrigals reveal Cabezón's knowledge of foreign, especially Franco-Flemish, polyphonic music (e.g., Lasso's *Susanne un jour,* Willaert's *Anchor che col partire,* Verdelot's *Ultimi miei sospiri,* etc.). His elaborated, Josquin-influenced contrapuntal technique appears even more intricate in his four- and five-part settings, where he develops beautifully imaginative *glosas*.[5] His *diferencias* (which strongly influenced English virginalists, as Kastner once noticed) are enriched by expressive harmonies and musical rhetoric patterns, making him one of the most important composers of his time.[6]

The earliest repertoire specifically intended for the harpsichord is found in Francisco de Tejada's *Libro de música de clavicímbalo* (1721), a collection of dances, some popular and typically Spanish (e.g., *Marizápalos, tonadilla, canarios*), some bearing descriptive names such as *Gitanilla* (Gipsy girl), and others courtly, with a significant presence of the French minuet.[7] His simple, uncluttered style exemplifies the secular repertoire commonly played on the harpsichord – entertaining and easy to execute, in accordance with the eighteenth-century *galant* spirit.

The four volumes of keyboard music collected by Antoni Martín i Coll from the early eighteenth century mainly contain organ works, but all the secular repertoire, with no specific organ registrations, and no liturgical

Example 9.1 Antonio de Cabezón, *Diferencias sobre la Gallarda Milanesa, Obras de música para tecla, harpa y vihuela* (1578), mm. 1–18

use, could as well be played on the harpsichord. This is the case with his *tocatas alegres de Corelli*, canciones, minuets, dances (*zarabande*), *folías*, *canarios*, and transcriptions from stage works by Lully and others.[8] How much improvisation and harmonic filling was added in performance is not known. The same is true of the works by Joan Cabanilles (1644–1712) on an ostinato bass or dance rhythm, such as his *gallardas* and *xácara*, which are well suited to the harpsichord.[9]

The favorite early eighteenth-century genre, the sonata, encompasses the oldest repertoire intended solely for the harpsichord. The work of Vicente Rodríguez (1690–1760), Cabanilles's heir, is regarded as its earliest dated evidence.[10] His *Toccatas para címbalo* are preserved in a 1744 manuscript containing one *pastorela* and thirty *tocatas*, called *sonatas* in the source, proof that the two terms were then interchangeable in Spain.[11] His pieces are arranged by key, in chromatic ascending order from the tonics of D-Dorian to Db major an octave above, and display great formal and stylistic variety, indicating that they were written over many years, during which Rodríguez honed his skills in the use of the tonal system and the blossoming *style galant*.[12] Some sonatas (nos. 1, 2, 23) are in three movements connected by motivic links, reminiscent of the early baroque ensemble sonata. Others are extended single-movement works in a freer toccata style, mixing late-baroque pseudo-polyphonic voicing and long episodes displaying the newer hand-crossing technique. Rodríguez calls for this in twenty sonatas, perhaps because it was such a novelty, but such passages are not as picturesque and timely placed as in Albero or Soler; rather, they often sound stagnant and repetitious, halting the musical flow.

Example 9.2a Vicente Rodríguez, Sonata 20, *Toccatas para címbalo* (1744), mm. 1–9

Example 9.2b Vicente Rodríguez, Sonata 20, *Toccatas para címbalo* (1744), mm. 64–72

Typical of Rodríguez is the extended *Fortspinnung* of a motif (Sonata 25, 240 bars) or cell (Sonata 16, 283 bars). The influence of the Italian concerto is recognizable in the melodic gestures of the Adagio of Sonata 27 and in the Largos of the three-tempo sonatas. Analysis of Rodríguez's fourteen two-section sonatas clearly reveals the sundry stylistic trends upon which he draws, including *Fortspinnung* and early *galant* phrase articulation (e.g., nos. 5, 8, 10, 15, 17–21, 24, 26, 29, and 30).[13] An interesting example of such a mixture can be found in Sonata 20. Its chromatic theme is stated in imitation but is written in a danceable 3/4 meter and connected to a decorated countersubject (see Examples 9.2a and 9.2b).

Fortspinnung and driving rhythms can be found throughout, even in the cross-hand leaps in the left hand, but the chromatic theme reappears, expanded and enriched, until a surprising cadential phrase is repeated three times in a downward sequence, thus producing a lively *galant* atmosphere.

Cantabile themes articulated in four-bar phrases can be found in Sonatas 19, 21, and 24; and in five-bar groups in Sonata 30, sequentially repeated over a romanesca progression, shown in Example 9.3.[14]

Other sonatas in this collection feature a two-movement prelude–toccata format – either a slow, improvisational part followed by fast tempo in fugato style (as in Sonatas 9 and 27) or a solemn Grave preceding the Allegro (Sonatas 6 and 9), reflecting Rodríguez's own view of the French overture.

The same slow–fast pattern was used by Rodríguez's Catalan contemporary, José Elías (ca. 1687–1755).[15] His twelve sonatas, actually called *tocatas*, are written in a graceful *style galant*, very unlike those of his colleague.[16] They reveal the assimilation of Italian stylistic traits such as the *stile concertante* (e.g., the Allegros of nos. 5, 6, and especially 11),

Example 9.3 Vicente Rodríguez, Sonata 30, *Toccatas para címbalo* (1744), mm.1–16

certain melodic contours, the use of *pastorela*, the da capo aria form, or the Grave–Allegro pattern drawn from Corelli's *sonata da chiesa*. Even when the copyist added organ directions to the titles, such as *Partido* or *Registro Ygual*, these toccatas fit the harpsichord because of their light two-part voicing, often with a simple "trommel bass," and repeated full chords, as in the Grave from Toccata 11.[17] Some feature late-baroque rhythms, rich chromaticism and frequent repeated notes (e.g., nos. 4 and 10), while others make use of the lyrical dotted rhythms of the siciliana typical of the *pastorela* (e.g., Allegros from nos. 2 and 9, Graves from nos. 7 and 8). A distinctive aspect of Elías's style is an exuberant, richly ornamented right-hand melody line over a simple texture in the left, as seen in the Grave movements of nos. 1, 2, 3, and 5.

Perhaps the oldest Spanish harpsichord sonata is the only surviving work by Pere Rabassa (1683–1767), which also attests to the Italian-style influence.[18] It is in four movements, Giusto – Allegro – Adagio – Allegro, like a baroque ensemble sonata, with a 12/8 gigue-like opening Allegro in Corelli fashion. Idiomatic harpsichord writing is especially apparent in the Adagio, with full chords suggesting that arpeggios are used, and in the second Allegro, quite similar to Rodríguez's Sonata 29.

Among the Madrid court musicians who were active alongside Domenico Scarlatti, then Queen María Bárbara's teacher, Sebastián Albero (1722–1756) stands out.[19] His works have come to us in two manuscripts: *Obras para clavicordio o piano forte*, dedicated to King Ferdinand VI, with six three-movement works (Recercata – Fugue – Sonata); and the *Sonatas para clavicordio* codex, with its two groups of fourteen sonatas plus a fugue (nos. 15 and 30).[20]

Albero adhered to a predominantly old-style Spanish prototype, the *tiento* (i.e., fugue), *intento*, or *partido*, which remained the favorite organ genre throughout the eighteenth century. His very extended fugues (some are 300 to 500 measures in length) follow Elías's model, the learned Iberian *tiento* heritage being updated by the use of long themes embellished with *galant* elements in a tonal language (where, according to Koch, "dissonance need not be prepared"), as opposed to the modal *tiento*. This was actually the mixture Elías hinted at when he called his 1749 collection *Obras entre el antiguo y moderno estilo*.[21] Like Elías, Albero makes extensive use of chromatic passages, chords, and modulations; counterpoint is also treated freely, going as far as using a 3/8 dance meter (perhaps inspired by Scarlatti's Sonata K30, Fuga) and hemiolias.[22] This is the case with the *Fuga prima*, in which a rhythmic theme, first stated six times in tonic and dominant, reappears throughout, alternating with modulating sequential passages and left-hand broken chords, always based on motifs derived from the theme. Some of these, containing the Phrygian cadence VIb–V, stress the use of a Spanish folk device, to which Soler often resorted as well.

The *recercada* genre had disappeared from Spain after Diego Ortiz's sixteenth-century *recercadas* for viola da gamba. Clearly, Albero was trying to resurrect the genre of a prelude-like, free-tempo work, and his *recercata* is quite close to Louis Couperin's *prélude non mesuré*, as well as to the virtuoso baroque toccata, in that he uses a brilliant improvisational style unknown to Spanish composers at this time.[23] The same can also be detected in the short preludes included by Antonio Soler in his major treatise, *Llave de la modulación* (1762).[24] Thus, Albero's music embodies three different styles: the *phantasticus* (improvisational) in his *recercatas*, the learned (imitative) in his fugues, and the *galant* in his sonatas. His six sonatas in the Madrid source are in two-part form, the second part opening with striking surprises, thus avoiding shallow repetition. There are almost no hand crossings (except for those few in nos. 4 and 6, plus nos. 1, 5, 13, and 18 from the Venice source), as the composer is seeking musical substance rather than mere virtuosity. The early *galant* style dominates, and the episodic structure is built on motivic repetition. The Sonata no. 2 fully displays Albero's concertante style, as does the opening of no. 4, a type of allemande quite similar to Rodríguez's no. 2. No. 6 is a fine example of Albero's expressive style (Example 9.4a), its similarities with Scarlatti's notwithstanding.[25]

The use of folk rhythms (no. 1, m. 21) and guitar-like repeated chords (no. 4, m. 28; no. 5, m. 26; no. 6, m. 22) is also noteworthy. The Andantes display an intensely expressive singing style as, for instance, in no. 6 or in no. 3 (Example 9.4b), where a repeated motif on a descending chromatic bass (F–Eb–D–Db–C) and the contrasting tonalities F minor and Bb minor produce the effect of a heartfelt lament.

Another major figure is José de Nebra (1702–1768).[26] A dozen movements of his sonatas have been uncovered so far. These include some that

Example 9.4a Sebastian Albero, Sonata 6, *Obras para clavicordio o piano forte*, mm. 31–46

Example 9.4b Sebastian Albero, Sonata 3, *Obras para clavicordio o piano forte*, mm. 33–43

have not been fully documented as being written by the composer, plus an unfinished Grave. Nebra's works are in a late-baroque style mixed with early *galant* elements (Tocatas 1E and 2E, and Tocata 1A, 4A) and aspects of Italian music (Tocata 5E).[27] Melodic patterns from Tocata 2E are quite similar to Elías's Grave movements from Tocatas 1, 2, and 3, as well as to his Allegro from Tocata 8. While Nebra uses a closed-type two-part form, he introduces unexpected key contrasts and new expressive themes in the second section, as in his Tocata 1E in G major. Here, after the introductory D major cadence, an effusive, languid D minor subject is stated (m. 20). Its opening motif appears in imitation three times in each hand – a typical *stile antico* feature – and is then repeated twice more, with variations, in F major (m. 25) and D minor (m. 29), before leading to the D major closing section (m. 33). Notice his use of the Phrygian interval, with its contrasting folk modal character.

The best-known mid-eighteenth-century figure is undoubtedly Antonio Soler (1729–1783).[28] His work embodies the consolidation of new stylistic trends and the adoption of the classical sonata form. Out of more than 130 surviving sonatas, only a selection of twenty-seven was published during his time (London, ca. 1796).[29] A detailed chronology is hard to pinpoint, as most sonatas have come to us as undated manuscripts.[30] They display an impressive variety of forms and styles.[31] Most are single-movement works, but Soler also wrote a few with two,

Example 9.5 Antonio Soler, Sonata in C minor, R48, mm. 6–15

Example 9.6 Antonio Soler, Sonata in C minor, R100, mm. 9–21

three, or four movements, although it remains difficult to ascertain if all were originally multimovement. Examples of two-part form abound, revealing a mixture of late-baroque style (and powerfully driving *Fortspinnung*), usually in triple meter, with *galant* motifs and ornamentation, sequential progressions, virtuoso passages, and hand crossings. Here, Soler appears at his most inspired and original. The polyphonic legacy is present in the movements expressly written in this style (e.g., the *intentos* from Sonatas nos. 63 to 68/III), as well as in the numerous sonatas opening with an imitative theme statement (nos. 5, 6, 9, 14, 18, etc.).[32] A folk flavor is occasionally achieved by resorting to ostinatos, particularly on the Phrygian cadence (VIb–V), as in *Sonatas* no. 18 (m. 8), no. 19 (mm. 13, 46), and no. 48 (Example 9.5, mm. 10–12).

Some sonatas come close to the orchestral *Sturm und Drang* style (e.g., nos. 10, 48), while others are lighter and more playful (nos. 25, 37, 49, and 56); some are quasi-folksongs (nos. 53, 58, and 60); a few have a military character (nos. 1 and 22); and several use stylized folk dances, such as the bolero rhythms of nos. 4 (mm. 1, 21), 73 (m. 57), and 86 (m. 2) or 90 (mm. 1 and 11). The Andantes exhibit an intimate singing style (nos. 16, 68), now languid (no. 18, 20), now agitated, again in the *empfindsamer Stil* (nos. 75, 77, 79). Rich harmonies are exquisitely combined in no. 100 (see Example 9.6) to create a plaintive lament, also resorting to such typical

Andalusian folk music resources as the insistent Phrygian interval (A♭–G; m. 5) and guitar imitation, with *rasgueado* (strumming) on a diminished seventh chord and its *punteado* (i.e., finger picking) answer given to the left hand (mm. 9–10).

In multimovement sonatas, one can notice the adoption of the classical sonata format, as well as the inclusion of *galant* traits, such as a slower harmonic rhythm and frequent use of Alberti bass patterns. Earlier lively folk elements yield to transparency and clarity, typical of the early classical style. Based on dated sources, these sonatas are believed to have come from Soler's final years.

An especially interesting figure is Manuel Blasco de Nebra (1750–1784), organist at Seville Cathedral and José de Nebra's nephew.[33] Twenty-four sonatas and six *pastorelas* of his survive, out of a known total of 172 attributed to him, revealing a very interesting and original style, with a lyrical and emotional quality that sets him apart from his colleagues.[34] The six pieces discovered in Osuna are single movements in a simple and elegant *style galant*. All other sonatas, except 11MO and 12MO, are in two movements, Adagio (or Andante) and Allegro (or Presto).[35] Blasco de Nebra merges folk elements with his own peculiar manner of articulating the melody in long, profusely ornamented phrases, full of winding and irregular motifs, in a fascinating combination of the *galant* and *Empfindsamkeit*. He is fond of repeating a motif or phrase with charming variants or unexpected harmonic and melodic turns. His Adagios are intensely expressive (3Ma, 5Ma), subtly lamenting (2MO, 6MO, 1Ma), or display a delicate, intimate lyricism (2Ma; 3MO, third theme) and a funeral march character (2MO; 4Ma; 5MO, second theme, which is also the opening Allegro theme).[36] Some Allegros feature a late-baroque rhythmic drive in a danceable gigue meter, with motivic repetitions typical of Scarlatti and Soler (3MO, 4MO, 11MO, 2Ma). Blasco de Nebra also employs vigorous Spanish folk traits, some of which burst into and contrast with the more meditative first themes. The four-note arpeggiated appoggiaturas, recalling the French *arpègement figuré* (2Ma, Allegro, m. 19; 1MO, m. 26), emulate guitar strumming (see Example 9.7). The short grace notes conjure up the sharp sound of castanet clicks, which are usually associated to the downward melodic tetrachord in the melody of Phrygian ostinatos, as in 1MO, m. 26 (i.e., D–C♯–B–A♯), 4MO, m. 14 (F♯–E♭), and 9MO, m. 9 (C♯–B♭). Such augmented seconds also contribute to an exotic, Middle Eastern sound.

Joaquín Montero (1740?–ca. 1815) published *Seis sonatas para clave y fuerte piano* in 1790, also in two movements, Adagio – Allegro. His style is reminiscent of that of his predecessor Blasco de Nebra, such as the embellished melodic contours on a siciliana, 6/8 dotted rhythm (Sonata 1). However, Montero's style is simpler, less ornamented, often featuring

Example 9.7 Manuel Blasco de Nebra, Sonata 1 from E-MO Ms. 2998, mm. 26–39

triplets and unexpected passages in parallel octaves, divided between two hands, creating a playful rustic character (e.g., Sonata 2/I, m. 4).[37] The *galant* style dominates, rhythmically varied motifs unfolding with irregular articulation and emphasizing majestic dotted rhythms (Sonatas 2 and 4) that evoke a symphonic style (Sonata 6).

Besides the cited works, repertoire from the Catalan region is of remarkable interest, especially that of the organists of Montserrat Monastery, such as Anselm Viola (1738–1798). Sixteen sonatas of his are preserved; five bear the title *para clarines*, indicating performance on the organ.[38] The others connect Soler's *galant* compositional style to the Iberian organ tradition, with frequent fanfares and horn-call motifs as well as bass-line passages in broken octaves (e.g. nos. 11 and 13), not unlike those of Cabanilles and Elías. Some sonatas feature regular phrases in a light two-part texture, with frequent use of the Alberti bass – or its shortened two-note version (nos. 1, 3, 7, 9). Others are more virtuosic in character, with a thicker texture (Nos. 2, 8, 10, 12). This is evident in some of the fifteen known sonatas by Felip Rodríguez (1759–1814).[39] Other notable works by Catalan composers are twenty-one single-movement sonatas by Manuel Espona (1747–1779); eight sonatas published by Narcís Casanoves (1747–1799), which are also single-movement works, although some might be followed by a rondo; twenty-two sonatas by Francés Mariner (1720–1789); ten works by his nephew, Carles Baguer (1768–1808); or the collection of twenty-three single-movement sonatas by Josep Gallés (1758–1836).[40] The most relevant sonatas in the Aragonese area are those by Juan Moreno y Polo (1711–1776), now recognized as the real author of the Sonata 121, once attributed to Soler; the six by Mariano Cosuenda (1737–1801); and the seven attributed to José Ferrer (ca. 1745–1815).[41]

Despite generations of famous organists at the service of the Madrid royal chapel, which employed four players at the same time, little eighteenth-century keyboard repertoire from this chapel has survived. They include several sonatas and fugues, dated ca. 1746–1752, by Joaquín Oxinagas, which strongly resemble those of Albero.[42] This compositional approach was to be passed on to the next generation of composers, such as Jose Lidón (1768–1827) and Juan Sessé (1769–1801). Both were hired as court organists in 1768. Another applicant for the position was the Valencia organist, Manuel Narro (1729–1776), from whom a Concerto for Harpsichord and Orchestra in G major (1767) and fifteen sonatas survive.[43] Several harpsichord sonatas by Lidón have been recently discovered, including a *Sonata para clave en sol* and a *Sonata para órgano con trompeta real y clave*.[44] Sessé's surviving music consists of *Seis fugas para órgano y clave, Obra I* (1773) and the *Cuaderno primero de una colección de piezas de música para clavicordio, forte-piano y órgano. Obra 6ª* (1785?). We know of other lost works by Sesse from inventories or newspaper advertisements, such as his *Doce minuetos para clavicordio* (1776), *Ocho divertimentos para clave o forte-piano* (1790) or *Seis sonatas para clavicordio que pueden servir para órgano* (1777).[45] These provide evidence of the most popular genres as well as a flexible approach to instruments, their repertoires being interchangeable either between harpsichord and piano or between harpsichord and organ, unless idiomatic organ writing was used.[46]

Felix Máximo López (1742–1821) represents the end of the era of harpsichord composition in Spain, his works already featuring unmistakable indications for the fortepiano.[47] However his collection *Música de clave* contains seventeen sonatas idiomatically suited for the harpsichord. Symbolically, it opens with a *Pieza de clave* in a style that is old-fashioned for the time: a two-part texture, spirited baroque *Fortspinnung* in a dance-like 3/8 meter, with hand crossings and repeated notes. His other works use a more contemporary language, attesting to the reception of the classical Viennese style in Spain; in fact, eight of the sonatas are loose arrangements of seven Haydn symphonies.[48] López also wrote rondos, minuets, *pastorelas*, and two sets of six *Variaciones al minuet afandangado*.[49] In the second set he uses a mixture of classical features: the prelude (Preludio Largo) begins with dramatic French overture solemnity and *Sturm und Drang* harmonic tension. This contrasts with the minuet (*Allegro Moderato*), which takes on a light fandango air from its rhythmic pattern (three quarter-notes – four eighth-notes – one quarter-note). López's *Variaciones del fandango español* resemble the older fandangos by José de Nebra, José Martí, and Soler (R146).[50] It is jam-packed with typical folk elements like the *seguidilla* rhythmic pattern and its variants, frequent guitar and castanet imitations, alternating 3/4 and 6/8 meters, and Phrygian inflections, such as the extended Andalusian cadence in the last section, in which the Phrygian tetrachord is heard above a pedal (see mm. 156–160).[51] This piece, with its breathless, almost frantic pace and exhilarating gestures, effectively expresses the fury and fire of this famous dance, which has since become a symbol of Spanish music.

The illustrious history of the harpsichord in Spain spanned a period of more than two hundred years, beginning in the sixteenth century with the rich contrapuntal works in Henestrosa's book and those by Cabezón and reaching its full splendor with the virtuoso and idiomatic harpsichord music of the eighteenth. The repertoire encompassed a wide range of genres, national styles, keyboard techniques, and folk idioms, making Spanish harpsichord music one of the most important contributions to the repertoire.

Notes

1. Cabezón entered Queen Isabel's service in 1526 and was appointed *músico de cámara* at Charles V's court by 1538. When the Queen died (1539), Cabezón passed to the service of Prince Philip and his sisters, the infantas Maria and Juana, as *músico de tecla* (keyboard musician). In 1543 Cabezón was named organist of the chapel of Prince Philip. From 1548 to 1551 he accompanied the prince in his travels to Milan, Naples, Germany, the Netherlands, and later to London, when Philip married Mary Tudor.
2. See John Griffiths, "Venegas, Cabezón y las obras 'para tecla, harpa y vihuela,'" ed. Luisa Morales, in *Cinco siglos de música de tecla española. Five Centuries of Spanish Keyboard Music* (Almería: Asociación Cultural Leal, 2007), pp. 153–168.
3. See Miguel Angel Roig-Francolí, *Compositional Theory and Practice in Mid-Sixteenth-Century Spanish Instrumental Music: The Arte de tañer fantasia by Tomas de Santa Maria and the music of Antonio de Cabezón* (PhD diss., Indiana University, 1990).
4. See Maurice Esses, *Dance and Instrumental Diferencias in Spain during the 17th and Early 18th Centuries, Vol. 1, History and Background, Music and Dance,* Dance and Music Series 2 (Stuyvesant, NY: Pendragon Press, 1991), pp. 659–662.
5. See an updated review of Cabezón studies in J. Artigas and A. Ezquerro, "Antonio de Cabezón redivivo," *Anuario Musical* 69 (2014), pp. 5–50.
6. M. Santiago Kastner, *Contribución al estudio de la música española y portuguesa* (Lisbon: Atica, 1941), pp. 71–94. See Águeda Pedrero-Encabo,

"Estrategias compositivas de Cabezón en su glosado de *Ultimi miei sospiri* de Verdelot," *Revista de Musicología* 34, no. 2 (2011), pp. 317–332.

7. *Libro de música de clavicímbalo del Sr. Dn. Francisco de Tejada.* Source: E-Mn M815, facsimile in www.bne.es. See Esses, *Dance and Instrumental Diferencias,* Vol. 1, pp. 272–273.

8. See Esses, *Dance and Instrumental Diferencias,* Vol. 1, pp. 251–265; Louis Jambou, "Andrés Lorente, compositeur: essai d'identificacion de la tablature du ms. M1358 de la Bibliothèque Nationale de Madrid," *Melanges de la Casa de Velázquez* 12 (1976), pp. 251–270, and Jambou, "Transmisión, evolución y transformaciones musicales en Martín y Coll: de Cabezón y Lully a Martín y Coll," *Nasarre* 17, no. 1–2 (2001), pp. 305–330.

9. Cabanilles was appointed chief organist of Valencia Cathedral in 1666, a lifetime position. A major organ composer, he led the transformation from the late seventeenth-century baroque to the early eighteenth-century styles. These are found in a modern edition by Higinio Anglés, *Iohannis Cabanilles Opera Omnia,* Vol. 4 (Barcelona: Biblioteca de Catalunya, 1927).

10. Vicente Rodríguez Monllor was organist at the Valencia Cathedral from 1713 until his death. His organ pieces are located in the *Libro de organistas valencianos* (E-Bbc M1012), ed. Águeda Pedrero-Encabo, *Vicent Rodríguez: Obres per a orgue,* Compositors Valencians, 10 (Barcelona: Tritó, 2009). Some pieces, e.g. the *Fantasía de VIII tono,* by Rodríguez, and the *Tocata de 5º tono punto alto* (Anonym), are suited for the harpsichord.

11. *Libro de tocatas para címbalo 1744.* Modern edition by Almonte Howell, *Vicente Rodríguez Toccatas for harpsichord (Thirty Sonatas and a Pastorela, 1744),* Recent Researches in the Music of the Classical Era, vols. 22–23 (Madison, Wisconsin: A-R Editions, 1986).

12. Águeda Pedrero-Encabo, *La sonata para teclado: su configuración en España* (Universidad de Valladolid, 1997), pp. 83–197.

13. Águeda Pedrero-Encabo, "Los 30 *Essercizi* de Domenico Scarlatti y las 30 tocatas de Vicente Rodríguez: paralelismos y divergencias," *Revista de Musicología* 20, no. 1 (1997), pp. 373–392.

14. See Robert O. Gjerdingen, *Music in the Galant Style* (New York: Oxford University Press, 2007), pp. 25–43.

15. José Elías was appointed organist at Sant Pere de las Puelles in 1712, and at Sant Just i Pastor, Barcelona in 1715. On 1725 he became organist of the Descalzas Reales, Madrid. In 1761 he did not sign the approval of Soler's treatise *Llave de la modulación,* which suggests he had already died. See José Maria Llorens, *José Elías Obras completas,* Vol. 2A (Barcelona: Diputación Provincial, 1981).

16. Águeda Pedrero-Encabo, "Some Unpublished Works of José Elías," in *Music in Spain during the Eighteenth Century,* ed. J. Carreras and M. Boyd, second edition (Cambridge University Press, 2006), pp. 214–221.

17. The *Partido* calls for splitting the registration into two halves (between c^1 and $c\sharp^1$); *Registro igual* indicates undivided stops. *Josep Elíes. 24 Obres per a orgue,* Águeda Pedrero-Encabo, ed. (Barcelona: Tritó, 2008).

18. Rabassa was appointed chapel master at Vic Cathedral in 1713 and at Valencia Cathedral in 1714. In 1724 he moved to Seville Cathedral, where he remained until his death (1767). He also wrote a *Guía para los*

principiantes (ca. 1728–1738), one of the most important eighteenth-century composition treatises. The sonata itself is preserved as *Sonata* in a volume entitled *Libro de organistas valencianos* (see Appendix 5).

19. Albero had been organist at the Madrid royal chapel since 1746.

20. Here *clavicordio* refers to the harpsichord. The words *o pianoforte* look like a later addition, judging from the different ink color.

21. See Heinrich C. Koch, *Versuch einer Anleitung zur Composition*, Vol. 1 (Leipzig: Adam Friedrich Böhme, 1782), p. 155, cited in Leonard Ratner, *Classic Music: Expression, Form and Style* (New York: Schirmer, 1980), p. 23; José Elíes, *Obras de órgano entre el antiguo y moderno estilo* (Madrid, 1749), ed. José María Llorens; and José Elías, *Obras Completas*, Vol. 1A, B (Barcelona: Diputación Provincial, 1971, 1975).

22. From Domenico Scarlatti, *Essercizi per Gravicembalo* (London, 1738/9).

23. About Albero's style of writing recercatas, see W. Dean Sutcliffe, *The Keyboard Sonatas of Domenico Scarlatti and Eighteenth-Century Musical Style* (Cambridge: Cambridge University Press, 2003), pp. 211–212.

24. Antonio Soler, *Llave de la modulación y antigüedades de la música* (Madrid: Joaquín Ibarra, 1762), pp. 121–127: "Quatro Preludios para Aprender" and "Síguense otros quatro Preludios," facsimile in www.bne.es., Antonio Baciero, ed., in *Biblioteca española de música de teclado*, Vol. 4 (Madrid: Union Musical Española, 1979).

25. On the Albero–Scarlatti comparison, see Giorgio Pestelli, *Le sonate di Domenico Scarlatti proposta di un ordinamento cronologico* (Torino: Giappichelli, 1967), pp. 224–231; and W. Dean Sutcliffe, "Domenico Scarlatti and an Iberian Keyboard 'School': A Comparison with Albero," in Dinko Fabris and Paologiovanni Maione, eds., *Domenico Scarlatti: musica e storia* (Naples: Turchini, 2010), pp. 269–290. Also see Sutcliffe, *The Keyboard Sonatas of Domenico Scarlatti*, pp. 224–225.

26. Nebra was appointed organist at the Descalzas Reales in 1719 and at the royal chapel in 1724; by 1751 he was vice chapel master of the royal chapel. He had also worked as Infante don Gabriel's harpsichord teacher since 1761.

27. Numbering from the Escalas edition cited as E, numbering from the Alvarez edition cited as A. The Sonata in F major (E-3) has been attributed to Galuppi in a German source and edited in *Baldassare Galuppi (1706–1785) Le Opere Strumentali*. Serie Prima, La musica per tastiera, Vol. 5, Manoscritti da fonti tedesche e inglesi, Giorgio Dal Monte (Sonatas 1–12) and Nicolò Sari (Sonates 13–21) eds. (Padova: Armelin Musica, 2014), No. 9 "Sonata in Fa Maggiore" (R.A. 1.8.10).

28. Born in Olot in 1729, Soler entered the Escolanía de Montserrat by 1735. Between 1746 and 1752 he was chapel master either in Lérida or in Seo de Urgel. In 1752 he was appointed organist at the Escorial Monastery, becoming chapel master in 1759. From 1773 to 1783 he taught the Infante, Don Gabriel de Borbón.

29. *XXVII Sonatas para Clave, por el Padre Fray Antonio Soler, que ha impreso Robert Birchall*. It contains the Sonatas 1–27, ed. Samuel Rubio, *P. Antonio*

Soler. Sonatas para instrumentos de tecla, 7 vols. (Madrid: Unión Musical Española, 1957–1972), Vol. 1 (Sonatas 1–20), and Vol. 2 (Sonatas 21–27).

30. Available data in Enrique Igoa's doctoral dissertation: *La cuestión de la forma en las Sonatas de Antonio Soler* (PhD diss., Universidad Complutense de Madrid, 2013), pp. 88–90. http://eprints.ucm.es/24593/1/T35203.pdf. See also G. Truett Hollis, "'El diablo vestido de fraile': Some Unpublished Correspondence of Padre Soler," *Music in Spain during the Eighteenth Century*, second edition (Cambridge: Cambridge University Press, 2006), pp. 192–206.

31. See Igoa, *La cuestión de la forma*, 2013.

32. The sonatas are cited according to the numbering in the Rubio edition, the most complete to date, despite errors and alterations. See Samuel Rubio, *P. Antonio Soler. Sonatas para instrumentos de tecla*, 7 vols. (Madrid: Unión Musical Española, 1957–1972).

33. Blasco de Nebra was born in Seville and had studied in Madrid under his uncle, José de Nebra, for several years until 1766. He probably met Soler during this period. In 1768 he was appointed his father's assistant as Seville Cathedral organist; some ten years later he inherited this position.

34. The most detailed study on the musical style of Blasco de Nebra is W. Dean Sutcliffe, "The Keyboard Works of Manuel Blasco de Nebra," in M. Ángel Marín and Marius Bernadó, eds., *Instrumental Music in Late Eighteenth-Century Spain* (Kassel: Reichenberger, 2004), pp. 306–307.

35. The twelve sonatas from the Montserrat manuscript *E-MO* 2998 are cited as "MO" in the numbering.

36. The sonatas from the *Six sonatas para clave y fuerte piano. Obra primera. In Madrid* (ca. 1770–80) are cited as "Ma" in the numbering.

37. Montero was organist at San Pedro el Real, Seville. Ten minuets of his have come to us as well, edited by Antonio Ruiz-Pipó as *Diez minuetes para clave y fuerte piano* (Madrid: UME, 1973). See also Linton Powell, "The Sonatas of Manuel Blasco de Nebra and Joaquín Montero," *Music Review* 41, no. 3 (1980), pp. 197–206; Linton Powell, *A History of Spanish Piano Music* (Bloomington: Indiana University Press, 1980); and Linton Powell, "Dos caballeros de Sevilla: la música de tecla de Manuel Blasco de Nebra y Joaquín Montero," in *Claves y pianos españoles: interpretación y repertorio hasta 1830*, ed. Luisa Morales, in *Actas del I y II Symposium Internacional "Diego Fernández" de música de tecla española Vera-Mojácar 2000–2001* (FIMTE, El Ejido: Instituto de Estudios Almerienses, 2003), pp. 205–208.

38. *Anselm Viola. Compositor, pedagog, monjo de Montserrat*, ed. Luisa Cortada (Barcelona: Publicacions de l'Abadia de Montserrat, 1998), pp. 249–341. The "C" numbering is the order in which they appear in this edition.

39. "Obres musicals dels monjos del Monestir de Montserrat (1500–1800) Música Instrumental," in *Mestres de l'Escolanía de Montserrat*, Vol. 2, David Pujol, ed. (Barcelona: Monestir de Montserrat, 1936).

40. *Miguel Espona: Sonatas para clavicordio o clavecín*, Serie 2C, ed. [no name], (Mollerusa: Scala Aretina 2001). *Narcís Casanoves i Bertrán. 6 Sonates per a piano*, Daniel Codina, ed. (Barcelona: Publicacions de l'Abadía de Montserrat, 1997). See also a study of the sources by Daniel Codina,

"Aproximació a l'obra per a tecla del P. Narcís Casanoves (1747–1799)," in *Anuario Musical* 48 (1993), pp. 143–151. *Carles Baguer: Siete Sonatas*, ed. M. A. Ester Sala (Madrid: UME, 1976); *Tres Sinfonías para tecla*, Serie C: Música de Cámara, 14, M. A. Ester Sala, ed. (Barcelona: Instituto Español de Musicología, 1984). *Josep Gallés: Vint-I-Tres Sonates pera tecla*, ed. Bengt Johnsson (Barcelona: Institut d'Estudis Catalans, Societat Catalana de Musicologia, 1995). See Susanne Skyrm, "Las 23 sonatas para tecla del padre José Gallés," in *Claves y pianos españoles: interpretación y repertorio hasta 1830*, Luisa Morales, ed. (Instituto de Estudios Almerienses, 2003), pp. 209–216.

41. See Benjamin Lipkowitz, "The Villahermosa Manuscript: An Important Source of Late Eighteenth-Century Spanish Keyboard Music," *Music in Spain*, pp. 207–213; Dionisio Preciado, *José Ferrer: Sonatas para clave* (Madrid: Real Musical, 1979), and *Doce compositores aragoneses de tecla siglo XVIII* (Madrid: Editora nacional, 1983). See Luisa Morales, "Fuentes de la Sonata R121," in *Nuevas Perspectivas sobre la música para tecla de Antonio Soler*, L. Morales and M. Latcham, eds. (Almería: Ediciones Leal, 2016), pp. 63–176, and "Juan Moreno y Polo, Sebastián Tomás y Anónimos, Obras para tecla del siglo XVIII. Ms. del Monasterio de San Pedro de las Dueñas (León)," in *Tecla Aragonesa*, V, Luisa Morales, ed. (Zaragoza: Institución Fernando el Católico, 1997). See also Mariano Cosuenda, *Seis sonatas para clave*, Jesús Gonzalo López, ed. (Zaragoza: Instituto "Fernando el Católico," 1998), and the anthology *Early Spanish Keyboard Music: An Anthology in Three Volumes*, Vol. 3, B. Ife and R. Truby, eds. (Oxford: Oxford University Press, 1986).

42. Oxinagas was organist at the royal chapel in 1749. *Obras musicales de Joaquín Ojinaga*, José López-Calo, ed., in *Cuadernos de música* Vol. 2 (San Sebastián: Sociedad de Estudios Vascos, 1989).

43. *Manuel Narro (1729–1776). Concert per a clave i orquesta (1767)*, María Gembero, ed. (Barcelona, Tritó: 2003). *Manuel Narro Campos 1729–1776. Obras de tecla*, José Climent and Rodrigo Madrid, eds. (Valencia: RACV, 2000).

44. *José Lidón. La música para teclado*, Vol, 2, Dámaso García Fraile, ed. (Madrid: Sociedad Española de Musicología, 2004). Vol. 1 (2002) contains only organ works.

45. *Cuaderno tercero de una colección de piezas de música para clavicordio, forte-piano y órgano. Obra 8ª*, cited in Baltasar Saldoni: *Diccionario biográfico-bibliográfico de efemérides de músicos españoles, Tomo II* (Imprenta de D. Antonio Pérez Dubrull, Madrid, 1880), pp. 117–118, based on the advertisments of *Gaceta de Madrid*. See also Félix de Latassa y Ortin, *Biblioteca nueva de los escritores aragoneses que florecieron desde el año de 1795 hasta el de 1802*, Tomo VI (Oficina de Joaquín de Domingo, Pamplona, 1802), pp. 223–224.

46. See also "José Teixidor y Barceló: Sonata para clave o fortepiano (1794)," and "José Teixidor: Sonatas de clave," Raúl Angulo, ed., in *Ars Hispana* (Fundación Gustavo Bueno, 2010, 2012). Also, Joaquín Asiain: *Tres sonatas para forte-piano dedicadas a el serenísimo Príncipe de Parma. Variaciones*

para forte-piano o clave, in *Ars Hispania*, Raúl Angulo, ed. (Fundación Gustavo Bueno, 2013).

47. Félix Máximo López began as fourth organist at the royal chapel in 1775 and gradually advanced until he became first organist in 1805. See Alma Espinosa, *The Keyboard Works of Félix Máximo López: An Anthology* (Washington, DC: University Press of America, 1983).

48. López arranged seven sonatas for the harpsichord from Haydn Symphonies, some with significant variants and excisions. See Alma Espinosa, "Félix Máximo López, Franz Joseph Haydn, and the Art of Homage," *Early Keyboard Journal* 16–17 (1998–1999), pp. 143–151. The Haydn symphonies are cited in Alma Espinosa "Música de clave de Félix Máximo López: ¿Realmente para clave?," in *Claves y pianos españoles*, L. Morales, ed. (Almería: Leal, 2003), pp. 177–204.

49. See also Laura Cuervo, "Repertorio musical en nueve cuadernos manuscritos para piano en la Biblioteca Nacional de España [1800–1810]," *Revista de Musicología* 36 (2013), pp. 225–256.

50. Entitled *Fandango de España*, it was attributed to José Nebra and edited by Rosario Alvarez in *Obras inéditas para tecla* (Madrid: Sociedad Española de Musicología, 1984), p. 52; J. Martí, J. Teixidor, J.T. Murguía, J. Codina. *Obras para fortepiano*, Pedro González, ed. (Madrid: RCSMM, 1991).

51. See Guillermo Castro, "A vueltas con el fandango. Nuevos documentos de estudio y análisis de la evolución rítmica en el género del fandango," *Sinfonia Virtual* 24 (2013) www.sinfoniavirtual.com/flamenco/ritmica_fandango.pdf; Judith Etzion, "The Spanish Fandango: From 18th-Century 'Lasciviousness' to 19th-Century Exoticism," *Anuario Musical* 48 (1993), pp. 229–250.

Further Reading

Esses, Maurice. *Dance and Instrumental Diferencias in Spain during the 17th and Early 18th Centuries*. Stuyvesant, NY: Pendragon Press, 1991.

Águeda Pedrero-Encabo. *La sonata para teclado: su configuracion en España*. Valladolid: Universidad de Valladolid, 1997.

Powell, Linton. *A History of Spanish Piano Music*. Bloomington: Indiana Universiy Press, 1980.

Sutcliffe, W. Dean. *The Keyboard Sonatas of Domenico Scarlatti and Eighteenth-Century Musical Style*. Cambridge: Cambridge University Press, 2003.

10 Domenico Scarlatti in Portugal and Spain

JOÃO PEDRO D'ALVARENGA AND ÁGUEDA
PEDRERO-ENCABO

Scarlatti in Portugal

JOÃO PEDRO D'ALVARENGA

In *Baltasar and Blimunda*, a novel by the Nobel Prize-winning Portuguese writer José Saramago, the harpsichord music of Domenico Scarlatti (1685–1757) is presented as having a liberating and subversive power, so revealing is its spirit of innovation, tolerance, and openness to progress and modernity.[1] Such an optimistic view is much at odds with the persistently shadowy situation of the composer and his music in modern historiography.

With Ralph Kirkpatrick's classic monograph from 1953 – still a subject of consideration and debate more than sixty years after its publication – Domenico Scarlatti was awarded his place in modern musicological narrative.[2] That place, however, remains on the fringe, regularly visited but seldom fully explored. Jane Clark, arguably one of the most probing of the Scarlatti scholars, stated that "writing about the sonatas" – and we would add, "and their composer" – is "a field so full of pitfalls that anyone willing to risk an opinion is risking a great deal."[3] Few have taken this risk, even if the Scarlattian literature is limitless. Scarcity of secure first-hand documentary evidence and biographical data and the absence of musical autographs have been the major obstacles in assessing the composer and his output. The absolute contrast between Joel Sheveloff's and Roberto Pagano's entries for the last two editions of the *New Grove* elucidates the kind of concurrent approaches, as the first totally avoids conjecture, sticking to the known facts and leaving out second-hand anecdotal sources, while the latter takes these as convenient testimonies and indulges in a novelistic speculation to fill in the many missing details.[4] The apparent success of Pagano's approach to Domenico's biography lies in the centrality of the commonplace psychological plot of the overshadowing paternal figure, whose death finally allows the insecure son "to become properly himself" – an approach rooted in the "profound knowledge of Sicilian history and culture and an unrivaled awareness of the Sicilian 'psyche,'" as the author proudly admits, quoting one of his reviewers.[5]

A more serious and balanced narrative of Scarlatti's life, equally cover-
ing his entire career (while Kirkpatrick gave particular weight to Scarlatti's
years in Portugal and Spain), considering both his vocal and instrumental
output and avoiding conjectures about the composer's character and
psychology, is Malcolm Boyd's 1986 monograph.[6] However, the groundbreaking work in Scarlattian scholarship, even if received with mixed
feelings, is Dean Sutcliffe's 2003 book, which, while focusing on the sonatas
and problems of musical syntax and style, includes a comprehensive critical commentary on the existing literature, pinpointing the unsolved
issues and contradictions in the accounts of Domenico's life and career to
date.[7] Recent developments in the research of Scarlattian subjects has
centered on Domenico's Portuguese and Spanish periods, including new
biographical evidence and newly discovered Spanish sources for his keyboard works.[8]

Domenico Scarlatti's early career until late 1719 unfolded in Naples,
Florence, Venice, and Rome. It was not atypical for an eighteenth-century
Italian-born composer. He apparently had a precocious aptitude for keyboard performance and improvisation, seriously engaged in opera and
chamber vocal music composition, and held a number of prestigious
positions in noble households and major ecclesiastical institutions.
The commissioning of the *Applauso genetliaco* by the Portuguese ambassador extraordinary to Rome, Rodrigo Anes de Sá Almeida e Menezes, 3rd
Marquis of Fontes – a *serenata* sung on the night of 10 August 1714 on
a stage specially constructed at the Piazza Colonna facing the residence of
the Marquis – marked the turning point in Domenico's life. Five years
later, after having left his post as chapel master of the Cappella Giulia in
early September, he arrived in Lisbon on November 29, 1719, coming
overland. He had been expected "anxiously by the King," João V, and
then "impatiently," to be "the head, and director of all his music in the
Patriarchal Church" – a position that has been insistently mistaken for that
of chapel master.[9]

Following his arrival, on December 27, 1719, Domenico Scarlatti and
tenor Gaetano Mossi were assigned to the service of the *Infante* Dom
António (1695–1757), the King's younger brother, with the titles of
Maestro and Virtuoso, respectively.[10] No document allows us to conclude
that Scarlatti was in the direct service of the *Infanta* Maria Bárbara
(1711–1758), the King's eldest daughter, Princess of Asturias and later
Queen of Spain by marriage with Fernando VI, earlier than 1729.

Domenico Scarlatti certainly remained in Lisbon for more than three
whole years, from late 1719 to 1722. Between 1723 and late 1725 he
traveled in succession to Naples, possibly London, Paris, Rome, and once
again to Paris. He was probably in Lisbon in the year 1726, though no

record of his activity has so far emerged for this period, and he returned once more to Rome via Massa on February 2, 1727, passing one last time through Lisbon in late September 1729 before going permanently to Spain.[11] The first period he spent in Lisbon, between 1720 and 1722, corresponds to the one with the highest rate of documented compositional activity.[12] Reference should, however, be made to the paucity of sonatas by Scarlatti in eighteenth-century Portuguese sources of keyboard music, a situation that clearly contrasts with that in Spain, where many of his sonatas seem to have enjoyed a wide dissemination.[13] Nonetheless, documentary evidence, particularly from the late 1740s and early 1750s, suggests that Scarlatti sonatas were held in a high esteem in the circles most closely associated with the court and that copies from Madrid were then commissioned and received in Lisbon.[14]

It is quite possible that Domenico had acted as a kind of agent for King João V. This would explain many of his life decisions. Such a suspicion is particularly justified by a number of strange circumstances: His travels to Paris have left no trace except in official diplomatic correspondence; he was apparently not able to completely fulfill his functions as "composer of Italian music," having to be replaced by Giovanni Giorgi (d. 1762) as of late January 1725; and he unexpectedly moved to Spain – that is, to obscurity – under the king's command, to supervise Maria Bárbara, not only musically, it seems, but also politically. This can be judged from the fact that the Portuguese king, "in view of certain particular reasons," presented him for a knighthood in the Order of St James in 1738, also granting him by decree of June 10, 1739 an annuity of 400,000 *réis* to be debited to the accounts of the Lisbon Customs. As dedicatee, the king also presumably paid for the lavish London printing of the *Essercizi*. Moreover, since the Portuguese "particular" also means "reserved," or even "private," these rewards and the "particular reasons" certainly had nothing to do with music but rather with other types of services.[15] Scarlatti made at least two abortive attempts to return to Portugal, in 1744 and 1748. The reasons why he does not succeed in leaving Spain are, again, obscure. Alexandre de Gusmão, secretary to King João V, in a letter from late January 1748, says that he was "doing all the diligences to obtain permission for our Scarlatti to come to this country, as he much desires, but with little hope, because of several scruples that are presented, which will not be easy to overcome."[16] It is not clear what the impediments referred to by Gusmão were and who created them, but it seems that, contrary to his wishes, Scarlatti never managed to leave Spain after he had arrived in Seville in late 1729.

Scarlatti in Spain

ÁGUEDA PEDRERO-ENCABO

The sonatas of Domenico Scarlatti apparently circulated only through manuscript copies within Spain during the eighteenth century.[17] Most stayed within the confines of the royal court, from where they were spread by nearby organists, such as José Nebra, Sebastián Albero, or "Padre" Soler.[18] In fact, handwritten copies are the only evidence of the reception of early printed editions in Spain.[19] However, some Scarlatti sonatas were widely disseminated in Europe during his lifetime, through various editions and reprints in Paris, London, and Amsterdam.[20] Recent research has revealed that the Parisian publications were first, such as the *Pièces Choisi[e]s pour clavecin ou l'orgue. Opera Prima* (ca. 1737), probably being the earliest.[21] Scarlatti's reputation throughout Europe as a keyboard composer began with these editions, probably published in the following sequence: *Pièces Choisi[e]s* (Paris, 1737), *Pièces* (Paris, 1737), *Essercizi* (London: Fortier, 1738/9), Roseingrave (London: Cooke, 1739), and the Parisian Boivin I and Boivin II (ca. 1740–1742, comprising the same works as those in the Roseingrave edition).[22]

The *Essercizi* is undoubtedly the most significant of these collections, being a selection from which Scarlatti would have excluded the more conservative sonatas (e.g., K31–K42 in the edition by Roseingrave, who possibly obtained them in Italy from drafts given to him by the composer himself).[23] In fact, the *Essercizi* sonatas included in Venice, 1742 (K3, K10, K11, K12, and K17) offer earlier versions than those found in the Fortier edition.[24] This seems to confirm that these were transmitted individually, and that most were probably in circulation prior to the "official" versions in Fortier and the newly discovered manuscript in the *Orfeó Català* (1740).

A study of the *Orfeó Català* manuscript has revealed that it was copied in the Court of Madrid by José Alaguero, one of the copyists in the service of the Royal Chamber.[25] A comparative analysis of Alaguero's writing with other manuscripts containing Scarlatti's sonatas affirms that he was also the only copyist of all the volumes of Venice (including 1742 and 1749); the Parma series; the "Ayerbe manuscript;" and finally, two of the codices preserved in the Music Archive of the Cathedrals of Saragossa (*Libro 1º* and *Libro 2º*).[26] The Orfeó manuscript is also interesting because it presents a different order for the collection of sonatas-essercizi, and thus breaks with the pedagogical sequence that seems to be proposed in the Fortier edition.[27] Although only this second volume has been located, it is presumed that there was a first, since the Orfeó begins *in media res* with Sonata XVI. Its cover also has similar characteristics to the later Venetian codices, so it can be deduced that it was designed in two volumes (probably to emulate Roseingrave`s publication). The Orfeó original was probably Scarlatti's own draft; he would have been involved in the copying, but not the correcting.[28]

Recent research provides new data for Scarlatti's compositional activity prior to the aforementioned outpouring of publications, which actually ocurred when the composer had already been settled on the Iberian Peninsula for eighteen years.[29] One of the manuscripts preserved in the Bibliothèque de l'Arsenal in Paris offers interesting information about the early diffusion of some of the sonatas, like the famous Sonata K29.[30] This work, characterized by its exuberant and histrionic hand crossings, appears in the Paris source with only the most "natural" crossing of the hands, suggesting that it is an earlier version that predates the virtuosic displays found in Scarlatti's later revisions, such as the *Essercizi*, Orfeó manuscript, and Roseingrave/Boivin II prints.[31]

Also noteworthy in this source is Sonata K17, whose presence in an anonymous copyist fascicle reveals its connection with the workshop of the famous engraver "Roussel" (Claude, or his daughter, Louise).[32] The antiquity of this source has allowed us to place it in circulation in Paris at a very early stage, together with the Sonatas K9, K11, K29, K31, K39 and K66 made by the same copyist. It is possible that these sonatas were carried to Paris by Scarlatti himself in one of his documented trips to the French capital in 1724 or 1725, a possibility that has opened up a new area of research into the connection between Scarlatti and Rameau regarding the development of the innovative hand-crossing technique.[33]

As has been widely discussed, one of the most recognizable features of the Scarlattian style is the inspiration freely taken from Mediterranean folk and popular materials, especially dance rhythms. Scarlatti usually adopts a generic approach by reworking the impressions of sounds, rhythms, and gestures associated with the popular world, but in some cases it is possible to identify an actual dance rhythm. One well-known example is the recognizable *seguidilla* pattern in Sonata K380; another is the Portuguese fandango found in Sonata K492.[34]

Several sonatas from the earlier period also show Scarlatti's attraction to the rhythms and gestures of popular dance, such as Sonatas K5, K6, K7, K17, K26, K28, and K33. The imitation of guitar techniques can be found in Sonata K14 (as in the guitar-like *rasgueado* and the effect of the pedal on A) and in Sonata K24, with its passages of *rasgueados*, appoggiaturas and brilliant toccata-style hand crossings. In Sonata K29, the repeated chords that imitate the strumming guitar style are emphasized by the sonority of the Phrygian tetrachord with the augmented second, E-D♯-C-B.

Much has been written about the Scarlatti style (e.g., Kirkpatrick, Boyd, et al.), but new methodological approaches have allowed us to go beyond formalistic views, enabling us to expand our understanding of the rich stylistic features of the composer.[35] Sutcliffe, for example, offers a new vision in which Scarlatti's diverse musical languages are combined and contrasted within the same work.[36] This diversity, along with the development of a freer keyboard writing style and an original, expressive harmonic language, places Scarlatti as one of the most fascinating keyboard composers in the history of harpsichord music.

Notes

1. Portuguese original published as *Memorial do Convento* (Lisbon: Editorial Caminho, 1982); English translation by Giovanni Pontiero first published in 1987 (New York: Harcourt Brace Jovanovich).
2. Ralph Kirkpatrick, *Domenico Scarlatti* (Princeton: Princeton University Press, 1953).
3. Jane Clark, "Review of *Domenico Scarlatti: Master of Music* by Malcolm Boyd," *The Musical Times* 128, no. 1730 (1987), p. 209.
4. Joel Sheveloff, "(Giuseppe) Domenico Scarlatti," in *The New Grove Dictionary of Music and Musicians*, ed. Stanley Sadie (London: Macmillan, 1980), Vol. 16, pp. 568–578; Roberto Pagano (with contributions by Malcolm Boyd), "(Giuseppe) Domenico Scarlatti," in *Grove Music Online*, www.oxfordmusiconline.com/subscriber/article/grove/music/24708pg7, first published in *The New Grove Dictionary of Music and Musicians*, second edition, ed. Stanley Sadie and John Tyrrell (London: Macmillan, 2001), Vol. 22, pp. 398–402.
5. Roberto Pagano, *Scarlatti – Alessandro e Domenico: due vite in una* (Milan: Arnoldo Mondadori, 1985), p. 409; English translation by Frederik Hammond as *Alessandro and Domenico Scarlatti: Two Lives in One* (Hillsdale, NY: Pendragon Press, 2006), with references (not always elegant) to post-1985 scholarship; revised edition as *Alessandro e Domenico Scarlatti: Due vita in una*, 2 vols. (Lucca: Libreria Musicale Italiana, 2015); and Pagano, *Alessandro e Domenico*, rev. ed., p. xiv, quoting Malcolm Boyd, *Domenico Scarlatti: Master of Music* (London: Weidenfeld and Nicolson, 1986), p. 27.
6. Boyd, *Domenico Scarlatti*.
7. See W. Dean Sutcliffe, *The Keyboard Sonatas of Domenico Scarlatti and Eighteenth-Century Musical Style* (New York: Cambridge University Press, 2003), and Michael Talbot, "Review of *The Keyboard Sonatas of Domenico Scarlatti and Eighteenth-Century Musical Style* by W. Dean Sutcliffe," *Echo: A Music-Centered Journal* 6, no. 1 (2004), www.echo.ucla.edu/Volume6-issue1/reviews/talbot.html.
8. See João Pedro d'Alvarenga, "Domenico Scarlatti in the 1720s: Portugal, Travelling, and the Italianisation of the Portuguese Musical Scene," in *Domenico Scarlatti Adventures: Essays to Commemorate the 250th Anniversary of His Death*, ed. Massimiliano Sala and W. Dean Sutcliffe, *Ad Parnassum Studies* 3 (Bologna: Ut Orpheus Edizioni, 2008), pp. 17–68; Gerhard Doderer, "Aspectos novos em torno da estadia de Domenico

Scarlatti na corte de D. João V (1719–1727)," *Revista Portuguesa de Musicologia* 1 (1991), pp. 147–174; Doderer, "Some Remarks on Domenico Scarlatti's Portuguese Period (1719–1729)," in *Domenico Scarlatti: Musica e storia*, ed. Dinko Fabris and Paologiovanni Maione (Naples: Turchini Edizioni, 2010), pp. 225–247; Serguei N. Prozhoguin, "Rileggendo la lettera di Domenico Scarlatti," in *Domenico Scarlatti Adventures*, ed. Sala and Sutcliffe, pp. 69–154; and Prozhoguin, "Cinque Studi su Domenico Scarlatti," *Ad Parnassum: A Journal of Eighteenth- and Nineteenth-Century Instrumental Music* 8, no. 16 (2010), pp. 97–[198]. See note 17 for the references to studies on Spanish manuscript sources.

9. See Alvarenga, "Domenico Scarlatti in the 1720s," pp. 23–24, and 42–44.

10. See Alvarenga, "Domenico Scarlatti in the 1720s," p. 26.

11. On Scarlatti's stays in Lisbon and traveling years, see Alvarenga, "Domenico Scarlatti in the 1720s," especially pp. 21–38.

12. At least nine full-length *serenatas* and ten to thirteen sacred vocal works, including a four-choir *Te Deum* with full orchestral accompaniment for the year's end in 1721, two complete sets of responsories, and possibly also the ten-voice *Stabat mater*; see the list of works in Alvarenga, "Domenico Scarlatti in the 1720s," pp. 67–68 and p. 54 for the *Stabat mater*.

13. The only Scarlatti sonatas surviving in Portuguese sources are: K85, K82, K78/i, K94 in *P-Cug* MM 58; K50 in *P-Ln* MM 338; K98, K43 and K24 in *F-Pn* Vm^7 4874.

14. See Manuel Carlos de Brito, "Novos dados sobre a música no reinado de D. João V," in *Livro de Homenagem a Macario Santiago Kastner*, ed. Maria Fernanda Cidrais Rodrigues, Manuel Morais and Rui Vieira Nery (Lisbon: Fundação Calouste Gulbenkian, 1992), pp. 515–533, here pp. 526–527. The *Libro di tocate*, *P-Ln* F.C.R. 194.1, containing a hitherto unknown Sonata in A major and published in facsimile by Gerhard Doderer as *Domenico Scarlatti: Libro di tocate per cembalo* (Lisbon: Instituto Nacional de Investigação Científica, 1991), is almost certainly of Spanish provenance.

15. On these aspects of Domenico's life and career and especially his move to Spain, see also Jane Clark, "Farinelli as Queen of the Night," in *Eighteenth-Century Music* 2, no. 2 (2005), pp. 321–323, particularly p. 324. Marie-Thérèse Mandroux-França also wonders if the Parisian travels were not "a mission supported by João V"; see her "Journal d'une collection d'estampes 1724–1728," in Pierre-Jean Mariette, *Catalogues de la collection d'estampes de Jean V, roi de Portugal*, ed. J. Thuillier, M.-T. Mandroux-França, and M. Préaud, Vol. 1, *Préfaces – études – notes – index* (Lisbon, Paris: Fundação Calouste Gulbenkian, Bibliothèque Nationale de France, Fundação da Casa de Bragança, 2003), p. 316.

16. Alexandre de Gusmão, letter to the Arcediago de Oliveira, Lisbon, January 26, 1748, in *Alexandre de Gusmão: Cartas*, ed. Andrée Rocha (Lisbon: Imprensa Nacional-Casa da Moeda, 1981), p. 134.

17. For some of the important sources on this subject, see Malcom Boyd, *Domenico Scarlatti: Master of Music* (London: Weidenfeld and Nicolson, 1986), pp. 154–157; Joel Sheveloff, "Tercentenary Frustations," *The Musical Quarterly* 71, no. 4 (1985), pp. 399–436; W. Dean Sutcliffe, *The Keyboard Sonatas of Domenico Scarlatti*, p. 70; Maria A. Ester Sala, "Domenico

Scarlatti-Granados: noticia sobre la localización de un manuscrito de tecla extraviado," in *Livro de homenagem a Macario Santiago Kastner* eds. M. F. Cidrais, M. Morais and R. Veira Nery (Lisbon: Fundaçao Calouste Gulbenkian, 1992), pp. 16–252; Águeda Pedrero-Encabo, ed., *Domenico Scarlatti: Tres sonates inédites per a clavicèmbal* (Barcelona: Tritó, 2011); Laura Cuervo, "El manuscrito Ayerbe: una fuente española de las sonatas de Domenico Scarlatti de mediados del siglo XVIII," in *Ad Parnassum Studies* 13, no. 25 (2015), 1–26; and Celestino Yáñez, *Nuevas aportaciones para el estudio de las sonatas de Domenico Scarlatti. Los manuscritos del Archivo de Música de las Catedrales de Zaragoza*, 3 vols. (PhD diss., Universitat Autònoma de Barcelona, 2015).

18. Single copies are found in Montserrat, Valladolid, Tenerife, and País Vasco, some of which were altered to make them more idiomatic for the organ (see Boyd, *Domenico Scarlatti*, p. 190).

19. See Águeda Pedrero-Encabo, "Una nuova fonte degli 'Essercizi' di Domenico Scarlatti: il manoscritto Orféo Catalá (E-OC)," in *Fonti Musicali Italiane* (2012), pp. 151–173; and Boyd, *Domenico Scarlatti*, p. 156.

20. Boyd has remarked that only seventy-three of Scarlatti's ca. 550 sonatas were published during his lifetime (Boyd, *Domenico Scarlatti*, p. 159). See also Joel Sheveloff, *The Keyboard Music of Domenico Scarlatti: A Re-Evaluation of the Present State of Knowledge in the Light of the Sources* (Michigan: UMI Research Press, 1970), pp. 145–155.

21. *Pièces Choisi[e]s pour le clavecin ou l'orgue. Opera Prima* (Paris: Boivin, [1737]), RISM S 1196.

22. *Pièces pour le clavecin*, Paris: Boivin [1737] RISM S 1197; *Essercizi per gravicembalo*, London: [B. Fortier, 1738/1739], RISM S 1189; *XLII Suites de Pièces* [ed. by Roseingrave] London: Cooke [1739], RISM S 1190; *Pièces pour le clavecin*, 1er volumen, Paris: Boivin [1740], RISM S 1198. *Pièces pour le clavecin*, 2e volumen, Paris: Boivin [1742], RISM S 1199. Dates taken from Jean Duron, "La recepción de la obra de Domenico Scarlatti en Francia," in *Sevilla y corte: las artes y el lustro Real (1729–1733)*, ed. Nicolás Morales and Fernando Quiles García (Sevilla: Casa de Velázquez, 2010), pp. 318–319. About the date of the *Essercizi*, see Sergei N. Prozhoguin, "Cinque studi su Domenico Scarlatti," *Ad Parnassum Studies* 8, no. 16 (2010), p. 158.

23. Boyd, *Domenico Scarlatti*, p. 162.

24. The volumes housed in Zaragoza's Archive and in the Catalunya Library contain some sonatas-essercizi: K30 (*E-ZAc*, fuente 1); K6, K16, K12, K23, K17, and K14 (*E-ZAc*, fuente 3); K10 (*E-ZAc*, fuente 4); and K23, K16, K25, K27, K17, and K19 (E-Bbc M 1964). These confirm their circulation in Spain as individual works. The data are taken respectively from Yáñez, *Nuevas aportaciones*, Vol. 2. and Pedrero-Encabo, *Tres sonates*, pp. 24–28.

25. *Sonate, per cembalo/ del Sig^r. D^n. Domenico./ Scarlatti, &./1740*. It is housed in the Palau de la Música. Biblioteca del Orfeó Catalá (*E-Boc* MM 12-VI-17): http://mdc.cbuc.cat/cdm/compoundobject/collection/MMautors/id/995/rec/1/lang/ca. This source contaits fifteen sonatas-essercizi, in the following order: K20, K4, K8, K19, K27, K16, K26, K25, K23, K21, K28, K24, K18, K29, K30 (Pedrero-Encabo, "Una nuova fonte," pp. 155–156).

26. Alaguero was also the copyist of the two volumes with works of Sebastián Albero mentioned in Chapter 9. On recent discoveries about the Münster manuscripts and their copyists see Anthony Hart, "A Re-evaluation of the Keyboard Sonatas of Domenico Scarlatti in the Santini Collection in Münster," *Studi Musicali nuova serie*, 2 no. 1 (2011), pp. 49–66; Anthony Hart, "New Findings on the Possible Copyists and Owners of the Scarlatti Sonata Manuscripts in Münster: The Role of Antonino Reggio," *Early Music* 39, no. 1 (February, 2011), pp. 57–64.

27. Todd Decker, "The Essercizi and the editors," in *Domenico Scarlatti Adventures*, p. 310.

28. See Pedrero-Encabo, "Una nuova fonte," pp. 157–158.

29. Duron, "La recepción," pp. 313–328; and Prozhoguin,"Cinque studi," pp. 97–198.

30. Paris, Bibliothèque de l'Arsenal (*F-Pa*: Ms 6784.343); source description in Sheveloff, *The Keyboard Music*, pp. 97–100.

31. In this case, the early status of the source and the antiquity of the copy are fundamental, since later editions, such as Ambrose Pitman's *The Beauties of Dominico Scarlatti*, chose to remove certain hand crossings in order to make it easier to play. See Ambrose Pitman, *The Beauties of Dominico Scarlatti* (London, 1770?), Preface, p. 2, digitalized in: www.erato.uvt.nl /files/imglnks/usimg/8/84/IMSLP59390-PMLP121828-Scarlatti _-_Pitman_1785.pdf. This topic has been discussed by Pedrero-Encabo, "Playing Scarlatti: Keys and Questions about the Performance of Some Keyboard Sonatas through the Analysis of Early Sources," at the *2nd International Conference on Historical Keyboard Music: The Keyboard and Its Role in the Internationalisation of Music 1600–1800*, University of Edinburgh, July 19–21, 2013.

32. See Prozhoguin, "Cinque studi," pp. 160–161. Claude Roussel (1655?–1720s) was the printer of music collections such as the *Premier livre de pièces de clavecin* of Rameau (Paris, 1706). The best-known editions by Louise Roussel (1700–1774) are Rameau's *Pieces de clavessin avec une méthode* . . . (Paris, [1724]) and the *Nouvelles suites de pièces de clavecin* (Paris, [1727]).

33. On Scarlatti's travels to Paris, see note 8.

34. About the fandango of Scarlatti, see Guillermo Castro, "A vueltas con el fandango. Nuevos documentos de estudio y análisis de la evolución rítmica en el género del fandango," *Sinfonia Virtual* 24 (2013), p. 6: www .sinfoniavirtual.com/flamenco/ritmica_fandango.pdf; Guillermo Castro, "Rhythmic Evolution in the Spanish Fandango: Binary and Ternary Rhythms," in *The Global Reach of the Fandango in Music, Song and Dance: Spaniards, Indians, Africans and Gypsies*, ed. K. Meira Goldberg and Antoni Pizà (Newcastle: Cambridge Scholars Publishing, 2016), pp. 120–152. (This volume is a revised and translated edition of bilingual conference proceedings published by the Junta de Andalucía, Consejería de Cultura: Centro de Documentación Musical de Andalucía, *Música Oral del Sur*, Vol. 12 (2015). The bilingual proceedings may be accessed here: www .centrodedocumentacionmusicaldeandalucia.es/opencms/documentacion/ revistas/revistas-mos/musica-oral-del-sur-n12.html.) Although some

examples may be questionable, see also Jane Clark, "Domenico Scarlatti and Spanish Folk Music: A Performer's Re-appraisal," in *Early Music* 4, no. 1 (1976), pp. 19–21; Donna O'Steen Edwards, "Iberian Elements in the Sonatas of Domenico Scarlatti" (DMA diss., North Texas University, 1980); Rafael Puyana, "Influencias ibéricas y aspectos por investigar en la obra para clave de Domenico Scarlatti," in *España en la música de Occidente*, Actas del Congreso Internacional celebrado en Salamanca, 29 de octubre–5 de noviembre de 1985, 2 vols., ed. Ismael Fernández de la Cuesta, José López-Calo, and Emilio Casares (Madrid: Ministerio de Cultura, INAEM, 1987), Vol. 2, pp. 51–60; Emilia Fadini, "Domenico Scarlatti: integrazione tra lo stile andaluso e lo stile italiano," in *Domenico Scarlatti Adventures*, pp. 155–196. A recent approach can be found in Luisa Morales, "Sonatas-Bolero by Domenico Scarlatti," *Domenico Scarlatti en España*, in proceedings of the *FIMTE* Symposia 2006–2007, ed. Luisa Morales (Almería: Leal, 2009), pp. 313–325.

35. For other discussions about the stylistic approach, see Giorgio Pestelli, *Le sonate di Domenico Scarlatti: proposta di un ordinamento cronologico* (Torino: Giappicheli, 1967), although his proposed chronological ordering is not consistent; Pedrero-Encabo, "Domenico Scarlatti," *La sonata para teclado: su configuración en España* (Valladolid: Uva, 1997), pp. 202–226; Pedrero-Encabo, "Scarlatti, Domenico. III. Las sonatas para teclado;" in *Diccionario de la Música Española e Hispanoamericana*, eds. Emilio Casares Rodicio, Ismael Fernández de la Cuesta and José López-Calo (Madrid: SGAE, 2002), vol. 9, pp. 855–857; Rosalind Halton, "Domenico Scarlatti and His Cantabile Sonatas," *Musicology Australia* 25 (2002), pp. 22–48; Sara Gross Ceballos, "Scarlatti and María Bárbara: A Study of Musical Portraiture," in *Domenico Scarlatti Adventures*, pp. 197–223; and Rohan H. Stewart-MacDonald, "The Minor Mode as Archaic Signifier in the Solo Keyboard Works of Domenico Scarlatti and Muzio Clementi," in *Domenico Scarlatti Adventures*, pp. 401–443.

36. Sutcliffe, *The Keyboard Sonatas*, pp. 78–144; and Chris Willis, "One Man Show: Improvisation as Theatre in Domenico Scarlatti's Keyboard Sonatas," in *Domenico Scarlatti Adventures*, pp. 271–308. On the reception of Scarlatti by Haydn see Federico Celestini, "Die Scarlatti-Rezeption bei Haydn und die Entfaltung der Klaviertechnik in dessen frühen Klaviersonaten," *Studien zur Musikwissenschaft. Beihefte der Denkmäler der Tonkunst in Österreich* 47 (1999), pp. 95–127.

Further Reading

Boyd, Malcolm. *Domenico Scarlatti: Master of Music*. London: Weidenfeld and Nicolson, 1986.

Kirkpatrick, Ralph. *Domenico Scarlatti*. Princeton: Princeton University Press, 1953.

Pagano, Roberto. *Alessandro and Domenico Scarlatti: Two Lives in One*. Hillsdale, NY: Pendragon Press, 2006.

Sutcliffe, W. Dean. *The Keyboard Sonatas of Domenico Scarlatti and Eighteenth-Century Musical Style*. New York: Cambridge University Press, 2003.

11 Russia

MARINA RITZAREV

The idea of associating eighteenth-century Russian harpsichord music with the gorgeous collection of instruments in Saint Petersburg museums would be misleading.[1] Instruments as artifacts reflect many things, especially the great wealth of the Russian aristocracy and its desire to consume European culture. However, if we examine the relevant libraries and archives for all the available sources of Russian harpsichord music with the corresponding instruments of the period, we discover that the two groups do not match: compared to the number of instruments, there are relatively few collections of music.

Could it be that in Russia, expensive and beautiful instruments had a greater chance of survival than the music itself? Considering the many upheavals in Russian history, this might indeed be true, at least in some measure. Or perhaps the opposite is the case: aristocratic refugees tried to save cultural relics from potential revolutionary vandalism by taking old scores with them but were forced to leave the instruments behind. We can speculate about the reasons for this discrepancy, but the conclusion to be drawn from this investigation is that the harpsichord repertoire in eighteenth-century Russia was probably small in quantity. In fact, this chapter could list only approximately one dozen harpsichord pieces and another dozen works written optionally for harpsichord or fortepiano and thereby complete our discussion of the harpsichord culture in eighteenth-century Russia. However, by placing this phenomenon in historical, political, and cultural contexts, we can also ask why this is the case.

The history of instrumental music in Russia, beginning at the very birth of the Russian state and continuing with medieval Russia and its adoption of Christian Orthodoxy as its official religion, is long and complicated. At the outset, Russian Orthodoxy forbade the use of instruments in church, following the Hebrew tradition prohibiting them in synagogues, in remembrance of the destruction of the Second Temple. This fidelity to that tradition, however, also reflected immediate practical needs. In fact, instrumental music as part of religious ritual represented an evil for Orthodoxy, which had two principal rivals and enemies: pagan minstrels from within the country (i.e., *skomorokhi*) and the Roman Catholic Church from the outside.

Yet, from the viewpoint of Orthodoxy, it was a difficult struggle to eliminate instrumental music from the ritual without diminishing the attractiveness and influence of the Church. This went so far that in the middle of the seventeenth century the Church decided to persecute and exile the *skomorokhi* and destroy their instruments, church officials claiming that the instrumental culture growing within the Western Catholic Church was "Latin heresy." These and other factors contributed to the belated development of instrumental music in Russia and other Orthodox countries.[2]

However, what was forbidden for the Church and the general population was fully embraced at the courts of the Russian Tsars. The first keyboard instruments appeared there as early as the late sixteenth century, in 1586, during the reign of Tsar Fedor Ioannovich (1557–1598), a gift from Queen Elizabeth I of England to Tsarina Irina Fedorovna, brought to Russia by the Englishman Jerome Horsey, who later wrote: "The Emporis [*sic*] his sister invited to behold the same [gifts], admired especially at the organes and virgenalls, all gilt and enambled [*sic*], never seinge nor heeringe the like before, woundered and delighted at the lowd and musicall sound therof."[3] Of course, they served more as a precious toy rather than something that could reflect cultural tastes or tradition. Nevertheless, the beginning of instrumental music had been established. Gradually, keyboard instruments became a standard feature of secular court life, captivating high society with the possibilities of reproducing familiar songs and dance tunes in a new medium.[4] Remarkably, however, while plucked single-manual keyboard instruments were being imported, a number of shops making portable organs already existed in seventeenth-century Moscow, particularly within its German Quarter. These new Western instruments, however, did not push out traditional plucked instruments like the *gusli* or *bandura*, with their rich sound and textural possibilities.[5] These coexisted with keyboard instruments quite far into the eighteenth century.

Russia underwent enormous cultural changes and growth in the eighteenth century. The members of the aristocracy had experienced extremely hard times during the Petrine reign (1698–1725) and were especially devastated after being transferred to the new capital of Saint Petersburg from Moscow, where they had earned a living from their estates. The Petrine reforms, sometimes called the "Petrine revolution," drastically changed the social and cultural environment. One of the consequences, in light of the lack of an existing keyboard culture in seventeenth-century Russia, was that it was difficult if not impossible to develop anything even remotely comparable to that in Western Europe, particularly because there was nothing upon which to base the creation of an instrumental culture in general and the harpsichord in particular, a problem exacerbated by the lack of necessity, money, or resources. Concepts such as trained musicians, music printing, or teachers simply did not exist. Nevertheless, beginning with earlier Renaissance-baroque models, both spheres gradually gained momentum and progressed to a mature classicism by the end of the century.

This process was also accelerated by the Westernization of Russia after Saint Petersburg was founded, especially after the Tsar insisted on the development of a social life and court entertainments, both highly stimulating for secular music. Keyboard instruments, among other cultural novelties, spread throughout aristocratic circles, their variety widened with increasing imports from Europe. Among the scarce evidence for this development is a newspaper announcement of 1729 telling the readers that the organist of the St. Katharinen Church in Danzig (now Gdańsk, Poland), Theophil Andreas Volckmar (Volkmann), offered to music lovers a "large clavecin and large clavichord."[6] Nevertheless, the growth of instruments in the possession of the Russian aristocracy could still be counted only in single units, and no principal changes in repertoire took place; rather, it consisted of the same songs and dances. The only noticeable difference was in genres: New dances such as the minuet, bourrée, and siciliana made steady inroads into the Russian soundscape.

The earliest Russian collection of harpsichord music is a handwritten album bearing the name of its owner, Prince Dolgoruky, and the date 1724.[7] The collection contained a few keyboard pieces and several violin parts. Unfortunately, it is now lost, and we only know it from a description made by the musicologist Anatoly Drozdov in 1937, who saw it in Dmitrov – an ancient town near Moscow. Drozdov mentions minuets and "La sicilienne," and "L'Harmonieux Rondeau" in the French style among the works of the collection.[8]

From this weak piece of evidence, we might conclude that the harpsichord was used more for basso continuo in ensemble with other instruments or voice, rather than as a solo instrument. The same is true for our next example from this period: "Mezhdu delom bezdelie, ili Sobranie raznykh pesen s prilozhennymi tonami na tri golosa" ("Idleness Midst Labor, or a Collection of Various Songs with Music for Three Voices") by Gregory Teplov.[9] A series of new Russian songs, so-called *Rossiyskaya pesnya* in *galant* style, specifies that the accompaniment instrument was the harpsichord.

The fruits of the Petrine revolution began to be felt more strongly in the second third of the eighteenth century, namely from the 1730s, when several dozen Italian musicians arrived, thus establishing not only Italian opera but also an entire infrastructure of European music in Russian culture. This resulted in the development of an increased taste and desire for music, and more resources as well. To cite one example, the German harpsichordist Gertrude Koenig gave lessons to distinguished pupils at Empress Anna Ioannovna's court (r. 1730–1740).

From this point on, Russian cultural life in the eighteenth century developed under three main influences: Italian architecture, painting, cuisine, and music; French etiquette, literature, and fashion; and German military skills, science, crafts, and urbanism. Many foreigners found opportunities in the vibrant dynamic of building the new Westernized Russia. These and other factors contributed to the growing hunger for Western culture.

While there is little evidence to calculate the number of keyboard instruments in early eighteenth-century Russia, by the 1740s one gets the general impression that the harpsichord primarily remained at the imperial court and with the elite aristocracy, while the clavichord, although used in high society alongside the harpsichord, enjoyed broad popularity among the people. One reason for this was that the clavichord was portable, smaller in size, more affordable, and had a more singing sound. This preference can also probably be explained by the strong influence of German culture, and the close proximity of the Germanized Baltic countries. Beginning in about 1749, two instrument makers – organist Joachim Bernard Wilde and Lorenz Eckholm – frequently advertised all kinds of music services in the newspaper *Sankt-Peterburgskie vedomosti*. The harpsichord is remarkably absent from such announcements, but the clavichord appeared frequently and in various contexts, such as to be bought or sold, instrument repair, and music lessons. Interestingly, as late as 1773, Georg Simon Löhlein's *Clavier-Schule: oder Kurze und gründliche Anweisung zur Melodie und Harmonie, durchgehends mit practischen Beyspielen erkläret* was translated and published with the Russian title indicating the clavichord as principal instrument: *Klavikordnaya shkola, ili Kratkoe i osnovatel'noe pokazanie k soglasiu v melodii, prakticheskimi primerami iz'yasnennoe, sochinennoe gospodinom G.S. Leleynom*, despite it being aimed at all keyboard instruments.

From the 1780s, the fortepiano would come to dominate the market. However, if we list purely harpsichord works written in eighteenth-century Russia, we will discover that most of them – sonatas and concertos – were composed by foreign *Kapellmeisters* working at the Russian imperial court and the courts of the Russian aristocracy for their patrons and high-ranking students and aficionados. The period is concentrated within about three decades (from approximately the late 1750s to the mid-1780s), which we will survey in chronological order, following the succession of court *Kapellmeisters*.

The earliest composer to be mentioned is Giovanni Marco Rutini (1723–1797). He was in St. Petersburg with the Locatelli opera between 1757 and 1762.[10] He also served as the harpsichord teacher to the future Catherine II, although no traces of her musicality in her mature years have ever been noted. There are German editions of Rutini's harpsichord sonatas Opus 5 and Opus 6 from this period, published in Nuremberg, since music engraving and a market for harpsichord music in Russia had yet to be fully developed. However, because the number of music lovers and skillful amateurs among courtiers was growing, it is plausible that Rutini was in demand as performer and teacher and that his music became a musical staple of the Russian aristocracy. In 1760–1761 Rutini also served and probably lived at the exceptionally rich and musically developed court of Count Peter Borisovich Sheremeteff, a member of one of the most famous families among Russian aristocracy.[11]

Hermann Raupach (1728–1778), a German keyboard player and composer who served as clavicembalist in the Russian imperial court orchestra beginning in 1755 and also sought his fortune as an opera composer, probably composed some harpsichord pieces in Russia, such as his six sonatas for clavier and violin. He published these in 1762 in Paris and dedicated them to Count D. Golitsyn shortly after temporarily leaving his position in Russia, but it is possible that at least some were written prior to his departure.

The earliest works that can be confirmed as being composed and printed in Russia are six sonatas by Vincenzo Manfredini (1737–1799), his *VI sonate da clavicembalo / dedicate / alla sacra maesta imperiale / di / Caterina Seconda … da Vincenzo Manfredini …*, 1765.[12] Like Rutini, Manfredini, the brother of famous castrato Giuseppe Manfredini, arrived in Russia with the Locatelli company in 1757 or 1758. His career in Russia was initially associated with the court of Grand Duke Peter Fedorovich, future Emperor Peter III. Following Catherine the Great's ascent to the throne in 1762, Manfredini served as a court *Kapellmeister* at some point between the tenures of Francesco Araja (1709–ca. 1762–1770), who left Russia around 1762, and Baldassare Galuppi (1706–1785), who arrived in 1765. This might explain why Manfredini, perhaps looking for a chance to be appointed musical instructor to the heir to the throne, Grand Duke Pavel Petrovich, presented to his patron the six harpsichord sonatas mentioned above. Indeed, Manfredini was awarded 1,000 rubles, an amount comparable to the annual salary of second-rank court artists, and appointed music instructor to the Grand Duke.[13]

We can also assume that Manfredini composed some instructive pieces as well, although none survive. His position was of lower rank than the first *Kapellmeister*, who was also responsible for producing operas, and it appears that Manfredini remained in Russia for the sole purpose of being restored as the first *Kapellmeister* at the end of Galuppi's tenure. In the late 1760s Manfredini tried to establish public concerts in St. Petersburg with the help of his fellow musicians Gregory Teplov, Adam Olsufiev, and Lev Naryshkin, with whom he had played a decade earlier at the Oranienbaum musicales at the court of the Grand Duke Peter Fedorovich. For this, he engaged his talented student Elizabeth Teplova, Teplov's daughter, writing for her the Harpsichord Concerto in B♭ major (1768, published in The Hague and Amsterdam in 1769 and in London before 1786).[14]

Teplova and her two sisters were good musicians and belonged to the circle of youthful courtiers surrounding Grand Duke Pavel Petrovich. Manfredini's enterprise was a success, but it did not last long. In 1768, with the arrival of the international star Tommaso Traetta (1727–1779), who replaced Galuppi as *maître de chapel* and would serve at the Russian court between 1768–1775, Manfredini lost all hope of a permanent position and left Russia. It is reported that many years later, in 1798, Manfredini's faithful pupil, Emperor Paul the First, asked his former teacher to serve at his court again, alas too late: Manfredini arrived later that year but soon became ill and died in August 1799.[15]

While Manfredini was on the sidelines, Galuppi occupied the spotlight at the court of Catherine II from 1765 to 1768. Besides opera, conducting the court choir, and teaching, his duties included harpsichord recitals. These events were so remarkable that they were even mentioned in the court chronicles *Kamer-furiersky journal* (September 26, 1765 and April 11, 1766), which rarely reported on music. Jacob von Stählin (1709–1785), the Russified German academician employed by the Russian court as an expert in culture and the arts, wrote:

> This great musician's special manner of playing harpsichord, as well as the unusual accuracy in performance of his own compositions, which were first pleasurable news, returned every Wednesday in the late afternoon at the court chamber concerts held in the antechamber of the Empress's apartments. This aging virtuoso earned universal acclaim among the courtiers, and such gratitude on the part of Her Majesty the Empress that she deigned to send him a gift for winter time: a red velvet camisole with gold embroidery and lined with sable, the cap and the muff from the same precious fur.[16]

Although it is unclear whether Galuppi composed new sonatas in Saint Petersburg, it is noteworthy that in the winter of 1781–1782, some fourteen years after he left Russia, he received a visit from Grand Duke Pavel Petrovich and his spouse Grand Duchess Maria Fedorovna in Venice, the couple traveling incognito under the names Count and Countess Severnye (i.e., "Conti del Nord"). To acknowledge this important meeting,

Galuppi presented a set of sonatas to Maria Fedorovna. While it is possible that Galuppi added the dedication "in omaggio alla granduchessa di Russia Maria Feodorovna / Baldassare Galuppi" to his *Passatempo al cembalo*, there is no documented evidence to prove this, and it is still unclear which of Galuppi's sets of six sonatas can be connected to this event.[17]

The period of Tommaso Traetta's tenure, 1768–1775, seems to have been an unfavorable one for harpsichord music in Russia. There are, in fact, no mentions of his instrumental compositions at all. It probably could have been otherwise, were it not for the critical period for the Russian Empire when the Russian–Turkish war (1768–1775) coincided with Yemelyan Pugachev's Rebellion (1773–1774), the Plague Riot in Moscow (1771), and several dangerous pretenders to the throne, to mention a few of the most dramatic political and historical events. These might have resulted in the dearth of harpsichord publications during this period.

It could not have been a completely sterile musical era, however, because during these years, two young Russian composers, Maxim Berezovsky (ca. 1740–1777) and Dmitry Bortniansky (ca. 1752–1825), studied in Italy, the first with Padre Giovanni Battista Martini in Bologna and the second with Galuppi in Venice. As their preserved music reveals, Berezovsky and Bortniansky had full command of harpsichord and instrumental composition; those years in Italy would, in fact, be their only opportunity to study it or perfect their knowledge and skill. The fact that none of their harpsichord pieces from that period are known today does not in any way mean that they did not exist. Furthermore, not only did they learn much from their tutors but they also exploited every opportunity to connect with the many Russian aristocrats in Italy during that decade. A fine example is Berezovsky's Sonata for Harpsichord and Violin, written in Pisa in 1772 when Count Alexey Orloff was living in the city. It is also evidence that in the 1770s, Russian composers did write harpsichord music – although not necessarily in Russia.

These "silent-harpsichord" years in Russia were soon compensated for by the brilliant Giovanni Paisiello (1740–1816), whose work in Russia from 1776 to 1783 happily coincided with the genuine flourishing of arts resulting from the end of political troubles and the beginning of decades of stability in Russia. This period, however, also marks the beginning of the fortepiano epoch in Russia. Although Paisiello wrote most of his clavier compositions for this instrument, the harpsichord did not lose its noble admirers, first among them the young and talented Grand Duchess Maria Fedorovna (1759–1828), who became very fond of the instrument. In 1782, Paisiello wrote and published for her his *Regole per bene accompagnare il partimento, o sia il basso fondamentale sopra il cembalo: composta per Sua Altezza Imperiale la Gran Duchessa di tutte le Russie* and two *Concerti per cembalo con orchestra*: one for the Grand Duchess and another for the Empress's lady-in-waiting, Countess Ekaterina Alexeevna Senyavina. Thus, when Paisiello left Russia in 1783, a year before the end of his contract, Maria Fedorovna promised him a pension, and, in return, Paisiello promised to supply her with new sonatas. Although neither fulfilled their obligations, this provided a great opportunity to another composer – and this time a native Russian.[18]

Bortniansky returned from Italy to Russia in 1779 as a skilled and universally recognized *Kapellmeister* and in 1780 was appointed director of vocal music at the Russian Imperial Court Chapel. In 1784, after the end of Paisiello's vacations, he received the position as music teacher to the Grand Duchess and fully established himself at the court of the Grand Duke, becoming the natural candidate for this position when Paisiello decided not to resume his Russian service.

The first thing required of Bortniansky was to satisfy Maria Fedorovna's seemingly unquenchable thirst for harpsichord sonatas. Because of this, one and a half centuries later, almost every Soviet piano student between the ages of eleven and fourteen could play a sonata by a native Russian composer. In addition to harpsichord sonatas, Bortniansky wrote other keyboard compositions, mostly for fortepiano but also for clavichord. These were collected in a single bound manuscript collection known among Russian musicologists as "Maria Fedorovna's album." Of great potential importance to scholars of Russian music, it is now lost.

We know of this album, however, because it was carefully examined and described by Nikolai Findeizen, who also quoted incipits of all the pieces and fortunately succeeded in publishing the first three of eight sonatas for harpsichord.[19] Findeizen, the only person to have studied the collection in its entirety, noted Bortniansky's complete familiarity with European styles of the time and praised it for being melodically more attractive than the compositional styles of Clementi, Pleyel, or Dušek, even suggesting that it approached the qualities of Haydn and Mozart. He emphasized the melodic grace and charm and the presence of Russian and Ukrainian gestures and structural aspects in certain themes. Indeed, the surviving sonatas fully confirm Findeizen's evaluation. Influenced by the melodic style of French and Italian comic operas, they certainly belong to the 1780s, a generation after Galuppi's sonatas.[20]

Bortniansky's sonatas are written in the mature classical sonata-allegro form, and are excellent examples of the genre, especially because he often surprises the audience by avoiding textbook models. The same characteristics can be seen in the first movement (the only one that has survived) of Bortniansky's harpsichord concerto in D major.[21] Maria Fedorovna's collection also contained Bortniansky's three-movement harpsichord concerto in C major; this is now lost, but its incipits are in the music appendices of Findeizen's study.[22]

The 1790s witnessed the Russian publication of a few editions of Haydn's and Mozart's harpsichord pieces and arrangements, as well as those by little-known composers such as the German [?] Klose and the Italian [?] Kucci (or Cocchi). Of course, the harpsichord was still used as a continuo instrument, mainly with voice and violin.

Italian masters were also no longer the principal musicians in Russia during the late eighteenth century. There was, for example, the Bohemian Arnošt Vančura, or, as he was named in Russia, Baron Ernst von Wanczura (1750–1802). Between 1785 and 1794 he published his *Journal de musique pour le clavecin ou pianoforte dédié aux dames*. Von Wanczura arrived in Saint Petersburg as a harpsichord virtuoso no earlier than 1773, composed operas and symphonies, and served as an opera theater manager. One of his claims to fame was the ability to play the harpsichord with his hands reversed, the fingers pointing upwards, plus chin, nose, and elbows![23]

The German Johann Wilhelm Hässler (1747–1822, in Russia from 1792), became a key figure in the reorientation of Russian tastes from the Italian to Viennese schools. He was, in fact, the first to create in Russia the image of Haydn as a great, revered composer. After a short period serving as piano teacher to the Grand Duke Alexander Pavlovich (the future Emperor Alexander I), Hässler moved to Moscow where he remained until the end of his life. Reputed to be a pupil of Johann Christian Kittel – one of J. S. Bach's students and later Haydn's colleague – Hässler embodied for Russians the great German tradition. A charismatic authority in figured bass and piano performance, he contributed to the most popular clavier genres in Russia at the time: sonatas and variations on Russian themes. His works were widely published at the end of the 1790s and during the first two decades of the nineteenth century, in both St. Petersburg and Moscow, by Russian publishers such as Johann Daniel Gerstenberg (1758–1841), J. S. Kaestner, Weisgaerber, Schildbach, and others, as well as by the composer himself. Fortunately, some of his works, including those belonging to the nineteenth century, have been preserved in a handsomely bound volume from the collection of Tsar Alexander I. Its titles give a good idea of the typical Russian harpsichord and fortepiano repertoire of this era, such as *Chanson russe. Variée pour le pianoforte*, Op. 9; *Prélude et ariette variée*, Op. 10, *pour le clavecin ou pianoforte; Trois sonates pour le forte-piano*, Op. 14; *Sonatine in F-dur*, Op. 20, *pour deux clavecins ou fortepianos; Fantasie et Chanson russe* Opp. 19–24,

Variée pour le clavecin ou fortepiano; and *360 preludes* Op. 47 *pour le piano-forte dans tous les tons majeurs et mineurs.*[24]

Gerstenberg was a particularly prolific contributor as a publisher and enlightened advocate for the best-known and most popular genre for Russian composers, both noble amateurs and professionals, including "Russianized" foreigners: the variations on Russian folksongs. Others include Vasily Trutovsky's Variations on Russian songs (*Variatsii na russkie pesni dlya klavitsimbala ili fortepiano* (*sochinenia V. Trutovskogo. V Sanktpeterburge*, 1780); Vasily Karaouloff's *Trois airs russes variés pour le clavecin ou piano-forte* (1787); Hessler's [*sic*] Russian folksong with twelve variations for harpsichord or piano-forte (*Russkaya narodnaya pesnya s 12 peremenami dlya klavesina ili piano-forte* (*soch. g. Gesslera*, 1793); Parfeny d'Engalitchew's *Air russe avec variations pour le clavecin ou pianoforte … dédié à son altesse impériale madame la gande duchesse de toutes les Russies Elisabeth Alexiewna* (1798); B. Boehm's *Air russe varié et rondo pour le clavecin ou le piano-forte* (1798); and Chrétien-Fréderic Segekbach's *Douze variations d'un air russe pour clav ou p-f. Oeuv. 2* (1799).[25]

The polonaise was another popular genre in the Russian clavier repertoire of the 1790s, and nearly all of these were composed by Joseph (in Russian, "Osip") Kozlovsky (1757–1831). A self-described but nevertheless highly skilled amateur, since as a nobleman he could not be a professional musician, Kozlovsky could boast of a triple identity: Belorussian by birth, Polish geopolitically (since Belorussia was then part of the Polish-Lithuanian Commonwealth), and Russian by residence and service in the Russian army. His musical connections were no less interesting. He was a nephew and pupil of the above-mentioned Vasily Trutovsky (the court *guslist* and the composer of the first clavier variations on Russian songs) and eventually a teacher of the Polish diplomat, politician, and composer Michał Kleofas Ogiński, the author of the highly melancholic polonaise *Farewell to the Homeland*, written at the time of the suppression of the Kościuszko Uprising (1794) and Ogiński's own emigration to Paris shortly after the uprising was suppressed.

In summary, eighteenth-century Russian harpsichord music occupied an important and special niche among music for other keyboard instruments, such as the clavichord and fortepiano, and was at the top of the social hierarchy at the imperial court and at the palaces of the major aristocratic families. Harpsichord playing was considered the most noble pastime among female members of aristocratic families, and the possession of these instruments, with their warm and resonant sound and beautiful decorations often featuring gallant scenes, was a characteristic attribute of luxurious salons. The repertoire for the instrument consisted mostly of sonatas and concertos, usually provided by Italian court *Kapellmeisters*, as well as minor pieces and favorite Russian airs with variations. The harpsichord was of course also often used as basso continuo and in ensembles with violin (first listed) and voice, but as in all other countries, the music eventually outlived its medium and smoothly passed to fortepiano.

Postscript

Before concluding this chapter, brief mention must be made about the connections between Russian, Belorussian, and Ukrainian music cultures, a subject that has usually been ignored in Russian studies.

Thanks to the fundamental research of Olga Dadiomova on the subject, the musical world of eighteenth-century Belorussia can now be unveiled in all its richness, offering a different perspective on Russian music in general.[26] For example, in Nesvizhi alone during the 1750s–1780s we find Czech performers and *Kapellmeisters* such as Jan Dušek and Frantishek Erzhombka. Among the leading local musicians was Jan Dawid Holland (1746–1827), a Polish composer of German birth, who came to Belorussia from Hamburg.

Eighteenth-century Ukraine had a less promising and less clear relationship with the harpsichord. To begin with, Ukraine did not exist as a country at this time. It was called Malorossia (Little Russia) and was brutally divided between Russia, Poland, Austria-Hungary, and Turkey.

Nevertheless, it cannot be said that the harpsichord was a complete stranger to Ukrainian music, and the crumbs of evidence regarding the instrument lead us to the city of Lviv and to the highly musical court of Count Kirill Razumovsky (father of Andrei Razumovsky) in Glukhiv as head of Malorossia in 1750–1764.[27] In addition, there was a short-lived Academy of Music in Kremenchug (in which a class of a few students was taught by Giuseppe Sarti in 1788–1789) that also implies the existence of amateur music making. It would be more accurate, however, to conclude that these were really enclaves of Russian culture, rather than something that could be considered native eighteenth-century Ukrainian music. That said, it should be noted that the rich and fascinating legacy of Ukrainian songs and dances has attracted the interest of European musicians since the seventeenth century. No wonder that traces of some Ukrainian dances and songs in harpsichord music can be found in Polish and German collections, both probably based on the Lviv influence.[28] Indeed, Lviv was (and still is) a cultural center, even boasting of Johann Philipp Kirnberger having lived there between 1741 and 1750 – as a harpsichordist.[29]

Notes

1. The two largest instrument collections in Russia can be found in Saint Petersburg, at the Saint Petersburg Museum of Music, Sheremetev Palace, and in the Glinka National Museum Consortium of Musical Culture in Moscow, www.glinka.museum/en/.

2. For further details, see Marina Ritzarev, *Eighteenth-Century Russian Music* (Farnham: Ashgate, 2006, rep. 2016, 2017).

3. J. Horsey, *Russia at the Close of the Sixteenth Century. Comprising the Treatise "Of the Russe common wealth," by Dr. Giles Fletcher, and the Travels of Sir Jerome Horsey, Knt., Now for the First Time Printed Entire from His Own Manuscript*, ed. Edward A. Bond (London: Printed for the Hakluyt Society, 1856), p. 217, quoted in N. Findeizen, *History of Music in Russia from Antiquity to 1800*, trans. Samuel William Pring, ed. and annotated by Miloš Velimirović and Claudia R. Jensen (Bloomington: Indiana University Press, 2008), Vol. 1, p. 192 and p. 367, fn. 302.

4. C. R. Jensen, *Musical Cultures in Seventeenth-Century Russia* (Bloomington: Indiana University Press, 2009), pp. 77–104.

5. The *gusli* is the ancient Russian multistring plucked instrument known from at least the sixth century BCE. The *bandura* is the Ukrainian plucked-string, folk instrument. It had five to twelve strings in the seventeenth and eighteenth centuries and can have as many as sixty-eight strings today.

6. P. Stolpyansky, *Muzyka i muzitsirovanie v starom Peterburge* (Leningrad: Muzyka, 1989), pp. 183–184.

7. It is difficult to establish which of the highly positioned Princes Dolgoruky (sometimes Dolgorukov), who came from a large, ancient, but not usually well-educated family, could be the owner. Vladimir Natanson suggested Vasily Lukich Dolgoruky (1672–1739), a highly educated diplomat who studied in Paris. See V. Natanson, *Proshloe russkogo pianizma* (Moscow: Muzyka, 1960), p. 51. Another Prince, Alexey Grigorievich Dolgorukov (?–1734) could be a candidate as well, since he was an educated statesman who spent some time in diplomatic missions in Italy, Malta, and Poland.

8. A. N. Drozdov, "Istoki russkogo pianizma," in *Sovetskaya muzyka* 8 (1938), pp. 41–57.

9. Gregory Teplov, *Mezhdu delom bezdelie, ili Sobranie raznykh pesen s prilozhennymi tonami na tri golosa* (St Petersburg: Akademia nauk, 1751–1759).

10. Giovanni Battista Locatelli (1713–1785), after going bankrupt in Germany, signed a contract with the Russian court and managed the Italian Company in St. Petersburg for five years (1757–1762).

11. G. Pestelli, *The Age of Mozart and Beethoven* (Cambridge: Cambridge University Press, 1984), p. 18; A. Porfirieva, *Muzykal'ny Peterburg: XVIII vek, entsiklopedichesky slovar'*, 5 vols. (St. Petersburg: Rossiyskiy Institut Istorii Iskusstv: Kompozitor, 1999), Vol. 3, p. 61.

12. Facsimile edition, A. M. Pernafelli, ed. (Milan: Edizioni Suvini Zerboni, 1975). See also *RISM* M 352, Vol. 5, p. 405.

13. The same opus was severely criticized the following year by the German composer and writer J. A. Hiller. See *Wöchentliche Nachrichten und Anmerkungen die Musik betreffend* 1, no. 17, October 21, 1766 (Leipzig:

Verl. der Zeitungs-Expedition), pp. [127]–131, quoted in R.-A. Mooser, *Annales de la musique et des musiciens en Russie au XVIIIe siècle*, 3 vols. (Genève: Ed. du Mont-Blanc, 1948–1951), Vol. 2, p. 39.

14. V. Manfredini, *Concert choisie pour le clavecin avec l'accompagnement des deux violons, taille, basse, deux hautbois ou fluttes, deux cors de chasse ad libitum.* (Den Haag: Burchard Hummel, 1769; Amsterdam: Johann Julius Hummel, 1769), *RISM* M 350, Vol. 5, p. 405; *A Favourite Concerto for the Harpsicord or Pianoforte with Accompaniments for Two Violins, Hautboys, or Flutes, Two Horns Ad Libitum, Tenor and Violoncello* (London: P. Evans, before 1786), *RISM* M 348, M 349, Vol. 5, p. 405); V. Manfredini, *Concerto in Si♭ per cembalo e orchestra*, A. Ton, ed. (Milano: Carisch, 1957).

15. Findeizen, *History of Music in Russia*, Vol. 2, p. 91.

16. J. von Stählin, *Nachrichten von der Musik in Russland, facs. ed. with commentary*, Ernst Stöckl (Leipzig: Edition Peters, 1982), p. 171. The original publication is J. von Stählin, "Nachrichten von der Musik in Russland," in M. J. Haigold, ed., *Beilagen zum Neuveranderten Russland* (Riga – Mietau, 1769); reprinted and quoted by J. A. Hiller, *Wöchentliche Nachrichten*, http://reader.digitale-sammlungen.de/resolve/display/bsb10527275.html (accessed 23 December 2016).

17. The autograph of this collection (found at Istituto musicale "Niccolò Paganini," Genova, shelf mark D-8-31) does not contain a dedication. Nevertheless, Franco Piva in his edition *Baldassare Galuppi, detto Il Buranello. Passatempo al cembalo, Music sonate. Trascrizione e revisione di Franco Piva* (Venezia: Instituto per la Collaborazione Culturale, 1964) related this opus to Galuppi's meeting with the Russian Grand Dukes. For more details see E. Antonenko, "Kistorii otnosheniy Baldassare Galuppi i russkogo imperatorskogo dvora," in *Nauchny vestnik Moskovskoy konservatorii* 1 (2011), pp. 92–104, http://nv.mosconsv.ru/wp-content/media/06_antonenko_ekaterina.pdf (accessed 23 December 2016).

18. For details of the pension and sonatas, see A. Weydemeyer, *Dvor i zamechatel'nye lyudi v Rossii vo vtoroy polovine XVIII stoletia*, 2 vols. (St. Petersburg: Einerling, 1846), and J. L. Hunt, *Paisiello: His Life as an Opera Composer* (New York: National Opera Association, 1975), p. 34.

19. Findeizen, *History of Music in Russia*, Vol. 2, pp. 205–208 (description of the collection); pp. 327–334 (incipits of the compositions); pp. 376–379 (fragments of two pieces).

20. *Dmitry Bortnyansky (1751–1825): The Russian Album*, recorded by Olga Martynova, harpsichord, Pratum Integrum Orchestra (CM 0052003); www.caromitis.com/eng/catalogue/cm0052003.html.

21. Published as D. Bortniansky, *Concerto di cembalo*, M. Stepanenko, ed. (Kiev: Muzychna Ukraina, 1985). Recorded and edited by P. Serbin in *Dmitry Bortnyansky (1751–1825): The Russian Album*.

22. Findeizen, *History of Music in Russia*, Nos. 81–83, Vol. 2, p. 331.

23. M. P. Pryashnikova, "Kompozitor i klavesinist ekaterininskoy epokhi Ernst Vanzhura," in E. R. Dashkova, *Portret v kontekste istorii* (Moscow: Moskovsky gumanitarny institut im. E. R. Dashkovoy, 2004), Vol. 21, p. 162.

24. A. Porfirieva, *Muzykal'ny Peterburg: XVIII vek*, Vol. 1, pp. 245–246.

25. All the names and titles are spelled here as they appear in Russian editions.
26. O. V. Dadiomova, *Muzykal'naya kul'tura gorodov Belorussii v XVIII veke* (Minsk: Navuka i tekhnika, 1992) and *Muzychnaya kul'tura Belorussii XVIII stagoddzya. Gistoryka-tearetychnae dasledavanne* (Minsk: Belaruskaya dzyarzhaunaya, akademia muzyki, 2002).
27. It was mentioned as early as the middle of the seventeenth century in a document from Bogdan Khmelnitsky's court (1652), as well as being sold in the Polonized West Ukrainian city of Lviv in 1667. See M. Stepanenko, "Klavir v istorii muzychnoy kul'tury Ukrainy XVI-XVII st.," in *Ukrains'ka musychna spadshchina: Stat'i. Materialy. Dokumenty. Vyp. 1* (Kiev: Muzychna Ukraina, 1989), p. 33.
28. A collection from the middle of the seventeenth century in the Krakow Jagellon Library (shelf mark 127/256) contains over two hundred keyboard pieces aimed for domestic music making and pedagogical repertoire, including songs, and religious and secular *kanty*. See Stepanenko, "Klavir v istorii," pp. 38–39). The owner of this collection was Kievan Metropolitan Kiprian Zhokhovs'ky.
29. The name of Timofey Belogradsky, a lutenist of Ukrainian origin and pupil of Silvius Leopold Weiss, is sometimes mentioned in connection with Ukrainian keyboard music, probably because lute music could also be performed on the harpsichord.

Further Reading

Findeizen, Nikolai. *History of Music in Russia from Antiquity to 1800*. Translated by Samuel William Pring, edited and annotated by Miloš Velimirović and Claudia R. Jensen. Bloomington: Indiana University Press, 2008.

Jensen, C. R. *Musical Cultures in Seventeenth-Century Russia*. Bloomington: Indiana University Press.

Ritzarev, Marina. *Eighteenth-Century Russian Music*. Farnham: Ashgate, 2006, reprinted New York: Routledge, 2016, 2017.

12 The Nordic and Baltic Countries

ANNA MARIA MCELWAIN

Introduction

This chapter will discuss the music for the harpsichord or other keyboard instruments used interchangeably with it in the countries surrounding the Baltic Sea. These include the most northern parts of Europe, as well as those on the southern coast of the sea; that is, the Baltic Countries that consisted of approximately present-day Estonia, Latvia, and Lithuania.[1] The Nordic Countries were united from 1397 until 1523 through the Kalmar Union, which consisted of Norway and Sweden with their Dependencies, and Denmark.[2] When the Union was dissolved, the Kingdom of Denmark consisted of Denmark and Norway until 1814 when Norway was ceded to the Kingdom of Sweden. Finland also belonged to Sweden until 1809, after which it became a Grand Duchy of the Russian Empire.

Compared with continental Europe, art music traditions in the Nordic and Baltic areas are relatively young. The music that used harpsichords revolved around royal courts. It has been easy to find harpsichord music from the Nordic countries, but the Baltic region is more challenging.[3]

Kingdom of Denmark

The Danish rulers of the Kingdom of Denmark enthusiastically promoted the performing arts, bringing musicians from abroad, encouraging native ones, and creating a welcoming atmosphere for the development of music.[4] Denmark, moreover, was the first Nordic country to produce art music independent of continental traditions, and Sweden followed its lead.[5]

Dieterich Buxtehude (ca. 1637–1707), although most often associated with Germany, was presumably born and educated in Denmark, in Helsingborg (present-day Sweden). He moved in 1668 to Germany to work as an organist in Lübeck, where he remained until his death and wrote most of his works.[6] Nevertheless, Buxtehude kept in close contact with Denmark and Sweden, and the influence of Danish folk music can be found in his cantatas.[7] In Denmark he wrote the cantata *Aperite mihi portas justitiae* (BuxWV 7), as well as a series of keyboard suites and variations notated in tabulature that were discovered in Nykøbing in 1939. The manuscript includes two sets of tunes that were popular in Scandinavia in the late seventeenth century.[8]

Denmark benefited from numerous German composers in return. Melchior Schildt (1592–1667), a student of Sweelinck's, was the court organist for King Christian IV (r. 1588–1648) from 1626 to 1629.[9] Among his surviving keyboard compositions is a *Pavana Lachrymae,* one of a multitude of keyboard arrangements of John Dowland's *Lachrymae.*[10] Matthias Weckmann (ca. 1616–1674) worked in the Danish royal chapel in Nykøbing during 1642–1646, but it is not known whether he composed any of his keyboard music during this time.[11]

Unlike Schildt and Weckmann, who spent only a short period in Denmark, Johann Adolph Scheibe (1708–1776) remained there and achieved significant status in Copenhagen; Det Musikalske Societet, the first musical society in the country, was founded under his influence. However, Frederick V (r. 1746–1766), the successor of Christian VI (r. 1730–1746), had a more secular view of the arts. Scheibe was fired from his post but opened a music school for children in Sønderborg and continued to compose, write, and translate Danish classical texts into German.[12] Among Scheibe's solo keyboard pieces are four concertos for harpsichord and approximately fourteen duo or trio sonatas, mostly for harpsichord obbligato with violin and/or traverso. Scheibe is also known for *Der critische Musikus* (1737–1740), an important publication with references to composers of his time.[13]

Yet another German émigré who influenced the musical scene in Denmark was Johann Abraham Peter Schulz (1747–1800), a pioneer of Danish music. As *Hofkapellmeister* and director of the Royal Theater (1787–1795) during the reign of Christian VII (r. 1766–1808), Schulz was responsible for several changes and innovations at the royal chapel, and presented stage works that dealt with political problems, such as land reform. He also established a benefit fund for widows of musicians and wrote a pedagogical treatise.[14] Among his most significant keyboard works are *Six diverses pièces pour le clavecin ou le piano-forte,* Op. 1 (1776) and a *Sonata per il clavicembalo solo,* Op. 2, in E♭ major (1778), both composed prior to his period in Copenhagen.[15] Schulz's student, Christoph Ernst Friedrich Weyse (1774–1842), became a notable native Danish composer of lieder and keyboard works.[16]

Hardenack Otto Conrad Zinck (1746–1832), also from Germany, first performed in Copenhagen in 1786. He was then offered a post as *Singmeister* in the court and spent the rest of his life in that city. Three years earlier, he had published his *Sechs Clavier-Sonaten* (1783), which were highly praised by contemporary critics and reflect the influence of his teacher Carl Philipp Emanuel Bach. His four volumes of *Compositioner for Sangen og Claveret / Compositionen fur den Gesang und das Clavier* (1791–1793) include sonatas and variations for keyboard.[17]

Even though the Copenhagen court was the musical center of Denmark, other venues provided opportunities for composers and performers. For example, Johan Daniel Berlin (1714–1787) came to Copenhagen at the age of nineteen, and later became town musician of Trondheim, Norway.[18] Berlin published his *Musicaliske Elementer* in 1744, making it the first Norwegian-language textbook on music theory and musical instruments. He also had an interest in instrument construction and built a *cembalo da gamba verticale* (viola da gamba with a keyboard); a piano with a pedal; a monochord; and a mechanism, now lost, which produced a version of his Hass harpsichord sensitive to touch, enabling him to play dynamics on the instrument.[19] Only a few of his thirty compositions survive.[20]

Erich Ove Friling (ca. 1772–1835) was born in Norway but is listed as a music dealer in Copenhagen in 1799. He sold scores and musical instruments, taught, and composed. His earlier compositions indicate the options of either *Claveer* or *Fortepiano*.[21] Israel Gottlieb Wernicke (1755–1836) was the son of the organist of Bergen Cathedral.[22] His compositions include an *Arietta con 50 variazioni: per il clavicembalo*, based on the folksong "Gestern Abend war Vetter Michael da." It seems to have been fashioned after Bach's Goldberg Variations, and includes canons, double and triple counterpoint, and even pizzicato chords with instructions to use the pedal on the pianoforte if not played on the clavier.

Kingdom of Sweden

It is notable that the era of the harpsichord and clavichord extended longer in Sweden than in most parts of Europe. Harpsichords were frequently mentioned in newspaper announcements up to 1800, and, unless specified for the fortepiano, Swedish keyboard literature was played on the harpsichord, clavichord, and square piano until the first half of the nineteenth century.

Like Denmark, Sweden maintained strong connections with German musicians. A prime example is the Düben family. Andreas Düben (ca. 1597–1662), an organist and composer, immigrated to Sweden in 1620, but few of his works have survived.[23] His son Gustaf Düben (ca. 1628–1690) was perhaps the best-known musician of the family: a member of the Swedish court orchestra, a friend of Buxtehude, and an avid music collector. Many original manuscripts and transcriptions of Buxtehude's works are held in the Düben Collection, one of the best-preserved collections of seventeenth-century music.[24] Nearly all of Gustaf Düben's compositions exist in manuscript.[25] Two of his sons, Gustav von Düben (bap. 1660, d. 1726) and Anders Düben (1673–1738) succeeded their father as *hovkapellmästare*, and took over the task of expanding their father's collection of music. Anders accompanied King Charles XII (r. 1697–1718) on his military campaigns during the Great Northern War (1700–1721) and wrote music accordingly. His few remaining keyboard pieces include the *Marche pour les Suédois* ("Marche of the Swedes", also known as *Marche de Narva*).[26]

During the reigns of Charles XII (r. 1697–1718) and his father Charles XI (r. 1660–1697), a German organist, Christian Ritter (ca. 1645/50–ca. 1717), worked at the court in Stockholm from 1680–1699. His surviving works include two keyboard suites (F♯ minor and C minor, the latter a Froberger-like lamento) and a sonatina in D minor, which, despite its title, is written in the style of a North German organ toccata.[27]

It was only after Sweden's liberation from Danish rule that its musical life was able to prosper independently, and eventually produced the greatest Nordic composer, Johan Helmich Roman (1694–1758). He wrote in most of the compositional genres of his time and was the first Nordic composer to compose secular instrumental compositions, but the only work published in Roman's lifetime was a collection of twelve sonatas for flute, violin, and harpsichord (1727).[28] He also composed pieces for voice and harpsichord and, most importantly for this chapter, twelve keyboard suites or *sonater*, each consisting of four to seven movements and revealing influences of Handel and Italian music.[29]

Another native Swedish composer from this period is Johann Joachim Agrell (1701–1765), but unlike Roman, Agrell spent most of his life abroad after his studies in Uppsala, in Kassel and Nuremberg, for example. Unfortunately, almost none of Agrell's compositions from Sweden have been preserved, but he did remain in contact with the country of his birth, dedicating his *Sei sonate per il cembalo solo* (Nuremberg, 1748) to Crown Prince Adolf Frederick. In this dedication Agrell mentions his dear homeland and regrets that fate had forced him to live abroad.

Nevertheless, most of Agrell's instrumental works were published during his lifetime, and Roman, among others, took an interest in his career and requested that all of Agrell's published works be sent to the Swedish royal chapel. Among his best-known instrumental pieces are his symphonies, at least twenty-two in number, and his numerous harpsichord concertos from the 1750s and 1760s.[30] In addition to Roman, Agrell was influenced by the Italian Fortunato Chelleri (1690–1757), who was the

Kapellmeister at the Kassel court and later joined the court in Stockholm. Chelleri stayed only for two years, however, because he was not able to tolerate the northern climate.[31]

The German harpsichordist and composer Conrad Friedrich Hurlebusch (1661–1765) came to Stockholm at the invitation of Frederick I (r. 1720–1751), but remained there only from 1722 to 1725, submitting his resignation because he did not receive the promised post as court organist.[32]

Although most musicians arriving in Sweden from Germany had a connection with the court, Baltzar Knölcke (ca. 1711–1754) became town musician in Ystad in 1730 and was cathedral organist in Linköping from 1739 until his death. He wrote sinfonias, chamber music, vocal music, and keyboard music, in a style reflecting the transitional period from the baroque to the *galant* styles.

Another German immigrant to Sweden, Hinrich (Henrik) Philip Johnsen (1716/1717–1779), arrived with Crown Prince Adolf Frederick's royal court orchestra in 1743. He became an organist at Klara Church in Stockholm, a court organist, a chief conductor of the French theater company, and a founding member of the Royal Swedish Academy of Music, where he was the first librarian and taught music theory. Among his harpsichord works are two concertos, six fugues for organ or harpsichord, and *Sei sonate per il cembalo* (1754), one-movement works similar to the sonatas of Domenico Scarlatti in form and virtuosity.[33]

The best known of Johnsen's pupils was Johan Wikmanson (1753–1800), a native Swede. Apart from studying mathematics and instrument construction in Copenhagen for two years, Wikmanson spent his life in Sweden, where he was the director of education and harmony and theory teacher at the Royal Academy of Music and one of the most famous organists in the country.[34] His keyboard compositions include a sonata with a short humorous movement *Hönshuset* ("Henhouse"), a *Divertissement på Södersfors*, and a cycle of pieces composed for his daughter (*Fragmenter för min lilla flicka*).[35]

Also carrying on Roman's legacy in Sweden was Ferdinand Zellbell the younger (1719–1780), a composer, organist, harpsichordist, violinist, and teacher. His most famous student, Olof Åhlström (1765–1835), composed two collections of sonatas for harpsichord or pianoforte with violin obbligato: *Trois sonates pour le clavecin avec l'accompagnement d'un violon ad libitum* and *Quatre sonates pour le clavecin avec l'accompagnement d'un violon ad libitum*. His solo keyboard works include sonatas, sonatinas, and individual pieces. However, Åhlström was best known as a music publisher. In 1788 he established *Musikaliska Tryckeriet*, the first large-scale musical printing press in Sweden, and was granted an exclusive royal privilege to engrave and print sheet music. Åhlström's *Musikaliskt Tidsfördrif* ("Musical Pastimes"), published between 1789 and 1834, contains a large variety of vocal and instrumental compositions and is therefore a good source of Swedish music from this period.[36]

During the "Gustavian period," King Gustav III (r. 1771–1792) sought to make Sweden, and especially its capital Stockholm, an internationally revered cultural center. He commissioned the first opera in Swedish, *Thetis och Pelée*, from Francesco Antonio Baldassare Uttini (1723–1795). An Italian active in Sweden from 1755, Uttini was a member of the Mingotti troupe, which was invited to perform operas for the court in Stockholm upon the invitation of Queen Lovisa Ulrika. During this time, he composed six harpsichord sonatas, remained the Queen's private *kapellmästare*, and was later appointed *hovkapellmästare*.[37]

German-born Joseph Martin Kraus (1756–1792) came to Sweden in 1778 and succeeded Uttini as the *hovkapellmästare*. In 1782 King Gustav III sent Kraus on a four-year tour of Europe to study and investigate musical currents, and upon his return he assumed numerous duties: as the only *kapellmästare* at the Royal Opera, the director of the concert activities of the royal court orchestra and many other concert series and theaters, director of the Royal Academy of Music, and in 1788 principal *hovkapellmästare* of the royal court orchestra. After the assassination of King Gustav III in 1792, Kraus composed the *Sorgemusik över Gustav III* for the royal funeral. This work brought an end to Kraus's career, which included the composition of almost two hundred works, including sonatas, rondos, variations, and dance music.

In addition to Kraus, the Gustavian court welcomed a multitude of other German composers, such as Georg Joseph Vogler (1749–1814), Johan Fredrik Grenser (1758–1794), and Johann Christian Friedrich Hæffner (1759–1833). Vogler's major keyboard contribution is a collection of fifteen works entitled *Pièces de clavecin*, which is a supplement to his *Clavér-schola* (Stockholm, 1798). The work is dedicated to his pupil, King Gustav IV Adolf (r. 1792–1809). The titles have a strongly Swedish flavor with references to Finland and Russia as well: *Min far han var en Vestgöthe han han: Chanson suedoise; Ak minan rakas linduisen: Air Finois; Höns gummans visa: Chanson suedoise; Marche de Charles XII auprès du Narva; Air russe; Marche des Chevaliers de l'Ordre des Seraphims en Suéde;* and *Quarndansen: Danse suedoise*. Other keyboard works from the Swedish period are a theme and variations in C major, which was printed in Åhlström's musical journal *Musikaliskt Tidsfördrif* (Vol. 1 no. 1, 1789); Variations on God save the King (1791); and six sonatas for two keyboards (1794).

Unlike Vogler, Grenser remained in Sweden and was a member of the royal court orchestra in Stockholm. Hæffner also remained in Sweden after his arrival in 1781 and became chief conductor of the royal court orchestra, *director musices* at Uppsala University, and the cathedral organist of the city. His keyboard works are mainly arrangements from various operas.

Finland

The Finnish composers worth mentioning flourished during the period in which the fortepiano began to replace the harpsichord. They include Thomas Byström (1772–1839) and Fredrik Emanuel Lithander (1777–1823), whose compositions were published in *Musikaliskt Tidsfördrif* (1798, 1799) and other Swedish musical journals. At least four of Lithander's ten siblings became composers, the best known being Carl Ludvig (1773–1843).

The Baltic Countries

The history of professional art music in the Baltic countries is brief, about one hundred years. Ties to Germany were strong: Even the de facto language of administration and education in the Baltic area was German. For example, the German-born Johann Valentin Meder (bap. 1649, d. 1719) was employed in Copenhagen, worked as *Kantor* in Reval during 1674–1680, and concluded his life as *Kantor* in Riga.[38] Thirteen of Meder's compositions can be found in the Düben collection in Uppsala, although none are for solo harpsichord. A Johann Fischer worked in Mitau (present-day Jelgava, Latvia) between 1690 and 1697, where he held a post in the court of Duke Friedrich Casimir of Kurland and may have written for the harpsichord, or at least used it as a continuo instrument.

Significant numbers of musical virtuosi performed in the Baltic cities of Mitau and Riga on their way from Western Europe to St. Petersburg during the eighteenth century. There were also close ties between Mitau and Riga and the University of Königsberg (present-day Kaliningrad, Russia). Johann Friedrich Hartknoch (1740–1789), a Latvian harpsichordist, founded a publishing house in Mitau with a branch office in Riga, which later became its main office. He would publish harpsichord compositions by Carl Philipp Emanuel Bach, Johann Christian Bach, Johann Christoph Bach, and the J. S. Bach student Johann Gottfried Müthel (1728–1788), who would emigrate to Riga in 1758 and remain there until the end of his life.[39] Müthel's known keyboard works include seven concertos, one for solo harpsichord and the rest for harpsichord and strings, nine sonatas, and a variety of smaller pieces. His duets for two keyboards in

C major and E♭ major, published in 1771, offer the option of fortepiano in the title. The first known example of this in the title of a published work, it demonstrates the rising popularity of the instrument during that era. These duets are played today on harpsichords, clavichords, and fortepianos.[40]

Hartknoch's publishing house in Riga published several harpsichord sonatas written by his student from Königsberg, Johann Friedrich Reichardt (1752–1814). Christian Wilhelm Podbielski (1740–1792), also from Königsberg, wrote for the harpsichord in traditional German rococo style: Six sonatas for the harpsichord were published in Riga by Hartknoch in 1783 and *Petites pièces pour le clavecin et pour le chant* in Königsberg in the same year.[41] Another of Harknoch's published composers was Johann Gottfried Wilhelm Palschau (1741–1815). He was born in Copenhagen as the son of Peter Jacob Palschau, who was originally from Holstein but worked in the Royal Opera orchestra in Copenhagen. Palschau toured throughout Europe from an early age and lived in Riga from about 1771 to 1777, studying with Müthel. Later, he relocated to St. Petersburg, where he focused entirely on writing for the keyboard. His works consist of two sonatas (Nuremberg, 1762), two concertos for harpsichord and strings (Riga, 1771, published by Hartknoch), and several sets of variations on Russian folk melodies, such as *Chanson russe variée* and *Air varié à quatre mains pour le clavecin ou piano-forte.* In some of his later keyboard works, Palschau specified fortepiano rather than harpsichord.[42]

Conclusion

As we have seen, we have sources of keyboard music from Sweden and Denmark, but next to nothing from the other Nordic and Baltic countries. Possible explanations may be the existence of established monarchies in Sweden and Denmark, which promoted music, and the fact that no battles were fought on Swedish soil, giving archives a better chance of surviving. The Düben collection mentioned earlier is a prime example.[43] Another invaluable source for Swedish music is the website of the Swedish Musical Heritage project, which contains almost a thousand biographical entries and extensive lists of compositions with the possibility to download scores or order hardcopies.[44]

The monarchs brought many musicians from abroad, mainly from Germany, and nurtured native composers as well, especially in Sweden. There are fewer sources in Norway, which was under Danish rule, and in Finland under Swedish rule. With regards to the Baltic countries, the lack of established monarchies, the constant wars and conflicts, plague epidemics, and fires took their toll on the musical archives of these countries.

The Soviet era might also have contributed to this dearth of musical evidence. Hopefully, later studies will be able to unearth more harpsichord treasures from the Nordic and especially the Baltic areas. Until then, we must enjoy what is within our reach.

Notes

Grateful acknowledgment is given to Anthony Marini (Sibelius Academy) and Anna Maria Pirttilä (University of Oulu) for their invaluable help.

1. Their location between Russia and Central Europe on the Baltic coast made these countries of strategic importance, and they were thus the sites of numerous battles and frequently changing borders and rulers.
2. Their dependencies included parts of Finland, Iceland, Greenland, the Faroe Islands, and the Northern Isles.
3. Frederick Key Smith, *Nordic Art Music: From the Middle Ages to the Third Millennium* (Westport, CT: Praeger, 2002), p. 1.
4. Musicians from mainly Germany, England, and Italy came to work in the court of Copenhagen.
5. Smith, *Nordic Art Music*, p. 2.
6. For biographical information of Buxtehude's earlier years in Denmark see Kerala Johnson Snyder, *Dieterich Buxtehude: Organist in Lübeck* (Rochester, NY: University of Rochester Press, 1987), pp. 3–35.
7. Gerald Cockshott, "Music in Denmark," *The Musical Times* 89, no. 1270 (December, 1948), pp. 363–365.
8. One is a folk tune known in Germany as *Kraut und Rüben*, part of the Quodlibet in J. S. Bach's Goldberg Variations (BWV998); the other is a ballet tune of French origin. See John Horton, *Scandinavian Music: A Short History* (London: Faber and Faber, 1963), pp. 62–64.
9. Christian Vestergaard-Pedersen, "Melchior Schildt I Danmark. En oversigt over tid og sted for hans ophold I årene 1626–1629," *Danish Yearbook of Musicology* 7 (1973–1976), pp. 237–246.
10. In W. Breig, *Lied- und Tanzvariationen der Sweelinck-Schule* (Mainz: Schott, 1970).
11. Geoffrey B. Sharp, "Matthias Weckmann 1619–1674," *The Musical Times* 115, no. 1582 (December, 1974), pp. 1039–1041.
12. Smith, *Nordic Art Music*, p. 22.
13. Johann Adolph Scheibe, *Der critische Musikus*, Vol. 1 (Hamburg, 1738), Vol. 2 (Hamburg, 1740), rev. (Leipzig, 1745).
14. *Gedanken über den Einfluss der Musik auf die Bildung eines Volks* (C. G. Prost: Copenhagen, 1790).
15. See Otto Rieß, "Johann Abraham Peter Schulz' Leben," *Sammelbände der Internationalen Musikgesellschaft* 15, no. 2. (January–March, 1914), pp. 169–270.
16. See Smith, *Nordic Art Music*, pp. 27–28.
17. Zinck studied with Carl Philipp Emanuel Bach in Hamburg around 1768–1769. His *Compositionen für den Gesang und das Clavier* (1791–1793) in four volumes consist of lieder as well as keyboard sonatas and variations.

18. Berlin was originally from Memel, Prussia (present-day Klaipėda, Lithuania), and thus could equally belong to our discussion of Baltic composers.
19. See Smith, *Nordic Art Music*, p. 8.
20. Berlin wrote six harpsichord concertos, as well as a concerto for his cembalo da gamba verticale, which are all lost.
21. Friling's earlier compositions giving "clavier" as an option with the "fortepiano" include *Caracteristiske Stykker för Fortepiano eller Klaveer* (1812).
22. Nanette Gomory Lunde, "Israel Gottlieb Wernicke: The Contrapuntist of Scandinavia," *SEHKS Early Keyboard Journal* 1 (1982–1983), pp. 56ff.
23. See Smith, *Nordic Art Music*, p. 7, and Horton, *Scandinavian Music*, p. 55.
24. The Düben collection was finally donated to the University of Uppsala in 1732 by Anders Düben. It contains the manuscripts and prints of 1,500 vocal compositions and over 300 instrumental works.
25. Smith, *Nordic Art Music*, p. 7.
26. Anders von Düben's career went from *hovkapellmästare* to *directeur* of music, and later to *hovmarsalk* (Marshal of the Royal court). He wrote vocal music for the Narva ballet, which celebrated Sweden's triumph at Narva, as well as instrumental dance music and strophic solo arias accompanied by one or two violins.
27. See Tobias Norlind, "Zur Biographie Christian Ritter's," *Sammelbände der Internationalen Musikgesellschaft* 12, no. 1. (October–December, 1910), pp. 94–99.
28. See Smith, *Nordic Art Music*, pp. 8–10. The sonatas were first printed in Stockholm in 1727.
29. Eva Nordernfelt-Åberg, "The Harpsichord in 18th-Century Sweden," *Early Music* 9, no. 1, "Plucked-String Issue" (January, 1981), p. 48.
30. They include three concertos for harpsichord and strings in F major, D major, and A major (1751); four concertos for harpsichord and strings in B major, D major, A major, and D major (the latter also for solo harpsichord); two concertos for harpsichord and strings in A major and F major; and three concertos for obbligato harpsichord, flute or violin, and strings in A major, Bb minor, and G major (1753).
31. Nordernfelt-Åberg, "The Harpsichord in 18th-Century Sweden," p. 48.
32. See Rainer Kahleyss, *Conrad Friedrich Hurlebusch (1691–1765): Sein Leben und Wirken* (Frankfurt: Haag & Herschen, 1984). Harpsichord compositions of Hurlebusch include *Opere scelte per il clavicembalo*, Op.1 (Amsterdam, ca. 1733), *Composizioni musicali per il cembalo, divise in 2 parti* (Hamburg, ?1735), and *VI sonate di cembalo*, Op. 5 (Amsterdam, 1755).
33. See Nordernfelt-Åberg, "The Harpsichord in 18th-Century Sweden," p. 51.
34. Smith, *Nordic Art Music*, p. 24.
35. *Divertissement på Södersfors and Fragmenter för min lilla flicka*, facsimile editions (Stockholm: Autographus musicus, 1984).
36. Cited in Carl Nisser, *Svensk instrumentalkomposition 1770–1830* (Stockholm: Bokförlaget Gothia, 1943).

37. See Lennart Hedwall, "Adolf Fredriks och Lovisa Ulrikas tid. Hovmusik och konsert Uttini," in Leif Jonsson and Anna Ivarsdotter-Johnson, eds., *Musiken i Sverige. Frihetstid och Gustaviansk tid 1720–1810* (Stockholm: Fischer, 1993), pp. 61–88.

38. Werner Braun, "Meder, Johann Valentin,'" *Neue Deutsche Biographie* 16 (1990), p. 596.

39. Gunter Hempel, "Hartknoch," in *Oxford Music Online: Grove Music Online*, www.oxfordmusiconline.com/grovemusic/view/10.1093/gmo /9781561592630.001.0001/omo-9781561592630-e-0000012474? rskey=9kWGeG&result=1.

40. Walter Salmen, "Johann Gottfried Müthel, der letzte Schüler Bachs," in *Festschrift Heinrich Besseler*, ed. E. Klemm (Leipzig: Deutscher Verlag für Musik, 1961), pp. 351–359.

41. Walter Salmen, "Reichardt, Johann Friedrich," *Neue Deutsche Biographie*, 21 (2003), pp. 295–296.

42. Ernst Stöckl (1993), *Musikgeschichte der Russlanddeutschen* (Dülmen: Laumann-Verlag, 1993), p. 47.

43. www2.musik.uu.se/duben/Duben.php.

44. www.swedishmusicalheritage.com/.

Further Reading

Horton, John. *Scandinavian Music: A Short History*. London: Faber and Faber, 1963.

Nordernfelt-Åberg, Eva. "The Harpsichord in 18th-Century Sweden." *Early Music* 9, no. 1,"Plucked-String Issue" (January, 1981), p. 48.

Smith, Frederick Key. *Nordic Art Music: From the Middle Ages to the Third Millennium*. Westport, CT: Praeger, 2002.

13 The Harpsichord in Colonial Spanish and Portuguese America

PEDRO PERSONE

The harpsichord has played a less than silent role in the Spanish and Portuguese Americas. Our intention here is to fill what gaps exist in our understanding and appreciation of the role of this instrument during the colonial era.[1]

On June 7, 1494, two years after the discovery of America and six years before the discovery of Brazil, Portugal and Spain signed a treaty in the village of Tordesillas in northern Spain, setting boundaries for their discovered lands outside of Europe.[2] The Portuguese were given rights to the Atlantic coast, and Spain was awarded the Caribbean and Pacific coast. The primary goal of both kingdoms was the exploitation of the resources of this territory, such as gold, silver, precious stones, wood, and other materials. The Catholic Church supported these colonial agendas, since it had its own: to plant its religious flag in the New World.

Among the religious orders that traveled to the Americas, the Jesuits stand out. The study of the presence of the harpsichord and its music in the Portuguese and Spanish colonial regions is inevitably linked to the expansion and influence of the Society of Jesus as it sought to convert native peoples, its missionaries arriving in the New World very soon after the creation of the Society. Jesuits arrived in Brazil in 1549, Peru in 1567, Mexico in 1572, and finally Paraguay in 1585.

Colonial Spanish America

Viceroyalty of Nueva España

Vast viceroyalties were established throughout Spanish America, their sovereignty extending even as far as the Philippines in Southeast Asia. The Viceroyalty of Nueva España (1519–1821) eventually included Arizona, California, Colorado, Nevada, New Mexico, and Utah in what would be become the United States and Costa Rica in Central America.[3]

Mexico

Mexico City was the capital of "New Spain." The palaces of the viceroys here and in other cities were centers of governmental authority, music being generally associated with official events and celebrations. However, much like the European courts, the palaces also supported nonofficial cultural activities, such as literature, theater, music, and social events, including balls.

Harpsichord Teaching

In 1524 the Flemish Franciscan Fray Pedro de Gante, or Pieter van der Moere (ca. 1479–1572), established a music school for the native Indians in Texcoco, Mexico.[4] Music instruction also took place in the cathedrals and convents. María Micaela and María Joaquina, daughters of Ignazio Gerusalemme (ca. 1707–1769) – or Ignacio Jerusalem y Stella – became music teachers at the Colegio de San Ignacio de Loyola and the La Encarnación convent; both had studied at the Colegio de San Miguel de Belém.[5] Throughout the eighteenth century, choirboys studied the harpsichord and the clavichord, as these instruments were deemed necessary for learning harmony.[6] They also had to learn other instruments, those who chose the organ in order to work in the college and cathedral being told that they should begin with the harpsichord.[7] The harpsichord also served as an instructional instrument for organists in the churches and convents and, following the Hispanic tradition, was also used to accompany religious music corresponding to the offices of Holy Week, especially the Lamentations of Jeremiah and the Miserere. The harpsichord thus became so essential in the colonies that Spanish rulers dispatched official guitar makers to their territories in the New World, since they knew how to construct clavichords, harpsichords, and monochords.[8]

Further evidence of the importance of the harpsichord as a pedagogical instrument can be seen in the number of instructional works that appeared in Mexico at the end of the Viceroyalty era. The *Leciones de clave y principios de armonía* by Benito Bails (1730–1797), published in Madrid in 1775, was advertised in the *Diario de México* in 1805.[9] There was also the *Teoría de los principios mas esenciales de la musica*, published in 1814, and Mariano Lopez de Elizalde's (n.d.) *Tratado de Música, y lecciones de clave* was published in Guadalajara in 1821.[10] Another study method can be found in the manuscript SMMS M3, housed in the Sutro Library of San Francisco, California.[11] It contains information on theoretical and practical aspects of keyboard instruments, such as the section "Diferentes evoluciones para manejar los dedos," which provides technical exercises, each presenting a specific rhythmic difficulty and its fingering.[12]

Harpsichordists

Mateo Tollis de la Roca (ca. 1710–1781) presented himself to the Cabildo of Mexico City as "harpsichord master" in 1756, arriving with the wife of Vicerei Agustín de Ahumada y Villalón (ca. 1715–1760), the Marquis de las Amarillas; he was subsequently appointed harpsichordist for the Cathedral of Mexico.[13] In 1757 he became assistant to Ignacio Jerusalem, master of the boys' choir, and rose to the position of head organist in 1761.

José Manuel Aldana (1730–1810), professor at the *Colégio de Infantes* at the Metropolitan Cathedral of Mexico, and José Mariano Elízaga (1786–1842), were other important figures in the history of Mexican music. Both lived during the period of transition between the end of Spanish domination and the early years of independent Mexico.[14]

Elízaga's father, José Maria, was a harpsichord teacher, and his son demonstrated his talents for the harpsichord and composition from childhood.[15] It is reported that when one of his father's students failed to execute an exercise correctly, the five-year-old Elízaga stepped in and played the exercise correctly, and the *Gaceta de México* published an article extolling his talents on October 30, 1792.[16] Elízaga then studied with Juan Joseph Echeverría, organist of the Cathedral of Morelia, and became so famous that he was soon invited to appear at the palace, earning support from the viceroy, Don Vicente de Gümes Pacheco de Padilla (1740–1799), Count of Revillagigedo, who financed a year of his studies at the *Colégio de Infantes*. Elízaga then returned to Morelia where he continued to study with José Maria Carrasco (n.d.), after which he returned to the capital to study with Mariano Soto Carrillo (1760–1807).[17] Later, at the end of the Viceroyalty of Nueva España, Elízaga taught fortepiano and had the opportunity to give lessons to "the distinguished *señorita* de Huarte," or Ana María Josefa Ramona de Huarte y Muñiz (1786–1861), who married Agustín Come Damián de Iturbide y Aram Buru (1783–1824).[18] When Agustín Iturbide became emperor Agustín I of Mexico on May 18, 1822, he appointed Elízaga "Master of the Imperial Chapel."[19] His *Elementos de música*, containing lessons for both harpsichord and fortepiano, was published the same year.[20]

Repertoire

There are few surviving sources of instrumental music from the Viceroyalty of Nueva España. Among these are the *Duodecimo Minuetti / Compost / Dal Sr. Carlo Piozzi*, housed in the Archivo Musical de la Biblioteca Turriana. This is notable considering the manuscript is the work of an Italian composer and not signed.[21] Among the other secular works found in this archive are nineteenth-century pieces for piano, or voice and piano, and reductions, parts, and excerpts of operas. The oldest collection, discovered in the 1970s by Thomas Stanford, features sonatas and minuets for solo keyboard and for violin and continuo, some pages identified by Stanford as coming from Arcangelo Corelli's *Sonate a violino e violone o cimbalo,* Op. 5. There is also a sonata by Antoine Mahaut (1719–ca. 1785) and pieces by Leonardo Leo (1694–1744).[22] In the *Quaderno Mayner* we find more works of Pozzi, and a handwritten collection of works for harpsichord or fortepiano used in Mexico City between the years 1804 and 1814.[23] It appears that the *Quaderno Mayner* was not used initially for the teaching of harpsichord or fortepiano, as there are few exercises and no fingering, but a few, such as the *Sonata quinta del Señor Aydem* [*sic*] by Haydn and sonatas of Luigi Boccherini (1743–1805), do demand a degree of technical and interpretative skill.[24] In any event, such works were preferably performed in private settings by wealthy families in early nineteenth-century Nueva España, including those of Soto Carrillo, Doña N. Terri, José Maria Horcasitas (1770–1800), Augustín Horcasitas (1784–?), and Manuel Antonio del Corral (1790–?).[25]

Guatemala

A choir existed to sing both Gregorian chant and polyphonic music in Guatemala from 1534 to 1563, in the bishopric of Francisco Marroquin (1499–1563). Sixteenth-century Guatemalan Chapel Masters included Hernando Franco (1532–1585), Pedro Bermúdez (1558–1605), Tomás Pascual (ca. 1595–1635), and Gaspar Fernandez (ca. 1565–1629); these are among the most important composers of Spanish America. The Portuguese Gaspar Fernandes arrived in Guatemala in 1599 to serve as organist and chapel master in the cathedral and became chapel master in Puebla de los Angeles in Mexico between 1606 and 1629, where he composed villancicos accompanied by continuo. A second golden era in Guatemalan music occurred in 1738, with choir directors and composers such as Manuel José de Quirós (?–1765), Rafael Antonio Castellanos (ca. 1725–1791), and Pedro Nolasco Estrada Aristondo (?–1804).[26]

Viceroyalty of Peru

As important as Nueva España, the Viceroyalty of Peru (1542–1824) was another wealthy center of culture that supported music.[27] Its territory included parts of Central America and practically all of South America, except the regions extending east of the Tordesillas meridian that were granted to Portugal in the Treaty of Tordesillas. These lands included only the eastern extremes of the South American continent and formed the beginning of what is now Brazil.

Venezuela

Little is known about the harpsichord in colonial Venezuela, which was part of the Viceroyalty of Peru. However, we have a document in which we learn that Captain Don Francisco Mijares de Solórzano (ca. 1611–1668) had a large harpsichord in his house in Caracas.[28]

Colombia

Among the notable figures in Colombia are Archbishop Baltasar Jaime Martínez Compañón (1737–1797), a great promoter of music in Bogotá and one of the leading intellectuals in colonial history, and the organist Agustín Valasco. He was hired in 1794 as a harpsichordist and harpist and to prepare the choir for performances in the city's churches, receiving two hundred pesos a year for his services.[29]

The segregation between native Indians and Spaniards resulted in separate musical organizations being set up within small villages, such as Bogotá and Tunja (Colombia), where the instrumentalists were exempt from taxes.[30] Maintaining their native traditional songs and dances, Indians were dancing and drinking *chincha* in Santa Fé in 1591, but they also sang Spanish songs accompanied by harpsichords and other instruments in the houses of the Spanish upper class.[31]

People in Santa Fé, Columbia, seem to have been accustomed to the harpsichord and clavichord. There is, for example, evidence of a harpsichord (or virginal) from Antwerp in that city during the late sixteenth century.[32] José Ignacio Perdomo Escobar claimed to own a harpsichord made in the seventeenth century by a *Criollo* builder from the village of Tasco, Boyacá, and the Colombian José Custodio Cayetano García Rovira (1780–1816) fluently played Haydn's sonatas on the harpsichord.[33] The same is true for the fortepiano. For example, the Marquesa de San Jorge of Santa Fé celebrated for weeks the arrival of her fortepiano, since everyone wanted to become familiar with the new instrument.[34]

Ecuador

The Flemish Franciscan monks Josse de Rickey Malina and Pierre Gosseal de Louvain arrived in Quito in 1534 and founded their convent in 1535. In addition to teaching indigenous children to read and write, Fray Josse taught them the art of chanting and to play musical instruments, including the harpsichord.[35] Some years later, in 1555, the Franciscans founded their first school, San Andrés.

Initially, the title of chapel master was only bestowed upon those ordained in Spain. Later the post of chapel master was offered to talented professional musicians, many of whom were *mestizos* or *creoles* – nationalized mixed castes that ranked beneath Iberian-born Spaniards. The first mestizo to become a teacher was Diego Lobato de Sosa Yarucpalla (ca. 1538–1614), who received this post because of his exceptional musicianship.[36]

Another important musical figure in Ecuador was Maria Ana de Paredes Flores y Jaramillo (1618–1645) or Santa Mariana de Jesus. People close to her said that her life, marked by mysticism, was influenced by another mystical nun, Marianna Francisca de Jesus Torres (1563–1635), who sang and played organ and harp.[37] Bermudez described some of Flores y Jaramillo's traits:

> From a young age [she] learned to read and write, to play vihuela, harpsichord and zither. In all these, she did well and also learned to sing since she had a good voice and all these natural graces she learned from the desire to be a nun of the Convent of Santa Clara of this City . . . sometimes she had a little leisure time that was often between nine and ten at night, or later, joining Doña Juana Caso, her niece, on the harpsichord, vihuela or guitar, sang in a very good voice some strophic songs to the divine.[38]

Peru

Cristobal de Molina (1529–1585), a musician accompanying the Spanish conquistador Francisco Pizarro Gozáles (1478–1541), also served as the harpsichord teacher to his *mestiza* daughter Francisca Pizarro Yupanqui (1534–1598).[39]

Monks in the Peruvian Jesuit Mission of Maynas also endowed the title *letrados* (literates) on deserving Indian musicians, thus flattering them with the suggestion that they were closer to the sacred.[40]

Harpsichords

A virginal built in 1581 by Hans Ruckers (ca. 1555–ca. 1623) was discovered in Peru in 1916, thus making it the oldest surviving instrument of the builder. Found near Cuzco on a farm belonging to the Marquis of Oropesa, a descendant of the Incas, it is now part of the instrument collection in the Metropolitan Museum of Art in New York.[41]

Customs documents from the Contaduría Mayor del Archivo Nacional Histórico between 1769 and 1799 record the entry of fifty musical instruments into Peru. They included harpsichords, pianos, organs, harps, flutes, and violins as well as sheet music. In 1787, "a harpsichord or English fortepiano" arrived in the port of Callao (Lima), and two treatises on music, published in Spain, followed shortly thereafter in Concepción and Santiago (Chile).[42]

Among the records of ships coming from Spain in the Registros del Fondo Real Aduana, in the Archivo General de la Nación del Perú, are found 302 musical instruments that entered Callao between 1772 and 1803. Among these were seven harpsichords, one taxed at 6,000 *reais de vellón* for the Count of San Carlos, and a *clavepiano*, an instrument that combined the mechanisms of harpsichord and fortepiano, on the frigate *La Ventura* in 1785.[43]

Harpsichordists

Juan de Pancorbo, an elder from Cusco, stated in his 1674 will that he had lent his harpsichord to the monastery of Santa Catalina.[44] Another example of the active musical life in Peru is the appraisal of the assets on April 20, 1799 of Doña Josefa Olavide y Jáuregui (1726–1799), sister of the Peruvian writer and politician Pablo Antonio José de Olavide y Jáuregui (1725–1803). In this are found a new French small harpsichord, an antique harpsichord, a large harpsichord made in Paris with built-in organ (*claviorganum*), and an antique harpsichord. Harpsichords were already being made in Lima but importing one from Europe could signify high social status rather than musical necessity.[45]

Repertoire

The largest shipment of musical scores to Peru was an order of more than five hundred pieces made in 1799 by the Galician merchant Antonio Helme, who planned to sell them in his shop on Pozuelo Street, Lima, along with the various instruments. We know that these pieces were not Spanish, but from other parts of Europe because they were classified as "foreign products." This is confirmed by the list of composers whose works were printed mainly in Antwerp, London, and Paris: Johann Christian Bach (1735–1782), Carl Friedrich Abel (1723–1787), Luigi Boccherini (1743–1805), Johann Anton Filtz (1733–1760), Carlo Giusepe Toeschi (1731–1788), and Christian Cannabich (1731–1798).[46]

Bolivia

An important collection of music was found in the Chiquitos Mission, in colonial times part of the Jesuit Republic of Paraguay. It contains musical scores from the libraries of the churches of San Rafael and Sant'Ana, two of the ten churches that were part of the Mission of the Chiquitos Indians.[47] Among the Jesuits responsible for the high musical level of the Chiquitos, the most important was the Swiss priest Martin Schmidt (1694–1772), a Jesuit musician and architect who first encountered the Chiquitos in 1730.[48]

Harpsichords

According to Julieta Alvarado, the first keyboard instruments that were brought to the region were of Flemish origin; their characteristics remained unchanged until the middle of the eighteenth century. This explains the similarity of harpsichord construction found in the old imperial villages of Potosí and Sucre, these being built in local workshops and demonstrating a consistent construction aesthetic that dominated the Amazonian-Andean region and reflected the unparalleled musical development there.[49]

There are at least two surviving harpsichords from the mission workshops.[50] One is decorated in chinoiserie, the other with a simple wood design. The natural keys on the two harpsichords are made of white bone. The black keys, or accidentals, on the harpsichord of the Museum of Charcas are tear-shaped and made of walnut inlaid with mother-of-pearl diamonds and squares. The harpsichord in the Santa Teresa Museum uses cedar for the sharp keys. The keyboard range is four octaves (in forty-five notes) from E/C to c^3 short octave. This range, common on Spanish keyboards, is typical of keyboard instruments in the Americas. The two harpsichords have three rosettes on the soundboard with no signature. The Charcas harpsichord, which features a drawer above the keyboard to hold harpsichord tools, is inscribed "De mi Sra. Dña. Petita Lemoine Año de 17 ..." This refers to a descendant of Jean-Baptiste Lemoine, a Frenchman who settled in Bolivia and had among his children Petrona (b. 1770), the subsequent owner of the harpsichord, who married the Galician Don Ramon García Pérez at the age of sixteen.[51]

Chile

Harpsichords and Harpsichordists

The harpsichord was present in Chile since the sixteenth century and was used in both sacred and secular contexts. In 1594 a harpsichord arrived in Concepción for the Incan princess Beatriz Clara Coya (1556–1600), wife of the governor Martín García Oñez de Loyola (1549–1598). In 1597 the sexton of Lima (Peru), Friar Antonio de Montearroyo, sent a harpsichord in exchange for one hundred masses for the convent of St. Augustine of Santiago.[52]

Thanks to the discovery of a handwritten source dated 1594, we have the first description and record in Chile outside of the religious sphere for the possession of a harpsichord, the purchase of materials for its repair, and its decoration. This instrument belonged to the above-mentioned Beatriz Clara Coya who purchased it just before returning to Peru in 1599.[53]

In 1701, a harpsichord was used for the continuo part in the debut of the opera *La púrpura de la rosa* by Tomas de Torrejón y Velasco (1644–1728), presented in the Palace of the Viceroyalty of Peru. A document dated September 1726 in the Archivo Histórico de la Provincia Mercedaria de Chile, Santiago tells us that the Convento de La Merced owned a clavichord in 1721.[54] We also learn in the Augustinian Archives that the San Agustín Convent of Santiago had a "large harpsichord since 1597."[55]

Maria Francisca Javiera Velaz de Medrano, the wife of the Governor, Gabriel Cano de Aponte (1665–1733), was reported to be a skillful keyboard performer, and, because of her influence, harpsichords came to the region. A French traveler wrote in 1709 that the local ladies played spinets, castanets, and tambourines, and by 1740, there were at least twenty harpsichords in Santiago, five in Concepción, and one in La Serena.[56] The cathedral in Concepción had, in addition to the organist, an instrumental ensemble consisting of one harpsichordist, one harpist, two violinists, fife, and percussion.[57] Around 1820, fortepianos started to arrive in Chile and began replacing the harpsichord.[58]

Argentina

Pedro de Mendoza (ca. 1499–1537), upon his arrival in Buenos Aires in 1536, brought together some expeditionaries like Nuño Gabriel who, upon arrival, began to teach the Indian children "songs against their vices."[59] Juan Gabriel Lezcano (Nuño's real name) was the only musician in the Mendoza fleet, and it was he who founded the first music school in this region.

Musical traces of the Italian organist and composer Domenico Zipoli (1688–1726) disappeared shortly after the publication of his *Sonate d'intavolatura per órgano e címbalo* in 1716 and were only rediscovered 217 years later in 1933.[60] It was not until 1941, however, that the Uruguayan musicologist Lauro Ayestarán (1913–1966) made the connection between the Italian organist, Domenico Zipoli, and the Jesuit, Domingos Zipoli, who came to South America. According to studies by Furlong and Ayestarán, in 1717 the Jesuit Zipoli arrived in Buenos Aires and later died in Santa Catalina, Córdoba in 1726.[61] It is not known precisely what prompted such a renowned Roman composer, one connected to Arcadia, the secret brotherhood movement in Rome, to embark on such a curious and dangerous undertaking, renouncing the path of glory to devote himself to the salvation of indigenous souls. Nevertheless, performances of Zipoli's works can be found from Argentina to Peru, and his music formed a significant part of the Concepción collection in Chiquitos.[62] Among the works left by Zipoli is his pedagogical *Principia elementa ab bene pulsandum organum et cimbalum,* a method for improvisation and performance that includes hundreds of pieces for both organ and harpsichord.[63]

Harpsichords and Harpsichordists

The Lézica family residence was a place of musical cultivation. The Indian Cristóbal Pirioby (1764–1794) served as harpsichord teacher to the Lézica daughter.[64] He was born in San Carlos (Paraguay), studied with Jesuit students, and married at the age of sixteen. He then moved to Buenos Aires, where he was acclaimed as a harpsichordist, changed his name to José Antonio Ortiz, and began to dress in the best European fashion.[65] Pirioby was in much demand by *Porteña* high society, to whom he offered lessons in singing, harpsichord, violin, and guitar. In front of his house hung a sign that read: "Harpsichord Master." He built harpsichords and other musical instruments and accumulated a rich musical library that included works of Haydn, Boccherini, Pleyel, Scarlatti, Stamitz, and others.[66] The posthumous inventory of Pirioby's instruments included two cedar harpsichords, one with hammers and the other with feathers (i.e., quills); a cedar spinet, stringed; three recently made guitars; and other instruments.[67]

The Harpsichord in Colonial Portuguese America

According to the aforementioned Treaty of Tordesillas, Portuguese America consisted of a relatively small portion of land on the Atlantic Coast. However, the Portuguese expanded their domains through actions known as *Entradas* and *Bandeiras*.[68] These expeditions extended the Brazilian territory to the north, east, and south.[69] Hundreds of settlements emerged along the paths of the *bandeirantes* expeditions, founding several Brazilian cities of today.

Jesuits in Brazil

Only nine years after the creation of the order of the Jesuits, Manuel da Nóbrega (1517–1570) came to Brazil as part of the fleet of Tomé de Souza (1503–1579) and established the first Jesuit presence in Brazil. The work of converting the Indians was not their only activity, but it was their main objective. With the intention of bringing their moral standards and cultural practices to the natives, the Jesuits needed to resort to broader civilizing methods that brought together indigenous and European cultures. As we have seen, the Jesuits realized that music would be an efficient means of converting and indoctrinating the Indians, who appreciated music, and of teaching the catechism.[70] As the missionary and Jesuit historian Guilhermo Furlong reminds us, the Indians' "unique capacity for music ... was, from California to Tierra del Fuego, as important as spiritual life."[71]

After twelve years of Jesuit activity on Brazilian soil, we find the arrival of harpsichords in the entourage of D. Pero Fernandes Sardinha (1496–1556), who settled in Salvador to create the first cathedral and to become the first Bishop in Brazil.[72] Unfortunately, Dom Sardinha was slaughtered by the Caetés tribe and, with his entourage, devoured in 1556.

In a letter to Ignatius of Loyola in 1554, the Jesuit Father José de Anchieta (1534–1597) reported on the transfer of their college to a new village, the mass being celebrated on 25 January in a poor little house and the Indians bringing their children to be taught by the Jesuits. Vocal instruction was the duty of Father Antonio Rodrigues (1514–1590), the first music master in the town of São Paulo, his importance emphasized by the fact that he was once entertained at a college party with ensembles of organ, harpsichord, and flute.[73] For New Year's Eve vespers in Bahia, Indian boys taught by Father Antonio Rodrigues played organ, harpsichord, and flutes, according to a 1565 letter from Father Antonio Blasques to the Provincial Governor.[74]

In Rio de Janeiro the Jesuits built their church and college in Morro do Castelo, coinciding with the founding of the city. Another important Jesuit institution was Fazenda Santa Cruz, eighty kilometers from Rio de Janeiro.[75] Thus, in addition to teaching the catechism, the Jesuits fulfilled another function: creating a quality educational network in urban centers. The noticeable difference between the music of the Jesuits in Portuguese and Spanish America is that Portuguese Americans kept written documents but few iconographic references and concentrated their activities in urban centers, as in the colleges of Rio de Janeiro and São Paulo and then later in the seventeenth century with the colleges of Pará and Maranhão.[76] In Spanish America there was more emphasis on sheet music, instruments, and keyboard instruction.[77]

The Portuguese also actively protected the Indians in the interior, keeping them as far as possible from the Europeans and trying to make them self-sufficient. For example, we read that "the ferocious Tupinambás boasted of being the best musicians of the vast Pindorama," and "among the Tupinambás musicians are many esteemed ... [and] exempt from being harmed."[78] In the chronicles of the itinerant Father Fernão Cardim (1549–1625), he writes about the harpsichords he found in various places along his travels in Bahia (Ilhéus and Porto Seguro), Pernambuco, Espírito Santo, Rio de Janeiro, and São Vicente during the years of 1583–1590.[79] Examples are as follows:

> When the priest visited the classes, he was received by the students with great joy and celebration. Some epigrams were recited and there was good music of singing, harpsichord and discantes.
>
> Day of the Kings (January 6, [16]84) some brothers renewed their vows. Then he said Solemne Mass with deacon and subdeacon, officiated at the corner of the organ by the Indians, with his flutes, harpsichord and discante.

In all these three villages there is a school of reading and writing, where the priests teach the Indian boys; some more skilled are also taught counting, singing and to play; all take to this well, and there are already many who play the flutes, violas, harpsichords.

In the procession there was good music of voices, flutes and organs. Upon a few steps were certain students, with their discantes and harpsichords, they said psalms, and some motets and also recited epigrams to the holy relics.

The next day, because it was the day of the eleven thousand virgins, there was a great party at the college ... The mass was officiated with Indians' a capella, with flutes, and some Cathedral singers, with organs, harpsichords and discantes.[80]

In southern Brazil, in what was known as the Jesuit Republic of Paraguay, Father Louis Berger (1590–1639), a French musician, painter and dancer, was the first to teach vocal and instrumental music to the natives, starting in 1626. Berger was quoted in his *Cartas Ânuas* as saying: "with his lute he converted multitudes of infidels."[81]

In 1639, Father Antonio Ruiz de Montoya (1585–1652) described the natives' love of music as taught by the priests and their commitment to learn the execution of sacred songs and the handling of musical instruments. These instruments, mostly produced by the natives themselves, were copied from European models.[82]

The French priest Jean Vaisseau (1583–1623) taught the natives musical notation and perfected their musical performance.[83] At that time, schools of music, choral singing, and dance were set up in all the missions. The Indians practiced the instruments daily, learned to sing by reading notes and became skilled musicians up to European standards. Upon the arrival of two French priests in Paraguay in 1628, the Indians performed ballets with music for two choirs, in the French style. Several instruments are mentioned, including a clavichord manufactured by the Indians.[84]

In the north of Brazil, a Luxemburg priest, Jean-Philipp Bettendorff (1625–1698), served as superior of the Mission of Maranhão, where someone other than a Jesuit played the harpsichord for a Novena of St. Francis of Assisi (ca. 1691).[85] Around this time in the south of Brazil, a Father Sepp arrived to teach, with a particular emphasis on music. In contrast to other Jesuits, Sepp's musical expertise was in the *stile moderno*, leading to a significant improvement in music produced in the missions by and for the Indians. We also learn that the "Prosecutor of the Company of Jesus" in the Netherlands, who came on the same ship with Sepp to Buenos Aires, purchased instruments, including a harpsichord and a spinet.[86]

Sepp also worked on music in the Yapeyú mission.[87] Upon his arrival, he and his Jesuit companions were welcomed by the natives of the mission with dances, theater, and music. Sepp was surprised and deeply pleased to see the taste and interest of the Guaraní for music, as well as being interested in developing their artistic activities. The only fault that Sepp noticed was that they were technically and stylistically backward, since the Indians were instructed by Spanish priests who knew only the ancient Renaissance polyphony while, for almost a century, Europe had embraced the baroque style. Sepp reported: "what it costs me to instruct the Indians in our European music, only the good God knows . . . and that differs from the old Spanish music (which they still have) as the day differs from the night."[88] Sepp's goals were to create a National School of Music in Yapeyú. From the beginning, the smaller villages could boast of four organists, four lutenists, flute players, harpsichordists, trumpeters, and other instrumentalists.[89]

Sepp relied on the scores he requested from the Order or what he knew from memory, but initially he had difficulties obtaining musical instruments. Those that he had brought from Europe were copied by the Indians themselves in the mission workshops. More than mere copyists, the captive Guaraní were true artists, building fine organs, *cítolas*, harpsichords, psalteries, bassoons, flutes, theorbos, and trumpets within various missions.[90] The coming of Sepp to southern South America made possible a rapid evolution in the arts and music within the missionary regions.

In 1759, the Jesuits were expelled from Brazil by the Marquis of Pombal, Sebastião José de Carvalho e Melo (1699–1782). In 1768, within the inventory of the Jesuits' property found on the Fazenda Santa Cruz, which was appropriated for the benefit of the Crown of Portugal, are found a harpsichord and a clavichord.[91] In the post-expulsion period, harpsichords are also mentioned in the inventories of the Belém da Cachoeira Seminary in Bahia; the Village of Reritiba, in Espírito Santo; and at the Fazenda de Santa Cruz, Rio de Janeiro. Although the College of Maranhão inventory does not mention harpsichords, a letter from Father Bernardo de Aguiar, rector of the college, states: "in the hand of Carlos José, organist of the college, was the harpsichord of the said college."[92] The Jesuits left behind twenty harpsichords, twenty spinets, and eleven clavichords at the time of their expulsion.[93]

Non-Jesuit Harpsichord Activity
The major Brazilian towns and cities grew along the Atlantic coast. Their hot and humid climate was not conducive to the preservation of the wood, metals, and fabrics, and attacks of termites, fungi, and oxidation meant that few instruments remained intact for long, nor did they survive into the present day.[94] However, we do have a record of a small organ and a *clavicembalo* brought in 1549 by the ship *O Licorno* that arrived in São Vicente (São Paulo) from Antwerp.[95]

Music in the seventeenth century was central not only in religious events other than those of the Jesuits but also in festive and political occasions. According to the testimony of Jorge Rodrigues, editor of the *Relaçam da aclamação*, the restoration of the Portuguese throne was celebrated in Rio de Janeiro in 1641. At the end of the seventeenth century, with the news of the abundance of gold in Minas Gerais, many people went to Rio de Janeiro, as the riches discovered in the lands of Minas Gerais came through the port of the city, resulting in considerable social, commercial, and economic development.[96]

Thus, in the transition from the seventeenth to eighteenth centuries, Rio de Janeiro, with its increasingly busy port, began to flex its muscles as an important commercial center, resulting in the importation of instruments, notably harpsichords. In the *Registro da carta régia* of 1721, in evaluating the genres for calculating and taking the *dízima* from Customs, we can note the presence of large harpsichords among other goods.[97]

Around 1690, Portuguese instrument construction began a significant expansion, due to the recovery of the kingdom's financial power, thanks to the exploitation of Brazilian gold and precious stones. With Portugal's recovered status and the accession to the throne of D. João V in 1706, political support was given to the arts. This resulted in a resurgence of Portuguese organ building and an increased interest in the harpsichord and, later, the fortepiano.[98] According to José Ramos Tinhorão, "the harpsichord would have been one of the instruments found in the possession of Peregrino of Nuno Marques Pereira on his visit to a music school in Salvador (Bahia) in the first decade of the eighteenth-century."[99]

In São Paulo, D. Luís Antônio de Souza Botelho Mourão (1722–1798), 4th Morgado de Mateus, began chronicling the presence of music in daily life. With this document, in which the harpsichord frequently appears in the cities of Santos, São Vicente, and São Paulo, we read about the "excellent music and beautiful instruments of violins, harpsichords and organ [and] good harpsichord, fiddle and organ music."[100] Polastre describes such instruments, including harpsichords, being played during the 1766 Feast of Our Lady of Amparo in São Vicente. She mentions that mulattos played harpsichord, horns, "aboares" (oboes), flutes, fiddles, and drums while traveling in canoes.[101]

With the rise of Rio de Janeiro as the capital of the Portuguese colony in 1763, the city became the political, economic, administrative and cultural center of Portuguese America. This resulted in a marked increase in the importation of cultural goods. For example, in 1766, a *Pauta das Avaliações* included many musical instruments and accessories, such as large and small harpsichords, and spinets.[102] The taxation on these was $19,200 for large harpsichords, $12,000 for the small ones, and $6,000 for "the smallest, or spinet." Similar values applied in the port of Santos in 1796.[103] In Santos, in 1784, Morgado de Mateus refers to a harpsichord and a clavichord. There is also mention of a harpsichord worth $48,000 in 1822.[104]

Unlike the gold rush in other countries, there was an intrinsic desire to settle in Villa Rica and its region. It is reported that *solfège* examples and various musical instruments were sold in many shops in Villa Rica (Minas Gerais); numerous editions of music and treatises, including those for harpsichord, regularly arrived from Portugal; and books coming from Lisbon found interested and avid consumers in Minas Gerais.[105] There is also mention of Silvestre José da Costa, who sang in a trio until 1778, after which he appears as a violinist, organist, harpsichordist, and double bass player.[106]

With music in full flower in Rio de Janeiro, it was not surprising that Sir George Staunton (1737–1801), while strolling through the city in 1792, witnessed women playing the harpsichord and the guitar through open doors and windows in the warm summer evenings.[107]

With the advances in the colony, it was very common for important families to dedicate themselves to making music. Some formed groups of amateurs, including singers and instrumentalists of excellent quality. According to Adrien Balbi, "João Leal was son of doctor Leal, and major of the General Staff. He is the best tenor of Rio de Janeiro, where they call him *Vacani*, because of the extraordinary talent that imitates the great Italian artist."[108] The exceptional musical talents within the Leal family spanned four generations. João Leal's father was one of the best doctors in Rio de Janeiro and a virtuoso on the violin. Seven of his sons studied at the University of Coimbra, where they graduated from several colleges, and they skillfully played music by Cimarosa, Rossini, Marcos Portugal, and other Italian and Brazilian masters.[109]

The 1798 posthumous inventory of the botanist Antônio Pereira Ferreira is proof that it was common to find harpsichords in the wealthiest residences of Rio de Janeiro during that time. One line item describes a "Fortepiano made in Rio de Janeiro ... appraised in the amount of ninety-five thousand réis," while another tells us that a "Small feathered harpsichord was appraised in the amount of twenty-two thousand réis."[110]

Brazil received various goods from Europe and Asia but only through Portuguese trade channels. Although industry in Brazil was banned, such prohibitions led the colony's merchants to circumvent these laws in order to keep their business alive by the use of contraband, which was not only permitted but also partially controlled by the government.[111] We can therefore assume that artisans in Brazil would also be able to disregard existing laws, and it is possible harpsichord and fortepiano builders existed in eighteenth-century Rio de Janeiro.[112]

There were, however, few harpsichord teachers in Rio de Janeiro. The most famous was José Maurício Nunes Garcia (1767–1830), a mulatto of humble origin who managed to become a priest and also assert himself as a composer. He was a pupil of Salvador José and learned to play the harpsichord practically by himself.[113] José Mauricio taught many ladies to play the harpsichord and in 1821 wrote a fortepiano method.[114]

The harpsichord and fortepiano coexisted for a time in early nineteenth-century Rio de Janeiro, as we see in the advertisements from this period. In 1810 an advertisement for a harpsichord for sale appeared in the Rio de Janeiro newspaper; it did not mention the builder, only its main features: "Whoever wants to buy a five-octave feathered harpsichord, with very good sound; you can go to Rua das Mangueiras No. 8."[115] On March 24, 1819, the *Gazeta do Rio de Janeiro* contained two sales announcements. The first reads: "One is to sell in the street of Violas No. 19, a new and modern fortepiano, also an orphica, instrument of new invention." In the second: "For sale, a feathered harpsichord of Mathias Boltheim [*sic*], in the street of the Alfandega No. 14, auction house."[116]

Repertoire

With the Jesuits' expulsion in 1759 came the disappearance of their musical scores. It wasn't until 1830 that music scores began being printed in Brazil, more than a century after Spanish America.[117] It seems very likely that some Indian composers wrote music prior to 1830, but because music was viewed as simply a practical item, it wouldn't have been signed.[118]

Manuel de Almeida Botelho (1721–?) was a Pernambucan who moved to Lisbon under the protection of the Marquis of Marialva.[119] Dom Domingos de Loreto Couto, an eighteenth-century historian from Pernambuco, tells us that Botelho composed cantilenas, *minuettes*, several sonatas, and toccatas for harpsichord.[120] Couto also comments that Father Antonio da Sylva Alcantara (1712–after 1757), a native of Recife, became a great musician and composed sonatas for violin, for harpsichord, and for cithara, all lost, unfortunately.[121]

Although the *XII Sonate da cimbalo di piano e forte detto volgarmente di Martelletti*, by Lodovico Giustini (1685–1743) was composed near Florence in 1732, it has direct connections to Brazil. The first collection for fortepiano, it was published because of the sponsorship of a Brazilian Bishop: the Carioca Dom João de Seyxas da Fonseca (1691–1758). According to the dedication, Seyxas, or Don Giovanni de Seyxas, was a musician of great talent and a skillful harpsichordist. The work was dedicated to D. Antonio de Bragança (1694–1757), second to the throne of Portugal, and an expert harpsichordist, like his niece Maria Bárbara, the student of Domenico Scarlatti (1685–1757).[122] This unusual set of connections between a relatively unknown composer (Giustini) from Pistoia, a small city near Florence, an important church authority originally from Brazil (Seixas), and a noble-born music lover from Portugal (D. Antonio), resulted in the departure point for the future of piano music.[123]

There are those who believe that the *25 Solfejos* that are part of the manuscript *Muzico e moderno systema para solfejar sem confuzão* (Recife, 1776) by Luís Álvares Pinto (ca. 1719–1789) were meant to be performed.[124] In the late 1980s, a craze occurred around a keyboard sonata in the Santa Cecilia Musical Society of Sabará (Minas Gerais). This work, the Sonata No. 2, *Sabará* (see Examples 13.1–13.3) by an unknown composer, has three movements and closely resembles the works of Italian authors writing during the stylistic transition of this era.[125]

The Portuguese Court Sheltered in Brazil

With the coming of Prince Regent D. João (1767–1826) and his court, great changes took place in Brazil. The Prince soon recognized the talents of the aforementioned José Mauricio, who went on to work as a chapel master, organist, harpsichordist, improviser, and admirable composer. Sigismund Neukomm (1778–1858) arrived in Brazil in 1817, and he developed a deep and lasting friendship with José Mauricio, whom he greatly admired.[126]

The idea of installing the Portuguese Court in Brazil had been considered several times, but it was only with the advances of Napoleon Bonaparte's (1769–1821) troops that the Prince Regent João, then King

Example 13.1 Anonymous, Sonata No. 2, *Sabará* (Santa Cecilia Musical Society of Sabará, Minas Gerais), movement I, mm. 1–6

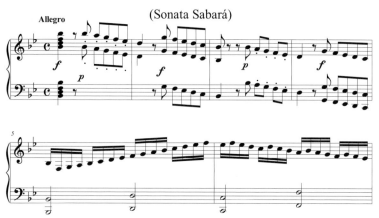

Example 13.2 Anonymous, Sonata No. 2, *Sabará*, movement II, mm. 1–6

Example 13.3 Anonymous, Sonata No. 2, *Sabará*, movement III, mm. 1–10

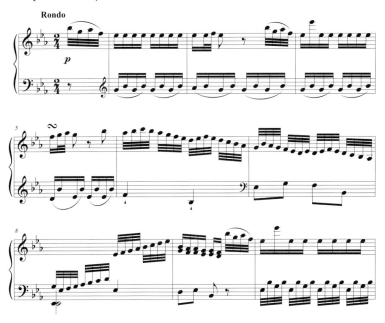

João VI, decided to escape to the South American country. D. Pedro de
Almeida Portugal (1754–1813), seeing the fragility of the kingdom, wrote
to the prince regent: "Your Royal Highness has a great empire in Brazil . . .
You must have all your Warships and every transport in Lisbon Square
assembled with haste."[127] The son of Dom João VI, Pedro married
Leopoldina of Habsburg (1797–1826), an excellent pianist and a student
of Leopold Koželuh (1747–1818). She brought with her to Brazil a vast
collection of scores. They are currently housed in the National Library of
Rio de Janeiro, in the Collection Thereza Christina.[128]

This brief report on the harpsichord in the Spanish and Portuguese Americas tells us that there are very many primary sources and instruments yet to be revealed. This vast field needs to be fully explored by both native and foreign harpsichordists and scholars. All are most welcome to join in the research of this fascinating subject.

Notes

All translations are the author's, unless otherwise noted.

1. In Spanish- and early Portuguese-speaking countries it is common to read the word "clavicórdio" in reference to the harpsichord or spinet, and "monocórdio" (or "manocórdio" and "monacórdio") for the clavichord. In this chapter, harpsichord will be used in place of clavicórdio and clavichord in place of monocórdio. For example, In the entry "Manicórdio" in the *Diccionario da Lingua Portugueza* composto pelo Padre D. Rafael Bluteau (1638–1734) reformado e accrescentado por Antonio de Moraes Silva (1755–1824), natural do Rio de Janeiro (Lisbon: Na Oficina de Simão Thaddeo Ferreira, Anno M.DCC.LXXXIX), p. 53, we read: "*Manicórdio, noun* (or before monochord) is a musical instrument of strings of wire, and keyboard, smaller than the Harpsichord, and Spinet, and the Fortepiano. We can understand this to be the clavichord."

2. Jorge Pimentel Cintra, "O Mapa das Cortes e as Fronteiras do Brasil," *Boletim de Ciências Geodésicas* 18, no. 3 (July–September, 2012), p. 422. The Treaty of Tordesillas divided the newly discovered lands outside Europe between Portugal and Spain along a meridian 370 leagues west of the island of Cabo Verde (on the west coast of Africa). This line of demarcation was halfway between Cabo Verde (already Portuguese) and the islands entered by Christopher Colombus on his first voyage. The lands to the east would belong to Portugal and the lands to the west to Spain.

3. See Gabriela Pellegrino and Maria Ligia Prado, *História da América Latina* (São Paulo: Editora Contexto, 2014), pp. 19–20.

4. See José-Antonio Guzmán-Bravo, "Mexico, Home of the First Musical Instrument Workshops in America," *Early Music* 6, no. 3 (July, 1978), pp. 350–355, here p. 350.

5. See Javier Marín Lopez, *Música y músicos entre dos mundos: La Catedral de México y sus libros de polifonía (Siglos XVI-XVIII)* (PhD diss., Universidad de Granada, 2007), p. 77.

6. See Jesús A. Ramos-Krittel, *Playing in the Cathedral: Music, Race, and Status in New Spain* (New York: Oxford University Press, 2016), p. 83.

7. See Faith S. Lanam, "Mothers, Niñas, and Nuns: The Professional Training of Young Female Musicians of Colonial Mexico," *American Musicological Society, Eighty-Second Annual Meeting*, November, 2016, pp. 53–54.

8. Francisco Barrio Lorenzot, *Compendio de los tres tomos de la compilación nueva de las ordenanzas de la M. Noble Insigne, y muy Leal, e Imperial* (Ciudad de Mexico: Secretaría de gobernación – Dirección de talleres gráficos, 1920), p. 85. Eduardo Areas and Jorge Rigueiro García write: "To become a professional *Violero*, it was necessary to demonstrate that one

mastered the construction of various instruments (clavichord, harpsichord, monochord, lute, bowed vihuela, harp and vihuelas of different sizes); if the candidate passed the examination, he was granted a license to establish a workshop," "La música colonial americana (siglos xvii y xviii): un espacio para el encuentro de dos mundos,"*Acta Académica,* 59 (2005), p. 7, www .academica.org/000–006/548. See also Javier Marín Lopez, *Música y músicos entre dos mundos: La Catedral de México y sus libros de polifonía (Siglos XVI–XVIII)* (PhD diss., University of Granada, 2007), p. 184.

9. This publication was a translation of *Leçons de clavecin et principes d'harmonie,* by Anton Bemetzrieder (1739–1817), published in Paris, 1771. See Jesús Herrera, *El Quaderno Mayner* (MA diss., Universidad Veracuzana, 2007), p. 56.

10. *Teoría de los principios mas esenciales de la musica que para instruccion y adelantamiento de sus discipulos, particularmente de clave, dispuso D. José Vicente Castro [?–1827], Ministro del Coro de la Metropolitana Iglesia de México,* 1814.

11. For details on *SMMS M3* see John Koegel, "New Sources of Music from Spain and Colonial Mexico at Sutro Library," *Notes* 55, no. 3 (March, 1999), p. 587. The unabridged manuscript, copied at the beginning of the nineteenth century, was purchased by Adolph Heinrich Joseph Sutro (1830–1898) in Mexico City between 1885 and 1889 and later taken to San Francisco.

12. Herrera, *El Quaderno Mayner*, p. 59.

13. See Lopez, *Música y músicos*, p. 190, and María Díez-Canedo Flores, "La flauta travesera en las dos orillas – Una sonata de flauta de Luis Misón en México," *Cuadernos de Música Iberoamericana* 14 (2007), pp. 57–58.

14. Jesús Herrera reports that there is a reference to Aldana in the *Diario de México* of 1806: "We know the merit in the vigüela of the American Pleyel Don Jose Aldana, who has been able to inspire his musical genius to his disciples." Herrera continues: "Apparently 'vigüela' seems to designate the violin, which puts Aldana within reach of teaching the harpsichord. Gabriel Saldívar included him among the great child prodigies in the history of music." See Jesús Herrera, "Carlo Pozzi: compositor europeo de música profana presente en la Catedral de México a fines del virreinato," *Heterofonía* 143 (July–December, 2010), p. 51.

15. Raúl W Capistrán Gracia, "Manuel Antonio Del Corral y José Mariano Elízaga," Ponencia presentada en el *4o. Congreso de Musicología Cima y Sima, Musicología en Acción* / CENIDIM. Museo de Arte Abstracto Felgueres. Zacatecas, Zac. p. 7, www.raulcapistrangracia.com/español-1/ ponencias-y-conferencias/.

16. See Gabriel Saldívar, "José Mariano Elízaga," *Heterfonía* 19, no. 4 (October–December, 1968), p. 41. See also Gabriel Saldívar. "Mariano Elízaga, Niño Prodigio," *Heterofonía* 106 (January–June, 1992), pp. 36–37. The article appeared in the *Gaceta de México*, October 30, 1792, t. V, núm. 21, pp. 181–183. For a full description, see Herrera, *El Quaderno Mayner*, pp. 52–53.

17. Carrillo, an admirer of Haydn, was a composer, pianist, and the leading piano teacher in Mexico City.

18. Capistrán Gracia, "Manuel Antonio Del Corral y José Mariano Elízaga," p. 7.
19. Jesús Herrera, *El Quaderno Mayner*, p. 53.
20. Herrera, *El Quaderno Mayner*, p. 53.
21. Jesús Herrera writes: "There is a microfilm copy in the Biblioteca Nacional de Antropología e Historia, in section 92: Archivo de Música Sacra de la Catedral Metropolitana, Mexico City, 1967 (selection of Thomas Stanford and Lincoln Spiess), roll I – Sonatas and minuetes. (9.4.51.I)." [9.4.51.I])]." Herrera, "Carlo Pozzi," p. 9.
22. See Herrera, "Carlo Pozzi," pp. 10, 11, 13, and 14.
23. Herrera, *El Quaderno Mayner*, p. 61.
24. See Karl Bellinghausen (1954–2017), *José Manuel Aldana. Vida y obra Signos, El arte y la investigación* (Mexico City: INBA-Dirección de Investigación y Documentación de las Artes, 1989), p. 152, and Herrera, *El Quaderno Mayner*, p. 113. Bellinghausen would later suggest that these sonatas were not works for solo harpsichord but rather keyboard pieces with the accompaniment of violin and likely written by an Italian composer. In 2004, Jacques Ogg, in research at the Biblioteca Miguel Lerdo de Tejada, Mexico City, recognized some movements as coming from the Opus 5 of Boccherini. Herrera, *El Quaderno Mayner*, p. 113.
25. For information on these families and performances, see Herrera, *El Quaderno Mayner*, p. 109; Tania Zelma Chávez-Náder, *New Perspectives on the Life and Music of the Mexican Composer Rodolfo Campodónico Morales (1864–1926): Study, Edition and Recordings of Six Rediscovered Piano Waltzes* (DMA diss., Arizona State University, 2009), p. 13. For a list of Corral's keyboard works, see Capistrán Gracia, "Manuel Antonio Del Corral y José Mariano Elízaga," pp. 2–3.
26. Francisco Martín Boniche Rosales, *Historia de la Música en Guatemala*, www.monografias.com/trabajos7/mugu/mugu.shtml.
27. Pellegrino and Prado, *História da América Latina*, p. 12.
28. José Antonio Calcaño, "La música colonial venezolana," *Revista Musical Chilena* 16, nos. 81–82 (July–December, 1962), p. 195.
29. *Libro de acuerdos desde el mes de 1794 [1794–1810], fol. 123v. (July 12, 1796)*; see Robert Stevenson, "Colonial Music in Colombia," *The Americas* 19, no. 2 (October, 1962), p. 134.
30. Egberto Bermudez, "La Música Colombiana: Pasado y Presente," in *A tres bandas: Mestizage, sincretismo e Hibridación en el espacio sonoro ibero Americano*, Alberto Recasens Berbarà, ed. (Madrid: Ediciones Akal, 2010), p. 248. This was also the case in the Jesuit missions on the Colombian and Venezuelan borders. Bermudez writes: "The dual scheme of a 'republic of Indians' separate from the 'republic of Spaniards' made it possible to replicate the cathedral musical organization in the small 'Indian villages' (especially around Bogotá and Tunja), where, according to the Royal Ordinances, the instrumentalists were exempt of tribute."
31. *Chincha*, a fermented drink usually made from maize, is a typical beverage in Spanish America.

32. See Egberto Bermudez, *La Música Colombiana*, 2010, pp. 248–249, and Egberto Bermudez, *La Música en el Arte Colonial de Colombia* (Bogotá: Fundación de Música, 1994), p. 91.

33. José Ignacio Perdomo Escobar, *Historia de la Música en Colombia* (Bogotá: Plaza & Janes, Editores, 1980), pp. 53 and 57.

34. Escobar, *Historia de la Música en Colombia*, p. 47.

35. Robert Stevenson, "Música en Quito," *Revista Musical Chilena* 16, Nos. 81–82 (July–December, 1962), p. 172.

36. Stevenson, "Música en Quito," p. 173, and Mario Godoy Aguirre, *Historia de la música del Ecuador* (Quito: Corporación Editora Nacional, Editorial Ecuador, 2005), p. 60.

37. Egberto Bermudez, "La vihuela de la iglesia de la Compania de Jesus de Quito," *Revista Musical Chilena* 179 (January–June, 1993), p. 73.

38. Bermudez, "La vihuela," pp. 73 and 75.

39. See María Gembero Ustárroz and Emilio Ros-Fábregas, eds., "Migraciones de Músicos entre España y América (Siglos XVI–XVII)," in *La Música y el Atlantico* (Granada: Universidad de Granada, 2007), p. 43.

40. Francismar Alex Lopes de Carvalho, "Mediadores do Sagrado: Os Auxiliares Indígenas dos Missionários nas Reduções Jesuíticas da Amazônia Ocidental (ca. 1638–1767)," *Revista de História* (São Paulo), no. 173 (July–December 2015), pp. 175–210.

41. Stewart Pollens, "Flemish Harpsichords and Virginals in the Metropolitan Museum of Art: An Analysis of Early Alteration and Restorations," in *Metropolitan Museum Journal* 32 (1997), p. 88.

42. Alejandro Vera, "Music, Eurocentrism and Identity: The Myth of the Discovery of America in Chilean Music History," *Advances in Historical Studies* 3 (2014), p. 307.

43. Alejandro Vera, "La circulación de la música en la América virreinal: el virreinato del Perú (siglo XVIII)," in *Anais do III SIMPOM 2014 – Simpósio Brasileiro de Pós-Graduandos em Música* (Rio de Janeiro, 2014), p. 11.

44. Geoffrey Baker, "Music in the Convents and Monasteries of Colonial Cuzco," *Revista de Música Latinoamericana* 24, no. 1 (Spring–Summer, 2003), p. 4.

45. Vera, "La circulación de la música en la América virreinal," pp. 12–13.

46. Vera, "La circulación de la música en la América virreinal," p. 13.

47. T. Frank Kennedy, "Colonial Music from the Episcopal Archive of Concepción, Bolivia," *Revista de Música Latinoamericana* 9, no. 1 (Spring–Summer, 1988), p. 1.

48. Kennedy, "Colonial Music from the Episcopal Archive of Concepción," p. 2.

49. Julieta Alvarado, "Los claves coloniales de Sucre y Potosí," *Anuario Musical* 58 (2003), pp. 197–199. Native instruments of Sucre and Potosí had fixed registers while those of original Flemish harpsichords could be changed. Alvarado also discovered keyboard instruments of Flemish origin among the belongings of missionary Father Anton Sepp von Rechegg (1655–1733).

50. Alvarado, "Los claves coloniales de Sucre y Potosí," p. 198.

51. Alvarado, "Los claves coloniales de Sucre y Potosí," pp. 198, 200, 202, and 203 respectively.

52. Alejandro Vera, "Musicología, historia y nacionalismo: escritos tradicionales y nuevas perspectivas sobre la música del Chile Colonial," *Acta Musicologica* 78, no. 2 (2006), p. 154.

53. Constanza Alruiz and Laura Fahrenkrog, "Construcción de instrumentos musicales en el Virreinato del Perú: vínculos y proyecciones con Santiago de Chile," *Resonancias* 22 (May, 2008), p. 57.

54. Alejandro Vera, "La música en el convento de La Merced de Santiago de Chile en la época colonial (siglos XVII–XVIII)," *Revista Musical Chilena* 58, no. 201 (2004), p 40.

55. Vera, "La música en el convento de La Merced," p. 40.

56. Samuel Claro Valdés and Jorge Urrutia Blondel, *Historia de Música en Chile* (Santiago: Editorial Orbe, 1973), p. 59.

57. Valdés and Blondel, *Historia de Música en Chile*, p. 60.

58. Valdés and Blondel, *Historia de Música en Chile*, p. 85.

59. Guilhermo Furlong, *Músicos argentinos durante la dominación hispánica* (Buenos Aires: Huerpes, 1944), p. 17.

60. Luis Szarán, *Domenico Zipoli, una vida, un enigma* (Nurnberg: Jesuitenmission, 2005), pp. 27–28.

61. See Vicente Gesualdo, "La Música en Argentina durante el periodo colonial," *Revista Musical Chilena*, 16, Nos. 81–82 (July–December, 1962), p. 128.

62. Gesualdo, "La Música en Argentina," p. 129.

63. See Domenico Zipoli, *Música para órgano y clave de las Reducciones Jesuiticas de America del Sur*, ed. Roberto Antonello and Luiz Zsarán (Nurnberg: Edition Missions Prokur S.J., 2000).

64. Gesualdo, "La Música en Argentina," p. 130.

65. Saul Gaona. *Lá creación musical em el Paraguay* (Asunción: Facultad de Arquitectura Diseño y Arte de la Universidad Nacional de Asunción, 2013), p. 36.

66. Luis Zsarán, *Diccionario de la Música en Paraguay* (Nurnberg: Jesuitenmission, 2007), p. 389.

67. Juan M. Boettner, *Música y músicos del Paraguay* (Asunción: Edicion de Autores Paraguayos, 1956), p. 61, www.portalguarani.com/1394_revista_digital_fa_re_mi_wwwmusicaparaguayaorgpy/14092_del_paraguay_profundo_n_1__revista_digital_fa_re_mi.html.

68. Carlos Eduardo Piassini, "A economia do Brasil colonial na perspectiva de livros diadáticos," *Revista Latino-Americana de História* 2, no. 6 (August, 2013), p. 842. The words "entradas," "bandeiras," and "monções" are used to refer generically to the various types of expeditions undertaken at the time of Colonial Brazil, for purposes as diverse as the simple exploration of the territory, the search for mineral wealth, the capture of indigenous or African slaves, and the attack and destruction of tribes or populations considered by colonials to be hostile or unwanted.

69. More specifically, official *Entradas* were expeditions organized by the government to survey and map the territory for Portugal. *Bandeiras*, on the other hand, were private initiatives to explore the territory beyond the Portuguese domains.

70. Marcos Tadeu Holler, *Uma História de Cantares de Sion na Terra dos Brasis: A Música na atuação dos Jesuítas na América Portuguesa (1549–1759)* (PhD diss., Unicamp, 2006), pp. 131–132.

71. See Daniela Ribeiro Pereira,"*Si soy misionero es porque canto, bailo y toco música": Para uma história social da música na Provincia Paracuaria (1609–1768)* (MA diss., *PUC-RS*, 2011), p. 20.

72. See Marcelo Fagerlande, ed., *O método de Pianoforte de José Mauricio Nunes Garcia*, facsimile (Rio de Janeiro: Relume-Dumará, 1995), p. 18.

73. Claudia Aparecida Polastre, *A música na cidade de São Paulo, 1765–1822* (PhD diss., USP, 2008), p. 29.

74. Holler, *Uma História de Cantares*, p. 116.

75. Mayra Pereira, *Do cravo ao pianoforte no Rio de Janeiro – um estudo documental* (MA diss., Universidade Federal do Rio de Janeiro, 2005), p. 67.

76. See Marcos Holler, "A música na atuação dos jesuítas na América Portuguesa," in *Anais 15º Congresso Anppom*, 2005, pp. 1132–1133.

77. As we noted in the section on Bolivia, more than five thousand colonial-period musical scores were left in the Jesuit missions of Chiquitos and Moxos.

78. Flausino Rodrigues Vale, *Elementos de folclore musical brasileiro* (São Paulo: Companhia Editora Nacional, 1978), citing Gabriel Soares de Souza (1540–1591), p. 17. "*Pindorama*" comes from the Tupi word 'Pind'ob' = palm tree + orama, meaning region or country of palm trees. The name was given by Ando-Peruvian and Pampian people.

79. Fernão Cardim was a Portuguese-born writer and Jesuit missionary, one of the first to describe the inhabitants and customs of Brazil. As a child, he entered the Society of Jesus. Already a Jesuit, he traveled to Brazil in 1583 as secretary of the visitor Cristóvão de Gouveia (1542–1622) and for the governor Manuel Teles Barreto (ca. 1520–1588). He traveled through Brazil and these adventures resulted in the *Narrativa epistolar de uma viagem e missão jesuítica pela Bahia, Ilheos, Porto Seguro, Pernambuco, Espirito Santo, Rio de Janeiro, S. Vicente, (S. Paulo) etc. desde o anno de 1583 ao de 1590, indo por visitador o P. Christovão de Gouvêa. Escripta em duas cartas ao P. Provincial em Portugal* later published as *Tratados da terra e da gente do Brasil*. Cardim eventually assumed the rectory of the College of Rio de Janeiro and became procurator of the province of Brazil (1598), returning to Europe the following year.

80. Fernão Cardim, *Narrativa epistolar* (Lisbon: Imprenssa Nacional, 1847), pp. 8, 31, 47, 61, and 77.

81. Jorge Hirt Preiss, *A música nas missões jesuíticas nos séculos XVII e XVIII* (Porto Alegre: Martins Livreiro-Editor, 1988), p. 20.

82. Preiss, *A música nas missões jesuíticas*, p. 27.

83. Vaisseau was formerly a musician at the court of Archduke Albert of Austria (1559–1621).

84. Rogério Budazs, "Sobre a música no Paraná, 1600–1850," in Manoel J. de Souza Neto, *A (des)construção da música na cultura paranaense* (Curitiba: Editora Quatro Ventos, 2004), p. 16.

85. Holler, *Uma história de Cantares,* p. 116.

86. Anton Sepp von Rechegg, *Viagem às missões jesuíticas e trabalhos apostólicos* (São Paulo: Livraria Martins Editora, 1972), pp. 75–76.
87. Located on the left bank of the Uruguay River, founded in 1626 by Father Roque Gonzáles (1576–1628). The mission covered the region where today are located the cities of Santana do Livramento, Alegrete, Quarai, and Uruguaiana (Rio Grande do Sul).
88. Sepp, *Viagem às missões e trabalhos*, 1972, p. 76.
89. Preiss, *A música nas missões jesuíticas*, pp. 21–27.
90. Preiss, *A música nas missões jesuíticas*, p. 45.
91. Mayra Pereira, *Do cravo ao pianoforte no Rio de Janeiro*, p. 139, citing a publication from 1894 titled *Treslado do autto de inventario da Real Fazenda de Santa Crus ebenz que nella seacham que fes o desembargador dos aggravos e juis do seqestro geral feito aos denominados jezuitas o Doutor Manoel Francisco da Silva e Veiga*. Pereira describes an inventory of the assets of the Santa Cruz Farm (Rio de Janeiro, 6 May 1768), published in Archivo do Districto Federal, No. 2, 1895.
92. Holler, *Uma história de Cantares*, pp. 116–117.
93. Holler, *Uma história de Cantares*, pp. 193–194.
94. See Carlos Penteado de Rezende, "Notas para uma história do piano no Brasil (século XIX)," *Revista Brasileira de Cultura* 6 (1970), pp. 13–14.
95. Polastre, *A música na cidade de São Paulo*, p. 71.
96. See Pereira, *Do cravo ao pianoforte no Rio de Janeiro*, p. 69.
97. Pereira, *Do cravo ao pianoforte no Rio de Janeiro*, p. 70. This document is the oldest recorded registry that refers to the entry of harpsichords in the port of Rio de Janeiro.
98. Pereira, *Do cravo ao pianoforte no Rio de Janeiro*, p. 66.
99. José Ramos Tinhorão, *História social da música popular brasileira* (São Paulo: Editora 34, 1998), p. 124, fn. 9.
100. Polastre, *A música na cidade de São Paulo*, p. 71 and p. 142.
101. Polastre, *A música na cidade de São Paulo*, p. 117.
102. For *Pauta das Avaliações das Fazendas, pelas quais se cobram os direitos da Dízima da Alfândega do Rio de Janeiro* see Pereira, *Do cravo ao pianoforte no Rio de Janeiro*, p. 71.
103. Polastre, *A música na cidade de São Paulo*, p. 205.
104. Polastre, *A música na cidade de São Paulo*, p. 71.
105. Francisco Curt Lange, "La Música en Villa Rica – Minas Gerais, Siglo XVIII," Parte I, *Revista Musical Chilena* (October–December 1967), 21, no. 102, p. 33.
106. Francisco Curt Lange, "La música en Villa Rica – Minas Gerais, siglo XVIII, Parte II," *Revista Musical Chilena* 22, no. 103 (January–March, 1968), p. 89.
107. Rezende, "Notas para uma História do Piano no Brasil," p. 25.
108. Adrien Balbi, *Essai statistique sur le Royaume de Portugal et d'Algarve*. Tome 2nd. (Paris: chez Rey et Gravier, 1822), p. 217.
109. Ayres de Andrade, *Francisco Manuel da Silva e seu tempo* (Rio de Janeiro: Edições Tempo Brasileiro, 1967), pp. 49–50.
110. Pereira, *Do cravo ao pianoforte no Rio de Janeiro*, p. 79.
111. Pereira, *Do cravo ao pianoforte no Rio de Janeiro*, p. 80.

112. Pereira, *Do cravo ao pianoforte no Rio de Janeiro,* p. 81.
113. Guilherme Theorodro Pereira de Mello, *A música no Brasil desde os tempos coloniaes até o primeiro decênio da Republica* (Salvador: Typographya de S. Joaquim, 1908), p. 160.
114. Marcelo Fagerlande, ed., *O método de pianoforte de José Mauricio Nunes Garcia,* facsimile (Rio de Janeiro: Relume-Dumará, 1995).
115. Pereira, *Do cravo ao pianoforte no Rio de Janeiro,* p. 84.
116. Pereira, *Do cravo ao pianoforte no Rio de Janeiro,* p. 86.
117. Paulo Castagna, "Dualidades nas propostas editoriais de música antiga brasileira," *Per Musi* 18 (2008), p. 7.
118. Budazs, "Sobre a música no Paraná," p. 18.
119. Rogério Budazs. *A Música no tempo de Gregório de Mattos* [1636–1696] (Curitiba: DeArtes/UFPR, 2004), pp. 8–10.
120. Dom Domingos Loreto Couto, *Desaggravos do Brasil e glorias de Pernambuco* (Rio de Janeiro: Officina Typographica da Biblioteca Nacional, 1904), p. 383.
121. Couto, *Desaggravos do Brasil,* pp. 374–375.
122. Pedro Persone, *The Earliest Piano Music: Lodovico Giustini (1685–1743) Sonate da cimbalo di piano, e forte, detto volgarmente di martelletti, Firenze, 1732* (Saarbrucken: VDM Verlag, 2008), pp. 26–27.
123. Persone, *The Earliest Piano Music,* pp. 10–17, 22–31, and 32–34.
124. For a modern transcription of this manuscript see, imslp.org/wiki/Muzico_e_moderno_systema_para_solfejar_sem_confuzão_(Pinto,_Lu%C3%ADs_Álvares).
125. Anon., Sonata No. 2, *Sabará* (Belo Horizonte: Editora Pontes, 2007), manuscript discovered by Domingos Sávio Lins Brandão.
126. Pedro Persone, *"O Piano era, então, ainda uma novidade": A Coleção Thereza Christina e sua performance* (Curitiba: Editora Prismas, 2014), p. 21.
127. Laurentino Gomes, *1808 – Como uma rainha louca, um príncipe medroso e uma corte corrupta enganaram Napoleão e mudaram a história de Portugal e do Brasil* (São Paulo: Editora Planeta, 2007), p. 47.
128. Persone,*"O Piano era, então, ainda uma novidade,"* p. 21.

Further Reading

Baker, Geoffrey. "Music in the Convents and Monasteries of Colonial Cuzco." *Revista de Música Latinoamericana* 24, no. 1 (Spring–Summer, 2003), pp. 1–41.
Béhague, Gerard. "Ecuadorian, Peruvian, and Brazilian Ethnomusicology: A General View." *Revista de Música Latinoamericana* 3, no. 1 (Spring–Summer, 1982), pp. 17–35.
Bermudez, Egberto. *La música en el arte colonial de Colombia.* Bogotá: Fundación de Música, 1994.
Chávez-Náder, Tania Zelma. *New Perspectives on the Life and Music of the Mexican Composer Rodolfo Campodónico Morales (1864–1926): Study, Edition and Recordings of Six Rediscovered Piano Waltzes.* DMA thesis, Arizona State University, 2009.

Escobar, José Ignacio Perdomo. *Historia de la Música en Colombia*. Fifth edition. Bogotá: Plaza & Janes, Editores, 1980.

Guzmán-Bravo, José-Antonio. "Mexico, Home of the First Musical Instrument Workshops in America." *Early Music* 6, no. 3 (July, 1978), pp. 350–355.

Kennedy, T. Frank. "Colonial Music from the Episcopal Archive of Concepción, Bolivia." *Revista de Música Latinoamericana* 9, no. 1 (Spring–Summer, 1988), pp. 1–17.

Lanam, Faith S. "Mothers, Niñas, and Nuns: The Professional Training of Young Female Musicians of Colonial Mexico." *American Musicological Society, Eighty-Second Annual Meeting*, November 3–6, 2016, pp. 53–54. www.ams-net.org/vancouver/abstracts.pdf.

Ramos-Krittel, Jesús A. *Playing in the Cathedral: Music, Race, and Status in New Spain*. New York: Oxford University Press, 2016.

Sepp von Rechegg, Anton (1655–1733). *Viagem às missões jesuíticas e trabalhos apostólicos*. São Paulo: Livraria Martins Editora, 1972.

Stevenson, Robert Murrel (1916–2012). "Colonial Music in Colombia." *The Americas* 19, no. 2 (October, 1962), pp. 121–136.

14 Bach, Handel, and the Harpsichord

ROBERT L. MARSHALL

Bach and Handel's relationship to the harpsichord entails several facets: their instruments, their performing careers, their roles as teachers, their continuo practice, and, of course, their music. This essay will be set out in the style of a parallel biography: juxtaposing the discussion of the two masters topic by topic, beginning with the instruments they owned and those for which they composed.

The Instruments

Documentary Evidence

Bach

At the time of their deaths, both Johann Sebastian Bach and George Frideric Handel had a number of harpsichords in their possession. The estate catalogue for Bach, drawn up by his surviving kin and their trustees shortly after his death on July 28, 1750, informs us that Bach owned no fewer than eight stringed keyboard instruments, five of them, at least nominally, harpsichords. They are listed, along with their assessed values, as follows:[1] "1 veneered *Clavecin*, which is to remain in the family if at all possible," value: 80 imperial thalers;[2] 3 *Clavesins*, each valued at 50 th; 1 *ditto,* smaller, value: 20 th; 2 *Lauten Wercke* each valued at 30 th; 1 *Spinettgen,* value 3 th." The monetary values most likely reflected the values of used instruments. A new, single-manual harpsichord in Saxony at the time fetched between sixty and a hundred thalers, a double-manual instrument between a hundred and two hundred thalers. The four used harpsichords valued at eighty or fifty thalers, therefore, were probably all two-manual instruments.[3]

Clavecin/Clavesin, of course, normally designated a harpsichord. Whether the term – presumably chosen by a nonmusician executor of the estate – in this instance was meant literally to specify a keyboard instrument with plucked strings or more broadly, perhaps the fortepiano, is not clear. What is known is that Bach in his later years was a sales agent for the organ builder Gottfried Silbermann and had sold (no doubt on commission) at least one – in Bach's words – "instrument called Piano et Forte" for the handsome sum of 115 thalers.[4] Regarding the two

Lautenwercke, J. S. Bach's one-time pupil Johann Friedrich Agricola reported in an editorial note published in the influential treatise, *Musica mechanica organoedi*, by Jacob Adlung, that he

> remembers, about the year 1740, in Leipzig, having seen and heard a lute harpsichord [*Lautenclavicymbel*] designed by Mr. Johann Sebastian Bach and executed by Mr. Zacharias Hildebrandt, which was of smaller size than the ordinary harpsichord, but in all other respects was like any other harpsichord. It had two [8-foot] choirs of gut strings, and a so-called little octave [*Octävchen,* i.e., 4-foot choir] of brass strings.[5]

The "smaller" *Clavesin* was probably a *Querspinett* (i.e., a trapezoid-shaped harpsichord, and presumably smaller than a virginal).

We learn from a later document that "during his lifetime," the composer had already given to his youngest son, Johann Christian, "3 *Clavire* nebst *Pedal*," and are informed further that at that time (November, 1750), the fifteen-year-old still had them.[6] These instruments undoubtedly referred to a two-manual pedal clavichord. As reported by Jacob Adlung, the term "clavier" was "often understood to mean primarily the clavichord."[7] Elsewhere Adlung explained how a pedalboard could be played together with the manuals of a clavichord in the manner of an organ.[8] Such an instrument, like the similarly constructed pedal harpsichord, primarily served for practicing or for domestic music making.[9] After close consideration of all the pertinent documentary evidence, Eberhard Spree concludes that "the designation '3 Clavire nebst Pedal' described an instrument consisting of three clavichords, each one comprised of strings, a resonance chamber, tangents and key levers. Two of them were operated with manuals and one with pedals."[10]

Handel

Regarding his harpsichord, Handel's last will and testament, dated June 1, 1750, records only the following: "I give and bequeath to Mr Christopher Smith my large Harpsicord [*sic*], my little House Organ, my Musick Books, and five hundred Pounds sterl:"[11]

Christopher Smith, Jr. (né Johann Christoph Schmidt, 1712–1795) was Handel's assistant. According to Otto Erich Deutsch, "Handel's large harpsichord, made by Johannes Ruckers in 1612, came into the King's possession through John Christopher Smith; the small one [not specifically mentioned in the will] made by Andreas Ruckers in 1651, is now [1954] in the Victoria and Albert Museum."[12]

Surviving Exemplars

Although the documentary sources reveal little about the instruments they enumerate, we in fact have more information about the harpsichords (or at least the types of harpsichords) that Bach and Handel probably knew and played – and perhaps owned – than is commonly assumed. Indeed, one or more of their personal harpsichords may still survive.

Handel

There is no longer any unambiguous trace of the "large harpsichord" that John Christopher Smith inherited after Handel's death in 1759. Moreover, according to Terence Best, nothing is known for certain about the harpsichords Handel owned, but, during his early years in England, he "must have played harpsichords by such makers as Hitchcock and Hermann Tabel, and undoubtedly some Ruckers."[13]

The claim that Handel owned a Ruckers instrument originated with the eighteenth-century music historian John Hawkins, who remarked that "Handel had a favorite Ruckers harpsichord, the keys whereof were hollowed like the bowl of a spoon." Best added that the 1651 Ruckers in the Victoria and Albert Museum "seems to show a connection with Smith" but that a 1612 Ruckers belonging to Queen Elizabeth II and housed in the Benton Fletcher Collection of Early Keyboard Instruments (Fenton House, Hampstead) was only "assumed" to be from Smith.[14]

Surveying the state of knowledge about Handel's harpsichords in 1993, Michael Cole wondered: "Might it be that 'large' implies not necessarily physical bulk or even two manuals but a keyboard with a full five octaves? If this were so, then it must be at least questioned whether the 'large' harpsichord could be synonymous with the Ruckers mentioned by Hawkins."[15] Cole's principal concern, however, was to call attention to a surviving instrument that, in the author's words, "bears an uncommon resemblance" to the harpsichord depicted in Philip Mercier's famous portrait of an informally dressed Handel, ca. 1730. The instrument at issue (now in the Bate Collection at Oxford University) is a single-manual harpsichord, of obscure provenance, with two sets of strings at 8-foot pitch. The maker was one William Smith, about whom little is known.

Smith's harpsichord has a GG–g^3 chromatic range, with "the same keys [viz., with "skunk-tail sharps," ivory naturals, black key-fronts], the characteristically carved end-blocks, the lockboard batten, and the nicely rounded crown on the spine adjacent, the color of the veneer, the same stop knob in the same place," as seen in the Mercier portrait.[16]

While never explicitly claiming that the surviving Smith instrument must be the very harpsichord visible in the portrait, Cole, after a close technical description entailing a comparison with a dozen other English instruments from the period, demonstrates that the resemblance could hardly be greater. If the instrument in the portrait and the one in the Bate collection are not one and the same, then it seems reasonable to consider them identical twins.

Handel, finally, also owned (or at least had at his disposal) a combination organ/harpsichord connected to a single keyboard that had been made in the 1730s to his specifications for use in his oratorio performances (see below).

Bach

Precisely one harpsichord of Thuringian provenance and dating from the first decades of the eighteenth century is known to have survived. It is no doubt the type of instrument that Bach and Handel would have been familiar with during their formative years. The unique exemplar, dating from ca. 1715 and by an anonymous builder, is now in the possession of the Bachhaus in Eisenach. It is a single-manual instrument with two 8-foot registers and a four-octave C–c^3 compass. Equipped with a transposing mechanism that shifts the keyboard up a minor third, it could play in any tuning from *Tiefkammerton* to *Chorton*.[17]

More intriguing and altogether controversial is the so-called "Bach Harpsichord," presently housed in the *Musikinstrumenten-Museum*, Berlin (Staatliches Institut für Musikforschung, Preußischer Kulturbesitz). Wilhelm Rust, the principal editor of the Bach-Gesellschaft complete edition, first described the instrument in 1860.[18]

He reported that it had belonged to the Voss family since the late eighteenth century, at the time was owned by Count Carl Otto von Voss (1786–1864) in Berlin, and that it had frequently been played by Wilhelm Friedemann Bach.[19] The Royal Instrument Collection in Berlin, following the advice of Philipp Spitta and under the impression that the harpsichord once belonged to J. S. Bach, acquired it from the Voss family in 1890. Some thirty-five years later, however, the noted scholar Georg Kinsky, in an influential article published in the *Bach-Jahrbuch* 1924, debunked that idea as a baseless myth.[20]

More recent research, however, begun in the 1980s, has nourished a plausible claim that the instrument may indeed have once belonged to J. S. Bach. Dieter Krickeberg and Horst Rase determined that the unsigned harpsichord almost certainly came from the workshop of the Thuringian builder, Johann Heinrich Harrass (1665–1714) of Großbreitenbach bei Sondershausen and could be dated to the early eighteenth century.[21] A two-manual harpsichord with a five-octave range (FF–f^3), it originally featured an unusual disposition: 16- and 4-foot registers on the lower manual; 8-foot register and buff stop on the upper manual, along with a shove coupler.[22] Jacob Adlung, who was a personal acquaintance of

J. S. Bach's, describes exactly such an instrument – perhaps exactly this instrument – in his organ treatise, which, although published posthumously, in 1768, was in fact completed in 1726.[23] If the instrument indeed had been built as described (i.e., with a five-octave, FF–f³ compass) before the death of J. H. Harrass in 1714, then it would be an unusually early example of a harpsichord featuring an "F orientation" rather than the far more typical "C orientation." Assuming that Bach indeed once owned this instrument, it seems plausible that he would have acquired it before he left Weimar (and Thuringia) in 1717 for Cöthen, in Anhalt, at the time a foreign country. Since the F orientation only became standard toward the end of Bach's life, however, the instrument may have in fact been the work of Harrass's son, Johann Martin (1671–1746).[24]

Siegbert Rampe adds:

> The simple exterior appearance of the instrument along with both its original and later disposition indicate that it was owned by a musician – not a wealthy aristocrat . . . a musician who would have wanted the three-course design, . . . one capable of producing, with limited means, a large number of tone colors.
> The musician may well have designed the instrument himself and later had it expanded.[25]

Perhaps that musician was indeed J. S. Bach. If so, perhaps the Harrass harpsichord was one of the *Clavesins* mentioned in the estate catalogue with a value of 50 thalers. In that event, Friedemann may have inherited it after Sebastian's death in 1750. Rampe, for unstated reasons, believes that the instrument was not one of those included in the estate catalogue, but rather that Friedemann took possession of the instrument in 1733 when he left the paternal home. He speculates further that Friedemann, at some point after settling in Berlin in 1774 and desperate for funds, sold the harpsichord to Count von Voss, as he is known to have done with his father's musical manuscripts.[26]

In the year 1719, Bach traveled to Berlin to take delivery of a harpsichord and escort it back to Cöthen. The instrument has not survived, but it is described in a later Cöthen court inventory as "das große Clavecin oder Flügel mit 2 Clavituren von Michael Mietke in Berlin, 1719"; that is, a "grand" two-manual harpsichord by the maker Michael Mietke (ca. 1670–1729?).[27] Two Mietke harpsichords are preserved, however, both now in the Charlottenburg Palace, Berlin: a white single-manual (once belonging to Princess Sophie Charlotte, r. 1701–1705) with two 8-foot registers and a range originally of GG, AA–c³, and a black two-manual instrument with 8-foot and 4-foot registers on the lower manual, an 8-foot register on the upper, and originally with a range of FF, GG, AA–c³.[28] Sheridan Germann suggests that Bach may have played the single-manual instrument when he visited Berlin in 1719; Mary Oleskiewicz suggests that it could just as well have been the two-manual black instrument.[29]

Bach's Tuning, Temperament, Pitch, and Keyboard Preferences

Tuning

On the final page of the obituary for J. S. Bach, written by C. P. E. Bach and J. F. Agricola (1754), the authors report that "In the tuning of harpsichords, [Bach] achieved so correct and pure a temperament that all the tonalities sounded pure and agreeable. He knew of no tonalities that, because of impure intonation, one must avoid."[30] In a letter to Johann Nicolaus Forkel, Bach's first biographer, Philipp Emanuel attested further that "no one could tune and quill his instruments to please him. He did everything himself."[31] Forkel elaborates on this point, commenting in his biography that the tuning "never cost him above a quarter of an hour."[32]

As for the objective of the tuning, the Berlin theorist Friedrich Wilhelm Marpurg reported that "Mr. Kirnberger has ... told me ... about how the famous Joh. Seb. Bach ... confided to him the tuning of his clavier, and how that master expressly required of him that he tune all the thirds sharp."[33] Johann Philipp Kirnberger was a student of Bach's from 1739 to 1741.

Temperament

Bach's exact preferences regarding temperament cannot be completely known since, as David Ledbetter points out, his views "changed and developed over the course of his career." Ledbetter suggests that Bach's later Weimar works probably used something like Werckmeister III described in the later treatises of Andreas Werckmeister and Johann Georg Neidhardt. The wide thirds and narrow fifths described in Werckmeister's treatise, *Erweiterte und verbesserte Orgel-Probe* (1698), seem particularly relevant for the *Well-Tempered Clavier*. Bach in general probably wanted a temperament in which "every key could be used equally as a tonic (i.e., with no Pythagorean thirds), but at the same time preserved something of the evolutionary nature of the collection in a subtly shaded inequality."[34]

Pitch

The pitch of Bach's harpsichords, like their temperament, varied not only from place to place but also from genre to genre.[35] In a solo composition or in a chamber work with stringed instruments, all the instruments could obviously be tuned according to the taste of the player(s). In a chamber work with woodwinds, on the other hand, the harpsichord had to accommodate the normally low tuning of those instruments. At Weimar the chamber pitch at the court chapel was usually tuned to a^1 = ca. 415 Hz, the so-called "high French opera pitch." This was presumably the normal pitch for the harpsichord located in the court chapel, as well. But for chamber music performances at court the pitch was probably lowered to a^1 = ca. 392 Hz, the so-called "low French opera pitch" (known in Germany as *Tiefkammerton*, or low chamber pitch), which in the early eighteenth century was the usual pitch for French woodwind instruments.

In Cöthen, too, the normal pitch alternatives were evidently a^1 = ca. 392 Hz (the "low French opera pitch") or a^1 = ca. 406 Hz (the so-called "low French chamber pitch"), that is, about one and a half or two equally tempered semitones below a^1 = 440 Hz. Since the same low French opera pitch (a^1 = 392 Hz) was used in Dresden and in Berlin, where Michael Mietke built his keyboard instruments, is one to conclude that Bach's keyboard works from the Cöthen period would have been performed more than a whole tone lower than modern concert pitch? Not necessarily: The Mietke harpsichord belonged to the court. Bach's own harpsichords for his private use and instruction could have been tuned to whatever pitch level the composer wished. Of course, had he rehearsed ensemble works like the Brandenburg Concertos at home, the tuning of the harpsichord on those occasions would have had to accommodate that of the wind instruments (i.e., presumably a^1 = 392 Hz).

In Leipzig, finally, surviving woodwind instruments reveal that the pitch norms there centered variously on a^1 = 391 Hz, a^1 = 404–405 Hz, and a^1 = 410–414 Hz.[36] Once again, whatever this might imply about the pitch standard Bach adopted for performances of his harpsichord concertos and chamber compositions with the Collegium Musicum need not necessarily apply to the way he intended instruments to be tuned for the solo harpsichord works of the *Klavierübung*.

Keyboard Design

Agricola, who had been a pupil of Bach's from 1738 to 1741, informs us in his annotations to Adlung's organ treatise that

> It is good to have the manuals [i.e., the length of the keys] as short as possible ... As far as the width of the keys is concerned, it is known that particularly in Brandenburg the keys are made narrower than elsewhere, but

no man yet has got his fingers stuck between the semitones ... The semitones must anyway be a little narrower at the top than at the bottom. That is how the late Capellmeister Bach required them to be.[37]

The music itself unambiguously reveals the compass and the number of manuals Bach and Handel required from the harpsichords they must have had at their disposal at various times, which they probably assumed would be available to anyone who wished to play their works.

Handel

The vast majority of Handel's harpsichord compositions were written early in his career: for the most part either during his Hamburg years (1703–1706) or his first years in London (1712–1720). Terence Best conjectures that the Suite in C (HWV 443) and the Partita in D (HWV450), "may well be Handel's earliest surviving keyboard works ... written in his boyhood in Halle" (i.e., before 1703).[38] Both works have a C–c^3 range – the same range limit effectively observed in all the works that Best believes were written during his Hamburg years.[39] Handel's English harpsichord pieces, largely composed between 1712 and 1718 (much of it published between 1720 and 1735), remain within a GG–d^3 compass.

Handel only occasionally calls for a two-manual instrument. The F major chaconne (HWV485), a work assigned by Best to the Hamburg years, exploits echo effects between two manuals. A Sonata in G major (HWV579) with a G–c^3 compass, perhaps written for the electress of Hanover during Handel's sojourn there (1710–1712), features both alternating phrases for two manuals along with passages in which the right hand plays manual I, while the left hand, simultaneously, plays manual II. (The electress herself, incidentally, attested that she had shown Handel a harpsichord made in Düsseldorf that he liked).[40] Handel requires a two-manual instrument in two airs (HWV466 and 470) datable to ca. 1710–1720, which, however, according to Donald Burrows, may have been intended for the organ.[41] Handel does not require two manuals for any of his major English harpsichord compositions.

Bach

With but one exception Bach's pre-Cöthen keyboard compositions remain within the four-octave compass C–c^3. The single exception, the "Aria Variata all Man. Italiana" (BWV989) extends the range down to AA. Like most of the keyboard pieces in the early manuscript sources, the "aria variata" does not specify an instrument. The genre of the work, however, a set of secular variations, along with the extension of the compass below C, makes it a virtual certainty that the composition was intended for a stringed keyboard, presumably the harpsichord.

George B. Stauffer has suggested that an early version of the Chromatic Fantasia (BWV903a), with its low AA – a note removed in the final version – may, like the extensive cadenza of the early version of the first movement of Brandenburg Concerto No. 5, have been intended for the Mietke harpsichord mentioned previously. Stauffer also notes that the English Suite No. 1 in A (BWV806) and the E major Invention (BWV777), among other works, call for AA – strong indications that the range of Bach's Cöthen instrument probably extended down to that pitch. But, unlike the Mietke instruments in Charlottenburg Palace with their upper limit of c^3, Prince Leopold's instrument must have been custom designed to include a high d^3 – a note demanded in the early as well as later versions of the Chromatic Fantasia.[42]

Unlike the suites, the works belonging to Bach's systematic, pedagogical keyboard collections from the Cöthen period largely stay within the normal $C-c^3$ compass. Perhaps, as Alfred Dürr has suggested, this restriction reflects the range limitations of the instruments played by Bach's students and family members rather than necessarily that of Bach's own instrument.[43] Nor can it be a coincidence that the elaborate title pages on the autograph scores of both the *Well-Tempered Clavier* I (BWV846–869) and the Inventions and Sinfonias (BWV772–801), dated 1722 and 1723, respectively, specify no particular instrument but simply the generic *clavier*. Bach, no doubt, purposely left the choice among harpsichord, clavichord, and organ *manualiter* to the discretion and available resources of the player.[44]

Both the first and last volumes of Bach's monumental *Klavierübung* – containing, respectively, the six partitas (1726–1731), and the Goldberg Variations (1741) – require a $GG-d^3$ compass. The Goldberg Variations, like the two works included in Part II of the *Klavierübung* (1735) – the Italian Concerto (BWV971) and the Ouverture in B minor (BWV831) – famously prescribe a two-manual harpsichord. Curiously, the compass of the Italian Concerto is restricted to $AA-c^3$ and deliberately avoids d^3.

Stauffer conjectures that since the $GG-d^3$ range appears in Bach's harpsichord works for the first time in the partitas of *Klavierübung* I, the composer may well have acquired an instrument with that compass at about that time.[45] Could it have been the Harrass instrument, which Adlung may have seen *chez* Bach shortly before describing it in his organ treatise, whose manuscript he completed in just that year? Chronological coincidence, admittedly, is not proof.

Bach, finally, requires e^3 in the mirror fugue of the *Art of Fugue*. The pitch f^3 (along with e^3) appears only once in his works: in the second movement of the Triple Concerto in A minor (BWV1044) – a work, transmitted only in a copyist's manuscript, whose authenticity is uncertain.[46]

The publication of the four parts of the *Klavierübung* between 1726 and 1741 more or less coincided with Bach's activities with the Leipzig Collegium Musicum, the reputable music-making association consisting of professional musicians and university students that Bach directed from 1729 to 1737 and sporadically again from 1739 on. Bach's concertos for one or more harpsichords along with most of his surviving chamber works with obbligato harpsichord may well have been composed (or arranged for their current instrumentation) during the same years. The compass of their harpsichord parts suggests that Bach had at his disposal one instrument (no doubt his own) with a range from GG to d^3, but that the other harpsichords available for the concertos with multiple solo parts each had a C–d^3 compass. The presence of *piano* and *forte* dynamics in the second and third harpsichord parts of the Triple Concerto in D minor (BWV1063), however, argue that they were equipped with a second manual.

Among the numerous concerts offered by the Collegium Musicum, one is of particular interest. In June 1733 a local newspaper announced that "Bach's Collegium Musicum . . . [will present] a fine concert . . . with a new harpsichord [*Clavicymbel*] such as had not been heard here before."[47] Speculation abounds about the nature of this unprecedented instrument: that it was a lute harpsichord, a harpsichord with a lute stop, that it had a 16-foot register, or perhaps that it was a fortepiano from the workshop of Gottfried Silbermann.[48]

Keyboard Playing

Bach and Handel were both recognized from their youth as extraordinary keyboard virtuosi. The legends and anecdotes about their triumphs abound in contemporary accounts and early biographies. More enlightening, however, is what witnesses reported about the style and character of their playing.

Handel[49]

An amusing anecdote, reported by one Denis Nolhac, recounts that in January 1707 he heard Handel perform in Rome for the papal musicians.

> Handel went to a harpsichord, with his hat under his arm . . . he played the instrument so skillfully that everyone was very surprised, and because Handel

was a Saxon, and therefore a Lutheran, that made them suspect that his skill was supernatural. I even heard some saying that holding on to his hat had something to do with it . . . [H]aving moved close to Handel to watch him play, I told him . . . of the ridiculous suspicions of these Signori Virtuosi. A moment later, as if by accident, he dropped his hat, relaxed and played much better than before.[50]

A few years later, the dowager Electress Sophia of Hanover, writing to her grand-daughter in June 1710 about the recently arrived Saxon, observed that he "surpasses everyone who has ever been heard in harpsichord playing and composition."[51] Another ear-witness, Johann Mattheson, who had been Handel's colleague in Hamburg, recalled in his *Grundlage einer Ehrenpforte* (1740) that in the year 1703 he and Handel had traveled to Lübeck in order to hear Buxtehude. Once there, they played "almost every organ and harpsichord, and by reason of our playing made a particular decision, . . . namely, that he should play only the organ, and I the harpsichord."[52] This is corroboration, perhaps, of the verdict that was about to be reached a few years later regarding the legendary contest between Handel and Domenico Scarlatti in Rome.

Some doubt exists as to the veracity of that anecdote, which was first cited by Handel's first biographer John Mainwaring, who tells us that the contest took place under the auspices of Cardinal Ottoboni; Scarlatti was proclaimed the victor at the harpsichord and Handel the better organist. Mainwaring characterizes their playing as follows:

> No two persons ever arrived at such perfection on their respective instruments, yet it is remarkable that there was a total difference in their manner.
>
> The characteristic excellence of Scarlatti seems to have consisted in a certain elegance and delicacy of expression. Handel had an uncommon brilliancy and command of finger: but what distinguished him from all other players who possessed these same qualities, was that amazing fullness, force, and energy, which he joined with them. And this observation may be applied with as much justice to his compositions as to his playing.[53]

Despite having largely abandoned the composition of harpsichord music by 1720, Handel remained active as a virtuoso throughout his life, acclaimed in particular for his improvisations. Indeed, at least one contemporary report, from the year 1753 (i.e., after Handel's ultimately unsuccessful eye operation), claimed that his "playing is beyond what even *he* ever did."[54] In December 1755, Handel is reported to have offered an entertainment at the home of his friend Anne Donnellan, playing and displaying her newly acquired harpsichord built by Jacob Kirckman.[55]

John Hawkins claimed that Handel's improvisations "stole on the ear in a slow and solemn progression; the harmony close wrought, and as full as could possibly be expressed; the passages concatenated with stupendous art, the whole at the same time being perfectly intelligible, and carrying the appearance of great simplicity."[56] Charles Burney, for his part, claimed to have heard the composer in his later years "when his hand was then so fat, that the knuckles, which usually appear convex, were like those of a child, dinted in, so as to be rendered concave." However, his touch was "so smooth, and the tone of the instrument so much cherished, that his fingers seemed to grow to the keys. They were so curved and compact, when he played, that no motion, and scarcely the fingers themselves, could be discovered."[57]

Bach

Considerably more is known about Bach's harpsichord playing than about Handel's. This is hardly surprising: Keyboard music played a far greater role in Bach's creative life than in Handel's. Moreover, Bach had dozens of private students throughout his career, many of whom testified about their mentor's keyboard playing and teaching methods.

Although Bach's numerous organ recitals are amply documented, only a single instance is recorded of him specifically playing the harpsichord in public. The occasion was not a famous recital but rather the performance of a newly composed cantata: the *Trauer-Ode* (BWV198), written in October 1727 for the funeral service for Queen Christiane Eberhardine. According to a chronicler, it was "composed in the Italian style, with *Clave di Cembalo*, which Mr. Bach himself played."[58] The harpsichord part, ironically, consists only of the basso continuo line – an indication that on this occasion Bach conducted the ensemble from the keyboard, a practice more typical of Handel.

At Bach's command performance at the court of Frederick the Great in Potsdam in May 1747, the composer was famously asked to improvise a fugue on the theme that would soon become the basis of the *Musical Offering*. Bach's improvisation was performed not on a harpsichord, however, but rather, as commanded, on one of the king's Silbermann fortepianos. Bach offered an equally legendary solo performance exactly thirty years earlier, in 1717, in Dresden. A contest was to take place between him and the renowned French virtuoso Louis Marchand. After Marchand failed to appear, Bach performed alone. According to Bach's advocate, Johann Abraham Birnbaum, writing in 1739, the contest was to have been "a trial of their respective talents at the clavier."[59] The size of the gathering, characterized in the obituary of 1754 as "a large company of persons of high rank," along with the fact that Marchand was famous as a *claveciniste*, leave no doubt that Bach must have played a large harpsichord.[60]

Drawing on interviews and correspondence with Bach's sons, as well as information contained in J. J. Quantz's flute treatise, Johann Nicolaus

Forkel devotes an entire chapter of his Bach biography to a description of Bach's keyboard technique. He reports:

> Bach is said to have played with so easy and small a motion of the fingers that it was hardly perceptible. Only the first joints of the fingers were in motion; the hand retained even in the most difficult passages its rounded form; the fingers rose very little from the keys . . . Still less did the other parts of his body take any share in his play . . . He rendered all his fingers, of both hands, equally strong and serviceable, so that he was able to execute not only chords and all running passages, but also single and double shakes with equal ease and delicacy. He was a perfect master even of those passages in which, while some fingers perform a shake, the others, on the same hand, have to continue the melody.[61]

Forkel also praised Bach's "beautiful touch . . . the clearness and precision in connecting the successive tones . . . the new mode of fingering . . . the equal development and practice of all fingers of both hands."[62]

Bach's reputation as an innovator in the extensive use of the thumb comes to us from C. P. E. Bach's enormously influential treatise, published in 1753: "My late father . . . heard great men in his youth who did not use the thumb except when it was necessary for large stretches." The son explains that as a consequence of changes in taste, the father "was obliged to think out a much more complete use of the fingers, and especially to use the thumb (which apart from other uses is quite indispensable especially in the difficult keys) . . . Thus it was raised suddenly from its former idleness to the position of principal Finger . . . [It] enables one to bring out all kinds of things at the proper time."[63]

Philipp Emanuel's famous claim about his father's decisive role in the modern use of the thumb has been sharply challenged in recent decades. Mark Kroll, for example, declares that "it is simply not true that the thumb was not used in keyboard playing prior to J. S. Bach. 'Modern' fingerings for scales (i.e., RH 1–2–3–1–2–3–4; LH 5–4–3–2–1–3–2–1), as well as many other possible finger combinations, can be found as early as the sixteenth century." Kroll emphasizes that the historical approach to fingering in actual practice was quite pragmatic. He quotes M. de St. Lambert's "practical and reasonable view," expressed in his *Principes du clavecin* (Paris, 1702), that "each [player] need only seek a fingering that is comfortable and graceful," and cheerfully cites Michael Praetorius's sarcastic assertion in *Syntagma musicum* (1619) that "this [excessive preoccupation with proper fingering] is not worth talking about: let a player run up and down the keyboard with his first, middle, or third finger, indeed even with his nose if that will help him, as long as it enables him to make everything clear, correct, and pleasant to hear."[64]

At all events, the validity of C. P. E. Bach's priority claim on behalf of his father in the use of the thumb and the development of modern keyboard

Example 14.1 J. S. Bach, *Applicatio*, BWV994

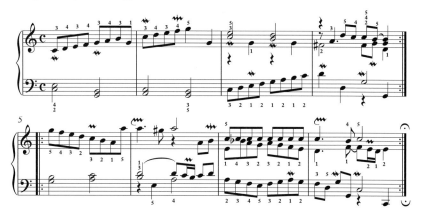

Example 14.2 J. S. Bach, Prelude in C major, BWV870a, with original fingering, mm. 1–5

technique cannot be resolved here. Suffice it to report that Bach's fingering method is exemplified in his own handwriting in two short pedagogical items entered into the *Klavierbüchlein* for his son Wilhelm Friedemann. The first, an exercise in C major called *Applicatio* (BWV994), reveals that Bach in fact was still teaching traditional finger-crossing techniques such as 3–4–3–4–3–4 in ascending and 3–2–3–2–3–2 in descending scalar patterns in the right hand, along with an ascending 3–2–1–2–1–2–1–2 pattern in the left hand.

More informative than Bach's autograph is a copy in the hand of his pupil, Johann Caspar Vogler. The manuscript, housed in the Staatsbibliothek zu Berlin, preserves an early version of the C major prelude and "fugetta" from the *Well-Tempered Clavier* II (BWV870a) that is replete with copious fingerings.[65]

Reasonably assuming that the fingerings represented Bach's intentions, Quentin Faulkner subjected it to a close analysis. He finds among its notable features, along with the equal employment of all fingers – including the thumb – in general, the frequent use of the same finger on two notes in succession, especially among the outer fingers and, occasionally, the modern device of passing the fingers over the thumb. Faulkner's conclusion proposes "two fundamental principles": Bach's use of the thumb (1) in the presence of numerous accidentals and (2) as a pivot finger for the "smooth execution of scale passages that extend beyond a five-note compass."[66]

Keyboard Teaching

Handel

Johann Mattheson observed that during his Hamburg years (1703–1706), Handel had "very many students."[67] It is likely, then, that many of his surviving keyboard compositions, which are known to be early works, were written in connection with his teaching. The composer, however, whose students were mainly amateurs (often aristocratic women), passionately disliked the activity. He once told a London visitor, "After I had left [Hamburg] . . . no power on earth could have moved me to take up teaching duties again – except Anne, the flower of all princesses."[68] The reference is to Princess Anne (1709–1759), the talented daughter of the future King George II, whom Handel instructed in thoroughbass and composition for about ten years (1724–1734).[69] He later gave lessons to Anne's sister, Louisa (1724–1751) and is known to have composed two suites for her (HWV447 and 452) in 1738/9, possibly his very last keyboard compositions. Another likely student of his was the later Duke of Chandos, James Brydges (1674–1744). Nothing is known, unfortunately, about the specifics of Handel's teaching method beyond what can be inferred from the passagework, figurations, and other technical challenges he incorporated into his compositions, especially the preludes and variation sets.

Bach

Once again, we are much better informed in the case of Bach. His pupils, in contrast to Handel's, were mostly aspiring professional musicians; and it is therefore hardly surprising that he was deeply committed to teaching. The earliest testimony about Bach as a teacher appears in a letter written in 1712 by his Weimar student, Philipp David Kräuter. Reporting to his sponsors in Augsburg, Kräuter declared, "it is assuredly six hours per day of guidance that I am receiving, primarily in composition and on the keyboard, at times on other instruments."[70] Ernst Ludwig Gerber, in his indispensable biographical dictionary of musicians (1790), described the experience of his father Heinrich Nicolaus Gerber as a pupil of Bach's for several years, beginning in 1724. According to the son:

> At the first lesson [Bach] set his Inventions before him. When he had studied these through to Bach's satisfaction, there followed a series of suites, then the *Well-Tempered Clavier*. This latter work Bach played altogether three times through for him with his unmatchable art, and my father counted these among his happiest hours, when Bach, under the pretext of not feeling in the mood to teach, sat himself at one of his fine instruments and thus turned these hours into minutes.[71]

The sequence Inventions–Suites–*Well-Tempered Clavier* has governed the teaching of Bach's keyboard works ever since. Equally notable is the testimony that Bach performed these works on "one of his fine instruments" – among them, quite likely, one of the instruments listed at the time of the composer's death in the estate catalogue. We are still left to wonder, however, which instrument(s) he chose for these demonstrations: the clavichord, one suspects, for the Inventions; the harpsichord, presumably, not only for the Suites but also (despite its rigorous restriction to the usual C–c^3 organ compass) for the *Well-Tempered Clavier*.

Forkel filled in the preliminary stages Bach prescribed for less proficient students:

> The first thing [Bach] did was to teach his scholars his peculiar mode of touching the instrument ... For this purpose, he made them practice, for months together, nothing but isolated exercises for all the fingers of both hands, with constant regard to this clear and clean touch. Under some months, none could get excused from these exercises; and, according to his firm opinion, they ought to be continued, at least, for from six to twelve months. But if he found that anyone, after some months of practice, began to lose patience, he was so obliging as to write little connected pieces, in which those exercises were combined together ... With this exercise of the fingers, either in single passages or in little pieces composed on purpose, was combined the practice of all the ornaments in both hands. Hereupon he immediately set his scholars to his own greater compositions, which ... would give them the best means of exercising their strength. In order to lessen the difficulties, he made use of an excellent method: first to play to them the whole piece, which they were to study, saying, "so it must sound."[72]

Continuo Playing

Handel

Handel conducted and accompanied his operas and oratorios from the keyboard – a practice he just as likely followed in the performance of his secular cantatas and other ensemble works during his Italian years. In fact, not long after beginning his professional life as a musician (initially as a second violinist) at the Hamburg opera, he served as well as an accompanist, substituting for the director, Reinhard Keiser. The most notorious event dating from that time was his duel with Mattheson, precipitated when Handel refused to yield up the keyboard accompaniment during a performance of Mattheson's opera, *Cleopatra*, to the composer.[73]

Despite this unpleasantness, Mattheson observed decades later: "the renowned Handel has often played [ex tempore] accompaniments in his stage performances, where the solo harpsichord especially excelled."[74] A case in point occurred in 1711 when Handel conducted *Rinaldo*, his first opera written for England, from the harpsichord. An early account of the premiere noted that "Mr. Handel . . . accompanied the voices himself on the Harpsichord in the Orchestre, and performed his Part in the Overture, wherein his Execution seemed as astonishing as his Genius in the Composition."[75] For the aria "Vo' far guerra," the score at some points in the A section contains blank spaces between phrases that Handel filled in with improvised harpsichord interpolations. Elsewhere he invented appropriate accompaniments while the singer either executed a flourish or sustained a long note.

For Handel, then, keyboard accompaniment, at least in his own music (and on at least one occasion), entailed considerably more than playing modest chords.

Another eminent musician who witnessed Handel in the opera pit was Johann Joachim Quantz, who attended a performance of *Admeto* during his visit to London in 1727. He relates in his autobiography: "All together, under *Händel's* conducting, made an extremely good effect . . . Only few solo instrumentalists were there . . . e.g. Händel, as is well known, on the harpsichord and organ."[76] The sources for Handel's English oratorio performances contain at least two keyboard continuo parts; the second part was usually played by Handel's longtime assistant John Christopher Smith, Jr. Beginning in 1732, the composer usually conducted, apparently, from a keyboard outfitted with a device that enabled him to play both the organ and the harpsichord from the same harpsichord console via a tracker action. Burney claimed that it was "first contrived in this country for Handel himself at his Oratorios; but to convey them to so great a distance from the instrument, without rendering the touch impractically heavy, required uncommon ingenuity and mechanical resources."[77] From 1735 on Handel typically performed an organ concerto during the intermission, each time featuring a newly improvised solo part. Nonetheless, the autographs indicate that, in Winton Dean's words, "despite the limelight focused on the organ, there is no doubt that Handel accompanied the greater part of the oratorios on the harpsichord, which was by far the more important instrument of the two."[78]

For the lessons he gave Princess Anne, Handel wrote out a comprehensive course of instruction in musical composition. One extant manuscript, dating from ca. 1724–1726, includes a section containing twenty-four thoroughbass exercises that illustrated, in musical notation alone, the treatment of the various harmonies: root position, thirds, suspensions, sevenths, octaves, ninths, pedal points. The manuscript, however, lacks both verbal explanations and any notation of the recommended right-hand realization of the figured bass.[79]

A recently discovered autograph transcription of Handel's cantata "Crudel tiranno amor" (1721) reveals, however, that he called for "big, multi-note chords in both hands" along with frequent octave doublings in the bass.[80]

Bach

Bach expected the harmonic realization of the continuo part in his instrumental ensemble and secular vocal music to be played on a harpsichord. Moreover, like Handel, he expected the realizations to be, at the least, full-textured in four parts and, if possible, imaginative. With regard to instrumental chamber music this often meant extemporaneously introducing contrapuntal ideas, including completely new melodies, into the right-hand realization. Lorenz Mizler, a former Bach pupil, writing in 1738, observed that Bach "accompanies every thorough bass to a solo so that one thinks it is a piece of concerted music and as if the melody he plays in the right hand were written beforehand."[81] Similarly, the Stuttgart court musician Johann Friedrich Daube attested that

> [when Bach] played, the [written-out] upper voice had to shine. By his exceedingly adroit accompaniment he gave it life when it had none. He knew how to imitate it so cleverly, with either the right hand or the left, and how to introduce an unexpected countertheme against it, so that the listener would have sworn that everything had been conscientiously written out. At the same time, the regular accompaniment was very little curtailed. In general his accompanying was always like a *concertante* part most conscientiously worked out and added as a companion to the upper voice so that at the appropriate time the upper voice

would shine. This right was even given at times to the bass, without slighting the upper voice.[82]

Ernst Ludwig Gerber's description of his father's two-year course of keyboard lessons with Bach (see above) includes the following: "The conclusion of the instruction was thoroughbass, for which Bach chose the Albinoni violin solos ... My father executed these basses according to Bach's fashion, particularly in the singing of the voices. This accompaniment was itself so beautiful that no principal voice could have added to the pleasure it gave me."[83]

The manuscript, finally, of Heinrich Nicolaus Gerber's continuo realization for Albinoni's Violin Sonata in A minor, Op. 6, no. 6, survives, along with Bach's corrections. Philipp Spitta published a transcription of it in the appendix of his Bach biography (helpfully including the original violin part and the figured bass numbers, which were not included in Gerber's manuscript).[84]

As for church music, a late witness to Bach's continuo practice, Johann Christian Kittel (1732–1809) – evidently Bach's last pupil (having studied with him from 1748 onwards) – recalled that "When Sebastian Bach performed a piece of church music, one of his most capable pupils always had to ('so musste allemal') accompany on the harpsichord ... No one dared put forth a meager thoroughbass accompaniment. Nevertheless, one always had to be prepared to have Bach's hands and fingers intervene among the hands and fingers of the player and, without getting in the way of the latter, furnish the accompaniment with masses of harmonies that made an even greater impression than the unsuspected close proximity of the teacher."[85]

Such "masses of harmonies" appear in the written-out accompaniment passages in the solo part of the Harpsichord Concerto in F major (BWV1047), an arrangement of the Brandenburg Concerto No. 4. As David Schulenberg observes, they contain "chords up to seven parts during the ritornellos" and offer an example of what he dubs Bach's "full-voiced" manner of continuo realization. He plausibly suggests that the obbligato harpsichord part in the second movement of Bach's Flute Sonata in B minor (BWV1030) is another such written-out continuo realization, and points out as well that while the sixteenth-note rests in measures 2 and 4 "allow the keyboard to avoid anticipating the resolution of the short appoggiaturas in the flute part ... these rests do not prevent unison doublings on $c\sharp^2$ and $d\sharp^2$, violating a directive of Quantz."[86]

Kittel's account bears witness not only to Bach's predilection for "full-voiced" continuo realizations: it also reveals that, at least during Kittel's time in Leipzig, a harpsichord was employed – seemingly as a matter of course ("so musste allemal") – in the performance of a church composition. In fact, a harpsichord was apparently part of Bach's church music performances from the beginning of his Leipzig tenure. Bach himself attested, in a May 1727 letter of recommendation for his pupil, Friedrich Gottlieb Wild: "During the four years that he has lived here . . . [Wild] has helped to adorn our church music with his well-learned accomplishments on the *Flute traversière* and the *Clavecin*."[87] Bach became Thomaskantor in May 1723; Wild therefore must have played for him from the beginning of his Leipzig tenure.

Over the course of at least a decade before he had settled in Leipzig, Bach had composed some thirty church compositions. Most were written during his last three years in Weimar (1714–1717); that is, after he had received the title of concertmaster and was instructed to "perform new works monthly."[88] Still retaining the post of court organist, Bach presumably directed the performances of these works from the organ console while simultaneously realizing the continuo part.[89]

The Leipzig churches, however, where Bach's sacred music was performed, engaged full-time organists, leaving the Thomaskantor free to conduct the musicians face-to-face. For the vast majority of Bach's church compositions, the organist realized the continuo from a transposed figured bass part usually marked "Continuo" (but occasionally "Organo"). The transposition reflected the fact that the Leipzig organs were pitched a whole tone higher than the woodwinds, with which Bach aligned the notation of the strings and vocal parts.

In addition to the organ part, at least one – often two – untransposed continuo parts exist for a church composition. Usually marked "Continuo," they were intended for the reinforcing bass-line instruments: cello, contrabass, bassoon. Occasionally the heading of a continuo part reads "Cembalo" and at times contains thoroughbass figures as well. Moreover, the principal Leipzig churches regularly maintained harpsichords in the choir loft. After considering the array of documentary and musical source evidence, Laurence Dreyfus concluded, in a comprehensive study of Bach's continuo practice, that Bach in Leipzig must have employed both the organ and the harpsichord – a practice he calls "dual accompaniment" – for the rendition of the continuo. Moreover, both instruments, to an unknowable extent, may have realized the continuo figures simultaneously. Like Handel's practice in his London oratorios, then, Bach in Leipzig evidently employed two keyboard players in his church music performances: the church

organist at the console and one of his advanced students at the
harpsichord.[90]

Harpsichord Music

As mentioned previously, although Handel continued to perform on the
harpsichord in his later years, he effectively abandoned the composition of
new harpsichord music after 1720. Bach, in contrast, despite occasional
interruptions dictated by the circumstances of his employment, composed
keyboard music throughout his life. Handel's most significant harpsichord
works, the so-called Eight Great Suites (HWV426–433), appeared in
London in November 1720, "printed for the Author." In 1733 John
Walsh published a second volume of *Suites de pièces* (HWV434–442),
which were culled from much earlier compositions. A volume of Six
Fugues or Voluntaries for the Organ or Harpsichord followed in 1735.
Decades after Handel's death (ca. 1793) Samuel Arnold published a so-
called "fourth collection" (or "Third Set of Lessons for the Harpsichord").
It included the two suites Handel had composed for Princess Louisa
(HWV447, 452).

In dramatic contrast to Handel's creative arc, Bach's greatest achieve-
ments as a keyboard composer date from the years after 1717 and belong
to two distinct periods. During his six years as court *Kapellmeister* in
Cöthen (1717–1723) Bach completed the English and French Suites, the
Well-Tempered Clavier I (1722) and the Two- and Three-Part Inventions
and Sinfonias (1723). After a three-year hiatus, during which he was
obliged to devote himself almost exclusively to composing church music,
Bach resumed the composition of ambitious collections of keyboard
music. The year 1726 marked the initiation of the landmark publications
that over the decade 1731–1741 would eventually encompass the four
parts of the *Klavierübung*. Bach may have intended to publish further
keyboard collections as parts of the *Klavierübung* series: The *Well-
Tempered Clavier* II (BWV870–93), and the so-called Great Eighteen
Organ Chorales (BWV651–68), were both essentially completed at
about the same time, ca. 1742. The *Art of Fugue* (BWV1080) too, like
the Great Eighteen largely but not quite finished at the time of Bach's
death, may have been conceived as a part – perhaps as the capstone – of
the *Klavierübung* project.

Handel

Handel's extant solo keyboard works occupy almost two hundred numbers
(426–612) in the *Händel Werke-Verzeichnis* (HWV).[91] But that number

may not reflect the full extent of his harpsichord music. According to a catalogue appended to Mainwaring's biography, "a great quantity of Music ... was made in Italy and Germany. How much of it is yet in being, is not known. Two chests-full were left at Hamburgh [*sic*], besides some at Hanover, and some at Hall [i.e., Halle]."[92]

In their entirety, Handel's keyboard works encompass a total of fifteen keys: C, c, D, d, E, e, F, f, f♯, G, g, A, a, B♭, b; they extend from F minor, on the flat side, to E major on the sharp side and remain within the traditional boundaries of four sharps or flats. They altogether avoid tonics on the chromatic pitches A♭, E♭, and D♭. The absence of the key of E♭ is perhaps surprising. (By comparison the fifteen keys represented in Bach's Two and Three-Part Inventions and Sinfonias include E♭ major but avoid F♯ minor). Handel's most chromatic keys – A, E, f, and f♯ – all appear among the Eight Great Suites, the keys of A major and F minor occupying the beginning and ending of the collection.

From the outset, the popular harpsichord genres of dance suite and variation are well represented. In contrast to the works later published in London, Handel's early suites more often than not contain all four of the traditional German suite dances: allemande, courante, sarabande, gigue; they normally appear in direct, unbroken sequence. The suites frequently begin with a prelude that features the typical scalar passagework, sequential patterns, and complementary rhythmic motives familiar from the German keyboard and organ tradition. Such a composition is the Suite in C (HWV 443), considered by Terence Best to date from Handel's Halle period.[93] Not infrequently a variations movement – often, as in the same work, a chaconne or *passacaille* featuring increasingly virtuosic keyboard pyrotechnics – concludes the suite. Such movements may have been designed as challenging exercises for his students – as well as to display the composer's own virtuosity. Handel continued to include such challenging variations movements in his London publications.

Handel's suites contain few modish dances – the so-called *Galanterien*. The gavotte makes an occasional appearance, and several suites conclude with a minuet. Along with multimovement suites, a number of independent movements survive from the early period: specifically, single dances, airs, and preludes – the latter often notated, in the French manner, as half-note or whole-note chords to be elaborated by the player.

After having completely abandoned keyboard composition during his Italian sojourn (1706–1710), Handel gradually resumed the activity after he settled in London. Like Bach, then, his keyboard works belong to two separate periods, but in Handel's case both date to the early part of his career: the Hamburg years, 1703–1706, and the early London years, 1712–1720.

During the year 1717–1718, while living as a house guest of James Brydges, the Earl of Carnarvon and future Duke of Chandos, Handel brought his keyboard oeuvre to its zenith, reworking much of his early keyboard music as well as composing new suites and at least eleven fugues. The stimulus to this renewed commitment was provided not only by his possibly having taken on the earl as a student but especially by having learned that pirated copies of his keyboard works were about to be published in Amsterdam. Motivated by this provocation, Handel saw to the publication in 1720 of his *Suites de Pièces pour le Clavecin ... PREMIER VOLUME ... printed for the Author.*[94] The title clearly implies that a further volume was intended. A composer's preface explains, moreover, that he had "been obliged to publish Some of the following Lessons because Surrepticious and incorrect Copies of them had got Abroad."[95]

The suites published in the 1720 collection constitute Handel's magnum opus in the domain of harpsichord music, notable not only for their high quality of craftsmanship, richness of invention, and expressive power but also for the freedom with which the composer treats the traditional formal conventions of the genre.

Only one of the eight suites – Suite No. 4 in E minor (HWV429) – presents all four of the conventional dances in their normal order. Otherwise, only Suite 7 in G minor (HWV432) includes a sarabande, while Suites 6 in F♯ minor (HWV 431) and 8 in F minor (HWV433) contain neither allemande nor courante. The conventional dances of the E minor suite are preceded, however, not by a conventional prelude but, unconventionally, by a fugue. However, the opening work, Suite No. 1 in A major (HWV426), traditionally initiates the collection with an old-fashioned prelude that opens with an auspicious, resonant AA–A octave pedal point – much like the opening sonority of the C major prelude that launches the *Well-Tempered Clavier* II. The A major prelude also features massive chord passages in both hands notated in whole notes. The G minor suite, for its part, begins with a genuine French overture.

Suite No. 2 in F major (HWV427), finally, is not a suite at all but rather an Italian church sonata consisting of two pairs of slow–fast movements: the opening adagio a highly florid adagio in the style of an aria, the closing movement an allegro fugue. It is one of the five full-fledged fugues that Handel included in the collection; they compensate in a sense for the absence of the minuet, bourrée, gavotte, and other *Galanterien*.

Two suites conclude with sets of variations. No. 5 in E major (HWV430) ends with the famous "Harmonious Blacksmith" variations – a flamboyant virtuoso showpiece consisting of systematically accelerating note values driving toward a climactic conclusion. The G minor suite, for its part, ends with a *passacaille* – actually based on sixteen iterations of a four-measure chordal progression (like Bach's chaconne for unaccompanied violin) rather than a ground bass theme; it, too, features accelerating note values along with increasing chromaticism for climactic effect. Suite No. 3 in D minor (HWV428) balances a toccata and fugue opening movement with an extravagantly florid "air" followed by five variations, or "doubles." The suite's conclusion, however, is provided by a vigorous presto, binary in form but a concerto in style (i.e., punctuated by an authoritative and incisive ritornello motive).

Handel's edition was, in the words of Andrew Talle, "an international bestseller," frequently reprinted not only in London but also in Paris and Amsterdam. Talle, in fact, argues that Bach borrowed the theme of the allemande of Partita No. 2 in C minor, BWV826, first published in 1727 as part of the *Klavierübung*, from the allemande of Handel's D minor suite. If so, that would suggest that Bach acquired a copy of the first volume of Handel's *Suites de pièces pour le clavecin*, presumably at the Leipzig fair, shortly after he had settled in the city and perhaps was motivated by the success of Handel's bestselling volume to launch a similar enterprise himself.[96]

The nine compositions appearing in the next collection of Handel's keyboard music, published by John Walsh ca. 1733 under the title *Suites de pièces pour le clavecin ... Second Volume* (HWV434–442), were clearly compiled from defective sources. Handel's active participation in its preparation, therefore – beyond presumably having given Walsh his permission to publish it – is altogether doubtful. He may, however, have had a hand in selecting and ordering the pieces. The six interior suites of the collection (HWV436–441) are conventional dance suites. The second of two suites in D minor (HWV437) is the most familiar work in the collection owing to its sarabande whose two variations are based on a tune closely related to the well-known "Lascia ch'io pianga" aria from *Rinaldo* (1711) – a clue perhaps to its dating.

The final position of the volume is occupied by an enormous chaconne in G major (HWV442), a work presumably written early in Handel's Hamburg period. Its sixty-two rather mechanical, and ultimately tedious, variations over an eight-measure ground bass (identical to the first eight bass notes of the Goldberg theme) may well have been conceived as teaching material. The piece is best understood as a repository of stereo-typical motivic and finger patterns.

The first work in the 1733 collection is a three-movement miscellany in B♭ (HWV 434). It begins with an opening prelude consisting of whole- and half-note chords alternating with passagework. The second movement is an energetic etude labeled "Sonata." The finale, arguably the most attractive movement in the volume, is a set of five variations on an "aria" – the

Example 14.3a G. F. Handel, Fugue in G minor, HWV605, mm. 1–5

Example 14.3b J. S. Bach, Fugue in B minor on a Theme of Corelli, BWV579, mm. 1–5

Example 14.3c G. F. Handel, "He smote all the first-born of Egypt," from *Israel in Egypt*, mm. 1–5

Example 14.3d G. F. Handel, Fugue in A minor, HWV609, mm. 1–6

Example 14.3e G. F. Handel, "They loathed to drink of the river," from *Israel in Egypt*, mm. 1–4

Example 14.3f J. S. Bach, Fugue in A minor, BWV889/2, mm. 1–4

theme that would serve as the basis for Johannes Brahms's *Variations and Fugue on a Theme by Handel*, Op. 24.

The volume of *Six Fugues or Voluntaries for the Organ or Harpsichord* (HWV605–10) published by Walsh in 1735 apparently contains the fugues composed during Handel's early London years (1711/12–18) but unlike the five that were incorporated into the 1720 collection of suites had not yet been published. While eschewing elaborate contrapuntal artifice, they maintain the integrity and independence of the part writing.

The subjects of all six fugues – each beginning (as it happens) on the fifth degree – are concise and memorable. Those for the fugues in G minor (HWV605) and B♭ (HWV607) are double subjects: the initial idea is immediately and consistently answered by a complementary countersubject. The double subject, an Italian feature, appears at times in the works of the young Bach as well, for example in the *manualiter* toccatas in F♯ minor (BWV912a), D minor (BWV913), and E minor (BWV914). The double subject of Bach's Fugue in B minor on a Theme of Corelli (BWV579), based on Corelli's Trio Sonata, Op. 3, No. 4 (1689), bears a striking resemblance to the double subject of Handel's G minor fugue. Handel later adapted it for the chorus "He smote all the first-born" from *Israel in Egypt* (1739). He also reused the A minor fugue subject (HWV609, transposed to G minor) for the chorus "They loathed to drink of the river" in the same oratorio. With its dramatic opening and concluding chromatic scalar descent, the subject's resemblance to that of the A minor fugue from the *Well-Tempered Clavier II* (BWV889, completed ca. 1742) is unmistakable – and perhaps not coincidental.

In the year 1738/39 Handel composed two attractive suites for his student, the Princess Louisa (HWV447, 452). Modest in scale and in their technical demands, and consisting only of the four traditional dance movements, they form a retrospective epilogue to Handel's career as a harpsichord composer.

Bach

Bach's monumental and systematic collections of keyboard music have stood at the center of the serious keyboard player's repertoire since the composer's lifetime and, beginning in the nineteenth century, have occupied an ever more prominent position in the life of the concert hall. The literature devoted to them, already "oceanic," continues steadily to grow.[97]

The expected presentation at this juncture of an extensive review of J. S. Bach's stylistic development as a composer of harpsichord music will not be forthcoming. The present author has already published such a survey containing whatever original perceptions he has to offer on the subject;[98] and adding a few hundred words, or even a few thousand words, within the limited format of the present volume would serve little purpose. Much like Louis Marchand, he recognizes the futility of taking on that daunting challenge. After all, the encyclopedic compendium *Bachs Klavier- und Orgelwerke*, published about a decade ago, containing contributions by fifteen eminent authorities, is over a thousand pages long; David Ledbetter's study devoted exclusively to the *Well-Tempered Clavier* fills more than four hundred pages. Perhaps a few final observations contemplating Bach's relationship to the harpsichord could be of some interest here.

As arguably the greatest composer for the instrument in history (not to mention his status for many as the greatest composer in history *tout court*), it is fair to wonder exactly what the harpsichord meant to Johann Sebastian Bach and what purpose it served for him in his artistic mission. Like the organ, but far more intimate, the harpsichord (and perhaps the clavichord as well) was very likely his vehicle – his "instrument." Improvising at the keyboard stimulated his imagination. More significantly, composing for keyboard instruments and performing his works at the keyboard gave him absolute autonomy, and enabled the personal, direct expression, and communication, of his musical ideas. Writing for and performing at the keyboard allowed him to explore and convey, by himself, the full range of his musical imagination: from the most introspective and private to the most flamboyant and extroverted. As he wrote on the title page of his six compositions for unaccompanied violin, very likely aware of the pun created by the (deliberately?) ungrammatical Italian: *Sei solo* (six solo[s], or rather: you are alone).

Upon reflection, it is not at all surprising that Bach's keyboard works – more, perhaps, than his contributions to other genres – probe the limits. To a profound degree they are demonstrations (in the sense of experiments) as they test the limits of the tonal system, the tuning system, contrapuntal and harmonic limits, the physical limits of players, the technological limits of instruments.

On the latter point, Bach's keen interest in musical instruments no doubt accounts for his activity in the development of the lute harpsichord, on the one hand, and the fortepiano, on the other. He shared this commitment with one of his relatives, his cousin Johann Nicolaus Bach (1669–1753), the town and university organist at Jena, and a builder of lute harpsichords whose instruments earned the praise of Jacob Adlung.[99]

Bach's criticism and ultimate endorsement of Gottfried Silbermann's fortepianos is well known. But he is also credited with having invented a "viola pomposa," perhaps identical – perhaps not – to the violoncello piccolo called for in a number of cantatas. His prescriptions for the mysterious *corno da tirarsi* and/or *tromba da tirarsi* in other cantatas attest at the least to his interest in – and need for – trumpets and horns capable of playing chromatics.

In probing limits, Bach not only explores and demonstrates them: In the end he conquers, "domesticates," them, brings them under control, in order then to expand them. His favorite strategy of expansion, as is well known, is synthesis: uniting, fusing, national traditions (French, Italian, and German) and/or historical traditions (*stile antico, stile modern, style*

galant), homophony and polyphony, functional tonality and modal counterpoint – often enough in the same works.

But in the final analysis, Bach's "experiments" were not merely the
product of abstract intellectual speculation. Their larger purpose, one
suspects, was to extend the range and depth of musical expression. From
the beginning, Bach's keyboard compositions were more than well-crafted,
exemplary representatives of prevailing conventions and genres. They
were in addition highly individual "character pieces." Consider the programmatic *Capriccio on the Absence of the Beloved Brother*, BWV992.
Presumably composed by 1705, it is certainly the most famous keyboard
composition from Bach's early years.[100] In addition to its explicit literary
program – a feature unique among Bach's keyboard works – the *Capriccio*
is notable for its tonal audacity, progressing at one point in the second
movement (a depiction of "the various casualties that could befall the
friend abroad") via the circle of fifths from the tonic G minor to the key
of B♭ minor. This is harmonic and tonal exploration with a personal,
expressive, poignant purpose.

At the other end of his career we find what is arguably Bach's greatest
harpsichord composition: the Goldberg Variations (BWV988), published
in 1741 as the final part of the *Klavierübung*. Like the two volumes of the
Well-Tempered Clavier, it is, as a totality, encyclopedic in its far-reaching
survey of styles, genres, and compositional techniques – all investigated, as
is Bach's wont, according to a single unifying principle: the contrast pair of
prelude and fugue in the one instance, theme and variations, along with
canonic art, in the other.

As individual numbers, however, what is striking, and moving, about
the constituent members of the *Well-Tempered Clavier* and the Goldbergs
is their intensely individual character. They are "character pieces" in the
most literal sense: giving expression to every mood and emotional state
from uninhibited exhibitionism to the deepest, most sorrowful, most
personal introspection.

To study, practice and ultimately play one of Johann Sebastian Bach's
masterpieces at the harpsichord (or any other keyboard instrument) is to
become his intimate partner – one-on-one – sharing the bold compositional forays and privy to the heights and depths of expression, all fortunately set down in notation and preserved for posterity.[101]

Notes

1. An English translation of the estate catalogue appears in *The New Bach
   Reader*, ed. Hans T. David and Arthur Mendel, rev. Christoph Wolff
   (New York: W. W. Norton, 1998), pp. 250–256, especially pp. 251–252.

2. A *Reichsthaler* (imperial thaler) was worth about $100 in today's US currency.

3. See Siegbert Rampe, "Cembalo (Spinett und Virginal)," *Das Neue Bach-Lexikon: Das Bach-Handburch*, Vol. 6 (Laaber: Laaber-Verlag, 2016), pp. 171–172.

4. See Christoph Wolff, *Johann Sebastian Bach: The Learned Musician* (New York: W. W. Norton, 2000), p. 412.

5. Howard Schott reasonably suggests that one of the two lute harpsichords listed in Bach's estate catalogue would have been the instrument heard by Agricola, who had studied with Bach from 1739 to 1741. See "Bach, Johann Sebastian," in *The Harpsichord and Clavichord: An Encyclopedia*, ed. Igor Kipnis (New York: Routledge, 2007), p. 23. The other was the work, perhaps, of his cousin, Johann Nicolaus Bach (1669–1753).

6. *The New Bach Reader*, pp. 255–256.

7. Jacob Adlung, *Anleitung zur musikalischen Gelahrtheit (Erfurt, 1758)*, p. 568, facs. edition, ed. Hans Joachim Moser (Kassel: Bärenreiter Verlag, 1953).

8. Jacob Adlung, *Musica mechanica organoedi (Berlin, 1768)*, Vol. 2, pp. 158–62, facs. edition, ed. Christhard Mahrenholz (Kassel: Bärenreiter Verlag, 1961).

9. See Robert L. Marshall, "Organ or 'Klavier'? Instrumental Prescriptions in the Sources of Bach's Keyboard Works," in *J. S. Bach as Organist: His Instruments, Music, and Performance Practices*, ed. George Stauffer and Ernest May (Bloomington: Indiana University Press, 1986), pp. 212–239 (esp. pp. 220–221). Reprinted in Marshall, *The Music of Johann Sebastian Bach: The Sources, the Style, the Significance* (New York: Schirmer Books, 1989), pp. 271–293 (280–281). See also Joel Speerstra, *Bach and the Pedal Clavichord: An Organist's Guide* (Rochester: University of Rochester Press, 2004), pp. 26 and 46.

10. Eberhard Spree, *Die verwitwete Frau Capellmeisterin Bach. Studie über die Verteilung des Nachlasses von Johann Sebastian Bach* (PhD diss., Hochschule für Musik Carl Maria von Weber, Dresden, 2017), pp. 116–117.

11. *Handel: A Documentary Biography*, ed. Otto Erich Deutsch (New York: W. W. Norton, 1954), p. 691.

12. *Handel: A Documentary Biography*, p. 692.

13. Terence Best, "Handel," in *The Harpsichord and Clavichord*, ed. Igor Kipnis (New York: Routledge, 2007), p. 217.

14. "Handel," in *The Harpsichord and Clavichord*, p. 217.

15. Michael Cole, "A Handel Harpsichord," *Early Music* 21, no. 1 (1993), pp. 99–109, esp. p.104.

16. Cole: "A Handel Harpsichord," pp. 99 and 106. Cole reproduces an image of the Smith harpsichord (p. 99), as well as a close-up photograph of its keyboard (p. 100) and a photo of the instrument shown in the Mercier Handel portrait (p. 101). Reproductions of Mercier's Handel portrait can be found at www.allabouthandel.com/portraits-of-handel/portrait-of-handel-by-philip-mercier/.

17. See Rampe, *Das Neue Bach-Lexikon*, p. 172, which includes a photograph of the instrument. A closer description of the instrument, along with a wider discussion of German harpsichords in the Bach era, appears in John Koster, "The Harpsichord Culture in Bach's Environs," in *Bach Perspectives* 4, ed. David Schulenberg (Lincoln, NE: University of Nebraska Press, 1999), pp. 57–77, esp. p. 61.

18. See the *Bach-Gesellschaft* edition, Vol. 9, *Kammermusik*: Works for flute, violin, or gamba and harpsichord or continuo (Leipzig: Breitkopf & Härtel, 1860), Foreword, p. xiv. A modern photograph of the instrument, which currently has the catalogue number 5614, is posted on the website of the Musikinstrumenten-Museum: https://en.wikipedia.org/wiki/ Berlin_Musical_Instrument_Museum#/media/File:Bach_Cembalo.jpg.

19. Friedemann Bach is known to have sold or given manuscripts of his father's music to his Berlin patron (the father of Rust's informant), Count Otto Carl Friedrich von Voss (1755–1823).

20. Georg Kinsky, "Zur Echtheitsfrage des Berliner Bach-Flügels," in *Bach-Jahrbuch* 1924, pp. 128–138.

21. Dieter Krickeberg and Horst Rase, "Beiträge zur Kenntnis des mittel- und norddteuschen Cembalobaus um 1700," in *Studia organologica: Festschrift für John Henry van der Meer*, ed. Friedemann Hellwig (Tutzing: Hans Schneider, 1987), pp. 285–310.

22. Kinsky, "Zur Echtheitsfrage, p. 288.

23. Adlung, *Anleitung*, 2, p. 110; also Rampe, "Bach Cembalo," in *Das Neue Bach-Lexikon*, pp. 106–108, esp. p. 107.

24. Re the F versus C keyboard orientations, see Alfred Dürr, "Tastenumfang und Chronologie in Bachs Klavierwerken," in *Festschrfit Georg von Dadelsen zum 60. Geburtstag*, ed. Thomas Kohlhase and Volker Scherliess (Stuttgart: Hänssler, 1978), p. 74. Dürr based his description on Friedrich Ernst, *Der Flügel Joh. Seb. Bachs* (Frankfurt, London, 1955).

25. Rampe, "Bach Cembalo," p. 108.

26. Rampe, "Bach Cembalo," p. 107.

27. For the Cöthen court inventory, see *Bach-Dokumente, Band 2: Fremdschriftliche und Gedrucke Dokumente zur Lebensgeschichte Johann Sebastian Bachs 1685–1750*, ed. Werner Neumann and Hans-Joachim Schulze (Kassel: Bärenreiter, 1969), pp. 73–74. The commonly reported death year for Mietke – 1719 – is incorrect. He was alive in 1726 and described as "the late Mietke" ("seel. Mietke") in November 1729. See Dieter Krickeberg, "Michael Mietke – ein Cembalobauer aus dem Umkreis von Johann Sebastian Bach," *Cöthener Bach-Hefte* 3 (1985), pp. 47–56, esp. p. 49.

28. A thorough description of the instruments appears in Sheridan Germann, "The Mietkes, the Margrave and Bach," in *Bach, Handel, Scarlatti: Tercentenary Essays*, ed. Peter Williams (Cambridge: Cambridge University Press, 1985), pp. 119–148.

29. Germann, "The Mietkes, the Margrave," p. 121. For more on the possible connections between the Mietke harpsichords in the Charlottenburg Palace and both J. S. and C. P. E. Bach, see Mary Oleskiewicz, "Keyboards, Music Rooms, and the Bach Family at the Court of Frederick the Great," in *Bach*

Perspectives 11: J. S. Bach and His Sons, ed. Mary Oleskiewicz (Urbana: University of Illinois Press, 2017), pp. 24–82, esp. pp. 35–36, and n. 37.

30. *The New Bach Reader*, p. 307.
31. *The New Bach Reader*, p. 396.
32. *The New Bach Reader*, p. 436.
33. *The New Bach Reader*, p. 368.
34. David Ledbetter, *Bach's Well-Tempered Clavier: The 48 Preludes and Fugues* (New Haven: Yale University Press, 2002), pp. 41–45.
35. Bruce Haynes devotes an entire chapter to "Sebastian Bach and Pitch" in his *A History of Performing Pitch: The History of "A"* (Lanham, MD: Scarecrow, 2000).
36. Haynes, *History of Performing Pitch*. See also, Mary Oleskiewicz, "The Trio in Bach's Musical Offering: A Salute to Frederick's Tastes and Quantz's Flutes?" in *Bach Perspectives 4*, esp. pp. 96–98.
37. *The New Bach Reader*, p. 365. Sheridan Germann observes in this connection that the extant harpsichords by Michael Mietke are the only ones of Brandenburg origin known and that they "fulfill [Agricola's – and Bach's] criteria admirably." See Germann, "The Mietkes, the Margrave," pp. 119–148, esp. pp. 128–129.
38. *Händel: Keyboard Works IV: Miscellaneous Suites and Pieces, Second Part*, ed. Terence Best (Kassel: Bärenreiter, 1975), Preface, p. vii.
39. Namely, the first eighteen compositions appearing in his volume (*Keyboard Works IV*). The courante of the C minor suite (HWV 445) contains a single GG as octave reinforcement at the final cadence.
40. In a letter of August 1710, cited in Best, "Handel," p. 217.
41. Donald Burrows, *Handel*, second edition (New York: Oxford University Press, 2012), p. 575.
42. See George B. Stauffer, "J. S. Bach's Harpsichords," in *Festa Musicologica: Essays in Honor of George J. Buelow. Festschrift Series, No. 1*, ed. Thomas J. Mathiesen and Benito V. Rivera (Stuyvesant, NY: Pendragon Press, 1995), pp. 289–318, esp. pp. 294–295. See also Stauffer, "'This fantasia … never had its like': On the Enigma and Chronology of Bach's Chromatic Fantasia and Fugue in D Minor, BWV 903," in *Bach Studies*, ed. Don O. Franklin (Cambridge: Cambridge University Press, 1989), pp. 160–182, esp. pp. 176 and 180.
43. Dürr, "Tastenumfang und Chronologie in Bachs Klavierwerken," p. 77.
44. See Marshall, "Organ or 'Klavier'?" p. 234.
45. Dürr, "Tastenumfang und Chronologie in Bachs Klavierwerken," pp. 85–86; Stauffer, "J. S. Bach's Harpsichords," pp. 303–304.
46. Dürr, "Tastenumfang und Chronologie in Bachs Klavierwerken," pp. 86–87. The required compass in the *Well-Tempered Clavier* 2, incidentally, extends from AA to d$\flat^3$.
47. *The New Bach Reader*, p. 156.
48. Stauffer evaluates all these possibilities, in Stauffer, "J. S. Bach's Harpsichords," pp. 298–300.
49. The Handel discussions in this essay, particularly the present section, have benefited from Ellen T. Harris's valuable suggestions, for which the author expresses his thanks.

50. See *George Frideric Handel: Collected Documents, Volume I 1609–1725*, ed. Donald Burrows et al. (Cambridge: Cambridge University Press, 2013), pp. 74–75.
51. Burrows, *Handel*, p. 52.
52. Deutsch, *Handel: A Documentary Biography*, p. 502.
53. Deutsch, *Handel: A Documentary Biography*, p. 18.
54. Cited in Ellen T. Harris, *George Frideric Handel: A Life with Friends* (New York: W. W. Norton, 2014), p. 329.
55. Deutsch, *Handel: A Documentary Biography*, pp. 766–767.
56. Cited by Winton Dean in "Handel, George Frideric," *New Grove Dictionary of Music and Musicians* (London: Macmillan, 1980), Vol. 8, p. 104.
57. Charles Burney, *An Account of the Musical Performances . . . in Commemoration of Handel* (London, 1785) quoted in Donald Burrows, *Handel*, p. 502.
58. *The New Bach Reader*, p. 136.
59. *The New Bach Reader*, p. 79.
60. For comment in the obituary, see *The New Bach Reader*, p. 301. No fewer than twenty accounts of the 1717 "noncontest" circulated before the publication of Forkel's biography in 1802. They differ in many particulars; they all agree, however, in failing to specify the instrument Bach had played on that notorious occasion. Presumably it was too obvious to mention. See Werner Breig, "Bach und Marchand in Dresden: Eine überlierferungskritische Studie," *Bach-Jahrbuch* 1998, pp. 7–18.
61. *The New Bach Reader*, p 433. Those last remarks effectively describe Variation 28 from the Goldberg Variations.
62. *The New Bach Reader*, p. 434.
63. *The New Bach Reader*, pp. 359–360.
64. Mark Kroll, *Playing the Harpsichord Expressively: A Practical and Historical Guide* (Lanham, MD: The Scarecrow Press, 2004), pp. 48–49.
65. Staatsbibliothek zu Berlin, Stiftung Preussischer Kulturbestiz, Berlin, Germany, shelfmark Mus. Ms. Bach P 1089.
66. Quentin Faulkner, *J. S. Bach's Keyboard Technique: A Historical Introduction* (St. Louis: Concordia Publishing House, 1984), pp. 23–24, 33. A transcription of the entire composition, BWV870a, with its fingering, appears on pp. 27–29.
67. Johann Mattheson, *Grundlage einer Ehrenpforte* (Hamburg, 1740), cited in Deutsch, *Handel: A Documentary Biography*, p. 503.
68. Reported by one Jacob Wilhelm Lustig, quoted here after *Georg Friedrich Händel: Composition Lessons from the Autograph Collection in the Fitzwilliam Museum Cambridge. Hallische Händel-Ausgabe, Supplement Band 1*, ed. Alfred Mann (Kassel: Bärenreiter, 1978), p. 11.
69. Mann, *Georg Friedrich Händel: Composition Lessons*.
70. *The New Bach Reader*, p. 318.
71. *The New Bach Reader*, p. 322.
72. *The New Bach Reader,* p. 453.
73. Mattheson, *Ehrenpforte* (1740) and his *Georg Friderich Händels Lebensbeschreibung* (1761), both cited in Deutsch, *Handel: A Documentary Biography*, p. 13.

74. Deutsch, *Handel: A Documentary Biography*, p. 431.
75. Deutsch, *Handel: A Documentary Biography*, p. 644.
76. Deutsch, *Handel: A Documentary Biography*, p. 754.
77. Quoted in Winton Dean, *Handel's Dramatic Oratorios and Masques* (London: Oxford University Press, 1959), p. 109.
78. The secco recitatives were invariably accompanied by the harpsichord. See Winton Dean, *Handel's Dramatic Oratorios*, pp. 109–112.
79. Mann offers a complete transcription of the manuscript along with extensive analytical commentary in *Georg Friedrich Händel: Composition Lessons*. See also the practical edition with commentary in David Ledbetter, *Continuo Playing According to Handel: His Figured Bass Exercises*, Oxford Early Music Series 12 (Oxford: Oxford University Press, 1990).
80. See Harris, *George Frideric Handel: A Life*, p. 144.
81. *The New Bach Reader*, p. 328.
82. *The New Bach Reader*, p. 362. Hans-Joachim Schulze suggests that Daube probably never heard J. S. Bach perform but based his description on information ultimately deriving from C. P. E. Bach. See *Bach-Dokumente, Band 3: Dokumente zum Nachwirken Johann Sebastian Bachs 1750–1800*, ed. Hans-Joachim Schulze (Kassel: Bärenreiter, 1952), p. 111.
83. *The New Bach Reader*, p. 322.
84. Philipp Spitta, *Johann Sebastian Bach*, trans. Clara Bell and J. A. Fuller-Maitland (reprint, New York: Dover Publications, 1951), Vol. 2, p. 293, fn. 195, and Vol. 3, pp. 388–398.
85. Johann Christian Kittel, *Der angehende praktische Organist* (Erfurt, 1809), quoted after Laurence Dreyfus, *Bach's Continuo Group* (Cambridge, MA: Harvard University Press, 1987), p. 28. Dreyfus points out (p. 229, fn. 52) that Hans David and Arthur Mendel, in *The Bach Reader* (originally published in 1945, second edition 1966), following Spitta, omitted the opening clause of Kittel's paragraph, which reads in the original, "Wenn Seb. Bach eine Kirchenmusik aufführte," etc. The words are also absent in *The New Bach Reader*, p. 323.
86. David Schulenberg, "'Towards the Most Elegant Taste': Developments in Keyboard Accompaniment from J. S. to C. P. E. Bach," in *The Keyboard in Baroque Europe*, ed. Christopher Hogwood (Cambridge: Cambridge University Press, 2003), pp. 157–158.
87. *The New Bach Reader*, p. 135.
88. *The New Bach Reader*, p. 70.
89. Supporting this assumption are the following considerations: The list of members of the court capelle for the period 1714–1716 mentions no other keyboard player. (See *The New Bach Reader*, p. 71.) Moreover, the surviving performing parts for several Weimar church cantatas contain no separate organ parts, whereas the continuo figures were entered in the corresponding autograph scores (Dreyfus, *Bach's Continuo Group*, p. 231, fn. 51). A harpsichord, nonetheless, was located in the Himmelsburg chapel during Bach's Weimar tenure. See Reinhold Jauernig, "Johann Sebastian Bach in Weimar," in *Johann Sebastian Bach in Thüringen* (Weimar, 1950), ed. Heinrich Besseler and Günther Kraft, pp. 49–105, esp. p. 70.

90. Dreyfus, *Bach's Continuo Group*, chapter 2, pp. 10–72. The organists at the Leipzig churches during Bach's tenure are identified by name in Christoph Wolff, *Johann Sebastian Bach: The Learned Musician*, p. 252.
91. An overview of Handel's keyboard music with presumed dates and other information appears in Burrows, *Handel*, pp. 572–577.
92. John Mainwaring, *Memoirs of the Life of the Late George Frederic Handel*, new foreword by J. Merrill Knapp (New York: Da Capo Press, 1980), p. 149.
93. See Best, *Händel Keyboard Works IV*, Foreword, p. vii.
94. Burrows, *Handel*, p. 105.
95. Burrows, *Handel*, pp. 124–125.
96. Andrew Talle, *J. S. Bach's Keyboard Partitas and Their Early Audience* (PhD diss., Harvard University, 2003), pp. 64–66.
97. Among the notable publications of recent decades the following deserve special mention: Paul Badura-Skoda, *Interpreting Bach at the Keyboard* (1993); Joseph Kerman, *The Art of Fugue: Bach Fugues for Keyboard, 1715–1750* (2005); David Ledbetter, *Bach's Well-Tempered Clavier: The 48 Preludes and Fugues* (2002); Siegbert Rampe, ed., *Bachs Klavier- und Orgelwerke* (2007–2008); David Schulenberg, *The Keyboard Music of J. S. Bach*, second edition (New York: Routledge, 2006); Joel Speerstra, *Bach and the Pedal Clavichord: An Organist's Guide* (2004); Talle, *J. S. Bach's Keyboard Partitas and Their Early Audience*.
98. See the chapter "Johann Sebastian Bach," in *Eighteenth-Century Keyboard Music*, ed. Robert L. Marshall, second edition (New York: Routledge, 2003), pp. 68–123.
99. Adlung, *Musica mechanica organoedi*, 2, pp. 135f.
100. On the dating of the *Capriccio*, see Robert Hill, *The Möller Manuscript and the Andreas Bach Book: Two Keyboard Anthologies from the Circle of the Young Johann Sebastian Bach* (PhD diss., Harvard University, 1987), pp. 123–127.
101. The author is indebted to Don Franklin, Ellen T. Harris, Mark Kroll, Andrew Talle, and Martin Zepf for their valuable suggestions, and to Eberhard Spree for sharing with him a prepublication version of his dissertation.

Further Reading

Burrows, Donald. *Handel*. Second edition. New York: Oxford University Press, 2012.

Burrows, Donald, et al., eds. *George Frideric Handel: Collected Documents, Volume I: 1609–1725*. Cambridge: Cambridge University Press, 2013.

David, Hans T. and Arthur Mendel, revised by Christoph Wolff. *The New Bach Reader*. New York: W. W. Norton, 1998.

Ledbetter, David. *Continuo Playing According to Handel: His Figured Bass Exercises*. Oxford Early Music Series 12. Oxford: Oxford University Press, 1990.

Marshall, Robert. *The Music of Johann Sebastian Bach: The Sources, the Style, the Significance*. New York: Schirmer Books, 1989.

"Johann Sebastian Bach," in *Eighteenth-Century Keyboard Music*, edited by Robert L. Marshall. Second edition. New York: Routledge, 2003.

Wolff, Christoph. *Johann Sebastian Bach: The Learned Musician*. New York: W. W. Norton, 2000.

15 The Harpsichord in Ensemble

MARK KROLL

The harpsichord could serve a number of different roles in an ensemble. One is as a basso continuo instrument, in which the harpsichordist improvises a part from either a figured or unfigured bass or from the score itself. Another is as an obbligato instrument, to play a part fully written out by the composer. These two roles could often overlap. Compositions that were predominantly written with a figured bass could feature obbligato passages at various points in the work, and sections of basso continuo are to be found in pieces with composed keyboard parts. This chapter will be divided into two sections, the first focusing on the harpsichord as a basso continuo instrument, and the second, for want of a better term, "accompanied keyboard music"; that is, compositions with written-out harpsichord parts.[1]

The Harpsichord as a Basso Continuo Instrument

The addition of a keyboard player to a vocal or instrumental ensemble would seem to serve an obvious and practical musical purpose, even when it is not indicated in the music, since the ten fingers of the keyboard player could help the singers with intonation, keep the ensemble together, reinforce the rhythm, and perhaps also enliven the composition or contrapuntal texture with improvised embellishments or imitative passages. This was probably a frequent practice even in those eras where there is little if any documentation to prove the presence of a keyboard, such as in the *a capella* choral literature of the fourteenth and fifteenth centuries.

The practice of playing a keyboard part from open score begins to appear more frequently in the sixteenth century.[2] For example, in 1553 Diego Ortiz describes three methods by which the clavier and viol (or violone) might play in ensemble.[3] Ortiz calls the first *Fantasia*, in which the keyboard player merely improvises a part. In the second, to be used above a plainchant, the "harpsichord should play what is written for the bass, accompanying with consonances and some counterpoint appropriate to the *Recercada* the *violone* is playing." Ortiz also suggests that what the harpsichord plays "should be made up of well-ordered consonances, then the *violone* should enter playing some charming passages; when the *violone* plays some runs or long notes then the harpsichord should answer appropriately, and together they should play some fugues, with regard and respect for one another." With the third method, Ortiz tells us that the keyboard could perform all the parts of an apparently unaccompanied madrigal or motet and adorn it with diminutions or imitative passages, while the viol played one of the other melodies. In other words, the keyboard player performs from score but with a greater freedom than merely reproducing one or more of the separate parts.

Ortiz has thus set the stage for the creation of the basso continuo, which gradually developed into the notation of figured bass, a system of numbers and symbols used to indicate the intervals to be played over a given bass line. There was, however, considerable resistance to the use of figured bass rather than playing from score during Ortiz's time and in the succeeding generation of composers and theorists. Girolamo Diruta, in the second part of his *Il Transilvano* (1609), preferred that his students make a score out of multivoiced compositions and play from that, explaining: "it will be impossible for the one playing the *Basso continuato* not to commit errors. He will never play all the parts of the composition and always achieve a harmony. So . . . do not give in to this laziness, make an open score of the music and play all parts."[4] Adriano Banchieri, in his *Conclusioni del suono del organa* (Bologna, 1609) also accused keyboard players who choose to play from a figured bass rather than from a score of "sheer laziness."[5]

The practice of playing from score was also common among French keyboardists during the first half of the seventeenth-century. This early preference for score reduction over figured-bass realization persisted among all national styles, long after the use of figures became the standard mode of playing a basso continuo. Girolamo Frescobaldi remained a proponent of the older method throughout his career.[6] Heinrich Schütz, in the preface to his *Cantiones sacrae* (1625), complained that "the publisher . . . wrested this basso continuo from me," and maintained his conservative approach even as late as 1648, when he tells us in the preface to the *Geistliche Chormusik* that he "originally composed [the work] without basso continuo," because organists should not be "discouraged by transcribing [the music] into tablature or score . . . to achieve all the more its desired effect."[7]

Nevertheless, the early Italian monodists and opera composers, such as Jacopo Peri, Giulio Caccini and, a bit later, Claudio Monteverdi, embraced the new system, as did Bernardo Strozzi, who summarized this position in the preface to the third volume of his *Concerti ecclesiastici*, which was never published but quoted and translated by Michael Praetorius in his *Syntagma musicum III* (1619). Here Strozzi tells us that figures were invented so that "one could play correctly, without mistakes and conform as much as possible to the composer's composition . . . I have heard – also tried to reproduce myself – how some people performed motets of Palestrina . . . by means of such figures, so convincingly that it appeared to the listeners that the piece had been transcribed into a complete score." Strozzi also mentions that

> the score of all the parts was created in an earlier time, and one was supposed to be able to play from it accurately as written . . . but because it is so difficult and tedious to play from it competently, and because the people who invented and taught it are dead, or at the very least quite old, whoever thinks this is necessary should spare himself the trouble, due to this shortage of old masters.[8]

Composers and theorists in Germany, France, and England, such as Johann Staden, Nicolas Fleury, and Roger North, also adopted the use of figured bass. Praetorius's own instructions in his *Syntagma musicum* are characteristically clear and worth repeating at length here and elsewhere in this section.

Praetorius begins with a description of the basso continuo, and offers a brief history of the genre as well:

> The *Bassus generalis* or *continuo* is so called because it continues from the beginning of the piece to the end and, as principal part, contains within itself the entire motet or concerto. It is quite common in Italy, especially in the works of the outstanding composer Lodovico Viadana, the superb creator of this new art, who devised and published the method of having, one, two, three, or four voices sing to the sole accompaniment of an organ, regal, or other fundamental instrument. It is therefore necessary that such a thoroughbass and *continuo* part for the organist or lutenist, etc. be available as a foundation.[9]

Praetorius continues with various rules and performance suggestions, or "qualifications" for the "organist [these apply to harpsichord as well, of course] who wishes to play from a thoroughbass":

1. He must understand counterpoint, or at least be able to sing perfectly, recognize proportions and the beat or meter correctly, know how to resolve dissonances into consonances in all keys, different major and minor thirds and sixths properly, and to take other similar things into account.
2. He must have a good grasp of staff notation and be well practiced on the keys or frets of his instrument, regardless of whether it is an organ, regal, lute, theorbo, or similar chord-playing instrument.
3. He must have a discriminating ear so that he can interact with the singer, that is, the person singing the concerted part, when the parts are put together.[10]

Praetorius also addresses the conservatives who disapprove of the new figured-bass system: "I have heard that the best organists among us today have little regard for these figures, too, and that they have made thousands of dissonances because they did not want to pay any attention to them."[11]

With these and other comments Praetorious has essentially summarized, relatively early in the century, almost all the rules of playing the basso continuo. They would be used, expanded upon, and described in numerous well-known and oft-cited treatises published in the seventeenth and eighteenth centuries, the most important of which are available in facsimiles or translations and are listed in the further reading. I will offer here a brief discussion and synthesis of the rules as described by selected authors concerning differing approaches and national styles.

The Art of Basso Continuo Realization

It should be emphasized at the outset that, according to these writers and my own fifty years of experience as a continuo performer, the function of the harpsichordist in ensemble is not merely to produce harmonies by realizing figures and following certain rules. The true art of basso continuo performance is to provide a tasteful and useful accompaniment, one that supports the other players and enhances the interpretation of a work. The harpsichordist therefore serves as the de facto conductor of the ensemble, using the harpsichord's incisive attack and distinctive sonorities to provide a steady beat. He or she also helps to shape dynamic nuances and changes in color or texture by varying the number of notes in the realization, and the speed and direction of the arpeggiation; adds nonchord tones and ornaments to enrich the harmonies; imitates the melodic lines to a greater or lesser degree; and adapts the realization to conform to different national styles and practices.[12]

Nevertheless, composers and theorists of the period did specify a number of basic rules to follow. Their comments, however, could sometimes be contradictory, vary considerably between different national styles, or be subject to a large degree of flexibility and personal preference, but harpsichordists must be completely familiar with them if they hope to produce a historically informed basso continuo realization. The following offers a representative summary of these rules.

Voice Leading

The proscription against parallel fifths and octaves, the *bête noir* of voice-leading rules, was not rigidly applied to figured-bass realization. Praetorious writes: "It is far more important that the organist look carefully at what voices are to sing than to watch out for parallel fifths and octaves."[13] According to Viadana: "the organ part is never under any obligation to avoid two fifths or two octaves, but those parts which are sung by the voices are."[14]

The French writer M. de Saint-Lambert, always a pragmatic theorist, reminds the reader: "since Music is made just for the ear, a mistake that does not offend in the least is not a mistake."[15] Regarding parallel fifths and octaves in particular, he observes: "one is not too scrupulous about having them in the Accompaniment when one accompanies in a large Musical Ensemble – in which the clamor of the other Instruments covers the Harpsichord in such a way that one cannot judge whether or not it makes mistakes."[16] In other words, as I have often told my students: "if you can't hear it, it is not wrong." That said, St. Lambert does caution: "when one accompanies a single voice, one cannot adhere too religiously to correctness . . . for then everything is exposed, and the Critics will let you get away with nothing."[17]

The Italian Lorenzo Penna is a bit more conservative, especially when it comes to the soprano and bass parts. Writing in 1672, he warns the player: "Two consecutive Octaves are to be avoided, and two Fifths, and their compounds, either by step or leap; which Rule applies principally to the extreme parts."[18]

Follow the Melodic Line?

Harpsichordists are sometimes tempted to take the path of least resistance by doubling the melodic line(s), but this was generally frowned upon. Francesco Gasparini was adamant: "One must never play note for note the vocal part or other upper composed part for the violin, etc."[19] Most writers, however, allowed a more flexible approach, as did Pier Francesco Tosi in his *Opinioni dei cantori antichi e moderni* of 1723.[20]

Number of Parts

A four-voice accompaniment was considered the default sonority throughout the seventeenth and eighteenth centuries, but this was often neither practical nor desirable in basso continuo, since, as we have noted, different types of music demand different dynamics, colors, and textures. The player was therefore urged to exercise considerable discretion, as Quantz writes: "The general rule of thorough-bass is that you always play in four parts; yet if you wish to accompany well, a better effect is often produced if you do not bind yourself very strictly to this rule, and if you leave out some parts, or even double the bass an octave higher with the right hand."[21] C. P. E. Bach, Quantz's colleague at the court of Frederick the Great, concurred: "A consistent four-part accompaniment is rare."[22]

Changing the Bass Line or Figures, Adjusting the Texture

As should now be apparent, flexibility lies at the core of basso continuo realization. This is true even for the written figures and bass line, which, contrary to what some might believe, were never sacrosanct or immutable. According to Saint-Lambert, the harpsichordist "may even raise or lower the entire Bass by an Octave for several successive measures – either to conform further to the character of the singing voice; or to take best advantage of the quality of his Instrument (which often resonates better in one range of the Keyboard than in another); or, lastly, to free up the hands or to bring [them] closer together [if they happen to be] too encumbered or too separated."[23]

Octave doubling was also a useful tool for C. P. E. Bach: "A simple octave doubling of the bass by the left hand also has a penetrating effect; it is indispensable, when the notes are not rapid and are easily played."[24]

Adding, removing or changing figures is also a hallmark of this practical and flexible approach, Saint-Lambert suggesting that the accompanist may even sometimes change the chords assigned to the notes when he decides that others are better.[25]

Making a texture thinner or thicker for musical or technical reasons as described above was also acknowledged as a common and useful practice during this era. Turning again to Saint-Lambert:

> When the measure is so hurried that the Accompanist cannot comfortably play all of the notes, he then can be content to play & accompany just the first note of each measure – and thus leave it for the *Basses* de *Viole* or the *Violon* to play all the notes; they can do this much more easily, since they have no accompaniment to combine with . . . Contrary to what we have just said, when the Basses are little burdened with notes & drag on too much for the liking of the Accompanist, he may then add other notes to embellish further.

This, St. Lambert explains, should only be done if the accompanist "is certain that this will do no harm to the Air, nor above all to the solo part." He continues by emphasizing one of the cardinal rules of basso continuo performance: "For the Accompaniment is only made to support the voice, & not to stifle or disfigure it by a noisy clamor."[26]

It should be mentioned again, however, that there were probably as many styles of basso continuo as there were harpsichordists and organists. Gasparini, for example, claimed that taking such liberties as described by St. Lambert were not proper in a basso continuo realization: "I do not approve of the diminution of the bass itself because it is very easy to miss or depart from the intention of the composer and from the proper spirit of the composition – and to offend the singer." At the same time, he makes the clear distinction between soloist and accompanist: "he who accompanies must take pride in the title of a good, solid accompanist, not of a spirited and agile performer. He may suit his fancy and unleash his brilliance when he plays alone, not when he accompanies."[27] These words of warning, which can be found in other commentaries on the subject, should be carefully followed by all basso continuo players.

Imitation

Melodic imitation is another core element of a skilled and sophisticated basso continuo realization. According to Praetorious, the player may use it when

> the singer becomes tired and short of breath after executing many different runs, beautiful divisions, *groppi, tremoletti*, and *trilli*, he begins to sing the following notes in a simple and unadorned fashion. At this point the organist can introduce fine, skilled divisions, etc. – but only in his right hand – and attempt to imitate the singer's runs, divisions, and variations, etc, which were previously performed.[28]

Penna and Adam Heinichen agree. Penna writes: "In the Ritornelli, or in the pauses designed to rest the singer, the Organist should play something after his own fancy, imitating the Arietta, or other gay pieces just sung."[29] Heinichen offers a more detailed explanation of the technique:

> the second class of embellishments concludes with imitation, which differs from said embellishments in that it does not depend like the former on our own ideas but must be taken from the notated composition itself. Therefore, imitation in this context results if an accompanist seeks to imitate a composer's melodic motive or invention in places where the composer himself HAS NOT USED IT [original caps].[30]

There were, of course, almost as many views on the subject of embellishment and imitation as there were writers. Roger North, for example, cautioned against changing the bass line, but approved of imitation:

> It is not allow'd a tho-base part to break and adorne while he accompanys, but to touch the accords only as may be figured, or the composition requires. Yet there is a difference in the management when the upper parts move slow, and when they devide, or when they are full, or pause. In the latter case, somewhat more airey may be putt in, and often there is occasion to fill more or less.[31]

Viadana also told the keyboardist "to play the organ part simply," and in particular with the left hand, but encouraged imitation and embellishment, although "in such a manner that the singer or singers are not covered or confused by too much movement."[32]

Dynamic Inflections and Arpeggiation

As we have seen, the arpeggiation of chords is an essential tool with which to adjust dynamics, accents and musical syntax. Both Nicolo Pasquali and St. Lambert describe the technique. Pasquali writes: "Care must be taken not to strike abruptly, but in the *Harpeggio* Way, laying down the Fingers in the Chords *Harp-like. i.e.,* one after another; sometimes *slow,* other times *quick,* according as the Words express either common, tender or passionate *Matters.*"[33]

St. Lambert calls arpeggiation "one of the most suitable embellishments for Accompaniment with the Harpsichord ... Even when one does not double Parts, one still should arpeggiate them. One could repeat a single chord even several times, by arpeggiating it first in ascending & then in descending."[34]

An interesting comment about arpeggiation in large or noisy ensembles comes from C. P. E. Bach, who writes: "in intermezzos and comic operas with much noisy action and other works for theater where the action often occurs backstage, constant or frequent arpeggiation must be resorted to so that the singer and accompanist will hear each other clearly at all times."[35]

Registration

The harpsichordist can also create dynamic inflections by adjusting not only the texture but also the registration, as Saint-Lambert describes: "For extremely delicate voices, one could (as we have said) either disengage a stop or two on the Harpsichord, or else leave out one note from each chord – thus reducing the Accompaniment to two Parts."[36]

C. P. E. Bach's explanation of the use of registration to enhance dynamic contrast on a single-manual instrument is particularly detailed:

> Of all the instruments that are used in the playing of thorough bass the single-manual harpsichord is the most perplexing with regard to forte and piano ... some resort to a highly detached touch in order to express a piano, but ... it is better to reduce the volume by using the right hand less fequently over passing tones ... [on] the two-manual harpsichord fortissimo and forte are played on the louder manual ... a simple octave doubling of the bass also has a penetrating effect ... in the piano both hands use the softer manual ... in a mezzo forte, the left hand may play the bass as written on the louder manual while the right accompanies on the softer.[37]

Acciaccatura

A special and valuable addition to the harpsichordist's arsenal of basso continuo techniques is the acciaccatura, a nonharmonic tone played as quickly as possible before or simultaneously with the chord itself. Gasparini colorfully compares it to the harmless bite of an insect or animal:

> In breaking a full chord as I have described, one can touch fleetingly in the right hand on the semitone just below the upper octave ... play it with a certain quickness, in the form of a mordent, sounded on, or rather a little before the beat and released immediately, so that it adds a certain grace rather than offending the ear. It is called a mordent [*mordente,* "biting"] because of its

resemblance to the bite of a small animal that releases its hold as soon as it bites, and so does no harm.[38]

Mid-eighteenth-century composers such as Francesco Geminiani and his student Charles Avison (1709–1770) were no strangers to the acciaccatura. Geminiani challenged: "no Performer therefore should flatter himself that he is able to accompany well till he is Master of this delicate and admirable Secret."[39] Avison wrote that the acciaccatura and the "dropping or sprinkling Notes, are indeed some of the peculiar Beauties" of the harpsichord.[40]

National Styles

It would be tempting to claim that the Germans preferred a rich, contrapuntal texture in their basso continuo realizations, that the Italians added virtuoso passagework, and the French advocated discreet embellishment. Although there are elements of truth in these statements, such generalizations would be misleading since, as I have mentioned previously, there were as many exceptions to the rules as there were composers and writers. Nevertheless, contemporary commentators were indeed aware of the differences in national styles, such as Lecerf de La Viéville, whom we met in the chapter on France. He writes:

> All that is generally heard in the Italian music is a thorough-bass accompaniment unceasingly varied, this variation being often a kind of breaking of chords, and an arpeggiation, which throws dust in the eyes of those who know no better . . . an accompaniment . . . ought to be subordinate to the melody, and not overpower it. The voice ought to stand out and attract the main attention; just the opposite happens here . . . the thorough-bass accompaniment . . . rattles so loudly that the voice is smothered.[41]

The usually pro-Italian Rousseau found good things to say about both styles of continuo realization. His comments on playing arpeggios are particularly valuable for today's performers:

> In Italian recitativo secco play each chord fully but only once; do not restrike or rearpeggiate unless the strings are also accompanying. Play the chords short and add no ornaments. The Italians like to hear nothing from the accompaniment in such recitative. But for French recitative sustain the chords, arpeggiate gracefully and continually from top to bottom, and fill out the sounds as you can.[42]

The Proper Accompanist

Despite the differences described above, not to mention the nationalistic chauvinism of people like Lecerf, there was unanimous opinion about the essential characteristics of a good accompaniment and a good accompanist.

The most important were taste, discretion, and a proper understanding of the harpsichordist's role in an ensemble. That is, as noted by St. Lambert, Geminiani, and many others, the player should never forget that he is an accompanist and not a soloist. Praetorius, for example, warned against musicians "bumping" into one another, musically speaking, or trying to become "the cock of the roost":

> When several instruments are present in an ensemble they must watch each other and leave room to prevent bumping into each other, so to speak ... each must wait his turn to display, one after another, his *schertzi, trilli,* and accents. They must not warble among themselves like a flock of sparrows, each trying to shriek and crow the highest and loudest to prove himself the cock of the roost.[43]

Saint-Lambert obviously knew some accompanists who fancied themselves soloists:

> There are those Accompanists who have such a good opinion of themselves that (believing themselves to be worth more than the rest of the Ensemble) they strive to outshine all of the Players. They burden the Thoroughbass with divisions; they embellish the Accompaniments, & do a hundred other things that perhaps are very lovely in themselves – but which are at the time extremely detrimental to the Ensemble, & just serve to show the vain conceit of the Musician who produces them. Whoever plays in Ensemble ought to play for the honor & the perfection of the Ensemble, & not for his own personal honor. It is no longer an Ensemble when everyone plays just for himself.[44]

Geminiani expanded on his disapproval of ego displays: "If an Accompanyer thinks of nothing else but the satisfying his own Whim and Caprice, he may perhaps be said to play well, but will certainly be said to accompany ill."[45]

Writers also gave the following good advice still relevant today: Harpsichordists should carefully prepare the accompaniment beforehand by studying not only the figures, but all the parts; that is, to practice. Viadana advised the organist to "first cast an eye over the concerto which is to be sung, since, by understanding the nature of the music, he will always execute the accompaniment better."[46] Penna added: "Be careful as soon you have the part from which you to play, to understand its character, in order to be able to accompany it suitably."[47] Some advice was highly practical: Make sure accompanists can see the people with whom they are playing. Or, as Marco da Gagliano wrote in the preface to *La Dafne*: "First, ensure the instruments that accompany the voices are situated in a place so as to be able to see the singer's face so that, hearing each other better, they might play together."[48]

In summary, it is accurate to say that the art of basso continuo playing is not merely a practice but indeed an art. Rather than realizing the figured bass with unvarying chords, as is too often found in commercial editions of baroque music, harpsichordists who follow the advice of the composers, players, and theorists of the seventeenth and eighteenth centuries, and listen carefully to the performers they are accompanying, can become an important member of the ensemble – if not the most important.

Accompanied Keyboard Music

In this section we examine representative examples of accompanied keyboard music, organized by national styles.[49] A more extensive list can be found in Appendix 6.

Italy

Early examples of the genre were composed by Dario Castello (ca. 1590–ca. 1658) and Biagio Marini (1594–1663). Castello's *Sonate concertate in stil moderno per sonare nell' organo overo spineta, con diversi istrumenti. A due e tre voci con basso continuo* was published in Venice in 1629 with separate parts, presumably to accompany the keyboard score. Marini's *Sonata per l'organo e violino o cornetto, sonate, symphonie, canzoni, passemezzi, etc.*, Op. 8 (1626), indicated that the soprano part could be played by a violin, or a trombone an octave lower. The most notable composer in this group was Girolamo Frescobaldi (1583–1643). His *Toccata per spinettina e violino* (*Primo libro delle canzoni a 1, 2, 3, 4 voci*, Rome, 1628) belongs to the category in which the basso continuo passages in figured or unfigured bass alternate with obbligato sections. The toccata opens with nine measures of solo violin accompanied by the basso continuo. These are followed, somewhat unusually, by an extended section for solo harpsichord (i.e., marked "Violino tace, Spinettina sola"). However, Frescobaldi has also written a separate bass part that reinforces the principal notes of the harpsichordist's left hand, indicating that a performance was to include a separate bass instrument, such as a viola da gamba or violone.

The violin reenters at measure 25 ("Segue Spinettina, e violino"), its various motives imitated by the right and left hands of the harpsichordist. The work continues in a similar manner, although one finds brief passages of basso continuo and even several measures in which the bass instrument assumes a solo role. The work concludes with a brilliant passage in virtuoso toccata style for both instruments (see Example 15.1).

Example 15.1 G. Frescobaldi, *Toccata per spinettina e violino*, mm. 83–85

A number of examples of "Italian" accompanied keyboard music of the eighteenth century were written by composers who were born in Italy but spent much of their careers abroad. Felice Giardini (1716–1796) moved to London around 1751, when he published his only work in the genre, the *Sei sonate di cembalo con violino ò flauto traverso*, Op. 3. They consist of five two-movement works and a concluding four-movement sonata (Allegro – Grazioso – Allegro Staccato – Minuet, with variations). It is notable that the opening of each sonata would be indistinguishable from other basso continuo sonatas: a solo melodic line accompanied by a figured bass. However, despite this apparently irresistible nod to the "violino solo" genre by the virtuoso violinist-composer, the remainder of the work falls comfortably into the category of the accompanied keyboard sonata. The violin serves a secondary role, and the harpsichord is fully developed, including occasional hand crossings, although basso continuo passages do reappear at various points in each work, perhaps to allow Giardini to briefly showcase his skills.

Tommaso Giordani (ca. 1733–1806) spent even more time outside of his native Italy than Giardini, mostly in London and Dublin. His *Quarttete pour le clavecin, flûte, violon et violoncello* (published by W. Haveisen of Frankfurt-am-Main in 1775) consists of two movements, Allegro and Rondo Allegro. Once again, the keyboard player begins with basso continuo (here for the first seven measures), after which the part alternates frequently between figured bass and obbligato. The instrumental parts, however, do not serve an accompaniment role but are independent and fully developed. The writing is, as expected, in the early classical style, including extensive use of the so-called Alberti bass in the keyboard player's left hand.

Antonio Rosetti (ca. 1750–1792), another Italian émigré, spent most of his career in Germany and Paris. The title page of his six accompanied sonatas (*Sonate per cembalo o piano-forte con accompagnato d'un violino*, Op. 6 (Venice, ca. 1785) specified the piano, but the harpsichord was certainly a possible choice during this transitional period between the two keyboard instruments. What is most notable here is that Rosetti, like almost all composers of music with an obbligato keyboard part, was well aware of the inherent balance problems in music of this style, in which the harpsichord (or for that matter, the early piano) could easily be overpowered by the accompanying instrument(s). Rosetti addresses the problem by often indicating a quieter dynamic marking for the violin. For example, in the first movement of the first sonata, a passage for the violin is marked *piano*, while the keyboard is given a *forte*. In the second sonata, the opening movement features the solo keyboard at *forte*, and the violin enters four measures later at *piano*.

The French composer Louis-Gabriel Guillemain (1705–1770) also expressed this concern about balance, while confirming the concept of *ad libitum* practices, in the "avertissement" to his *Pièces de clavecin en sonates avec accompagnement de violon*, Op. 13 (Paris, 1745): "When I composed these sonatas, my first idea was to leave them as harpsichord solos without accompaniment, having noticed often that the violin covered [the harpsichord] a little too much . . . if one wishes, perform these sonatas with, or without accompaniment; they lose nothing of their melody, since the harpsichord part is self-sufficient."[50]

In 1777, another Frenchman, C.-J. Mathon de la Cour (1738–1793), editor of the *Almanach musical*, also addressed this issue. He first comments on the nature of the genre: "It would seem that sonatas of this kind ought to be classified as trios; they nevertheless retain the name sonatas because the harpsichord part predominates, and the accompanying parts are not obbligato – or at least they are only written to make the harpsichord shine."

He then colorfully places the questions of dynamic balance in accompanied keyboard music within the context of court etiquette, or *politesse*:

> We cannot resist pointing out here that the harpsichord is the only creature in this world that has been able to claim sufficient respect from other instruments to keep them in their place and cause itself to be *accompanied* in the full sense of the term. Voices, even the most beautiful ones, lack this privileged position: they are covered mercilessly, and all the nuances are hidden from us without scruple; but as soon as it is a question of accompanying a harpsichord, you see submissive and timid instrumentalists softening their sounds like courtiers in the presence of their master, before whom they dare not utter a word without having read permission in his eyes.[51]

France

The accompanied keyboard sonata in France indeed has a particularly rich history. The *Pièces de clavecin en sonates avec accompagnement de violon*, Op. 3 (n.d.) of Jean-Joseph Cassanea Mondonville (1711–1772) has often been credited with being the first French accompanied keyboard sonata, but this is something of an exaggeration.

François Couperin (1668–1733), for example, implies in the preface to his *Concerts royaux* (1722) that these ostensibly solo compositions could also be played with other instruments, telling us that he intended to perform them with his colleagues, the violinist François Duval, the oboist Pierre (or Anne) Philidor, the gambist Alarius [Hilaire Alarius Verloge], and bassoonist Pierre Dubois for his regular Sunday "petits Concerts de chambre" for Louis XIV in 1714 and 1715.[52] Several decades earlier, Elisabeth-Claude Jacquet de La Guerre (1665–1729) indicated the same flexibility in her second volume of harpsichord pieces, the *Pièces de clavecin qui peuvent se jouer sur le violon* (Paris, 1707), and instrumental parts were issued for several of Gaspard Le Roux's (1660–1707?) *Pièces de clavecin* (1705).

Nevertheless, Mondonville's six sonatas, Opus 3 can be considered the first work in France belonging to the genre in which the harpsichord part is (almost) completely written out. There are, however, a few curious passages in the second movement of the fifth sonata that feature a figured bass, but their function seems somewhat ambiguous, since the left hand of the keyboard is written out (see Example 15.2). One possibility is that the right-hand arpeggios written out in the opening measures of this section

Example 15.2 Joseph Cassanea Mondonville, *Pièces de clavecin en sonates avec accompagnement de violon*, Op. 3, Sonata V, Aria, mm. 1–12

should be continued with the harmony indicated by the figures. However, because the use of figures does not appear in any other sonata, a definitive interpretation is elusive.

All six sonatas are divided into three movements. Those in Sonatas II and IV are designated Allegro – Aria – Giga; Sonata I begins with an Overture, followed by Aria and Giga; the movements of Sonatas III and V are Allegro – Aria – Allegro; and Sonata VI has Concerto – Larghetto – Giga. Throughout, Mondonville establishes a pattern that would be followed by the majority of composers writing music in this genre: that is, as the title describes, a keyboard work accompanied by one or more instruments (in this case, the violin). The keyboard writing is brilliant throughout, and assumes the dominant role, while the violin serves a secondary function, at least in the outer movements.

A good example is the first movement of the first sonata, in which the violin essentially doubles the right hand of the harpsichord. In the Allegro that follows the opening overture, the harpsichord has an extended solo passage, the violin reentering nine measures later and, in general, serving as an accompaniment. This is equally true of the third movement, Giga, of this sonata, if not more so. Here the violin is definitely subservient, serving only to reinforce the strong beats of the harpsichord parts, which again is virtuosic, including passages that involve hand crossings. The violin is given a more prominent role in the second movements of Opus 3. Those in the first five sonatas are titled "Aria," while the sixth, a Largehetto, features contrapuntal and virtuoso writing for both instruments.

Mondonville's later *Pièces de clavecin avec voix ou violon*, Op. 5 (1748), which follow a similar compositional plan, are made all the more notable by the inclusion not only of an accompanying violin but a vocal line provided with complete sacred texts in each of the eight separate multi-movement works. In his preface, moreover, Mondonville underscores the flexible nature of the accompanied keyboard genre, telling us that the specified instruments (or voices) could be interchanged with others or omitted entirely, writing: "the voice part could be played on the violin" and "lacking a violin or voice, the accompaniment could be used for the entire piece."[53] Jean-Philippe Rameau (1683–1764), in his well-known *Pièces de clavecin en concerts* (1741), a work inspired by the success of Mondonville's Opus 3, said the same in his preface:

> The success of recently published sonatas which have come out as harpsichord pieces with a violin part, has given me the idea of following much the same plan in the new harpsichord pieces which I am venturing to bring out today. I have given them the form of little suites for harpsichord, violin or flute, and viol or second violin . . . these pieces lose nothing by being played on the harpsichord alone.[54]

As previously mentioned, this would be true for almost all accompanied keyboard sonatas published in France after Mondonville and Rameau. Notable examples are the *Sonates en quatuor . . . avec . . . deux violons, une basse, et deux cors ad libitum*, Op. 3 (1779) of Claude-Benigne Balbastre (1727–1799), which includes *ad libitum* parts for two horns; and Étienne-Nicholas Méhul's (1763–1817) *Trois sonates pour le clavecin ou le forte-piano avec accompagnement d'un violon*, Op. 2 (ca. 1788), the announcement of its publication specifying that the violin part was "ad. lib."[55] Not surprisingly for a work of this vintage, the basso continuo is completely absent. The violin occupies a decidedly subservient role and is, in fact, dispensed with entirely in the second sonata.

Germany and Austria

Georg Philipp Telemann (1681–1767), a prolific composer in every genre, made a number of notable contributions to the accompanied keyboard literature. Four particularly impressive examples can be found in his *Essercizi musici, overo dodeci soli e dodeci trii à diversi stromenti*. Among the notable features of these pieces, which he dubbed "trios," is the inclusion of a separate basso continuo part.

Trio X (TWV42: Es3), for example, is scored for oboe, obbligato harpsichord, and continuo. In its four movements (Largo – Vivace – Mesto – Vivace), the oboe part is anything but a "submissive and timid" courtier, as described by Mathon de la Cour. In the first movement, the two instruments enter together, the oboe with a sustained note lasting more than two measures, accompanied by a rocking arpeggio figure in the harpsichord. This pattern is then repeated in the dominant, after which the instruments engage in imitation through various keys, the harpsichord occasionally accompanying the oboe. The figured bass is independent in a number of sections, implying the use of a second harpsichord, although it is not impossible for the solo harpsichordist to assume the basso continuo role as well. The two instruments are given virtuoso passagework in the second movement, and the third movement opens with a dotted figure in the harpsichord, answered by a contrasting, plaintive "sigh" motive in the oboe. The final movement, again opening with the harpsichord, here playing a rousing *chasse* figure over the first three measures, continues throughout with virtuoso, extroverted writing for both instruments (see Example 15.3).

J. S. Bach was, of course, no stranger to the genre. Prime examples are the six violin sonatas (BWV1001–1006) and three viola da gamba sonatas (BWV1027–1029), although these are written more in the form of trio sonatas in which the harpsichordist plays one melody in the right hand and bass line in the left, and they will therefore not be considered here.

Example 15.3 G. P. Telemann, *Essercizi musici, overo dodeci soli e dodeci trii à diversi stromenti,* Trio X (TWV42: Es3), Movement IV, mm. 30–34

Bach's sons were active practitioners in the art of the accompanied harpsichord sonata. One of C. P. E. Bach's (1714–1788) most distinctive works in this genre is his *Sonata a cembalo e violino* in B minor, W76, the first movement in particular. It begins with an extended virtuosic, almost hysterical section for solo harpsichord that is answered ten measures later by a completely different *affect* in the violin, a plaintive melody in the true *empfindsamer Stil*. One finds brief sections of figured bass in all three movements, but the sonata overall is a tour-de-force for two fully independent instruments, which are at times in direct contrast to each other.

Two other interesting works by C. P. E. Bach featuring an obbligato harpsichord are the "Two Trios," W161, published in 1751. Both feature the *ad libitum* practice in which the upper voice could be played by the keyboard. The full title is *Zwey Trio; das erste für zwo Violinen und Bass, das zweyre für 1 Querflöte, 1 Violine und Bass, bey welchem beyden aber die eine den Oberstimmen auch auf dem Flügel gespielt werden kann.*

Another contribution of the Bach family to the genre are the *Sechs Sonaten für das Clavier, mit Begleitung einer Flöte oder Violino* by J. C. F. Bach (1732–1795). These are bright three-movement works in the early classical style and do not use basso continuo. The only possible accompanied work of W. F. Bach (1710–1784), the so-called "Sonata for Viola and Harpsichord," cannot be authenticated.[56] Johann Christian Bach (1735–1782) will be considered below in the section on England.

Two final German works are worthy of mention in this section, although they were written by little-known composers: Johann Pfeiffer (1697–1761) and Joseph Schuster (1748–1812).[57] Pfeiffer's "Sonata for Viola da Gamba and Concertizing Harpsichord" is one of a small number of accompanied sonatas that feature this instrumental combination. In four movements, it concludes with a Tempo di Bourée. Schuster's six *Divertimenti da camera a cembalo e violin di Giuseppe Schuster*, three-movement works in the early classical style, without basso continuo, were known by Mozart, who wrote to his father from Munich on October 6, 1777: "I enclose six duets *à clavicembalo e violino* by Schuster for my sister. I have played them often here, and they are not bad. If I stay here I shall compose six in the same *gusto*, for they are very popular here."[58]

England

One of the most prolific English composers of accompanied sonatas was Charles Avison. He published three separate collections, titled: *Six Sonatas for the Harpsichord, with Acompanyments for Two Violins and Violoncello*, Op. 5; *Six Sonatas for the Harpsichord, with Acompanyments, for two Violins and a Violoncello*, Op. 7; and *Six Sonatas for the Harpsichord, with Acompanyments for two Violins and a Violoncello*, Op. 8. His model was Rameau's *Pièces de clavecin en concert*, which had been published in England in 1750 and given their English premiere by Avison in Newcastle in 1751. Avison was a great admirer of "foreign" composers, Geminiani in particular, but also Domenico Scarlatti, C. P. E. Bach, and Rameau, as he states in the "Advertisement" for Opus 8: "Among the various Productions of foreign Composers for the Harpsichord, the Sonatas of SCARLATTI, RAMEAU AND CARLO-BACH have their *peculiar* Beauties. The *fine Fancy* of the Italian – the *spirited Science* of the Frenchman – and the German's *diffusive Expression* are the distinguishing Signatures of their Music." Unlike Rameau, however, Avison scored his sonatas, as the titles indicate, for harpsichord, two violins and cello. The bowed instruments are secondary to the harpsichord throughout, and serve to merely reinforce the melodic lines of the keyboard. Avison makes his intentions in this regard clear in the "Advertisement" to Op. 7: "The accompanying Violins which are intended to enforce the Expression of the Harpsichord, should also be kept always subservient to it."

Avison also addresses the ever-present problem of balance inherent in the genre, writing in the "Advertisement" to Opus 5: "The Violin Parts of these Sonatas being intended for Assistants only, the *Forte* or *Rinforza*, i.e. the Strength or Increase of them, ought not to overpower the Harpsichord."

Among the numerous works J. C. Bach composed for obbligato harpsichord and instruments are the *Six Sonatas for the Harpsichord or Piano Forte: With an Accompagnament for a Violin*, Op. 10 (WarbB2, London 1773). They are all two-movement pieces in which the harpsichord assumed the predominant role, with some virtuoso keyboard writing that is similar to that of his father and older brothers. The violin is decidedly secondary throughout. J. C. Bach's choice of music for the opening measures of the first sonata of this collection, in B♭ major, is particularly notable: they are a direct quotation of the opening passage from his father's *Partita in B♭ major* (BWV825), which Johann Christian alters with dotted rhythms in *galant* style.

A sonata for obbligato harpsichord and viola da gamba ascribed to G. F. Handel has been known for many years, but its authenticity is not certain. However, recent research, including the examination of a manuscript held at the University of Lund, which has the title "Concerto," seems to add weight to Handel's authorship. If it is indeed authentic, it was probably composed early in Handel's career, perhaps when he was in Italy.

Spain and the United States

Luigi Boccherini (1743–1805) was born in Italy, but his extended residence in Spain qualifies him for this section. His *Six sonates pour le clavecin avec l'accompagnement d'un violon*, composed before he moved to Spain, was published in Paris in 1769, and the manuscript held at the Parma Conservatory bears the title "Opera V. 1768." These works are the exception to the rule. That is, they are not written in the accompanied harpsichord style as described in this chapter. Rather, both parts are given equal prominence and solo roles, so much so that it is fair to categorize these pieces as full-blown sonatas for violin and keyboard. Four of the sonatas are in three movements, and numbers III and V have two.

Rayner Taylor (ca. 1747/48–1825) is even less well known than Pfeiffer and Schuster. Born in England, Taylor spent a considerable amount of time in the United States, from ca. 1773 to1778 and ca. 1792 to 1825. His *Six Sonatas for Harpsichord or Piano Forte with an Accompaniment for a Violin*, Op. 2 are composed in the expected accompanied keyboard sonata format, but there are a few distinguishing characteristics. One is the use of numerous dynamic markings, ranging from *pianissimo* to *fortissimo*. Another is the instruction to the violin in the second movement of the sixth sonata to use the mute ("con sordino").

Notes

1. Another possible category – the harpsichord concerto – will not be considered here, since this is not an ensemble work per se, but rather a composition in which the harpsichordist serves the role of a soloist accompanied by instruments.
2. For an excellent discussion of this issue, see James Ladewig, "The Use of Open Score as a Solo Keyboard Notation in Italy ca. 1530–1714," in *Essays in Honor of John F. Ohl, A Compendium of American Musicology* (Evanston: Northwestern University Press, 2001), pp. 75–91.
3. Diego Ortiz, *Tratado de glosas sobre clausulas y otros generos de puntos en la musica de violones* (1553), cited and translated in Giulia Nuti, *The Performance of Italian Basso Continuo* (Aldershot: Ashgate, 2007), pp. 8–10.
4. Girolamo Diruta, *Il Transilvano. Dialogo sopra il vero modo di sonar organi, & istromenti da penna, Seconda parte del Transilvano* (Venice: Giacomo Vincenti, 1609), in Murray C. Bradshaw and Edward J. Soehnlen, eds., *Girolamo Diruta "The Transylvanian" (Il Transilvano)*, (Henryville/ Binningen: Institute of Mediaeval Music, 1984), Vol. II (1609), p. 144.
5. Cited in Gregory S. Johnston, "Keyboard Accompaniment in the Early Baroque: An Alternative to Basso Continuo," in *Early Music* 26, no. 1 (February, 1998), pp. 51–60, 63 and 64, here pp. 51–52.
6. See Ladewig, "The Use of Open Score as a Solo Keyboard Notation in Italy," pp. 76 and 79.
7. Johnston, "Keyboard Accompaniment," p. 56.
8. Translated in Jeffery T. Kite-Powell, Michael Praetorius, *Syntagma musicum III* (Oxford: Oxford University Press, 2004), pp. 137–138. Another version of these comments appears in Robert Donington, *The Interpretation of Early Music* (New York: St. Martin's Press, 1974), p. 306.
9. Kite-Powell, *Syntagma musicum III*, p. 133.
10. Kite-Powell, *Syntagma musicum III*, p. 135.
11. Kite-Powell, *Syntagma musicum III*, p. 137.
12. The violoncello, frequently a member of the continuo group, shared many of these duties, such as that of the conductor. For example, Corrette wrote: "the violoncello holds the reins at a concert." See Michele Corrette, *Méthode pour apprendre le violoncelle*, Op. 24, p. 46, cited in Valerie Walden, *One Hundred Years of Violoncello* (Cambridge: Cambridge University Press, 1998), p. 245. For a full discussion of the role of the cello in accompaniment, see Walden, *One Hundred Years*, chapter 8, pp. 241–269.
13. Translated in Kite-Powell, *Syntagma musicum III*, p. 144.

14. Translated in Oliver Strunk, *Source Readings in Music History* (New York: W. W. Norton, 1950), p. 422.
15. M. de Saint-Lambert, *Nouveau traité de l'accompagnement du clavecin, de l'orgue, et des autres instruments* (Paris: Ballard, 1707), chapter 8, p. 61, rule 13, trans. and ed. John S. Powell as *A New Treatise on Accompaniment with the Harpsichord, the Organ, and with Other Instruments* (Bloomington and Indianapolis: Indiana University Press, 1991), p. 106.
16. Saint-Lambert, *A New Treatise on Accompaniment,* (chapter 8, rule 10, p. 60 in original), p. 105.
17. Saint-Lambert, *A New Treatise on Accompaniment,* (chapter 8, rule 10, p. 60 in original), p. 105.
18. Lorenzo Penna, *Li primi albori musicali*, Bologna, 1672, Book 3, chapter 1, rule 10, trans. in Franck Thomas Arnold, *The Art of Accompaniment from a Thorough-Bass as Practised in the 17th and 18th centuries*, 2 vols. (New York: Dover Publications, 1965), p. 136.
19. Francesco Gasparini, *The Practical Harmonist at the Harpsichord*, trans. Frank S. Stillings, ed. David L. Burrow (New Haven: Yale University Press, 1963), p. 89.
20. This is best expressed in the 1757 translation of Tosi by J. F. Agricola, *Anleitung zur Singkunst* (Berlin; George Ludewig Winter, 1757), pp. 187–188.
21. Johann Joachim Quantz, *Versuch einer Anweisung die Flote traversiere zu spielen* (Berlin: Johann Friedrich Voss, 1752), trans. Edward R. Reilly as *Playing the Flute* (New York: Schirmer Books, 1966), p. 251.
22. C. P. E. Bach, *Versuch über die wahre Art das Clavier zu spielen*, 2 vols. (Berlin, 1753/1762), trans. W. J. Mitchell as *Essay on the True Art of Playing Keyboard Instruments* (New York: W. W. Norton, 1949), p. 388.
23. Saint-Lambert, *A New Treatise on Accompaniment,* (ch. 8, rule 6, p. 59 in original), p. 103.
24. C. P. E Bach, *Essay on the True Art of Playing Keyboard Instruments*, p. 369.
25. See Saint-Lambert, *A New Treatise on Accompaniment*, p. 62.
26. Saint-Lambert, *A New Treatise on Accompaniment,* (ch. 8, rules 4 and 5, pp. 58–59 in original), pp. 101–102.
27. Gasparini, *The Practical Harmonist*, p. 90.
28. Kite-Powell, *Syntagma musicum III*, p. 144.
29. Lorenzo Penna, *Li primi albori musicali* (Bologna, 1672), chapter 14, trans. Arnold, *The Art of Accompaniment from a Thorough-Bass*, p. 148.
30. Johann David Heinichen, *Der General-Baß in der Composition*, pp. 578–579, trans. George J. Buelow, *Thorough-Bass Accompaniment According to Johann David Heinichen* (Berkeley: University of California Press, 1966), p. 188.
31. John Wilson, *Roger North on Music; Being a Selection from His Essay Written during the Years c. 1695–1728* (London: Novello, 1959), p. 249.
32. Lodovico Grossi da Viadana, *Centro concerti ecclesiastici*, Preface, trans. Strunk, *Source Readings*, p. 421.
33. Nicolo Pasquali, *Thorough-Bass Made Easy* (Edinburgh: R. Bremner, 1757), p. 47.

34. Saint-Lambert, *A New Treatise on Accompaniment*, (ch. 8, rules 7 and 8, p. 62 in original) p. 110.

35. C. P. E. Bach, *Essay on the True Art of Playing Keyboard Instruments*, p. 422.

36. Saint-Lambert, *A New Treatise on Accompaniment*, (ch. 8, rule 2, pp. 61–62 in original), pp. 108–109.

37. C. P. E. Bach, *Essay on the True Art of Playing Keyboard Instruments*, pp. 368–369.

38. Gasparini, *The Practical Harmonist*, p. 80.

39. Francesco Geminiani, *Treatise on Good Taste in the Art of Music* (London, 1744), preface, p. 4.

40. Charles Avison, *An Essay on Musical Expression* (London: C. Davis, 1753), pp. 134–135.

41. Lecerf de La Viéville, "Comparaison," in *Histoire* (Amsterdam, 1725), Vol. 1, p. 297, trans. in Donington, *The Interpretation*, pp. 369–370.

42. Peter Williams, *Figured Bass Accompaniment*, 2 vols. (Edinburgh: Edinburgh University Press, 1970), Vol. 1, p. 55, citing Rousseau, 1782, "Accompagnement."

43. Kite-Powell, *Syntagma musicum III*, p. 153.

44. Saint-Lambert, *A New Treatise on Accompaniment*, (ch. 8, rule 5, pp. 58–59 in original), pp. 102–103.

45. Francesco Geminiani, from the *Art of Accompaniment*, trans. Nuti, *The Performance of Italian Basso Continuo*, p. 128.

46. Lodovico Viadana, *Concerti ecclesiastici,* Venice, 1602, preface, rule 3, trans. Strunk, *Source Readings*, p. 421.

47. Lorenzo Penna, *Li primi albori,* Book 3, chapter 20, rule 1, trans. Arnold, *The Art of Accompaniment from a Thorough-Bass*, p. 151.

48. Nuti, *The Performance of Italian Basso Continuo*, p. 28.

49. For further details, see William S. Newman, "Concerning the Accompanied Clavier Sonata," *The Musical Quarterly* 33, no. 3 (July, 1947), pp. 327–349; Mary Cyr, "Origins and Performance of Accompanied Keyboard Music in France," *The Musical Times* (Autumn, 2015), pp. 7–26; Ronald R. Kidd, "The Emergence of Chamber Music with Obligato Keyboard in England," *Acta Musicologica* 44, no. 1 (January–June, 1972), pp. 122–144; and David Fuller, "Accompanied Keyboard Music," *The Musical Quarterly* 60, no. 2 (April, 1974), pp. 222–245.

50. Cited in Cyr, "Origins," p. 22.

51. Cited in Bruce Gustafson and David Fuller, *A Catalogue of French Harpsichord Music 1699–1780* (Oxford: Clarendon Press, 1990), p. 5.

52. See Cyr, "Origins," pp. 13–14.

53. J. J. Mondonville, *Pièces de clavecin avec voix ou violon*, Op. 5, preface.

54. Jean-Philippe Rameau, *Pièces de clavecin en concerts*, ed. Erwin R. Jacobi (Kassel: Bärenreiter, 1961), preface, p. xv.

55. It was announced in the *Calendier musical universel* of 1788–1789 (p. 242) as: "Trois sonates pour le clavecin, violon ad. lib par M. Mèhul, oeuvre 2ème."

56. The manuscript of the viola sonata is found at the Library of Congress, part of manuscript M412A2B15, and titled "Elf Trio von Em. Bach and 3 Trii von Friedemann Bach. No. 161."

57. Pfeiffer was born in Nuremberg and in 1720 became a violinist in the Court orchestra at Weimar. In 1734 he was appointed *Kapellmeister* in Bayreuth, where he remained until his death. Schuster was born in Dresden and studied with Giovanni Battista Martini in Italy, where he enjoyed considerable success as an opera composer.

58. *Letters of Wolfgang Amadeus Mozart*, selected and edited by Hans Mersmann, trans. M. M. Bozman (New York: Dover Publications, 1972), p. 36.

Further Reading

Primary Sources

Avison, Charles. *An Essay on Musical Expression*. London: C. Davis, 1753.

Bach, C. P. E. *Versuch über die wahre Art das Clavier zu spielen*. 2 volumes. Berlin, 1753/1762). English translation by W. J. Mitchell as *Essay on the True Art of Playing Keyboard Instruments*. New York: W. W. Norton, 1949.

Bach, J. S. *Precepts and Principles for Playing the Thorough-Bass or Accompanying in Four Parts*. Translated by Pamela L. Poulin. Oxford: Clarendon Press, 1994.

D'Anglebert, Jean-Henry. "Principes de l'Accompagnement," in *Pièces de clavecin*. Paris: [author], 1689. Modern edition *J.-H. D'Anglebert, Pièces de clavecin*. Edited by K. Gilbert. Paris: Heugel, 1975.

Delair, D[enis]. *Traité d'accompagnement pour le théorbe, et le clavessin*. Paris: Author, 1690. Translated and edited by Charlotte Mattax as *Accompaniment on the Theorbo & Harpsichord: Denis Delair's Treatise of 1690*. Bloomington and Indianapolis: Indiana University Press, 1991.

Diruta, Girolamo. *Il Transilvano. Dialogo sopra il vero modo di sonar organi, & istromenti da penna, Seconda parte del Transilvano* (Venice: Giacomo Vincenti, 1609). Translated and edited by Murray C. Bradshaw and Edward J. Soehnlen as *Girolamo Diruta "The Transylvanian" (Il Transilvano)*, Vol. 2 (1609). Henryville/Binningen: Institute of Mediaeval Music, 1984.

Geminiani, Francesco. *The Art of Accompaniment*. 2 volumes. London: John Johnson, 1753.
   A Treatise of Good Taste in the Art of Music. London, 1744.

Heinichen, Johann David. *Gründliche Anweisung ... Zu vollkommener Erlernung de General-Basses*. Hamburg: Benjamin Schiller, 1711. Translated by Benedikt Brilmayer and Casey Mongoven. New York: Pendragon Press, 2012.

Lampe, John Frederck. *A Plain and Compendious Method of Teaching Thorough Bass*. London: J. Wilcox, 1737. Facsimile. New York: Broude Brothers, 1969.

Locke, Matthew. *Melothesis, or, Certain General Rules for Playing Upon A Continued Bass*. London: J. Carr, 1673. Facsimile. New York: Broude, 1975.

Mattheson, Johann. *Grosse Generalbass-Schule*. Hamburg: J. C. Kissnersbuchladen, 1731.

Muffat, Georg. *An Essay on Thoroughbass*. Edited with an Introduction by Hellmut Federhofer. American Institute of Musicology. Tübingen: C. L. Schultheiss and Chr. Gulde, 1961.

Pasquali, Nicolo. *Thorough-Bass Made Easy*. Edinburgh: R. Bremner, 1757.

Penna, Lorenzo. *Li primi albori per li principianti della musica figurate*. Bologna: Giacomo Monti, 1672.

Praetorius, Michael. *Syntagma musicum III*. Translated by Jeffery T. Kite-Powell. London: Oxford University Press, 2004.

Quantz, Johann Joachim. *Versuch einer Anweisung die Flote traversiere zu spielen*. Berlin: Johann Friedrich Voss, 1752. Translated by Edward R. Reilly. New York: Schirmer Books, 1966.

Roussier, P.-J. *Traité des accords*. Paris: Bailleux, 1764. Facsimile. Geneva: Minkoff, 1972.

Saint-Lambert, Monsieur de. *Nouveau traité de l'accompagnement du clavecin, de l'orgue, et des autres instruments*. Paris: Ballard, 1707. Translated and edited by John S. Powell as *A New Treatise on Accompaniment with the Harpsichord, the Organ, and with Other Instruments*. Bloomington and Indianapolis: Indiana University Press, 1991.

Telemann, Georg Philip. *Untericht im Generalbass Spielen ...* Hamburg: Michael Christian Bock, 1773.

Tosi, Pier Francesco. *Opinioni de' cantori antichi, e moderni*. Bolgna: L. dalla Volpe, 1723. English translation by J. E. Galliard as *Observations on the Florid Song*. London: J. Wilcox, 1743.

Viadana, Lodovico. *Cento concerti ecclesiastici. Preface*. Venice: Giacomo Vincenti, 1602. Modern edition Leipzig: Breitkopf & Härtel, 1964.

Secondary Sources

Arnold, Franck Thomas. *The Art of Accompaniment from a Thorough-Bass as Practised in the 17th and 18th Centuries*. 2 volumes. New York: Dover Publications, 1965.

Buelow, George J. *Thorough-Bass Accompaniment According to Johann David Heinichen*. Berkeley: University of California Press, 1966.

Christensen, Jesper Boje. *Eighteenth-Century Continuo Playing: A Historical Guide to the Basics*. Kassel: Bärenreiter, 2002.

Donington, Robert. *The Interpretation of Early Music*. New York: St. Martin's Press, 1974.

Dreyfus, Laurence. *Bach's Continuo Group: Players and Practices in His Vocal Works*. Cambridge: Harvard University Press, 1987.

Espinosa, Alma. "More on the Figured-Bass Accompaniment in Bach's Time: Friedrich Erhard Niedt and 'The Musical Guide.'" *Bach* 12, no. 1 (January, 1981), pp. 13–22. Published by Riemenschneider Bach Institute, Berea, Ohio.

Gasparini, Francesco. *The Practical Harmonist at the Harpsichord*. Translated by Frank S. Stillings, edited by David L. Burrow. New Haven: Yale University Press, 1963.

Goede, Thérèse de. "From Dissonance to Note-Cluster: The Application of Musical-Rhetorical Figures and Dissonances to Thoroughbass

Accompaniment of Early 17th-Century Italian Vocal Solo Music." *Early Music* 33, no. 2 (May, 2005), pp. 233–250.

Gudger, William D. "Playing Organ Continuo in Handel's Messiah." *The American Organist* 19, no. 2 (February, 1985), pp. 91–92.

Keller, Hermann. *Thoroughbass Method.* Translated and edited by Carl Parrish. New York: W. W. Norton, 1965.

Mann, Alfred. *Georg Friedrich Händel: Composition Lessons from the Autograph Collection in the Fitzwilliam Museum, Cambridge. Hallische Händel-Ausgabe,* Supplement Volume Kassel: Bärenreiter, 1978.

Nuti, Giulia. *The Performance of Italian Basso Continuo.* Aldershot: Ashgate, 2007.

Rose, Gloria. "A Fresh Clue from Gasparini on Embellished Figured-Bass Accompaniment." *The Musical Times* 107, no. 1475 (January, 1966), pp. 28–29.

Strunk, Oliver. *Source Readings in Music History.* New York: W. W. Norton, 1950.

Williams, Peter. *Figured Bass Accompaniment.* 2 volumes. Edinburgh: Edinburgh University Press, 1970.

Wilson, John. *Roger North on Music; Being a Selection from his Essay written during the years c. 1695–1728.* London: Novello, 1959.

16 Contemporary Harpsichord Music

LARRY PALMER

In the Beginning

Creativity will always express itself! Newly returned to the musical scene, the "ancient" harpsichord soon attracted living composers – at first a few, then others in ever-increasing numbers. Less than five years after two Parisian firms, Érard and Pleyel, and the musical instrument restorer Louis Tomasini each constructed their first "modern" harpsichord and displayed them at the Paris Exposition of 1889, composer Francis Thomé (1850–1909) dedicated *Rigodon, pièce de clavecin,* Op. 97, to "his friend Louis Diémer," a piano professor at the Paris Conservatoire; he played both the eighteenth-century Taskin harpsichord borrowed from the builder's descendants and the newly built harpsichords at the Exposition.

Jules Massenet included a harpsichord in the scoring of his opera *Thérèse* (1907) – probably the first twentieth-century use of the instrument in an orchestral score. As for solo harpsichord works, it now appears that the harpsichord's first twentieth-century piece to appear in print came from the pen of French organist Henri Mulet (1878–1967), whose *Petit Lied très facile pour clavecin ou piano,* truly a miniature at only thirty-four measures, was published in 1910.[1]

More substantial is Mario Castelnuovo-Tedesco's three-movement *English Suite* (1909), first conceived when the fourteen-year-old Italian was a student in Florence. Thirty-one years later, in 1940, Castelnuovo-Tedesco (1895–1968), by then a resident of the United States, transcribed his early work from memory for the harpsichordist Ralph Kirkpatrick. A printed score "for piano or harpsichord" was published by Mills Music (New York) in 1962.[2]

Within the next two decades, Ferruccio Busoni, Ottorino Respighi, Richard Strauss, Gabriel Pierné, and Manuel de Falla included the harpsichord in their orchestral scores, and Busoni, whose home in Berlin was graced by the long-term loan of an American-built Dolmetsch–Chickering harpsichord, wrote a lone solo work, his *Sonatina ad usum infantis* "per cembalo composità" in 1915. Published in 1916, this work has both originality and charm, but, strangely, the composer allows his compass to descend to a low E, a semitone below the range available on the preferred instrument, and, like many subsequent works for harpsichord, this piece would benefit greatly from a damper pedal – a device not found on the historic instrument.[3]

Two Early Masterpieces, First Recordings, and Several Other Endeavors

On 25 June 1923, the first staged performance of Falla's puppet opera *El retablo de maese Pedro* took place in the Paris music room of the Princesse de Polignac.[4] It was an event with far-reaching significance: Wanda

Figure 16.1 Wanda Landowska, Unsigned Caricature, gift of Momo Aldrich, Larry Palmer Collection.

Landowska (1879–1959), the most widely known advocate for the twentieth-century revival of the harpsichord and its most celebrated artist (see Figure 16.1), was engaged to play the prominent harpsichord part.

On this occasion, both the player and her instrument impressed the youthful composer Francis Poulenc, who was in attendance. Subsequently each composer presented Mme. Landowska with a concerto: Falla in 1926, Poulenc in 1929. These two major works, the Spanish master's chamber piece for harpsichord, flute, oboe, clarinet, violin, and cello, and the Frenchman's jaunty *Concert Champêtre* for harpsichord and full symphonic ensemble both rank highly among the twentieth century's most important (and popular) pieces for the revived instrument.

Landowska never recorded the Falla concerto, but Falla himself did, on both harpsichord and piano.[5] As for Landowska's recording of Poulenc's *Concert Champêtre* (a 1948 broadcast performance conducted by Leopold Stokowski), it remains, despite some flawed orchestral moments, the most definitive and individual among the plethora of subsequent recordings.[6] A later disc from Landowska's student Rafael Puyana comes closest to his teacher's rhythmically stimulating and joyful rendition.[7] Both of these recorded performances employed a Pleyel instrument equipped with foot pedals for quick, and frequent, changes of the instrument's ample variety of tonal colors.[8]

The 1920s saw the first commercial recordings of contemporary music for harpsichord. Two of Landowska's own compositions, *Bourrées d'Auvergne I and II* were committed to disc during her earliest recording sessions at the Victor Studios in Camden, New Jersey (USA), in 1923 and 1928. Slightly earlier, in 1920, the British virtuosa Violet Gordon Woodhouse (1871–1948) included three English folk dances during *her* pioneering recording venture: *Newcastle, Heddon of Fawsley,* and *Step Back* as arranged by the folksong collector Cecil Sharp – totaling nearly three minutes of music!

Equally of short of duration, and dedicated to Woodhouse, is the 1919 *Dance for Harpsichord* (or piano) by Frederick Delius (1862–1934), yet another work that requires major adjustments if it is to sound convincing on the harpsichord. Two years later, Dutch composer Alexander Voormolen (1895–1980), a student of Maurice Ravel, composed his *Suite de claveçin* (Ouverture – Gigue – Sicilienne – Toccatina) – of approximately eight minutes in duration.

More Concertos

Organist and composer Hugo Distler (1908–1942) was a leading talent of the German organ scene with its growing appreciation of music from the early baroque period, as well as a renewed interest in historic keyboard instruments, both original and those which copied the baroque style. A unique composition by the young composer is his *Concerto for Harpsichord and String Orchestra*, Op. 14 (1931) – a work both spicy and appealing. With a tonal pallette that has hints of Hindemith and Stravinsky as well as a rollicking third movement based on the song *Ei du feiner Reiter* by the early German master Samuel Scheidt, it is a challenging piece but one that rewards the required technical effort with scintillating and fresh music. A fourth movement (Allegro Spiritoso e Scherzando), deleted from the published score by the composer, is preserved in the Distler Archive in Lübeck. The Nazi cultural police chose to censor Distler's magnum opus by including it in their "degenerate art" category, thereby outlawing any further performances in the Reich after it was performed to great acclaim during a 1936 festival of German church music in Berlin.

The Czech composer Bohuslav Martinů (1890–1959) also produced an elegant and tuneful *Concerto for Harpsichord and Small Orchestra* (1935) during his sojourn in Paris. Composed for the harpsichordist Marcelle de Lacour, it is particularly noteworthy for its employment of piano as continuo instrument supporting the harpsichord's solo, a reversal of the more usual instrumental roles!

Frank Martin (1890–1974), a Swiss composer who spent much of his career in Holland, composed two major works for harpsichord and orchestra. The twenty-minute *Concert pour clavecin et petit orchestre* (1952) is a graceful addition to the concert repertoire, but pride of place goes to Martin's earlier work from 1945, the *Petite symphonie concertante* for three solo instruments – harp, harpsichord, and piano – and two string orchestras. Commissioned by, and dedicated to Paul Sacher, conductor of the Basel Chamber Orchestra, Martin's pleasing work maintains a place in the active concert repertoire.

From the United Kingdom: Charming Works by Howells and Leigh

Herbert Howells (1892–1983) composed the twelve short pieces that comprise *Lambert's Clavichord* as a tribute to the noted photographer and instrument maker Herbert Lambert of Bath. With the 1927 publication of this set, his Opus 41, the British composer earned a place in musical history: These charming neo-Elizabethan miniatures are the first published modern works for clavichord. During a 1974 interview with the composer, I inquired if they might be played on the harpsichord. Dr. Howells replied that he often performed them on the piano and gave his permission to play them on any available keyboard instrument.

Another audience-friendly work is an eight-minute *Concertino for Harpsichord and Strings* (1934) by Walter Leigh (1905–1942). One wishes that this piece were much longer, for its three short movements (Allegro – Andante – Allegro Vivace) never fail to charm listeners. Perhaps the best solution might be to play it twice!

A Prolific Commissioner of New Music: Sylvia Marlowe

More than any other member of her generation, Sylvia Marlowe (1908–1981) increased the significant contributions of major American composers to the literature of her chosen instrument. Considering the Pleyel harpsichord a "vehicle for modern music, even swing," the keyboardist, largely a self-taught harpsichordist, built her career as a popular radio performer, playing more than 1,500 broadcast concerts, many of them in two series – *Lavender and New Lace* and *New Portraits of Old Masters*. For these programs, Marlowe performed standard harpsichord repertoire as well as instrumental foxtrots based on such popular harpsichord classics as Rameau's *Tambourin* ("18th-century Barrelhouse"), Daquin's *Le Coucou* ("Cookoo-Cuckoo"), Mozart's Turkish March ("Mr. Mozart Meanders"), and Haydn's D major Sonata ("Haydn Seeks"). Her broadcasts introduced the sounds of the harpsichord to vast numbers of new listeners.

Marlowe also appeared as an entertainer, revolving with her harpsichord on a rotating platform at the Rainbow Room, a New York City nightclub. This close association with dancing may have been the major influence that led Marlowe to commission her first serious contemporary work: She heard Vittorio Rieti's *Second Avenue Waltzes for Two Pianos* and fell in love with them. This infatuation led to her commissioning the ensemble work Partita for Flute, Oboe, String Quartet and Obbligato Harpsichord from Rieti (1898–1994) in 1945. It was premiered in 1951 and followed by three more Rieti pieces for Marlowe's collection: *Sonata all'antica* for solo harpsichord (1946), Concerto for Harpsichord and Orchestra (1955/1957), and *Alla Francesca* (1961).[9]

More works from Alan Hovhaness (1911–2000), Paul des Marais (1927–2013), Carlos Surinach (1915–1997), Ben Weber (1916–1979), and Alexei Haieff (1914–1994) joined the Marlowe playlist, but her most distinguished and honored commission was the *Sonata for Flute, Oboe, Cello, and Harpsichord* (1952) by Elliott Carter (1908–2012), a work in three intellectually stimulating and aurally attractive movements.

The composer stated that his idea was "to stress as much as possible the vast and wonderful array of tone colors available on the modern harpsichord," and to that end he provided detailed instructions for a large John Challis instrument with pedals that operated the changing of the harpsichord's registers.[10] The sonata's first movement (Risoluto) begins vigorously with an arresting gesture from the harpsichord and proceeds as one continual diminuendo from this initial energy. The second movement (Lento) commences with a single note (G), arches through a contrasting middle section that employs the composer's signature technique of metric modulation, and returns to the initial lone G. The final movement (Allegro), in a rollicking 6/8 meter, is the most challenging in terms of ensemble. Marlowe reported that it required more than forty rehearsals to prepare this demanding work for performance. Carter's quartet was awarded the prestigious Walter W. Naumburg Musical Foundation Award in 1956.

As different from the Carter as any work could be, *Lovers (A Narrative in Ten Scenes)* by Ned Rorem (b. 1924) consists of short musical vignettes portraying the events of a day in the life of a young couple; it is scored for four players: harpsichord; oboe/English horn; cello; and a percussionist on tympani, vibraphone, xylophone, glockenspiel, and chimes. This is programmatic music, attractive and appealing even though the harpsichord writing, while manageable, is quite pianistic with thick chords and large leaps. Again, the harpsichordist often longs for a sustaining pedal! *Quartet* and *Lovers* have the same relationship in Marlowe's repertoire as did Falla's concerto and Poulenc's *Concert Champêtre* in Landowska's: One critically regarded work rarely played contrasts with an audience-pleasing piece heard much more frequently.

In 1960 Marlowe recorded the disc *Six Americans*: works by Ben Weber, Arthur Berger, John Lessard, and Rieti, as well as three pieces originally for the piano: Harold Shapero's Sonata in D, and two works, Sonata No. 4 and *Portrait of Nicolas de Chatelain*, by Marlowe's longtime advocate, the music critic and composer Virgil Thomson. Interestingly, the adapted works fit the harpsichord at least as well as Rieti's and Lessard's piano-inspired creations.

With one of her most unusual projects, it would seem possible that no other performer introduced as many young listeners to the harpsichord as Marlowe did: Her children's record *Said the Piano to the Harpsichord* presented the story of a rivalry between the two instruments.[11] Included in the musical illustrations was not only an improbable bit of Chopin (played first on the piano, then repeated a second time on the harpsichord!) but also one of the more charming of new works, Douglas Moore's short arrangement of *The Old Gray Mare* (1948) in which both keyboard instruments, ancient and modern, ultimately played together as friends. At least one of those fortunate young persons who succumbed to the antique instrument's charm, Richard Kingston (b. 1947), would eventually grow up to become one of America's foremost harpsichord makers in the second half of the century. He credits his early infatuation with his life-long love to Marlowe's record and the harpsichord "licks" from the television serial *The Addams Family*.[12]

Patroness of the Avant-Garde: Antoinette Vischer

Another determined champion for new music, the Swiss harpsichordist Antoinette Vischer (1909–1973), commissioned an extraordinary collection of harpsichord works by a stellar group of modernist composers. Outstanding among this group of thirty-eight creators are Bohuslav Martinů, Maurice Ohana, Hans Werner Henze, Earle Brown, Luciano Berio, Cathy Berberian, Duke Ellington, Boris Blacher, Isang Yun, Mauricio Kagel, John Cage, and György Ligeti, whose *Continuum* is frequently cited as the most original among all twentieth-century works for solo harpsichord (see Figure 16.2).[13] Both unusual and effective, this four-minute composition is basically an expanding tremolando that builds to a mighty climax that then subsides to a single fast-repeated high pitch. Totally unexpected from a composer whose organ music often relied on crashing tone clusters, this sensitive music is extraordinarily well crafted to display both the tonal resources of the harpsichord and the technical prowess of an executant.

Martinů, cited earlier for his Harpsichord Concerto, composed a solo *Sonate pour claveçin* for Mme. Vischer in 1958, less than a year before his death. Three connected short movements display both a welcome knowledge of the instrument's tonal possibilities and an audible nostalgia for the Czech homeland from which he had spent so many years as an expatriate. (Musical references to the Dvorak Cello Concerto and the bells of Prague are heard, and the vigorous final section of the *Sonate* ends softly, leaving a sense of quiet resignation.)

Cathy Berberian's dramatic chance music from 1969, *Morsicat(h)y* bears a title that is a four-way pun dealing with death by biting, a mosquito, Morse Code, and the composer's abbreviated name. This type of "regulated improvisation" requires the player to create a score by employing specified metrics: The right hand is to simulate mosquito sounds while the left hand attempts to swat the "audible" insect away. The printed "score" includes a sample sketch, but the work is, in a sense, no longer authentically performable since the piece depends on reciprocal communication with its composer. Using rhythms determined by

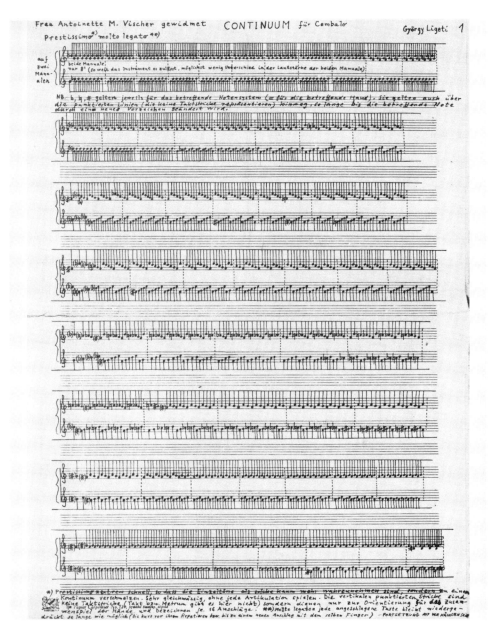

Figure 16.2 Ligeti's manuscript of *Continuum* (Antoinette Vischer Collection, Paul Sacher Foundation, Basel), courtesy of Dr. Simon Obert, Curator of the Antoinette Vischer Collection at the Sacher Foundation.

telegraphy's Morse Code, the player is expected to create snippets of music with pitches derived from a chart provided in the score. But the text to be set to these pitches was to be determined by sending a postcard to the composer (several copies of an addressed card were included in a pocket on the inside back cover of the publication), who would then respond with a message to be translated into the required musical gestures. Unfortunately, Berberian (1925–1983), talented singer and wife of composer Luciano Berio, is no longer answering written requests. One of the last truly *authentic* performances thus occurred during a harpsichord recital at Southern Methodist University in Dallas, when Marilyn Saker, a harpsichord major in the Master's degree program, chose Berberian's work as part of her group of pieces by women composers. She sent the obligatory request and received the promised response (dated 5 October 1982). Unforgettable was the graphic and vivid sonic explosion at the mimed destruction of the eponymous (imaginary) mosquito in a final smashing gesture that provided a loud dissonant tone cluster in the lowest range of the harpsichord! This type of "chance music," or improvised dramatic performance, was a hallmark of its period.

A similar Vischer commission, Mauricio Kagel's *Recitativarie (for Singing Female Harpsichordist)* begins with a very slow procession to the instrument (with the artist's hands held aloft in a prayerful position), a panorama meant to mimic Wanda Landowska's carefully choreographed entrance to a concert stage. When the music finally begins, Kagel (1931–2008) combines short excerpts from Chopin piano pieces and snippets from Bach cantatas, complete with nonsensical texts – surrealistic, and entirely typical of avant-garde performance expectations of the era.

The most extreme of Vischer's happenings was undoubtedly John Cage and Lejaren Hiller's *HPSCHD* (pronounced *harpsichord*), first experienced on 16 May 1969 at the University of Illinois, Champaign-Urbana. Lasting from 7:30 p.m. until midnight, the music comprised twenty-minute solos for one to seven harpsichords and magnetic tapes played on fifty-two amplified monaural machines. These musical materials were to be used in whole or part, in any combination, with or without interruptions. Both players and instruments formed varied groups: David Tudor played an electronic harpsichord; the begetter of the event, Madame Vischer, and Philip Corner shared one Neupert two-manual instrument; William Brooks played a Challis single; Ronald Peters, a Brueggeman double; Yuji Takahashi, a Dowd double; and the young pianist/composer Neely Bruce, one by Hubbard. In addition to playing his/her own solo, each harpsichordist was free to play any of the others (according to a note in the program).[14]

Reviewing the subsequent Nonesuch vinyl recording of *HPSCHD*, record critic and harpsichordist Igor Kipnis commented, "At first noisy, this 'experience' ultimately becomes one of tedium and almost unrelieved boredom. Personally, I find the New York Subway offers as much sonic anarchy, and at least there you are getting from one place to another."[15]

Vischer's extensive list of new works for the harpsichord practically guarantees that she will not be forgotten. Her friend, the distinguished Swiss author and playwright Friedrich Dürrenmatt, wrote:

> Antoinette Vischer has gone down in the annals of musical history in the most legitimate manner: as patroness. She caused the modern and ultra-modern composers of our time to interest themselves in an old-fashioned instrument – the harpsichord. As a result, the old-fashioned instrument became modern, and its abstract quality suited modern music.
>
> By commissioning compositions for it, Vischer led modern music on to new paths. The manner in which she did this proves how consciously she proceeded . . . She knew whom she was ordering from, and was supplied with what she wanted: musical portraits by composers of themselves, in that they had to occupy themselves with apparently unfamiliar tasks. Thus, through the wiles of a woman once again, something new was born.[16]

Meanwhile, in the UK

On the other side of the English Channel, British composer Peter Maxwell Davies (1934–2016) offered his own version of an avant-garde happening, albeit one that was four hours shorter than *HPSCHD*. With a duration of thirty intense minutes, *Eight Songs for a Mad King* requires a male singer of extraordinary vocal prowess as well as virtuoso histrionic ability (the vocal line ranges from a falsetto high B all the way down to the lowest basso profundo sounds). Scored for an instrumental ensemble of six players: flute (piccolo), clarinet, percussion (21 different instruments), keyboard (harpsichord, piano, and dulcimer), violin, and cello, Davies's music ranges from swoops and screams to recognizable quotations from Handel's *Messiah* as he portrays King George III's descent into madness. Premiered at Queen Elizabeth Hall in London on April 22, 1969, this solo cantata/happening predated Cage's extravaganza by twenty-four days and managed to accomplish nearly as much musical chaos in 240 minutes less performing time.

Harrison, Persichetti and a Recital by Kirkpatrick

Born in Portland, Oregon, Lou Harrison (1917–2003) was truly an American original. Before moving to New York City in 1943 he composed a series of six sonatas for harpsichord. With spare, often two-voiced textures, and by suggesting the replacement of equal tempered tuning with the more distinctive baroque unequal tunings, Harrison had already set himself apart from the mainstream.

In his own words about these path-breaking works:

The first [of the sonatas] dates from the mid-1930s but the set was not completed until the early 1940s, and they were published in 1943. The original impulse came from two sources, as the *Sonatas* themselves have probably already made clear ... the first of these was my intense admiration for Manuel de Falla and especially for his use of the harpsichord in several instances including the famous *Concerto*. This was, in my own feelings, perhaps erroneously embedded in a matrix of feeling which concerned California.
The "Mission Period" style of life, artifacts, and the feelings intrigued me very much. [It was] the Works Progress Administration period and the dominant impulse was "Regionalism." Thus the *Cembalo Sonatas* reflect "nights in the Gardens of Spain," "Flamenco" as well as [American] Indian Dances, and Provincial "Baroquery" in the West.[17]

On occasion, Sylvia Marlowe had programmed individual selections from Harrison's sonatas, but the complete set formed an integral part of a "Recital of Twentieth-Century Harpsichord Music" presented at the University of California, Berkeley, on 21 January 1961, by the era's most prominent American harpsichordist, celebrated Yale professor Ralph Kirkpatrick (1911–1984). Other offerings heard on his program entirely devoted to contemporary works included the premiere of *Set of Four* by Henry Cowell (1897–1965), from whom Kirkpatrick had specifically requested left-hand octave trills to demonstrate the technical prowess of his oversized hands (an attribute the recitalist proudly noted in his introductory commentary to the published score), plus additional pieces composed for him by Ernst Lévy (*Fantasie Symphonique* [1939]) and Peter Mieg (*Le voyage à Montfort* [1956]). Completing the extensive list were compositions by Halsey Stevens, Vincent Persichetti, and David Kraehenbuehl. Delius's *Dance* served as the single gesture to music from earlier in the century.

In notes to the program, the artist wrote: "[Pieces by] Douglas Allanbrook [*Sonata Number One*] and Daniel Pinkham [*Epitaph for Janet Fairbank*] were written by composers who are themselves accomplished harpsichordists, and the pieces of Mel Powell (*Recitative and Toccata Percossa*) and David Kraehenbuehl (*Toccate per Cembalo*) were written respectively for my former pupils Fernando Valenti and Robert Conant."[18]

Of particular interest was the inclusion of a single movement (the first: Andante sostenuto–Allegro) from Sonata, Op. 52, by Vincent Persichetti (1915–1987). This piece, written for Fernando Valenti and premiered by him at New York's Town Hall in 1951, remains, in my opinion, the most appealing of all the ten essays in sonata form produced by this genial composer. After a thirty-year hiatus, Persichetti resumed his composing for harpsichord, producing a bumper crop of three sonatas in 1981, two more the following year, and one each in the years 1983, 1984, 1985, and 1987. The composer's additional solo harpsichord pieces *Parable XXIV*, Op. 153 and *Serenade* No. 15, Op. 161 are also splendid additions to the repertoire.

Earlier in his illustrious career, Ralph Kirkpatrick had toured extensively with the violinist Alexander Schneider. At their New York Town Hall concert of 30 November 1945, the artists premiered one of the most distinguished contributions to the twentieth-century duo repertoire, *Sonatina for Violin and Harpsichord* by Walter Piston (1894–1976). Subsequently their performance of this beautifully crafted work was recorded for Columbia Records as the first disc in a Modern American Music Series. Another major contemporary work in Kirkpatrick's wide-ranging concert offerings was the *Concerto for Harpsichord and Orchestra* by his Yale University faculty colleague Quincy Porter (1897–1966). This was the newest work to be heard on Kirkpatrick's December 1960 concerts with the Cleveland Orchestra (Robert Shaw, conducting) – the first evenings in the orchestra's forty-two-year history at which a harpsichordist appeared as assisting artist on regular subscription concerts by this renowned ensemble. Such a tardy debut was sweetened by the presentation of three concertos as the first half of the program: Porter's new single-movement work, J. S. Bach's Concerto in A major, BWV1055, and the iconic twentieth-century concerto of Manuel de Falla. An equally important concert debutant shared the Severance Hall stage on those evenings: a just-completed 1960 two-manual harpsichord by the Boston master-builder William Dowd, on loan for these performances from Cleveland's Unitarian Church (where Assistant Conductor Shaw was Director of Music).

Contributions from Four Major Composers

Among the twentieth-century's more famous composers such as Igor Stravinsky, Béla Bartók, Paul Hindemith, and Benjamin Britten, only Bartók might be considered to have joined the harpsichord's list of composers. The Hungarian master suggests in the preface to Volumes III–VI of his *Mikrokosmos* (for piano) that certain pieces might be suited for performance at the harpsichord. Stravinsky, the most celebrated international composer of the century, had planned to write a harpsichord concerto during the 1920s, but nothing for harpsichord materialized from his pen until he gave the instrument a major role in the score of his neoclassical opera *The Rake's Progress* (1951). Not only does the harpsichord fill its classic role as keyboard continuo instrument, it becomes, as well, an aural, vibrant character in the spine-chilling climactic card game scene that seals the leading protagonist's fate. Hindemith, a fine violist, who had made concert tours with harpsichordist Alice Ehlers, would have seemed to be a "natural" match for the instrument considering his contrapuntal and linear style of composing, but he, too, restricted his use of the harpsichord to brief appearances in two late operas: the 1952 revision of *Cardillac* and his 1960 opus *The Long Christmas Dinner*. Britten pursued a similar path, utilizing the instrument in his operatic adaptation of Shakespeare's *A Midsummer Night's Dream* (1960), and once again in the late cantata *Phaedra* (1975).

Mid-Century Music from France, Hungary, and the United States

A work popular with harpsichordists during the second half of the twentieth century is a set of six insect portraits, *L'insectarium* by Jean Françaix (1912–1997). These clever, if sometimes unwieldy, musical portrayals of centipede, ladybug, water spider, sea flea, beetle, and ant were completed in 1953. Since the composer dedicated his score to Wanda Landowska (who was at this time a resident of the United States, well ensconced in her Connecticut home), it was fitting that the premiere performance should be given by one of her students, the Belgian harpsichordist Aimée van de Wiele, at the Abbaye de Royaumont on 14 July 1957. A second popular score by Françaix is the compact, five-movement Concerto for Harpsichord and Instrumental Ensemble (flute and strings). Neoclassical in its clarity, and typical of its composer in charm and wittiness, the work dates from 1959.

Another pleasant piece is *Concertino for Harpsichord and Orchestra* (1949) by the Hungarian composer Ferenc Farkas (1905–2000), whose spicy tonal palette may have evolved from a mingling of his studies with the Italian colorist Ottorino Respighi and an equal admiration for the Viennese composers of the early twentieth-century. This worthwhile twenty-minute work displays a classic three-movement concerto design: Allegro – Andante – Allegro.

"Seldom in a long life of record-reviewing have I been so utterly beguiled, captivated, seduced, entertained, and generally delighted by a new piece as by Lester Trimble's *Four Fragments from the Canterbury Tales*," began Alfred Frankenstein's review of the first recording of this elegant 1956 work scored for high voice, flute, clarinet, and harpsichord.[19] Trimble (1923–1986) set Geoffrey Chaucer's poetic Middle English descriptions of a "Knyght," a "Yong Squier," and the "Wyf of Biside Bathe" and prefaced these beguiling musical portraits with the scene-setting opening lines from the medieval classic: "Whan that Aprille with his shoures soote ..." as "Prolog." The music that brings these ancient texts into the present is precisely as lovely and satisfying as inferred by the critic's words. A performance for the National Convention of the American Guild of Organists in Dallas (1972) offered this gem as part of a harpsichord-centered program. Commendations of this selection were relayed to the performers through several subsequent decades of these biennial national gatherings. Trimble's hauntingly lovely piece is one that "got everything" just right.

"The Harpsichord on the Contemporary Scene: Roots for a Tradition"

In 1958 Stoddard Lincoln wrote an article for the *Bulletin of the American Composers' Alliance* in which he laid out some basic suggestions on ways to write successfully for the harpsichord. Lincoln (1925–2007) had studied harpsichord with both Kirkpatrick and Valenti (who taught at the Juilliard School in New York), and his comments ring true today, more than half a century later. After advising his target audience to study keyboard works from their successful professional ancestors from the baroque era and explaining in clear detail why so many pianistic passages are not equally effective when transferred to the harpsichord, Mr. Lincoln paid tribute to some exemplary living composers. Leading the short list was Vincent Persichetti, highly commended for his harpsichord sonata. Later in the essay Lincoln commented that pianists usually write the best piano music, and, therefore, harpsichordists will almost certainly serve a similar function when they choose to write for their own instrument; a special commendation in this category was given to Daniel Pinkham (a Landowska student), and further kudos went to Robert Parris and to Persichetti, cited as "pianists who have taken the time to familiarize themselves with the harpsichord and its capabilities."

Other composers and works put forward as good examples: Howells and his *Lambert's Clavichord* pieces; Henry Cowell's *Set of Four*; the concertos of Poulenc, Leigh, Martin, and Falla; and, as an unanticipated addition to the list, the German composer Kurt Hessenberg (1908–1994), a colleague of the organist and harpsichordist Helmut Walcha, who was praised particularly for the clarity of his writing in his *Ten Short Preludes* (*Zehn kleine Präludien*, 1945). From Sylvia Marlowe's group of commissioned composers, the author chose to recommend works by John Lessard and Elliott Carter.

Concluding his article, Lincoln declared, "The harpsichordist is eager to play new works . . . and any harpsichordist [would be] eager to work with the composer in the hope that a fine-sounding work will result."[20]

New Music Promoted by Harpsichord Societies and Competitions

In 1980, early music received a special boost of grassroots support with the creation of the Southeastern Historical Keyboard Society (SEHKS). During that same year, there began an ongoing conversation concerning the future viability of the harpsichord as a vital musical instrument, initiated by the Society's founder and first president, George Lucktenberg (a professor at Converse College in Spartanburg, South Carolina) and a generous wealthy harpsichord enthusiast. Their ongoing discussions led to the establishment of the Aliénor Harpsichord Composition Competitions, dedicated to the fostering of new music. The first of these events occurred in 1982 as part of the society's annual conference in Tallahassee, Florida. Aliénor's goal was, and is, to encourage harpsichord music with varying degrees of difficulty: keyboard and ensemble music suitable for both amateur and professional players. Usually organized to occur every four years, nine competitions have been held, resulting in a total of more than 750 new scores, submitted from all parts of the globe. Harpsichordist Elaine Funaro, invited by Dr. Lucktenberg to perform one of the submitted works for the final round of that earliest competition, succeeded him as Aliénor director. Some of the compositions she has recorded or included in subsequent recital programs include works by American composers Edwin McLean, Thomas Donahue, Timothy Tikker, Tom Robin Harris, Dan Locklair, Albert Glinsky, Rudy Davenport, Mark Janello, Paul Whetstone, Asako Hirabayashi, Jeremy Beck, Janine Johnson, Kent Halliday, Glenn Spring, and James Dorsa, as well as works from Penka Kouneva (Bulgaria), Nicole Clément (France), Isaac Nagao (Japan), and Stephen Yates (Australia).

In 1984 a companion society, the Midwestern Historical Keyboard Society (MHKS) was founded by Nanette Lunde of Eau Claire, Wisconsin. The two geographical entities worked well together, often holding joint meetings in various parts of the country. Ultimately both groups merged in 2010 to form the Historical Keyboard Society of North America (HKSNA), with Aliénor director Funaro as its first president.

An Indispensable Book: *Harpsichord and Clavichord Music of the Twentieth Century* by Frances Bedford

The amazing breadth and depth of modern composition for the harpsichord is perhaps nowhere so immediately apparent, or so completely overwhelming, as it appears in this huge volume published in 1993. Even for one well versed in this repertoire, it is mind-boggling to experience the sheer size of this hefty hardbound tome. A 54-page introductory section prefaces a 608-page catalog of works for harpsichord in every category from solo works to opera scores. The 24-page index of composers for harpsichord comprises 2,256 names – and of course only includes composers active before 1993.

When invited to contribute a foreword to this impressive publication, I accepted with pleasure. The final paragraph of that introductory essay reads:

> What has been written for the harpsichord and clavichord in our century, as detailed in Bedford's carefully researched book, is significant, diverse, and quite staggering in its quantity. Considering that before the revival of the harpsichord no obsolete instrument had ever made a successful return to viable concert life, one might even call this outpouring of new music amazing.
> The bibliography of this music documents an active period in the harpsichord revival. Best of all, by providing users with such practical details as publication data, duration, and level of difficulty, this book will aid new generations of players in exploring the repertoire. This valuable resource for such an exploration is Frances Bedford's enduring contribution to the harpsichord and clavichord revival.

On to the Twenty-First Century

So, A.B. (after Bedford), how is one to proceed without a guide? Researching historical documents is surely more accurate than attempting to keep up with a constantly expanding repertoire of new pieces or daring to predict which ones might be standard fare, beloved classics, or totally forgotten for future audiences. Thus, in an effort to acknowledge and include as wide a perspective on the various styles and musical personalities encountered by those brave and adventurous souls who seek the new, newer, and newest compositions, I contacted a small group of colleagues comprising a dozen harpsichord-savvy persons known to have an appreciation for new music. Each was invited to submit a list of favorite contemporary harpsichord pieces. Nine responded, most of them with the suggested ten items (several with more, one with less); so, including my own list of ten, we assembled a repertoire of nearly one hundred titles for inclusion in this current essay. Interestingly, both the Falla and Poulenc concertos appeared on seven of the ten lists; and, only slightly less-cited, Ligeti achieved six of ten for his solo work, *Continuum*. Is it not indicative of this composer's genius, that, having produced only three harpsichord compositions with a total duration of slightly less than fourteen minutes, he garnered the highest consensus in the solo harpsichord category?[21]

Perhaps we could continue this ongoing survey by investigating repertoire selections made by one of the more distinguished performer/composer figures of the present, Jukka Tiensuu (b. 1948). His composition *Fantango* (1984) appeared on two of the top-ten lists, and we have the composer's own performance of it on his compact disc *The Fantastic Harpsichord* (Finlandia FACD357). Fantasy, indeed, beginning with the accompanying booklet in which the photograph of the artist displays only his head, which, reminiscent of the biblical John the Baptist following Salome's dance at the court of King Herod, seems to be equally separated from his body, although in this case, still open-eyed and resting benignly across the keyboards of a double-manual harpsichord rather than on a silver platter. Other "fantastical" works in this program are from Iannis Xenakis, Salvatore Sciarrino, and Kaija Saariaho (b. 1952), whose 1984–1986 *Jardin secret II*, a highly regarded piece that includes taped electronic and human sounds, was another title submitted for our tally of new works. To provide a welcome contrast, Tiensuu wisely included works from the baroque by Michel Corrette and Antonio Soler as aural palette cleansers.

Second in this trio of Tiensuu recordings, *The Exuberant Harpsichord* (Finlandia, FACD 367) fulfills the promise of its title with brilliant readings of all three Ligeti solo pieces, plus Erik Bergman's *Energien* (1970), Anneli Arho's *Minos'* (1978), Esa-Pekka Salonen's *YTA IIb* (1985–1987), and Usko Meriläinen's *Zimbal* (1972), François-Bernard Mâche's *Korwar* (1972), and, as contrast, two "ancient pieces" by Thomas Morley.

A third disc in the trilogy, *The Frivolous Harpsichord* (Ondine, ODE 891–2) presents shorter dance-inspired pieces by William Albright, Naji Hakim, Dan Locklair, Penka Kouneya, Dave Brubeck, Erkki Salmenhaara, Jyrki Linjama, John Cage, Mauricio Kagel, Roberto Sierra, Franzpeter Goebels, Tonino Tesei, François Couperin, Domenico Scarlatti, and Tiensuu's own *Veto*. Frivolous it may be, but this vast variety from Fandango to Ragtime and the Blues is exciting, too. It also reminds us of the contributions that some great jazz and pop artists have made to the furthering of harpsichord sounds and awareness in our centuries.[22]

Popular Concertos by Gorecki and Glass

The Polish modernist composer Henryk Gorecki (1933–2010) described his nine-minute, two-movement *Concerto for Harpsichord and (Solo) Strings* (1980) as a "prank." Influenced by the vitality of Polish folk music, this short and athletic minimalist work is dedicated to harpsichordist Elizabeth Chojnacka, who reported that each of her many performances of the compact piece resulted in an enthusiastic audience's demand for an encore; thus, this work should be considered a rousing popular success.

Philip Glass (b. 1937) also contributed a delightful audience favorite with his twenty-three-minute *Concerto for Harpsichord* (2002). Three movements with obvious groundings in baroque concerto form and content but still of the new century with its jazzy 7/8 metered finale, it was premiered (on short notice) by Jillon Stoppels Dupree, who credited the composer as particularly sensitive to instrumental balances, always seeking to allow an unamplified harpsichord to be heard. She commented that when the first rehearsal demonstrated an overly heavy scoring for the lyrical second movement (the longest of the three), Glass immediately decided to reduce the orchestration to one player on a part.[23]

Moderate Modernism: A Gentler Music

Elizabeth Chojnacka was also the dedicatee of a well-thought-out and atmospheric solo piece, *Rain Dreaming* by Toru Takemitsu (1930–1996). However, this particular commission from the Aliénor Competition Awards received its first performance by SEHKS president George Lucktenberg during that Society's 1986 meeting in Washington, DC.

Henri Dutilleux (1916–2013) did not support "aesthetic terrorism" but rather forged his own more individual way with colorfully evocative music. *Les Citations* for oboe, double bass, harpsichord, and percussion was a two-movement work begun in 1985, to which Dutilleux was adding movements until his death. His "citations" were quotations from modern composers Benjamin Britten and Jehan Alain, and Clément Janequin from the early sixteenth century, thus spanning both geographic and temporal boundaries for his musical inspiration.[24]

British composer Stephen Dodgson (1924–2013) was known particularly for the high quality of his compositions utilizing plucked-string instruments (guitar, harp, and harpsichord). That the latter instrument inspired many pieces might coincide with his choice for a life partner, the harpsichordist Jane Clark. Of his solo works the best known are five volumes, each comprising six *Inventions* (1955–1985) and the larger-scale *Sonata-Divisions* (1982), dedicated to his wife. My own favorite is *Carillon for Two Harpsichords* (1967), and not far behind that scintillating work on the hit parade are several delightful movements from the *First Suite for Clavichord*: "Second Air," "Tambourin," and "Last Fanfare" – all three of which are equally at home on a harpsichord.

Some Personal Commissions

In 1961 young Neely Bruce (b. 1944), a first-year student at the University of Rochester's Eastman School of Music, was the first composer from whom I received a harpsichord piece (*Nine Variations on an Original Theme*). The next appeared as an unsolicited manuscript that arrived in my Southern Methodist University mailbox: Rudy Shackelford's *Le Tombeau de Stravinsky* (1970). A commission to Stephen Dodgson resulted in his *Duo for Harp and Harpsichord*; two pleas to organist/composer colleague Gerald Near (b. 1942) resulted in his lovely *Triptych*, and a stunning Concerto for Harpsichord and String Orchestra (1980). Others included Ross Lee Finney's sole work for harpsichord, *Hexachord for Harpsichord* (1984), and nine works by Rudy Davenport (b. 1948), culminating in his poignant *Songs of the Bride for Soprano, Oboe, and Harpsichord*. Treasured and oft-performed works by Glenn Spring (b. 1939), first encountered in 1990, include the captivating miniatures *Trifles* and *Bela Bagatelles* and the longer works *In Memoriam Georgia O'Keeffe*, *Images from Wallace Stevens* (for violin and harpsichord) and a 2006 suite, *Hommages*, comprising Spring's moving tributes to composers he thought of as mentors: Schumann, Bartók, Debussy, Stravinsky, and Mahler.[25]

Quite a lot of worthwhile works have been published during the first two decades of the twenty-first century. Among them are William Bolcom's (b. 1938) *Le fantôme du clavecin* (2005), a modern evocation of the French *ordre* comprising nine movements, and, in 2015, his charming miniature, *The Vicarage Garden*. From Frank Ferko (b. 1950), *Triptych* (2000) – toccata, theme and five variations culminating in a fine four-voice fugue. Timothy Broege (b. 1947) quotes Dowland's *Lachrymae* in his *A Sad Pavan*, excerpted from *Songs Without Words* for winds, voice, and harpsichord.

Shadow Journey: Twenty-First-Century Music for Harpsichord

The British Harpsichord Society, founded in 2002, launched its first contemporary music competition one decade later. *Shadow Journey* is the title of the compact disc recording that comprises the top choices from the more than ninety submissions representing eighteen countries. Included as well is a representative piece from each of the three final-round adjudicators: Larry Goves, Rob Keeley, and Gary Carpenter. The winning composers, Alessandro Ponti, Patrick John Jones, Aled Smith, Ivan Bozicevic, Gavin Wayte, Enno Kastens, Jung Sun Kang, Junhae Lee, Thomas Donahue, Jürgen Kraus, and Satoru Ikeda, might well be among the early representatives in a twenty-first-century successor to the Bedford Catalog. Stay tuned!

A Trio of Women Composers

Léonie Jenkins (1925–2000) pursued a fulltime career in medicine but also found time to enjoy her other love, music. *The Elements for Two Harpsichords* was first performed publicly in 1994. Six short movements depict Earth, Metal, Water, Wood, and Fire, prefaced by a musical representation of The Void, which returns, referenced in the work's final measures.

Ellen Taaffe Zwilich (b. 1939), the first woman to earn a Juilliard doctorate (DMA) in composition (1975) and to be awarded the Pulitzer Prize in Music (1983), wrote her *Fantasy for Harpsichord* in that same year.

Another brilliant composer who also holds a doctorate from Juilliard, Victoria Bond (b. 1945) seems to have created the perfect companion piece for Françaix's insects! Her *Peculiar Plants for Harpsichord*, winner of the 2009 Walter Hinrichsen award from the publishing firm C. F. Peters, is a compellingly dramatic set of pieces with accompanying poetry by the work's dedicatee, harpsichordist Kenneth Cooper, and the composer. The introductory verse ends with this quatrain:

> Music is the fourth dimension,
> and deserves our full attention;
> so we gave our plants a voice,
> making harpsichord the choice.

Twenty-two minutes of music and clever verse form vivid auditory portrayals of the Strangler Fig, Venus Flytrap, Creeping Moss, Blushing Violet, Deadly Nightshade, Ghost Orchid, and Ragweed!

A Postscript from Vincent Persichetti

> I don't miss an orchestra when I'm composing for harpsichord. Most of the harpsichord players I know aren't very active. They spend their time playing

figured bass, accompanying other instruments. I try to give them something else to do. They can play as loud as an orchestra, be whatever they want to be. Meanwhile I am on to another ... *Harpsichord Sonata*. Don't worry, you certainly do not have to play them all at once ... I love the medium. Do you?[26]

Yes, Vincent, you may rest in peace: I *do* love the harpsichord! And I continue to seek out new music for this queen of instruments. There is always something new and exciting, for "Creativity will always express itself."[27]

Notes

1. A complete facsimile of the original publication was reprinted in *The Diapason* (January, 2011), p. 12.
2. See Palmer, "Mario Castelnuovo-Tedesco's English Suite for Harpsichord at 100," *The Diapason* (December, 2009), pp. 36–37.
3. In 1974 the present writer recorded the work for the Musical Heritage Society, *The Harpsichord Now and Then*, MHS 3222.
4. Michael de Cossart, *The Food of Love: Princesse Edmond de Polignac (1865–1943) and Her Salon* (London: Hamish Hamilton, 1978), pp. 147, 148.
5. These were recorded on 2 and 4 June 1930, Studio Albert, Paris; and reissued on CD, EMI Composers in Person disc 18 of a set of 22 (copyright 2008). The performers were Manuel de Falla, keyboards; Marcel Moyse, flute; George Bonneau, oboe; Emile Gedeau, clarinet; Marcel Darrieux, violin; and August Cruque, cello.
6. Available on Music and Arts, CD-8212, Berkeley, CA, 1994.
7. Recording available on LP, Philips 6505-001.
8. Poulenc's later work, a 1935 *Suite française d'après Claude Gervaise* for harpsichord and wind ensemble of ten instruments, is a charming twelve-minute arrangement based on incidental music for a play. The balance between solo instrument and collaborators is better in this chamber piece than in the concerto.
9. Editor's comment: Mark Kroll has recently released a CD of almost all of Rieti's solo and chamber music for harpsichord, with Marina Minkin, harpsichord, Carol Lieberman, violin and other instrumentalists on New World Records, 80764. He has also recorded two CDs of American harpsichord music for Albany records that feature the music of Piston, Starer, Zwilich, Read, Harrison, Singleton, Catalbiano, Trimble, Antonou, Hovhannes and others. See *American Harpsichord Music of the 20th Century* (Albany Records, TROY 457) and *The Contemporary Harpsichord* (Albany Records, TROY 668).
10. See Else Stone and Kurt Stone, eds., *The Writings of Eliott Carter* (Bloomington: Indiana University Press, 1977), p. 272, and also the preface to the publication of this work.
11. Young Peoples Records, Inc., YPR-411 (1948).

12. See Larry Palmer, *Harpsichord in America* (Bloomington: Indiana University Press, 1989), and the essay "Lavender and New Lace: Sylvia Marlowe and the Twentieth-Century Harpsichord Repertoire," *Contemporary Music Review* 20, no. 1 (2001), pp. 117–124.

13. For dates and other information about the composers mentioned in this chapter, see Frances Bedford, *Harpsichord and Clavichord Music of the Twentieth Century* (Berkeley, CA: Fallen Leaf Press, 1993), *passim*.

14. Vischer's collection of manuscripts and photographs is archived in the Paul Sacher Foundation, Basel, and described in a book by Ule Troxler: *Antoinette Vischer: Dokumente zu einem Leben für das Cembalo*, Basel: Birkhäuser, 1976. This volume includes a complete facsimile of the Ligeti *Continuum* manuscript as well as notational material for Duke Ellington's *A Single Petal of a Rose*.

15. Igor Kipnis, in *Stereo Review* (May, 1970), p. 121.

16. Troxler, *Antoinette Vischer*, p. 10. Dürrenmatt's paragraph, dated 24 December 1966, formed part of the program notes for Vischer's first major recording of works from her collection.

17. Letter from Harrison to the author, dated 11 September 1979.

18. Program notes by Ralph Kirkpatrick, reprinted in *A Recital of Twentieth Century Harpsichord Music* (recorded 1961), Music and Arts CD-977 (1997).

19. Review from *High Fidelity Magazine*, reprinted on the inside front cover of the C. F. Peters score, 66068p (1967).

20. Stoddard Lincoln, "The Harpsichord on the Contemporary Scene: Roots for a Tradition," *Bulletin of the American Composers' Alliance* 7, no. 2 (1958), pp. 18–22.

21. Ligeti's two additional pieces, both dating from 1978 – *Hungarian Rock* and *Passacaglia Ungharese* – also made the list.

22. Duke Ellington, Dave Brubeck, Eubie Blake, Don Angle, Rosemary Clooney, Mitch Miller, among others.

23. Notes to CD 0030, *The Concerto Project*, Philip Glass, Volume II, produced by Orange Mountain Music.

24. Editor's note: The full title is *Les Citations, Diptych for oboe, harpsichord, double bass and percussion*. Mark Kroll's recent recording of the final and complete version of this work with the Boston Symphony Chamber Players – *Profanes et Sacrées: 20th-Century French Chamber Music* (BSO Classics 1102) – was nominated for a Grammy Award.

25. For more complete information, see Larry Palmer "Some Sins of Commission," *The Diapason* (September, 2005), pp. 19–21.

26. Letter to the author, November 5, 1983, quoted in L. Palmer: "Vincent Persichetti: Words to Mark His 70th Birthday," *The Diapason* (June, 1985), p. 8.

27. Thanks to the colleagues who contributed their top-ten lists: Professor Barbara Baird; Professor and Harpsichordist-scholar Mark Kroll; Composer-keyboardist Timothy Broege; Harpsichordist-scholar Jane Clark; Berlin Musik Museum Curator Martin Elste; Harpsichord recitalist and Aliénor director Elaine Funaro; Recitalists-recording artists

Christopher D. Lewis and Andreas Skouras; and Robert Tifft of Southern Methodist University's Bridwell Library staff.

Further Reading

Bedford, Frances. *Harpsichord and Clavichord Music of the Twentieth Century.* Berkeley, CA: Fallen Leaf Press, 1993.

Palmer, Larry. *Harpsichord in America.* Bloomington: Indiana University Press, 1989.

Stone, Else and Kurt Stone, eds. *The Writings of Eliott Carter.* Bloomington: Indiana University Press, 1977

17 Tuning and Temperament

PAUL POLETTI

During the centuries in which the harpsichord enjoyed its preeminence, musical instruments were divided into two broad categories: *perfect* instruments, being the voice, unfretted bowed strings, and, to a lesser extent, woodwinds, all of which have either completely or partly flexible intonation; and *imperfect* instruments, including all keyboard instruments, the harp, and fretted strings, which have fixed intonation. A number of historical texts indicate that musicians playing perfect instruments were expected to adjust the notes of a concord so as to produce pure harmonic relationships with the bass regardless of the harmony or tonality.[1] By contrast, "imperfect" instruments had to be subjected to an intentional detuning of the primary consonances (i.e., a *temperament*) because an immutable gamut of only twelve notes per octave is grossly inadequate to produce pure intervals in all tonalities. Historical authors often described temperament as a taking away from one consonance in order to give to another (i.e., robbing one of its absolute purity in order to bring another into the realm of tolerable impurity). It is important to realize that a temperament was almost always viewed as a necessary evil and not an ideal, at least until the widespread adoption of equal temperament (hereinafter ET) in the mid-nineteenth century erased the notion that pure consonances were the model for proper intonation.

In contrast to the wide variety in harpsichord construction according to time and place, temperament practice was surprisingly consistent throughout Europe, albeit with a few minor anomalies. After the abandonment of Pythagorean tuning during the early Renaissance, and up to the general adoption of equal temperament towards the end of the eighteenth century, the most widely used systems were regular and modified meantone temperaments.[2] In the late seventeenth and early eighteenth centuries, German theorists also developed a type of "rational" circulating temperament which aimed at offering the freedom of ET while yet retaining better purity in the central tonalities (i.e., those with few accidentals). Each of these three broad families will be dealt with in greater detail here below, in roughly chronological order.

Regular Meantone Temperaments

Unbeknownst to most Western musicians and listeners of today, the modern major third of ET is much wider than the acoustically correct natural third and therefore quite seriously discordant, a situation which we accept without complaint simply because we have been programmed to do so through constant exposure. It is almost as badly out of tune as the very wide medieval Pythagorean "third" (properly called a "ditone"), and correcting this fault was the impetus for the development of regular meantone temperaments. They produce the maximum number of identically sized major thirds, which are either absolutely pure or very close to pure, depending upon the system. Eight thirds are good, stretching from E♭-G to E-G♯ (by fifths), while the remaining four are so wide as to be unbearable. This means that only six major tonalities are available (from B♭ to A), since at either extreme the tonality lacks either the dominant or subdominant triad. Likewise, accidental notes are restricted to a single harmonic function (i.e., a sharp cannot be used as a flat and vice versa); the usual assignation of black keys on the keyboard was C♯, E♭, F♯, G♯, and B♭. These good thirds are achieved by making eleven fifths considerably narrower than pure, all by the same amount, leaving the last "fifth" (actually, a diminished sixth, usually G♯-E♭) far too wide to be usable. Additionally, there are nine good minor thirds, from C-E♭ to G♯-B♮, and three exceedingly narrow, though their harshness is not so noticeable as with the bad major thirds. Though the situation for minor tonalities might appear to be better, it is actually far worse; one minor triad is lost to the bad fifth (G♯-B-E♭) and most of the rest of the tonalities lack tolerable dominant or subdominant triads, leaving only three usable minor keys: G, D, and A minor. The seriously discordant consonances were referred to as "wolves," since their wailing quality is evocative of wolves howling together in the forest. While today it is customary to use the term only in regard to the one sour fifth, Praetorius said "our predecessors called f-g♯ 'the wolf,' since these two notes form a completely false minor third."[3]

It is important to note that in all regular meantone systems, there is no variation whatsoever in the size of any properly spelled interval, either consonant or dissonant, and therefore all usable tonalities sound identical, both melodically and harmonically. Theoretically, meantone fifths are narrowed by a specific fraction of the syntonic comma, the purity of the major (and minor) thirds being defined by the chosen fraction.[4] One-quarter comma produces pure major thirds and slightly wide minor thirds. Larger fractions (one-third, two-ninths) will result in worse sounding fifths, slightly narrow major thirds and purer minor thirds, while smaller fractions (one-fifth, one-sixth, etc.) improve the sound of the fifths slightly but result in both major and minor thirds that are somewhat impure.

While there are some sparse indications that meantone systems were already being developed in the late fifteenth century, the first precise description of any meantone system was Zarlino's presentation of two-sevenths comma (1558), with major thirds slightly narrower than pure.[5] A number of extant tuning recipes call for pure major thirds, including those of Praetorius (1619), Mersenne (1636), Printz (1696), Douwes (1699), van Blankenburg (1739), Bédos (1778), and Hook (ca. 1795), but others failed to specify the exact size of the thirds, such as Aaron (1516) and Denis (1643). Lanfranco (1533) and a number of later English sources (Malcolm, 1721; Wood, ca. 1730; and Holder/Keller/Prelleur, 1731) specifically called for major thirds "as sharp as the ear will bear," a quality which is difficult to determine today as our modern ears have become so inured to the sound of ET.[6] The widest "good" major third for which there is documentary evidence is Sorge's assertion (1748) that Silbermann tuned his organs in one-sixth-comma meantone. In any event, the advantages gained by employing slightly wide major thirds are minuscule, primarily being a marginal improvement in the quality of the fifths. One-quarter-comma meantone also has an overly wide diatonic semitone (117 cents), a problem alluded to by Muffat (1698); the correct natural proportion of 16/15 (112 cents) is found in one-fifth-comma meantone.[7] Regarding the fundamental problem of the wolf intervals, though, no known historical meantone variation offered any real remedy, and even if the fifths were to be tempered by as little as one-seventh comma, the four wolf thirds remain slightly wider than a Pythagorean ditone and the wolf fifth is still quite uncomfortably wide.

For the uninitiated listener, the musical effect of a meantone temperament can be quite dramatic. The sound of the relatively narrow pure major third is at once both foreign and strangely compelling. Since the acoustical conditions which create the harmoniousness of a major third do not exist in ET, the music at once acquires an additional pallette of harmonic color to which we are unaccustomed, often described as a ringing, "bell-like" quality. Dissonant harmonies, such as a diminished seventh chord, also acquire an extra pungency and sense of urgency. The overly wide leading tones also increase the dramatic effect of cadential progressions, both melodically and harmonically. These effects can be heard to great advantage in any appropriate piece, but they are absolutely essential to certain bodies of literature, such as that of the English virginalists and much Italian music of the sixteenth and seventeenth centuries. To the experienced listener, such music sounds flat and lifeless when performed in any other type of temperament.

Loosening the Bonds of Regular Meantone Temperaments

A number of contrivances can be employed in order to more or less free the musician from the constraints of regular meantone. A simple expedient is to retune an accidental as its enharmonic, for example, E♭ as D♯ if one needs the good third B-D♯ in E minor. In fact, retuning only one key would make both accidentals available, albeit in different places on the keyboard. The ease and rapidity with which individual notes of a harpsichord can be retuned makes this solution appear to be self-evident, and many modern musicians do indeed use it, especially in continuo playing where one is often free to choose where the third of any harmony is realized. However, this trick comes at a cost, since retuning any note to its enharmonic equivalent also perturbs the normal distribution of usable fifths, something which the musician must keep well in mind. In the worst case, it can introduce two additional wolf fifths, such as retuning B♭ as an A♯, which would spoil the normally good fifths of E♭-B♭ and B♭-F.

A very common historical solution was the construction of instruments with "subsemitones" or divided accidental keys. Subsemitones expand the keyboard's gamut beyond twelve notes per octave by providing the extra keys, jacks, and strings for some of the most commonly needed enharmonic pairs, such as G♯/A♭ and E♭/D♯. The earliest known keyboard with subsemitones was on an organ in Cesna Cathedral (ca. 1468), followed shortly thereafter by the organ in Lucca Cathedral (1480).[8] Organs and harpsichords with subsemitones are known to have been made in Germany, Holland, France, and England as well.

During the sixteenth and early seventeenth century, the idea of sub-semitones was carried to such an extreme that a distinct subclass of harpsichord was created, known alternatively as *cembalo cromatico* or *archicembalo*, having anywhere from nineteen to thirty-one keys per octave. A number of different tuning systems were proposed, including expanded pure intonation schemes and microtonal equal divisions of the octave, but one common method was simply to extend regular meantone to the point where even the naturals had enharmonic equivalents, such as B♯, C♭, E♯, and F♭. Zarlino was known to have owned a *cembalo cromatico*, probably with twenty-four tones, and an example of a thirty-one-toned instrument still exists today.[9] Mersenne highly praised the idea of such augmented keyboards, claiming that they allowed the imperfect instruments to achieve what was normal for the perfect instruments; his eighteen-tone design was refined by J. A. Ban for a harpsichord built in Haarlem in 1639.[10]

While Mersenne believed that the initial awkwardness of playing upon an extended gamut keyboard would quickly disappear as the hand became accustomed to it, others, including both Schlick and Werckmeister, strongly derided even a small number of subsemitones as an unnecessary and confusing impediment. Although once quite common, only a very few such instruments have survived into modern times, often in an altered state due to a later rebuild in which a new keyboard was made without subsemitones and the extra strings were used to expand the total range of the instrument. This dearth of surviving originals has contributed greatly to an underappreciation of the extent to which such instruments most likely affected historical temperament practice, as any work written with subsemitones and an extension of either meantone or pure intonation in mind would now give a false impression that a more forgiving twelve-toned temperament was intended. Even if a modern performer were to determine that the presence of an extended gamut keyboard was the most likely in historical terms, the problem remains that very few modern instruments are so equipped, leading to an inevitable application of the wrong temperament.

Meantone Modifications

Another widely used method of escaping the bonds of regular meantone was to tamper with its uniform structure in order to eliminate the wolf fifth and, to a lesser degree, take some of the bite out of the wolf thirds. This was accomplished by replacing the narrow fifths toward either extreme of the chain with fifths which were less narrow, completely pure, or wider than pure.[11] The extent to which any such system mitigated the limitations of regular meantone depended upon two factors: the quality of the central "good" major thirds and the number of regular meantone fifths retained in the central chain. The wider the primary thirds and the shorter the central chain, the less restrictive the temperament. In such heavily modified schemes, an approximation of true harmonic circulation appears to have been the aim, as the worst major thirds are narrowed sufficiently so as to become almost completely inoffensive. Other systems seem to have been designed to enable bass-line circulation only, without ever stumbling upon a bad fifth, using pure or close to pure initial thirds and a long central chain of regular-sized fifths. In these temperaments, full triadic circulation was still out of the question, as a number of major thirds remain so badly out of tune as to be essentially unusable. This sort of temperament was especially suited to continuo playing, since the bass, which often moves by fourths or fifths, could be played without caution, and the occasional sour major third could be omitted from the right-hand realization, leaving it to be properly intoned by the flexible melody instruments.[12]

Meantone modifications also differ from regular meantones in one very significant way: their irregular structures create variations in triad quality among the different tonalities, though not all do so to the same degree. Systems with a longer central chain remain closer to the monochromatic texture of regular meantone, with a central core of identical "good" keys and any variation confined to the transitional and "bad" keys. Systems with a shorter central chain, sometimes as few as the first four fifths demarcated by the initial major third (usually C–E), have a more gradual transition from the best tonality to the more piquant keys with a qualitative hierarchy among the "good" tonalities as well. It is most likely the use of such meantone modifications that led to the idea that the irregular temperament was related to key *affect*, and not the use of rational circulating temperaments such as those proposed by Werckmeister, as is commonly assumed today (see below).

Most meantone modifications have come down to us as imprecise tuning recipes which are open to interpretation. Essential factors, such as the exact size of the initial third(s), the sourness of any bad thirds and the tempering of the irregular fifths, are often described in vague terms such as "as sharp as the ear will bear," "less tempered than the others," "closer to pure, "not quite pure," and "somewhat wider than pure." Thus even the knowledgeable modern musician or tuner with considerable experience with historical temperaments and the relevant musical literature may well be able to derive a variety of interpretations without departing from a literal reading of the text. While this might appear to present a problem of questionable authenticity for the modern musician, we must not forget that the imprecision of the text would have presented a similar freedom of interpretation to the contemporary reader as well, and therefore this inherent flexibility accurately represents the historical reality. It may even have been the case that such imprecision was by design, allowing a certain degree of variation in order to adapt to the musical requirements of the moment.

Until recently, modern authors considered meantone modifications to be largely a French phenomenon of the late seventeenth and eighteenth centuries, since the majority of such descriptions are found in French literature, including those of Chaumont (1695), St. Vincent (1712), Rameau (1726), d'Alembert (1752), Corette (1753), and Rousseau (1767), systems referred to with the catch-all term "*temperament ordinaire.*" However, instructions for systems of this nature can also be found in other countries from the early sixteenth to the beginning of the nineteenth centuries. In fact, the first truly complete step-by-step tempering instruction of any kind anywhere is, structurally speaking, a modified meantone (Schlick, 1511), though some musicologists prefer to view it as a transitional step from Pythagorean tuning towards regular meantone. As usual, Schlick's instructions are imprecise, and some modern authors choose to interpret them as allowing for full circulation.

A century after Schlick, Praetorius (1619) mentioned that some tuners were widening the fifths F♯-C♯-G♯ of an otherwise regular meantone in order to mollify the bad thirds, though he disapproved of the practice. No complete tuning instruction for a modified meantone appeared in German until Werckmeister's second printing of his brief treatise on figured bass (1698). This temperament is worthy of special mention for several reasons. First, while the work was specifically intended for the "incipient" player, Werckmeister makes no mention whatsoever of his previously published (1681/91) rational circulating organ temperaments (discussed below), for which he is most famous today, all of which are significantly simpler in structure and far easier to execute. Secondly, this tuning instruction was republished in full by Mizler in 1737, who felt it would be "both pleasing and useful for many [of his readers]" (i.e., the members of his exclusive correspondence society, which included J. S. Bach, Graun, Handel, Telemann, Schröter, and Sorge, among others).[13] Thirdly, despite its later publication date, it might be seen as an indication of a practice of circulating temperaments on the harpsichord in Germany which preceded Werckmeister's rational organ temperaments (see below). Finally, it was the first unequal temperament to be presented in modern literature on the performance of music according to historical practices, appearing as a footnote in F. T. Arnold's groundbreaking work on realizing figured bass in 1931.[14] Despite all of the above, this very fine and flexible temperament has lamentably remained almost entirely ignored and unused by modern harpsichordists until quite recently.

Additional instructions for modified meantone that have survived include two anonymous manuscripts, one in the Padua conservatory (mid-eighteenth century?) and another in the British library, as well as two English systems attributed to Avison (ca. 1750) and Handel (ca. 1780).[15] Another intriguing indication of meantone modification as standard practice in eighteenth-century England is found in Tiberius Cavallo's article promoting the adoption of ET (1788) in which he described how "harpsichords and organs are commonly tuned at present."[16] While his hierarchical list of key quality might seem too vague to provide any solid information, it is actually surprisingly easy to distill a reasonably reliable reconstruction, which seems to have been a rather typical modified mean-tone. Finally, although it was too late to be of much importance to the harpsichord, Young's temperament of 1801 is also properly a modified meantone due to the logic of its construction and, as such, may well be a further indication of a general practice in England during the preceding decades.[17]

Rational Circulating Temperaments

Rational circulating temperaments are essentially a German phenomenon of the late seventeenth and early eighteenth centuries. While their aim is to enable either quasi or full circulation, they do so not through the makeshift solutions of meantone modifications but rather through a conscious manipulation of the total amount of tempering around the circle of fifths. This total is divided into fractional parts distributed among the fifths in such a way that the best major thirds remain in the natural keys (again, usually centered around C major), with a gradual transition to the worst thirds in the distant tonalities. The contrast between the best and worst tonalities is often significantly less than in a modified meantone, since the intention is usually, although not always, to enable the full use of all keys (i.e., with tolerable thirds as well as fifths). As a consequence, the qualitative contrast between best and worst keys is greatly reduced, and differences between closely related tonalities are quite subtle.

Andreas Werckmeister seems to have been the first to use such an approach, offering two such systems in his *Orgelprobe* (1681) and again in his *Musicalische Temperatur* (1691). Both were designed to enable circulation, but not to the same extent; the first was for those who often played in the distant tonalities (*modos fictos*) and the second for those who remained primarily in the natural keys (*regular-modos*), a distinction reflected in the latter's purer thirds in the natural keys and more strident thirds in the distant keys. A third temperament given in 1691 provided yet another option for remote keys, one which moved closer yet to the logical conclusion of ET. All three were presented as tables listing the amount of tempering for fifths and major thirds in fractions of a generic "comma," but step-by-step tuning instructions were only given for the *regular-modos* design. Despite this, modern musicologists/musicians have focused almost exclusively on the *modos fictus* design, which is now generally known as "Werckmeister III" from the order in which it appeared in 1691.

Werckmeister's rational temperaments are often characterized today as a radical new development that ostensibly freed composers from the limitations of regular meantone for the first time. However, he stated several times that his intent was to allow the organ to perform pieces in *modos fictos* in accordance with current practice.[18] It was a stubborn adherence to regular quarter-comma meantone among organ builders, as well as their use of subsemitones as a stop-gap solution, which Werckmeister repeatedly and vehemently criticized and tried to correct with his rational temperaments. Taken altogether, this might well imply that *stringed* keyboard instruments were already being tempered in a more flexible manner, most likely some sort of modified meantone similar to that which he himself would later recommend for continuo playing, as mentioned above.

Werckmeister's real contributions to the history of temperament lay not so much in these rational temperaments themselves but more in his new simplified method for constructing and evaluating such systems. He employed a generic "comma" which simultaneously stood for both the Pythagorean and syntonic commas as well as one-half of the diesis, even though it was mathematically equal to none of them. He divided this ersatz comma by a small integer – either three or four, depending upon the temperament – and used this fractional portion as a basic unit for quantifying the tempering of both fifths and major thirds. Neidhardt, despite being far more proficient mathematically, adopted and improved upon Werckmeister's method, dividing the generic comma by twelve and providing an evaluation of minor thirds as well as major, a method which was adopted in turn by Sorge. Though both of these later authors were fully aware of this method's inherent inaccuracies, they apparently found it a small price to pay for the ease of design it offered. The inevitable incongruities were easily accounted for when the temperament was finally represented with mathematical precision (i.e., in monochord lengths). Using geometry and a compass to mark out his monochord, Werckmeister replaced his ersatz comma with the syntonic, leaving the small discrepancy to be disappeared among the ostensibly "pure" fifths, while Neidhardt and Sorge, both of whom employed mathematical calculation, used the Pythagorean comma, causing their qualitative evaluations of thirds to be slightly erroneous.

Another ubiquitous modern misconception about rational circulating temperaments in general and those of Werckmeister in particular is the idea that unequal circulating systems were clearly preferred over ET during the eighteenth century due to their subtle acoustic differences between tonalities. Such differences supposedly formed an essential part of the various musical elements a composer had at his disposal which together formed the *Affecten-Lehre*, the knowledge of how to evoke certain emotional responses through music. Many today believe that such unequal circulating systems were generally referred to as "well-tempered" (*wohl temperirt*), a term supposedly coined by Werckmeister for his rational circulating systems. J. S. Bach's use of the same term in the title of his famous collection supposedly indicates that he, too, wanted a subtly unequal temperament, not the ET universally assumed by nineteenth- and early twentieth-century musicologists.

While this narrative rests upon a solid foundation (i.e., the idea that some historical authors – though by no means all – held that unequal temperaments increased emotive capability), the basic premise that *wohl temperirt* was generally understood as specifically meaning "unequal" does not stand up to a careful examination of the source literature. Werckmeister's own use of the term is sporadic, and, when taken altogether, his only consistent requirement was that a "well-tempered" keyboard allow for completely unrestricted circulation without resorting to subsemitones.[19] While his own schemes are indeed unequal, he mentioned ET as a possibility a number of times, and, in his last work, published posthumously, he specifically stated that "if the temperament were arranged such that all the fifths were tempered by one-twelfth comma and an accurate ear were to realize it on a keyboard instrument, a well-tempered harmony throughout the entire circle and in all keys would certainly result."[20] Beyond Werckmeister, a thorough search of the major works from the larger corpus of eighteenth-century German temperament literature turns up only a handful of occurrences of "*wohl temperirt*," none of which could be construed as deviating from his usage in any way. The question of Bach's temperament will be dealt with separately below.

After Werckmeister, the most important authors were Neidhardt and Sorge. Neidhardt's first publication (1706) was dedicated solely to ET, but his later works of 1724 and 1734 provided a methodical exploration of the possible permutations for unequal circulating temperaments using Werckmeister's generic comma method. Neidhardt also expanded on Werckmeister's *regular/fictus* options by providing a short list of four temperaments intended for different social milieus: a village, a small city, a large city, and the court. The village temperament favored the natural keys at the expense of the distant keys, while the other designs represented an incremental progression towards ET, the latter being recommended for the court, presumably in relation to the harmonic sophistication of the musical literature which would have been performed in each setting. Sorge's various mid-century publications consistently recommended ET while nonetheless offering several subtly unequal alternatives.

It is difficult to judge the degree to which any of these rational circulating systems were ever put into practice in eighteenth-century Germany. To the extent that unequal temperaments were preferred over ET, differences in key color probably only formed a partial motivation.[21] A more compelling reason may have been simply to allow the most often used keys to remain somewhat purer than the seldom used keys, as Werckmeister repeatedly stated. Both Neidhardt and Sorge mentioned that wind instruments, which were normally made to be either pure or close to pure in their home key, worked better with such unequal systems precisely for this reason. Additionally, the unequal schemes are all easier to implement than ET since they inevitably contain at least a small number of pure fifths.

Several other temperaments are also often considered to be rationally circulating, including schemes proposed by Young, Vallotti, and Kirnberger. Young's primary temperament is better characterized as a modified meantone (as described above), but it is often misrepresented in modern texts as a rational circulating scheme which departs slightly from Young's own monochord values. He also provided another system which he claimed would provide "nearly the same effect," with six identically tempered fifths from C to F♯ and the remaining fifths pure. Both of his proposals, however, are too late to have any real significance for harpsichord literature. Young's second scheme is often conflated with that of Vallotti, a temperament which enjoys a modern overpopularity which is greatly disproportionate to its true historical significance. While it was mentioned by Tartini (1754) as well as in an obscure English tract on physics (1781),[22] Vallotti's own description remained in manuscript form until the twentieth century. A similar situation exists with Kirnberger. His first system, published in 1771, is not a temperament at all but a rather crude combination of Pythagorean and just tuning, in which the comma is borne by only two fifths, D-A-E, making them both far too sour to be usable. Kirnberger begrudgingly recognized this problem in a private communication with Forkel, admitting that the comma could also be distributed among the first four fifths (C to E), a system known today as "Kirnberger III." Here again, both systems are too late to have much relevance for the harpsichord, especially the latter, which was not published until the late nineteenth century.

Equal Temperament

Needless to say, ET is the most rational of all circulating temperaments, and, in that sense, it is indeed the "best and simplest," as it was called in the title of Neidhardt's first publication (1706). ET has been present in the Western musical tradition at least since the Renaissance as a common (though not the only) tuning for fretted string instruments, both plucked and bowed. Numerous historical authors mentioned the problem of using keyboard instruments with the lute and the viol due to the difference in tempering, and eliminating such conflicts was one of the main arguments of those advocating ET for keyboards.

An episode reported by the organist and harpsichord maker Jean Denis in his 1636 treatise on tuning meantone is at once amusing and informative. Denis had attended a private concert for which the harpsichord had been tuned in ET, and afterwards he was asked what he thought of the new temperament. His said that it was "very harsh and coarse to the ear," and when his hosts suggested that it was simply a question of his ear becoming accustomed to these unfamiliar sounds, he retorted that if they were to offer him a supper of rotten meat and vinegar, they could not claim that his disgust was merely due to an unfamiliarity with these new flavors. The harpsichordist then turned to the ease of playing with the lute and the viol, but Denis countered that it would be much better to try to perfect those instruments so that they, too, could produce proper major and minor semitones, as on the keyboard when tuned in the normal (i.e. meantone) manner. In any event, Denis's report proves that some were already trying ET on keyboard instruments in France during the first half of the seventeenth century and obviously finding it quite acceptable.[23]

Nonetheless, no further indication of ET in France has survived until Rameau's famous recommendation in 1737, in which he abandoned his earlier preference for modified meantone. His comments are particularly interesting, for not only did he say that those who thought that differences in key quality caused differences in affect were mistaken, but he went even further, claiming that such differences "displeased the ear" and distracted it from its proper task of following "the intertwining of the keys."[24] D'Alembert later (1752) stated that most musicians had not heeded Rameau's suggestion and kept to the tradition of *temperament ordinaire*. This conservative approach was reaffirmed by Rousseau (1767) and Mercadier de Belesta (1776), and the use of *ordinaire* may well have continued up to the fall of the Ancien Régime. In Italy, Frescobaldi may also have been an ET advocate, at least if Doni's disparaging remarks can be believed, and it is commonly assumed today that Froberger brought the practice back to Austria after his studies with Frescobaldi in Rome. However, in the case of both composers, the possibility cannot be excluded that they were composing for keyboards with subsemitones tuned in extended meantone.

In Germany during the late seventeenth and early eighteenth centuries, there was a notable flurry of interest in ET in the hopes that it might resolve the peculiar problem of combining *Chorton* (A = 465 Hz) organs with *Kammerton* (A = 415 Hz) orchestral instruments. This situation usually required the organist to transpose his part down by a whole step (usually at sight), causing him to collide with the harmonic limits of meantone even more often than when playing alone. While Neidhardt clearly preferred ET, in 1734 he reported that many who had tried it found it wanting due to the sourness of the major thirds, the size of the half steps, and "a lack – so they say – of variety in the tempering of the major thirds and the conse-quent heightening of emotion," injecting a hint of personal incredulity that key *affect* was the result of acoustical differences.[25] In 1731, Mattheson also spoke very favorably of ET, though he admitted that most musicians would find it difficult if not impossible to play in tune with keyboard instruments tuned in ET as their ears were so accustomed to just intonation. He thought the only way to overcome this tendency would be to raise an entire generation of musicians from childhood hearing nothing but ET, though he had no idea how that might be accomplished.[26] As the century wore on, however, musicians did slowly adapt, and ET soon became the standard recommendation in both theoretical and practical works, includ-ing those of Sorge, Marpurg, and others. By 1757, the general view had changed so much that the Braunschweig harpsichord and clavichord maker Bartold Fritz could state that the best possible keyboard tempera-ment was unequivocally that in which no difference whatsoever could be detected among the various tonalities.[27] His brief treatise on tuning offered a simplified though flawed method for realizing the same. His second edition, published in the same year, was dedicated to the "famous virtuoso" C. P. E. Bach, who Fritz claimed had praised his treatise for providing "all that is possible and necessary" on the topic.[28]

A Case Apart: Bach's *Well-Tempered Clavier*

Until the revival of unequal temperaments in the second half of the twen-tieth century, musicologists were unanimous in assuming that Bach's famous collection of preludes and fugues in all major and minor keys had been written specifically to demonstrate the advantages of ET. During the last half-century, that opinion has been reversed completely, and now it is more or less taken as an established fact that Bach used some kind of subtly irregular system, either a very smooth modified meantone or a rational circulating scheme. Much of this new-found conviction rests upon the widespread mythology surrounding the term *"wohl temperirt"* discussed above. Dozens of authors have presented a variety of solutions based upon justifications ranging from a partial statistical analysis of the perceptibility of major-third quality (Barnes, 1976)[29] to numerical symbolism (Kellner, 1975).[30] A recent flurry of proposals has been based upon the hypothesis that the ornamental loops across the title page of the Bach's original manuscript are actually a cryptic instruction for reproducing his temperament.[31]

Unfortunately, there is just as little objective evidence to support this new approach as there was for the traditional assumption of ET, and all the various modern proposals, no matter how convincingly argued, remain confined to the realm of conjecture. Only a few vague comments regarding Bach's practice have come down to us, all secondhand, and none of them can be taken as conclusively supporting or excluding either manner of tempering. A number of modern authors have turned to the music itself to support their proposals, citing specific points where their particular temperament intensifies the listening experience. However, the fact that they can all provide different examples proves that there is no inherent bias towards any one particular temperament hidden within the musical structure itself.

The truth is that just about *any* unequal temperament which adheres reasonably well to the general outlines of the larger corpus of eighteenth-century German temperament theory will undoubtedly cause subtle variations in the qualities of various harmonic structures which would be absent in ET. While each set of examples may well be compelling in its own right, ultimately such subjective impressions prove nothing about Bach's actual practice, and any performer who chooses to use ET should in no way be criticized as being "inauthentic" for that reason alone. Perhaps the last word on the subject is best left to Marpurg, who, in writing about unequal temperaments in 1776, perfectly anticipated the modern quest for the chimera of "Bach's lost temperament":

> There's only one kind of equal temperament, whereas there are innumerable unequal temperaments possible. This opens up an abundant wellspring of variation for the speculative musician, and since every musician will happily invent his own, it follows that from time to time we will be presented with a new type of unequal temperament, and everyone will consider his to be the best.[32]

Notes

1. For an excellent selection of historical comments on the difference between keyboard and nonkeyboard intonation, see Bruce Haynes, "Beyond Temperament: Non-Keyboard Intonation in the 17th and 18th Centuries," *Early Music* 19, no. 3 (1991), pp. 357–381.
2. Pythagorean tuning is not a temperament because no consonance is intentionally detuned; the entire gamut is defined by an unbroken chain of pure fifths. While the major and minor thirds are seriously out of tune, they were not considered to be among the consonant intervals.
3. Michael Praetorius, *Syntagma musicum, Band II: De Organographia* (Wolfenbüttel, 1618), p. 155 [author's translation].

4. The syntonic comma is the difference between the interval formed by the first and last pitch classes of a chain of four contiguous fiths and a pure major third, the latter being narrower by about 22 cents.

5. See Mark Lindley, "Fifteenth-Century Evidence for Meantone Temperament," *Proceedings of the Royal Musical Association* 102 (1975–1976), pp. 37–51.

6. For complete information on these and other sources cited in the text, see the list of further reading.

7. See Haynes, "Beyond Temperament," p 367.

8. Patrizio Barbieri, *Enharmonic Instruments and Music, 1470–1900* (Latina: Il Levante Libreria Editrice, 2008), p. 21.

9. The instrument, built by Vitus de Trasuntinis in Venice in 1606, bears the title "Clavemusicum omnitonum modulis diatonicis, cromaticis, et enearmos [*sic*]." It is preserved in the collection of the *Museo internazionale e biblioteca della musica di Bologna*, inventory number 1766.

10. Barbieri, *Enharmonic Instruments and Music*, p. 36.

11. A fifth tempered by a given amount will sound identical regardless of whether the tempering is wide or narrow.

12. Robert Smith describes this process in detail at the end of his somewhat impenetrable tome on regular meantone temperaments, finishing off with this rather amusing exception to the rule: "It appears also from the reasons above, that no voice-part ought to be played on the organ, unless to assist an imperfect singer, and keep him from making worse concords with the base and other parts than the organ itself does." See Robert Smith, *Harmonics, or the Philosophy of Musical Sounds* (Cambridge, 1749), pp. 240–244, here p. 244.

13. Lorenz Mizler, *Musikalische Bibliothek oder Gründliche Nachricht nebst unpartheyischem Urtheil von alten und neuen musikalischen Schriften und Büchern*, Vol.1, pt. 2 (Leipzig, 1737), pp. 49–68, here p. 50.

14. F. T. Arnold, *The Art of Accompaniment from a Thorough-Bass as Practised in the XVIIth & XVIIIth Centuries*, Vol. 2 (London: Oxford University Press, 1931), pp. 204–205.

15. The title of the British Library source is "*How to Tune an Organ, Harpsichord, Virginal or Espìneta*," Anonymous, *GB-Lbl*, MS harleian 4160, ca. 1698.

16. Tiberius Cavallo, "Of the Temperament of those Musical Instruments, in Which the Tones, Keys, or Frets, Are Fixed, as in the Harpsichord, Organ, Guitar, &c.," *Philosophical Transactions of the Royal Society of London* 78 (London: 1788), pp. 234–258, here p. 252.

17. Modern writers often impose an ahistorical interpretation on Young's instructions by assuming a division of the Pythagorean comma, but his monochord numbers confirm that his "comma" was the syntonic. Young also leaves four fifths as mathematically undefined "gap fillers," which, by definition, excludes his system from the rational circulating family.

18. For instance, on the title pages of both the 1681 and 1691 works, Werckmeister tells us that he gives instructions for tempering so that "according to current practice, one hears a pleasing and tolerable harmony in all the tonalities with accidentals." In the introduction to the chapter on temperament in *Orgelprobe* (p. 16), he says it is important that a new organ

be tempered "such that one can have a tolerable harmony in all keys (since these days most of the pieces or songs are set in tonalities with accidentals)."

19. This conclusion is based upon a careful reading by this author of all ten of Werckmeister's surviving works in German.

20. A. Werckmeister, *Musicalische Paradoxal-Discourse* (Quidlinberg, 1707), p. 110 [author's translation].

21. For an exhaustive examination of the topic of key *affect* that traces the idea back to its roots long before the eighteenth century, see Rita Steblin, *A History of Key Characteristics in the Eighteenth and Early Nineteenth Centuries*, second edition (Rochester: University of Rochester Press, 2002).

22. W. Jones, *Physiological Disquisitions, or Discourses on Natural Philosophy of the Elements*, London, 1781.

23. Jean Denis, *Traité de l'accord de l'espinette* (Paris: 1643/1650), p. 12. English translation in *Treatise on Harpsichord Tuning by Jean Denis*, trans. and ed. Vincent J Panetta, Jr. (Cambridge, 1987), p. 68. Panetta points out the Mersenne's comments on ET in various publications are almost identical, word for word, to those of Denis, suggesting that he had used Denis's *Traité* as a source.

24. Jean-Philippe Rameau, *Génération harmonique, ou traité de musique théorique et pratique* (Paris: Prault fils, 1737), pp. 94–105, here p. 104.

25. J. G. Neidhardt, *Gäntzlich erschöpfte, Mathematische Abtheilungen des Diatonsich-Chromatischen, temperirten Canonis monochordi* (Königsberg/Leipzig: Andre, 1734), p. 40.

26. See Johann Matthesson, *Grosse General-Baß-Schule oder der exemplarischen Organisten-Probe* (Hamburg: 1731), p. 144.

27. See Bartold Fritz, *Anweisung, wie man Claviere, Clavecins, und Orgeln, nach einer mechanischen Art, in allen zwölf Tönen gleich rein stimmen könne* (Leipzig: Breitkopf, 1757), pp. 1–2.

28. Fritz, *Anweisung*, foreword to second printing.

29. John Barnes, "Bach's Keyboard Temperament: Internal Evidence from the Well-Tempered Clavier," *Early Music*, Vol. 7, no. 2 (April 1979), pp. 236–249.

30. Herbert Anton Kellner, "Wie stimme ich selbst mein Cembalo," *Das Musikinstrument*, Vol. 19 (Verlag des Musikinstrument, 1976).

31. Bradley Lehman, "Bach's Extraordinary Temperament: Our Rosetta Stone," *Early Music* 33, nos. 1 and 2 (2005), pp. 3–23 and 211–231, respectively.

32. F. W. Marpurg, *Versuch über die musikalische Temperatur* (Breslau: Korn, 1776), p. 183.

Further Reading

Barnes, J. "Bach's Keyboard Temperament." *Early Music* 7, no. 2, 1979, pp. 236–249.

Haynes, Bruce. *A History of Performing Pitch. The Story of "A."* Lanham, MD: Scarecrow Press, 2002.

Hook, James. *The Preceptor for the Piano-Forte, Organ or Harpsichord*. London, ca. 1795.

Hunt, Edgar. "Corrette on Stringing and Tuning." *The English Harpsichord Magazine* 2, no. 5, 1979.

Lindley, M. "Mersenne on Keyboard Tuning." *Journal of Music Theory* 24, no. 2,1980, pp. 166–203.

Malcolm, Alexander. *A Treatise of Musick*. Edinburgh: 1721.

McGeary, Thomas. "Early Eighteenth-Century English Harpsichord Tuning and Stringing," *The English Harpsichord Magazine* 3, no. 2, 1982, pp. 18–22.

Neidhardt, J. G. *Beste und Leichteste Temperatur des Monochordi*. Jena: Beilcken, 1706.

    Sectio Canonis Harmonici. Königsberg: Eckarts, 1724.

    Gäntzlich erschöpfte, Mathematische Abtheilungen des Diatonsich-Chromatischen, temperirten Canonis monochordi. Königsberg and Leipzig: Eckarts, 1734.

Printz, W. C. *Phrynis Mitilenaeus oder Satyrischer Componist*. Dresden and Leipzig, 1696.

Rameau, Jean-Philippe. *Nouveau Systême de Musique Theorique*. Paris: L'Imprimerie de Jean-Baptiste-Christophe Ballard, 1726.

Rousseau, Jean-Jacques. "Temperament" (pp. 499–507) and "Ton" (pp. 515–517). *Dictionnaire de Musique*. Paris, 1768.

Schlick, Arnolt. *Spiegel der Orgelmacher vn Organisten*. Mainz: Peter Schöffer the younger, 1511. English translation and edition by Elizabeth Berry Barber. Buren: Fritz Knuff, 1980.

Sorge, J. A. *Anweisung zur Stimmung und Temperatur sowohl der Orgelwerke, als auch andere Instrumente, sonderlich des Claviers*. Hamburg: 1744.

    Gespräch zwischen einem Musico theoretico und einem Studioso Musices. Lobenstein, 1748.

    Ausfürliche und deutliche Anweisung zur Rational-Rechnung und der damit verknüpfften Ausmessung und Abtheilung des Monochords. Lobenstein, 1749.

    Zuverlässige Anweisung, Claviere und Orgeln behörig zu temperiren und zu stimmen. Leipzig, 1758.

van Blankenburg, Quirnus. *Elementa musica of nieuw licht tot het welverstaan van de musiec*. s'Gravenhage, 1739.

Werckmeister, Andreas. *Orgelprobe*. Frankfurt and Leipzig: 1681

    Musicalische Temperatur. Frankfurt and Leipzig: 1691.

Young, Thomas. "Outlines of Experiments and Inquiries Respecting Sound and Light." *Philosophical Transactions of the Royal Society of London* 90, 1800, pp. 106–150.

Appendices

Appendix 1: Chronological List of Harpsichord Composers from the Netherlands and Northern Germany Discussed in Chapter 4

NORTHERN AND SOUTHERN NETHERLANDS

Jan Pieterszoon Sweelinck (1562–1621)
Peeter Cornet (ca. 1575–1633)
Anthoni van Noordt (ca. 1619–1675)
Pieter Bustijn (1649–1729)
Quirinus van Blankenburg (1654–1739)
Jean-Baptiste (John) Loeillet (1680–1730)
Conrad Friedrich Hurlebusch (1691–1765)
Rynoldus Popma van Oevering (1692–ca. 1781)
Gerardus Havingha (1696–1753)
Josse Boutmy (1697–1779)
Joseph-Hector Fiocco (1703–1741)
Jacob Wilhelm Lustig (1706–1796)
Johan Nicolaas Lentz (1720?–1782)
Guillaume Boutmy (1723–1791)
Christian Ernst Graf (Graaf) (1723–1804)
Johann August Just (ca. 1750–1791)

NORTHERN GERMANY

Melchior Schildt (1592–1667)
Heinrich Scheidemann (ca. 1595–1663)
Franz Tunder (1614–1667)
Matthias Weckmann (1616–1674)
Christian Flor (1626–1697)
Dieterich Buxtehude (ca. 1637–1707)
Johann Adam Reincken (1643–1722)
Georg Böhm (1661–1733)

Appendix 2: Recommended Editions to Accompany Chapter 4

Blankenburg, Q. van. *Verzamelde klavierstukken.* Muziek uit de Republiek 1 / *Collected Keyboard Pieces* / Music from the Dutch Republic 1. Rudolf Rasch, ed. Utrecht: Koninklijke Vereniging voor Nederlandse Muziekgeschiedenis, 2001.

Clavicimbal- en orgelboek der gereformeerde psalmen en kerkzangen. Facsimile edition, Rein Verhagen. Erve Muziek, Gorssel 2013.

Böhm, Georg. *Sämtliche Werke für Klavier/Cembalo.* Klaus Beckmann, ed. Wiesbaden: Breitkopf & Härtel, 1985.

    Sämtliche Orgelwerke. Klaus Beckmann, ed. Breitkopf & Härtel, Wiesbaden 1986.

Boutmy, J. and G. *Opere per clavicembalo: Sonate – Suites.* Laura Cerutti, ed. Padua: Armelin Musica, 1997.

Bustyn, P. *IX Suittes pour le clavessin.* Facsimile edition. Albert Clement, ed. Exempla Musica Zelandica I. Middelburg: Koninklijk Zeeuwsch Genootschap der Wetenschappen, 1992/2011.

Buxtehude, D. *VI Suittes, divers airs avec leurs variations et fugues pour le clavessin, Amsterdam 1710.* Pieter Dirksen, ed. Muziek uit de Republiek 2 / Music from the Dutch Republic 2. Utrecht: Koninklijke Vereniging voor Nederlandse Muziekgeschiedenis, 2004.

    Keyboard Works, Part 3: Preludes, Toccatas, Fugues, and Canzonas for Organ (Manualiter), Harpsichord or Clavichord. Christoph Wolff, ed. Dieterich Buxtehude, The Collected Works, Volume 17. New York: The Broude Trust, 2016.

    Keyboard Works, Part 4: Suites and Variations for Harpsichord or Clavichord. Christoph Wolff, ed. Dieterich Buxtehude, The Collected Works, Volume 18. New York: The Broude Trust, 2016.

Cornet, P. *Complete Keyboard Music.* Pieter Dirksen and Jean Ferrard, eds. Monumenta Musica Neerlandica XVII. Utrecht: Koninklijke Vereniging voor Nederlandse Muziekgeschiedenis, 2001.

Dutch Keyboard Music of the 16th and 17th centuries. Alan Curtis, ed. Monumenta Musica Neerlandica III Utrecht: Koninklijke Vereniging voor Nederlandse Muziekgeschiedenis, 1961.

Flor, C. *Dreizehn & Ein Choral für Clavier nach den Handschriften der Ratsbücherei Lüneburg.* Jörg Jacobi, ed. Bremen: Edition Baroque, 2004.

    Zehn Suiten für Clavier nach der Handschrift Mus.ant.pract. 1198 der Ratsbücherei Lüneburg. Jörg Jacobi, ed. Bremen: Edition Baroque, 2006.

Havingha, G. *VIII Suites, gecomponeerd voor de clavecymbal off spinet.* Facsimile edition. Clemens Romijn, ed. Utrecht: STIMU, Utrecht 1990.

    Het klavierboek van Quirijn en Jacoba Elizabeth Bambeek van Strijen (1752), Rasch, R. (ed.) Muziek uit de Republiek 5 / *The Keyboard Book of Quirijn and Jacoba Elizabeth van Bambeek van Strijen (1752).* Music from the Dutch Republic 5. Utrecht: Koninklijke Vereniging voor Nederlandse Muziekgeschiedenis, 2001.

Hill, Robert, ed. *Keyboard Music from the Andreas Bach Book and the Möller Manuscript.* Cambridge, MA: Harvard University Press, 1991.

Hurlebusch, C. F. *Compositioni musicali per il cembalo, divise in due parti.* Max Seiffert, ed. Amsterdam: Alsbach, 1912.

    Klavierboek Anna Maria van Eijl. Frits Noske, ed. Amsterdam: Vereniging voor Nederlandse Muziekgeschiedenis, 1959.

Loeillet, J. [M. Baptist Lully], *Lessons for the Harpsichord or Spinet. Almands, Corants, Sarabands, Airs, Minuets & Jiggs.* Facsimile edition. Alamire: Peer 1989.

    Six Suits of Lessons for the Harpsichord or Spinnet. In Most of the Key's with Variety of Passages and Variations Throughout the Work. Facsimile edition. Alamire: Peer 1989.

Lübeck, V. (Sr. and Jr.), *Neue Ausgabe sämtlicher Orgel- und Clavierwerke I–II / New Edition of the Complete Organ and Keyboard Works.* 2 volumes. Siegbert Rampe, ed. Kassel: Bärenreiter, 2003–2004.

Lustig, J. W. *Sonates pour le clavecin, Première partie (gravées par Mme Leclair) 1742.* Facsimile edition. Geneva: Minkoff, 1986.

XXIV Capricetten voor 't clavier. Harald Vogel, ed. Muziek uit de Republiek 9 / Music from the Dutch Republic 9. Utrecht: Koninklijke Vereniging voor Nederlandse Muziekgeschiedenis, 2008.

Noordt, A. van. *Tabulatuurboeck van psalmen en fantasyen (1659).* Jan van Biezen, ed. Monumenta Musica Neerlandica XI. Amsterdam: Vereniging voor Nederlandse Muziekgeschiedenis, 1976.

Psalm Variations from Lynar B7. Pieter Dirksen, ed. Utrecht: Koninklijke Vereniging voor Nederlandse Muziekgeschiedenis, 1996.

Reincken, J. A. *Sämtliche Werke für Klavier/Cembalo.* Klaus Beckmann, ed. Wiesbaden: Breitkopf & Härtel, 1982.

Scheidemann, H. *Sämtliche Werke für Clavier (Cembalo).* Pieter Dirksen, ed. Wiesbaden: Breitkopf & Härtel, 2000.

Scheidemann, H., Schop, J. et. al. *Ausgewählte Stücke aus dem Celler Clavierbuch (um 1662).* Martin Böcker, ed. Wiesbaden: Breitkopf & Härtel, 1990.

Schildt, M., Scheidemann, H., Radeck, J. R., Anonym, *Keyboard Music "The Voigtländer-tablatur."* Henrik Glahn, ed. Music in Denmark at the Time of Christian IV 3. Copenhagen: Engstrøm & Sødring, 1988.

Speuy, H. *Psalm Preludes for Organ or Harpsichord.* Frits Noske, ed. Amsterdam: Heuwekemeijer, 1963.

Strunck, D. *Sämtliche Orgelwerke / Complete Organ Works.* Klaus Beckmann, ed. Mainz: Schott, 2006.

Strunck, N. A., *Sämtliche Orgelwerke / Complete Organ Works.* Klaus Beckmann, ed. Mainz: Schott, 2007.

Sweelinck, J. P. *Sämtliche Werke für Tasteninstrumente / Complete Keyboard Works.* Harald Vogel and Pieter Dirksen, eds. Wiesbaden: Breitkopf & Härtel, 2004–2007.

Sämtliche Orgel- und Clavierwerke / Complete Organ and Keyboard Works. Siegbert Rampe, ed. Kassel: Bärenreiter, ongoing series from 2003.

Weckmann, M. *Sämtliche Freie Orgel- und Clavierwerke / Complete Free Organ and Keyboard Works.* Siegbert Rampe, ed. Kassel: Bärenreiter, 1991.

Zuid-Nederlandse Klavecimbelmuziek. Drie handschriften uit het Rijksarchief Antwerpen: Arendonk, Dimpna Isabella en Maria Therese Reijnders / Harpichord Music of the Southern Low Countries. Three Manuscripts from the National Archives in Antwerp: Arendonk, Dimpna Isabella and Maria Therese Reijnders. Godelieve Spiessens, Irène Cornelis, eds. Monumenta Flandriae Musica 4 Leuven: Alamire, 1998.

Appendix 3: Principal Editions Cited in Chapter 5

Ebner, Wolfgang [and Georg Muffat]. *Sämtliche Werke für Clavier (Orgel),* 2 volumes. Siegbert Rampe, ed. Kassel: Bärenreiter, 2003–2004.

Fischer, Johann Caspar Ferdinand. *Sämtliche Werke für Tasteninstrument.* Ernst von Werra, ed. Leipzig: Breitkopf & Härtel, 1901.

Froberger, Johann Jacob. Bärenreiter, *Complete Works*, 7 volumes. Siegbert Rampe, ed. Kassel: 1993–2015.

Froberger, Johann Jacob. *Complete Suites and Tombeaus.* Pieter Dirksen, ed. 2017.

Hassler, Hans Leo. *Variationen "Ich ging einmal spatieren" für Cembalo.* Georges Kiss, ed. Mainz: Schott, 1971.

Kerll, Johann Caspar. *The Collected Works for Keyboard.* C. David Harris, ed. New York: Broude, 1995.

Kindermann, Johann Erasmus. *Ausgewählte Werke II.* Felix Schreiber and Bertha Antonia Wallner, eds. Leipzig: Breitkopf & Härtel, 1924.

Krieger, Johann and Johann Philipp. *Sämtliche Orgel- und Clavierwerke*, 2 volumes. Siegbert Rampe and Helene Lerch, eds. Kassel: Bärenreiter, 1999.

Muffat, Georg. *Vier Partiten für Cembalo.* Markus Eberhardt, ed. Magdeburg: Walhall, 2014.

Muffat, Georg [and Wolfgang Ebner]. *Sämtliche Werke für Clavier* (Orgel), 2 volumes. Siegbert Rampe, ed. Kassel. Bärenreiter, 2003–2004.

Muffat, Gottlieb. *The 32 Ricercaten and 19 Canzonas*, 3 volumes. Erich Benedikt, ed. Vienna: Doblinger, 2003.

   Zwei Suiten. Raimund Schächer, ed. Stuttgart: Cornetto Verlag, 2008

   Componimenti musicali (1739) for Harpsichord. Christopher Hogwood, ed. Bologna: Ut Orpheus, 2009.

Pachelbel, Johann. *Klavierwerke … Nebst beigefügten Stücken von W. H. Pachelbel.* Max Seiffert, ed. Leipzig: Breitkopf & Härtel, 1901–1902.

   Hexachordum Apollonis. Hans Joachim Moser and Traugott Fedtke, eds. Kassel: Bärenreiter 1958.

   Complete Works for Keyboard Instruments, Vol. 6, *Ciaconas, Fantasias, Suites*; Vol. 7, *Chorale Partitas*; Vol. 8, *Arias with Variations*. Michael Belotti, ed. Colfax: Wayne Leupold Editions 2011–2018.

Poglietti, Alessandro. *Composizioni per il cembalo.* Emilia Fadini, ed. Milan: Ricordi, 1984.

Richter, Ferdinand Tobias. *Clavierwerke.* Markus Eberhardt, ed. Magdeburg: Walhall, 2009.

Schultheiss, Benedikt. *Muth- und Geist-Ermuntrender Clavier-Lust.* Richard Hudson, ed. Neuhausen-Stuttgart: Hänsseler, 1993.

Steigleder, Johann Ulrich. *Tabulatur Buch Dass Vatter Vnser 1627.* Jörg Jacobi, ed. Bremen: Edition Baroque, 2006.

Techelmann, Franz Matthias. Suiten für Tasteninstumente von und um Franz Mathias Techelmann c. 1649–1714. Herwig Knaus, ed. Graz: Akademische Verlagsanstalt, 1996.

Appendix 4: Modern and Facsimile Editions Cited in Chapter 6

Balbastre, Claude-Benigne (1727–1799)
   Pièces de clavecin, premier livre (1759).
      Modern edition. Paris; Heugel, 1974, ed. Alan Curtis.

Facsimile edition. *Pièces de clavecin, premier livre,* New York: Broude, Performers edition 26424.

Boismortier, Joseph Bodin de (1689–1755)

Quatre suites de pièces de clavecin, Op. 59 (1736).

Modern edition. *Quatre suites de pièces de clavecin,* Munich: F. E. C. Leuckart, 1959/1972, ed. Erwin Jacobi.

Chambonnières, Jacques Champion de (ca. 1601/2–1672)

Pièces de clavecin.

Modern edition. *Oeuvres Complets,* New York: Broude, 1967, eds. Paul Brunold and André Tessier, trans. Denise Restou.

Clérambault, Louis-Nicolas. *I.^{e r}* (1676–1749)

Ier Livre de pièces de clavecin (first edition, 1702; 2nd edition, 1704).

Facsimile edition. New York: Broude, Performers Facsimiles 24522.

Corrette, Michel. (1709–1795)

Premier Livre de pièces de clavecin, Op. 22 (1734).

Facsimile edition. Geneva: Minkoff, 1982.

Couperin, Armand-Louis (1727–1789)

Pièces de clavecin (1751).

Modern edition. *Selected Works for Keyboard.* Madison: A-R Editions, 1975, ed. David Fuller.

Facsimile edition. *Pièces de clavecin,* New York: Broude, Performers Edition 17341.

Couperin, François (1668–1733)

Pièces de clavecin, Premier livre (1713).

Modern edition. Paris: Heugel, 1982, ed. Kenneth Gilbert.

Modern edition. Kassel: Bärenreiter, 2016, ed. Denis Herlin.

Facsimile edition. Courlay: Fuzeau, 1988.

Second livre de pièces de clavecin (1717).

Modern edition. Paris: Heugel, 1984, ed. Kenneth Gilbert.

Modern edition. Kassel: Bärenreiter, 2018, ed. Denis Herlin.

Facsimile edition. Courlay: Fuzeau, 1990.

Troisième livre de pièces de clavecin (1722).

Modern edition. Paris: Heugel, 1971, ed. Kenneth Gilbert.

Facsimile edition. Courlay: Fuzeau, 1988.

Quatrième livre de pièces de clavecin (1730).

Modern edition. Paris: Heugel, 1971, ed. Kenneth Gilbert.

Facsimile edition. Courlay: Fuzeau, 1987.

L'art de toucher le clavecin (1716, rev. 1717).

Modern edition. New York: Alfred Publishing Co., 1974, ed. and trans. Margery Halford.

Facsimile edition. Courlay: Fuzeau, 1996 (1717 edition).

Couperin, Louis (ca. 1626–1661)

Pièces de clavecin.

Modern edition. *Pièces de clavecin,* Monaco: Éditions de L'Oiseau-Lyre, 1959, ed. Thurston Dart.

Modern edition. *Pièces de clavecin,* Paris: Heugel, 1988, ed. Alan Curtis.

Dagincour, François (1684–1758)

Pièces de clavecin … premier livre (1733).

Dandrieu, Jean-François (ca. 1682–1738)

Livre de clavecin[I] (1704).

Livre de clavecin [II] (ca. 1704–1720).

Livre de pièces de clavecin (first book of maturity, 1724).

Second livre de pièces de clavecin (1728).

Troisième livre de pièces de clavecin (1734).

> Modern edition. *Jean-François Dandrieu: Trois Livres de clavecin*, Paris: Schola Cantorum, 1973, eds. Pauline Aubert and Brigitte François-Sappey.

> Modern edition. *Music for Harpsichord*, University Park, PA: The Pennsylvania State University Press, ed. John White.

> Facsimile edition. *Les Caractères de la Guerre*. Courlay: Fuzeau, 1989.

D'Anglebert, Jean-Henry (1629–1691)

Pièces de clavecin (1689).

Daquin, Louis-Claude (1694–1772)

Ier Livre de pièces de clavecin (1735).

> Modern edition. *Pièces de clavecin*. London: Faber, 1983, ed. Christopher Hogwood.

> Facsimile edition. Geneva: Minkoff, 1982.

De Mars, M.^{R} (1702–1774)

Premier livre de de pièces de clavecin (1735).

> Facsimile edition. Geneva: Minkoff, 1982.

Duphly, Jacques. (1715–1789)

Pièces de clavecin (1744).

Second livre de pièces de clavecin (1748).

Troisième livre de pièces de clavecin (1756).

Quatrième livre de pièces de clavecin (1768).

> Modern edition. *Pièces pour clavecin*. Paris: Heugel, 1967, ed. Françoise Petit.

> Facsimile edition. Books I–IV, New York: Broude, Performers Facsimiles 65, 66, 67, and 69.

Forqueray, Antoine "Le Père" (1671/2–1745) and Jean-Baptiste (-Antoine) "Le Fils" (1699–1782)

Pieces de viole … mises en pièces de clavecin … livre premier (1747).

> Modern edition. *Pièces de clavecin*. Paris: Heugel, 1970, L.P. 17, ed. Colin Tilney.

Foucquet, Pierre-Claude (1694/5–1772)

Les caractères de la paix, pièces de clavecin, Op. 1 (1749).

Second livre de pièces de clavecin (1751).

Gravier, M.^{R} L'abbé (fl. 1759–1762)

Six sonates pour le clavecin [1759].

> Facsimile edition. Geneva: Minkoff, 1982.

Jacquet de La Guerre, Elisabeth-Claude (b. 1665–1667, d. 1729)

Pièces de clavecin (1687).

Pièces de clavecin qui peuvent se joüer sur le viollon (1707).

> Modern edition. *The Collected Works for Harpsichord*. New York, Broude, 2008, ed. Arthur Lawrence.

Le Roux, Gaspard (d. 1707)
  Pièces de clavecin (1705)
    Modern edition: *Gaspard Le Roux: Pieces for Harpsichord*, New York: Alpeg
      Editions, 1959, ed. Albert Fuller.
Marchand, Louis (1669–1732)
  [Livre premier,] Pièces de clavecin (1699).
  Livre second, pièces de clavecin (1702).
    Facsimile edition. New York: Broude, Performers Facsimiles 17 and 18.
Rameau, Jean-Philippe (1683–1764)
  Premier livre de pièces de clavecin (1706).
  Pièces de clavessin (1724).
  Nouvelles suites de pièces de clavecin (ca. 1729–1730).
    Modern edition. *Pièces de clavecin,* Kassel: Bärenreiter, 1958, ed. Erwin R.
      Jacobi.
    Facsimile edition. *Premier livre de pièces de clavecin*, New York: Broude, 1986,
      ed. R. Peter Wolf.
    Facsimile edition. *Nouvelles suites de pièces de clavecin*, Courlaty: Fuzeau, 1987.
Royer, Joseph Nicolas Pancrace (ca. 1705–1755)
  Pièces de clavecin, premier livre (1746).
    Facsimile edition. Pièces de clavecin, premier livre, New York: Broude,
      Performers Edition, 68112.
Simon, Simon (ca. 1735–after 1780)
  Pièces de clavecin, Op. 1 (1761)
Siret, Nicolas (1663–1754)
  Pièces de clavecin [First Book] (ca. 1710–1715).
  Second livre de pièces de clavecin (1719).

Appendix 5: Composers, Works, and Sources Cited in Chapter 9

Albero, Sebastián (de). *Obras para clavicordio o piano forte*
  PRIMARY SOURCE: E-Mc 4/1727(2), facsimile in www.rcsm.eu.
  MODERN EDITION:
  Nueva Biblioteca española de teclado: siglos XVI al XVIII, Antonio Baciero,
    editor. 7 vols. Madrid: UME, 1986.
  Treinta sonatas para clavicordio
  PRIMARY SOURCE: *I-Vnm It.IV,197b (=9768),* facsimile in internet.culturale.it.
  MODERN EDITIONS:
    Sebastián de Albero, 30 Sonatas for Harpsichord, Ryan Layne Whitney editor.
      lulu.com, 2015.
    Sebastián Albero, Treinta Sonatas, Raúl
      Angulo, editor. Madrid: Ars Hispana, 2017.
Blasco de Nebra, Manuel. *Six sonatas para clave y fuerte piano. Obra primera. In
  Madrid* (ca. 1770–80).
  PRIMARY SOURCE: *E-Mn* M/2238 and *E-Mn* M/2239, facsimile in www.bne.

MODERN EDITION: *Manuel Blasco de Nebra, Seis Sonatas para Clave y Fuerte Piano*, Robert Parris, editor. Madrid: UME, 1964.

Seis pastorelas y doce sonatas

PRIMARY SOURCE: *E-MO* 2998 (also including the *Obra primera*)

MODERN EDITION:

6 *pastorelas y* 12 *sonatas para fuerte piano*, Bengt Johnsson, editor. Egtved: Denmark, 1984.

Cabezón, Antonio de. *Obras de Música para tecla, harpa y vihuela de Antonio de Cabeçon, musico de la Camara y Capilla del Rey Don Philippe nuestro Señor. Recopiladas y puestas en cifra por Hernando de Cabeçon, su hijo* [...] (Madrid: Francisco Sánchez, 1578).

PRIMARY SOURCE: *E-Mn.*, facsimile in bdh.bne.es.

MODERN EDITIONS:

Antonio de Cabezón, Selected Works for Keyboard. Gerhard Doderer and Miguel Bernal Ripoll, editors. 4 volumes. Kassel: Bärenreiter, 2010.

Antonio de Cabezón Obras de música para tecla, arpa y vihuela, de Antonio de Cabeçon ... recopiladas y puestas en cifra por Hernando de Cabeçon su hijo. Madrid, 1578. Javier Artigas, Gustavo Delgado, Antonio Ezquerro et al. editors. 4 volumes. Madrid: Consejo Superior de Investigaciones Científicas, Institución Fernando El Católico, 2010.

Antonio de Cabezón Obras de música para tecla, arpa y vihuela.

Volume 1, Claudio Astronio, editor. Bologna: Ut Orpheus, 2001.

Volume 2, Paolo Erdas, editor. Bologna: Ut Orpheus, 2011.

Henestrosa, Luis Venegas de. *Libro de cifra nueva para tecla, harpa y vihuela* (Alcalá de Henares: Ioan de Brocar, 1557).

PRIMARY SOURCE: *E-Mn R/6497*, facsimile in bdh.bne.es.

MODERN EDITION:

Monumentos de la música española, Volumes 2–3. Higinio Anglés, editor. Barcelona: Instituto Español de Musicología, 1944; reprint 1984.

López, Félix Máximo. *Música de clave*

PRIMARY SOURCE: *E-Mn M/1234.* Facsimile in bdh.bne.es.

MODERN EDITIONS:

"Félix Máximo López, Integral de la música para clave y pianoforte." *Antologías. Música para piano.*" Alberto Cobo, editor. Madrid: ICCMU, 2000.

Variaciones al minuet afandangado

PRIMARY SOURCE: *E-Mn M/1742.* Facsimile in bdh.bne.es.

MODERN EDITIONS:

Dos juegos de variaciones sobre el "minué afandangado" para forte piano, Genoveva Gálvez, editor. Madrid: Sedem, 2000.

Variaciones al Minuet afandangado Charles-François Dumonchau-Félix Máximo López, Antoni Pons Seguí, editor. Madrid: Ars Hispana, 2013.

Montero, Joaquín *S[eis sonatas] para clave [y fuerte piano] d[edicada] a la Rl. Socie [dad Bascongada]/compu[esto] por Joach[in Montero] organista en la [parroquial iglesia de] Sn. Pedro el Rl. [de] Sevilla.*

PRIMARY SOURCE: *E-Boc PM 12-V-10.* Facsimile in mdc.cbuc.cat.

MODERN EDITIONS:

Joaquín Montero, Diez minuetes para clave y fuerte piano. Antonio RuizPipó, editor. Madrid: Unión Musical Española, 1973.

Seis sonatas para clave y fuerte piano, Op.1. Linton Powell, editor. Madrid: Unión Musical Española, 1977.

Seis sonatas para clave y fuerte piano, Op.1. Transcribed by Alex Coblentz. www.independent.academia.edu/AlexCoblentz

Nebra, José De. Uncatalogued manuscripts from Morella (Castellón) and Real Colegio Seminario del Corpus Christi.

MODERN EDITIONS:

"Joseph Nebra: Tocatas y sonata para órgano o clave." *Tecla Aragonesa*, Volume 1. Román Escalas, editor. Zaragoza: Institución Fernando el Católico, 1987)

"Joseph Nebra: Tocatas y sonata para órgano o clave," *Tecla Aragonesa* Volume 3. Salúd Álvarez, editor. Zaragoza: Institución Fernando el Católico, 1995.

Rabassa, Pedro. *Sonata* in *Libro de organistas valencianos*

PRIMARY SOURCE: *E-Bbc* M1012

MODERN EDITIONS:

Pere Rabassa Sonata pera clavicèmbal. Águeda Pedrero-Encabo and Bernat Cabré i Cercós, editors. Barcelona: Tritó, 2006.

Rodríguez Monllor, Vicente. *Libro de tocatas para címbalo repartidas por todos los puntos de un diapasón, Con la advertencia, que por todas las teclas blancas están por tercera menor, y tercera mayor a exepción [sic] de las negras, que por lo desafinado de los Terminos no están mas, que por el que menos disuena. Compuesto por M. Visente Rodriguez presbítero Organista Principal de la Metropolitana Yglesia de Valencia. Año 1744.*

PRIMARY SOURCE: *E-Boc* PM 12-VII-1. Facsimile in mdc.cbuc.cat.

MODERN EDITION:

Vicente Rodríguez Toccatas for harpsichord (Thirty Sonatas and a Pastorela, 1744), Recent Researches in the Music of the Classical Era, Almonte Howell, editor. Volumes XXII–XXIII. Madison, Wisconsin: A-R Editions, 1986.

Soler, Antonio. *XXVII sonatas para clave, por el Padre Fray Antonio Soler, que ha impreso Robert Birchall.* Núm. 133. New Benet Street.

PRIMARY SOURCE: *GB-Cfm: MU MS. 48 (32-F-18).*

Sonatas del Pe. Padre Soler que hizo para la diversión del Serenissimo Señor Infante Don Gabriel obra 7ª y 8ª año 1786.

PRIMARY SOURCE: *E-Boc* Ms 58. Facsimile in mdc.cbuc.cat.

Toccate nº XII per cembalo composte dal Padre Antonio Soler discepolo di Domenico Scarlati.

PRIMARY SOURCE: *E-Mc* 3/429. Facsimile in rcsmm.eu.

Keyboard Works by Domenico Scarlatti, Antonio Soler and Alessandro Scarlatti, with other unidentified Works.

PRIMARY SOURCE: *US-NYpm: Cary 703 Record ID:* 316355. Facsimile in: www.themorgan.org/music/manuscript/316355.

MODERN EDITIONS:

> *P. Antonio Soler. Sonatas para instrumentos de tecla.* Samuel Rubio, editor. 7
> Volumes. Madrid: Unión Musical Española, 1957–1972.

> *Antonio Soler, Sonatas for Piano.* Frederick Marvin, editor. 4 Volumes. London:
> Mills Music Ltd, 1957–1968.

> *Early Spanish Keyboard Music, Vol. III.* Barry Ife and Roy Truby, editors. Oxford:
> Oxford University Press, 1986.

> *Antonio Soler. 14 Sonatas for Keyboard from the Fitzwilliam Collection.* Kenneth
> Gilbert, editor. London: Faber Music Limited, 1987.

Appendix 6: Select List of Compositions with Written-Out Harpsichord Parts to Accompany Chapter 15

Identifying remarks: opus numbers, catalogue numbers, dates of composition or publication, keys, and specified instrumentation

Abel, C. F.

> Op. 2 (Violin or Flute)
> Op. 5 (Violin or Flute, Violoncello)
> Op. 13 (Violin)

Avison, Charles

> Op. 5 (Two Violins and Violoncello)
> Op. 7 (Two Violins and Violoncello)
> Op. 8 (Two Violins and Violoncello)

Bach, C. P. E.

> W75–78 (Violin)
> W83–87 (Flute)
> W88 (Viola or Viola da Gamba)
> W93–95 (Flute, Viola, Violoncello)
> W161 "Two Trios" (No. 1 Two Violins; No. 2 Flute and Violin)

Bach, J. C.

> Op. 2 (Violin or Flute and Violoncello)
> Op. 10 (Violin; versions of two sonatas for Viola da Gamba: Warb
>   B2b in B-flat major, and Warb B4b in G major)
> Op. 16 (German Flute or Violin, version of no. 6 for Viola da Gamba))
> Op. 18 (German Flute or Violin)
> Op. 22 (Violin, Oboe, Flute, Tenor [i.e., Viola], Violoncello)

Bach, J. C. F.

> B 15-B 20 (Flute or Violin)
> B 31 and 32 (Violin and Viola)

Balbastre, Claude

> Op. 3 (Two Violins, Bass, Two Horns *ad libitum*)

Beauvarlet-Charpentier, J. J.

> Op. 2 (Violin)

Boccherini, Luigi

> Op. 5 (Violin)

Boismortier, Joseph Bodin de
    Op. 80 (Flute)
Castello, Dario
    Sonata, 1629 (Diverse Instruments)
Clementi, Muzio
    Op. 2 (German Flute or Violin)
    Op. 3 (Flute or Violin)
Corrette, Michel
    Op. 25 (Violin)
Couperin, A.-L.
    Op. 2 (Violin)
    Op. 3 (Violin and Violoncello)
Frescobaldi, Girolamo
    Toccata, 1628 (Violin, Violone)
Garth, John
    Op. 2 (Two Violins, Violoncello)
Giardini, Felice
    Op. 3 (Violin)
Giordani, Tommaso
    Op. 3 (Flute, Violin, Violoncello)
Graun, Johann Gottlieb
    GraunWV: A:XV:2 and A:XV:10 (Two Trios, Viola da Gamba and Basso Continuo)
    GraunWV: Av:XV:50 (Viola da Gamba)
Guglielmi, Pietro
    Op. 2 (Two Violins and Violoncello)
Guillemain, Louis-Gabriel
    Op. 13 (Violin)
Handel, G. F.
    RISM: S-L Saml. Wenster U:1 (Viola da Gamba)
Jackson, William
    Op. 2 (Violin)
Jacquet de La Guerre, Elisabeth-Claude
    1707 (Violin)
Marini, Biagio
    Sonata, 1626 (Violin, Trombone)
Méhul, Étienne-Nicholas
    Op. 2 (Violin)
Mondonville, Jean-Joseph Cassanea
    Op. 3 (Violin)
    Op. 5 (Voice or Violin)
Pfeiffer, Johann
    WoO (Viola da Gamba)
Rameau, J. P.
    WoO, 1741 (Violin, or Flute and Viola da Gamba or Second Violin)

Rosetti, Antonio
 Op. 6 (Violin)
Schaffrath, Christoph
 Op. 1 (Violin)
Schobert, Johann
 Op. 1 (Violin)
 Op. 2 (Violin)
 Op. 3 (Violin)
 Op. 7 (Two Violins and Bass)
Schuster, Joseph
 WoO (Violin)
Simon, Simon
 Op. 1 (Violin)
Tapray, Jean-François
 Op. 1, 1758 (Three Violins and Violoncello)
 Op. 1, later version, 1770 (Violin)
 Op. 5 (Violin and Viola)
Taylor, Rayner
 Op. 2 (Violin)
Telemann, G. P.
 Essercizi Musici:
  TWV 42: G6 (Viola da Gamba, Basso Continuo)
  TWV 42: A6 (Flute, Basso Continuo)
  TWV 42: B4 (Recorder, Basso Continuo)
  TWV 42: Es3 (Oboe, Basso Continuo)
Wagenseil, Georg Christoph
 WoO, ca. 1760-61 (Two Violins, Violoncello)
Wanhal, Johann
 ca. 1795 (Clarinet or Violin)

Glossary

Allemande – a dance in duple meter, usually beginning with an upbeat

Bon goût – the French term for "good taste"

Canzona – a contrapuntal genre that usually begins with a standard rhythmic pattern

Chorale prelude – composition for organ, usually based on a Lutheran chorale melody

Comma – the term used in tuning systems to indicate deviations from a pure interval

Courante/Corrente – a dance in either 3/2 or 3/4 meter

Double manual – a harpsichord with two keyboards

Fantasia – a style of keyboard composition that is typically free and not based on a fixed form or melodic motive, but can also be imitative or dance-like

Galliard – a fast dance in triple meter

Gigue – a fast dance in either 6/8 or 6/4 meter

Ground – a repeating or ostinato bass line, or the name of a composition with such a bass line

Cembalo – the name for harpsichord in Germany and Italy

Clavecin – the name for harpsichord in France

Hz – standard acoustical symbol for "Hertz," a unit of frequency

Lessons – English term used for various styles and collections of keyboard compositions

Pavan – a slow dance in duple meter

Sarabande – a slow, serious dance in triple meter, usually with an emphasis on the second beat

Toccata – a style of composition to be performed relatively freely, despite the notated rhythms

Tombeau – a composition written in honor or memory of a deceased person

Ricercare – an imitative genre, the name is derived from the Latin "to seek" or "to search out"

Registration – the combination of stops on an organ or harpsichord

Index

Note: Dates of living persons have not been included. An alternative version of this index, organized thematically, can be found online at www.cambridge.org/9781107156074.